THE MEDITERRANEAN IN THE ELEVENTH CENTURY

A MEDITERRANEAN SOCIETY

PUBLISHED UNDER THE AUSPICES OF THE

Near Eastern Center
University of California
Los Angeles

S. D. GOITEIN

A Mediterranean Society

THE JEWISH COMMUNITIES OF THE ARAB WORLD
AS PORTRAYED IN THE DOCUMENTS OF THE CAIRO GENIZA

VOLUME II

The Community

UNIVERSITY OF CALIFORNIA PRESS
Berkeley • Los Angeles • London • 1971

UNIVERSITY OF CALIFORNIA PRESS
BERKELEY AND LOS ANGELES, CALIFORNIA
UNIVERSITY OF CALIFORNIA PRESS, LTD.
LONDON, ENGLAND

ISBN: 0-520-01867-2
LIBRARY OF CONGRESS CATALOG CARD NUMBER: 67-22430

PRINTED IN THE UNITED STATES OF AMERICA

In loving memory of my mother

Frida Goitein nee *Braunschweiger*
(1870–1920)

"When Rav Joseph [who was blind] heard
the steps of his mother, he said to
his students: 'Let me stand up; I
perceive the Presence of God approaching.' "

Qiddushin, 31*b*

Preface

This volume of *A Mediterranean Society* explores the nature of medieval religious democracy using the rich documentation left by a community living on the crossroads of three continents and representing contacts the three religions had with one another. Like the preceding volume, *Economic Foundations,* this study is based on the documents of the Cairo Geniza (described in the Introduction to volume I). As a rule, it refers to previous research on the history of the period concerned (950-1250) only when these documents seem to demand some qualification of its results.

Several institutions and offices of a very specific character are treated here and, because of their many-sided and varying functions, appear in each of the three chapters of this volume. When the reader is confronted with unfamiliar terms, such as "Gaon" or "Nagid," "yeshiva" or "muqaddam," he is advised to make copious use of the Index. Each part of the book deals only with those aspects of an institution or an office which are relevant to its subject.

I wish to express my gratitude to the distinguished colleagues—friends, and others whom I do not know personally—for their encouraging and illuminating reviews on volume I. A comprehensive glossary of the Arabic and Hebrew terms mentioned and explained in this book (missed by some readers), as well as cumulative indexes of Geniza texts and general topics, will be included in volume III. As announced in the Preface to volume I, a companion volume, called *Mediterranean People: Letters and Documents from the Cairo Geniza, Translated into English,* will be published after the publication of the third and final volume of the present work.

Unlike volume I, this volume does not contain an index of Geniza texts. Such an index would have comprised at least forty pages, but would have been of only temporary value since the sources cited here are included in the final, cumulative index now in preparation for inclusion in volume III. Moreover, this volume is divided into more than sixty sections and subsections (see Contents) so that anyone wishing to make sure whether a certain source is included would be able to find out in a matter of minutes.

As in volume I, and for the same reason, no bibliography is attached, but the reader will find copious references to scientific literature in the lists of abbreviations and, of course, in the Notes.

Readers using the Notes are advised that cross references to chapter, section, and note refer also to the relevant text. It has been found that this method is more expedient than references simply to pages. A page in this volume contains an average of at least five different topics, each based on one or several sources. Since the chapter and section numbers appear in the heading of each page, a desired topic is found quicker by reference to them and to the note mentioning the sources than merely to a page number.

By its very nature, this volume tries to penetrate deeper into the inner life of the Geniza society, and I feel I need to present my credentials.

I do not believe that I would have been able to understand these ancient parchments properly (I mean not only philologically, but also psychologically) had it not been for the many years of ethnolinguistic research I carried out among Yemenites, those most Jewish and most Arab of all Jews. They consist of two markedly distinct groups: the educated townsmen, mostly highlanders, persons of a thoroughly Mediterranean type—no barrier being felt between them and a European; and the primitive villagers from remote regions, mostly lowlanders, often people of great charm, especially the women—but from another planet. Despite the differences in time, location, and historical circumstances, familiarity with these two types of Oriental people helped to throw light into many a dark corner of the Geniza world.

Second, and strange, as it may sound, I derived much profit for the understanding of the communal texts discussed in this volume from my experience as senior education officer to the British Mandatory Government of Palestine during its woeful last decade (1938-1948). My office was a curious blend of administrative, pedagogical, and diplomatic activities and provided many insights into the workings of public bodies of different character and size. One of my many duties was care of the schools of Oriental Jews. Following the outbreak of World War II, these schools had lost most of their means of maintenance, but, by statute, were not eligible for government assistance unless they had attained certain educational standards. Whether my work with these institutions contributed anything to the improvement of their administration and teaching, I do not know (assistance they got, anyhow). That it was an excellent opportunity for me to become familiar with traditional Oriental education and the persons and bodies running it, about this, there is little doubt.

Last, and strangest of all, I believe I would have missed many aspects of the Geniza documents had I not been granted the opportunity of observing the American scene for many years. Authoritarian Germany, where I spent my childhood and youth, and the Jewish society in Palestine and later Israel, with its socialist, welfare, and protectionist tendencies, which saw most of my working life, were utterly different from the Geniza society, which was loosely organized and competitive in every respect. This vigorous free-enterprise society of the United States, which is not without petty jealousies and often cheap public honors, its endless fund-raising campaigns and all that goes with them, its general involvement in public affairs and deep concern (or lip service, as the case may be) for the underdog—all proved to be extremely instructive. We do not wear turbans here; but, while reading many a Geniza document one feels quite at home.

In conclusion, I wish to reiterate what I have said repeatedly in public and in private: I regard this book and similar publications of mine solely as preparatory stages leading to the main task of Geniza research, the systematic edition of the original texts with full translations, commentaries, and facsimiles. As a matter of fact, most of my time during the last eighteen years has been devoted to the preparation of such an undertaking. But while it was difficult—and possible only under extreme privation—to produce a volume like the one presented here without adequate financial aid, it goes without saying that a comprehensive program of text editions cannot be carried out unless provided with proper means. A powerful foundation, institution, or a Maecenas should find here an opportunity for a *monumentum aere perennius.* Despite the difficult times through which we live at present, I confidently hope that the findings presented in this book will convince some readers that the sources on which they are based deserve to be brought to the knowledge of the scholarly world.

When my mother, who had never known illness in her life, was carried away by the all-European meningitis epidemic of 1920, I put the quotation from the Talmud, printed in the Dedication, on her tombstone. (It is still there, in the deserted Jewish cemetery of Frankfurt am Main, a few steps beyond the elaborate tomb of Paul Ehrlich, the inventor of Salvarsan and Nobel prizewinner.) It gives me deep satisfaction that now, exactly fifty years later, I am able to revive the memory of that unusual woman: beautiful and well read, of stern principles, but unbounded kindness, steeped in the romantic idealism of the nineteenth century—and always silent and enigmatic.

April 3, 1970 S. D. Goitein

Contents of Volumes I and III

Contents

Abbreviations and Symbols

The abbreviations and symbols listed in *Med. Soc.,* I, xix–xxvi, are used in this volume.

A plus sign after the shelf mark of a Geniza manuscript means that the document has been edited and published or is included in S. D. Goitein's *India Book* or M. Michael's *Nahray* (see *Med. Soc.,* I, xxii and xxiv). A plus sign within parentheses after the shelf mark means that the relevant text has been edited only in part or has been translated in Goitein, *Education* (see *Med. Soc.,* I, xxi). Publication data on the edition or the serial number of the document in *India Book* or *Nahray* is supplied at the first appearance of the relevant shelf mark and is to be found in Shaked, *Bibliography* (see *Med. Soc.,* I, xxv [edited texts only as far as published prior to 1964]). An asterisk after the shelf mark of a manuscript means that the document is translated in S. D. Goitein, *Mediterranean People* (see p. vii, above).

Additional abbreviations, not used in volume I:

Abramson, *Bamerkazim*	S. Abramson, *Ba-merkazīm uva-tfūṣōt bi-tqūfat ha-ge'ōnīm.* Jerusalem, 1965.
Baedeker, *Ägypten,* 1928	Karl Baedeker, *Ägypten und der Sudan.* Leipzig, 1928.
Benjamin of Tudela, ed. Adler	*The Itinerary of Benjamin of Tudela,* ed. M. N. Adler. London, 1907. The pages of the English translation are cited.
Dinur, *Yisrael ba-Gola*	B. Dinur, *Yisrael ba-Gola.* Tel Aviv, 1968. Vols. I, i–iv, II, i–iii.
Fattal, *Non-Musulmans en pays d'Islam*	A. Fattal, *Le statut légal des non-Musulmans en pays d'Islam.* Beirut, 1958.

Harkavy, *Responsen der Geonim*	A. Harkavy, *Responsen der Geonim.* Berlin, 1887.
Hirschberg, *The Jews in North Africa*	H. Z. (J. W.) Hirschberg, *A History of the Jews in North Africa* (Heb.). Jerusalem, 1965. 2 vols.
Mahler, *Chronologie*	Eduard Mahler, *Handbuch der jüdischen Chronologie.* Leipzig, 1916.
Meinardus, *Orthodox Copts*	Otto Meinardus, "The Attitudes of the Orthodox Copts towards the Islamic State . . . ," *Ostkirchliche Studien,* 13 (1964), 153–170.
MGWJ	*Monatsschrift für die Geschichte und Wissenschaft des Judentums.*
Rabbinic Anthology	C. G. Montefiore and H. Loewe, *A Rabbinic Anthology.* Meridian Books [1938].
Samuel b. Eli	S. Assaf, *A Collection of Letters by Samuel b. Eli and His Contemporaries* (Heb.). Jerusalem, 1930.
Schechter, *Saadyana*	S. Schechter, *Saadyana.* Cambridge, 1903.
Sefer ha-Yishuv	*Sefer ha-Yishuv,* Vol. II, ed. S. Assaf and L. A. Mayer (Heb.). Jerusalem, 1944.
Steinschneider, *Arabische Literatur der Juden*	M. Steinschneider, *Die arabische Literatur der Juden.* Frankfurt, 1902.
Tritton, *Muslim Education*	A. S. Tritton, *Materials on Muslim Education in the Middle Ages.* London, 1957.
Tyan, *Organisation judiciaire*	Emile Tyan, *L'Organisation judiciaire en pays d'Islam.* Leiden, 1960.

Appendixes A–C in this volume are cited in chapter v, section C, and elsewhere when they occur frequently by letter and number. For example, A1 means Appendix A, section 1.

Articles whose author is not indicated are written by S. D. Goitein.

A MEDITERRANEAN SOCIETY

Map of Medieval Egypt

CHAPTER V

Communal Organization and Institutions

INTRODUCTION: *The Functioning of a Medieval Democracy*

The Christians and Jews living under Islam during the High Middle Ages formed communities of a very specific character. They were not citizens of the principalities in which they happened to live but were "protected" subjects, that is, their life, property, and honor were safeguarded and the free exercise of their religion was permitted, as long as they paid their poll tax and submitted humbly to the restrictions imposed on them by Islam.[1] The administration of their own affairs was left to themselves. Thus, they formed a state not only within the state, but beyond the state, because they owed loyalty to the heads and to the central bodies of their respective denominations, even though these were found in a foreign, or even hostile, country. On the other hand, a caliph or sultan ruling over a considerable number of non-Muslims, or even a government official in charge of a city or a smaller locality, would find it advantageous to recognize a representative dignitary or one or more notables who would form a connecting link between a subject minority and himself and who could be held responsible whenever convenient. The ecumenical, territorial, and local religious and semireligious authorities of the various denominations thus served, as a rule, also as their official or semiofficial secular heads. The ecumenical or territorial leaders would appoint, or confirm the election of, local representatives wielding both religious and temporal authority.

Since the machinery of the state itself was loose in those days, the coercive power of the denominational communities was even weaker. Nevertheless, the cohesiveness of comparatively small groups, living under the pressure of a majority of another faith, and the greater dedication of its members, largely compensated for this weakness.

In one, perhaps the most important, respect the Christian and Jewish communities were even stronger than the amorphous masses of Muslims. They had carried over from Hellenistic and Roman times civic forms of communal organization which gave the individual member opportunity to be active in the life of the congregation. The pre-Christian Jewish congregation grew out of the unique needs of a religion that had abolished sacrifices and offerings everywhere except in the Temple of Jerusalem. Prayer, as well as the study of the Holy Scriptures and the religious law, became a concern for everyone and had to be organized on a local basis. Thus, there arose the Synagogue (lit., the Assembly), the mother of the church. When Palestine and most of the Near East came under Greek, and later Roman, domination, the trappings of secular corporation were added to what had originally been a brotherhood of intrinsically religious character. The result was a public institution of enormous vitality, developing in many different shades inside both Judaism and Christianity. This asset of a long-standing tradition was enhanced by the tangible effect that the rise of a Middle Eastern bourgeoisie in early Islamic times had on the non-Muslim population. Christians and Jews now belonged largely to the middle class of merchants and skilled artisans, of government officials and agents, and to the very prominent medical profession. These well-educated and experienced men took a lively interest in the affairs of their community and strove hard for the honors bestowed on meritorious members. In addition to this rivalry there often prevailed a marked tension between the notables, who derived their influential position in the community from their connection with the government or from their riches, and the rank and file, which insisted on having its full share in the decisions affecting the activities of the Church or the Synagogue.

The concerns of the community were manifold. There were questions of religious dogma and ritual practice. Similarly, the upkeep of the houses of worship and the seats of religious learning, as well as the appointment and payment of the various community officials, required much attention. Furthermore, law in those days was personal rather than territorial; an individual was judged according to the law of the denomination to which he belonged.[2] Almost the entire field of family law and also cases of inheritance and commercial transactions were handled by the courts of the various religious communities. Criminal law was the preserve of the state. Since Muslim juridical organization did not know the institution of a public prosecutor, however, it was left to the officials of the Church or the Synagogue to seek redress in case of an infringement of the rights of their coreligionists, or when unruly members of their own flock could not be kept in line by the use of whatever powers of coercion were at the disposal of the religious authorities. It is natural that Christians and Jews often applied to government courts, sometimes even in cases of communal strife and dissensions arising from their own religious tenets or ritual. This turning to government jurisdiction resulted in an interesting interplay of the various laws invoked. In everyday life, however, the ordinary citizen arranged his affairs before the denominational courts, which were also cheaper (and perhaps less corrupt). All in all, juridical autonomy was one of the most essential aspects of Christian and Jewish life in the countries of Islam during the High Middle Ages.

Finally, the social services, in our day the responsibility of state and local authorities, had to be provided in those times by the Church and the Synagogue. The education of children whose parents or other relatives were unable to bear the costs, the care of orphans and widows, of the poor and the old, the ill and the disabled, needy travelers and foreigners, and, last but not least, the ransoming of captives—all were works of charity, expected to be carried out by each denomination for its own members. This entailed much organization, often transcending the limits of a locality or even a country, and required a spirit of devotion to the common good, both of which made for closely knit communities despite wide geographical dispersion.

The heyday of the Middle Eastern bourgeoisie of the tenth through the thirteenth centuries also saw the blooming of communal life of Christians and Jews under Islam. At the end of this period, when the region succumbed to military feudalism and its corollary, Muslim clericalism, most of the ancient communal institutions waned or disintegrated altogether. The very detailed information to be gathered from the documents of the Geniza about Jewish public life should form useful material for comparison of all the numerous and prosperous non-Muslim communities in medieval times. Moreover, it also had some bearing on the history of the Muslim middle class, which has not yet been sufficiently studied. It may well be that a closer scrutiny of all the sources concerned may one day reveal that certain traits of community life, which we are inclined to attribute to the special circumstances of minority groups, were indeed characteristic of the period studied in this book in general. It applies in particular to the question of municipal corporation, to which much attention has lately been paid.[3]

The essence of a religious democracy is well defined in the book of Deuteronomy 1:13, where Moses says to the Children of Israel: "Get you wise and capable men, who are well-known among your tribes, and I will make them heads over you." It is left to the people to agree on suitable representatives, but the spiritual leader makes the final choice. Referring to this verse, a tenth-century head of a yeshiva, who was also a prominent scholar, wrote this legal opinion, which may be summarized as follows:

It has been asked why it is written: "Thou shalt establish judges and officers in all thy gates" (Deuteronomy 1:18)—in the singular and not in the plural. The answer is this: The verse is addressed to the spiritual leader, on whom it is incumbent to appoint judges in Israel, just as Moses has said: (here follows Deuteronomy 1:13, quoted above). Without the appointment by Moses, the election by the people was not valid. Even Joshua's office, although he was chosen by God, was complete only after his investiture by Moses. The same is true of Saul and Samuel. All this proves that installment in an office is incomplete unless it is done by the spiritual leader of any given period. In the absence of such leadership, however, each community is at liberty to make its own choice.[4]

The basic attitude expressed in the responsum summarized dominated Jewish public life during the Geniza period. The local or territorial communities acted largely according to their own lights, but were always eager to receive sanction and approval from some higher spiritual authority.

Modern democracy functions in an extremely formal and legalistic way. Each and every step, such as the election of representatives or the fixing of a budget, is preceded or accompanied by the exact description of the procedures, by the promulgation of laws and bylaws, and the taking and counting of votes. It lies, however, in the very nature of things that, in reality, masses can be guided only by a comparatively limited number of leaders and that the laws represent the condensed expression of the powers actually ruling a people. The society reflected in the Geniza records (much as similar societies not only under Islam but in contemporary Christendom as well) was far less legalistically minded, or, rather, did not feel the necessity of making laws because it had the safe guidance of the Law of God. The modern historian would commit a grave error if he assumed that legalistic procedures were the only ways of securing and safeguarding the participation of the populace in the conduct of its affairs. Although formal decisions taken by public bodies were by no means entirely absent, the Geniza people had many other ways for making its will prevail. It must be conceded that, because of its comparatively limited size, the Jewish community was, to a certain extent, exceptional: everyone could be, and normally was, present in the synagogue when public affairs were discussed and decided upon. Constant surveillance and action by a whole congregation were possible and, as we see, took place regularly. Still, it is my hope that this factual and detailed account of the functioning of the Jewish public body during the Geniza period will be conducive toward a balanced view of medieval religious democracy in general.[5]

A. ECUMENICAL AND TERRITORIAL AUTHORITIES

1. *The Gaon, or Head of the Academy, and the "Head of the Diaspora"*

The eternal struggle between authority and freedom can be mitigated by rival authorities (such as legislature, administration, and judiciary), by the leadership's need to have recourse to the led ("no taxation without representation"), and by the uniting force of an idea, such as the striving for a new social order or the service of God. The Jewish community represented in the Cairo Geniza records derived its very raison d'être from its unfaltering allegiance to its religion, while the other factors making for an intensive community life, divided authority and a lively reciprocity between the leader and the led, were likewise present.

The highest authority of the Jewish community was the yeshiva, represented by its head, the Gaon. Yeshiva is habitually rendered in English as "academy." For the period under discussion, rightly called the gaonic period, the medieval "collegium" would be a more suitable equivalent. The yeshiva combined the functions of a seat of learning, a high court, and a parliament (see below, chap. vi, sec. 7). It wielded absolute authority inasmuch as it interpreted the Law of God from whose decisions there was no appeal. In view of this, it is strange that there should have been three such bodies and not one: two in Iraq (Babylonia) and one in Palestine. The Babylonian yeshivas originally had their seats in two different localities, Sura and Pumbedita, but each retained its name after moving to the capital, Baghdad. This tripartition went back to the third century A.D. but should not be compared with the various denominations of the Eastern

Church, which also originated in pre-Islamic times. The latter were based on dogmatic schisms, that is, they denied to one another the possession of correct belief, whereas the three Jewish ecclesiastical councils recognized one another as equally orthodox and differed only in matters of ritual and legal usage. To give just two, but rather tangible, examples: According to the Babylonian rite, the six yearly holidays were celebrated for two days each, whereas they were observed for only one day each by the Palestinians. The Palestinian family law decreed that half the dowry of a woman who died childless reverted to her family, a practice not accepted by the Babylonians. All these differences between the "Easterners" and the "Westerners"—as the Babylonians and Palestinians, respectively, were called—were listed in special collections; this type of literature was later much developed in Islam where similar conditions prevailed.[1]

Although the centuries preceding and following the Arab conquest of the Middle East are the most obscure in Jewish history, it can be said with reasonable certainty that the Jewish communities of the countries included in the Byzantine empire followed the Palestinian academy, while those living under Persian rule were administered from Babylonia. The yeshivas of Babylonia divided among themselves the provinces of the Persian empire according to mutual agreement. In early Islamic times, when Egypt and North Africa became colonial areas for immigrants from the East, and when, starting in the tenth century, owing to the beginning of the devastation of Iraq, many members of its middle class moved westward, the geographical division between "Easterners" and "Westerners" became entirely blurred. In many towns, there were now two Jewish congregations, a "Palestinian" and a "Babylonian." This was true not only of cities like Old Cairo, Alexandria, Damascus, and Ramle, the administrative capital of Palestine, but also of smaller towns like al-Mahalla in Lower Egypt, Baniyas in Palestine, and Palmyra in Syria.[2]

As a corollary, in towns like Old Cairo, Alexandria, Ramle, Damascus, and Aleppo, a differentiation was made between the "large," or main, and the "small," or minor, synagogue. We are most probably right in assuming that the main synagogue in these formerly Byzantine towns was the Palestinian. For Alexandria and Ramle this is known to be true and for Old Cairo it can be inferred. As for Damascus, the Muslim historians assert that only one synagogue was included in the treaty that delivered the city into the hands of the Arab conquerors (together with fourteen churches), which means that only one was in existence in Byzantine times. A Geniza document from 933 refers to "the small, namely, the Babylonian synagogue."[3]

In most of the larger cities there also existed a community of Karaites (lit., "Bible readers"), a Jewish sect that disapproved of the teachings of the Talmud. They differed from the majority of the Jews, the so-called Rabbanites, that is, the followers of the rabbis or teachers of the Talmud, as markedly as one Christian church from another. The religious aspect of this schism is discussed in *Med. Soc.,* Volume III, chapter x. As a social group, the Karaites presented a strange picture. On the one hand, many of the richest Jews and of those connected with the government (such as the Tustaris, often referred to in this book) belonged to this sect. On the other hand, nowhere in Judaism do we find such outspoken condemnation of wealth and the wealthy and of the easy life of the diaspora as in the pages of the early Karaites. These writers preached rigorous ascetism and called for immediate emigration to the Holy Land (where, in those centuries, life was hard anyhow). This contrast has found full expression in the Geniza documents. While in stern Palestine militant Karaites and Rabbanites were constantly at loggerheads—a state of affairs which engendered government interference more than once—in easygoing Egypt, friendly relations prevailed between the members of the high bourgeoisie belonging to the two denominations. Intermarriage was frequent, so common indeed that the Geniza has preserved not only actual marriage contracts between two such parties, but formularies showing how such "mixed marriages" should be arranged so as not to hurt the religious sensitivities of either husband or wife. The Karaites did not recognize the religious authority of the Gaons since they represented rabbinic Judaism, but they felt themselves to be, acted like, and were regarded as full members of the Jewish community. (In this respect, the Karaites of the Geniza period differed considerably from those in czarist Russia and its successor states. The well-integrated Karaites in the state of Israel have all come from Egypt.) The Gaons of Jerusalem and Baghdad freely applied to Karaite notables for help, both pecuniary and other (such as intercession with the government or aid in the settlement of communal strife). That aid was readily granted is proved by the gaonic correspondence in which praise is lavished on meritorious Karaites and God's blessing is called upon them.[4]

It was different with the Samaritans, familiar to everyone from the New Testament. This sect, which had already seceded from the main body of Judaism in the time of the Second Temple (indeed, had never fully belonged to it), did not recognize the Jewish religious authorities. Occasionally, a Samaritan would turn to a Rabbanite congregation for help or would join it outright. The Samaritan who signed a record of the rabbinical court in Damietta in January, 1106, had probably adopted the Jewish faith. We have two letters from a Samaritan carpenter, who possessed some Hebrew learning, in which he describes himself in moving terms as a Kohen and foreigner in great distress. He asked not for alms, but for work, emphasizing that he could make "chests, bedsteads, doors and beams" (whereas each of these categories was usually made by craftsmen who specialized in one or the other). He requested that "the head carpenter" be instructed to accept him (presumably during the restoration of the synagogue of the Palestinians in the 1030's) for the members of his own sect were too worldly minded to pay attention to a needy coreligionist. He is alluding to the fact, known otherwise, that a section of the small Samaritan community had become prosperous and had quickly assimilated themselves to the Muslim environment. While the documents mentioned contain about all the nonliterary Geniza texts tell us about relations with Samaritans, they yield considerable information about Karaites. Still, these references are too spotty for a complete inside story of this colorful sect. Thus, with a few exceptions, the picture of Jewish communal life, as drawn from Geniza material, of necessity is confined to the Rabbanites, the followers of the yeshivas, and their Gaons.[5]

The adherence of a congregation to one of the two Rabbanite rites or, rather, to one of the three yeshivas, was expressed by no means solely by its ritual and law. It also had an administrative aspect. A close relationship existed between the central seats of Jewish learning and the individual communities attached to them. On recommendation by their congregations the local leaders were appointed by the heads of the academies and were regarded as their deputies. A *ḥāvēr*, or member of the academy, was usually chosen for the task. Thus, "ḥāvēr" in the Geniza documents is to a large extent equivalent to "rabbi," with the important qualification that, as a rule, he served not only as spiritual leader, but also as president of his congregation. During most of the first half of the eleventh century the leader of the Rabbanite community of Old Cairo was described as *khalīfa* (cf. caliph), or representative, of the Gaon of Jerusalem. Incidentally, the contemporary bishop of Tunisia was designated by the same Arabic term. An official of the synagogue of the Palestinians, writing to the same Gaon, constantly uses the term "your synagogue."[6] Similarly, "the congregations [plural!] praying in the synagogue of the Babylonians" in Old Cairo, in addressing the head of an academy in Baghdad, refer to their synagogue as "the one that bears the name of your yeshiva."[7] In legal documents of the eleventh century, the court in the synagogue of the Palestinians describes itself as acting on behalf of the High Court of the yeshiva of Jerusalem and its head; we again find the same reference a hundred years later, when the yeshiva itself had moved to Cairo.[8] When a Gaon died, the communal officials had to be reinstated by his successor.[9] In short, while it would be incorrect to speak about a Jewish clergy, in those times the Synagogue, not unlike the Church, was organized in a comparatively authoritarian manner.

The ties linking a congregation to a yeshiva could last for many generations despite the immense distances separating the two. A Gaon writing from Iraq to Spain in 953 mentions that religious and legal queries sent from Spain to his great-grandfather and to his grandfather (who between them had been in office for forty years) and even to the Gaons preceding them were still in his hands.[10] It is no exaggeration to say that in most of the Gaonic letters preserved in their entirety the addressees are reminded of the long-standing bonds between the yeshiva and their own forebears or predecessors. Moreover, the Geniza material enables us to actually follow up such relations between a yeshiva and local leaders during two or more generations not only with regard to larger cities, such as Old Cairo and Alexandria in Egypt, Qayrawān in Tunisia, and Fez and Sijilmāsa in Morocco, but also to smaller towns, such as Gabes in Tunisia.

Although the yeshivas recognized the orthodoxy of their sister institutions, they insisted that a community should follow at one time only the guidance of one, that is, queries should not be submitted simultaneously to two. When the scholars of Qayrawān once addressed both Babylonian yeshivas with the same question, they received a stern rebuff: since decisions depended on reasoning, the yeshivas could arrive at different conclusions with the result that their rulings, instead of serving as a guide, could create confusion and discord (ninth century).[11] Public appeals, however, were held in one and the same congregation for all three yeshivas simultaneously, with the lion's share going to the one in closest contact with the donors, as evident from various letters referring to the same North African city.[12] The maintenance of yeshivas, as of other religious or educational institutions, or even of single scholars, was a matter of religious duty and piety and not only one of specific indebtedness.

The prestige of a yeshiva depended on the scholarship and other personal qualities of the man or the men who stood at its head. When a particularly brilliant and energetic Gaon graced a yeshiva, communities were induced to transfer their allegiance to him. References to such occurrences are by no means rare. When a faction in the

Palestinian congregation of Old Cairo was dissatisfied with the Gaon of Jerusalem, at a time when Hay (d. 1038), one of the greatest Gaons, led one of the two yeshivas of Baghdad, a warning was sounded that the congregation concerned might disavow "the authority of Palestine."[13] Since factional shifts affected the finances of a yeshiva, they often brought strong reactions, still recognizable in the gaonic correspondence, especially of the tenth and eleventh centuries.

When assuming office, a Gaon would issue a pastoral circular outlining his own religious and communal program and, where the circumstances called for it, make comments on the situation and needs of the congregation addressed. When Saadya, a native of the Fayyūm in middle Egypt, became Gaon in Baghdad in May, 928, he sent a circular to Córdoba, Seville, and five other cities in Spain, and probably to other countries as well.[14] But only the circular and a letter preceding it sent to Old Cairo have been preserved. In the letter, the head of the academy promises to seek redress for the grievances of the addressees by approaching the central government in Baghdad through the influential Jewish court bankers residing in that city. We have to bear in mind that during the twenties of the tenth century utmost disorder prevailed in Egypt, and at that time the country was administered, albeit rather diffidently, from Baghdad.[15] Besides this reference to the specific needs of the community addressed, the letter, written in highly stylized Hebrew, is devoted to two subjects: God's grace manifested in revealing his written and oral law and the Gaon's general concern for his flock, "for without an army there is no king and, without students, scholars have no splendor."[16]

The pastoral circular contained thirty points, of which the following are of general interest. Men should fear God even in times of affluence, a clear indication of the generally prosperous state of at least a section of the community at that time. No one should separate himself from the congregational activities and duties. Supererogatory fasts and prayers had less value than the avoidance of a single sin. Although this preference for moral and religious punctiliousness over ritual is familiar to the Bible reader from the Prophets (quoted, of course, in the circular), the special emphasis laid on it reflects the general attitude of the medieval devotee, to whom hard, supererogatory works represented the essence of religious perfection. The circular concludes with two admonitions referring to the academy itself: one, to support the students of the sacred law, and another, to address all queries with regard to religious and legal matters to the Gaon and his school.[17]

The first and most tangible bond between the central seats of Jewish higher learning and the widely dispersed communities was the obligation of the latter to contribute to the upkeep of the former. Many gaonic letters contain solicitations, sometimes in the form of urgent appeals or even of more or less veiled threats. Some modern Jewish scholars who have dealt with this material have felt rather uneasy about it finding it somewhat undignified. The reason for their judgment is to be found in the scholars themselves, however, for all of whom were from continental Europe, where universities and colleges are usually maintained by the state. In Anglo-Saxon countries, the finest institutions of higher learning are or used to be the so-called private universities, that is, public institutions maintained largely through private means. A Gaon soliciting funds was as natural a social phenomenon in the Jewish middle class society of the High Middle Ages, as a president or vice-chancellor doing the same in the United States or in England in our own day. The difference is, of course, that most of the relevant Geniza material comes from the late tenth through the twelfth centuries, when both Iraq and Palestine were laid waste by almost continuous warfare and other disorders and the yeshivas often found themselves in utmost penury and distress. Of Iraq, once the richest of all Islamic countries, a tenth-century Gaon writes: "There is no country in the world in which destitution is as rampant as here in Babylonia." In his letter, he requests the addressees, scholars living in Spain, Morocco, or France, to send their contributions via the yeshiva's representative in Qayrawān, Tunisia, to its honorary treasurer in Baghdad, who, most characteristically for this period, also happened to be a Tunisian.[18] There is no need for quotations to prove the desolate state of Palestine in this period; references to its mounting devastation long before the advent of the Crusaders are made throughout this book.

Glowing descriptions of the splendor of the Babylonian yeshivas also exist, however, and letters of solicitation were not confined to times of distress. By chance, the Geniza has preserved copies of a dossier of letters sent by a Gaon of Baghdad to Yemen and Yamāma, that is, to southwest and central Arabia. The letters show that the yeshiva had representatives in many small places all over the country, that it was well informed about each of these men, and that the communities sent their donations regularly. They also reveal the different types of donations made,[19] a subject that is detailed in many other letters as well. First, there were fixed yearly contributions that were collected by each community even when, for one reason or other, it was impossible to forward them, so that we read repeatedly about such voluntary taxes having accumulated during the years.[20] They were called "the fixed charge" or "the fifth," a term identical with the one for contributions made to Muslim sectarian chiefs.[21] The letters often emphasize that donations to the yeshiva were as meritorious as those made to the Temple of Jerusalem. Indeed, one gets the impression that a very ancient custom persisted in these yearly consignments. In addition, special collections were made in the communities from time to time.[22]

Private generosity was another, and perhaps no less important, source of income for the yeshivas. In times of danger or distress, as well as on festive occasions such as holidays or family celebrations, vows of donations for the houses of learning were pronounced, and bequests were sometimes conferred upon them. Finally, it was customary to stipulate fines not for the benefit of one of the parties to the contract, but for pious purposes, including the maintenance of the yeshivas.

The Geniza also provides us with considerable information regarding the aid given to the Palestinian academy, first while it had its seat in Jerusalem and then after it had moved to Cairo in 1127. Gifts were made not only to the institution as such, but in addition to its more prominent members individually. They consisted not only of cash, but also of precious robes and other textiles, of Oriental spices and other goods that could easily be converted into money. Letters of thanks have been preserved from which we learn that these presents were sent regularly. It was also expected that each community would address the yeshiva at least once a year. In the early days of their rule over Egypt the Fatimid caliphs granted substantial stipends to the Gaons of Jerusalem. Joshiah Gaon, referring to the changed attitude of al-Ḥākim, writes around 1013: "At the time we derived our livelihood from the government we did not trouble you with requests."[23]

The comparatively strong control exercised by the academies over even remote communities is to be explained by the fact that many local leaders had themselves pursued their postgraduate studies there and their loyalty to their alma mater was like that of modern alumni. Some, or perhaps the majority, of the students had benefited from the academy's funds. The following incident may illustrate the situation. A scholar from Egypt on his way to Baghdad, where he intended to continue his studies, was detained in Mosul. He had sent "a student and servant" of his to the Iraqian capital to determine whether it was safe for him to enter it, but meanwhile he had run short of cash. The Gaon answers: Had he known of the writer's intention to come, he would have borne the cost of his entire journey, and, of course, his sojourn in Baghdad would be at the expense of the yeshiva.[24]

Most of the letters of the Gaons conclude with the admonition that the addressees should submit all their queries to the academy. This standing request had a double purpose. It was intended to assert the prerogative of the yeshiva as the highest authority in all dogmatic, ritual, and legal matters, and it also served as a reminder to the local scholars to keep up with their studies. The teaching method in the yeshiva required the student's preparation of a given text, on the basis of which he was expected to ask questions to be discussed in the assembly of the scholars. Since study was not confined to school, but was obligatory for one's lifetime, the method pursued orally in the yeshiva was later on continued in writing. Many of the questions to the Gaons which have come down to us are entirely theoretical. They were prompted by the zeal of study, not by the need for the clarification of actual cases.

Still, a large share of the questions submitted to the yeshivas was concerned with practical problems, ritual, legal, dogmatic, and communal. These queries were discussed by the member scholars, but, as far as we know, unlike the yeshivas in Hellenistic and Roman times, neither the half-yearly conventions of the Babylonian schools, nor the autumnal assemblies on the Mount of Olives or other meetings of the Jerusalem yeshiva took formal votes. The Gaons certainly had to give consideration to the opinions of the other members of the academy and occasionally referred to them. Their responsa, or answers, were styled in the form of personal, authoritative statements, however, and sometimes heavenly inspiration was claimed ("Thus I was shown from Heaven"). Occasionally, the second in rank, the president of the court, would sign for the Gaon,[25] or (in Jerusalem) a reply would be issued by the Gaon and the "Third" jointly (the president of the Jewish high court of Palestine had his seat in Ramle, the administrative center of the country).[26] But such cases were exceptional and noted as such. Any scholar of recognized standing could be approached for a legal opinion and the same case could be submitted to several experts, but their responsa were personal judgments, not official resolutions.[27]

The Gaons would insist on the strict execution of their decisions, if necessary with the help of the Muslim government. We find such a statement even in a letter to Egypt by the Babylonian Gaon Samuel b. Eli (in office 1164-1193) written at a time when Egypt had its own Gaon.[28] It seems, too, that the various boards of the academy, which consisted of three, seven, or ten members, had only consultative and administrative functions, but the ultimate decisions rested with the head of the school. A settlement made in the Palestinian yeshiva in 1042, according to which all decisions had to be made by a committee of five, seems to have been exceptional. Referring to it, Solomon b. Judah, the Gaon affected, writes: "I have only the name, but not the power, of my office."[29] The Gaon promoted or demoted the members of the academy and could expel undesirable elements altogether.[30] He vigorously interfered in the internal affairs of the communities under his control, upholding the authority of the leaders appointed by him (but admonishing them not to misuse their position) and restricting their opponents, if necessary, by outright excommunication. We have numerous examples for this in the letters of various Palestinian Gaons, in particular in those of Solomon b. Judah, who died in 1051 after having been in office for at least twenty-five years. About a hundred of his epistles have been preserved, completely or in part, and have attracted the attention of the scholars from the very outset of Geniza research. Yet, a good number of them are still unpublished. It would be erroneous to ascribe these close connections between the Gaon of Jerusalem and the Egyptian congregations simply to geographical proximity and to the fact that Palestine and Egypt formed parts of the Fatimid empire. As the rich correspondence from Qayrawān shows, the Gaons of Baghdad insisted strongly on asserting their authority in a remote country like Tunisia, which was separated from them by more than one political boundary.

The Gaons were not elected as a rule, but followed each other according to a complicated system of precedence, the president of the High Court attached to the yeshiva normally being the successor designate. Scions of a number of gaonic families would accede to the office after having served for many years in other capacities. Sometimes, especially in Iraq, meritorious scholars, hailing from as far away as Spain or Morocco, or even a provincial town in Tunisia, would be elevated to the rank of Gaon.[31] Naṭrōnay of the Sura yeshiva succeeded his father more than fifty years after his parent's death and after eight other Gaons had "ruled" (the term used in the sources) in between. Despite his short term of office (853-858) he has left a large number of responsa, some of which are of lasting importance. Dōsā, the son of the great Saadya, had to wait seventy-one years until his turn came; he still managed to be in office for four years and was able to report about his good health to his admirers in Qayrawān.[32] In Palestine, in 1063, Elijah ha-Kohen b. Solomon followed his father after an interval of almost forty years, while we find him signing documents as "Sixth" in 1037 and as "Fourth" in 1045; he was "Third" in 1051 and became president of the High Court some years later. In order to insure smooth transition, the incumbent Gaon and his son would mention the Gaon designate, *me 'uttād,* in public prayer by this title, a practice also followed by Solomon b. Judah (and his son Abraham) for his rival and successor Daniel b. Azarya.[33]

The Gaons seem to have groomed their sons for succession by making them clerks (scribes) of the yeshiva, a capacity in which the young men trained themselves in formulating responsa and also had opportunity to correspond with all the leaders and scholars of the communities connected with their fathers. They thus became known to everyone who counted and could also prove their mettle within the yeshiva itself. Evyatar, the son of the Palestinian Gaon Elijah ha-Kohen just mentioned and later himself a prominent Gaon, wrote letters for his father while still only "Fourth" and, in the same capacity, signed a responsum together with him which was sent from Jerusalem to Mayence (Mainz) in Germany. Abraham, a son of the Gaon Solomon b. Judah, represented his old father both in letters, many of which have been preserved, and as a personal emissary to the communities of Egypt and Syria, but, as far as our sources go, never advanced to more than "Fourth."[34] Samuel b. Ḥofnī, whose responsum on the nature of a religious democracy is rendered above (p. 4), appointed his son Israel officially as clerk of the Sura yeshiva and mentioned him as such in his correspondence. Israel added greetings in his own name to letters sent by his (then very old) father in 1004 and 1008, but succeeded him as Gaon only in 1017, the octogenarian Dōsā b. Saadya holding office in between.[35] A special case was Hay, who for many years signed responsa jointly with his equally eminent father Sherira (whose history of Jewish learning, originally a responsum sent to Qayrawān, forms the basis of our knowledge of the Babylonian schools). Hay was president of the High Court and Gaon designate; as such he acted for his father, who like himself reached a very old age (both died in their late nineties). As far as we know, Hay was also the only Gaon who attained office immediately after the death of his father.

The elaborate system of succession did not always work smoothly. Literary sources, as well as the Geniza records, show that sometimes vigorous contests were fought over the gaonate when a vacancy occurred and occasionally even against an incumbent Gaon. These contests, albeit sometimes unsavory, with bans and counterbans pronounced and other undignified measures taken, acted in general as a wholesome counterbalance to family rule and clerical despotism.

The scales were often tipped by the lay leaders or by the community at large, whose influence was as pronounced in the Synagogue as in the Eastern Church. When the pilgrims from all over the Jewish world, assembled on the Mount of Olives east of Jerusalem in September, 1038, were dissatisfied with the handling of communal affairs by the old Gaon Solomon b. Judah, "they passed to the mansion of the Shuway' family, took a Torah scroll and prayed over Nathan b. Abraham as Gaon. The subsequent Saturday they assembled in Ramle in Nathan's Hall [where he used to officiate as supreme judge], with no one remaining in the synagogues [which were under the jurisdiction of Solomon] and asked Nathan to deliver the sermon and to expound the Scripture [the prerogative of the Gaon]."[36] The agreement of 1042, reached in the Palestinian academy after this contest between the two Gaons (see n. 29), was made in the name of "the academy and the elders of the community." In a complaint submitted to the caliph al-Mustanṣir during the communal strife, one party, styling itself "the Rabbanite Jews," stated that the governor of Ramle had no right to coerce them to follow a Gaon whom they had not "chosen" and with whom they were not "satisfied." After his reinstitution, Solomon b. Judah, the Gaon involved, declared that he owed his office neither to family connections nor to his own wisdom or riches (all of which he professed not to possess), but solely to "the will of God and the people."[37]

Since the Gaon had judicial and administrative authority over the Jewish community, it is natural that the government reserved itself the right to confirm him in his office. When al-Ẓāhir, the fourth Fatimid ruler of Egypt (1021-1036), ascended the throne, a Gaon of Jerusalem asked his friends in Fustat to obtain for him a letter of installment; the diplomas issued by the preceding three caliphs were still in the possession of the yeshiva. A fragmentary, but highly interesting, Geniza document in Arabic characters, which was aimed at securing such a letter of installment from the Fatimid government, serves to conclude this survey. The details preserved give a fairly complete idea of the Gaon's competence: (1) The Gaon has jurisdiction over only the Rabbanite persuasion (to the exclusion of the Karaites and Samaritans). (2) He is the highest authority on religious law and is entitled to expound it in public lectures. (3) In particular, he supervises all matters of marriage and divorce. (4) He is the guardian of the religious and moral conduct of all the members of the community. (5) He has the right to impose or to cancel an excommunication. (6) He appoints and dismisses preachers, cantors, and religious slaughterers. (7) He (appoints and) defines the competence of judges and supervises them as well as the trustees of the courts (who were in charge of the property of orphans or litigants confided to them). (8) His official title is *ra's al-mathība,* head of the academy, and his son has certain prerogatives. (9) The Rabbanite community owes obedience to his legal decisions, as well as to his administrative dispositions. (10) He may delegate his authority over a certain city or country to any person chosen by him.[38]

While the gaonate was a force that penetrated the whole fabric of life of the Jewish community during the Geniza period, the secular head of the Jews, the so-called "head of the Diaspora," whose seat was in Baghdad, had only limited importance. Under Roman and Persian rules, respectively, a patriarch acted in Palestine as the representative of the Jews, and an exilarch, or "head of the Diaspora" performed the same function in Babylonia. Both derived their lineage from King David. The former office was abolished by the Byzantine emperors early in the fifth century, but the dignity of the Babylonian exilarch continued to exist and even attained new splendor under the caliphs. The Muslims, like the Jews and Christians before them, regarded David, the reputed author of the Book of Psalms, as one of the great prophets, and, with their respect for lineage, ranked the scions of such an ancient and noble line very highly, according to one reference, even above the catholicus, or head of the very important Nestorian Church. By the time of the Geniza records, however, the rule of the caliphs themselves had become confined to a few districts in Iraq—as far as they ruled at all—while the homage paid to them by Muslim rulers was of a purely honorary character. Similarly, the head of the Diaspora exercised direct control over only a part of the Jewish communities in the lands of the Eastern caliphate, whereas in the countries represented in the Geniza, the territorial Jewish leaders accepted his "suzerainty," if at all, only as a matter of form. As far as they were concerned, dispensing of honorific titles seems to have been his main function.[39]

In this period of the preponderance of the yeshivas an exilarch could attain ecumenical status only when he was a scholar of rank or took over outrightly the presidency of a yeshiva himself. This happened, for example, when, in 1038, after the demise of the great Hay, the exilarch Hezekiah b. David was chosen as his successor. As far as we are able to judge from his letters, Hezekiah did not assume the title of Gaon, but acted as one, since he answered questions of religious law and exhorted his correspondents to submit their queries to and to support the scholars attached to him.[40] In 1120 we again find an exilarch at the head of a school.[41] Of particular interest is the patent of confirmation issued in 1161 by the exilarch of Baghdad Daniel b. Ḥisday for the Egyptian Gaon Nethanel ha-Levi. The lengthy document has acquired some renown because it was restored from three fragments preserved in New York, Cambridge (England), and Leningrad.[42] The confirmation had been sought by the head of the school in Cairo, because there existed a certain rivalry between him and the Gaon in Damascus as to who was the true successor to the Palestinian Gaon. (Jerusalem was occupied at that time by the Crusaders.) In the letter of confirmation, the exilarch presented his own credentials at length by stating that he had covered the whole field of talmudic studies then usually pursued and by emphasizing that, on God's command, he had established a "high yeshiva" himself. Clearly, in propping up the authority of the Egyptian Gaon he had first to prove his own competence. It should be noted that documents issued in Fustat around 1090 in the name of the "High Court of the Rēsh Gālūthā" refer not to the exilarch of Baghdad but to David b. Daniel b. Azarya, who is soon to be discussed.[43] The same holds true of a letter from Ascalon, Palestine, mentioning, inter alia, instructions given by the Rōsh ha-Gōlā (the Hebrew form of the title) to an official of the synagogue in that city.[44]

It is hardly necessary to mention that the office of the exilarch was occasionally hotly contested among various members of the House of David. Since the caliph reserved for himself the right to confirm the appointment, it is natural that the Jewish courtiers and higher government officials had a say in the matter. To such occurrences known thus far the following might be added, one from February, 1069, a time for which we have very little information about the exilarchate. A Muslim scholar, whose autograph diary has come down to us, makes the following entry during that month: "Dissension has risen to its highest point among the Jews; they wanted to appoint one particular man among the sons of David, but Ibn Faḍlān opposed them and wished to seat another one; they are still disputing about that." The notable referred to, Abū 'Alī II Ibn Faḍlān (who should not be confounded with his namesake and presumable grandfather who was involved in events of the year 998), was the senior Jewish government officer at that time. When a Muslim fanatic induced the caliph to stop the work of the non-Muslim officials in 1058, Ibn Faḍlān and his Christian counterpart were ordered to stay home together with their coreligionist underlings. But soon the government needed their services again. This explains why in 1069 we find Ibn Faḍlān having decisive influence on the election of an exilarch.[45]

The family of the exilarchs, which had been prominent for so long a time, was large and ramified and it is not surprising that some of its more ambitious members should have tried to make capital of their dignity as "princes of the House of David" (Heb. *nāsī*). We find them everywhere, often trying to assume authority, even in faraway Yemen.[46] In 1051, one particularly gifted Davidite, Daniel b. Azarya, became head of the Palestinian academy, and a few decades later his son David tried to establish an exilarchate in Egypt, extending over the whole Fatimid empire. It is characteristic of this state of affairs that Daniel b. Azarya himself, in a pastoral letter, emphasizes that no member of the House of David, and not even of his own household at that, was authorized to hold any public office except when appoint by himself.[47] In official documents written in Fustat in 1088 and the subsequent years, David b. Daniel was entitled "the great nāsī, the nāsi of all [the diasporas of] Israel." [48]

By the end of the twelfth century we find nāsīs in Cairo, Alexandria, and the Egyptian countryside. Others had their seat in Damascus, Aleppo, and Mosul. Members of the Mosul branch resided temporarily in Egypt, and a number of their letters have been preserved. Their doyen, Solomon b. Yīshay (Jesse), appearing in documents and letters written in and around 1237, had no official standing in the Jewish community of Egypt, but, being a scholar and much sought after preacher, he was influential and was addressed by the same titles as the exilarch David b. Daniel one hundred and fifty years before him.[49] Although sometimes receiving emoluments from the community, the nāsīs were of no real consequence, except when they were scholarly persons of renown. Their role may be compared with that of the Alids, or descendants of the Prophet Muhammad, in the contemporary Muslim society.

Thus, the Jewish community, as it appears to us through the Geniza, had more than one communal authority, and these authorities were dependent on their followers in different ways. The allegiance of a congregation to a Gaon and other leaders was expressed in a public prayer for their welfare inserted into the service. These prayers were by no means mere formularies, but contained specific references, for example, to the Gaon's family or to his foes.[50] The dispensing with this prayer indicated a break. As is well known, the Church, and later on Islam, followed a similar procedure. When a Coptic priest ceased mentioning the patriarch's name at the Holy Eucharist, he demonstrated that he no longer recognized him as legitimately installed.[51] The Muslim Friday service was the occasion for making a city's loyalties known. The yeshivas, on their side, held public prayers for the welfare of dedicated community leaders at the holy places in Jerusalem or the sacred shrines in Babylonia. These prayers, too, had a "political" connotation, as they indicated who was regarded as the legitimate local representative of the Gaon. Moreover, at these prayers, any person included was mentioned by his official or honorary title or titles, conferred upon him by the yeshiva. The public prayer was thus the occasion for the formal conveyance of honors or privileges. "We prayed for him as a member" in an Arabic letter from the beginning of the eleventh century means that the person was officially recognized as a member of the yeshiva, and, as such, was qualified to serve as the spiritual (and temporal) leader of a local community.[52]

Besides the synagogue service, there were many other occasions for the expression of allegiance to an ecumenical or territorial authority. At a public lecture it was customary for the lecturer to open with an exordium in which he would "take permission" from the authority to which he owed loyalty, the idea being that only the latter had the right to give an authoritative explanation of the Holy Scriptures. At weddings and banquets, a similar symbolic request for permission to say grace was pronounced, since the Gaon, if present, would have been honored to say the benediction concluding a feast.[53] Finally, scores of documents have been found bearing the remark that they were written in the name of the leader, or leaders (such as "the Gate" [the court] of the yeshiva) to whom communal allegiance was due, for the judges or other persons issuing the documents were regarded as deputies of the man or institution in power at the time. The common term for all these various expressions of loyalty—whether in the synagogue, at a banquet, or in the courtroom—was *reshūth,* literally, "taking permission."

Of the many hundreds of documents bearing such an authorization the most impressive is perhaps the bill of manumission given on Monday, October 17, 1132, to the slave girl Ashū in the city of Mangalore on the Malabar coast of India. Her former proprietor (and, I suspect, later husband) Abraham Yijū, a Tunisian merchant, industrialist, scholar, and poet, who has left about eighty items of his in the Geniza, wrote this document in his own exquisite hand, introducing it thus: "In the city of Mangalore . . . , the royal city, which is situated on the Great Sea and which is under the jurisdiction of our Lord Daniel, the great prince, the head of the Diaspora of all Israel, the son of our lord Ḥisday, the great prince . . . , and also under the jurisdiction of our Gaon Maṣlīaḥ ha-Kohen, the head of the yeshiva Ge' ōn Ya 'aqōv [the Palestinian academy], the son of Solomon, the head of the yeshiva . . . ." A Jewish court in India thus issues in 1132 a document for a local girl and a merchant from Tunisia in the name of the exilarch of Baghdad and of the Palestinian Gaon, who, at that time, had his seat in Cairo. To make the geographical diversity complete: the deed is preserved today in the Institute of the Peoples of Asia in Leningrad.[54]

Incidentally, such references to the personalities or institutions under whose authority a document was issued are our main source for the chronology of Jewish history under Islam during the High Middle Ages.[55]

The double loyalty expressed in the Mangalore document reflected practical considerations: The Jewish merchant colonies on the west coast of India originated partly in Iraq and Iran and partly in the countries of the Mediterranean basin. Therefore, the documents issued by their courts had to pay homage to the Jewish authorities predominant in each of these two areas. The same was true of the Jews of Yemen, who, since olden times, had been in closest contact with the Iraqian yeshivoth, but became, in the wake of the lively India trade, even more attached to their coreligionists in Egypt and the countries adjacent to it. From Aden in the south to Sa 'da in the north public prayers used to be said over the exilarch of Baghdad and Gaon Maṣlīaḥ of Cairo. The harmony was disrupted when an ambitious relative of the head of the Diaspora arrived in Aden in 1134 and claimed exclusive authority for the exilarch (and himself, of course, as the latter's local representative).[56]

The Aden controversy of 1134, which is reflected in several Geniza documents, shows that the custom of "taking permission," while conducive in general to communal cohesiveness, was apt to lead to confusion in times of discord. Therefore, there were congregations that tried to do away with these time-honored symbols of unity altogether. The Geniza contains much material about this contest for and against the reshūth. After the death of Moses Maimonides, his son Abraham attained the leadership of the Jews of Egypt at a very tender age, whereupon he met with strong opposition. Many people stayed away from the synagogues and opened private prayer assemblies because they objected to the reshūth pronounced in his name. In order to restore peace, a statute was adopted, to be valid for thirty years, abolishing the custom of reshūth and excommunicating anyone establishing a private place of prayer.[57] This statute must have been rescinded not long after its adoption, for less than ten years after the death of Moses Maimonides we find his son Abraham regularly referred to as the head of the community in the preambles to legal documents and this remained the case with regard to his descendants and successors throughout the thirteenth and fourteenth centuries. The lesser the importance of these leaders became, the more bombastic grew the honorific epithets heaped on them. In this late period, nine lines of titles were nothing exceptional in a reshūth preceding an ordinary legal document.[58] Another aspect of this custom is discussed in the section on life in the synagogue (chap. v, sec. D, 2).

Even a cursory reading of the correspondence of the Gaons reveals the diocesan organization of the Jewish community. The official title title of Ephraim b. Shemarya, so often mentioned in these pages, was "permanent court [i.e., judge] for Fustat and all its districts."[59] The Gaons always insisted that all contributions be sent to them through an acknowledged leader in charge of a district or a country, that all letters to the yeshiva likewise be forwarded solely through him, and that he be revered and honored and his instructions followed without wavering. In the letters to south Arabia, referred to above (p. 11), places hundreds of miles nearer Baghdad than San 'a, the capital of Yemen, were advised to send their donations and letters solely through the judges (the biblical word *shōfēṭ* is used) in that city. In a letter to another Oriental community, dated 1152, a local dignitary, who himself had been in charge of a smaller district, is reinstated and the ban on him lifted, after he had consented to submit to the authority of the *allūf* (as a distinguished member of the Babylonian yeshiva was called) in command of the diocese concerned.[60] The queries addressed to the yeshiva even by prominent local scholars were scrutinized and screened by the district authority before being forwarded to their final destination.

Two letters written by a ḥāvēr, or member of the Palestinian academy, who headed communities in northern Syria, strikingly illustrate the manifold duties incumbent on a district authority. He appointed local judges and other community officials, dealt with all public affairs, both internal and external, and acted himself as a judge and a religious leader, and he had to collect all the dues of the yeshiva. He was not a local man, but had come to the place with his family by sea (most probably from a port in Palestine to one in northern Syria).[61]

These functions were not always combined in one person. As the example of Qayrawān, about which we are particularly well informed, shows, the district representation of a yeshiva could be tripartite: a public figure, usually connected with the government, whose influence was strong enough to ensure generous donations and to watch over the proper conduct of communal affairs; a treasurer, who did the actual collecting and forwarding of the sums donated; and a prominent scholar, who presided over the local court and conducted, also partly supervised, the legal and religious (as differing from the business) correspondence with the yeshiva.[62]

The question whether this diocesan organization developed spontaneously, whether it was influenced by the model of the Church, or whether it went back to an ancient, pre-Christian trait of Jewish community life, lies outside the scope of this book.[63] It stands to reason, however, that the development of the institution of territorial heads of the Jewish communities discussed in the following section, grew at least partly out of the diocesan organization of the gaonate.

2. *The Territorial Heads of the Jewish Community. The Nagid*

There is hardly a public institution about which the Geniza has provided so much new material as that of the heads of the Jewish community in the Fatimid and Ayyubid kingdoms. There is also hardly one that has been so thoroughly misrepresented by modern historical research.

The reason for this deficiency is to be sought in the fact that the dignity of Nagid (pronounced *nagheed*), as the territorial head of the Jewish community was called in Hebrew, was described by the Jewish authors of the sixteenth and seventeenth centuries in terms suited to the period immediately preceding its abolition in 1517. Their accounts were corroborated by those of Muslim authors writing in late Mamluk times. This double testimony was so impressive that most historians dealing with the subject were inclined to interpret the new material emerging from the Cairo Geniza in the light of the later developments reflected in the literary sources. Characteristic in this respect is this statement of Jacob Mann, the greatest authority on Geniza research: "From the Fatimid regime (969) to the conquest of the country by the Turks (1517) Egyptian Jewry was strongly organized under the Nagid, who was the chief of the Rabbanites, Karaites and Samaritans alike, recognized by the government as Ra'īs al-Yahūd." [1]

In reality the situation was far more complicated. The title "Nagid" does not appear in Egypt until about 1065, almost a hundred years after the Fatimid conquest, and it was not in continuous use even after its inception. Only from the beginning of the thirteenth century did the Hebrew title "Nagid" become permanently attached to that of Ra'īs al-Yahūd, "The head of the Jews." In general, we have to distinguish between the title and the office, and, as far as the office is concerned, we have to keep in mind that the combination of the task of representing the Jewish community before the government with that of exercising its highest legal and religious authority developed in Egypt under very specific historical circumstances. Disregard of these considerations led to the confusion still prevailing in Jewish historiography about this most important institution.[2]

Nagid is a biblical word, usually translated as prince or leader. As title, it is an abbreviation of such high-sounding phrases as "Prince of the Diaspora," "Prince of the People of the Lord [or: of Israel]," or "Prince of Princes."[3] As far as we are able to see, the first to have borne this title was Abraham b. 'Aṭā', physician in attendance to Bādis and his son al-Mu'izz, the rulers of Tunisia and some adjacent territories, during the first half of the eleventh century.[4] Abraham b. 'Aṭā' used his influential position to protect his coreligionists in a period that witnessed a general increase in fanaticism and disorders in that country. Moreover, he was a staunch supporter of the Jewish seats of learning in Baghdad, in particular of their great leader, Hay Gaon (d. 1038), and in recognition of his many merits Hay conferred on him, in spring 1015, the title Nagid. Abraham's father, 'Aṭā', or Nathan (both mean "gift," the first in Arabic, the second in Hebrew), already had occupied a similar position of communal leader, but with the more modest, and more widely used, title "head of the congregations."[5] The title Nagid was not entirely new, it had already been given by an Iraqi yeshiva to a prominent lay member (who was, however, of a family of Gaons) around 900. It was common practice that titles borne first by dignitaries of, or connected with, the academies of Baghdad or Jerusalem, were later on bestowed also on meritorious persons abroad.[6] Thus the title "Prince of the Diaspora" as designation for the leader of the Jewish community of a country, was by no means created in opposition to the office of the exilarch, the "head of the Diaspora," but grew organically from the way in which the yeshivas were used to confer honorary epithets.[7]

Ibn 'Aṭā's successor, Jacob b. Amram, is called in a legal document, written in Fustat, 1041–1042, "Prince of the Diaspora," but is simply addressed as "the Nagid" in letters, even official letters addressed to him from the community of Palermo, Sicily, or from the exilarch of Baghdad.[8] His activities, as known to us through various Geniza letters, resemble in many respects those of the Egyptian Nagids at their height, known to us from later times. He was a powerful protector of his flock, a stern keeper of law and morals in the community, an administrator of justice whose impartiality was famous, and a shield for the weak. The scholars ate "at his tables" and were honored by him with embroidered silk robes (the embroidery probably contained the

Nagid's name—like the robes of honor bestowed by Muslim rulers or by the Jewish exilarchs in Babylonia in pre-Islamic times).[9] He personally attended to the lawsuits between prominent members of the community, trying to bring about reconciliation, while the rabbinical courts dealt with the strictly juridical issues of the cases. Unlike Egypt, however, which had good, but not outstanding, Jewish scholars, the Nagids of Qayrawān are mentioned in both documents and letters always after such towering figures of rabbinical scholarship as Hananel b. Hushiel or Jacob b. Nissim. Clearly, they never represented the highest religious and legal authority of the Jews of Tunisia.

It is not excluded that Jacob b. Amram's family was of European origin (just like that of Hushiel). For in one Geniza letter we read that instead of making the annual appeal for the academy of Jerusalem, the Nagid arranged for a big collection for a Rūmī relative who had been robbed while traveling between Salerno and Bari in southern Italy. (The letter assures us that the Jerusalem appeal was carried through anyway, albeit belatedly.)[10] Around 1060, when the Nagid had fallen into disgrace with the ruler and had to quit the country he lived "beyond the sea," west or north of Tunisia. This could have been Muslim Spain, but also Christian Europe. The Tunisian merchants in Egypt kept their allegiance to him, organized a levy for the exile (but the money was lost in shipwreck), and paid heed to his instructions. But in Tunisia the office of Nagid had come to an end. It had a short sequel in Sicily, when the western part of the island was dominated by Ayyūb, the son of Tamīm, the Zīrid ruler of Tunisia (ca. 1064). "He appointed Zakkār b. 'Ammār as Nagid over the Jews . . . because he administered also most of his own affairs." [11]

Samuel Ibn Nagrela, the Jewish vizier of Granada, Spain, received the title Nagid in or around 1027 (most probably also from Hay Gaon). It became part of his proper name in his lifetime; he is known in Jewish history and Hebrew literature simply as Samuel ha-Nagid.[12] With his son Joseph (or, rather, Yehōsēf), who was killed in 1066, the title lapsed in Spain, as it did simultaneously in Tunisia.[13]

At exactly the same time the title makes its appearance in Egypt, where it was held by the scholar and court physician Judah b. Saadya, his more prominent brother Mevōrākh, and the latter's son Moses.[14] The latest document referring to Mevōrākh as Nagid is dated 1111, and a private letter reports that he died on March 30, 1112. The documents issued under the authority of his son range from March, 1115, to December, 1124.[15] Besides these three men, whose terms of service covered (with interruptions) a period of about fifty years, we know of only one [16] other Nagid in Fatimid times, the illustrious Samuel b. Hananya (1140–1159), who is sometimes confused with his still more famous Spanish namesake. His predecessor in the leadership of the Jews of Egypt, the Palestinian Gaon Maṣlīaḥ (1127–1139), and his successors, the Gaons Nethanel and Sar Shalom, were, as their title implies, heads of schools. The long-standing controversy, whether Maimonides (arrived in Egypt around 1165, died 1204) was Nagid or not, is entirely futile. There is no doubt that he was appointed by the government at some time as "head of the Jews," but he never bore the title Nagid, most probably because he did not care to and because no one was willing to confer it on him.[17] He was followed by his son Abraham in his office as Ra'īs, who, in documents from December, 1213, is regularly styled Nagid.[18] We can only surmise the reason for this change. Abraham was embarrassingly young when he took office, and met with much opposition, particularly with regard to his pietistic and ascetic reforms. Perhaps the title was secured for him by his partisans in order to strengthen his position. In any case, the abundant wealth of Geniza material from his period enables us to observe how it became absolutely de rigueur to issue a legal document in any part of Egypt as under the authority of the Nagid. Since Abraham Maimonides was followed by at least four [19] Nagids from his offspring during a period of over 170 years, it is natural that the title became identified with the office, and as such passed into literary usage.

Sporadically, and specified by the name of the country for which they were responsible, Nagids were found also in Yemen on the one hand, and in Syria and Palestine on the other. While the Geniza has preserved rich information about the former, we know hardly more than the names of the latter. It is therefore premature to surmise under which circumstances the Syro-Palestinian version of the dignity came into being and of what type it was. As for Yemen, our sources are indicative enough. Owing to the growing importance of the India trade, the Jewish representative of the merchants in Aden became a powerful figure in those parts. One of them, Maḍmūn b. Japheth b. Bundār, was honored by the head of the Diaspora of Baghdad with the title "Prince of the Land of Yemen," which after his death in 1151 was bestowed also on his son Ḥalfōn (d. 1172) . A tombstone of a Nagid Ḥalfōn, son of a Nagid Maḍmūn (presumably their descendants) bears the date August, 1248. They were preceded by a Shemarya b. David, a maecenas of poets and scholars (Hebrew Shemarya has the same meaning as Arabic Maḍmūn: "Protected by God"). The series of Yemenite Nagids concludes with David b. Amram, the author of the Great Midrash, the most renowned piece of Yemenite Jewish scholarship.[20]

Thus, we see that as far as the Fatimid and early Ayyubid periods are concerned the leadership of the Jewish territorial communities was by no means confined to persons bearing the title Nagid. There is no need to repeat here the passages dealing with the office of the Ra'īs al-Yahūd, or "head of the Jews," in the late Muslim handbooks of administration, for most of these passages are available, conveniently collected, in an English translation.[21]

The office of the Ra'īs (or Rayyis, as the word is spelled in the Geniza records) is described by the Muslim scholars of the fourteenth and fifteenth centuries as corresponding to that of the patriarch of the Christians. He was to be selected from the Rabbanite majority, but was to represent the minority groups of the Karaites and Samaritans as well.[22] His function was to "join the Jews together and to prevent their separation" and to serve them as legal authority and judge in conformity with their laws and customs. In particular he had to watch over the proper procedures in matters of marriage and divorce as well as of excommunication. He was responsible for law and order in the community, and also for the observation of the restrictions imposed by the Islamic state on its non-Muslim subjects. The wearing of discriminatory badges and the prohibition of the erection of new houses of worship are especially emphasized. The Rayyis was to be pious and learned and a man of absolute integrity. He was expected to be able to expound the Hebrew Scriptures and was entitled to do so in whatever synagogue he chose. He was appointed by the government after the community had agreed upon the candidate acceptable to it.

In this section I explore how far the reality revealed in the Geniza records corresponds to the description summarized above and when and under what circumstances this specific brand of the office of the Rayyis came into being.

Almost all the modern historians who have discussed this office seem to assume that it was created by the Muslim successor states in order to make the Jewish communities incorporated in them independent of authorities outside their own jurisdiction. According to this theory the Fatimids did not want their Jewish subjects paying allegiance to the "head of the Diaspora" in Sunnite Baghdad, and when Tunisia was on the way to breaking away from the Fatimids, a separate Nagid was immediately installed there. Such assumptions are in conformity with the modern idea of a state but disregard the medieval deference to supraterritorial communities based on religion. No Muslim source known to the present writer supports these assumptions, while the facts reflected in the Geniza records point to the contrary conclusion. The strongest bonds of cooperation existed between the Jews living within the borders of the Fatimid empire and the Jewish academies of Baghdad, and as far as we have documents about the appointment of the heads of the community in Egypt, we see that they were installed by and received honorary titles from the head of the Diaspora who had his seat in Iraq and even more from the yeshivas there. The origin of the office of the Nagid, like that of the Christian patriarchs with which it was compared by the Muslim authors, is to be sought in developments taking place inside the community that it represented. While saying this, I am not unaware of the fact (alluded to on the first page of this chapter) that everywhere, even in a small town, the Muslim authorities found it convenient to recognize a prominent member of a "protected" community as its responsible representative. But this was simply a requirement of administrative expediency, not a question of "independence from Baghdad."

The Jewish Diaspora was led by the yeshivas of Palestine and Iraq and organized in territorial units which may be characterized briefly as dioceses. Egypt was no exception. The first man in charge of Jewish communal affairs there, mentioned in the Geniza documents after the Fatimid conquest, was a ḥāvēr, or member, of the Palestinian academy.[23] He was succeeded by Shemarya b. Elhanan, a prominent scholar who had been a high-ranking official of the Babylonian academy and was styled "president of the High Court of all Israel." [24] Despite his allegiance to the Babylonian yeshiva he was in charge also of the Palestinian community in the Egyptian capital. As founder of a rabbinical college in Old Cairo he won fame from Spain to Iraq and was hailed in poems in his honor as the leader of his time. Like his father, he was *rāv rōsh,* which should not be translated as "chief rabbi," but "grand mufti," meaning that he was the highest-ranking scholar in the country authorized to give legal opinions. Shortly after his death the funeral of a popular cantor on December 31, 1011, was the occasion for an extraordinary occurrence. A large crowd had turned out to pay him the last honor. This obviously aroused the ire of the Muslim mobs. It was a time when the persecution of the Christians, instigated by the Fatimid caliph al-Ḥākim a few years before, had reached its height and had whetted the appetite of mischief-makers. The funeral cortege was attacked, its participants were beaten and robbed, and twenty-three of the more prominent members of the community were thrown into prison and condemned to death by both the qadi and the governor of the city. But the caliph intervened unexpectedly (al-Ḥākim loved to do the unexpected). The imprisoned were dismissed and strong warnings were sent to the stations of the government post and to the Muslim population of Alexandria and other towns to refrain from any acts of violence against the Jews. This event appeared to those affected to be caused by a miraculous heavenly intervention and was commemorated in a Hebrew scroll, of which several copies have been preserved. Had there been in existence at that time any official Jewish leader in addition to the recently deceased Shemarya, he would have acted in that situation of dire predicament, or his absence had to be explained. But there was none.[25]

Shemarya was succeeded by his son Elhanan both as head of the Old Cairene school and as leader of the Egyptian Jews. In the first capacity he was called "head of the scholars of all Israel," that is, high-ranking member of the Babylonian academy with full juridical powers in his diocese, and in the second, "The elder of the Diaspora."[26] Like his father he was also recognized by the Palestinian community of Old Cairo and handled the legal cases in provincial towns as well.[27] Collections were taken for his college in Damascus and in Acre, Palestine, most probably in the Babylonian congregations there.[28] As long as the relations between the caliph and his non-Muslim subjects were normal, he, or rather his college, was also in receipt of a government grant, which shows that he had some official standing.[29]

For the period extending from Elhanan's death (ca. 1025) to the middle of the ten sixties, the Geniza is particularly rich in documents and letters dealing with public life. In none does there appear an official head of the Jews in the Fatimid empire.[30] The paramount authority is the yeshiva of Jerusalem, and, as long as the great Hay Gaon lived, also that of Baghdad. The Gaon appoints the higher community officials in Old Cairo and other towns and addresses even smaller places in matters concerning public affairs.[31] The chief judges of the Palestinians in Old Cairo during this period appear also as leaders of the Rabbanite Jews in general, and as heads of the whole Egyptian diocese. Letters from the Rīf seeking their guidance and help have been preserved,[32] and when a local leader writes to the ḥāvēr of Fustat that he and his congregation pray for him all the time, on Sabbaths and holidays, he means to say that he recognizes the ḥāvēr's seniority.[33] It is, however, the Gaon of Jerusalem who is responsible to the central government for the appointment of the Jewish judges following his rite in the Egyptian capital,[34] and it is he who upholds his own authority over the local officials against the heads of the Jewish community in Fustat.[35]

Quite a number of high-standing Jewish personalities used their influential position to protect or promote their brethren during this first century of Fatimid rule. It is perhaps worthy to note that the most prominent of them, Abū Sa'd al-Tustarī, who for some time wielded utmost power over the empire, was a member of the Karaite minority group. Nowhere is it stated that these powerful men had any official standing in the community. As far as our sources show, all legal authority was exercised in the name of the Gaons, or heads of the yeshivas.[36]

Things changed in the ten sixties when the Jerusalem yeshiva was much weakened by the rivalry between the nāsīs from the royal house of David, who had come from Iraq, and the priestly Gaons of Palestine. Moreover, in 1071 Jerusalem was conquered by the Seljuks, and the yeshiva had to move into exile, first to Tyre on the Lebanese coast and later on to Damascus. In these times of eclipse of the central Jewish authority there happened to be in Egypt a family that combined noble descent and a tradition of scholarship and piety with an influential position at court. The distinguished position of the brothers Judah and Mevōrākh, sons of Saadya, mentioned above, was expressed by their bearing the highest titles from the yeshivas of both Palestine and Babylonia; from around 1065, Judah, and some time after his death, Mevōrākh were honored also with the epithet Nagid. Their leadership was by no means undisputed. It was challenged by the same nāsī David b. Daniel who had claimed the gaonate in Jerusalem. By 1095, however, Mevōrākh was firmly established as the highest authority of the Jews in the Fatimid realm. He occupied this position uncontested until his death in a plague on March 30, 1112, and was succeeded by his son Moses without any opposition. Our sources expressly state that Mevōrākh was appointed by the government and show him in close cooperation with al-Malik al-Afḍal, the mighty viceroy and actual ruler. Many letters addressed to him and others emanating from his office reveal his manifold activities as communal leader, and numerous documents issued under his authority (instead of that of the yeshiva) have been preserved. In a letter addressed to him he is described as installed in his office by God. The nāsī (probably a Davidite living in Egypt) is quoted in it as declaring that no one except God was above the Nagid. Mevōrākh is to be regarded as the initiator of the office of the head of the Jews in its double function as representative of the Jewish community before the Fatimid government and as highest legal and religious authority for the Jews themselves, and as such he appeared to later generations.[37]

It would be entirely improper to assume that there had been Nagids of the type of Mevōrākh before him but that, by mere chance, they had left no traces. We possess an enormous number of letters and documents from the eleventh century—dated documents for practically every year from 1002. This material reveals to us, positively, how the community functioned, and negatively, that while the head of the Jews was duly mentioned as the highest religious authority in legal documents of the time of Mevōrākh and later, nothing of the kind appears in documents preceding him. Jewish historiography must finally be prepared to give up preconceived theories in the face of the facts disclosed to us by the Cairo Geniza.

From the time of Mevōrākh to the end of the classical Geniza period there is a constant flow of sources about the leadership of the Jews in Egypt and the adjacent countries. It is possible therefore to form a concrete idea about the nature and the scope of this office during that time.

On the subject of the appointment of a rayyis, it would be inconsistent with the spirit of the age to expect formal elections, followed immediately by an official installation by government. Things were far less formal and far more intricate. The rayyis had to seek support from three different sources: the Jewish local and territorial communities that would accept him as their leader; the Jewish ecumenical authorities who would acknowledge him and confer on him "a new name" and some additional honorary titles; and finally the government that was to confirm him officially in his position. The sequence in which these three were obtained depended entirely on the circumstances. Thus a usurper of the dignity of Nagid assures the Jewish public that he had been recognized by the head of the Diaspora, by the government, and subsequently also by the Gaon of Palestine. He clearly lacked the one most vital support, that of his community, which knew only too well his deficiencies.[38] The significant wish, "May God turn the hearts of all Israel to you," or similar phrases are to be found in letters to leaders whose authority was contested,[39] and at the inauguration of a Nagid who succeeded his father (as in the case of Moses b. Mevōrākh or David b. Abraham Maimonides) the biblical statement concerning King Solomon "and all Israel listened to him" was recited.[40] In the only known Muslim document of the installation of a Jewish community leader by the government during our period the action was taken after he had been in office for eight years.[41] Although Mevōrākh's brother Judah was styled

Nagid and so referred to in letters, he himself received this title only some time after he had been made rayyis. Obviously, the Jewish ecumenical authority that conferred this title was slow in recognizing him.[42]

The informal way in which the appointment of a Nagid by the government was secured is well exemplified by a document from the thirteenth century. It refers to David Maimonides who took office in 1237 at the tender age of sixteen, which, by the way, shows how quickly this dignity, after it had become well established under his father Abraham, had become a hallowed, hereditary institution. A few notables had talked to all the persons of consequence in the government, and the latter accepted the proposal with enthusiasm. The official responsible for such matters demanded only that ten elders appear before him so that he could sound out the opinion of the community. The document goes on to say that the persons who had taken the initiative were assembled together with the Davidite nāsī and the judges in the synagogue of the Palestinians and asks nine persons listed by name to join them there without delay, together with whomever they could get hold of. The list is comprised of a man called "The Pride of the State," presumably a government official, some physicians and merchants, and also a veteran schoolmaster.[43]

Appointment was normally for a lifetime. The office of the rayyis was partly a political one, however, and therefore exposed to the ups and downs of politics, both of the state and of the Jewish community. As alluded to above, Mevōrākh himself had to cede his place for some time to the exilarch David b. Daniel. Several documents written around 1090 and signed by the most prominent members of the community were issued under the authority of the latter and there are letters congratulating Mevōrākh after his return to power.[44] The court physician and head of the Jews Abū Manṣūr Samuel b. Hananya (1140–1159) fell into disgrace for a time through the intrigues of the impostor Zuṭṭā.[45] Earlier, he had been in danger of losing his position to another rival, a member of the family of the two Gaons who came to power after him.[46] Samuel's successor in both his professional and public functions, the Gaon Nethanel ha-Levi, had ceded his dignity to another rayyis before the spring of 1169, but lived on comfortably at least another fifteen years on a generous pension granted him by his former master. Evidently, when he retired from the service of the caliph, he also resigned his post as leader of the Jewish community.[47] His brother Sar Shalom ha-Levi held the office in 1170 and again in 1177 through 1195 (at least), but he was replaced in 1171 by Maimonides for a number of years. Whether this change was connected with the fall of the Fatimids in 1171 cannot as yet be determined.[48] Nor do we know why Maimonides ceased to be the official head of the Egyptian Jews for so long a period. When Maimonides was reappointed at the end of his life, an enthusiastic pupil congratulated him saying that his acceptance of the office was an honor for the Jewish people and for the dignity of the rayyis, but a catastrophe for scholarship.[49] The family of the ha-Levi brothers, with whom Maimonides had competed for leadership almost from the time he set foot on the soil of Egypt, tried to dislodge his son Abraham after he had succeeded his father. As we have seen, however, during most of his time in office, legal documents written in Egypt regularly bear his name.[50]

Turning now to the rights and duties of the rayyis, we discern as the most conspicuous aspect of his office his capacity as highest juridical authority of the community. He appoints the chief judges, while the appointments of the other community officials are made by the latter with his approval, and in certain cases by him directly. The vast change brought into the public life of the Jews of Egypt and Palestine in the last third of the eleventh century is best exemplified by the fact that the courts in Old Cairo and in other places no longer describe themselves as appointed by the yeshiva, but by "our lord" Mevōrākh, or, during the latter's eclipse, by his rival, the exilarch.[51] Long years after Mevōrākh's death the two chief judges of Old Cairo describe themselves as installed by the late Nagid (and as reinstalled by his son and successor).[52] Soon it became habitual to name in every document the head under whose authority it was issued.

As the many relevant Geniza records prove, the appointment and supervision of the community officials outside the capital must have been one of the main concerns and headaches of the Nagids. In those days, a large section of the Jewish population was still living in small towns or villages. The administrative districts, although fixed by custom, were by no means rigidly defined. Thus, each new appointment required a careful description of the appointee's district. Encroachments by ambitious community leaders, or *muqaddams,* must have been common. Furthermore, in one and the same place more than one functionary was normally in office, and in this respect, too, the exact definition of everyone's duties and prerogatives required the Nagid's attention. Similarly, the relation between the judges in charge of a district and the local heads had to be regulated. Naturally, there were sometimes complaints about the scholarly competence of the persons appointed or their capacity to guide the community.

Often we read about officials leaving their posts because they were inadequately paid or because payments were in arrears. Others left in the wake of communal strife. It seems to have been the Nagids' policy to persuade the congregations to take their former leaders back. We read about visits of the highest Jewish dignitary to communities outside the capital and even of his spending the High Holidays there and leading the congregation during a part of the service in one of them. This was probably regarded as the bestowal of a high honor by the community.[53]

Although the rayyis was the supreme judge, he normally did not give judgments in person. Anyone dissatisfied with the handling of his case by a local court could submit a petition to him (often through a high-standing person) whereupon the rayyis would instruct the court or the local community, or both, how to deal with the complaint. An early example of this procedure may be studied in a letter of the Nagid Judah, Mevōrākh's elder brother.[54] A widow in a little town, who happened to be the sister of an influential banker, was about to be deprived of her rights in her late husband's house by her in-laws. The Nagid, having been approached by her brother, wrote to the congregation (women and children included!) and to the local judge that the case be settled either by compromise, preferably, or by an oath to be taken by the widow. Under no circumstances should action on the case be delayed.

This type of legal procedure pervaded the whole fabric of community life, as it appears to us in the Geniza papers. It is almost unnecessary to observe that the same form of juridical organization prevailed in contemporary Islam. A party who felt itself wronged would apply to the caliph (or to whomever happened to be the actual ruler) for a rescript in his favor, whereupon a qadi would deal with the matter in the spirit of the caliph's ruling. Thus, in the case of the widow just mentioned, her brother, the influential banker, had already obtained a caliphal rescript to a qadi but was prepared not to use it, provided the Jewish authorities redressed his sister's grievance with reasonable expediency. It is hard to say whether the Nagid's position in the judiciary system owed to Muslim influence, or whether he had simply adopted the role of the Gaon, whom he had replaced in the leadership of the Jewish community. Since pre-Christian times, the head of the yeshiva was seconded by the president of the High Court, and, as we learn from the Geniza, the Gaon followed the same procedure of giving instructions to the court or courts under his jurisdiction, as was later done by the Nagid with regard to the judges he himself appointed.[55] It is not impossible that both the Jewish and Muslim procedures were inspired by Roman precedents.

The Nagid's coercive power had its main root in his personal position of influence with the government. Both the community as a whole and its individual members needed him whenever they were in trouble. He was the "savior of a people with little power," as we read in one petition to a Nagid.[56] His *hayba,* the respect paid him, was his most effective instrument of ruling. He could punish recalcitrant offenders with a temporary ban or with total excommunication. But as long as the Nagid was held in high esteem by the government, from Mevōrākh to Abraham Maimonides, little use was made of this extreme means of disciplinary action. Only in later centuries, when the position of the protected minorities and with it that of their leaders had deteriorated irreparably, even small transgressions were threatened or punished with excommunication. This is the reason that the right to pronounce the ban is so prominent in the description of the office of the rayyis in the Muslim sources, which are all later than our period.

No police or prisons were at the disposal of the head of the Jews. Whenever we read about *raqqāṣīn,* or policemen, sent by a Nagid, the context implies that they were members of the state police (which Jews could join in those days). It was normally the Nagid, however, who ordered or gave permission to turn over a coreligionist to the state authorities. Because of the legal position of the minority groups this was almost an act of extradition.[57]

The Nagid's role of peacemaker in his community was not confined to matters of a purely legal character. He had to occupy himself with a wide variety of disputes, which he tried to settle by mediation, by instructions to his officials, or through intervention by the government. A few examples suffice. An old and ailing muqaddam and his two brothers, who had become purveyors for the government and the army upon the recommendation of the Nagid and shared with their handicapped brother the burdens of the community, were menaced in their position by the competition of two Syro-Palestinian silk-dyers. A tax-farmer complains that newcomers from Tyre, Lebanon, were outbidding him.[58] Another tax-farmer, one in the fertile Fayyūm district who had neglected to make formal arrangements with his partners in the relevant government office, was cheated of his share, and, being unable to meet his commitments, was taken into custody. "God forbid," he writes to the Nagid from the prison, "that such wrongs should be done in your days."[59] A silk-weaver who owed money to his employer but wanted to quit his job asks the Nagid to instruct his judges to permit him to pay in installments, as the arrangement of settlements for insolvent debtors was in general of deep concern to the head of the Jewish community.[60] A long-standing feud within the noble family of the ʿAmmānīs in Alexandria was concluded by a ṣulḥa, or peace settlement, through the intervention of Abraham Maimonides. In a letter of thanks, one member of the family writes to him: "Everything crooked and difficult becomes straightened out in your days. For you, our Lord, are really the light of Israel, and the position of all of us has improved owing to you."[61] It was the personal prestige of the rayyis which gave him authority and made him valuable to his coreligionists.

Matters of religious dogma and ritual occupy little room in the Nagids' correspondence, if we disregard their general concern with the observance of the religious law and the study of the sacred writings. Of Mevōrākh his judges remark that he did not allow any change in the customary liturgy (or, rather, liturgies) to anyone, not even to his son and successor designate.[62] Such remarks, however, are rare. The responsa of Maimonides and his son Abraham are, of course, full of religious matters, but these masters were approached in their capacity as scholars rather than as rayyis al-Yahūd. In any case, no rayyis had absolute authority in the interpretation and application of the law. After having rebuked the persons concerned for mishandling a case, Abraham Maimonides writes in a responsum: "If, however, anyone, and were it the youngest of students, would prove that my decision is wrong, I shall accept the correct ruling." The interpretation of the law was a matter of knowledge and reasoning, not of any official authority.[63]

The responsum just quoted dealt with a case of family law. Matters of marriage and divorce, as well as of alimony, wills, and guardianships, were the particular prerogative of the Nagid, as also stated in the Muslim handbooks of administration. No foreigner or other person of uncertain family status could marry without a permit certified by the Nagid. Although a Jewish marriage or divorce did not require the presence of a priest, again and again it is emphasized in the Geniza records that only officials installed by the Nagid for the purpose were entitled to perform these functions. In many cases we find the Nagid attending to family disputes in person.

He did so as protector of the weak, which must have been his most time-consuming preoccupation, to judge on the basis of the material preserved. He was "the judge of the widows and father of the orphans," "the hope of the poor and the shield of the oppressed."[64] Alongside serious matters, such as the neglect or desertion of wives and children, the ransoming of captives, or the education of orphans, many petty requests were submitted to him, as when a poor woman wished to have a new veil, *miqna'a,* for the holidays and asks the Nagid to appoint a man to make a collection for this purpose. "To whom shall I apply, if not to you," she writes, as if she were herself wondering about her troubling the Nagid for such a trifle.[65] A pilgrim running out of funds, a debtor unable to meet his commitments, a poor man in a little town who did not earn as much "as a drink of water," but who had to pay the doctor for his sick wife and children—these and countless others turned to the Nagids for help.[66] Nor would the latter disdain to attend to even seemingly minute requests. By chance, the Geniza has preserved rescripts in the handwritings of both Maimonides and his son Abraham, dealing with small sums of a few dirhems.[67] When we read in one letter that the Nagid Mevōrākh (whose main vocation, we remember, was that of physician and counsellor to the viceroy of Egypt) had no time even to eat a piece of bread, we do not wonder.[68] It is perhaps appropriate to keep in mind that pious Muslim rulers showed the same indefatigable consideration for small requests addressed to them.

Many petitions submitted to the rayyis contained complaints about oppression by government officials or other torts for which redress was to be made by the government. With this we approach another field of the rayyis' activities (most characteristically neglected in the Muslim descriptions of the office), his role as protector of his coreligionists. Whether in a large city like Alexandria, or in a small place in the Delta, the Nagid was expected to act against rapacious officials either by intervention with the central government, or by talking things over with the local authorities on the occasion of a visit.[69] When a Jew was murdered and his belongings taken away, it was not the police who were trusted to take matters into their hands, but the rayyis who was requested to see to it that the lost goods were retrieved.[70] When pirates from Tripoli, Lebanon, captured some prominent persons, the rayyis had to approach the commander of the imperial fleet in order to rescue the captives.[71] Once, Jewish merchants from Tunisia, who had traveled on an Italian ship to Sicily, were robbed clean there by the sailors. As soon as the victims arrived in Alexandria, their business correspondent in that city wrote a letter to the Jewish representative of the merchants in Old Cairo asking him to introduce them to the Nagid. Clearly, it was expected that the Nagid would find means to secure compensation even in a foreign, Christian country.[72] Occasionally, we read similar requests addressed to prominent public figures other than the Nagid. Thus, it was perhaps not so much his official standing as head of the Jews but his personal influence that counted. Still, it seems that major grievances were brought before the rayyis.

The Muslim sources emphasize the duty of the rayyis "to protect the Muslims from the Jews," that is, to see to it that the discriminatory laws against non-Muslims, like wearing distinctive signs on one's clothing, be observed. This again reflects a later and more fanatic time, regarding which we read in Muslim historians that the Coptic patriarch and the head of the Jews solemnly undertook actually to excommunicate any member of their respective communities not complying with the discriminatory laws. In the records from the classical Geniza period we find no trace of such measures originating from the rayyis. At most he warns against any actions that could lead to friction with people of other faiths.

It has often been stated that the rayyis was in charge of the collection of the *jāliya,* the poll tax incumbent on non-Muslims, an assertion not borne out by the immense Geniza material bearing on the subject. The poll tax was normally collected by government officials, either directly or through tax-farmers. In some respects, however, the jāliya presented a major concern to the rayyis. The old rule of Muslim law that indigent persons were exempted from this tax was no longer observed in this period. Whoever was unable to pay was imprisoned and otherwise maltreated to the point of facing death. It was up to the community and above all the rayyis to guard the poor from that predicament. It seems also that the rayyis, like any other communal leader, was occasionally consulted regarding the estimate of a person's financial capacity. Finally, in the case of a poor community, the rayyis sometimes must have taken care of the tax for all members, coming to an agreement with the more capable members concerning their share and making good for the insufficient or lacking contributions through donations or public funds. For example, in the fourteenth century when Old Cairo had become a desolate place, the Nagid ruled at one point that the tax would be paid temporarily out of a fund destined for orphans and widows.[73] In another letter by the same Nagid to that impoverished community he warns them as follows: "No one from this office will come out to you this time. The tax collection will be carried out by the director of finance, the muqaddam [who would help with the estimate] and the government banker. So let every one of you be prepared to pay the tax and the fines [for the arrears]."[74] Incidentally, concerning these matters we need not rely on information provided by the Geniza, rich as it is. Had the rayyis been in charge of the poll tax, the Muslim handbooks of administration would not have failed to note this most important detail.

One wonders what material benefits a rayyis derived from his office. As in most other matters, we should not expect to find any fixed and formal arrangements. Everything depended on the community leader's personal position. If he was a physician and courtier, as indeed most of the rayyises happened to be, he would be in receipt of a pension from his patron and probably also of remunerations from his other patients. Like any affluent person he would possess land, from which he derived additional income. Several documents to this effect have been preserved. In one it is alleged that a Nagid possessed large stores of grain in a village at a time of famine.[75] As it was usual to send presents to scholars, a Nagid would be honored in the same way, and so, incidentally, was the Christian patriarch.[76] When the leader of the community was also head of a school, as with the Gaon Maṣlīaḥ, the other Gaons, and Maimonides, he would receive substantial donations destined for himself and his pupils.[77] A collection made by the Tunisian Jews in Egypt for their Nagid who had gone into exile was in all likelihood an extraordinary measure aimed at assisting a man in distress, for that Nagid had been famous for his riches and his lavish generosity.[78]

We hear of taxes imposed by and collected for a rayyis only with regard to the impostors David b. Daniel and Zuṭṭā. The latter was charged with "taking shoes from the barefoot." As we know from a document and a letter, he forced community officials to make a yearly contribution to him in return for their appointments.[79] This practice was common in Muslim society, and the exilarch of Baghdad also derived fixed revenues from the community, such as fees for animals slaughtered, marriage contracts, and bills of divorce (as reported by an Arabic writer of the ninth century).[80] Nothing of the kind is known thus far for the Egyptian rayyis. Maimonides' insistence on the postulate that public office should be honorary was not mere theory. That he himself groaned under its load is known from his letters. But he served as head of the Jews for comparatively short periods. His son Abraham, who did so during most of his life, was destroyed by it. The threefold task of Nagid, physician of the court (which included also regular turns at the government hospital), and religious reformer (who based his activity on wide-scale writing) was too much for him. The Geniza has preserved about seventy-odd autographs of his, showing the incredible variety of small official business to which he had to attend in person. Abraham died at the young age of fifty one, leaving his important and much needed work of religious reform (as well as his literary magnum opus) uncompleted. Thus Abraham Maimonides, the most representative Nagid after Mevōrākh, became a victim of the deficiencies of this time-consuming office.[81]

The history of the Nagids of the Mamluk period, descendants of Abraham Maimonides and others, falls outside the scope of this book. The Geniza material for these Nagids has not yet been studied in full.[82]

B. THE LOCAL COMMUNITY

1. *Its Composition and Organization*

Name and general character.—The mainstay of the Jewish faith and people was the local community, centering on one or two synagogues. It was called "the holy congregation," a postbiblical version of "a kingdom of priests and a holy nation" (Exodus 19:6). This designation was already in use in pre-Islamic times and then during the entire Geniza period, from the time of the few Hebrew papyruses preserved down to our latest papers written in Arabic language, and no difference was made in this respect between congregations in important cities, such as Jerusalem, Old Cairo, or Alexandria, and those found in the smaller towns of Palestine, Egypt, or Asia Minor. Occasionally, high-sounding epithets, like "the assembly of God," were employed. Often, a congregation is referred to simply as "Israel," because the local cell represented the whole body of the community.[1]

There was a strong feeling that next to God, as revealed in his Law, it was the people that wielded the highest authority. The bearers of dignities regarded themselves as installed by both.[2] The communal officials would be chosen and resolutions adopted by the community as a whole, and not only by the leading notables, although the latter, naturally, made the main decisions. A man who considered himself wronged would appeal to "Israel," that is, the local congregation assembled for prayer, a custom of deep significance for both legal procedure and life in the synagogue (see sec. D, 2, and chap, vii, sec. B, 3, below). The local community acted as judge or rather as jury, in particular when it was small and without a spiritual leader of higher rank. A document from spring, 1020, opens with these words: "This happened in our presence, we, the community of Syracuse [Sicily] constituted as a court." At approximately the same time a similar phrase was used in a letter addressed by the *qāhāl,* or congregation, of Ṣahrajt in Lower Egypt to the

Jewish chief justice in Fustat regarding a legal matter settled by it in partial accordance with his instructions. Two hundred years later we find this note about a defaulting debtor brought before the congregation of Minyat Ziftā (about which we shall presently hear more): "I presented him to the qāhāl, and they imposed on him a 'conditional ban,' " two other times in the short note the qāhāl being referred to as dealing with the case.[3]

Marriage contracts were regularly superscribed with good wishes for the congregation, in addition to those for the young couple (but, strange as it may sound, never any for their families).[4] Often we do find letters with the community addressed first, while the spiritual and secular leaders are mentioned in the second place or only in the introduction. The practice would be followed even when the congregation addressed included a renowned rabbinical authority and a Nagid (as in the case of a letter by the congregation of Palermo, Sicily, to that of al-Mahdiyya, Tunisia), or in statements of a purely legal character (as in a letter addressed in 1028 by the community of Tyre, Lebanon, to that of Aleppo, or one sent in 1034 from Old Cairo to al-Qayrawān). Such letters were written with utmost care in both script and style and were preceded by long exordiums praising the piety, justice, charity, and learnedness in which a Jewish community was supposed to excel. As a rule, the various groups of which a congregation was composed were mentioned individually.[5]

An ecumenical or territorial authority, while instructing his representatives about specific matters, such as help for a needy person, a legal case, or an appointment, would extend greetings to the community, often specifying the various groups and classes of people of which it consisted. Reading the Geniza letters side by side with the epistles in the second book of the Maccabees, the Talmud, or the New Testament, one has the impression of an old tradition handed down through the centuries (cf., e.g, Paul's Epistle to the Philippians, where the "saints in Christ" are addressed first and the bishops and deacons "together" with them). Only the flowery style of the introductions, although invariably written in Hebrew, might have been influenced by the Arabic predilection for exuberance.

Everyone, women and children not excluded, was regarded as belonging to the congregation. In accordance with the notions of decency prevailing in those days, women were rarely mentioned expressly but referred to in such general terms as "the rest of the people." There are, however, letters in which the public spirit of women (and girls) is lauded together with, or before, that of the men of a community, and as late a Nagid as David II Maimonides (around

1400) extended his greetings "to the whole congregation, both men and women." An envoy of the Jerusalem yeshiva, thanking for hospitality enjoyed, sends warmest regards to "all the community of al-Maḥalla the Great, young and old, children and women," and the Nagid Judah b. Saadya addressing another community in Lower Egypt does the same.[6]

Local variations, as well as considerations of style, entailed differences in the series of groups described as forming a congregation and in the order in which they appear. The following list presents a cross section through the material preserved: (1) judges and scholars in general; (2) the elders, usually meaning "the renowned elders," that is, the acknowledged community leaders; (3) other notables, normally persons bearing one or more honorific titles; (4) cantors (see chap. vi, sec. 10); (5) *parnāsīm,* the honorary or paid officials in charge of the public welfare services; (6) heads of the families (usually praised for their generous giving); (7) teachers and scribes; (8) young men ("in the splendor of their appearance"); (9) the rest of the community, minor and of age (i.e., children and women). Sometimes, important professional groups, like government officials, physicians, representatives of merchants, or the merchants in general, would be mentioned separately.[7]

Although Jewish (and Muslim) law, unlike the Roman, did not recognize public bodies as legal personalities, the qāhāl or *jamā'a,* as the Jewish local community was called in Hebrew and Arabic, respectively, does appear as such in our documents. An agreement with an official states that he would have no legal claims against the jamā'a should he fail to comply with any of the stipulations mentioned in the document.[8] An ordinance regulating the pilgrimage to the highly revered synagogue of Dammūh declares that the holy congregation (of Old Cairo) has appointed a certain person "as its representative" in all matters affecting that ancient sanctuary.[9] A contract of lease of a building belonging to the great synagogue in Ramle, Palestine, states that "the people of the synagogue" have leased the place and stipulated such and such conditions.[10]

It seems, however, that the idea of formal membership in the congregation was alien to those times. Therefore, strictly speaking, a statute or resolution was binding only on persons who had either signed it or attended its solemn promulgation (making a symbolic act of *qinyān,* or purchase, which validated also private transactions). At least, this was the legal opinion of Maimonides and his court, preserved in the Geniza together with the statute to which it referred.[11] Consequently, documents often are issued not in the name of the community as such, but by the undersigned in their capacity as witnesses either to the unanimous agreement of the whole congregation,[12] or to the fact that only those specified were in accord with the contents.[13] When, during an emergency, a declaration of the qāhāl in a town lists eighteen contributors, but is signed by only seven (or nine), the signatories clearly acted only as witnesses to a legal document.[14]

The financial obligations of the individual toward the community and the benefits derived by him from it are studied in section C. In this respect, too, the solidarity of the qāhāl was very real, but hardly formal. It was expressed in terms of religious injunctions, not of constitutional rights and duties. The law and ethics of religion were complemented by local custom, which was often referred to in, and occasionally reinforced by, written testimonies bearing witness to its age-old and general acceptance. From time to time, however, there arose situations that demanded more formal procedures. We shall presently see which ways were adopted to meet this need.

Large, medium-sized, and small communities.—By size and function, three types of local communities can clearly be discerned. In the capital cities the highest juridical and religious authorities had their seats and there alone a thorough religious and secular education was available. Everything was decided there. The capital was the country. This was fully so in Egypt, while in Palestine, Ramle, the administrative center, shared certain privileges with Jerusalem, the Holy City. In Tunisia, the seaport al-Mahdiyya stood in a similar relationship to Qayrawān and took over its role entirely after the sack of 1057.

Second in rank were the communities in maritime cities of larger size, such as Alexandria, Damietta, Ascalon, or Tyre, or in inland district centers, like al-Maḥalla or Minyat Ziftā in the Nile Delta, or Qūṣ in Upper Egypt. These centers also partly took care of the communities of the third type, located in the numerous smaller places, which, as a rule, were unable to maintain full panels of religious and communal officials. The geographical boundaries and administrative competence of the various district authorities were by no means static, but, as repeatedly shown in this volume, constantly had to be reapportioned and adapted to the personalities in charge and to the whims of public opinion.

There is no need to deal specifically with the congregations in the capitals and the maritime cities, since the major part of the material assembled in this volume refers to them. They, too, were by no means very populous. For Fustat we have voluminous data that would allow us to arrive at a fairly correct estimate. But these data have not yet been collected in their entirety, nor processed statistically. Calculations of the size of the Jewish community of Fustat during the twelfth and thirteenth centuries are provided below (pp. 139 ff). For the general population, too, modest figures have been proposed.[15]

Minyat Ziftā, example of a middle-sized community

As an example of a middle-sized community in a district center I choose Minyat Ziftā, the smallest of those mentioned above, because the amount of Geniza material referring to that place makes it possible to present it in its entirety with reasonable completeness. As to the size of the community in Minyat Ziftā, anyone engaged in population estimates of times and places for which we possess only haphazard information is aware of the precariousness of such computations. Certain conclusions might be drawn from the available items. Only one out of six elders signing a document in Minyat Ziftā, together with the presiding judge, in July, 1156, was identical with one out of five doing the same two years earlier, in July, 1154. The art of writing (as opposed to that of reading) was not common in the Middle Ages. The presence of ten persons (none of whom was a brother of another) able to understand the legal procedures involved and to properly sign a document induces us to assume that the community was not too limited in size.[16] Similarly, a letter addressed to the Nagid Abraham Maimonides in December, 1219-January, 1220, recommending the appointment (or confirmation) of the son of a former judge, is signed by seven individuals, besides the scribe. Since the letter emphasizes that another person in the little town was vehemently opposed to their candidate, it must be assumed for sure that another letter, signed by other elders from Minyat Ziftā, was sent to the Nagid at approximately the same time.[17] Finally, on a statement about contributions to a public appeal written in summer, 1266, when the community had already much declined, seven signatures and traces of at least two others are visible.[18]

Another indication of the size of the community in Minyat Ziftā may be abstracted from the following: When the Jewish authorities in the capital once sent a scholar to the provincial center to summon its judge Shabbetay b. Abraham (dated documents: March, 1135, through May, 1178 [19]), he found the town ravaged by a plague; all the members of the judge's family, twelve or thirteen persons, were dangerously ill; every week there were ten to twelve cases of mourning in the congregation, and it was hardly possible to find the requisite ten males able to perform the burial rites.[20] Had the community been exceedingly small, say, counting around thirty families, the writer certainly would have expressed himself differently, using, for example, the biblical phrase: "There was not a house where one was not dead" (Exodus 12:30). One should also bear in mind that in descriptions of plagues by Muslim historians one frequently reads that there was not a single man left able to properly bury the dead.

From a private letter of Shabbetay's father and predecessor, Abraham b. Shabbetay, we learn that the poor of the town assembled regularly before the judge (who would examine whether they were still eligible for public assistance) and that several social service officers took care of them. The letter also mentions a Karaite congregation in the locality.[21] In 1928, before the present population explosion, Minyat Ziftā, as it is called today, comprised about sixteen thousand inhabitants, including a conspicuous Jewish community.[22] The Spanish traveler Benjamin of Tudela reports that (shortly before 1168) five hundred Jews lived in Minyat Ziftā, giving the same number for al-Maḥalla, while such important caravan towns as Bilbays and Qūṣ had only three hundred.[23] All these details taken together lead to the conclusion that a likely estimate of the size of the population of a medieval Jewish community in a town of the Egyptian Rīf might be from sixty to ninety families with from three hundred to five hundred souls.

The economic activities of a middle-sized community were varied. The merchants from the capital and other places came to buy flax and indigo, the staple exports of Egypt, as well as sesame, a crop seemingly specific to the environment of Minyat Ziftā.[24] Traveling agents sold many types of silk and raw silk, which were partly used by the local industry and partly resold to the smaller places in the environment.[25] Jewish women wove materials characterized as "Rīf work," [26] while other textiles, of higher quality, as indicated by the prices, were also sent from Minyat Ziftā to the capital.[27] The little town had a *dār wakāla,* or trade center administered by a representative of merchants, and the story of one of its businessmen who traveled as far as Damascus and died there forms the subject of a query addressed to Moses Maimonides.[28]

"Sugar kitchens" and the production of potions and sweet beverages (or beer) must have been of special importance; both gave rise to petitions to the authorities in the capital on behalf of the local community, in addition to being referred to repeatedly in letters and documents.[29] The sale of raw sugar, *qand,* was, around 1150, in the hand of a local governor, *qā'id,* who charged the sugar "cooks" twice and more its normal price. The Nagid was asked to obtain a caliphal rescript stopping that high-handed practice.[30] A letter requesting protection against an outsider *sharābī,* or preparer of potions, and his two partners is discussed presently.

In addition to the occupations mentioned, the community in Minyat Ziftā comprised a government official with the title "Trusted by the Dynasty," two physicians, and two tax-farmers mentioned together in one document, a veterinary (who was sometime president of the congregation), a druggist, a silversmith, a well-to-do dyer, and three partners operating a tannery.[31] The professions of most of the signatories on documents are not known to us since it was not customary to specify them. Thus, the plethora of occupations in that medium-sized community was certainly far more differentiated than evident from the occasional references it is possible to assemble here. As country people, Jews in Minyat Ziftā sent honey and poultry to the capital, whether as presents or on a commercial basis is not stated.[32]

The economic strength (and public spirit) of a community may be gauged from its contributions to appeals for general causes. Around 1155, out of a total of 226-1/8 dinars donated toward the ransom of captives by ten Egyptian congregations (besides the capital and Alexandria where separate collections were made), Minyat Ziftā contributed 37 dinars, the second largest sum, al-Maḥalla being in the lead with 44 dinars. The payments were made by the contributors in silver coins, forty of which, as stated in the document, were worth a dinar.[33] With this total of 1,480 dirhems may be compared a contribution of 1,020-3/4 dirhems, made on behalf of the hard-pressed Cairo community 110 years later.[34] When Moses Maimonides was asked by a refugee from Morocco to provide him and his son with the sums needed for the payment of the poll tax, he wrote a letter to the community of Minyat Ziftā asking them to take care of it—a request that certainly was fulfilled.[35] A similar demand, paired with others, in favor of a learned silk-weaver and disciple of Abraham Maimonides was addressed to a notable in Minyat Ziftā by the district judge of al-Maḥalla.[36] The sums involved in transactions made in the town, or the fact that a woman possessed at least two houses there, also point to a certain degree of prosperity.[37] On the other hand, the humble amounts obtained in the weekly collections in the synagogue (1-1/2–3-1/4 dirhems in 1236) should not be rated as economic indicators; those collections were perfunctory acts of religious observance, not true works of philanthropy.[38]

On the subject of communal and spiritual life, the first Jewish judge and communal leader of Minyat Ziftā about whom we have some detailed knowledge, the Abraham b. Shabbetay mentioned earlier, was a member of the Jerusalem academy and a learned man. Parts of two valuable manuscripts copied by him, one in 1091 in Tyre (where the academy then had its seat) and one in 1093, are still preserved.[39] In October, 1106, he signed a document in Fustat and in June, 1107, another in Cairo; in October, 1125, he is referred to as judge in Minyat Ziftā. Thus, as often with judges in smaller towns, he had had a smaller position in the capital before being appointed to a judgeship in the province.[40] He must have taken up his post after 1110, for we have a fragment from that year of an interesting marriage contract written in Minyat Ziftā by another judge whose handwriting (betraying him as a Palestinian) and signature are known from another fragment.[41] A namesake of Abraham b. Shabbetay, who also had a Palestinian hand and wrote and signed a marriage contract in Fustat in 1063, might very well have been the grandfather of our judge. (The upper part of this document is preserved in Philadelphia, the lower in Cambridge, England.)[42]

A pastoral circular sent by Abraham b. Shabbetay to six congregations in smaller places around Minyat Ziftā reveals the extent of his parish.[43] In a long letter to the Nagid Moses b. Mevōrākh, which betrays him as an excellent Hebraist, Abraham congratulates the addressee in his own name and in that of the community on the downfall of a dangerous rival at the court, also a notorious Jew-baiter, and sends greetings from his son, the future judge, to the Nagid's mother ("my son kisses the hands of . . ."). Such intimacy, uncommon in an official letter, suggests that Shabbetay, while studying in Fustat, had probably been put up by the old lady or received from her other kindnesses (such as the payment of fees for the tutoring of a grandchild—a type of "charity" favored by well-to-do grandmothers).[44]

A personal letter by Abraham b. Shabbetay permits us some glimpses into the life of the provincial town. The judge used to sublet a section of his house to distinguished visitors. One was an official who came from Alexandria to Minyat Ziftā for an inspection, of which the writer was very apprehensive for some unnamed reason. Another visitor was even worse: he took to gambling so that the judge, in order to avoid a scandal, finally had to ask him to leave the house. 'Anān, the leader of the local Karaites, excommunicated the gambler, but the gambler—no doubt himself of some scholarly standing—retorted with a counterban. But he had to quit soon. "Had he remained one day longer, the government would have seized and lashed him with shoes."[45]

The correspondence of Shabbetay, Abraham's son, who served as judge and spiritual leader in Minyat Ziftā for over forty years, illustrates important aspects of communal life in a district center. The protection of the members of his parish from the overreaching of rapacious tax collectors—(a constant plague in Minyat Ziftā as everywhere)—required the intervention of influential persons in the capital. In a letter of thanks to one such notable Shabbetay praises the polite and considerate behavior of a government *mushārif,* or tax assayer, who had toured the district, and now asks the addressee to follow up the exercise of his *jāh,* or influence, when that official returns to Cairo and draws up the final lists.[46] Even more significant is a letter addressed to a high official with the title *thiqat al-mulk,* "confident of the rulers," written in 1169, at the time when the famous Saladin, who was then with Nūr al-dīn's army in Egypt, was all powerful in the country. A Jew from Damascus (who probably had accompanied the Syrian army and thus was personally known to Saladin) tried to use his influence on the factual ruler to unseat the old and ailing judge and replace him by one of his own favorites.[47] Shabbetay's plea must have been successful since we find him issuing documents in Minyat Ziftā in 1175 and 1178, showing that he remained in office at least nine years after the attempt to oust him.[48] A fragment of a letter of his to the chief judge in Fustat shows that it must have been customary for the district judges to present themselves frequently to their superiors in the capital, for Shabbetay apologizes for having not done so for five months because of illness.[49] In exceptional instances, as while lodging a complaint against an oppressive governor, the district judge would address the Nagid directly.[50] His correspondence with his fellow judges and the documents issued or validated by him reveal his day-to-day occupation, especially with family matters, cases of inheritance, and contracts related to economic life.[51]

Two other judges, or *muqaddam*s, as they were preferably called then, of Minyat Ziftā are known from the times of Moses and Abraham Maimonides. By that time a population shift must have occurred. Minyat Ziftā is situated on the western bank of the Damietta arm of the Nile, while on the opposite, eastern, bank is found Minyat (now Mīt) Ghamr, a community that has also provided the Geniza with a considerable amount of material. As the smaller place, Minyat Ghamr was normally under the jurisdiction of the Jewish judge of Minyat Ziftā, just as, normally, a Muslim notary in the latter town would take care of the sale of a house in the former.[52] At the beginning of the thirteenth century, the Jewish muqaddam took his seat in Minyat Ghamr, as evident from a document written and signed there by the judge Moses b. Peraḥyā in April, 1226, and from a letter of his to the Nagid Abraham Maimonides, in which he announced that he had left Minyat Ghamr and taken residence in Minyat Ziftā (where he was still active as judge in his old age).[53] A strongly worded letter to him by the Nagid, addressing him as muqaddam of both localities, admonishes him to delegate some of his functions to one of his deserving relatives, since he could not simultaneously be in two places.[54]

A letter by a muqaddam of Minyat Ghamr which is the epitome of local politics and of central administrative practices shows the two places again united, with the stipulation that only some of the functions (and revenues) of Minyat Ziftā were to go to the writer. According to him, "all" members of that community had expressed their satisfaction with him and asked the Nagid to confer on him the *taqdima,* or leadership, in full. Meanwhile, however, it had been given to another candidate, obviously with a larger following. At the same time the Nagid had joined to Minyat Ghamr the "eastern rural district," including the townlet of Ashmūm, in exchange for Minyat Ziftā. There, too, a rival muqaddam was more popular than our writer, with the effect that the new appointment brought to the complainant more trouble and waste of time than income. He requested therefore, that Minyat Ziftā be restored to him in full, and that he would like to retain also a third townlet, Malīj, for which he had held letters of appointment for years. The writer emphasized that he was a man with few relatives and only weak supporters. The Nagid was his protector, but needed to be reminded from time to time of the unsatisfactory situation.[55]

The final eclipse of Minyat Ziftā is evident from a number of documents that prove that a professional judge no longer stood at the head of the community. One letter reveals that a perfumer, with a good hand in both Hebrew and Arabic, had taken his place, another that a physician, who wanted also to replace a schoolteacher who had temporarily been forced to leave the town, had done so.[56] The latter incident is a particular sign of decline, since earlier the town had boasted of a full staff of juridical, religious, and educational personnel. A report on the excommunication of a defaulting debtor in Minyat Ziftā by a visiting judge or the imposition of a "conditional ban" on another debtor by "the community" as such also shows that a scholarly spiritual leader was no longer in the town.[57] Nor is the signature of one affixed to the important statement about the contribution of Minyat Ziftā to the United Appeal of 1266, cited above.

Indeed, that document said that the community had been reduced to utmost poverty.

Ṣahrajt, a village community

One of the six smaller places under the jurisdiction of the judge of Minyat Ziftā at the time of its flourishing around 1125 was Ṣahrajt, a big village situated on the eastern bank of the Nile south of Minyat Ghamr.[58] It serves as an example of a community of the third type, the very small one. The price of a house, paid by a brother to his two sisters and amounting to 10 dinars only, is indicative of the living standards in a rural environment.[59] The congregation possessed no proper synagogue building, only "a place of prayer."[60] It was headed by a layman or, mostly, a cantor, who also did the work of a public notary.[61] The knowledge of the law (or the desire to adhere to it) was not always too developed in such persons. A letter from the rabbinical court of Fustat censures a cantor of Ṣahrajt for having issued a marriage certificate to a divorced woman before the termination of the three-month waiting period prescribed by Jewish (and Muslim) law.[62] More complicated cases of divorce had to be submitted to the court in the capital. A power of attorney given by a divorcée in Ṣahrajt for such a case in November, 1060, is preserved in its entirety and betrays a reasonable degree of command of legal practice and parlance.[63] In this case the scribe must have been the local teacher, as is evident from a letter written by the same man recommending a colleague to the head of the community in Fustat.[64] A little later we find another teacher in Ṣahrajt.[65] Whether the functions of a cantor, schoolteacher, notary, and ritual slaughterer were occasionally or regularly combined in one hand is not evident from the Geniza material on Ṣahrajt, but we have repeated references to such combinations with regard to other small places.[66]

In general, the members of a community of so small a size were not true villagers. Because of the mobility of the population, its composition was perhaps not too different from that of a larger place. People from the capital and even from abroad stayed in Ṣahrajt, and a Ṣahrajt family emigrated to Byzantium (where father and son died, a wife survived, and a brother living in Fustat are mentioned in the letter reporting these details).[67] When we find that more difficult legal cases were decided in the capital, as noted above, or were settled by a judge from there visiting the little town, we should bear in mind that similar procedures were followed with regard to far larger communities.[68]

The scribe of Ṣahrajt whose exquisite hand is lauded in *Med. Soc.,*

I, 51, was a member of the Jerusalem academy and had acquired that rank shortly before settling in the Egyptian Rīf.[69] The work of another scribe from there who calls himself a teacher is still preserved; the man for whom the work was done, a native of Manbij in northern Syria, most probably also lived in Ṣahrajt.[70] The letters sent from the little town or addressed there presuppose a high standard of the knowledge of Hebrew.[71] The "place for prayer" must have been roomy enough to accommodate an audience listening to an elaborate sermon by Elhanan b. Shemarya of Fustat and paying him well for it.[72] Contributions for the ransom of captives were solicited from the small community in 1028, and, we may assume, certainly made.[73]

Population shifts

All Geniza papers of some length written in, or addressed to, Ṣahrajt originated in the eleventh century. From the twelfth and thirteenth centuries we know only that it belonged to the district of the muqaddam of Minyat Ziftā. Thus, it seems that Ṣahrajt was affected by a population shift like that experienced by Minyat Ziftā itself, only about a century earlier. No general conclusions should be drawn from the fortunes of these two communities. The town of Bilbays, situated on the caravan route from Cairo to Palestine, was the seat of a Jewish district judge at the time of Moses and Abraham Maimonides and their successors; more than twenty documents written there are known from the thirteenth century alone and even after the forceful conversion of its Jews to Islam and its synagogue to a mosque in 1301, reported by a later Jewish historian, it must have contained a sizable Jewish community.[74] But only sporadic references to the community of Bilbays have been found with regard to the first half of the twelfth century—for example, that it belonged to the district of Minyat Ziftā—and I do not know of a single dated document written there during the eleventh century. It will be possible to gain a comprehensive view of the developments in Egypt only after the seventy-five or so communities represented in the Geniza are scrutinized in a way similar to that tried here and, of course, after the infinitely more copious materials referring to Old and New Cairo and Alexandria are brought under control. The task will be completed only after similar work is done for the Mediterranean communities at large.

Congregation v. community.—In the preceding pages the terms "congregation" and "community" have been used interchangeably, although we are accustomed to applying the former to a group centering in a house of worship and the latter to a larger body of people living in a town or a district. This ambiguity was unavoidable because the Hebrew and Arabic terms used in our sources have both meanings. In this fact is reflected a reality to be faced in the Geniza records during the entire period.

As explained, there existed in most larger towns two synagogues, a "Palestinian" and a "Babylonian." Originally, these congregations had been formed mainly by persons coming from the countries of the former Byzantine empire on the one hand and those from the land of the Eastern caliphate on the other. By the time of the High Middle Ages, however, adherence to one of the two rites had become largely a matter of personal taste and decision with the result that the two synagogues had to compete with each other for new members. The Geniza reveals to us in detail how this was done. The Iraqis with their centuries-old experience of soliciting funds for their renowned seats of learning had the Gaons of Baghdad shower extravagant honorary titles on the many foreigners who flocked to the capital of Egypt from the four corners of the earth.[75] The Palestinians, albeit reluctantly, followed suit, but also had other feathers in their cap. They boasted of having the most precious Bible codices (some of which are still preserved in libraries), as well as magnificent Torah scrolls and beautiful sitting carpets. In addition, they pointed out that for various reasons their service was more attractive, since their Scripture readings were so much shorter than those of the Babylonians and were chanted by boys, so that parents who were eager to have their children participate actively in the service would certainly prefer the congregation of the Palestinians. On the other hand, the Babylonians tried to impart splendor to their service by entrusting the Scripture readings to excellent cantors.[76]

By the end of the twelfth century, the Babylonian rite (that of the "Diaspora") had been accepted almost everywhere. When Moses Maimonides became established in Egypt, he tried, for the sake of unity, to abolish the peculiarities of the Palestinians altogether. He was not successful, though; on the contrary, at the time of his son and successor Abraham the specific customs of the Palestinian synagogue of Old Cairo were reconfirmed by a solemn pact.[77]

It is natural that such competition would sometimes lead to friction among the leaders of the respective congregations or even among its members. "We, the two congregations [the text says: synagogues] have come together and united and made peace between ourselves," says an old, but unfortunately much damaged fragment, which at least indicates that peace had not prevailed before.[78] The rivalries among the community leaders, especially during the first half of the eleventh century, have been described by Jacob Mann in much detail.[79] It is, however, most remarkable that as soon as the Geniza lifts the veil from their obscure history *the two congregations appear throughout as belonging to one local community.* This is expressed first in the astonishing fact that the public chest was administered in common. As a rule, donations were made and fines stipulated or imposed for the benefit of the two synagogues in equal shares. "The Rabbanites living in Miṣr [Fustat]" were addressed by "Their brethren, the Rabbanites living in Ramle," in this way, although there were Palestinian and Iraqian synagogues in both cities and the matters discussed concerned religious ritual.[80]

Objects such as books, Torah scrolls, lamps, carpets, and other precious textiles were donated to the individual synagogues, but the far larger gifts destined for the social services (including the emoluments of community officials) were pooled for the benefit of the local community as a whole. Many accounts show that current expenditure was made for the two synagogues together and often by one and the same official. Property dedicated to charitable purposes was described as forming a part of the *qōdesh* ("the holy," see below), in Arabic *aḥbās al-Yahūd,* both meaning "Jewish pious foundations."[81] Even when the individual synagogue buildings were affected, as with the renovations undertaken after the demolition at the time of the caliph al-Ḥākim, a united appeal was made and the funds collected were distributed in equal shares.[82]

This cooperation was not entirely confined to the Rabbanite community. We read about a woman bequeathing her share in a house to poor ill persons of the two denominations, *ṭā'ifatayn.*[83] A public fast and united appeal, where Rabbanites and Karaites were expected to convene in one house of worship, is referred to in one letter, and reports about joint collections actually carried out have been preserved. The title "pride of the two denominations," given to a notable who, like many others, benefited by his liberality both Karaites and Rabbanites, illustrates the situation.[84]

Moreover, although the Palestinian and Babylonian congregations had their own chief judges and juridical courts, in more important matters the two chief judges and their assistants sat on the same bench. The appointments of the puisne judges outside the capital were regularly made by the two in common. In particularly delicate litigations, such as one concerned with a large inheritance, the chief

Jewish judge of Cairo (which was still regarded as a suburb of Old Cairo) would also be asked to participate—and preside, if his rank at the yeshiva was higher than that of his colleagues. These orderly procedures operated in full from the time of the Nagid Mevōrākh, but the tendency to have only one supreme juridical authority in a town is evident from the earliest documents at our disposal.[85] Even the beadles, who by their very task were attached to one building, had functions related to the community as a whole.[86]

Finally, the two congregations would gather in a synagogue or other place to listen to a guest preacher or at some other special occasion. We read about such gatherings regarding various cities, and occasionally, Karaites would also join in. Benjamin of Tudela reports that in Fustat the two congregations would join in prayer on Pentecost (the holiday celebrating the promulgation of the Ten Commandments on Mount Sinai) and on the Feast of the Rejoicing of the Law (when the yearly lections were completed and a new round started). According to Benjamin this was a custom fortified by statute. One would like to know the relationship between this custom and the Muslim communal prayer on the two yearly holidays, when the entire male population of a city would unite in a service held on a square outside the city.[87]

In view of this situation we are not surprised to find Geniza letters issued in the name of, or addressed to the community of Old Cairo or of other cities, although these cities contained more than one congregation. A noble woman in distress writes simply to the qāhāl of Old Cairo.[88] The same expression is used in two documents with regard to Alexandria, which also harbored a Palestinian and a Babylonian congregation.[89] We have letters sent by the joint congregations of the Egyptian capital (one including also that of New Cairo), by those of Alexandria, of Ramle, Palestine, and Tyre, Lebanon, and to the joint congregations of al-Mahdiyya and Constantinople.[90] A statute promulgated by the congregations of the Rabbanites in Old Cairo is discussed presently.

It is doubtful whether the replacement of the congregation by the local community is to be regarded as a sign of transition from a "hierocratic" to a democratic way of public organization.[91] As we shall see presently, the two elements, the hierocratic and the democratic, were present in both the Palestinian and Babylonian schools. The change is to be explained by specific historical circumstances. By the beginning of the eleventh century the conflict between the two schools had lost most of its acrimony. The strife around the fixing of the calendar, which was as severe in the Synagogue as it had been in the Church, had died down. A son of a Palestinian Gaon could now study under a Gaon of Baghdad. Honorific titles conferred by a Babylonian yeshiva were publicized in Palestine with the permission of the Gaon of Jerusalem. The Palestinian authorities were quoting the writings of the Babylonian schools as frequently as their own, while graduates from the Babylonian yeshivas living in Egypt were eager also to acquire a diploma from Jerusalem. The differences in ritual still gave occasion to bickerings, but these are recorded as exceptional cases.[92]

On the other hand, the eleventh century was fraught with emergencies calling for concerted action. It began with the demolition of the houses of worship under al-Ḥākim. There followed a long series of calamities that affected the country as a whole, while the minority groups were, as usual, no less hard hit. The Muslim sources have much to tell us about civil war, famine, and the breakdown of public order, resulting even in the pillage of the caliph's palaces. The lists of synagogue furnishings from this period suffice to testify that the houses of worship were not spared. In addition, we have direct testimony to the same effect. "I am unable to describe how I and my friends were afflicted when we heard what happened to the synagogue of the Palestinians," writes a merchant from Alexandria to a business friend in Old Cairo around 1070.[93] Events outside Egypt also required the utmost exertion for the common good. As a result of the invasions of the bedouins into Tunisia and of the Seljuks into Syria and Palestine, and later of the massacres perpetuated by the Crusaders in Europe and in the Holy Land, refugees were pouring in from all these countries, and the never ending necessity of ransoming prisoners of war or of persons captured by pirates presented a major challenge during most of the period. The newly created dignity of the Nagid, or head of the Jews, contributed much to the furthering of unity. As a matter of fact, the replacement of the congregation by the local community was nothing more than a return to the situation prior to the schism between "Easterners" and "Westerners." In Talmudic times, our sources know of no other communal organization except that of "the sons of a town," that is, of coreligionists living in one place.

Plenary assembly and representative bodies.—Each community or congregation, large or small, was headed by an official appointed or approved by a Jewish ecumenical or territorial authority and accredited in one way or another by the local governor or chief of police. His authority, although backed by the state and the highest representatives of the synagogue, was by no means absolute. He had to have the approval, confidence, and cooperation of the people. Otherwise he faced trouble and even dismissal. At his appointment the community granted him obedience, but it was never forgotten that he was its "servant."

A few examples illustrate this blending of hierocratic and democratic elements in Jewish community life. One of the most prominent Jewish judges in Old Cairo during the twelfth century, although reappointed by a new Nagid, described his situation to a colleague in Damascus as follows: "By the grace of God, the holy congregations love me and are pleased with my service and show me great favor. Praise be to the Almighty who let me find favor in their eyes so that they put me into office. My Nagid also likes me and bestows favors on me." Clearly, acceptance by the community was vital to this man at least as much as the approval of the Nagid.[94] The influential role of the laity in the selection of a Gaon has been pointed out above (p. 16).

In reply to a complaint by the Palestinian congregation of Alexandria about their chief judge, whose father and grandfather had preceded him in office, Solomon b. Judah, the Gaon of Jerusalem, emphasizes that he would by no means force them to retain him: "He is your son and it is from you that he derives his livelihood."[95] This letter, written in Arabic, is the more remarkable as it was followed by another letter in Hebrew, where the Gaon reiterates that the yeshiva would never appoint any one against the will of the congregation, but that, to the best of his knowledge, the disputed official had the confidence of the majority, which regarded him as a better scholar than even his father (who was then still alive and had recommended him).[96] As a matter of fact, the man retained his post for decades after his father's death, albeit not without opposition, according to various other Geniza documents relevant to him.

Once, when the synagogue building in Hebron, Palestine, had to be replaced by another, perhaps because an earthquake had made it unsafe, the executive had the following to report: "As soon as that piece of land had been bought, all agreed to pull the synagogue down and to erect a new one. On Sabbath, when all were assembled, I said to them: Do not say that the demolition of this place is being done on the order of one man. It is being done on the order of all of you. Then all said: Yes, we have decided on this unanimously. On the next morning, they began with the work of demolition and building." When the two synagogues of Alexandria were about to choose a new spiritual leader (approximately two hundred years after the correspondence referred to in the preceding paragraph) first "the community was consulted" about the prospective candidate (who was known in the city), and, after "they had said: yes," some twenty-five elders convened to decide how to proceed in the matter.[97]

References to plenary deliberations of the community are made not only when matters of major importance, like the two just mentioned, were up for decision. They were common even with regard to cases of civil law involving only a few persons. The custom of addressing letters dealing with such cases to the community as a whole was not merely a matter of courtesy. They were actually read out in public, as we learn both from requests made to the effect and from reports that it had been done.[98] It is also characteristic that sometimes letters were thus divulged which by their very nature were confidential (like the opinion of a higher authority about a community servant), or, quite the opposite, were withheld from the assembly against its wish.[99]

We have to keep in mind that in those days the population of a town was comparatively small and the local Jewish communities were even smaller. The full participation of all members in the discussion of public affairs did not present technical difficulties; on the contrary, it was natural. Since everyone attended service at least on Saturday, and mostly during the week as well, especially on Monday and Thursday, it was almost impossible not to bring before the congregation matters that were in any way regarded as being of public concern.

It seems, however, that the simple procedure of taking votes, although suggested by a biblical injunction and actually in use in early talmudic times, was unknown during the Geniza period. Decisions were made in such a way that a subject was first discussed in public and a statement then drawn up in writing and read out to the plenary assembly.[100] Unanimous consent was either explicitly stated, or the document was simply made out in the name of the community. Thus, the statute to be discussed opens with the following words: "Text of the statute adopted by the community of the Rabbanites living in Old Cairo." Disagreement was indicated by specifying those adhering to a resolution.[101]

The finances of the community were not left entirely to the discretion of the representatives and officials dealing with them. As we learn from one document, the accounts were displayed in the synagogue for the duration of four months and everyone was not only allowed, but obliged, to bring any objection he had before the court. This procedure explains why numerous accounts of public revenue and expenditure found in the Geniza are written in large and calligraphic characters (see sec. C, below).

All the same, the regular business of a community could not be transacted by a crowd, small though it might be. It was entrusted to a board of "elders." This important institution, referred to in hundreds of Geniza records, appears in an early Hebrew papyrus where the head of the synagogue, the elders of the synagogue, and the holy congregation are mentioned side by side.[102] It is hardly necessary to emphasize that this institution of the "elders" was not confined to the Jewish communities of the Islamic world. Just as we find elders active in Fustat and Damietta, Egypt, in Ramle and Baniyas, Palestine, or Qayrawān and Zawīlat al-Mahdiyya, Tunisia, so do we find them at the same time and in the same capacity in the communities of Speyer, Worms, Mayence, and Cologne, Germany.

The duties of the elders are well defined in the statute just alluded to, in which it was resolved that a board of ten elders should assist Ephraim b. Shemarya, head of the community in Old Cairo, as follows: *(a)* sit with him as judges of the court; *(b)* share with him the burden of all the needs of the community; *(c)* support him in the enforcement of religious duties; *(d)* help him protect public morality; *(e)* deal appropriately with those who live in a way disapproved by religion; *(f)* consider the letters addressed by the heads of the academy to the community and answer them after deliberation in the general assembly.[103]

The number ten has some significance in Jewish law, for a minimum of ten persons was required for a service to be regarded as communal; it constituted a public body. We find nine elders signing a declaration "in the presence" of the same Ephraim in August, 1038, and ten signing a legal deed together with another head of a congregation in Old Cairo in 1034. As late as 1208, a statute is signed by ten. The community in Jerusalem, and the small congregation in the townlet of Qalyūb were represented by the same number around 1050 and in 1195, respectively.[104] Even an official letter signed by the Gaon Solomon b. Judah and his son Abraham includes another eight signatories.[105] A list of ten prominent persons found on a slip of paper contained probably the names of candidates proposed at one time for a board of elders.[106] The jamā'a, or Jewish community, of Syracuse, Sicily, in an Arabic undertaking given to the bishop of

Cefalù at Christmastime 1187 was represented by ten (in addition to the scribe).[107] The government, too, expected ten notables to speak for the Jewish community at a time of trouble (around 1085) or on the occasion of the installation of a new Nagid (1237).[108]

A board of ten elders, so widely attested both geographically and chronologically, is expressly mentioned as religiously recommendable in a (fragmentary) pastoral letter of a dignitary from the house of David: "We shall select ten elders out of your notables and strengthen their arms so that they may lead the people, as it is incumbent on us to appoint elders and judges."[109]

We should not expect, however, that everywhere and at all times was this number adhered to. In the second decade of the eleventh century, the Ephraim mentioned earlier headed a board of seven; in the third decade, we find documents signed by that number, and the same holds true of an important statute written in 1205. "The seven best men of the town" was the standing designation for a municipal or congregational council in talmudic and later Hebrew literature, and this might have had some influence on the formation of boards of seven.[110] In a responsum, Maimonides states expressly that the number was not compulsory. A committee of three led the two Jewish congregations of Alexandria after the death of their chief rabbi and before the election of another. Three is the number of judges required by a Jewish court and suggested itself as the minimum number of members for a communal committee during a period of transition.[111]

Occasionally, we find councils of elders of considerable size. An eleventh-century Gaon of Jerusalem appoints, or approves the election of, sixteen elders, each mentioned by name (the list includes groups of three and two brothers, respectively). According to his letter, their duty was to assist the executive as judges and "in all matters of Israel" and to "strengthen his hand" in every worthy cause.[112] The letters issued in the name of local communities bear signatures in widely varying numbers, amounting to fifteen in Gaza, Palestine, and more than twenty in Palermo, Sicily.[113] Clearly, anyone of consequence who was prepared to exert himself for the public good could become an elder—provided he had the necessary following.

Formal appointments of elders by a Gaon or Nagid have been mentioned. One source speaks of joint action by the plenary assembly and the appointed local or district executive.[114] We are certainly right in assuming that no fixed and general rule was observed. Most likely, the ecumenical or territorial authority intervened only when communal strife made a decision from above imperative. In most cases, the bestowal of an honorary title on an elder was sufficient proof of the Gaon's approval.

In their capacity as representatives of the community the elders issued and received letters, signed contracts, made appointments, and promulgated statutes.[115] They did this either alone or (mostly) in conjunction with the muqaddam, or appointed executive, sometimes also appearing together with the community as a whole.[116] Their most important fields of activities were the social services and the judiciary, many of them serving as parnāsīm (social service officers), or as assistant judges. Special prayers were said for their well-being on the High Holidays, as for the ecumenical Jewish authorities. When the list of eulogized elders contained names not favored by the community, the latter would not fail to express its dissatisfaction.[117]

From these elders, who were honorary officials designated by the Hebrew term zāqēn ("old man," as Greek *presbyter),* are to be discerned the notables, sometimes informally called "noted elders," *al-shuyūkh al-mash-hūrīn,* or outrightly by the modern Arabic term *zu 'amā',* "leaders."[118] The latter formed the upper layer of the Jewish (and Muslim or Christian) middle class and probably had the last word in selecting community officials and in other decisions affecting the community.[119] Not everyone, however, belonging to this class acted as an "elder," and the official elders, it seems, were not always rich or influential.

These notables often acted as de facto representatives of the community with the central or local governments, using their influence for seeking redress of iniquities or for obtaining special favors. Many Geniza papers illustrate this situation (which was not confined to the Muslim world and the Middle Ages, as some historians seem to believe), and numerous examples are provided throughout this book. As a typical instance, the long letter of the community in Palermo to the one in al-Mahdiyya, repeatedly referred to before, may be summarized here. It is almost entirely devoted to the praise of just such a self-appointed representative, a Spanish Jew, called Khalaf (in Hebrew Ḥayyīm) b. Jacob, who, together with his son, was very influential with the Muslim authorities in Sicily. They succeeded in releasing from prison many persons who had been cast there because of their inability to pay the poll tax and in reducing the tax for many others. Once, when several ships foundered on their way to Egypt, and the government, as usual, laid its hand on the salvaged goods, the Spanish merchant extricated from it not only the goods belonging to the local Jews, but also those of coreligionists living abroad, while less fortunate people had to witness their merchandise sold by the government in public auction. Another time, the Muslim authorities wished to appropriate large sections of the Christian and Jewish cemeteries for some building projects. Again, it was Khalaf who averted this disaster from befalling the Jews, while the Christians had to ransom theirs with heavy payments. Finally, some large-scale litigation between coreligionists, which became a menace when brought before the Muslim courts, was settled through the good services of the foreigner. All this was done by him, as the letter emphasizes, without any material benefit accruing to himself and without charging anyone in the community a penny. Still, the letter (whose concluding part is mostly lost) must have had some practical purpose. Perhaps Khalaf wanted to open a warehouse for foreign merchants in al-Mahdiyya. We find him, indeed, in that city in and around 1030, acting as the representative of the great Ibn 'Awkal of Old Cairo. Be that as it may, Khalaf b. Jacob illustrates well the role of these self-appointed representatives (or "redeemers and faithful shepherds," as the letter calls them) of a much-harrassed minority group.[120]

Age groups, social classes, and factions.—The word for "old man" or "elder," in addition to the two meanings discussed, had in both Arabic and Hebrew a third and rather general sense, namely, that of a respectable person. Thus, one would speak of the *elder* Ḥasan, Mr. Japheth, the *young man* (Japheth was regarded as the Hebrew equivalent of Ḥasan, both meaning "handsome") ; or a person would be characterized as "the elder, the young man" (*al-shaykh ha-baḥūr*).[121] Similarly, the term "the young men," *baḥūrīm* in Hebrew and *ṣibyān* in Arabic, designated both an age group and a social class, although it was used more frequently in the former sense. One should beware of assigning too low an age to the top limit of the "age group" thus referred to. A merchant, who had traveled to both Sicily and India, or a silk worker, who had been married twice, could still belong to the "young men," and one letter even speaks of "ṣibyān from Aleppo, young and old." [122] We have already seen that in letters to a community greetings would be extended to the "young men" as a separate group.[123]

These "young men" were active in community life. When a congregation in Old Cairo was once divided with regard to a guest cantor from Ramle, Palestine, whom the elders of that city had banned, the youth supported him, and, to make things worse, "many sided with the baḥūrīm, for this generation is very corrupt, as it is written: The lad will behave insolently against the aged [Isaiah 3:5]."

A letter of the elders of Ramle itself complains about opposition by "ignorant, uncouth youngsters from the lowest ranks of the society."[124] According to a report from Old Cairo, the *shubbān yisrāel,* the youth, were enticed by a guest preacher, who expounded the Holy Scriptures in the way of mystical allegory, "which should not be listened to, let alone be believed."[125] A person in Gaza, Palestine, had complained that the local leader had incited ṣibyān al-yahūd, "the boys of the congregation," against him, a charge mentioned but strongly denied in the letter.[126] Troubles with the ṣibyān "who take delight in things which the Creator dislikes" are reported to his Nagid by a judge from an Egyptian town.[127] A petition, signed by twenty-six persons, opposed by seven, with three out of town, emphasized that only respectable elders, *rijāl shuyūkh,* no youth, *ṣabī,* were among the signatories. Owing to the fragmentary state of the manuscript, the nature of the dissension that gave rise to the petition cannot be ascertained.[128] In a letter seemingly addressed to the merchant prince and communal leader Ibn 'Awkal, his correspondent, a man in a similar position, describes how in his place "the elders began to make peace and to win over the hearts" and expresses the hope that God may "sow peace" (Zechariah 8:12) and "turn the hearts of fathers to their children and the hearts of children to their fathers" (Malachi 4:5; in the Hebrew text 3:24). Thus, we see that the conflict between "elders" and "young men" in medieval Muslim society, which has begun to be revealed by recent research, had its counterpart within the Jewish community.[129]

In some Geniza letters, the group revolting against the elders clearly constitutes a social class. A judge from Alexandria reports around 1180 that a notable had accused him before Muslim authorities of having organized dyers, oyster-gatherers, and other "poor stuff," named them his helpers (*anṣār*) and made them rule over the elders. Against this, the writer claims that he had always tried to cooperate with the notables, or "the great," as he also calls them, using a Hebrew expression. The people opposed to the elders he designates as "the public," "the community [al-jamā'a]" or simply "the Jews."[130] The Jewish oyster-gatherers of Alexandria are described in a Geniza letter as people of low standing; later, in Mamluk times, the Muslim fisherfolk of Alexandria, when severely oppressed, took the law into their own hands, lynching the governor of the city and his deputy.[131] Here, the Jewish oystermen appear together with the dyers as revolting against their own notables. In another long letter from Alexandria describing communal strife (unfortunately only the right half is preserved), cobblers are mentioned as one group belonging to the dissatisfied. In a similar letter from Old Cairo, potters are the representatives of the lower class whom a demagogue could easily bribe.[132]

In a particularly interesting but much damaged letter, a Cairene dignitary describes the unsatisfactory situation in Alexandria to his brother, one of the leading Jewish notables in the capital. Again, the local muqaddam is accused of being too lenient with the common people. He would use his influence with the local government in order to get them freed when they were put in prison after a brawl, and would not even have them fined. He continues:

> On Monday there arrived people who were reported to have brought with them a letter from the Prince of Princes [the Nagid Mevōrākh, around 1100]. They assembled crowds everywhere, exhibited the letter . . . and cried it out in the markets and in the houses. This was too much for me. I went to the chief of the police and demanded that the letter should be treated according to the established custom . . . , namely to be read out in the synagogue, so that the high orders contained in it could be obeyed. Divulging it in the markets and in the open places should be stopped. Even if this were a public letter [and not one addressed to certain persons], it should have been treated in this way. When my lord Fakhr al-Mulk—may God make his victories glorious—[the governor of Alexandria] receives a letter from his highness [the Nagid], he kisses it and puts it on his eyes, but the Jews drag it from one place to another.[133]

Incidentally, a very effective letter from the Nagid Mevōrākh to the amir of Alexandria is mentioned in another Geniza paper.[134] In any event, we see that the Cairene notable uses the word "Jews" in the meaning of the common as against the "better" people, when wishing to emphasize that low-class Jews treated a letter from the highest Jewish authority with less respect than the Muslim amir. This usage reminds the reader of Muslim literature of Arabic authors speaking contemptuously of "Arabs," meaning the bedouins and their like, or of Ottoman Turkish writers who deride "Turks," meaning Anatolian peasants.[135]

The conflicts between age groups and social classes occupied the Geniza records less than those between the various factions in the higher ranks of the society. The appointed executive needed the approval and cooperation of the community. Since it is difficult to please everyone, the muqaddam had to secure for himself a following among those favoring him or connected with him by family or other ties. Naturally, this tended to arouse misgivings in those who did not belong to the preferred group. Even in a small town, there would often be found a scholar equaling the appointed community leader in learning and religious authority or even outshining him. If he also possessed enough ambition and stamina, there would soon rally around him a faction demanding his appointment, and communal strife became inevitable.

Local dissensions were often intertwined with contests for ecumenical or territorial leadership. Rival Gaons or Nagids would seek followers and supporters in each and every town and congregation, giving would-be local leaders and troublemakers an excellent opportunity to try their fortune. Moreover, factions were formed by persons hailing from the same town or country who had settled in foreign parts. Because of the mobility of Mediterranean society in the High Middle Ages, this was an extremely common phenomenon.

Modern Jewish scholars who have dealt with these "dissensions" have been somewhat uneasy and unhappy about them. We should think of them rather as party politics inherent in any essentially democratic society. The modern Arabic word for political party, *ḥizb,* is already in use in the Geniza records to designate a faction, and the verb derived from it means "organizing, or forming, a party." [136] The term *'aṣabiyya,* esprit de corps, dedicated following the central idea of Ibn Khaldūn's philosophy of history (written in 1377), appears in our papers in the same sense. The following passage, written by the brother of the Davidite Daniel b. Azarya, who had obtained the gaonate of Jerusalem in 1051 after much strife, is characteristic: "You mentioned that a settlement was reached between 'Allūn [the ḥāvēr who was head of the Palestinians in Old Cairo] and my brother, the rayyis. I was happy about this, not for the just mentioned, the ḥāvēr, but for my brother, because by fighting against him, he ['Allūn] attains publicity [the text says: "a market"] and creates for himself a following *('aṣabiyya).*" [137] Just as in modern election campaigns politicians hurl the most objectionable invectives against each other without taking them too much to heart after the polls have made their decision, so in the Geniza records at the time of dissension, *maḥlōqeth,* the language used is strong, but as soon as peace, *shālōm,* is restored, the same persons become extremely polite and deferential to one another. (The two terms are always expressed in Hebrew, perhaps because the phenomenon described is timeless, or at least pre-Islamic). In the passage quoted above, the Rayyis, or *"head,"* was nicknamed "The Tail" in letters going "to all countries, East and West," but the same Mr. 'Allūn referred to as his adversary addresses him, after he had become Gaon, in the most glowing terms of reverence.[138]

Since everyone of consequence seems to have known everyone else, at least in the countries stretching from Tunisia to Palestine, interest in these communal dissensions was widespread. We learn about them almost exclusively through letters going from one country or town to another. Hearty congratulations were extended when peace was restored, sometimes mixed with the somehow skeptical hope that it should last.[139] Even more frequent are admonitions to put an end to a situation unworthy of members of the academy (which most communal leaders were); for "bickering among scholars is the delight of the common people." [140]

Where it was impossible to restore peace, the democratic right of secession was invoked. The dissatisfied party would withdraw from community life and refrain from "going down" to synagogue, as happened both in large cities and in small towns. While the secessionists could easily satisfy their religious needs by renting a room and forming a congregation by themselves, the local community would be seriously affected by their withdrawal,[141] for its financial means, especially funds for charitable purposes, were obtained largely through donations given and vows made in the course of the service. The failure of a considerable part of the community to appear at the service upset the whole budget. Therefore, in particularly grave cases, strong measures up to excommunication were taken by the community, or a caliphal rescript was obtained by the dissenters for their protection.[142] The disruption of the unity of a congregation also affected the proper functioning of its judiciary, an aspect that involved the government and invited its interference (see chap. vii, sec. B, 1, below). All in all, it seems that such secessions were of an ephemeral character. As far as our knowledge goes, no new congregations of permanent duration were founded during the Geniza period.

Statutes and economic measures.—The idea of legislation was foreign to the society studied in this book. Laws were given by God, and any new problem requiring legislative measures was liable to be solved by the scholars in charge of the interpretation of the sacred law. Questions regarding communal life were submitted to the Gaons and rabbis for decision just as were those regarding ritual or civil cases. Nevertheless, Jewish law itself, as it had developed during Hellenistic and Roman times, made provisions for the creation of statutes (called *taqqānā*) either "by the scholars," or "by the many," the latter being styled "the one that is irrevocable" and "given with the consent of God," formulas found also in a taqqānā preserved in the Geniza.[143] The idea behind such expressions is that the agreement of men represented the will of God (*vox populi vox dei*), or as the Muslim lawyers formulated it later in a saying ascribed to their Prophet: "My community will never be unanimous in the disobedience to God."

Formal resolutions adopted by a community and put into writing must have been comparatively common, since an Arabic verb *taqqan,* to make a taqqānā, was derived from the Hebrew term. Most characteristically no Arabic word is found in our sources for the idea of statute, presumably because the idea itself was foreign to the Muslim society of those days. Like other documents that were regarded as being of permanent value, statutes were not normally relegated to the Geniza and therefore only few have survived. Still, the material in hand gives some idea of the character and scope of communal legislation.

We have already read about the statute that defined the duties of ten elders elected to assist Ephraim b. Shemarya, then chief judge of the Rabbanite community of Old Cairo. In a similar enactment of July, 1028, the same community renews its allegiance to that leader, who had been appointed and reappointed by several Gaons years before. A still earlier taqqānā regulated the supervision of two slaughterhouses and the distribution of the revenue derived from them.[144] Settlements after communal strife were made in writing, sometimes in Hebrew as well as in Arabic, in order to safeguard both their sacred and public character.[145]

Around 1180, a community in a provincial town of Egypt opposed by a taqqānā an attempt by the impostor Zuṭṭā to levy a yearly contribution on their local judge against the renewal of his appointment. In the same document they also resolved not to accept any other judge sent to them by that Nagid. A resolution adopted on May 19, 1208, is so fragmentary that we are able to discern only that it dealt with the relationships with the Muslim authorities.[146] Statutes resolved upon by the Jewish community of Alexandria not to appoint as judge in that city a scholar from France or Byzantium or at least anyone who was not fluent in Arabic are discussed in *Med. Soc.*, I, 67.

Some statutes took the form of the pronouncement of a ban on anyone not complying with their provisions. Thus, we have a large fragment of regulations with regard to the tenants of houses belonging to the communal chest. Another statute imposes a ban on men and women dying silk materials in their homes and thus depriving the *ḍāmin,* who had farmed out the taxes due from that industry, of his legal income.[147]

In general, economic measures were a major concern of the community. The Talmud already discusses the problem of to what extent foreigners were obliged to share the financial burden of the local people. In the Geniza papers, it seems to relate mainly to the obligation to contribute to the *jāliya,* or poll tax, incumbent on indigent persons. Since the foreigners had already paid at home (otherwise they would not have been allowed to travel), it was reasonable not to trouble them with the local jāliya at all. There were circumstances, however, that induced some congregations to deviate from this rule. The Jewish (and also, it seems, the Muslim) population of the main port of Egypt, Alexandria, included many poor. Attempts were therefore made to have the foreigners share the welfare burden. A letter from one Sicilian merchant to another regrets that the addressee was squeezed dry, although "foreigners normally pay nothing or little." Another very long letter from Alexandria written by a Maghrebi is devoted wholly to this matter, but unfortunately not clear to us in its entirety. A delegation of thirty-five foreigners, headed by the writer, had approached the qadi and made a certain contribution in order to avoid further molestation. After a second complaint to the qadi, the local community took new measures. They reduced payments scheduled to be paid by the foreigners to one-half with a view to forcing them to contribute, and spread disparaging rumors against the leader of the Maghrebis. Since practically everyone coming from the West arrived in Alexandria, the matter was important enough for the promulgation of a ban by the Gaon of Jerusalem on anyone "hurting foreigners" by impelling them to make contributions not incumbent on them or by otherwise wronging them. A letter from Sicily urges Judah b. Moses Ibn Sighmār, the representative of the Maghrebis in Egypt, to work for the implementation of that ban, so that both old-timers originating from the Maghreb and newcomers could live peacefully in the land of the Nile.[148]

Another question that cropped up was the protection of inhabitants from economic competition by newcomers. The steps taken in the interest of local craftsmen against the competition of aliens are discussed in *Med. Soc.* I, 85. A letter by the judge Shabbetay b. Abraham of Minyat Ziftā vividly illustrates similar efforts with regard to commercial rivalry. An outsider from Cairo with two partners had opened a store of medical potions, thereby doing harm to "the Jews," that is, to the local community (as the letter emphasizes four times, although it seems that mainly the judge's own son was affected). The local community was unable to tackle the situation, particularly since a son of its leader was involved. The judge reports that he approached the chief of police, the qadi, and the "elders" (meaning probably the Muslim notables) and now asks two prominent men in Cairo directly to take up the matter with the person concerned.[149] When a rich man from Sfax, Tunisia, settled in Mazara, Sicily, around 1064, bought there a house for himself for 300 dinars and sent for his wife to join him (definite proof that he intended to stay in the island), the local Jews, who dreaded his competition, informed the Norman ruler of the arrival of the undesirable newcomer.[150]

Still, nothing has been found thus far in the Geniza papers comparable with an institution developed among European Jews and rightly explained by the students of history as fitting into the general structure of feudal society: the so-called *ḥerem ha-yishūv,* the denial of admission to any newcomer, except with special permission.[151] It is not only the silence of the Geniza records in this respect which is instructive. We have a very interesting letter indicating that the institution was foreign to the Mediterranean world. In this letter, a scholar strongly dissuades another from traveling to a country that would take "three years" to reach. (In *The Arabian Nights,* too, it takes over two years to get to a distant place.) Against the expectations of the addressee, the Jewish scholars there were of no greater erudition than a local scholar quoted by name. On the other hand, the language and manners there were foreign and barbarous and the Jews did not permit a coreligionist from abroad to stay longer than one month if he was engaged in business. The reference to scholars and the refusal of admission points to Germany as the country alluded to.[152]

In general, then, we see that statutes and formal enactments of a public body, although not frequently found in the Geniza, were by no means unknown. In these matters, as in others, the society reflected in the Geniza records somehow held the middle ground between Greco-Roman corporational life and the seeming paucity of communal organization in the Muslim society of the period.

2. *The Officials of the Community*

The muqaddam, or appointed executive.—The main figure of Jewish community life during the Geniza period was the muqaddam (lit., "the one put at the head," the superior), the religious and temporal head appointed with the consent of the community by the Jewish central authorities and accredited by the local representatives of the government. Some uncertainty has prevailed thus far concerning the nature of this office and its relationship to other offices in the community. Nevertheless, the Geniza contains sufficient material to enable us to gain clarity about this matter.[1]

The term "muqaddam" had been well known from Spanish Jewish history. When it made its appearance in the Geniza documents as well, a connection was naturally sought between the two. As late as 1950 it was suggested that the institution was brought to the East by Spanish Jews.[2] In reality, the office of the muqaddam was well established in Egypt by the end of the eleventh century, whereas in Spain muqaddams are mentioned frequently only during the thirteenth and fourteenth centuries. In Spain they appear regularly in the plural as elders forming boards consisting of four to twenty-five members and representing the local communities. Thus, no direct connection should be assumed between these two institutions.[3]

In order to arrive at a correct understanding of the term "muqaddam" as it was used in the East during the Geniza period, we have to keep in mind (*a*) that it appears there both in the specific sense defined above and in the general meaning of "leader," and (*b*) that the post of appointed executive could be held by persons of different professions, such as a ḥāvēr, or member of the Jerusalem academy, a judge, a cantor, a scribe, or even a layman with some Jewish learning. Consequently, we find persons styled muqaddam who did not hold the position of an appointed community leader at all, while on the other hand others who did occupy it were identified by their profession or by another characteristic. In other cases, both the profession and the position were indicated; for example, the sender of a magnificently written letter from the townlet of Malīj signs thus: "The ḥāvēr, muqaddam of Malīj."[4] Since this fluent terminology has led to a certain confusion, some details are given to explain the situation.

When the Spanish Jewish poet Judah ha-Levi, on the way to the Holy Land, passed some months in Alexandria in fall, 1140, and spring, 1141, he was called by the Muslims there "muqaddam of the Jews," although he did not, of course, hold any official position.[5] In a contract dated 1099, a beadle is threatened with immediate dismissal if he showed lack of respect against the members of the congregation or the muqaddams, meaning here anyone holding an office in the synagogue. Maimonides uses the word in the same sense.[6] The verb *taqaddam,* "to be appointed as head," simply could mean "to lead a congregation in prayer," said of an honored guest or of community officials taking up this duty in turn.[7]

On the other hand, even in our oldest documents we find the verb *qaddam* used in the technical sense of appointing to a post in the service of the community, and by the end of the eleventh century, in the documents issued under the authority of the Nagid Mevōrākh, the term "muqaddam" had become accepted as denoting a person in charge of a local community.[8] Since normally any larger community was headed by a judge, the Arab term designated such a person, as when, in a letter from Aden, around 1130, respects are paid to the Gaon, the muqaddams, meaning the three Jewish judges of the Egyptian capital, the cantors, and scholars of the Gaon's entourage.[9] Persons mentioned in a text first as judges, or puisne judges (*nā'ib*), or members of the academy, are later on referred to as muqaddams.[10] When we find a circular addressed to the muqaddams and puisne judges of the Egyptian countryside, we should not take this to indicate the existence of a judge *and* a muqaddam side by side, but rather that there were many places in which the latter office was held by persons who were not qualified judges.[11] On the other hand, in a city like Damascus or Old Cairo, when muqaddams and judges are mentioned together, we have to remember that the former word also designated the head of a synagogue.[12]

In short, the office of the appointed head of a local community was not always designated by the term "muqaddam." In fact the office was in existence long before the term became common in our sources. It may be that the Arabic title adopted this specific meaning in the last third of the eleventh century for the same reason that gave rise to the office of Nagid: the eclipse of the gaonate of Palestine and with it the necessity to regulate the communal service on a territorial basis. Licensing by the Nagid's representatives, the Jewish chief judges in the Egyptian capital, gradually replaced the diploma of the yeshiva.

Most of the judges and other muqaddams whose origin is referred to in our sources were foreigners or at least not natives of the town or district where they served. Palestine and Iraq, northwest Africa and Spain, Byzantium, and later also France provided most of the spiritual and communal leaders. This fact was perhaps due to the preference of the Egyptian Jews for more practical ways of life (a tendency that seems to have prevailed until modern times). When we find in smaller towns mostly outsiders as muqaddams, there was perhaps, in addition, a definite policy at work which intended to keep the appointee as far as possible independent of the local coteries. Many of our records refer to muqaddams new in the town, and in one letter the local people do not want him also as teacher, because they did not regard him as a permanent resident.[13]

Reference has been made to letters of appointment even with regard to a community in a small town. Such a letter has been preserved. It concerns Ephraim b. Shemarya, the head of the Palestinians and, during extended periods, of the Rabbanites at large, in Old Cairo. It is dated July, 1028, and represents the renewal of a long-standing allegiance. At that time, of course, public officials were appointed by the Great Sanhedrin (as the yeshiva of Jerusalem was called) through its presidents, the Gaons. Accordingly, the document, after having stated the desires of the community to comply with the commandments of God who had chosen Jerusalem (quoting Deuteronomy 17:8–10) and to follow the traditions of the Jewish faith, makes mention of the fact that Ephraim had been appointed by three successive Gaons to serve as judge, community leader, and religious authority, and given the title ḥāvēr, or member of the academy, by each of them. The new Gaon (Solomon b. Judah) had renewed all these prerogatives and Ephraim had displayed under him the same praiseworthy conduct and dedication as under his predecessors. Therefore, the community saw fit to accept his leadership in the future also and to obey him, as described by the law (quoting Deuteronomy 16:18).[14]

In the document just discussed, the allegiance of the local community was expressed long after the central authority had made the appointment. The opposite procedure can be observed in another document, written exactly two hundred years later (1228 or about that date). Anatoli of Marseille, the Jewish chief judge of Alexandria, had died, and the local congregations had agreed on the election of another French rabbi, who had already served them as acting judge for three years. Now a notable in Old Cairo is requested to secure the approval of the Nagid. Incidentally, in many documents the head of the Alexandrian Jewish community is referred to as muqaddam.[15]

A muqaddam over a city or an entire district needed a written certificate by the local governor or the caliph himself confirming his appointment. A man who had been transferred by the yeshiva from Egypt to a district in northern Syria (which comprised towns as distant from each other as Baalbek in present-day Lebanon and Raqqa east of the Euphrates) recounts that he had already seen the local governor four times and had been exceedingly well received by him, but had not yet taken from him the certificate of installment because he did not cherish the new place and was not sure whether he would remain. At a change of government a new certificate had to be secured (as was true of all other offices). A petition to this effect with regard to "Joseph, the Aaronite" (that is Joseph ha-Kohen, father and predecessor of Yeshū'ā, the muqaddam of Alexandria [see sec. B, 1. nn. 95, 96]) has been preserved. The badly mutilated fragment states that the incumbent had been successively appointed by three former Gaons mentioned by name, and had been reappointed by the present Gaon, "Solomon of Fez" (i.e., Solomon b. Judah). Joseph was to continue as the highest Jewish authority in the city with regard to cases of civil law, marriage and divorce, religious ritual, and appointment or dismissal of cantors (presumably also other communal officials; there is a gap in the manuscript); no one had the right to change his decisions except the Gaon who had appointed him. The Arabic script and style of the petition are identical with those of the document aimed at obtaining a letter of installment or confirmation for a Gaon (see sec. A, 1, n. 38, above). Both must have been written in 1036, when al-Mustanṣir became caliph, the only change of government during the incumbency of Solomon b. Judah.[16]

Just as there was no rigid procedure at the appointment of a muqaddam so did his duties and prerogatives depend largely on local conditions and on his own qualities and qualifications. We have noticed this in the complaint of the muqaddam of Minyat Ziftā. Still, a common pattern emerges from our variegated records. The duties of a muqaddam are well defined in three letters referring to an "excellent member of the academy," who had to leave his post in al-Maḥalla because of the dissatisfaction of his flock.[17] He had to administer all the affairs of the community, big and small, a task that included the maintenance of peace and unity within the congregation and its representation before the local state authorities; to decide all questions related to religious law and ritual; to expound the Scriptures and to teach the adults; to supervise the education of the young. His most substantial duty was to preside over the local law court and to perform all functions regarding marriage and divorce. He would also normally lead the congregation in prayer, but, unless he was a professional cantor, would leave most of the chanting and singing to others. The liturgy was still fluid at that time, and he would make decisions in this matter as well or ask a higher authority for guidance.[18] In addition, he would also serve as one of the local scribes, draw up legal documents, and write official letters. The handwriting of many a muqaddam is known to us, since much of the fruit of their labors has been preserved.

From these letters regarding al-Maḥalla, as well as other similar ones, it is evident that the muqaddam was empowered to make unilateral decisions solely in cases of religious law and ritual, where he was supposed to interpret the sacred writings authoritatively. But in communal as well as in legal matters (which were decided mostly by settlement rather than by formal judgments) he had to consult the elders and the community. In the smaller towns of the Rīf, where muqaddams were chosen because of a strong personality and the ability to restrain the unruly rather than for scholarship, their religious authority too was occasionally challenged. "This muqaddam," writes a scholarly schoolmaster from a small town to his friend in Old Cairo, "is not good enough to be an inferior, let alone a superior" and then goes on to give examples of the latter's mismanagement of the religious law (both, by the way, were Palestinians).[19] A muqaddam of Hebron, Palestine, complains to the judge of Old Cairo who had appointed him that he was not always obeyed even in matters pertaining to religion. About a similar grievance we shall read presently.[20]

A muqaddam had also to be a good fund-raiser, since communal revenue consisted to a large extent of voluntary contributions. A physician who was also a muqaddam assured his friend that he would not extort money from him, although both his vocation and avocation had trained him in this art.[21] Another substantial, and certainly not always pleasant, duty was the assistance of government officials or tax-farmers in the assessment of the poll tax incumbent on the members of the congregation. On the other hand, such a task was liable to strengthen the assessor's position.

The emoluments of the muqaddam are better treated together with those of other communal officials, since they differed from those of others in quantity rather than in nature, but were as varied. We frequently read that muqaddams (and others) leave their posts in a smaller town or rural district because they were not paid sufficiently or were not paid at all. Sometimes the parting official speaks about his parish in friendly and even loving terms, certainly because he realized that poverty rather than bad will was the source of their default. Thus, in a letter to the Nagid Mevōrākh, a muqaddam (and cantor) expresses his gratitude to the local community, young and old, for its attachment and writes that he would have preferred to stay until a substitute was sent by the Nagid, but that he was unable to do so since the income from his post sufficed only for his own maintenance, but not for that of his family (which had remained in the city).[22] Another muqaddam, a professional scribe, writes that he could not remain at his post because he did not derive from it the benefits normally connected with such a position, but would stay on until he completed a Torah scroll he had promised to write for the community.[23] In other letters, though, as in the one about Minyat Ghamr referred to above (p. 49), the complaints are bitter, and there is a general outcry against the *ḥāmās* (Heb.) *al-Rīf,* the sufferings endured by the more scholarly muqaddams in the congregations of the Egyptian countryside. Some stories in such Geniza letters recall *The Diaries of a Country Judge* of the modern Egyptian writer Tawfīq al-Ḥakīm, as when a muqaddam complains that the widow of the chief cantor threatened to accuse him before the local chief of police of being the cause of her husband's prolonged illness and death (he calls her Zeresh, the name of the wife of the notorious Haman of the book of Esther).[24]

Conditions in the smaller communities thus prevailing, the Jewish authorities in Old Cairo were anxious to strengthen the authority of the muqaddams. In an enormous letter issued by the two judges of the capital in the name of the Nagid Mevōrākh, a circuit judge is strongly rebuked for having given judgment in a town in the absence of the local muqaddam and for having taken other actions without consulting him (and the elders).[25] When a community leader, upon returning from a trip to the capital, found that the son of a scholar had married four couples, writing their marriage contracts and performing the weddings, he respectfully asks the chief judge to send him a letter explaining whether or not the action of the scholar's son was permissible—a polite form of announcing that something very improper had been done.[26] It is well known that Maimonides and his court published in January, 1187, a solemn prohibition against anyone, except the muqaddam, performing a wedding in specified provincial towns. A similar ban was pronounced in 1235 for Alexandria, and the Nagid Abraham Maimonides restated the position with regard to the provincial towns.[27]

A detailed thirteenth-century document from al-Maḥalla shows how seriously these matters were taken in later times and how careful scholars had become not to trespass on the rights of the local muqaddam. The document states that a certain scholar had never made a public appearance without announcing on that occasion that he was acting under permission from the head of the community. Specifically, he had performed a wedding ceremony solely at the urgent request of the head.[28] On the other hand, we also find a muqaddam complaining of being neglected by the central authorities. The unique letter suggests the reason for the neglect. The writer points out his own incompetence and limited knowledge, as well as his lack of books. It was therefore exceedingly difficult for him to decide any but routine questions (as an example of a case that he was unable to tackle he mentions an affair with a male and a female proselyte). Like others with little authority he had made much use of bans and temporary excommunication, but to no avail. The community did not accept his religious guidance. The letter is addressed to the judge of (New) Cairo who at that time had precedence over the other Jewish judges in the capital.[29] Naturally, overbearing communal leaders, so frequently castigated in the Talmud, are not absent from the Geniza records either. In a letter to a Nagid, written by the local scribe, a muqaddam is credited with boasting of "beating the people with shoes," treating them with utmost contempt.[30]

In addition to material gain, it was the social position and prestige connected with the office of the muqaddam which made it attractive for both professionals and laymen. To be sure, according to the pious Nagid Abraham Maimonides, neither should be aimed at. "It is not proper and it is not permissible," he writes, "for a muqaddam, or for the person who appoints him, or those over whom he had been appointed, to believe that the purpose of his office is to make profit from public funds or to gain an honored position. All this is merely incidental. The basic aim is the gain of the community in religiosity and welfare. This is the essence of a religious office, all the rest is incidental."[31]

The head of the congregation(s).—"Muqaddam," as we have seen, was the name of an office, not a title. Therefore, it is found only exceptionally as a family name and is never attached to the name of a person's father.[32] The opposite was the case with the "head of the congregation" or "congregations," *rōsh ha-qāhāl* or *ha-qehillōt.* It is extremely common as a title of honor following the name of a person's father or that of a person addressed in a letter or mentioned in a document, but we hear next to nothing about the activities specific to a person styled in this way.[33]

Clearly, at various times and in different places the title was given to holders of diverse positions in the community. In a letter sent to Manbij, far up in northern Syria, a scholar is addressed as "rōsh ha-qāhāl," but in the address, which is written in Arabic letters, he is called "the tax-farmer of the market and judge of the Jews."[34] Three cases of heads of congregations being or becoming judges have been noted for the eleventh century in Old Cairo.[35] When Maimonides mentions in one of his responsa that the congregations used to rise and remain standing while the head of the academy or the head of the congregation was reciting the Holy Scriptures, he was certainly using the term "head of the congregation" to mean a scholar appointed as community leader.[36]

On the other hand, there are many instances where the rōsh haquāhāl is differentiated from the scholarly executive. In an old letter written on parchment, sent from al-Mahdiyya, Tunisia, to the ḥāvēr Ephraim (of Old Cairo) a message is given to a head of the congregations there. The same appellation is found in an approximately contemporary letter addressed to the president of the Jewish court in Aleppo, Syria.[37] Around 1100, a document is signed in a little town by a rōsh ha-qāhāl together with the appointed judge, and the contents of the document clearly indicate that the judge, and not the rōsh ha-qāhāl, was in charge of the communal affairs. In addition, the shaky, awkward handwriting of the rōsh ha-qāhāl betrays an untutored person.[38] With few exceptions, most of the heads of congregations appearing in the Geniza records after 1050 are known to us only by name.

With some hesitation, a sketch of the historical development of this common term is attempted here. It is highly probable that the head of the congregation of the Geniza period replaced the ancient head of the synagogue *(rōsh ha-keneset,* Greek *archi-synagogos),* for the latter term is entirely absent from our records. As evident from the Talmud, the head of the synagogue was a layman inferior in rank to the scholar appointed as community leader, and indeed to any scholar.[39] In the Hebrew papyruses, the old title was still in full use,[40] but by the tenth century it had become obsolete, perhaps because it carried with it the connotation of laity, which was shunned in a period when everyone wanted to be regarded as a religious scholar. The new title was neutral and, as shown by the examples given above, could be borne by both judges and laymen. In the tenth and early eleventh centuries the term seems to have designated presidents of the congregations, for we find persons so styled mentioned in memorial lists together with Gaons and judges or using this title regularly after their signatures.[41] In Yemen and North Africa, the diocesan representative of the yeshivas was designated as head of the congregations.[42]

During the same period, however, it had become customary that only a scholar qualifying as member of the yeshiva could lead a large congregation, while toward the end of the eleventh century, we find that only a muqaddam, or appointee of the Nagid or his representatives, could fill this post. We never hear of a clash (or an act of cooperation) between a muqaddam and a rōsh ha-qāhāl. Thus, it would be out of place to regard the latter as a representative of the local people as opposed to the scholarly executive. We have also to keep in mind that no Arabic equivalent exists for this term.[43] It therefore seems that by the end of the eleventh century the title of head of the congregation had become merely an honorary one given to meritorious members of the congregation, perhaps to those having some prerogatives in the synagogue, as held by the ancient archi-synagogos, for example, the assignment to members and guests of the reading of various parts of the service. No express mention of this aspect has been found thus far. Only in small places that had no muqaddam does the head of the congregation appear as the man in charge of the community.[44]

We sporadically find other terms referring to leaders of congregations or local communities. In 1240, the *qayyim,* or superintendent of the "small synagogue" in Alexandria, possessed a house in Cairo, and, rather strangely, also seems to have lived there. *Qayyim* is a Muslim title referring to the administration of a mosque or other religious institution and was in later times transferred to that of a synagogue.[45] A person called *shaykh al-yahūd,* elder (i.e., head) of the Jews of Ascalon, Palestine, is mentioned early in the twelfth century, and a letter from Qūṣ in Upper Egypt, written about a hundred years later, speaks somewhat derisively of a perfumer "who says of himself that he is shaykh al-yahūd." By the fourteenth century the term designated the head of the community in Old Cairo who was responsible to the government for the payment of the poll tax.[46]

All in all, it seems that despite the prominent role of the elders and the plenary assembly in the conduct of the affairs of the community, the need was not felt to have a formally elected president as a counterweight against the appointed executive. In any event, the head of the congregation(s), although often mentioned in the Geniza records, seems not to have had such a role.

The social service officers and the "trustees of the court."—The *parnāsīm,* who were in charge of the communal property and the social services, are mentioned in the Geniza documents more frequently than any other officials. The very fact that the Hebrew term is often rendered in an Arabicized form *(firnās,* pl. *farānisa)* illustrates the popularity of that office.[47] The *parnās* of the Geniza period differs very much from his successor in European Jewry. He was not "a leader" or a president of a congregation, but an official of lower rank who served mostly in an honorary capacity, but who sometimes was in receipt of emoluments. As revealed by the greetings extended in official letters to various groups of the community, the social service officers were ranked after the scholars, elders, notables, and cantors. A combination such as "the parnās, the beadle" sounds strange to anyone familiar with the regular Hebrew usage, but occurs in the

Geniza more than once and was perfectly appropriate at a time and place where the beadle was higher and the parnās lower ranked than was true elsewhere. When Benjamin of Tudela visited "the Synagogue of Moses," the holy shrine of Dammūh on the southwestern outskirts of Fustat, he found it under the care of a scholarly old man whom he describes as "parnās and beadle," presumably an expression he had learned on his travels.[48]

The field of social services was the one in which respectable members of the community who did not excel in scholarship found rich opportunity for making their contribution to the common good. We find well-to-do and influential persons serving as parnāsīm. Through a happy coincidence, the Geniza has preserved dozens of letters and legal deeds relating to two parnāsīm, one called Eli ha-Kohen b. Yaḥyā (or Ḥayyīm or Ḥiyyā, all having the connotation "Life"), in Arabic 'Allūn b. Ya'īsh (which means "May he live"), and one 'Ullā ha-Levi b. Joseph, in Arabic Ṣā'id b. Munajjā (the Arabic was supposed to render the meaning of the Hebrew names) of Damascus, both living in Old Cairo in the same period. Of the former we have documents dated from 1057 through 1107 and of the latter from 1084 through 1117. Both were assistant members of the rabbinical court and as such signed many records. They were also trustees of the court (see below), and in this capacity too wrote and signed entries in the record books. 'Ullā was active in the Mediterranean as well as in the India trade and a wide variety of merchandise was handled by him as shown in his correspondence. He dealt chiefly in silk, corals, glass, brocade and other robes, and such Western goods as saffron, ambergris, and scammony, and oriental products, in particular brazilwood. In addition to his manifold duties as parnās, he was also a trustee of the yeshiva of Jerusalem. His colleague Eli held a position of confidence both with the yeshiva and the Nagids Judah and Mevōrākh and for some time also with the latter's bitter opponent, the exilarch David b. Daniel. The numerous letters addressed to him from Jerusalem, Ramle, and Ascalon show him as a rallying point for the Palestinians, while he was also closely connected with the Tunisians who had emigrated to Egypt. The two parnāsīm often acted together; on one occasion we find them signing a long list of needy persons to whom loaves were to be distributed by the community for the duration of a month.[49]

This short sketch was intended to give an idea of the type of persons serving as parnāsīm. As far as we are able to judge, they usually came from the upper middle class. At least, this was so during the earlier part of the classical Geniza period. Although many are known to us, none seems to have been honored with the title head of the congregation. An assertion to the contrary is based on a faulty reconstruction of a damaged text.[50]

All our sources point to the fact that in each congregation several parnāsīm were active simultaneously, a circumstance that was in accordance with Jewish law which required that no public office involving the handling of money should be held by fewer than two persons.[51] The Palestinians in Old Cairo at one time had seven parnāsīm, at another "more than four" (including one physician) and once exactly four, but even in a provincial town the judge would be assisted by several parnāsīm.[52] In the letters addressed to the Eli mentioned a few lines above, greetings are usually extended to two or more of his colleagues.[53]

A certain number of social service officers was required also because of the many different tasks incumbent on them (see sec. C, below). The administration and maintenance of the houses belonging to the community and the distribution of the revenue gained from them were sufficient to occupy more than one person. Since the parnāsīm were busy people engaged in gaining their livelihood, they would take turns, one "collector" soliciting contributions one week and another during the next, and so forth.[54] A distinguished visitor, a proselyte, or an indigent person from a good family (especially if he was a scholar) was assigned to a certain parnās who was expected to look after him personally. Jews living in a remote village would confide their affairs to a parnās in Fustat, probably because they had no access to a higher official.[55] Occasionally, a parnās had to travel in order to raise funds, for example, for the ransom of captives, or to accompany a scholar for the same purpose.[56]

Finally, in a large city like Old Cairo, a number of parnāsīm, originating from different countries, was desirable in order to meet the requirements of its cosmopolitan population. We find there parnāsīm of the Rūm (Europeans), of people from Jerusalem, from Damietta (most probably after the conquest of that town by the Crusaders in November, 1219) and even from the island of Crete (from which Jews might have migrated in large numbers after it had fallen to the Venetians in 1204). One of the chores of the parnāsīm was the assessment of the frequently changing needs of each indigent household, and this of course could be done more easily by a man closely acquainted with the background of the families concerned.[57]

The activities of the various social service officers were normally coordinated by the local judge or muqaddam. In addition, we find a "head of the parnāsīm," who presumably performed a similar task.

in 1090, such a head parnās gives a loan of 5 dinars (to be repaid in fifteen monthly installments) to a person known as "the poet"; in 1145, such an official takes a loan of 11 dinars from a "young man" (to be repaid in eleven monthly installments) and grants, two months later, a loan of 30 good silver pieces to a goldsmith.[58] In all these cases it seems that the loans were made on behalf of the public chest. Since an institution was not a legal personality, all financial transactions had to be made in the name of the parnāsīm personally. Our assumption is proved in the second example by the fact that the loan taken by the parnās was repaid by a man who had farmed out the revenue from houses belonging to the community, while in the first example it is more than probable that such was the case in view of similar occurrences.

With respect to the appointment of the parnāsīm, we find in one document that the ḥāvēr, the member of the yeshiva appointed as executive, "established" them in concert with the community, an arrangement to be expected in a society that, as we so often had opportunity to observe, displayed both a hierocratic and a democratic character.[59]

Until approximately 1150, we do not read anything in our records about material gains accruing to a parnās from his service to the community. This lack of information may or may not reflect the actual situation. From the second half of the twelfth century, the financial reports occasionally contain the item "cost of the collection of revenue," which suggests that honorary social officials were assisted or replaced by paid ones. Similarly, in these later times, a parnās distributing clothing would receive for himself and sometimes for members of his family a piece of clothing as well. This development is perhaps indicative of growing poverty rather than of a decline in public spirit. Besides, the practice that a person administering public funds should be remunerated out of those funds is attested as customary in an ancient Hebrew source.[60]

Another public office, often connected with that of the parnās, was that of the "trustee [of the court]," *ne'emān (bēth-dīn)*. Despite its frequency, no Arabic equivalent of the Hebrew term appears in our sources, which probably means that it designated an essentially Jewish institution. From its Aramaic designation, *hēmān*, an Arabic plural was derived and also an Arabic name for the office, *haymana*.[61]

Like the parnās, the trustee had manifold duties. Insolvent debtors deposited with him gold and silver vessels, books, and other valuables as collateral, until they were able to meet their obligations. With the consent of the depositor and under supervision of the court he could place such objects with other persons as a safeguard. Husbands traveling abroad empowered him to cash sums due them or left him money for the maintenance of their families during their absence. The alimonies due separated wives or divorcées with small children would be paid through him and he was often in charge of the estates of orphans or of foreigners who died far away from their families. He gave loans to needy people against collaterals deposited with him. The accumulated value of such deposits was sometimes very considerable. When in 1168 Old Cairo was sacked and burned, a trustee held collaterals worth ten thousand dinars, which perished in the general disaster. From another document referring to the same man, we learn that loans used to be given "through him," meaning that he served as a kind of banking institution.[62] He was called *al-firnās al-ma'arrī yedī'a al-jubaylī,* "the parnās from Ma'arra, known as the man from Jubayl," both towns in northern Syria. We remember that the Old Cairene parnās 'Ullā, who figures in so many documents, hailed from Damascus. Several parnāsīm and trustees of the court of Old Cairo were natives of Jerusalem and many bankers appearing in the Geniza papers have the family name Ḥalabī, meaning "of Aleppo." One is reminded of the remark of the tenth-century Muslim geographer al-Muqaddasī that banking was a favorite occupation of the Syrian Jews.[63]

A trustee of the court was a highly respected member of the community. Therefore, a person who had such a man as father would be referred to in official documents and in letters addressed to him as "the son of the trustee." In a court record dated May 28, 1207, three such persons are mentioned, two appearing as guardians of orphans, and the third as one of the two witnesses to the legal procedure, which means that the sons held positions of trust similar to those of their fathers. An Arabic approximate equivalent of this title has been found thus far only with regard to a person living in the tenth century.[64]

Many functions incumbent on a trustee of the court, such as the payment of alimony to a divorced woman, were fulfilled by a parnās. Although intrinsically different, the first being a juridical official and the latter a social one, in actuality they often rendered the same services.[65]

In a document from Ascalon, Palestine, written around 1100, the firnās is the head of the local community and a very arrogant one. "The neck of any person living in this town, whether foreign or native," he reportedly would say, "is beneath my foot."[66] Similarly, a letter from the same time speaks of the son of *the* parnās of Bilbays, the town on the caravan road between Cairo and Ascalon mentioned before.[67] This usage corresponds to that in talmudic literature, where alongside the plural parnāsīm in the sense of social service officers, appears the singular in the meaning of leader and head of a community. In the Geniza records this usage is definitely exceptional.

The synagogue beadle and messenger of the court.—The synagogue attendant, *shammāsh,* Arabic *khādim,* was not the minor official that a sexton of a church or a beadle in a synagogue is today. Various reasons account for the difference. The service of the sanctuary of God was regarded as an honored privilege. In a letter of appointment it is compared with the function of the Levites in the Temple of Jerusalem.[68] From another document we learn that in a small town a pious citizen rented a house and dedicated it as a synagogue on condition that he have the privilege "to clean and to serve it."[69] Similarly, in Islam, the work of the *farrāsh* (lit., the one who spreads the carpets), or attendant of the mosque, was often done by a high-standing person as an expression of reverence and love of God.[70]

Furthermore, as other letters of appointment state, the beadle's duties comprised not only the maintenance of the synagogue property, but also "the service of Israel, both women and men" (synagogue of the Palestinians), or the service "of the muqaddams and the other members of the synagogue" (Babylonians).[71] He was the community's factotum and was indeed called in some places, "servant of the community."[72] He served as messenger and assistant clerk of the court, and, in connection with this task, as attorney, trustee, cashier, and in other capacities. Therefore, he had an intimate knowledge of all that was going on in the community. It seems, too, that beadles more often than not were rather well-to-do. At least, we see them giving loans, some of no small size. Even the trustee with whom valuables worth ten thousand dinars had been deposited in 1168 was a "servant of the sanctuary."[73] The shammāsh of those days resembled perhaps his Christian namesake (*shammās* in Arabic), who was a deacon or a clerk of the church.

In his delightful book, *Jewish Life in the Middle Ages,* Israel Abrahams, having in mind the late Middle Ages (which for the Jews in some parts of Europe lasted until the end of the nineteenth century) describes the position of the shammāsh within the community as follows: "This functionary rapidly became ruler of the synagogue. His functions were so varied, his duties placed him in possession of such detailed information of the members' private affairs, his presence so permeated the synagogue and the home on public and private occasions, that the Shamash [Abrahams' spelling], instead of serving the congregation, became its master."[74]

The statement made in the last sentence is echoed in a Geniza letter addressed around 1105 to the Nagid Mevōrākh. The writer, after having listed various grievances against the beadle of the synagogue of the Iraqis in Old Cairo, concludes: "He has not the appearance of a servant, but that of a rayyis [head]."[75] The position of the shammāsh in the Geniza period differed, however, from that described in Abrahams' book, since the office as such was regarded in those days with more respect and the functions of the beadle, in accordance with the wider scope of Jewish community life under Islam, were then even more varied.

At the appointment of a shammāsh, an inventory of the books, scrolls, and furnishings of the synagogue, such as gold and silver ornaments, lamps, precious textiles, carpets and mats, was drawn up and all items confided to his care. He was responsible for their maintenance and preservation—a task that required in those insecure times both vigilance and resourcefulness. He was also in charge of their cleaning and of smaller repairs, for which he submitted monthly accounts. In particular, he tended to the appropriate illumination of the place during the night, in order to enable laymen and scholars to pursue their studies. In one document this appears as his most essential duty.[76]

We frequently find beadles assisting the social service officers or doing their work. In a letter of appointment, a beadle of the Babylonians is required to help the parnās Eli, whom we have met before, in collecting and distributing loaves of bread to the poor.[77] In various documents beadles collect the rents from houses or other property belonging to the community.[78] If he had sufficient means, a beadle would farm out the revenue from pious foundations.[79]

In his capacity as messenger of the court, the shammāsh delivered summons and other communications to the parties and had to be on hand during the sessions. In addition, he had to take down the depositions and pleas made by the persons appearing in court as they were repeated to him by the presiding judge. In one letter of appointment the beadle is threatened with immediate dismissal if he made any changes in the texts dictated to him;[80] but it is doubtful whether this function was common, for most of the rough copies of court records actually found in the Geniza are in the handwriting of scribes and judges known to us. We should remember, however, that the Geniza chamber was attached to the synagogue of the Palestinians, while the letter of appointment referred to was issued for that of the Babylonians, where perhaps other practices prevailed. In any case, a Geniza letter shows that even in a small town a beadle would have a good hand—betraying continuous training. Thus we are not astonished to find in a city like al-Mahdiyya a beadle (who was writing letters for a woman) serving as an accomplished scribe.[81]

The close connection with the courts gave the beadles opportunities for many different jobs. From a document issued in Cairo in 1094 we learn that a shammāsh who was charged with the delivery of a bill of divorce to a woman living in Palestine had retained it for three years; as he explained in court, he had always delayed in that way in order to give the couple opportunity to be reconciled (a rather high-handed way of forcing happiness upon others).[82] In 1098, a husband deposits the trousseau of his wife with a beadle until a settlement is reached.[83] A silk-weaver appoints a beadle as executor of his will, a physician makes another his attorney against a debtor, and a rich woman does the same in a matter of inheritance. We could cite more instances for this.[84]

In only one example thus far has a beadle been found performing police duties. He had caught a man and confined him in his house, because it was Passover week when the courts did not sit. On the concluding holiday, however, when the beadle was, of course, busy in the synagogue, the accused escaped through a window.[85] This event happened in April, 1028, to a beadle of the Babylonians in Old Cairo. Perhaps in this respect, too, the Babylonians had their own traditions. It is well known that in the lands of the Eastern caliphate, the authorities of the minority groups were sometimes permitted to imprison or to inflict corporal punishment on their members.

In his book, Israel Abrahams surmises that in the period of the Gaons the offices of the beadle and that of the messenger of the court were not combined in one person. Others held a different opinion. The answer to this and similar questions is that no rigid and unified system prevailed with regard to this communal institution as to others. In one letter of appointment, the service of the court appears as one of the most substantial duties of the beadle. In others, it is not even mentioned. Normally, a number of beadles served a community at one and the same time, and at one point there were five in the Egyptian capital. Thus they could divide the various duties among themselves.[86]

The beadle lived in the synagogue compound. One letter of appointment makes it incumbent on him to be present there "together with his boys."[87] Sometimes his family encroached on the synagogue property, as when we read in the complaint to the Nagid Mevōrākh that the beadle of the Babylonians lived "in the synagogue" with his brothers and their families, altogether about fifteen individuals. They acted as if the compound was their own property even to the extent of playing with pigeons on the roofs. (According to *The Arabian Nights* breeding carrier pigeons on one's roof was a sport of people of low class.)[88]

In this letter, as well as in another addressed by the same man to the Nagid in reference to the same matter, the assertion is made that the deputy judge in charge of that synagogue, also called muqaddam, did nothing without consulting the beadle. That official had become so confident of his position that he would refuse to obey orders inconvenient for him even if they were conveyed to him in the name of the Nagid.[89] Similarly, in a letter written much later, a shammāsh is charged with having brought an unworthy preacher to the synagogue.[90] The actual scope of an office was obviously defined by the personality of its holder rather than by hard and fast rules.

The position of a shammāsh was even more fortified if he remained in office for a long time. The beadle of the Babylonians, against whom such strong representations were made before the Nagid Mevōrākh, was appointed in 1099, but still at his post in June, 1127, many years after the Nagid had died. Regarding a beadle of the Palestinians, we have documents dated from 1159 to December, 1188, and his son, who served in the synagogue of the Babylonians, did so for a still longer period (documents dated 1186 through 1223, probably even 1183 through 1227). Since the preservation of documents is a matter of mere chance, the beadles most probably served for far longer periods than those indicated here.[91]

Female caretakers of synagogues are mentioned in *Med. Soc.*, I, 130. Meanwhile I have found an interesting document referring to a *khādima,* or female caretaker, whose husband was not a beadle. An Egyptian story in *The Arabian Nights* speaks repeatedly of an old woman in charge of a church.[92]

Other officials.—Most of the professionals discussed in chapters vi and vii have to be regarded as community officials, since they were often in receipt of emoluments from the community or derived benefits from it. Scholars and judges, cantors and preachers, the officials connected with the observance of the dietary laws (the slaughterer, and the "guards" of meat, milk, and cheese), as well as the scribes, either appear on the payrolls or were assigned other sources of public revenue. They, together with those described in this section, formed the large body of the servants of the community. Here I mention some classes of employees of minor importance.

Medical care was not the concern of the community, but was left to pious foundations. When we read that a Nagid granted a physician the exclusive right of carrying out the circumcision of the newly born in the villages of a section of the Egyptian countryside, there must have been a special reason for it—perhaps a mishap that had occurred at a circumcision there, or, more likely, because the Nagid wanted to provide a livelihood for an otherwise unsuccessful medical man.[93] For the performance of a circumcision a fee was paid. It was therefore regarded as a privilege for the Nagid to grant.[94] In one instance, it was given to a newly appointed notary to the exclusion of all other community officials. But laymen, too, learned this skill and practiced it gratuitously as an act of religious piety.[95]

Police and other security services were the prerogative of the state. Only the night watchmen, *ṭawwāfīn,* Heb. *meshōṭeṭē layla,* regularly appear as receivers of emoluments. They were Jewish, for they are always listed as individuals by name, while the occasional payments made to the members of the district police, qadis, and the like were noted only with the designation of the office of the persons remunerated.[96] Moreover, we have the will of a night watchman made in 1150 before a Jewish court.[97]

In the Hebrew "Scroll of Egypt" of 1012, in which the mad caliph al-Ḥākim is still praised as a prince of justice, one of his particular merits is the appointment of "trustworthy witnesses" as night watchmen.[98] The words in quotation marks designate respectable and reliable persons whose witness is accepted in a Muslim court of justice. The passage suggests that the guardians of security during the night often happened to be a menace to it. Perhaps for this reason the minorities in the course of time obtained the right to provide night watchmen of their own in the quarters predominantly inhabited by them. As suggested by a document from a provincial town, the *ṭawwāfīn* were paid by the proprietors of houses, who sometimes delegated this duty to the tenants,[99] and it explains why emoluments from the community to night watchmen were rather low. They represented only an additional help.

Similarly, the funeral personnel, such as washers of the dead, bearers of the coffins, and diggers of graves, were normally paid by relatives of the deceased, but sometimes appear also as receivers of wages or loaves of bread from the community.

We do not yet know the function of persons designated in Hebrew as *mashmīʿa,* herald. He could hardly be a kind of town crier, since here one would have expected an Arabic rather than a Hebrew term. Perhaps he acted as a solicitor of contributions to the synagogue, who announced the pledges in a loud voice.[100]

Persons called *murahhiṭ,* writers, and perhaps also singers, of liturgical poetry and their families appear not infrequently in the list of beneficiaries of the community chest. This important medieval calling would certainly have been even more conspicuous in the genuine records, had not the cantors fulfilled a similar task.[101]

Several community officials bearing Greek or Latin titles occur in ancient Geniza records. Because of their sporadic mention their exact functions during our period cannot be ascertained, although the meaning of the words concerned is well known.[102]

Public service and the principle of heredity.—In Arabic, as well as in Hebrew, the notion of public service was expressed by the same word as in English, namely, service. With a pun on I Kings 12:7 ("be a slave to this people today . . .") a Palestinian patriarch was credited with saying to two scholars who shunned public office: "You imagine it is rule that I give you; no, it is servitude."[103] This usage was applied to the highest as well as to the lowest office and appears in a laudatory context, as expressing the writer's exertion for the common weal, and in a pejorative sense, as a censure of the dependence on emoluments that were not much different from the recourse to public charity.[104]

One basic aspect of Jewish attitude toward public office, that regarding it as instituted by heavenly decree, is expressed in this talmudic saying: "Even the lowest irrigation official has been appointed by God."[105] This attitude is illustrated by a famous passage of Paul's epistle to the Romans (13:1): "There is no power but that of God; therefore, the powers that be are ordained by God." In a letter to the Jewish community of Old Cairo, written in summer, 1040, the Baghdad exilarch and Gaon Hezekiah elaborates this point by emphasizing the charismatic character of public office. Just as there are propitious times and places, so are there human beings chosen or rejected by God. Public office is like prophecy; he on whom God has bestowed the spirit, whom he has anointed as bearer of good tidings (Isaiah 61:1), he is the elected. Once the choice has been made, absolute obedience is due him.[106] When, during strife in a community, a speaker claimed that Jeroboam, the rebel (I Kings 12), "was better" than the anointed from the house of David because he was followed by the majority of the people of Israel, the nāsī attacked retorted that Korah, too, had rallied a multitude against Moses (Numbers 16), but everyone knew what happened to him and his company.[107]

All the same, the idea of the service of the people is represented in the Geniza with greater frequency. The Palestinian Gaon Solomon b. Judah, in a letter to Ephraim b. Shemarya of Old Cairo lauds him as serving the people with all his heart and all his soul and all his might—using the biblical phrase that refers to the service of God.[108] While reprimanding the same leader for quarreling with another, he writes: "These times are not like those that have passed, when each of you was his own lord; now you belong to God and to Israel."[109] Similarly a community official says in a letter from Acre, Palestine, sent almost immediately after its conquest by the Crusaders: "No one has ever been dedicated to the service of Israel more than I have been throughout my life."[110] A scholar from Ascalon, in retiring from public service, describes himself as a servant of the local community, although he never derived any material gain from his office.[111]

Normally, of course, public office was sought for gaining one's livelihood. "No man does service except for remuneration," states Solomon b. Judah, the Gaon of Jerusalem.[112] In an application to a Nagid of Yemen, the writer describes himself as being fit for nothing except the service of the community.[113] Disappointment with regard to the expectation of receiving a steady income from that source was only too frequent, as we have already seen with regard to the muqaddams in smaller places. There were other complaints. A man from Tunisia seeking a livelihood asks a friend to obtain work for him, "any work except the service of the people, for I am frail and skinny, and the service of men is exacting."[114] Another writer, a cantor in a small town, complains bitterly about his lack of opportunity for further study and about doing nothing but jingling off prayers. "All my life I have been tossed around in serving the Jews, being constantly occupied with the care of foreigners and the poll tax for the poor, playing around and trifling."[115]

Unhappy relations with the community were another and rather common cause of dissatisfaction. A remarkable, but unfortunately much damaged, letter contains among other telling passages the following:

I am most miserable. Some envy me, others despise me; others, again, are hostile. I have trouble from them all. God is my witness, would I know any profitable occupation bringing two dinars a month, I would not have touched the service of the Jews. Now, letters have their pitfalls; so please excuse me for writing this. You remember that I have come here at your advice, "if it displeases you, I shall go back" [cf. Numbers 22:34]. . . . They have torn my honor to pieces . . . I sit alone in my house, which is empty of everything. "But God is there" [Ezekiel 35:10].[116]

Community officials had to please their superiors and the influential, but at the same time had to take heed lest they offend the common people. In a letter addressed most probably to Maimonides a cantor excuses himself for being unable to do a certain service for him, since he had to officiate at a circumcision ceremony for a poor man. It was absolutely impossible for him to absent himself, "lest people say that I was staying away because he is poor. 'Had he been rich, I would have come and served him.' You know how our people are."[117]

Many documents illustrate the relationship between the public servant and the ecumenical or territorial authorities who had appointed or approved him. It was reciprocal. On the one hand, when a Gaon or a Nagid was faced with a rival, he had to secure for himself the allegiance of his appointees. In numerous letters we find solicitations in this sense, or assurances of loyalty by officials, or excuses and explanations in case the writer had faltered in his loyalty. A document in which officials from six small towns and villages in Upper Galilee reaffirmed their support of a certain Gaon is headed, with a pun on Exodus 21:5, by the words: "I love my lord, I will not go out free."[118]

The most characteristic aspect of public service in the Geniza letters was the absence of rigid limits of demarcation between the various offices. "The mark of the mediaeval, as opposed to the Roman, system is its fluidity. No category is clearly defined. Whatever class you belong to, you are constantly found performing the functions of another class."[119] This remark, made in a book on Byzantine maritime law, also applies to the situation reflected in the Geniza records. A judge, a social service officer, a cantor, a scribe, each had his specific qualifications and duties. All the same he would often be called upon to do another man's work. Precisely because of this fluidity, however, we frequently find a muqaddam, a cantor, a teacher, or a ritual slaughterer jealously guarding the privileges derived from his respective office.

When a public servant had a son who was able and willing to succeed him, it was regarded as proper to give him his father's post. How much father and son were regarded, so to speak, as one person is drastically shown in the following remark of an old cantor complaining to a Nagid that his post was taken by someone other than his son. He lived in the synagogue compound and whenever he heard the voice of the other cantor, his illness grew worse. "It is in fitting with your sense of justice that any one should *retain* his position. If my son is treated like this during my lifetime, what will happen to him after my demise?"[120]

In order to secure his son's succession, an official would have him work as his assistant and, as he grew older, as his substitute, a practice found in all ranks, from the head of a yeshiva down to a beadle.[121] Prudent persons went even a step further. The attendant of the tomb of Ezra, the most popular Jewish place of pilgrimage in Iraq, obtained certificates from both the Gaon Samuel b. Eli and an exilarch promising that his son would succeed him. When, after his death, some opposition prevailed, these certificates stood his son in good stead, according to the letter of another Gaon who confirmed him in his office on the basis of the promises mentioned.[122]

Contracts of appointment have been found of even a beadle or a religious slaughterer which refer to the fact that the father of the appointee had served in the same capacity. In one such contract, though, it is stated with much emphasis that another son would have no share in the services of the slaughterhouses, not even as a guard, because the community was not satisfied with his demeanor. Thus, succession to one's father's post was by no means automatic.[123]

Moreover, the principle of heredity was superseded by that of seniority and precedence, especially with regard to the Gaons or heads of schools, but it applied also to the lower ranks. Thus, after an ambitious cantor from Baghdad had sojourned for years in Tunisia and Spain, he was informed by a childhood friend, a Gaon, that all the older ḥazzānīn had died and that it was now his turn to become the muqaddam, or chief of the cantors.[124] A similar procedure seems to have been in force with regard to the appointment of beadles.

When an official had no male offspring, or had a son who was not inclined to follow his father's profession, he would look for a suitable son-in-law as his successor.[125] Naturally, a son-in-law, too, sometimes had other plans and strived for a higher position than that occupied by his father-in-law.[126]

In Jewish, as in Muslim, society, the principle of heredity was particularly effective with regard to the families of judges. Because of the importance of this phenomenon special attention is paid to it in studying the judiciary system. The material on the lower ranks scrutinized thus far seems to indicate that the privilege of succession was less often exercised than one would expect in view of its general acceptance by both social custom and Jewish legal theory. Perhaps the wider range of occupations open to Jews during the Geniza period induced younger people to look for jobs other than those held by their fathers. Moreover, the free enterprise society of that time looked down on income derived from service and salary. An inquiry into the finances of the community will help us understand the background of this attitude.

C. THE SOCIAL SERVICES

1. *Their General Character and Organization*

Even an affluent society dedicated to the ideal of free enterprise cannot do without social services. Free education for all, Social Security, aid to the unemployed, Medicare—all taken for granted in the United States of America—are cases in point. In a time and a society in which poverty and ill health were rampant and in which the imperfection of technology and the lawlessness of man made life precarious, there was an even greater need for public assistance to the faltering individual. The governments, whether central or local, did not feel themselves called upon to meet this need. As far as the Muslim majority was concerned, charity was semipublic: members of the ruling class or otherwise wealthy people, after having drained the population, often returned to it a part of the spoils in the form of pious foundations, or other charitable works, made to save the donor on the Day of Judgment. Muslim philanthropy, although strangely individualistic and seemingly lacking the impetus of communal cooperation and popular effort, was an impressive aspect of Islamic society during its periods of efflorescence. Interfaith charity, however, albeit not entirely unknown, was of little, if any, practical importance. The religious minorities had to look after themselves. They were burdened with supplying all the social services provided in our society by the states, municipalities, and other public bodies. How the Jewish communities of the Mediterranean area and, in particular that of Fustat, acquitted themselves of this noble and arduous task is revealed in detail by the documents of the Cairo Geniza.[1]

These communities had no statutory power to impose taxes on their members. Membership itself was not compulsory. In fact, there was strong inducement and often direct encouragement to join the ranks of the ruling religion. Hence, all charitable work had to be done on a purely voluntary basis. Under these circumstances the communal services of the Geniza period, their vigor, scope, and continuity, command our respect. Since not only the needy, but the community officials as well, depended on voluntary contributions, the members of the community had a most effective means of expressing their satisfaction or dissatisfaction with the conduct of public affairs and those conducting them. Thus the very character of public finances and social services safeguarded the participation of the community at large and provided it with a broad "democratic" base.

Sources of information.—Our knowledge of the nature and functioning of the social services is derived largely from lists of recipients and of contributors and from documents relating to houses and other communal property and the use made of their revenue. Records of the second type are mostly self-explanatory and are often dated. In order to enable the reader to evaluate these sources on his own, descriptions of 184 such documents are included in Appendix A.

The interpretation of the lists preserved is far more difficult. Only very few are dated and rarely do they have a heading explaining their purpose. Even where a superscription is provided, understanding it correctly is by no means easy and to do so often requires careful examination in connection with other relevant Geniza material. Thus the "List of Taxpayers" printed in Gottheil-Worrell's edition of Geniza fragments from the Freer Collection (pp. 66 ff.) is not what it was taken to be by the editors and other scholars who have made use of it; rather it is a list of persons who vowed donations in order to enable the poor to pay their poll tax.

Fortunately, the handwriting of the more prominent scribes active in Old Cairo between approximately 1015 and 1265 is known, and so it is possible to fix the period to which many an undated list belongs. Moreover, numerous names mentioned in the lists reappear in the dated records about public buildings or in other dated or datable documents. Finally, the professions of the persons listed or other details given about them divulge the purpose of a list. Therefore, the two lists published in Jacob Mann's *The Jews in Egypt and in Palestine under the Fāṭimid Caliphs,* II, 246–247, cannot designate persons contributing to a public fund, as the editor believed, for they mention one man in prison, another permanently disabled, a third blind, as well as many foreigners, several beadles and cantors, and a schoolmaster. Mann was certainly impressed by the fact that in both lists there appears Nahray (b. Nissīm), an outstanding eleventh-century scholar, public leader, and businessman. Nahray, however, served for many years as jurisconsult of the Jewish community of Old Cairo and as such was included in its payroll. To us it seems strange that a personage of such high standing and a poor prisoner or a cripple should be listed on the same sheet. As we shall presently see, in the Geniza period this was the normal procedure.

Only few of these lists have been edited thus far.[2] I have scrutinized over four hundred more and tried to define their characters and fix their approximate dates. Appendix B describes the beneficiaries of the community chest, both officials and needy people of all descriptions, as well as the varied benefits they received. Appendix C shows how the funds financing these services were solicited and collected, as far as they were not derived from the revenue of real estate donated to the community, as specified in Appendix A. The three appendixes are arranged in approximately chronological order, while the tables therein attempt breakdowns of the types of documents included in each.

The interested reader will find in the appendixes many significant details that could not be used in the summary description of the social services provided in the text proper. They also reveal to him how I arrived at my conclusions and provide him with a means to check their validity. The 434 documents assembled in these appendixes are fairly representative, but by no means exhaustive, and for two reasons. Wherever you find in the Geniza ten documents of a certain type you can be sure that at least three or four others will turn up some day, especially in the huge collections of literary or semiliterary character which have never been screened completely. Moreover, it was difficult to draw a strict demarcation line between the materials to be included in the appendixes and those merely to be mentioned or alluded to. The Geniza has preserved a large number of requests for help and also of instructions by authorities on how to deal with such applications. Many aspects of privation and suffering, as well as the ways and means to overcome them by concerted action of the community, are echoed in the Geniza letters. The appendixes are restricted to material of a more formal and official nature and should be regarded as the main, but not as the exclusive, source of our information.

The student of the documents described in the appendixes should recognize the difference between *communal records,* those characterized by their content, headings, or postscripts as referring to a congregation at large, and *administrators' notes,* those that list the revenue and expenditure made solely by the official writing or dictating the document. Examples of the first type are A 24, 48–92, 98–100, 129, B 1, 2*a* + 52, 17–24, 29, 33, 38, 63, 65, 66, 71, 74–76, 85, 93, and most of C. Illustrative of the second are the many notes left by the cantor and administrator Japheth b. David b. Shekhanyā around 1040, the parnās Abu 'l-Bayān around 1180, and the teacher and court clerk Solomon b. Elijah about fifty years later.[3] Failure to make such a distinction may lead to unwarranted generalizations.

As explained in the chronological table in the Author's Note preceding the appendixes, we are fairly well informed about the first half of the eleventh century, then again about most of the twelfth (with notorious gaps concerning some shorter periods). Many documents, albeit often of inferior value, refer to the first half of the thirteenth century, a period of complete decay for the Fustat community. The historian should pay attention to this uneven distribution of information.

Desirous of covering the skeletons of those communal lists with flesh and sinews, I analyzed them in detail wherever advisable and possible, explored the circumstances under which they came into being, and tried to identify the more important or characteristic personalities occurring in them. In view of the wealth of information available, the description of the social services furnished on the following pages should be regarded as no more than spadework. I have also refrained from comparing the Geniza material with Islamic deeds and literary sources with respect to such pious foundations as hospitals, schools, and libraries, and the amounts of cash, loaves of bread, clothing, and other emoluments allocated to the persons employed in them. Most of these foundations were princely creations that flourished later than the Geniza documents. Even so, such a comparison might be fruitful. Since research in Islamic social services is itself still in a rather rudimentary stage, the comparative study recommended here wins by deferment.

Ecumenical aspects.—The most impressive aspect of Jewish philanthropy as reflected in the Geniza record is its ecumenical character. The principle "charity begins at home," or, as a Hebrew saying has it, "the poor of your town have precedence over those of another" was regarded as a religious injunction and is so referred to in Geniza letters.[4] The very existence of such an injunction shows that at the time it was pronounced much was done for the needy outside the local community. The character of the Jewish community, or, perhaps of Mediterranean society in general, precluded parochialism.

In the first place, the maintenance of the ecumenical seats of learning in Jerusalem and Baghdad was a major concern for all Jewish communities, large and small.[5] Local institutions of higher learning or even individual scholars could likewise count on the support of friends in other countries. In the course of my work on the India trade I have come across a number of letters proving that the Jewish merchants of Aden regularly sent gifts to both local and foreign scholars and divines in Egypt. Presents made to a scholar were regarded as an equivalent to the offerings on the altar in the ancient Temple of Jerusalem. It was the quality of the scholar, not his whereabouts, which mattered.[6]

A similar rule applied to the poor. Gifts were sent to localities in which the need was greatest. It seems strange to us that a merchant from Aden, a native of that south Arabian port, should dispatch to Old Cairo the very substantial sum of 20 dinars for the benefit of the poor of that city.[7] Since, however, the capital of Egypt was a refuge for the victims of persecution and misery who came from all over the world, so that the demands made on its Jewish inhabitants by far exceeded their financial capacity, others felt obliged to share part of the burden. The Geniza has preserved a letter from Najera in the kingdom of Castile, Spain, describing what that community had done for a woman whose husband had been killed and who had to be ransomed together with her two daughters, and admonishing other congregations to follow suit. When we find "the woman from Spain" in an ancient list of receivers of alms in Old Cairo, we should not jump to the conclusion that the unhappy widow from Najera is meant, but only note that such occurrences were common.[8] Similar requests were made in a letter from the community in Granada, Spain, and another from Arles in southern France.[9] The largest single group of needy people appearing in our lists was the foreigners and of them the largest group was persons coming from Europe.[10] Under such circumstances it was proper and natural that the wealthy merchants of Aden, whose livelihood depended on the prosperous trade between the Mediterranean area and India, should send their contributions to Old Cairo, and not only to the scholars living there but also to the poor.

In order to alleviate its burden, the community in the Egyptian capital would send help-seeking foreigners on to the provincial towns and villages. "Kindly take care of this man and his large family, as long as we are busy with collecting money for the poll tax of the poor. We have already paid for ninety of them. We have promised him to finance his return to the Land of Israel when he will come back from your place." This letter, sent from Old Cairo to a place in the Egyptian Rīf, illustrates the situation.[11] We have a letter in Maimonides' own hand in which he asks a notable in a provincial town to arrange for a collection to pay the poll tax for a Jewish scholar from Morocco and his son, and another communication in which help is sought for a young scholar whom Maimonides' son Abraham, the Nagid, had sent away to the country with a small sum of money.[12] This procedure was adopted particularly for ransom and support of persons who had fallen into the hands of pirates or foes; in either case great financial sacrifices were required. While Alexandria, the usual port of arrival of such captives, and Old Cairo, their normal destination, had to shoulder the main burden, we see from reports preserved in the Geniza that the smaller communities also made very substantial contributions. This is all the more remarkable since most of these captives came from Byzantium or other parts of Europe, and their liberators were not familiar with their language and social habits.[13]

Another concern of ecumenical scope was the support of the poor, the devout, and the scholars of the Holy City. The permanent state of anarchy in which Palestine found itself during the eleventh century and the crushing taxation imposed on the minorities (and perhaps also on other sections of the population) had a ruinous effect on the economy of the country. Financial aid to the Jewish community there, which had always been regarded as a religious duty, now became a dire necessity. The Geniza records deal with this subject far more than the published materials would indicate. Special collections, made for the purpose, were called *tafriqat al-maqādisa,* literally, the distribution (of the amounts due from the individual members of a local community) of (the sum to be sent to) the Jerusalemites, and were held, like the collections for the distribution of cash among the local poor, on, or, rather, shortly before the holidays.[14] A fund raiser would be sent from Jerusalem, someone other than the permanent envoy of the yeshiva who had to be a scholarly person and carried assignments additional to collecting money.[15]

The amounts collected in Egypt, Sicily, and the Maghreb in a joint Karaite-Rabbanite emergency campaign for Jerusalem, the payment of the debts of the Jewish community there to the Muslim moneylenders (C 4), are the largest raised in any public appeal in the Geniza with the exception of ransoms for captives and special impositions by the government. One has to bear in mind, of course, that the Jerusalem community had to take care of the many destitute persons visiting or taking their domicile in the Holy City and had to pay fixed contributions even in years when, because of war or other calamities, no pilgrims with means made their appearance.

At times a donor would earmark his contribution to Jerusalem for a special purpose. Thus the congregation in Bilbays in the Nile Delta entrusted "gold" to a traveler leaving for Jerusalem with the instruction to deliver one part of it to "the synagogue of the Yemenite" and one to "the rabbis" (dated 1214). These specifications find their explanation in other Geniza letters. We learn that a rabbi from Yemen had lived for a certain time in Bilbays (and married a wife there; it was not a happy marriage), but later settled in Jerusalem and founded a synagogue there.[16] "The rabbis" could be taken as a general term, but it is likely that the reference is to the newly arrived French rabbis, for a scholar from France had served as spiritual leader in that Egyptian town and later sent to that congregation a request for support from Jerusalem.[17]

Early in the eleventh century a house in Old Cairo was made a charitable foundation for the benefit of the poor in Jerusalem, to which other houses, destined for the same purpose, were added later. We are able to trace the history of this "Jerusalem compound" through almost two hundred years. Similarly, revenue from stores in Ramle, the administrative capital of Palestine, covered most of a yearly imposition to be paid by the Jews of Jerusalem during the early decades of the eleventh century. The hot springs of Tiberias, Palestine, attracted sick, poor people from many places, and donations for them were constantly solicited in Egypt. Jacob Mann published ten documents related to this charity, and there are more.[18]

Popular character.—Next to its ecumenical aspect, the most significant trait of Jewish charity as revealed by the Geniza is its popular character, the participation of the whole community. Public appeals were of two distinct types. When large amounts were needed for immediate payment, as for the ransom of captives, everyone in a position to do so had to make an extraordinary effort in accordance with his means, wherefore in the contributions to appeals of this type the gap between the rich and those less well endowed was very pronounced. Futhermore, on occasions such as the donation of wheat for holidays or fast days the affluent or more liberal or more religious by far outstripped the rest of the contributors. Finally, in cases of special urgency, but limited scope, for instance, when a foreigner had to be supplied quickly with travel expenses, often no general appeals were made, but a number of notables put the money needed together.

In contrast with these "oligarchic" ways of philanthropy, the breakdown of types of documents at the end of Appendix C reveals the surprising facts that in many collections participation must have been fairly general, and also that the sums donated were closely similar. Persons known from other sources as important government officials, great merchants, or physicians would give only 1 or even ½ dirhem, while the bulk of the contributors would vow ½ or ¼ dirhem. We must always keep in mind that many of the lists are either imperfectly preserved or limited in scope by their very purpose (a frequent example: payments by, or solicitation of, persons who had not yet contributed). When the list C 39, with about 105, mostly prospective, contributors, notes only *one* dyer, while the contemporary C 46, which is incomplete, has *fourteen* of them (out of 127 names accompanied by amounts), it is evident that not only the long, but incompletely preserved list C 46, but also the apparently intact C 39 represents only a fraction of the members of the Rabbanite community of Fustat. We must therefore assume that certain types of collections were practically all comprising, comparable with the payment of membership fees in a modern congregation.

In the most extensive list preserved (C 55), which is preceded by an explanatory introduction, it is correct to assume that all capable members contributed, and the pledges listed show that this was actually so. That "urgent appeal" concerned wax candles for the illumination of a synagogue and the houses of the poor. (Candles were given to 32 persons out of a community of "less than 200" adult males.) In an appeal of this type one would expect that each participant would give according to his means and wishes. But this was not true. Everyone, high and low, from the Nagid Abraham Maimonides to a cook or a tailor paid 1 dirhem per adult male in his household. Only sugar factories and taverns were taxed higher as specifically profitable undertakings.

The identity of characteristic names proves that the strictly "egalitarian" list C 32 was contemporary with C 33, where *six* different levels of contributions are to be discerned, and the same holds true for the long and detailed lists C 46 and 47 as compared with C 41 and other simultaneous records. It is thus evident that for certain types of charity comparatively small sums were solicited, but everyone was expected to contribute. This principle seems to have applied to the weekly collections for the *mezōnōt,* or food (read: bread) for the poor, from which in later times other communal expenses were also paid, and to the contributions for the payment of the poll tax for those who were unable to pay it in full or at all. Above we also had the strange case of the appeal for wax candles, which, as the ninth entry in the breakdown of the types of documents at the end of Appendix B shows, must have been a quite regular feature (presumably before holidays). The preamble to that document (C 55) says expressly: "We shall shoulder it with united forces," *naḥmilhā yad wāḥida,* meaning that the payments will be in equal shares.

Popular participation expressed itself not only in monetary contributions. Everyone wanted to have a say in the use of funds and see for himself how they were used. The preamble of the drive just mentioned and the numerous appeals to congregations preserved (of which C 92–96 are good examples) illustrate the all-comprising publicity of communal philanthropy. Even a Nagid giving an order of payment from a public fund would state that it was made "with the consent of the community." [19] Most of the communal accounts and many of the lists of recipients or donors are written in large, calligraphic characters, because they were destined for display in the synagogue, all members being invited to scrutinize them. One document even states that everyone was not only entitled but religiously bound to advise the court of any inaccuracy to be found in the report, which, for this purpose, remained suspended for four months.[20]

The popular scope of medieval philanthropy had its root in religion, the belief that charity was one of the foremost religious duties and the safest path to the atonement of sins and to salvation. We are therefore not surprised to find men styled "The Pious" and a woman called "The Ascetic" prominent as donors.[21]

The community chest.—In cities with more than one synagogue, donations were sometimes made and houses acquired for individual synagogues, but the social services were usually communal, comprising all the coreligionists living in one place, rather than congregational.[22] In the capital of Egypt, which in those days consisted of two different cities, Old Cairo (Fustat) and the newly founded Cairo, even the payrolls of the various synagogues sometimes appear combined in one list.[23]

The property and assets of the community were called *qōdesh,* "the holy," a designation going back to ancient times when the treasury of the nation was stored in the precincts of the Temple of Jerusalem. The term conveyed the idea that anything dedicated to the common good was given to God, an idea familiar also to contemporary Islam where *māl al-muslimīn,* "belonging to the Muslims," was synonymous with *māl Allāh,* "belonging to God." From *qōdesh* was derived a verb (also in Judeo-Arabic: *aqdas*) meaning, literally, dedicate to a holy purpose. This usage strongly emphasized the religious character of charity and certainly was not without influence on the minds of the givers.[24]

The qōdesh was an idea, not an institution. There was no treasury to which all revenue was paid and from which all expenses were drawn. The organization of charity and other communal needs, such as the payment of officials and the maintenance and administration of buildings, was far more complicated. The income of the community consisted of regular collections, special appeals, miscellaneous items like fines or wills, revenue from the slaughterhouses and, in particular, of rents from the many buildings turned into charitable foundations. While certain types of expenditure were met regularly by such specific sources of revenue as the distribution of bread by weekly collections or the maintenance of buildings by the rent raised from them, many other types were not. Therefore, in orders of payment on account of the community chest, the source from which the expenditure was to be made had to be indicated, expressly or by implication.[25]

A beautiful illustration of this state of affairs is a report on daily expenses made for a distinguished sick foreigner in the course of two weeks. Every day he received one or two chickens, potions, and other food, and there were expenses for bandages, laundry, and lighting. As compensation for his expenses the man looking after him received (*a*) payments from a parnās administering (or, rather, farming the rent from) houses belonging to the community, (*b*) contributions from individuals, the largest one amounting to 5 dirhems, (*c*) the proceeds of a collection made especially for that purpose in the two synagogues of Fustat, which brought, however, only 7 dirhems, and, finally (*d*) a dinar weighing 23 qīrāṭs and worth 35-½ dirhems from the Nagid (Samuel b. Hananya).[26]

When a tenant in a communal building was in arrears with his rent, a teacher to whom this revenue was assigned failed to receive the fee due him for a boy sent by the community to his school. When a poor man was erroneously left out of a collection, the then head of the Jewish community had to give a special order to a social services officer to immediately find another source for the 5 dirhems allocated to the unhappy man who certainly had lodged a complaint. These examples could easily be multiplied.[27]

Similarly, donations or fines destined for the communal chest had to be earmarked for a specific use before being turned over to the relevant official. "I still owe the qōdesh 20-½ dinars out of a sum that I had pledged voluntarily. These shall be taken from the rent of the house that Isma'īl the Clothier has leased from me, every year 1 dinar for wheat and 1 for clothing," we read in the draft of an enormous document, apparently written by a man setting out on a long journey. We may assume the parnās in charge of the distribution of clothing and the one doling out wheat were informed of that obligation imposed on the lessee.[28] Houses were often given to "the poor" without any further specification. Many times, however, the purpose of the charitable foundation was indicated (see sec. 3, below).

This cumbersome system of financing the social services had its source partly in the general technical imperfections of medieval administration. The accumulation of public funds in one treasury was to some extent avoided in order to preserve them from the overreaching of rapacious government officials. Only in a sixteenth-century account does Arabic *khizāna,* "treasury," seem to denote a box in which all revenue was deposited and from which all expenditure was made. That account is written in the Hebrew language, and the writer, although using that Arabic word and dating according to Muslim months, apparently was a European, to judge from his spelling of Arabic names.[29]

Religious scruples, too, were involved in this splitting of communal revenue and earmarking of its various units for specific purposes, namely, the apprehension that one might use funds donated for one charity for the financing of another. The Talmud tells the story of a scholarly almoner who by mistake distributed money given for the poor in general as a special bonus on the feast of Purim and, having qualms about the propriety of his action, restituted the total amount from his own pocket.[30] It was precisely with regard to this religious injunction against "mixing the charities" that the authorities appearing in later Geniza documents were not always particularly successful. Even the instructions of the pious Nagid Abraham Maimonides contain examples of such occurrences, as when he assigned to a Maghrebi traveler money collected for a person from an Egyptian locality (B 78). The same account, written by Solomon b. Elijah, contains the following entry: "On the eve of the New Year I took a loan of 7 dirhems from the money of the wife of Faraḥ, given in trust to me by the Nagid, for the purchase of 10 pounds of olive oil for the synagogue of the Palestinians." At the time of the Nagid Joshua, Abraham's great-grandson, the impoverishment of the Fustat community had reached such a degree that once he had to order them to take from the item "Food for the Poor" 150 dirhems that had been advanced by five notables for the payment of the poll tax; everyone objecting to this extraordinary measure and refusing to contribute to the collection for "Food" under these circumstances would be excommunicated![31]

The community chest, although not a legal person in the strict sense, appears in the Geniza letters as party to a contract, and orders of payment were issued on it.[32] Its administration varied according to the times and the local conditions. As a rule it was in the hands of "the trustworthy elders in charge of public property and communal affairs," as the representatives of the community were called.[33] Contracts of lease of public property or agreements related to it were written in the names of the elders, or, as other legally valid documents, signed by three persons, usually including a judge.[34] Occasionally, a parnās would appear as the leaser, perhaps an imitation of the Muslim practice. The Geniza has preserved a contract—in Arabic characters, of course—where one of the administrators of the mosques of Cairo leases a small garden house to one 'Alī b. Ḥassān b. Ma'ālī al-Ṭarābulusī (of Tripoli), who could have been a Muslim, Christian, or Jew, but since his contract was found in the Geniza, most probably was Jewish.[35]

An expenditure from the community chest required the witness of at least two representatives of the community. Since people were busy with their own affairs, a parnās normally had several elders at his disposal, from whom he could choose one to assist him in a transaction. In one account a welfare officer mentions five different persons with whose knowledge he had carried out minor repairs in houses belonging to the community or made other payments for it.[36] The procedure adopted for larger expenditures is well illustrated in the document A 20. The parnās, who had farmed out the revenue from the house or houses dedicated to the poor of Jerusalem, had made all expenses for the very considerable repairs (the equivalent of about two months' revenue) in the presence of one responsible elder, who was assisted by another. Then the two elders testified to the transactions before three judges, whose signatures ratified the accounts.

In the time of the Mishnah (first and second centuries A.D.), the position of public trust inherent in the task of almoners was regarded so highly that daughters of almoners were qualified to marry into the priestly aristocracy. It is one of the surprises of the Geniza that it contains a statement by a judge to the effect that a certain perfumer had been in charge of the weekly collections for the poor in the course of the year 1161. Did the perfumer need that certificate for himself (perhaps for a lawsuit), or was a daughter of his about to marry into a particularly fastidious family? We may perhaps know some day.[37]

As long as Jewish community life in Egypt was fairly genuine and healthy, during the eleventh and twelfth centuries, the executive and legal aspects of public administration were kept apart reasonably well. The elders and the parnāsīm estimated the requirements of each branch provided for by the community chest and took whatever action was necessary. The judges saw to it that everything was done according to the law, gave instructions wherever needed, and confirmed the transactions of the administrative officials after proper scrutiny. Whenever we have a neatly written document that bears no signature, it is fairly sure that the action proposed by the elders was not approved, and often we can surmise the circumstances that evoked doubts.[38] A long list written around 1100 which enumerates the proposed allocations for clothing, partly in kind and partly in cash, bears the following remark over the signature of three well-known judges: "We, the court, are of the opinion that what is found above needs further examination, although it was written according to the counsel and the dictation of elders." [39] Even in matters of orphans and widows, the particular preserve of the courts, the elders were regularly consulted on the amounts of alimonies and related matters.[40]

It is true that with regard to communal charity, as in all other matters, the official head of the Jews of Egypt was the highest authority with whom all ultimate decisions rested. His onerous preoccupation with this duty has been described on pages 36 ff., above. His task, however, was not the current conduct of the social services, but the supervision of the charitable foundations, redress of injustice, and amends for negligence. (His trouble grew over the fact that so many people felt themselves wronged or passed over.) [41] Only when the deep decline of Egyptian Jewry set in around the turn of the thirteenth century did the Jewish judge, like the Muslim qadi, become administrator of the public funds, making each and every decision. The amount of small paper work done in these matters by Abraham Maimonides is really appalling.[42] Yet even in the late thirteenth and throughout the fourteenth centuries we find lively participation of the laity in the administration of charities.[43] Thus the Jewish community of Fustat, as long as we are able to follow its functioning, faithfully preserved the popular character of its social services.

2. *Sources of Revenue and Types of Relief*

The very organization of the social services, as described, implied that each type of relief had its specific source of revenue. There was one big exception (in addition to some smaller ones): the income from houses and other real estate owned by the community which could be used for any purpose, if the donors had not stipulated otherwise. This source of revenue, which in the course of the twelfth century became the most important single item in the budget of the community of Fustat, is treated in section C, 3, below.

The ways of public finance of the Jewish communities were by no means uniform even within Egypt. Alexandria, about which we are comparatively well informed, adhered to a system entirely different from that of Fustat. There, as was common in later times in many Jewish congregations in Europe, the main item of communal revenue was "the slaughterhouse," that is, a tax on meat, the food of the more affluent. A letter to Solomon b. Elijah inquiring whether his father, the judge Elijah, would be prepared to become the spiritual leader of the two synagogues of Alexandria promises as his main (or sole) emolument the income from the slaughterhouses, while the orphans of his predecessor would receive 10 dirhems a week from the same source.[1] In another letter on the same matter to the same address the writer says: "The slaughterhouses are the city," meaning that they are the main source of revenue of the community.[2] The Alexandrian official who wrote the letter described in C 84 also received part of his remuneration from this item of revenue.

It stands to reason that Alexandria, which was closely connected with Palestine, followed Palestinian practices in this matter, as in many other respects. For in Ramle, too, we find that "the market" (an abbreviation for "the market where the animals are killed," as another document formulates it), or "the markets," composed a major part of the income of the religious dignitaries, the distribution of which looms large in the correspondence of the Gaon Solomon b. Judah.[3]

In contradistinction, revenue from the abattoirs was of little consequence in Fustat. The professional killers of animals were communal officials inasmuch as they were appointed to their posts by the religious authorities. But economically they were on their own. They leased the revenue from the community against a fixed weekly payment of comparatively small sums (7–8 dirhems). This whole matter of ritual killing, so strange to the modern mind, but essentially a modified form of sacrifice, is discussed below in connection with the professions of the divines.[4]

There was another, main feature of public charity in which Alexandria followed old Palestinian ways and differed entirely from Fustat: the *quppā (shel ṣedāqā)*. In later Hebrew this simply means alms box, and in modern Hebrew quppā is the window of a cashier in a bank or a store. The original meaning of the word, however, like that of its Arabic equivalent *quffa*, was "basket," in our case, the basket in which bread was collected for the poor and from which it was distributed to them.

The long life of this primitive method of relief for the destitute is probably to be explained by the scarcity of small coins prevalent throughout most of the period considered in this book. While change was hard to come by, it was easy to prepare at home a few more loaves of bread than the family needed and it also gave the woman of the house the opportunity to be continuously engaged in a meritorious work of piety. Technically this was possible because they made two types of bread, the flat, soft loaves that were eaten fresh, preferably warm from the oven, and another, hard variety, a kind of biscuit that could stand a long time. Thus, we find that an almoner could sell old bread that was left over from a distribution for a price not much less than new loaves (see B 77). I assume that on Friday, the traditional day of distribution (in Fustat there were two such days, Tuesday and Friday [see below]), bread of each type was given, the fresh and soft kind for consumption on the Sabbath and the hard biscuits for the rest of the week. I have not yet found this detail referred to in the Geniza, but the special collections of fresh loaves of bread "on Friday night and other nights," reported for Fustat, may point in this direction.[5]

The term "quppā" is never mentioned in connection with Fustat. Since we possess hundreds of records and letters referring to charity from that city, this can only mean that the institution characterized by that word did not exist there. Thus far the only list containing vows for the donation of quantities of bread found in the Geniza (C 53), I have attributed to Alexandria, and the specific circumstances through which it has come to Fustat have been explained in my description of the document. There are at least three other documents mentioning the quppā of Alexandria: a certificate from the year 1253, entitling an old man of a distinguished and pious family to receive weekly rations of bread from that source; [6] a letter of an administrator of that charity (n. 41, below); and, finally, a detailed and most interesting description by an Alexandrian judge of the tensions in the community during the early years of Saladin's reign. His opponent, the president of the congregation, threatened to discontinue the payment of his salary and, instead, have twenty persons deliver to him their weekly contributions to the quppā. Whether these contributions were meant to be in cash or kind, or partly in loaves and partly in money (as in C 53) is not evident from the text, but it seems more likely that loaves indeed were meant since that tyrant wanted to do harm to his adversary.[7] A quppā is also mentioned in a letter from Minyat Ziftā, but there definitely an alms box is intended.[8] Unless otherwise indicated, the following sketch of the types of relief and of their ways of financing is confined to Fustat.

Contributions to the public chest were made in two stages: the *pesīqā,* the assignment of a certain sum to a certain purpose by the community as a whole and by each contributor individually, and the *jibāya,* or the collection of the sums promised. The first term is Hebrew, although it appears often in an Arabicized form (*basīqa* and the like), and carries with it a religious connotation: it was a vow that had to be fulfilled. The second is Arabic, a term familiar also in commerce; a long interval, often two months or more, intervened between the "handshake" and the "collection" in commercial transactions.[9]

A pesīqā was arranged both for the regular budget of the community and for any particular need requiring attention. A contract with a beadle provides for the same emoluments as those granted to his predecessors, namely, in addition to the poll tax and "extras," for two pesīqās a year, which means that twice a year a number of persons would vow to contribute a certain sum for him.[10] One pesīqā was usually made on the Day of Atonement since, as explained before, charity was regarded as a means of expiation. In a letter to a friend in the capital, a schoolmaster in a small town reports the (poor) results of the vows made for him on that day; in another, a scholar is promised a "worthy" pesīqā, if he consents to settle in Alexandria.[11] The yearly payment of the poll tax for the poor, one of the main concerns of any minority group under Islam in those days, was covered by a pesīqā; so also were the contributions to the seats of learning.[12]

On the other hand, the most varied purposes were served by the same means. A man who was unable to meet his obligations reports that a pesīqā in his favor had brought a substantial sum, but more than a month had passed without his getting the money (and the creditors had become uneasy, presumably because they suspected the debtor had pocketed the proceeds himself).[13] An official of the caliphal mint, who had fled from the capital to Alexandria, expected to be granted a pesīqā there, but the community of that city was neither in a position nor in the mood to do so. A Palestinian cantor, who displayed his art in Alexandria, was also deeply disappointed: the pesīqā brought only 2 quarter dinars and 60 dirhems, of which hardly 10 had remained with him when he wrote his complaint.[14] A schoolmaster from Algeria who was forced to live in a small town in

Egypt traveled every year to Old Cairo to obtain a pesīqā there, which means that he sought a post, instead of teaching privately, but was not successful.[15]

No appeal could be made without authorization. This rule is evident from applications to Nagids and other dignitaries for permission to solicit funds and from a Nagid's note under a solicitation ordering a cantor to read it out in the synagogue.[16] Numerous letters, addressed by Nagids and Gaons to the community in Old Cairo, contain instructions to arrange a pesīqā, and there are answers promising to expedite the collection or explaining why it was impossible to arrange one.[17] Once such an appeal for an individual was under way, participation could be almost general (see C 68).

Pledges were invited not only in public, but also privately, by notables going from house to house and from store to store, as stated expressly in some documents[18] and proved by the lists of names unaccompanied by amounts and arranged according to business addresses or professions. It would be intriguing to know whether there was any competition in the display of liberality among the various professional groups. In accordance with the spirit of that age, there certainly did not exist any formal organization in this matter (so efficiently achieved in Jewish and other appeals in the United States in our days), but unofficial pressures perhaps proved to be no less effective, to judge by the many standard average sums donated by large numbers of people.

Women are occasionally referred to as contributors and even as heading drives, especially for the upkeep of synagogues, but one finds them less frequently than one would expect in view of their farreaching economic independence in those days.[19] Their field of charity was mainly private and personal.[20]

Weddings and other family events, besides being essentially religious ceremonies, received an additional halo by charitable collections. These were of two types: for needy people and for the cantors and other singers of religious songs that took the place of, or were probably additional to, the players of secular music, who are also mentioned in the Geniza (although not specifically in connection with weddings).[21]

Complaints that pledges to public appeals were not made good and admonitions to work for their speedy realization are not rare. The many lists forming complements or balances of collections, and, conversely those of beneficiaries who had not yet received their share, are living testimony to such occurrences.[22]

In order to expedite the realization of the pledges, perhaps also as a means to have as many members as possible participate in the meritorious work, several collectors at one time were employed who often also took care of the distribution. In one document showing the persons in charge each week, a bridegroom heads the list, perhaps as a special honor.[23] In a provincial town (Sunbāṭ), a merchant, while cashing his outstanding debts, also collected from his customers the sums due from them for the community chest, repeatedly called here *ṣibbūr,* "the public." [24]

The main item of revenue, the "Food," the funds raised for the semiweekly distribution of loaves of bread to the poor, usually brought more than was needed for the purpose implied in its name, and the surplus was used for other important needs, such as salaries.[25] This unusual procedure comes up again when dealing with the subject of salaries. Since the weekly collection was the backbone of recurrent revenue, numerous documents refer to it, but it is not always easy to understand their purport. The following seems to have been the established procedure adhered to through the centuries: During or shortly after the High Holidays that initiate the Jewish calendar year the members of a congregation vowed how much they would contribute every week. A number of collectors (documents from the eleventh and thirteenth centuries mention by name eight to twelve at a time) would make the rounds every day except Saturday. On Sunday and Monday they would not collect much, but from Tuesday on the payments would be fuller and the service on Thursday morning was the occasion for trying to reach the weekly goal of contributions. The sums cashed in would be handed over to the parnāsīm, if they did not do the collecting themselves. The parnās would then draw up a list either of the individual donors or of the sums brought in by each assistant collector, and he would note—on the left side of his account or on a separate sheet—the sums paid to community officials and needy people or spent for other purposes.[26]

In addition to the weekly collection, whose main purpose was the distribution of bread to the needy, there was a recurrent appeal for wheat, which was also addressed to the community at large. While the weekly contributions were invariably in money, as proved by all the extant lists, the gifts for the distributions of wheat were made either in kind or in cash, and the gifts of wheat were obviously regarded as more appropriate and more meritorious since they are always listed first. There was another, striking difference between the collections for bread and those for wheat. Whereas bread collections consisted mostly in small standardized sums, wheat donations varied widely in amount. It seems, however, that to appeals issued close to one another in time the same persons made approximately the same contributions.[27] The frequency of these appeals and the quantities received by the beneficiaries are discussed in subsection 4*b*, below.

The amounts required for this charity must have been very large since the recipients of bread rations appear also in the lists of those partaking of the distributions of wheat. We might therefore be right in assuming that everyone who was able to do so was expected to contribute. The "Wheat Collection of Av [July-Aug.] 1178" lists 110 households making donations during two days. But it is more than probable that the drive was pursued throughout the whole period of mourning of the first nine days of Av, which culminates in the fast commemorating the destruction of the Temple of Jerusalem.[28]

A third regular collection was that for clothing the needy and the lower community officials. A booklet containing a report about one such appeal is entitled "Collection for the Clothing for the Year 1185–1186" (details in C 118). This evidence, however, should not induce us to assume that only one clothing drive a year was held. The lists referring to the handing out of articles of clothing suggest at least two yearly distributions. The sums of money required for this charity must have been high, so it stands to reason that several appeals were made in the course of a year.

In view of the widespread custom, common even among well-to-do people in those days, of acquiring and wearing used garments, one is surprised to find no reference to the collection of old clothes for the benefit of the poor. The answer is to be found in the lists relating to the distribution of wearing apparel, in that they show that the communal authorities were extremely anxious for persons of like social status to receive clothing of exactly the same type. Any attempt to distribute used garments would have led to endless jealousies and perhaps even to disorders.

The three appeals just surveyed provided only for the most basic needs. In addition, throughout the year, the congregation assembled in the synagogue responded to a vast range of requests. Some were mentioned above in connection with the explanation of the term pesīqā. Others are described in subsection 4, below, which specifies the beneficiaries of the community chest. "I possess no money except what I receive every Monday in the synagogue," writes a sick man who calls himself "the cantor, the son of the judge." "The Nagid promised me a week," writes another, meaning that all vows made during that period would go to him.[29] While the revenue from the charitable foundations assured a certain steadiness to the finances of the community, it was the constant demands on the liberality of the individual which kept the public spirit alive.

A frequently mentioned but perhaps not very substantial source of income of the community chest was fines stipulated in contracts or imposed by the courts. A glassmaker working at a melting furnace undertakes to pay 5 dinars in case he failed to comply with his contract.[30] A merchant whose case was heard in court on March 21, 1099, had not reappeared for the final hearing until Thursday, May 12, when he was informed that he would have to pay a fine of 5 dinars "for the poor of Miṣrayim [the Egyptian capital]," if he did not attend the session of the court on the subsequent Monday. (He did.)[31] A debtor who had to repay a loan of 100 dinars promised 10 if he were to be late in doing so.[32] A co-owner of a house stipulated 20 dinars for trespassing on the rights of his partners.[33] A husband and wife adhering to the Rabbanite and Karaite persuasions, respectively, undertake to give 30 dinars to the poor in the event one of them did not respect the religious susceptibilities of the other, and a husband who had behaved badly toward his wife was threatened with the unusually heavy fine of 40 dinars if the settlement reached after marital strife was breached.[34] The payments were to be made "to the two synagogues" or "to the court for the poor of Old Cairo." Or, in mixed marriages, "to the poor of the Karaites and the Rabbanites in equal shares," as found in the marriage contract of a rich Karaite widow who imposed on her future husband a fine of 100 dinars if he failed to follow any of the stipulations of the contract.[35] The same large fine was stipulated, only with the poor of the Rabbanites mentioned first, when a Rabbanite girl was married to the son of a Karaite notable.[36]

While it was common to will a house or part of a house to the qōdesh, comparatively few documents have thus far come to light in which a sum of money or other movable property was bequeathed for charitable purposes. We have a bequest of 2 thousand dinars to the community chest called *quppā shel ṣedāqa,* forming the object of a letter from Tyre, Lebanon, the case of a man in Tunisia leaving all his property to the poor, and that of a freedman giving one-quarter of his considerable belongings to the poor of his own town and another to those of the Rabbanite community of Jerusalem. All these are from the late tenth or the early eleventh century, which is perhaps not mere chance.[37] The businesswoman Wuḥsha willed 70 dinars to public charities, almost exactly 10 percent of the total cash left by her. Whether she, or her friend and religious adviser, the cantor Hillel b. Eli, had in mind Jacob's vow "I shall give You the tenth of all You grant me" (Genesis 28:33), I cannot say.[38] A physician (who had a son) left all his belongings, consisting of cash and medical books, to the holy synagogue of Dammūh (C 37). In a will made in Alexandria in January, 1143, a woman decrees that any money remaining after the payment of the burial expenses and of the sums bequeathed by her to relatives (with the exclusion of her son) should be given to the poor, but charged her executor with this task, not the officials of the community chest, while the court was to choose the charities worthy of consideration.[39]

To conclude this summary with an example that does not lack a certain humorous flavor: A woman in a little town had left to the community a valuable cloth of siglaton, a fabric highly cherished in the East and in Europe. Musing about what to do with this piece of public property, the elders decided to let each member of the congregation wear the precious garb one Sabbath. A learned judge, whose decision was requested in this matter, denounced the idea and suggested instead to sell the siglaton and to use the money to buy a book for the synagogue library or for repairs or lighting.[40]

In times of famine or other calamities causing scarcity of food the social officers could incur severe hardship and even dangers, a fact that is well illustrated in a complaint about calumniation and threat to his life addressed by an administrator of charities in Alexandria to the Nagid Abraham Maimonides around 1230. The Nagid had instructed the Jewish authorities in the Mediterranean port to store part of the wheat collected to meet impending emergencies. The administrator had acted accordingly with the result that only meager rations could be distributed. A rival scholar took advantage of the hardships and dissatisfaction of the poor, arranged a collection of his own, and immediately distributed the wheat that had accumulated. At the same time rumors were spread that the administrator had appropriated some of the victuals destined for the poor. The incitement against the unhappy public servant culminated in a nightly attack on him by a man who threatened to murder him if he did not distribute the accumulated reserves immediately and hand over the communal accounts to another, specified person. The administrator, who was backed by the acting judge, as well as by prominent scholars and notables, was urged to take legal action against his adversaries, but, as he explained in the letter, because of the precariousness of the situation, preferred to await a rescript of the Nagid or the return of the chief judge to Alexandria.

It should be noted that in many Geniza documents the population of Alexandria, Jewish and other, seemed particularly prone to discord and violence.[41]

3. *Charitable Foundations (Houses and Other Communal Property)*

During most of the Middle Ages, in western Europe and Byzantium as well as in the lands of Islam, charitable works and institutions of learning were maintained largely by the income from houses and other immovable property donated for the purpose. The Jewish community was no exception. The rich documentation found in the Geniza records on the subject furnishes a good deal of insight into the working of this outstanding institution of pious foundations in Islamic countries, the early development of which is rather obscure.[1]

A report about the history of the houses belonging to the synagogue of the Palestinians in Old Cairo up to 1039 makes mention of only eight houses and two stores. Two buildings and part of a third had been owed by the community from a time beyond the memory of the witnesses (A 3, ca. 1040). The first generation of public servants known to them by name, active around 960, acquired three additional buildings and two shops in the immediate vicinity of the synagogue, partly with the income from the older houses and partly with funds specifically collected for the purpose. In the next two generations an apartment was built on top of those two shops and five out of twenty-four shares in another house were bought; but most of the revenue was spent on the synagogue building itself. Three years after the completion of its renovation the synagogue and the houses belonging to it were damaged or demolished in the wake of the religious persecution under the caliph al-Ḥākim (ca. 1012). After the churches and synagogues were returned to their owners, many years passed until everything was restored. As before, signs were placed on the buildings stating to which synagogue they belonged and which caliphal authorization had been given for their ownership. Many constructions were carried out during the years 426-430 A.H. (Nov. 16, 1034–Oct. 2, 1038), for each of which exact accounts were publicly displayed. Such accounts, destined to be posted in the synagogue, have been found for these and the succeeding years through 1044 (A 4, 5, 6, 8, 9, 113-115, 117, 120-122). But the names of only two or three additional buildings appear in them.

A century later, during the second half of the twelfth century, the situation was entirely different. The accounts for the years 1181-1184 of one welfare officer alone contains details about twenty-nine houses and ten shops, while from other sources we know the names of ten other houses then in the possession of the Jewish community of the city (A 25-36). More than ninety such houses are mentioned in the accounts preserved from the years 1164 through 1215 (A 24-25), and numerous new items appear in later documents.

This large increase in the number of charitable foundations might have had its cause in specific circumstances, like the migration of wealthier families from Fustat to the more fashionable city and seat of the government, Fatimid Cairo, an exodus that precluded the profitable sale of old houses and made it more commendable to their proprietors to give them away as a pious deed. It seems, however, that in the Islamic population, too, there occurred from the twelfth century on a vast increase in the number and scope of charitable foundations. Thus, the marked changes discernible in our records might have owed to a general trend of the period rather than to causes specific to the Jewish community.

Naturally, the spiritual and communal leaders took the lead in this movement. A house often mentioned in the eighties of the twelfth century was that of "the Nagid," no doubt identical with that of "the Rayyis Abū Manṣūr," the Arabic name of the Nagid Samuel b. Hananya (1140-1159), prominent in the records of 1164 (A 24). His chancellor, the judge Nathan, also left a house to the community (A 28, 31, 35). We happen to have a document about its history. His wife had bequeathed to him half the house in which they lived and given the other half to the qōdesh (A 18). It is not surprising that the judge followed the example of his wife when his own hour of death drew near. A number of houses bear the names ʿAlam al-Dawla, Amīn al-Dawla, "Banner of the Dynasty," "Trustee of the Dynasty," and so on, that is, of persons connected in one way or another with the government. A parnās, physicians, and merchants are among the donors, but also a good number of artisans. Some of the most frequently mentioned houses are named after a glassmaker and a dyer, respectively. Many charitable foundations were established by women; we have to remember that even in families with modest means it was customary for a bride to be given a house or part of a house as her marriage portion.[2]

There were also certain types of property of which it is not stated how they were acquired by the community. Such, for example, were the "Oil House," the "Vinegar House," or the "Spinnery," and the hospices called *funduq,* an Arabic word meaning caravanserai, but derived from Greek *pandocheion,* a building attached to a church or a synagogue and set aside to harbor needy travelers.[3] We hear about "the" funduq or "the funduq on the Great Bazaar," as well as about "the small" and "the new" funduq and "the one between the two synagogues." Tenants paying monthly rents lived in the funduqs as well as in the buildings in which the commodities after which they were called had been produced or sold. A slaughterhouse and a *misṭāh,* an open space for the spreading of materials dyed or tanned, are also mentioned as forming part of the *aḥbās al-yahūd,* or properties of the Jewish community.[4]

The community chest shared many buildings with private persons, including Muslims and Christians,[5] sometimes because a donor earmarked only a part of his property for the qōdesh (A 18), but mainly because in those days many or most properties were divided up among various owners.

Normally, more than one tenant lived in a house belonging to a charitable foundation, as many as nine according to an account from the year 1040 or so (A 7), and twelve to fifteen parties shared the "House of the Glassmaker" in 1183 and the following years (A 30, 32, 43). It was not always possible to lease all the apartments available. The remark in A 6 (1042-1043), "empty this month," shows that vacancies already occurred at a time when the community owned comparatively few houses. In a later period we find vacancies in six out of fifteen houses, in three of them more than one, and in a fourth instance the whole building remained empty (A 43). Some accounts contain separate columns for unoccupied apartments.[6] Half-empty dwellings entailed not only loss of revenue, but also the threat of encroachment by the government, as well as special expenses.[7] Under these circumstances there is no wonder that rooms or apartments in the synagogue compound were rented also to non-Jews. An early example is found in A 10. Later on, the examples become frequent, including even a qadi, or Muslim judge. As it happened, he absconded without paying the rent (A 43).

Many accounts imply or state expressly that tenants were in arrears with their rent. The list A 117 is devoted entirely to delinquent tenants. In 1040-1041 the arrears amounted to one-third the total revenue from the communal houses (A 5). Tardiness in payments resulted sometimes in a reduction of the rent (A 142). There were other difficulties. A late statute for tenants, of which only the last four paragraphs have been preserved, makes the following points: *(a)* No excuse for nonpayment on time of the monthly rent is accepted. In case of want, "just as you beg for your food, beg for your rent." *(b)* The price fixed by three Jewish experts is definite and no unilateral adjustment is allowed. *(c)* The tenants are bound to show their contract with the charitable foundation (designated here by the Arabic term *waqf),* whenever requested. *(d)* No one is permitted to use the influence of Muslim acquaintances in order to obtain a lodging in the waqf or a rent lower than that stipulated by the experts. In the event of his failure to comply with the statute the tenant is threatened not with eviction but with excommunication, "which would bring damage to his person and to his property" (A 96).

Jewish as well as Muslim law provides that rents and wages are paid at the end of the periods for which they are due. In later times, however, when the community chest was in dire straits, the contracts it entered into show payments in advance for a full year and even for two years. In those contracts the rent was presumably lower than normal, and in one instance this is expressly stated.[8]

As to the administration of the qōdesh, we should not expect uniformity throughout the centuries. Usually several persons dealt simultaneously with the varied property of the community. The official specifically charged with this task and most frequently mentioned in connection with it was the parnās. The parnāsīm formed a kind of administrative board that received its instructions either from the chief parnās, where that office existed, or from the communal leader whatever his rank or title was at the time. The document A 3 mentions seven consecutive generations of such boards.[9] Cantors and beadles often did administrative work. Moreover, one or several properties were farmed out to professional collectors, even non-Jewish. In A 113 a cantor and a parnās cooperated, in A 148, a cantor, a beadle, and a Christian joined in collecting the revenue. The composite character of the administration of the pious foundations is obscured by the fact that most of our documents are notes by individual officials who listed only revenue and expenditure for which they were responsible and not those of the community at large.

In spring, 1150, the energetic Nagid Samuel b. Hananya appointed a general administrator for all the immobile and mobile property of the community, from its synagogues, books, silver ornaments, and precious textiles to its houses, orchards, and palm groves.[10] He even exempted the administrator from the supervision of the courts. This tough centralization had partly salutary effects, inasmuch as the new administrator started to resuscitate the properties that had fallen into disrepair or were entirely in ruins. But such plenipotentiary powers were not to the taste of the Jewish public and conflicted also to a certain extent with Jewish law which imparted to the courts the highest authority with regard to communal property. The office was abolished either by Samuel's immediate successor, the Gaon Nathanel b. Moses, or by Moses Maimonides during the first term of office (A 97). Yet, the reforms introduced by that administrator must have been far-reaching, for over a hundred years later, in 1252, his letter of appointment was submitted to the Nagid David, Maimonides' grandson, by some of the elders as forming the basis for all claims by or against the public chest (A 157).

The accounts of the collectors of revenue, partly drafts and partly clean copies, normally refer to one or to two months. There are also some for longer periods, such as four months (A 28, 33, 35) or five (A 6, 38). A summary of expenditure and revenue of six months coinciding with the second half of a Muslim year (A 24) seems to indicate that yearly accounts for buildings were made, at least in certain periods, according to the Muslim calendar and not the Jewish. Utmost caution is recommended for the use of these documents, since as a result of the predilection of the medieval scribe for variety, as well as for other reasons (such as the change of tenants), the same building not infrequently is referred to by two or three different designations. Moreover, in most cases only the actual receipts are listed, and it is not indicated whether they represent the rent due or only a fraction of it or, on the contrary, also contain the payments of arrears.

In A 25–36 where we have twelve reports by the same collector covering the comparatively short period of three years and seven months, we are on rather safe ground. Most of these records are in the handwriting of a well-known judge, which means that they represent official documents approved by, or at least submitted to, the relevant authority. Their scrutiny forms a good starting point for the study of the administration of the buildings belonging to the Jewish community chest of Old Cairo.

Since the idea of a central treasury was unknown, each collector served also as a paymaster. His balance sheet showed the revenue on the right side, and the expenditure on the left. The reason for this order of columns is, of course, that Arabic and Hebrew scripts run from right to left. Sometimes the revenue is written above the expenditure. According to the purpose of the account, the side devoted to revenue shows the payments of each tenant, or the total payment of each house, or the collector's total monthly revenue in general. In some accounts the arrears or additional payments of tenants are indicated. On the expenditure side, first place is taken by the maintenance of the buildings concerned, including a small tax called *ḥikr,* or lease (the idea being that the land was owned by the government), regular payments and gifts to watchmen and the keepers of compounds, expenses for rubbish removal and cleaning of cesspits and, above all, for repairs. In the half-yearly account A 24, the cost of repairs amounted to almost one-third the total revenue.

In addition to these expenses, countless items, changing every month, reveal the varied needs and social services of the community. In the first place, there was the expenditure for (olive, sesame, or linseed) oil for the lighting of places of worship, and for sundry other requirements. Second, payments for community officials and teachers (the latter received only small sums for the orphans and the children of the poor whom they happened to teach during the month concerned). Third, an odd variety of grants to needy of all kinds. Finally, where there was a cash balance, purses of dirhems or dinars, or bankers' notes, were handed over—not to a treasurer, for one did not exist—but to specified persons such as a parnās, a cantor, or a beadle; there were usually several individuals acting as treasurers during one month.

We have very definite information on the cost of the administration of the qōdesh. Many accounts, from 1164 through 1247, conclude with the item "collection," namely, the remuneration of the collector, who, as we know, had also to do a good deal of other work (A 24, 25, 32, 35, 38, 95). The collector's "fee" is invariably 10 percent of the revenue, which seems to be decent in view of the many-sided troubles the administrator had to face. Occasionally, in particular in times of trouble with government officials, when much extra work was required and when, without the collector's fault, the revenue was reduced, a special settlement with regard to the collector's compensation was made. We read about one reached "according to a decision of the elders." [11] A remuneration of only 5 percent (as in A 149*c*) is isolated as far as the administration of houses is concerned, but is paralleled by fees paid for the collection of contributions pledged at appeals.[12]

It is still premature—at any rate, I do not regard myself sufficiently competent—to assess the total revenue from the immovable property of the Jewish community chest as reflected in the Geniza records. The average total payments from the two groups of houses in A 25–36 (dated 1181–1184) amount to about 450 dirhems per month, which would give a yearly revenue of about 5,400 dirhems. With this may be compared the semiannual account of 1164 (A 24) amounting to 3,683 dirhems. In the second example we might have before us a report of only a part, albeit a considerable one, of the communal property. In the first example, we know positively that around 1181 the community possessed about twice as many houses as the number covered by the twelve accounts analyzed. We thus arrive at a yearly revenue of the qōdesh of about 10,000 dirhems. A number of uncertain factors, however, are involved in this computation. It should serve as an illustration, not be taken as fact.

Another question difficult to answer is the apportionment of the income from the religious endowments, that is, who were the actual beneficiaries and which percentage of the revenue did reach them. An analysis of the accounts A 25–36 (including A 43 which belongs to the same period) by Moshe Gil in his Ph.D. dissertation "The Institution of Charitable Foundations in the Light of the Cairo Geniza Documents" (University of Pennsylvania, 1970), produced these results:

Spent on	*Percentage of revenue*
Administration, maintenance, and repairs	29.6
Groundtax, cleaning, and watchmen	10.8
Total of upkeep of properties	40.4
Emoluments of officials and scholars	45.5
Synagogues (mainly for lighting)	8
Charity (mainly individual cases)	6.1
Total	100

As pointed out in the preceding paragraph, the accounts referred to concerned only about one-half the properties owned by the Jewish community of Fustat in the 1180's. Future research will have to examine the sporadic details available for the houses not included in A 25–36, 43, and will also consider whether communal officials and scholars not listed in these accounts were at that time in receipt of emoluments from the community. Anyhow, the very small percentage allotted to charity proper, as well as the fact that the cases noted mostly were those of persons with specific requirements, confirms the impression gained from subsection 2, above, that the needs of the mass of the poor were met by collections for bread, wheat, clothing, holidays, and other general appeals that were arranged at regular intervals or from time to time.

In view of this situation, it seems strange that the houses and other properties of the community should be regularly referred to as "the compound of the poor" or even "the property of the poor" (see e.g., A 41, 130, 143). The answer is to be found in the legal form of an endowment, which regularly stated, or, at least, implied that, should the persons or purposes for whose benefit the endowment was made cease to exist, "the poor" would become the ultimate beneficiaries. For God has promised us that there would always be a supply of poor people on earth (Deuteronomy 15:11). The same idea pervaded the Islamic waqf and it might even be that the formulation of Islamic endowment deeds influenced Jewish juridical practice. Before the law, the poor were ultimately the legal proprietors of the religious endowments, although, in fact only few would be their beneficiaries, except where they were made primary beneficiaries in express terms.

How long did the houses of the community chest survive its administration? While trying to answer this question, we are again confronted by the possibility that different buildings at different times might have had the same name, while one property might have changed its designation. Thus, one is tempted to identify the "House of the Dyer," prominent in the lists from around 1040, with the building bearing the same name in A 24 (1164) and in many of the accounts relating to 1181–1183. In 1042–1043 it brought a total of 18 dirhems per month (A 6) and in the 80's of the twelfth century an average of 16-½ dirhems. Dyeing, however, was a common Jewish profession. Therefore, despite the similarity of name and circumstances the identity is by no means sure. The compound dedicated to the poor of Jerusalem is referred to in our records over the span of two hundred years. It may well be, however, that several donations of houses were made for the same purpose during that long period. In any case, documents A 135 and 136 prove that stipends were regularly distributed from the revenue of these houses even during the years in which, because of the Crusaders, practically no Jews lived in Jerusalem (1099–1187). On the other hand, we learn from the documents of the 1040's that houses changed their names during a comparatively short period (for example, from "Little Cat" to "Camel," both names of persons). In legal documents we often meet with the formula "the house known *at present* under the designation X" (A 14). Therefore, the fact that, with the exception of the "House of the Dyer" and the compound of the Jerusalemites, we do not find in the 1180's any of the houses of the 1040's does not prove that all these had ceased to exist.

We can be relatively certain only in buildings of exceptionally rare names or in very special circumstances. The female name Muhra ("Filly") has been found thus far only twice in the Geniza, or perhaps only once: "The House of Muhra" appears in A 24 (1164), A 94 (1234), A 166; and in 1143 a Muhra, who may be identical with the donor of that building, made some testamentary dispositions in Alexandria.[13] 'Abla is a name well known in Arabic literature, for she was the beloved of 'Antara, the hero of a popular storybook. In the Geniza the name has been traced only once, in "The House of 'Abla," details about which are given in A 28 (1182) and A 94 (1234). The She-Camel (also a female nickname) donated her house in 1127 (A 128), which recurs in the lists A 24 (1164), A 39, A 45 (around 1215). "Lady Gazelle's" house, often referred to in the documents of 1181–1183, was still in such good repair in December, 1243, that it could be renovated at comparatively very low cost (A 155). The Ben Phinehas house occurs in at least sixteen documents between around 1125 (B 32) and 1215 (A 147). The house owned in common by the community chest and the Sharīf (a Muslim notable) is mentioned from 1181 (A 25) through 1247 (A 95), and "The Tower," the relic of a Roman fortification used as living quarters and storage house, is attested to for the same period. We see, therefore, that it was not at all exceptional for houses to remain in use by the qōdesh for sixty to ninety years. The period might actually have been far longer. Mention of a ruin has been found only once in the accounts I collected (A 30 and 35, both of which refer to 1183). But we have already read how "the ruins of the *heqdēsh*" were restored by an administrator appointed in 1150, seeming to indicate that, in the course of time, the Jewish charitable foundations did not fare better than other similar institutions in the Near East.

The Geniza also contains a reference to the fraudulent alienation of communal property by the authority to which it was entrusted. That reference, however, is found in the letter of an adversary and not substantiated by other sources.[14]

A comparison of the often referred to accounts of the 1180's with those made about forty years later shows a marked decline. The same houses bring less revenue, many rooms are unoccupied, and tenants abscond without paying. These changes are discussed in the context of the general development of the social services in the epilogue to this section.

One fact stands out clearly: during the second half of the twelfth and the first half of the thirteenth century, for which period we have comparatively rich documentation, the immovable properties, willed or donated to the community, yielded a large percentage of its regular revenue. It is a little strange to see the dead providing for the daily needs of the living. This phenomenon, however, is in conformity with a civilization in which people were eager to save their souls by special deeds of piety and where the younger generations were wont to look for the guidance and help of the older.

4. *The Beneficiaries of the Community Chest*

a. THE OFFICIALS

The minute division of labor characteristic of the Mediterranean society of the High Middle Ages required that persons devoting all or most of their time to the service of the community should be remunerated by an income provided by that community. On the other hand, the principle of free enterprise ingrained in this society, and perhaps also its organizational weakness, prevented an arrangement similar to that prevailing today, where one fixed salary covers all the recurrent emoluments received by a wage earner. The official of the Geniza period derived about a dozen different benefits from the community he served. Despite a certain regularity discernible in the salary scales and other types of income in the Geniza records, each employee seems to have worked under a special contract that also left considerable leeway for adapting the remuneration to performance.

One benefit, it seems, was granted to all officials, high and low: the community paid their poll tax to the Muslim government. Whether it was the beadle of a synagogue in 1075, or the Jewish chief judge of the capital in 1213, or a schoolteacher in a small town, payment of the poll tax was made or promised for all of them, and there are many other instances of this usage in our records.[1] As a matter of fact, this arrangement remained unchanged up to late Ottoman times.[2] In this respect the position of the ritual slaughterer was particularly noteworthy. He had to deliver to the community a part of his weekly income. But the community paid his poll tax.[3]

The payment of their poll tax by the community meant a great deal to people who were short of cash. It seems, however, that this benefit to community officials had more than financial significance. It went back to the talmudic precept that scholars—and, as a rule, only scholarly persons were appointed as community officials—should not share the burdens imposed on the public. In its turn, this injunction was based on a moral idea: "Learning makes one free: whosoever accepts the yoke of the Torah is exempted from the yoke of the rulers." [4]

With respect to salaries, various arrangements are evident in the documents. The differences are accounted for not so much by the change of time or place as the diversity of the sources from which the emoluments were paid. A muqaddam in Hebron, Palestine, complains that he had received neither a pesīqā, a special payment vowed to him by the community, nor a *mujāma'a,* a weekly salary.[5] We read about both very often in our sources. With equal frequency we find a monthly salary, in some cases paid to the same officials who appear in other records as receiving weekly wages. The reason for this duplication was technical. The rents for the houses belonging to the community were paid monthly; therefore, when the collector of the rents acted as paymaster, salaries were calculated on a monthly basis. On the other hand, when the wages were paid from the weekly contributions of the community members, the payrolls were made out weekly. Since most of the relevant lists are undated, it is difficult to say whether an official received both weekly and monthly payments at one and the same time, although duplication might well have occurred. A payment to a judge of 4 dirhems per month throughout a year (B 97) is feasible only if he had copious other sources of income.

On this subject a letter by the Gaon Sār Shālōm ha-Levi b. Moses (about 1176–1195) addressed to a provincial community is most instructive. In defining the rights of two clerics who had trespassed on each other's prebends, he writes that both would continue to receive *ṣibbūr,* a regular payment from the community, as well as a pesīqā; in addition, one was permitted to act as a teacher and as a religious slaughterer (there were other teachers, and also cantors in the little town), while only his rival was entitled to receive fees for writing deeds of marriage and divorce and other legal documents and for performing circumcisions. The tenor of the letter indicates that the payments of the community represented a subsidiary rather than the main means of sustenance for the two complainants.[6]

A pesīqā, or public appeal for officials, was usually arranged twice a year—on the High Holidays in the fall, and in the spring (on Passover [B 99])—as well as on special occasions. Thus, when an inspector sent by the chief judge in the capital found that the French rabbi in the Egyptian town of Bilbays was in dire circumstances, he addressed the community on the rabbi's behalf, which then vowed him 40 dirhems.[7] Naturally, a pesīqā was an excellent opportunity for the members of the congregation to manifest their estimate of the services of an official.

There were other such opportunities. The muqaddam of Hebron mentioned above complained that he received from the members of his congregation neither a gift (in money) nor a present (in kind, such as a piece of clothing).[8] Personalized support was religiously due the official in his capacity as a scholar, and because it was given in private, it had the advantage over the pesīqā, which was vowed publicly. The silver dirhems were delicately wrapped in a piece of paper before being handed over to the person honored.[9]

Most community officials, from the cantors down, appear also as recipients of loaves of bread, which were distributed twice a week, and also of wheat. They normally receive larger quantities than the needy persons listed with them. This usage is evident in all relevant lists beginning with the very first one (B 1), from the year 1026 or so, to one written about two hundred years later (B 47). The officials are either designated as such or known to us by their names from other sources.

The student of Muslim administrative practice is familiar with the fact that employees were paid partly in cash and partly in kind. This arrangement applied to a private teacher as well as to a soldier or an army officer. The *dīnār jayshī* the unit of soldier's pay, consisted of a quarter of one dinar in cash and certain quantities of wheat and oats.[10] It may be, however, that including cantors, beadles, inspectors of slaughterhouses and of milk production, night watchmen, and others, sometimes also parnāsīm, in the lists of the receivers of bread and flour was an old Jewish custom, the idea being that these categories of people were regarded as belonging to the poor. For, unlike the Muslim practice, where we find the heads and teachers of colleges, as well as librarians, in receipt of large numbers of loaves, and of meat and other victuals, from the charitable foundations, the Jewish spiritual leaders are not assigned such emoluments, either in the lists of receivers (Appendix B) or in those of expenditure from public funds (Appendix A). This difference between Muslim and Jewish practice needs further study.

No unified practice prevailed, it seems, in the distribution of clothing to officials. In some lists (B 25, 29, 33) cantors, beadles, and other lower officials and the parnās in charge of the distribution, received either a piece of clothing or a small monetary compensation. In one list written around 1200 (B 38), a judge, a cantor, a beadle, and the distributing parnās are assigned the very handsome sum of 45 *bakhāya* dirhems each, and as the parnās notes in a postscript that he had already received 22-½ dirhems for a *yūsufī* cloth, we may assume that the sum of 45 dirhems was sufficient for two articles of wearing apparel. It is noteworthy that the judge and the beadle, although receiving different salaries, are given identical sums for their clothing.[11]

Many documents suggest that community officials, and in particular beadles and cantors, lived in the synagogue compound. From some references the impression is given that free lodging was granted these officials, and one list states so explicitly.[12] Some late accounts, however, show them paying rents to the community chest like other tenants.[13] Perhaps the general decline of the community of Old Cairo in the thirteenth century contributed to this development. When we read that the community paid for repairs in "the room of the *dayyān* in the synagogue," the office of the judge rather than his living quarters was intended.[14]

An important benefit to officials was the payment by the community of school fees for their children. In most cases it is not indicated whether the boys referred to were orphans or not. In one account (B 44), however, we find on one page the beadle Maḥāsin receiving wages and loaves of bread, and on the reverse side his son is mentioned among the boys for whom school fees were paid to a teacher from the community chest. We cannot know, of course, how general this practice was; it forms an interesting parallel to practices accepted in our own day.

Although care for all widows and orphans was one of the main concerns of public charity, many of our lists show that special attention was paid to those of community officials. Particularly instructive in this respect is B 49 which contains payments just to officials and to the families of defunct employees. Various other documents point in the same direction, such as the one regarding the children of the chief rabbi of Alexandria, quoted above (subsection 2, n. 1), or the one in which the widow of a cantor is granted payment of fees for her boy to enable him to learn his father's profession.[15]

Did there exist anything resembling a pension for retired officials? Here again the copious accounts for the years between 1180 and 1220 prove to be instructive. In the dated lists for the years 1182–1184 (A 33, 35 [four entries], and a somewhat later account, A 43), the judge Jephthah (an exceedingly rare name) receives 20 dirhems per month.[16] In B 40, 41, 79–81, which are later by twenty years, his salary is 6-½ dirhems per week, about 28 a month; but after another period of twenty years, in A 76–79 (dated 1218) and B 46, 48 (the latter is dated 1219) he gets only 2-½ dirhems a week. The same development may be observed with regard to his colleague Manasse (b. Joseph). He and the judge Samuel b. Saadya receive 20 dirhems each month in 1181 (A 25, two entries). At that time Manasse had already attained his apogee, for he was in office as early as 1164 (A 24). Therefore, we are not astonished to find him receiving only 2-½ dirhems per week in the documents B 40, 41, where his younger colleague Jephthah received 6-½ dirhems.[17]

The data assembled in the preceding paragraph seem to indicate that in old age officials retired (wholly or partly) and received then only a fraction of their former emoluments, but it must be noted that express reference to the practice has not been found thus far, and in view of the composite character of the communal accounts the wide fluctuations in the payments made to the two judges might have had entirely different reasons. In general, we have to bear in mind that the terms "salary" and "wages" used here are to be taken with a grain of salt. In theory and practice, these regular payments were only "compensations for loss of time," [18] whereas work connected with each office and "honoraria" of various kinds constituted the main source of income. The dayyānīm, cantors, and beadles had regular functions at weddings and funerals, family events on which they probably made more cash than they received from the community chest. Judges normally were also notaries and scribes, and for each document they wrote appropriate fees were paid by the parties concerned. When the confidants of the aged Gaon Solomon b. Judah advised him to delegate some of his responsibilities to the president of his court, they suggested he let the president have half the revenue from the slaughterhouses and half that from the fees for issuing legal documents. Clearly, these were the main regular sources of income of the Jewish authorities in Palestine at that time (around 1040).[19] In all the lists surveyed in our appendixes A and B only one judge receives a decent minimum of a fixed salary: the French rabbi Anatoli of Marseille, who served in Old Cairo before becoming Jewish chief justice of Alexandria. According to A 43 his salary was 52 dirhems a month, as against 20 paid to the judge Jephthah and 13, that is, one-fourth of the Anatoli's salary, paid to a teacher. The reason for this exceptional treatment is easily understood. Documents were written mostly in the Arabic language of which the scholar from France did not have sufficient command. He therefore had to be compensated otherwise. Moreover, he possibly devoted more time to teaching adults than did his colleagues. In B 101 Anatoli receives a payment of 8 dirhems from a weekly collection, which would make only 32 dirhems a month. But this weekly emolument was probably additional to his monthly salary.

As is well known, Maimonides in his Code of Law insists on the old religious concept that public service, such as sitting in judgment or teaching adults, should be rendered gratuitously. The preceding pages have shown that this postulate was not unrealistic as it may appear to the modern historian. The salary paid by the community chest to public servants was no more than "a compensation for loss of time." Their real income came from a wide variety of other sources, a state of affairs that was in harmony with both the religious attitude and the spirit of free enterprise characteristic of the Jewish society of that period.

It should be noted that instances of gratuitous service to the community, like teaching adults, dispensing law, and performing religious functions, continued to exist well into the twentieth century, and not only in eastern Europe where traditional Jewish life persisted until World War II, but sporadically also elsewhere.[20]

b. THE NEEDY

"Had it not been for the mercy of Heaven and for my brother's son Joseph, I would have been forced to take recourse to Israel [i.e., public charity]. All my days I have been a burden on him and living on his money." Thus we read in a deathbed declaration, certainly made to fend off any claims by the government that the nephew might have inherited something from his uncle, but exemplifying at the same time quite a common situation.[21]

Anyone in distress was expected to turn first to his family. The loss of face that befell a clan unwilling or unable to support a faltering member was enough incentive for coming to his rescue, even where humanitarian or religious impulses did not inspire such action. There were, however, lonely people, foreigners and others, as well as indigent families consisting entirely of paupers. To these unfortunate people many different types of help were extended by the communities that left us their records in the Cairo Geniza.

Free bread.—First and foremost, there was the weekly distribution of bread, intended simply to keep body and soul together. The peoples of the Western world, particularly Americans, eat comparatively little bread. In the Middle East, up till recent times, bread was the main human fare. All other foods were combined (in both Arabic and Hebrew) in terms for which there is no equivalent in English and which mean "that which is taken together with bread." In both languages even verbs were formed to express this idea. In Arabic *adam,* in Hebrew *lippet,* means "taking something as food additional to bread." When a man had bread he had the main component of his meal. As Appendix B proves, bread was distributed with absolute regularity during the entire Geniza period and was the most conspicuous feature of public charity.

Study of the subject is best opened by examining the lists from November, 1107, and the period around it, for which we have at least ten items (B 17–24, 27–28, 31). We see here that twice a week, on Tuesday and Friday the Jewish community of Old Cairo used to distribute between 500 and 600 loaves of bread to about 140 persons or households, an average of about 4 loaves for each recipient. Carefully executed lists were kept for each distribution and at the end of the month the total expenditure was certified by two social service officers and the scribe who wrote the document (B 24). At that time a hundred pounds of bread cost half a dinar, or gold piece (B 19 [TS K 15, f. 5], B 24). The standard weight of one loaf of bread was 1 pound, which at that time in Egypt was equivalent to 437.5 grams, that is to say, not much less than the pound in use today in the United States and in England. When the number of recipients was higher than expected (or than provided for by the money available), the loaves were made substandard, as in B 24, where 500 pounds were distributed in 559 loaves.

Utmost care was taken to ensure that each household received exactly what it was entitled to, not less, but also not more, as proved by the changes in the rations discernible from week to week and even from a Tuesday to a Friday. During the first week of November, 1107, in nineteen out of ninety cases compared, the number of loaves distributed to a household was increased and in four reduced, making a total of twenty-three adjustments (see table 3 at the end of Appendix B). In the subsequent week there were three further reductions and one more increase. This meticulous care was perhaps prompted by religious scruples with regard to the "property of the poor" confided to its administrators. Anyhow, such minute surveillance must have entailed an enormous amount of work for the parnāsīm, or social service officers.

In each list, even of consecutive distributions, the names and other designations of the recipients appear in an entirely different order. The Rūm, that is, the poor from Europe, who in three instances are listed together as a separate group, appear in other rolls completely dispersed among the rest of the recipients. The arrangement of names indicates that the loaves were not distributed to the houses of the poor according to a geographical order, but that everyone picked up his share at a storeroom in the synagogue, and whoever came first was listed first. We may assume the Europeans were sometimes advised to appear together, since many of them might have been newcomers unable to explain their situation in the language of the country, or some of them might have been unknown to the parnāsīm and needed to be identified by their compatriots.

The unusually high percentage of Europeans (an average of 40 or more out of less than 140) suggests that the relief rolls around 1107 were exceptionally swollen in the wake of the bloody massacres perpetrated by the Crusaders. This assumption seems to be refuted by the carefully written list B 1, where we find, around 1026, 136 beneficiaries receiving a total of about 570 loaves, that is to say, the same numbers that we meet about eighty years later. It stands to reason, however, that this apparent similarity was merely fortuitous. A large part of the Jewish population (and with it the poor) probably moved from Old to New Cairo between 1026 and 1107, and only the influx of refugees from Europe and other countries created the similarity in number of beneficiaries from the weekly distribution of bread. Attention should also be paid to the fact that lists B 1 and B 2*a* + B 52 (which are two fragments of one sheet) represent only parts of more extensive documents. The decline of the community in Old Cairo during the thirteenth century seems to be evident from the quantities of bread distributed. It was 150 pounds in B 47 and 100 in B 50 (1241) and B 80 (see also B 79 and 81); and, naturally, the poorer sections of the population were slower in moving out of the Old City than those enjoying better material conditions.

How many loaves did each person receive? From B 1, where 121 households receive even numbers of loaves and only 10 uneven, it is evident that the normal ration was two loaves. One loaf was given to "a stranger" and one to "a Muslim," that is, people who normally did not partake in the distributions. Around 1107 many households received uneven numbers of loaves, although those with even numbers formed a large majority, and in several instances it is evident that a person got only one loaf each time, as when we find an item "Abraham, his sister and her mother—3" or "orphans—2" (B 24, col. II*b*). On the other hand, persons recognizable as community officials and certain others always received even numbers, which seems to indicate that the persons of these households received two loaves every Tuesday and Friday. Obviously, this was the norm, from which only in times of particular strain was an exception made.

Distributions of wheat.—Four loaves of bread weighing a total of about 1,750 grams, or about 4 pounds, is of course not sufficient food for one week. Here we have to keep in mind that the community also distributed wheat, which meant perhaps that, on special occasions, poor people, too, preferred to bake their own bread (or, rather, to have it prepared at home and baked by a *farrān).* Both the frequency and the scope of these distributions cannot yet be established fully. For the time being, we have explicit references only to the doling out of wheat before the Passover feast in springtime (C 82*a*; people baked their *matzot,* or unleavened bread, at home) and before the Little Fast (C 33, July, 1178). But there was certainly an even larger distribution before the Great Fast, or Day of Atonement, most of the time falling in September, and there might have been others before the remaining holidays and the minor fasts, for "the religious merit of a fast is acquired by giving alms," and holidays could be happy, as the Bible often reiterates, only when the poor were made happy, too.[22]

The unit of wheat handed out to one person was a quarter of a *wayba* (approximately 1 gallon weighing a little over 6 pounds) in B 26 and 35, and the double of this quantity in B 66 and 85. The detailed list B 66, like those of the distribution of loaves, indicates that certain families, especially of communal officials, received more than their number of members would have warranted.

Some proselytes, presumably Europeans of noble descent, were apportioned exceptionally high quantities of wheat. My surmise that these persons received special consideration because their eating habits were so different from those of the indigenous population[23] has received a certain degree of confirmation by a recent, unfortunately fragmentary, find. A proselyte expresses in beautiful Hebrew his thanks to a distinguished woman, who looked after him, for the fine bread she had sent and gives her instructions how to bake certain cakes ("put hot ginger in them"). In the introduction to his letter he says: "When I was holding an office in the vain religion that I followed before, I was served twelve dishes or more, I had every day [meat, wine, and so on, and] bread of exquisite taste. I tried [to obtain such bread] from the day I came to the land of Ishmael [Muslim countries], but was never entirely successful, until I found favor in your eyes. . . ."[24]

Taken together, the quantities of bread and wheat did not provide more than mere subsistence at starvation level. No wonder then, that the social service officers tried to supplement the meager rations provided by the public funds. In a letter of appointment made in June, 1099, the beadle of the synagogue of the Iraqis in Old Cairo was charged to help the parnās Eli, one of the signatories of B 24, "with the collection of bread on Friday and other nights."[25] This document shows that the parnās made a round on the eve of Sabbath and other nights, and when he found persons who had nothing to eat, he collected fresh bread from people having their supper and, with the help of the beadle, brought the loaves thus obtained to the needy.

It may be, however, that the lists analyzed were written at the time of famine or other public calamity. The year 1026 (see B 1, and 2*a* + B 52, which are fragments of one sheet) fell in a period of prolonged hunger and disorders notorious in Egyptian history.[26] The many documents made out in or around November, 1107, I linked with the Crusades because of the many refugees from Europe listed in them. It should be noted, though, that no Germanic names appear among them. The Rūm have either Hebrew names—women included (Egyptian Jewesses were never named after biblical heroines)—or bear Arabic names, certainly given to them by their environment for the sake of convenience. Occasionally there occur names of Greek or Romance origin, preserved in our lists no doubt because the Egyptian Jews were familiar with them (for example, *qalīnā* and *qalī qurī,* Greek *kale kore,* "pretty girl," and *sanyūr,* Romanesque *senior,* all in B 26). We are perhaps right in surmising that such detailed lists with changes every three or four days, like those discussed above, were drawn up only in times of scarcity. In normal years perhaps less strict procedures were adopted. Still, this assumption needs to be corroborated by express evidence.

Clothing.—The information about the distribution of clothing is varied, but incomplete. Document B 25 contains two lists of recipients, one numbering forty-four persons and the other thirty-seven, but it bears the mark "Leaf 3," which suggests that the fragment preserved is the concluding or middle part of accounts for two distributions amounting to at least three times as many beneficiaries as those whose names are preserved. All the other lists are either partial in character or also incomplete.

Distinguished persons received a *muqaddar,* literally, "valued," which, in a previous publication I took to mean that a special estimate was made for the needs of the beneficiary referred to.[27] Since then, I have found in the Geniza a craftsman described as a *muqaddarī,* or maker of muqaddars; thus, the term must denote a piece of clothing, although it seems not to be mentioned as such anywhere.[28] One of the meaning of muqaddar in Middle Arabic is "large," an appropriate designation for a garment. The assignment of a muqaddar is found in B 36 with regard to a respectable visitor from Benhā, Egypt, and in B 25 (approximately 1105) with reference to the parnās from Crete and "R. Isaac, the European," who might well be identical with Isaac Benveniste of Narbonne, France, who visited Old Cairo at that time. A letter in his hand reports that at nighttime his caravan was robbed by thieves who took among other valuables his good clothing and that he needed at least 8 gold pieces for replacing them.[29] A large quantity of muqaddars distributed at a time (to forty mostly communal officials, with one exception all male, and their families) has been found thus far only once (B 71, dated 1176). The allocation of a *thawb,* a gown that covered the whole body and whose standard price was 1 dinar, was entirely exceptional.[30]

It is no surprise that the types of clothing distributed were usually of a modest style. The lists mention either felt (B 29 and 33), or, in most cases, a piece of clothing called *jūkhāniyya.* This term, although occurring in the Geniza records more than two hundred times, has not yet been traced anywhere else; it is plausible that it was similar to, or identical with the fourteenth-century *jūkha,* a kind of cloak or raincoat, which al-Maqrīzī (d. 1442) reports as worn by Europeans and other foreigners, as well as by poor people in Cairo; only later, when prices had soared, had respectable persons also begun to use it.[31] E. Ashtor has rightly drawn attention to the fact that high-priced *jūkhāniyyas* made of silk, fine linen, or other costly fabrics appear in the lists of trousseaux.[32] Thus, the word, although derived from *jūkh,* (woolen) cloth, must designate the cut of the garment concerned, not its material. It probably was a robe with a hood, similar to the present-day Maghrebi burnous.

In B 33, fourteen persons receive a *fūṭa,* a sari-like cloth, the price of which varied widely in accordance with the material used. Respectable beneficiaries received pieces of cloth which they would have tailored for themselves according to their own taste *(shuqqa* [B 25 and 33]). Sometimes a piece of clothing was given to more than one person, "one jūkhaniyya to the orphans of Hiba, the son of the woman from Europe" (B 36), and in B 25, where *bayt,* "house," should perhaps not be taken as "wife, widow," for in the same list many women and widows are explicitly identified as such. Money as an alternative for clothing was sometimes given to more than one person too ("five dirhems to the shōmēr [chap. vi, 10 n. 37] and his son").

These monetary compensations had long puzzled me. For when we find, in A 34 (see also B 29 and 36), persons receiving "for clothing" 5, 4, and even 3, or 2 silver coins, we wonder what kind of clothing worth mentioning could be acquired with such small sums. The solution of this puzzle is to be sought in the technique of communal finances repeatedly referred to in these pages. The sums mentioned as distributed for clothing did not represent the whole amount a needy person received for a certain period, but only the share allotted to him by a particular collector during a certain month. Thus we find Sirb (an exceedingly rare name), the freedwoman, receiving a jūkhāniyya in fall, 1183 (B 36) and only a few months later getting 5 dirhems "on account of clothing" (A 34). The parnās in charge of the collection cashes 12 dirhems for clothing in one month, and one or two months later another 10 (A 34 and 35). It is also noteworthy that in A 34 the freedwoman receives the same sum as the wife of a parnās.

Most of the beneficiaries of this charity were women (B 25, 36, 64), in accordance with the talmudic injunction and the natural notion that female decency required proper clothing. In some lists (B 33 and 72) male persons form the majority. Clearly, there were two types of distributions of clothing, one destined mainly for the poor, and another for the many persons serving the community in one capacity or another.

Lodging.—As a rule, free lodging in the houses owned by the community was not among the benefits granted to needy people, at least not in later times. There is in A 149*a* an exception confirming the rule. The decision by the Nagid David I that a teacher was in principle entitled to free lodging (A 167) was futile since in the same letter he conceded that the person concerned paid rent to the community chest. Many poor families did live in houses belonging to pious foundations, as we know by the simple fact that many of the tenants of these houses appear in the lists of receivers of doles from the community. A closer study of the many references to prices of rents found in the Geniza records proves that many of these indigents were paying reduced rents.

Poll tax.—After food, clothing, and housing the most urgent need of a member of the minority groups under Islam was money for his jāliya, or poll tax. Failure to comply with this obligation entailed imprisonment, which, because of the bad state of the prisons in those times, could mean death. It is no exaggeration to say that the largest single group of requests for help preserved in the Geniza is that for assistance to pay the jāliya. This charity, which was regarded as tantamount to the greatest of all meritorious works, "the ransoming of the captives," was not left entirely to private initiative, and in certain periods it must have been the main object of communal efforts. A letter from Old Cairo referring to the payment of the poll tax for ninety persons as only a first installment was quoted above, and special collections made for that purpose were cited.[33] In a query addressed to Maimonides a case is reported where the funds collected for this purpose were confiscated by a Muslim official.[34] We even find the donation of a house for the help of persons unable to work and to earn the money for their poll tax (A 128).

The majority of people requiring assistance in this matter were not entirely destitute. Therefore, the community expected them to pay whatever they could and made up the rest. The long and highly interesting lists of working people, employees, and persons for whom security was given, paying sums ranging from 1/8 to 3/4 dinar (B 4-9, 55, 59), are to be taken as serving such a purpose. Lists of exclusively male persons of low standing (B 11, 53-54, 75) and of prisoners who could be ransomed with comparatively small sums (B 58, see B 96) must also refer to the payment of the poll tax for poor people by the community.[35]

Medical care.—No reference to a Jewish hospital has been found thus far in the Geniza. This is somewhat surprising, for many Jewish doctors are mentioned both by the Geniza and in Arabic sources as working in what could be called government hospitals, namely those erected by Muslim rulers, whereas Jewish patients are never mentioned in Geniza documents as making use of them.[36] On the other hand, our records from both the eleventh and the twelfth centuries reveal the existence of pious donations for medicines for the needy or for poor sick people in general.[37] Physicians treated indigent patients gratuitously—if the physicians could be reached by them. Both Maimonides and his great-great-grandson David II gave medical advice and help to poor persons with whom they had dealings in their capacity as heads of the Jews. Disabled persons of all descriptions are mentioned in heavy numbers in the lists of beneficiaries of the community chest. The blind, albeit not appearing in particularly large numbers, seem to have formed a special group, for in an instruction to an official with regard to one it is stated that the latter "is of the blind and gets his share with them" (B 57*a*).

Education.—Education, a big item in the family budget then as it is today, was furnished by the Jewish community for the poor and the orphans (mentioned in this sequence in an instruction by the Nagid Abraham Maimonides). Many references to this fact are found in our records, in particular, details about payments to teachers noted in monthly or weekly accounts. There was a change in educational policy insofar as during the eleventh and early twelfth centuries we read about special classes for orphans, and even of food supplied them there (B 52), while later on the children of the poor and the orphans were confided to different teachers to whom the community paid the fees. This change was attributable probably not to new pedagogical insight, but to the general decrease in the number of children in Old Cairo. From a letter addressed to a Nagid we may conclude that it was also customary to provide a minimum education for orphan girls at the expense of the community, and that books were donated to the synagogue for the use of orphans.[38]

Cash.—It is not easy to form an idea about the distribution of cash (or orders of payment [B 65]) to the needy. Ignoring cases of such help to travelers, foreigners, and other individuals, details about which abound in the Geniza,[39] we find direct references to the distribution of money to the poor before the Passover holiday,[40] and, in lieu of clothing[41] or wheat,[42] also to the blind (B 57*a* and 68) and sick (B 57*b*). The superscription heading the largest distribution of money (B 2*b*) has not been preserved, and one is at loss whether it marked a special occasion or was recurrent (certainly not more frequent than monthly).

In that early list B 2*b* (around 1025) forty-three out of forty-nine households receive 5 dirhems or a multiple of that sum, which thus must have been the unit per person in such a distribution. With this should be compared B 29 (around 1100), where twenty-two persons receive 5 dirhems, and four, 10 dirhems. Similarly, a sick man received a monthly payment of 5 dirhems around 1020 (B 57*b*) and a blind woman the same in 1159 (B 68). In three other lists, A 34 and 35, and B 36 (1180-1183), the groups receiving 5 dirhems are the largest. It is remarkable that such standard practices of charity should have remained in force for two centuries.[43]

An important help, I assume to elderly people particularly, must have been a fixed yearly share in the revenue from a house belonging to the community. The matter comes up in an elaborate letter addressed to Moses Maimonides,[44] and most probably the many payments made, according to our lists, by the administrators of pious foundations to persons not known otherwise as communal employees were largely of this type.

Another way of helping the indigent was to furnish tools for the exercise of their craft, as we read in the case of a very poor silkweaver.[45] Small loans from public funds are also mentioned.[46] The payment of the debts of an insolvent merchant by a number of well-to-do members of the community should be regarded as a type of mutual insurance of businessmen rather than a deed of charity—although, in the particular case reported, a dayyān supervised the action.[47]

Burial expenses.—Burial expenses, heavy in those times, as they are today in the United States (a corollary of free enterprise), were borne by the community when required by the circumstances. There was also a pious foundation for that purpose.[48] No communal funds were earmarked for the highly meritorious work of equipping a poor bride with a marriage portion. This delicate task, so prominent in Jewish charity elsewhere, was left to the families concerned or to private initiative. Appeals for orphan girls and the extremely poor were made directly to the community.[49]

Aid to travelers.—The Mediterranean people of those days, and the Jews in particular, were busy travelers. Lack of funds was an incentive rather than an impediment to travel, for the local communities would lodge, feed, and, if necessary, clothe the needy foreigner and finally expedite him to the next place able to take care of him. The Geniza abounds in references to this work of charity. In the lists of needy receiving bread, people from outside Old Cairo always form the largest single group. We do not hear much about lodging, because the community possessed houses that were rarely rented out in their entirety, as well as several funduqs, or caravanserais.[50] Items of expenditure such as "to a funduq for the lodging of people of Minyat Ghamr—4½ dirhems" (A 43, p. *b,* l. 28), are therefore exceptional.[51]

Once having arrived in a place like Old Cairo, the foreigner would remain for some time. In A 66-68, a traveler from Toledo, Spain, is in receipt of 5 to 6 dirhems a week (to which have to be added certainly lodging, as well as rations of bread and probably also of wheat) for at least five consecutive weeks. In several letters far longer periods are indicated. If the traveler took ill, a rather common occurrence, the community incurred serious expenses, especially if the patient happened to be a scholarly person. He had to be lodged in a private home, and his food, medicaments, and other needs supplied. The cantors, themselves, as the Geniza shows, often widely traveled persons, usually played host. An extremely interesting, but much damaged, account for one such learned and bedridden foreigner is superscribed "Month of Shevat," showing that the service was provided for a period longer than a month. An unfortunately very defective note addressed by the Nagid Abraham Maimonides to a committee of three in charge of hospitality, *ḍiyāfa,* also contains a reference to "every month."[52]

Finally, the visitor had to be dispatched to the next station on his journey. In the case of a distinguished guest, accompanied by a retinue, this was a large item of expenditure.[53] Sometimes the traveler was in a hurry to catch a caravan, wherefore the community would be asked by the Nagid recommending him to expedite the collection in his favor.[54] Occasionally, especially when a person of modest status was concerned, the authority taking care of his transportation would see to it that he reached his final destination. For example, after having arranged for the travel of a poor woman and her infant daughter from Old Cairo to Alexandria, the Nagid Abraham Maimonides asked the community in Alexandria to send her on to Palestine, where she had a grown-up daughter and some property.[55]

When a foreigner stayed on for a longer period or for good, work had to be found for him. The fact that so many teachers and cantors from foreign countries make their appearance in the Geniza documents might be partly attributable to the difficulty of finding other occupations for educated persons without means. In one case, and most appropriately, a newcomer was given the administration of a communal caravanserai. The relevant document states that he was assigned that post in preference to his compatriots arriving with him. (But he was a complete failure.)[56]

Naturally, the communities tried to regulate the influx of foreigners. A traveler on his way to Jerusalem "from the land of the Franks" and making a halt in Old Cairo, was requested by the yeshiva first to meet with the "distinguished member" Eli b. Amram, upon the receipt of whose report it would be decided whether the pilgrim was welcome in the Holy City. (He obviously intended to settle there.)[57] The same dignitary was approached for a cantor from Spain with little children, who was "exiled" from his country (for unstated reasons) and had found temporary refuge in a smaller place, but intended to travel to Fustat.[58] A letter dated 1208 reports about a Maghrebi who had sojourned in Sicily and had already been maintained by the Alexandrian community for one and a half years, but for whom no new pesīqā could be made since he had relatives in the city, obviously loath to assist him. A circular, signed by the Alexandrian dayyān and six notables requested "the communities" to receive him well, and now the writer of our letter, one of the signatories of the circular, asks the addressee, the cantor Abu 'l-Majd, who also served as one of the treasurers of the Fustat community, to take care of the foreigner at his arrival in the capital.[59]

Ransoming of captives.—The redeeming of captives was the cause of another, certainly the most costly, demand on public charity. A person captured by pirates first had to be ransomed, which cost 33⅓ dinars. Then he had to be given clothing, since his clothes were invariably taken by the pirates, and he also had to be maintained during his stay in the country and on his way back to his native town. A poll tax and a port duty (amounting in one instance to 2½ dinars) had to be paid to the Muslim government for him, and, of course, the fare of his return journey had to be found: one single captive cost the community more than the provision of bread for 150 persons during two months. How such an emergency was met is vividly illustrated in a letter from Alexandria. Five captives, still of tender age, had to be liberated from the hold of cruel captors. Everyone in the local community, men and women, boys and girls (as the letter emphasizes), ceased all their regular occupations and devoted themselves entirely to the collection of the ransom. Gold, silver, copper, flax, raw and spun (for many were flax spinners), household goods, and whatever had any value were brought together, until the young prisoners were freed. "The gentiles were astonished in the face of such sacrifices for entirely strange persons and said: 'Blessed is the people that is of such a condition. Yea, blessed is the people, whose God is the Lord' " (Psalm 144:15). The ecumenical aspect of this type of charity has been emphasized in subsection 1, above.[60]

On top of all these recurrent and often so exacting demands on private and communal generosity there occasionally occurred a disaster, the consequences of which could be overcome or mitigated only by extraordinary efforts. In the Geniza period we first have the destruction of the Christian and Jewish houses of worship in and around the year 1012, which took decades to rebuild; then came the devastation of Palestine by bedouins and Seljuks and, later on, the capture of Jerusalem by the Crusaders in 1099. The Geniza proves that the Jewish population of the Holy City was not entirely annihilated, as believed before, but that a refugee problem was created, to be solved in ways astonishingly similar to familiar procedures.[61] When Jerusalem was recaptured by Saladin in 1187, strenuous efforts were made to restore the Jewish houses of worship and learning. Finally, in 1265, when Sultan Baybars threatened to burn the Christians and Jews of Cairo, but converted the punishment into an exorbitant fine, the Jewish communities of the Egyptian Rīf exerted themselves in helping their brethren in the capital to bear a burden they were unable to shoulder alone. The Geniza has preserved a statement from a small town in the Delta, where eighteen persons brought together the very considerable sum of 1,020-¾ dirhems. The statement begins with the following words: "We, the congregation of Minyat Ziftā Jawād, make the following declaration: When, in the month of Av 1576 [1265], the decree of the King [that is, God] came upon us because of our many sins, necessitating a collection, we extracted strength from weakness and joined Israel in its tribulation, despite our inability to do so, our poverty and indigence."[62] The writers of this document certainly had in mind the talmudic maxim that charity practiced by poor people was particularly meritorious.

5. *Epilogue: An Appraisal of the Social Services*

Al-Muqaddasi, the renowned Muslim geographer, writing around 985, praises the people of Old Cairo for their spirit of charity and liberality. His praise, I presume, was meant for the Muslims of that city. But minority groups tend to compete with their environment in such matters, as may be observed in our own times nearer home.[1]

With this testimony, given at the beginning of the classical Geniza period, may be compared another one, given at its end. In a letter addressed to Fustat the Nagid Joshua (1310-1355) says: "The repute of the noble community for their works of charity and good deeds is great near and afar." These words do not represent merely an attempt at captivating the benevolence of the addressees, for on other occasions Joshua did not spare words of criticism and even reproach.[2] May I remark in passing that al-Muqaddasi and the Nagid use the same word for charity: *ṣadaqa-ṣedāqā.*

It should be noted also that Egypt, during the Fatimid and Ayyubid periods, served as a refuge for people in distress all over the world, as abundantly demonstrated in Appendix B. All this taken together permits us to conclude that the social services, as illustrated by the documents discussed, represent at least a good average of what was common usage in that respect in the High Middle Ages.

The vagaries of preservation must be blamed for a certain distortion of the picture to be abstracted from appendixes A-C. A disproportionally high percentage of our information dates from the thirteenth century, a period of complete decay for the Fustat Jewish community.[3] The decline set in during the twelfth century, presumably caused by the exodus to New Cairo and by other, secondary, circumstances, and was subsequently accelerated by a catastrophe of unusual proportions. Therefore, while examining the efficacy of the social services of the Fustat community one must always keep in mind that the records of the Geniza do not present us with a unified view, but tell us a story of continuous developments.

This story is incomplete by necessity since most of our lists are incomplete, that is, most of the documents were not intended to encompass the whole community, and those that were consisted of several leaves that have rarely been preserved in their entirety. Even when we have complete lists, as in the case of the recipients of loaves of bread in B 19-24 (see the remarks at the end of B 24), there are other circumstances that might limit the usefulness of a document as an instrument for drawing conclusions. For instance, it might have been written in time of emergency and under specific conditions, a possibility weighed above (p. 130). On the other hand, fragmentary sources often are apt to provide us with a wealth of information. Thus, even though none of the lists from the first third of the eleventh century are complete, they nevertheless tell us a story of no small dimensions about works of charity. Few lists of contributors are written as beautifully as C 1 and 2; since most of the notables of that period known to us from other sources are not included in the fragments preserved these documents can have listed only a fraction of the pledges actually made.[4] A fragmentary document (B 1) from the same time names 136 households in receipt of bread. The extant sheet enumerates 114 households on one side, and 22 on the verso, the end of the document. This sheet was the second of two pages and first was pasted to the first sheet as is still plainly evident. The lost sheet must have been covered with writing on both sides, the usual practice, giving room for details for about 225 households.[5] The total comes to about 350 households supported by the community in or around 1026, more than it did at any other time recognizable by us.

In order to be able to appreciate the efforts made for its fellowmen by such a medieval society we must know the numerical relationship between the breadwinners and the needy having recourse to public charity. A semblance of statistical completeness can be reached, of course, only where we have documents intended to comprise all the contributing members and where the main data contained in the missing leaves can be reconstructed with reasonable likelihood (as in the case of B 1, above). Such cases are C 30, written around 1155, and C 55, issued approximately eighty years later. In C 30 is represented a collection of unusual size and duration, no doubt for the ransom of captives, where everyone was forced to contribute. According to our calculations the list suggests a total of about 500 breadwinners.[6] At the same time the paupers assisted by the community comprised about

130 households (B 66: wheat to 103 persons, families, and groups; B 71: clothing and cash to over 130 parties, dated 1176; B 74, survey of 130 families).

A list of deaths occurring in the Rabbanite community of Fustat during four lunar months (December 27, 1125, through April 23, 1126) would be an important instrument for statistical purposes, if we could be sure that the first month was not exceptional. These are the facts:

	Total
First month: 23 adults, including one slave girl and one freedwoman; 5 children; 5 infants	33
Second month: 5 adults; 1 child; 1 infant (There is no entry for the first fourteen days of the month)	7
Third month: 5 adults, including 2 slave girls; 2 children (days not in strict order or omitted altogether)	7
Fourth month: 9 adults	9

The document clearly is a leaf from a book. It opens thus: "And Ephraim b. Abū Naṣr who used to recite the Song of Moses [Exodus 15] in the synagogue died; and also, on the same day, Sunday, the last day of Teveth, 1437 [Dec. 27, 1125], the mother of Abu 'l-Ḥasan who was a perfumer on the Great Bazaar; she had a sister and he had a son and a daughter." As this example shows, the list identifies the person concerned briefly and, in doubtful cases, states who the legal heirs are. Paupers with whom no problems of inheritance existed are referred to in a general way: "Infant boy of a glass maker, infant girl of a muleteer, a dyer from Rūm, a pauper living in the house of the qōdesh between the two synagogues, leaving a child." Additional leaves of that book of deaths may be found.[7]

In those days, unlike ours, the well-to-do families were large and those of the poor small. This fact was of influence on population statistics, but did not alleviate the burden of the contributors to public charity. The average size of the family of a breadwinner, including the old people who rarely were absent from a household, I have calculated as totaling 6 persons, while the average size of a family of paupers, many of whom were single old people, is estimated at only 2.5 persons (see the breakdown in B 74). Thus, the total Rabbanite Jewish population of Fustat around 1160 would have amounted to about 3,300 souls, approximately half the number 7,000 given by the traveler Benjamin of Tudela, who visited the city shortly before 1168. But in view of the uncertainty of the manuscript tradition of his book, many of his numbers, including that for Fustat, cannot be relied upon.[8]

Early in the thirteenth century radical changes in the size of the Jewish community of Fustat are discernible in the Geniza records. In a letter written at the time of the sultan al-Malik al-ʿĀdil (d. 1218), the Nagid Abraham Maimonides is accused of having urged "the whole community, almost 200 persons" to sign a petition to the sultan in his favor.[9] While a number written in such a context might lend itself to various interpretations, it must be regarded as reflecting a certain reality, for its recurs again in C 55, issued about twenty years later (around 1235). In an emergency appeal to the community a sum of 300-500 dirhems is requested, to which this note is attached: "But how can this be done, seeing that the number of male adults in Fustat today does not even reach 200" (each adult was expected to pay only 1 dirhem). The number of contributors was indeed "less than 200" (about 165 men, representing around 80 households). In the somewhat earlier list C 50 the names of 214 donators are still readable, and not many more were included, but here (C 50) several persons give together with unnamed others, and, unlike C 55, the younger members of a household do not appear. Therefore, in the interval between C 50 and C 55 an additional marked deterioration must have taken place. On the other hand the numerous communal accounts from that period (1220-1240) show a rather steady average of 35-45 relief recipients.[10]

What was the cause of this steep decline in the size of the community between C 30 and C 50 and 55? The pillage and conflagration of Fustat in December, 1168, which was often described as fatal to that city, seems not to have affected to an appreciable degree the quarters inhabited mainly by Jews. The fifty documents or so from the period 1168 to 1200 presented in appendixes A-C testify to a rather vigorous communal life. In B 74, which we assume dates from the beginning of the thirteenth century, around 135 households were still on the relief rolls of the Fustat community.

The turning point, it seems, was the devastating famine and plague of 1201–1202, so movingly described by contemporary Muslim writers [11] and referred to also in the Geniza documents. Perhaps half, if not more, of the Jewish population was wiped out, and since Fustat had already lost its role of leading city to New Cairo, it was unable to recover from that blow. Like the town itself, the Jewish community lingered on through the centuries. At the beginning of the fourteenth century there were still about 115 persons vowing donations for a foreigner on a single day (C 68), and 108 members made their yearly pledges in October, 1335 (C 69). The list C 78, written at a time when Egypt was under Ottoman rule, bears witness to a revival. But most of the donators were not local people as in the past, but immigrants or their descendants.

To come back to the quest for the numerical relationship between paupers and breadwinners, the survey has shown that, during the periods of the Nagids Samuel b. Hananya (1140–1159) and Abraham Maimonides (1205–1237), for both of which we possess comparatively rich documentation, there was one relief recipient to every four contributors to the charities of the Jewish community of Fustat—a very heavy load, especially if we remember that a paterfamilias usually presided over a large household. The achievements of the social services, as reflected in the Geniza documents, have to be judged in the light of these circumstances.

The most striking feature of these services was their conservatism. They all were rooted in pre-Islamic, talmudic institutions and betray their origin not only in their general character, but also in many details. Even the complaint so frequent in talmudic literature that pledges made in public were not made good recur again and again in the Geniza papers. Throughout the centuries two loaves of bread were given twice a week. The distributions of wheat, clothing, and cash remained the same all the time—as long as the impoverished community was able to bear the cost. We observe at least that they tried, albeit often unsuccessfully, to keep the old standards.

In his Code of Law, Maimonides enumerates eight degrees of charity, the highest being the help extended to a faltering member of the community through a gift, a loan, a partnership, or employment, which would spare him from needing public assistance.[12] There is ample evidence in the Geniza that Maimonides' admonition (which is based on a talmudic precept) was followed by many of his contemporaries.[13] It applied, though, mainly to relatives, friends, colleagues, or "sons of good families," who had not yet "uncovered their faces" by accepting alms or other relief in public. Those who had, belonged to the mass of *'aniyyīm* (Heb.), "the poor," who were almost a people by themselves, whom one was obliged to support, but who could not expect to be extricated from their poverty. God is the maker of rich and poor (Proverbs 22:2). "You must help the poor in proportion to his needs, but you are not obliged to make him rich." [14] Poverty is ordained by God; you may mitigate its evil consequences, but you cannot succeed in rooting it out altogether. This you must leave to the Creator (B 17, 19, 63: "List of the Poor—may God make them rich; may God help them"). When we have found that public charity supplied merely what we would regard as subsistence at starvation level, we must seek the causes first in the statistic revealing the large number of relief recipients as compared with that of breadwinners, and second in the fatalistic attitude toward poverty just described.

It should be remembered also that the motivation of charity was largely religious, a duty toward God rather than toward one's fellowman. Since there was no longer the Temple where one could express one's gratitude toward God or seek his forgiveness by sacrifices, gifts to the poor served as substitutes. This idea, so impressively expounded in talmudic and medieval literature, was taken literally and seriously. And I suspect that those long, calligraphic lists of contributors, which were suspended in the synagogue for public examination and also as incentive to further liberality, had an additional purpose: they were destined for God, who, while inspecting his synagogue, should see, black on white, what pious and charitable people were coming to pray in his house.

Last, but not least: private munificence competed with communal charity. With the exception of collections, made on extraordinary occasions, only relatively small sums were donated in response to public appeals or as regular contributions to a synagogue. Liberality was a virtue, best to be displayed in splendid isolation. While the basic needs of the mass of the poor were satisfied by the social services described in this section, special cases of want or misfortune—and how numerous they were!—as a rule sought relief in private help. The Geniza teems with letters illustrating this situation. They are discussed, together with some additional observations on the social notions of charity prevailing in those days, in *Med. Soc.,* Volume III, chapters viii and x.

D. WORSHIP

1. *The House of Worship*

a. ITS ARCHITECTURE

The architecture of the Christian or Jewish houses of worship under Islam cannot be discussed without noting the legal restrictions to which they were subjected. According to a proviso in one of the oldest sources of Muslim law no churches or synagogues were suffered in the new towns founded by the conquerors, an injunction that soon was understood to mean that no new non-Islamic houses of worship were to be erected anywhere in Islamic territory. This restriction is in force even today in states where Islamic religious law is state law. The tens of thousands of Americans who have worked in Saudi Arabia since the inception of the oil industry in that country have never been allowed to build a church for themselves.[1]

As a matter of fact, numerous churches and synagogues existed in Fustat and Baghdad at a time when the power of Islam was at its height, and even (New) Cairo, which was founded as late as 969, soon had its churches and synagogues.[2] Therefore, it has been said that the law banning non-Islamic houses of worship was honored more in the breach than in its execution,[3] but this statement is misleading. The more distinguished churches and monasteries in Fustat and Baghdad were pre-Islamic, while the new non-Muslim houses of devotion had to be modest and inconspicuous in order not to arouse the fanaticism of zealots. A Geniza letter reports, indeed, that the renovated part of a *kanīsa* (referring, it seems, to a church, and not a synagogue) had to be pulled down because it was higher than a nearby mosque.[4] The synagogue architecture as reflected in the Geniza records has to be judged in the light of this situation.

The most striking difference between the structure of a church or synagogue on the one hand and a mosque on the other was a gallery for women in the former. Islam was uneasy about the presence of women in the mosque and for the most part banished them from its houses of worship altogether. In the Temple of Jerusalem, it seems, women were separated from men only on special occasions of popular entertainment rather than during acts of devotion. But in the ancient synagogues of Galilee were found structures that have been interpreted by experts as women's galleries, and the American excavators of the magnificent synagogue of Sardis in Asia Minor provide the same explanation for their own finds. (The excavations are still in progress.) [5] This interpretation is corroborated by the testimony of the Cairo Geniza records. In the synagogues of both the Palestinians and Iraqians in Old Cairo, as well as in the holy shrine of Dammūh near Gizeh on the western bank of the Nile, there was a women's gallery, called *bayt al-nisā'*, "the place for women." It was reached by a staircase leading up from a special entrance, called *bāb al-sirr,* "the secret door," or bāb *al-nisā',* "women's door," which faced a side street leading to the thoroughfare, to which the main gate of the synagogue opened.

This separation, however, did not prevent women and men from meeting before, and, we may imagine, particularly after prayer. In a letter to a sick woman, a man (most probably a relative) refers to a conversation held "when I met you last in the synagogue,"[6] which could mean only: in the lane, or rather, court, fronting the building.

We have to keep in mind that the term "synagogue" included the whole compound surrounding and belonging to the house of worship.

Our records make mention of structural details in describing the final rebuilding of the synagogue of the Palestinians in 1039–1040 (almost thirty years after its demolition at the command of the caliph al-Ḥākim), as well as in accounts of repairs in this and other houses of worship. Occasional references to the subject are found in many Geniza records. The actual building of the synagogue of the Palestinians (in which the Geniza was preserved) was described in detail by that excellent traveler Jacob Saphir, who visited it in 1859 during its first "restoration," second by Alfred J. Butler in his book, *Ancient Coptic Churches of Egypt* ([Oxford, 1884], pp. 169–170), and finally by Jack Mosseri, a prominent member of the Cairene Jewish community who also sketched how the synagogue looked before 1890, when it was pulled down and replaced by another building.[7]

According to Butler, the main hall of the synagogue was about 65 feet long and 35 feet wide. It consisted of a nave and two aisles, the aisles, according to Saphir, divided from the nave by six columns on each side (just as in the synagogue of Sardis mentioned above, which was, however, approximately twice as large). This description tallies with the accounts of building materials acquired for the reconstruction of 1039–1040, and with other references in the Geniza records. The columns supported the women's gallery, which was made of timber. A large white column supported the middle part of the gallery between the southwestern ends of the two aisles, its large base still visible in Mosseri's sketch as "memorial stone." There is also a reference to columns within the women's gallery.

The repair of a glass window cost 1 dirhem in 1181. No other details about the number and look of the windows have been found thus far. The term used, *ṭāqa,* seems to indicate that at least their upper part was rounded.[8]

The synagogue of the Palestinians, as well as that of Minyat Ziftā in the Nile Delta, was covered with a *gamalūn,* or gable roof. The construction of a pitched roof over a comparatively broad room was less expensive than a durable flat ceiling; perhaps, also, it was found that it made for better acoustics. The nave of the Abū Sargah church, situated in the immediate vicinity of the synagogue of the Palestinians, was also covered with a pointed roof.

The holy ark, which contains the Torah scrolls, was a piece of masonry in front of the basilica, elevated and flanked by columns, like the sanctuary in the Coptic church. During the Geniza period it was called *hēkhāl.* The word is biblical Hebrew, but was not used in the talmudic period. Thus it stands to reason that the term, together with the architectural features, was borrowed from Coptic *haykal,* sanctuary, although the latter term was ultimately derived from the Hebrew Bible. In the synagogue of Hebron, which was rebuilt at the end of the eleventh century, the ark was situated between the two entrance gates. This arrangement goes back to the tripartite doorway (one main and two side entrances) found in the wall facing Jerusalem in the ancient synagogues of Galilee, such as those of Capernaum, Chorasin, and Beth Shearim. At that time, the ark was still a wooden chest and not a stone structure, and a tripartite portal was, of course, a common feature of Hellenistic architecture. It is not excluded that in the synagogue of the Palestinians in Old Cairo the wall facing Jerusalem originally had the same arrangement as that attested in a Geniza letter for the contemporary synagogue of Hebron, since the main street passed immediately before the northeastern wall. When, after the bitter experience of 1012, the synagogue was rebuilt, we may assume that the two entrances flanking the holy ark and opening to the main street were closed, and only one entrance, that on the southwest side opposite the holy ark, was left.

In a letter dated 1033 a man contributes 10 dinars for the erection of an ark in the synagogue of the Palestinians in Alexandria. An inscription from the same town, dated 1379, states that the donor had given the money for the columns and the lintel at the entrance of the ark sanctuary. A pair of curtains, described in one document as green divided the ark from the rest of the building, and a silver lamp was suspended "in" the ark, that is, between the chest containing the Torah scrolls and the curtains. Both features were common in the sanctuaries of the Coptic churches.

There is still another constructional detail that the synagogue seems to have borrowed from the church: the raised platform in the middle of the building, on which the Scripture lections and certain parts of the liturgy were read. Solemn processions, preceded by a particularly holy Torah scroll and moving from the ark to the platform and back, were ancient custom in the synagogue of the Palestinians.[9] In talmudic times reference is made frequently to a reader's platform, called *bēmā* (a Greek word), but this was a piece of wooden furniture that could be moved around. In the Geniza period, we have instead a fixed structure made of masonry, called *anbōl,* none other than the Latin-Greek-Coptic term *ambon(e)* still designating the same object in the Coptic church. To be sure, we also find the term in a Geniza letter with reference to a synagogue in Ascalon, Palestine, and a

Greek inscription from Side in Pamphylia (southern Asia Minor) mentions a Jewish ambon.[10] But the total silence of all the talmudic sources about such a central architectural feature of the synagogue building suggests that it was taken over from the church in a later period (approximately between A.D. 400 and 600). The Geniza also contains a reference to the *ṭāqat al-anbōl,* the niche in the platform, which was large enough to harbor a Torah scroll. There was perhaps no particular reason for mentioning the columns, although in the nearby Mu'allaqa church (pre-Islamic and still extant) the eleven columns of the ambon had symbolic meaning, representing the disciples of Jesus (twelve less Judas Iscariot).[11] Liturgical texts from the Geniza, edited recently, show that the anbōl was used for the chanting of special sections of the service and the reading of the lections, but not for the recitation of the regular prayers. Keeping in mind, too, that those liturgical texts contain such Greek words as *kyrios,* "Lord," and *eleison,* "have mercy"—familiar to the churchgoer up to the present day—one is inclined to assume that the introduction of the ambon into the synagogue meant more than merely the adoption of a structural detail.[12]

In general, the relationship of synagogue and church, as far as the architecture of the house of worship is concerned, was reciprocal: original Jewish, or rather Hellenistic-Jewish, features were taken over by the Christians, and, later on, came back to the Jews in a more developed form. It is worthy of note that "hēkhāl" has remained the term for the holy ark among the Oriental Jewish communities, while the foreign word "anbōl," although used throughout the Geniza period in both documentary and literary sources, passed entirely into oblivion.

Owing to the caprices of cultural shifts and language history the Muslim term for pulpit, *al-minbar,* became the generally used designation for the elevated platform in the synagogue in all *Christian* countries (pronounced *almemar* or similarly, while the Hebrew term *migdāl* remained confined to learned books). In the Geniza the word "al-minbar" practically never occurs. In the one case I have noted, it is used in the plural and in a way that shows that it did not belong to the daily speech of the Egyptian Jews in that time.[13]

Various sections of the synagogue of the Palestinians in Old Cairo, particularly the entrance to the ark and to the aisles, were decorated with exquisite woodwork. Much of it was still in its original place when Jacob Saphir and Alfred J. Butler visited the synagogue, and some remnants are preserved in the Arabic Museum in Cairo, as well as in the Louvre of Paris and other collections, in particular the

Israel Museum of Jerusalem, which possesses a door consisting of sixteen wooden panels and a board with a Hebrew inscription commemorating a person who died in his youth. The board was donated to the synagogue by his brother.[14] No reference to this important aspect of synagogue decoration has been found thus far in the Geniza records, with the exception, of course, of references to Jewish turners who produced such woodwork. The beautiful Hebrew script used in the engravings commemorating the donors as well as their names places the origin of the woodwork within the Geniza period, namely the eleventh through the thirteenth centuries.

Paul E. Kahle, in his book *The Cairo Geniza* reports as a fact (pp. 3–4) that the building housing the synagogue of the Palestinians was none else but the building of St. Michael's church which the Jacobite patriarch had sold to the Jews in 882 when he was forced to pay a tribute of twenty thousand dinars to the ruler of Egypt Aḥmad b. Ṭulūn. This view was shared by all scholars connected in any way with Geniza studies, including myself, and I still took it for granted when writing my article "The Synagogue Building and Its Furnishings," *Eretz-Israel* 7 (1964). Subsequent research, made during the printing of that article, convinced me, however, that this assumption was unfounded, and in a postscript to the English summary of that article I expressed the view that the church building was acquired by the Jewish newcomers from Iraq, who wished to have a synagogue of their own, whereas the synagogue of the Palestinians was the original and pre-Islamic Jewish place of worship.

An attentive reading of the Muslim antiquarians describing the churches and synagogues of Fustat confirms this opinion. Maqrīzī says (II, 494): "Michael, the patriarch of the Jacobites, sold the church in the vicinity of the Mu'allaqa [church] to the Jews," and Ibn Duqmāq describes (IV, 108) the synagogue of the Iraqians with exactly the same topographic definition as being "in the vicinity of the Mu'allaqa," while assigning another site to the synagogue of the Palestinians. According to Maqrīzī (II, 471), the door of the synagogue of the Palestinians bore an inscription carved in wood saying that it was built in the year 330 of the Seleucid era (A.D. 18–19) which, according to Maqrīzī's informants meant: prior to the destruction of the Temple of Jerusalem by Titus and 621 years before the rise of Islam. Various explanations for this date have been tried. Anyhow, local tradition clearly stated that the Palestinian synagogue was pre-Islamic and had been erected in gray antiquity whereas the Iraqian one had formerly been a church.

Butler confirms this view in his book on ancient Coptic churches

(I, 168–170), albeit without intending to do so, for he describes the building of the synagogue of the Palestinians as an example of the most ancient and primitive type of Coptic church. Naturally, the synagogue of the Palestinians did not serve as a model for church architecture. But, built during the Christian era of Egypt, it followed the pattern of the houses of worship then in vogue—as it did with regard to the details of ambon and ark discussed above. It preserved, however, the original plan in a purer form, because no substantial structural changes were necessary since the additional synagogues of the Iraqians and of the Karaites took care of the increase in population, the major part of which anyhow later moved to Cairo, the new capital nearby.

Butler regarded the wood carvings of dovelike birds, which were still in existence at the time of his visit, as an indication of the originally Christian character of the building. But much has been learned about wood carvings in the Fatimid period since Butler's time. Decorations with dovelike and other birds were common in secular as well as in religious buildings, and in general there was no marked difference in decorative wood carving among the various religions or between religious and secular purposes. In short, the synagogue of the Palestinians in Fustat must be regarded as a pre-Islamic building, much influenced by the Christian environment in its general layout and architectural details, but destined from the outset to serve as a Jewish house of worship.[15]

b. THE FURNISHINGS OF THE SYNAGOGUE

Unlike the mosque, where prayer is short and consists mostly of prostrations, genuflections, and other bodily movements, the service of the synagogue is protracted even on workdays and requires that the congregation be seated most of the time. According to the seating habits of that period, pews or chairs were not used for the purpose. Instead, the synagogue was covered with mats and carpets, while the individual members would bring in cushions to sit and to recline on.

In addition to occasional references, our knowledge of the synagogue furnishings during the Geniza period is derived mainly from inventories drawn up either when a new beadle was appointed or when the pieces remaining after a sack of the city or a similar disaster were counted. Such lists have been preserved from the years 1075, 1080, 1095–1096, 1099, 1159, 1181, and 1186. For the evaluation of these documents, not only their dates but also some other relevant facts have to be taken into consideration. It seems that the compound of the synagogue of the Palestinians, "the main synagogue," was better protected than that of the Babylonians; therefore, all or some of the metalwork and precious textiles belonging to the latter were often stored in the former. Also, a synagogue usually had more than one beadle, each seemingly responsible for only some of the furnishings.

Next to seating facilities, that is, mats and carpets, the illumination of the synagogue looms large in our documents. Monthly accounts of expenditure on olive and linseed oil are extremely common and could be used with profit by anyone studying the history of lighting. Detailed lists of the lighting appliances used are found in the records from the years 1075 and 1080, that is, shortly after the great sack of the Egyptian capital by the Turkish mercenaries, when even the palaces of the caliph were plundered and the fabulous "treasures of the Fatimids" were dispersed. A remark in a contemporary letter, "I was shocked when I learned what happened to the synagogue of the Palestinians," indicates that it did not escape the general devastation. Not a single silver lamp is mentioned in those lists, not even the one hanging in the holy ark according to an earlier document. On the other hand, the number and types of lighting implements referred to are rather impressive. In 1075, the synagogue of the Palestinians was illuminated by fifty-one large and small chandeliers, called *būqandalāt* i.e., *abū qandalāt),* a term not found thus far elsewhere, as well as by thirty bronze lamps. In 1080, the synagogue of the Babylonians possessed twenty-five lamps with grillwork —a type common in those days, according to the admirable study on the subject by D. S. Rice.[16] In addition, there were lamps in bronze and iron, three bronze "scorpions," or hooks, with "shells" (presumably implements similar to the latter-day Sabbath lamp), brass bowls, thirty "open" chandeliers and seventeen with grillwork, a chandelier with three "columns," that is, metal rods instead of chains, a chandelier with a long chain and a "scorpion," and, finally a *sanbūsaqa,* or triangle, as well as a hoop, both serving as bearers of candles.[17]

A hundred years later, in the list of 1181, no būqandalāt, or chandeliers, are mentioned anymore. "Saucers," *aṭbāq,* that is, flat lamps, were preferred at that time, presumably because they were easier to clean of oil rests than deep lamps. The Babylonian beadle received into his custody thirty-seven such "saucers," as well as "scorpions." Two silver lamps with chains of silver were among the treasures of the Babylonian synagogue preserved in the compound of the Palestinians in 1159.

The synagogues were particularly rich in precious textiles, which served mostly for the decoration of its walls and columns.[18] Murals, such as found at Dura-Europos, had already been banned from synagogues by the seventh century and there are references to the whitewashing of the Palestinian synagogue. On the other hand, hangings were a decoration common even in private homes. The material especially cherished was siglaton, a famous medieval fabric of heavy damask, which, in the synagogue inventories, is invariably of two colors, such as light green with blue-black, or white with black or red. Sometimes it was decorated with stripes of gold and silver. Brocade is also well represented. Of particular luxury were the covers for the Torah, the scroll containing the five books of Moses, and the Haftara, the lections from the Prophets. Naturally, a cover was spread over the *tēvā,* or desk on which the scrolls were laid, when they were chanted. The inventories include also other utensils, such as reading stools, *kursī,* and a prayer mantle, *īzār,* to be worn by the kohens while pronouncing the priestly blessing.

The most honored possessions of any synagogue were its Torah scrolls and books. In 1075, after the great sack of the Egyptian capital, there were eighteen Torah scrolls in the synagogue of the Palestinians, of which, however, some belonged to the Babylonians and to the holy shrines of Dammūh and Taṭay. No ornaments are mentioned at all, only three copper cases for the scrolls, while the rest were of wood. In 1159, an inventory notes cases of silver and of wood coated with silver, as well as many other silver ornaments, namely, "crowns" and "pomegranates," the latter being grillwork decorations covering the heads of the two rods on which a scroll is fastened. Most of these silver ornaments were either "burnt with gold" (gilded), or "glued with blackness" (embellished with niello work).[19] Processions in which the Torah scrolls, clad in precious textiles and crowned with their silver or gold ornaments, were carried from the holy ark to the anbōl, or central platform, and back formed one of the highlights of the synagogue service (see sec. D, 2, n. 9, below).

As for books, the synagogues were exceedingly eager to acquire old codices, written by famous scribes, or, at least, copies of such codices, designated as their "brothers." Utmost care was taken to read the Holy Scriptures in the correct pronunciation and with the traditional singsong or cantillation that fixed the tone appropriate for each word (cf. the neumes in the church music of the Middle Ages).[20] This could be done only with the help of authoritative and scrupulously exact texts. Comparing the booklists of 1080 with those from the years 1181 and 1186 we realize that a century was sufficient to consume most of the ancient stock. How much this appalling loss was the result of the conflagration of Old Cairo in December, 1168, or of general wear and tear, or of the lending out of books to judges, cantors, and teachers (about which we read in our records) cannot be determined. The many new codices dedicated to the synagogue of the Palestinians, as evident from the later lists, seem to point to a catastrophe destroying much of the old fund and requiring quick replacement. On the other hand, in the course of that century the synagogue was enriched by the most precious treasures: the manuscripts looted by the Crusaders at the conquest of Jerusalem in 1099 and sold by them afterward to the Jews of Egypt. Some of these treasures are still in existence, well preserved in public libraries in Europe, the United States, and Israel.

Since the synagogues had no pews or other furniture where one could keep one's own books used during the services and since Bible codices were heavy, the weekly Torah lections were copied separately in small booklets that could be carried easily by the worshipers. This custom gave the more opulent members of a congregation an opportunity to vie with each other in the acquisition of precious copies of holy texts. An outstanding example is the weekly lection of Numeri, chapters 13–15, written in 1106–1107, most probably in Fustat, by Isaac b. Abraham ha-Levi. It is remarkable both for its precious readings and its artistic execution. The talmudic injunction "beautify yourself before God with good works" was understood also in the sense that the things used in God's service should excel in beauty.[21]

c. THE SYNAGOGUE COMPOUND

"There is no instance of a sacred edifice standing clear and detached like an English church in its churchyard. A Coptic church outside never shows any outline: around it is huddled a mass of haphazard buildings which show that the architect's idea was concealment of the exterior rather than adornment." This "entanglement of the sacred fabric in other buildings, wall against wall," described by Butler as a distinctly Coptic peculiarity, was also characteristic of the synagogue during the period illustrated by the Geniza records.[22] The very term "the synagogue" was not confined to the place in which the prayers were held, but comprised the whole surrounding compound, all of it being its property. We read about a house adjoining, *mulāziq* (lit., "cleaving to") the synagogue, others adjacent to its vestibule, *dihlīz,* or to its *sukka* (hut for the Feast of Tabernacles), or to "the women's entrance." Mentioned is the living quarters, *sukn,* of a man, or the apartment, *ṭabaqa,* of another "in the synagogue," meaning, of course, one of the buildings in its immediate vicinity. Some letters have a synagogue as address. Since the synagogue complex bordered on more than one street, one would indicate also the street on which the living quarters of the addressee were situated. In a smaller locality, an upper story of the place of prayer might even house a workshop. Maimonides, who was asked whether this was proper, decided that the room immediately above the holy ark should not be used as a bedroom or as a workshop.[23] The synagogue compound had two special designations: *jiwār al-kanīs,* literally, "neighborhood of the synagogue," and *rub' al-kanīs,* which, although pronounced thus, seems not to have had the meaning "quarter," as in classical Arabic, but that of *rab',* "area, residence."

The clustering of houses around a synagogue or Coptic church served various purposes. It was a protective measure, aimed at concealing a building apt in times of tension to become a target of attacks by fanatics of the ruling religion. This defensive, negative aim was secondary, though, and of a later date. Originally, proximity to God's sanctuary was sought to derive blessing from it. "I want to live in the neighborhood of the synagogue" writes one man. A woman who was to be evicted from one of the houses adjoining the synagogue says in her complaint to a Nagid that her sole satisfaction in life was listening to the antiphonies carried over to her from the service. The officials of the synagogue lived "in" it, meaning in the surrounding buildings, just as the Coptic monks had their living quarters next to the church. Moreover, the synagogue compound served many needs that in ancient times and in small places were met by the synagogue building itself.

The rabbinical court held its sessions in the synagogue. Since an entry in an account mentions repairs "in the room of the judge in the synagogue," we may conclude that he had an office there or in one of the buildings adjoining it. Classes for schoolchildren, so far as they were not held in houses rented by teachers or in private houses, took place in synagogues. In those times schoolchildren were called "synagogue boys." Adults, too, studied in the synagogue, especially at night, on the Sabbath, and on holidays. Whether all these activities went on in the hall destined for communal prayer or in adjacent rooms or buildings is not evident from our sources in each individual case.[24]

The synagogue also served as a hospice for needy travelers and aliens. "I found two foreigners in the synagogue" writes a visitor of Bilbays in Lower Egypt. "The proselyte and the man from Aleppo, who live in the synagogue of the Babylonians," and "the woman whose dwelling place is in the synagogue of the Palestinians" are mentioned in lists of indigent persons. A schoolmaster from Tunisia and an old Maghrebi who was incapacitated by having been thrown from a mule lived in a synagogue in Alexandria. A textile merchant who was shipwrecked near Caesarea, Palestine, stayed in the synagogue of that town for five days, and there he spread out and dried his belongings. Even a man disabled by smallpox—he was from the land of Persia and, having lost his fortunes, had come to Egypt to look for a post as a communal official—was given shelter in the *kanīsiya,* as he calls the synagogue.[25] There is, as we have seen, even mention of a woman living "in the synagogue," leading to the conclusion that guest rooms or a special building in the synagogue compound no doubt harbored the travelers and foreigners. In the second half of the twelfth century and later we read about a funduq, or hospice, situated between the synagogues of the Palestinians and Babylonians and, later on, about two additional hospices.[26]

Since the distribution of bread and wheat to communal officials and to the needy was one of the main social services, it is natural that the community kept a storeroom for wheat.[27] The synagogue compound included a sukka, or hut to be used during the seven days of the Feast of Tabernacles. In crowded cities, where many people lived in apartments or possessed no courtyard where they could put up a festival booth of their own communal sukkas were a necessity. The same custom prevails throughout the United States today, with the difference, of course, that there these prefabricated structures are erected and taken apart every year, whereas in Fustat the communal sukka was a permanent building. Maybe it was also used during the rest of the year, perhaps for weddings and other festive occasions, when accommodation in private homes was not always sufficient, as were the Jewish "wedding houses" in the upper High Yemen, or the ancient Marriage House I saw in San Diego, California, or the Judentanzhaus, "dancing house of the Jews," in Rothenburg ob der Tauber, Germany.

Before prayer one was supposed to wash. Unlike drinking water, which was brought by carriers from the Nile, water for washing was supplied by subterranean structures referred to as wells. Even without express mention in a Geniza document, the existence of such a well in the synagogue courtyard could be assumed as certain.[28] Strange as it may seem to anyone familiar with traditional Jewish practices, no reference to a ritual bath could be traced thus far in any Geniza document referring to Egypt prior to 1200. Had it existed, it would have been mentioned somewhere, especially in the many accounts of repairs of buildings belonging to the community. This negative testimony of the Geniza is confirmed by the text of the famous "Statute," issued by Moses Maimonides and nine other scholars in spring, 1176. It states that, with very few exceptions, regular bathhouses and private arrangements comparable with modern showers were regarded by the Jewish women of Egypt as sufficient for the ritual requirements of the monthly purifications. This leniency was an abomination for Maimonides who had come from the far stricter Muslim West.[29] The reforms introduced by the Statute were very severe in nature and their impact is immediately recognizable in the Geniza records. In many marriage contracts issued after that date the two spouses promise to observe the so-called laws of purity under penalty, in the case of intentional transgression, of losing all their rights resulting from the contract. The "pool of the Iraqian synagogue," appearing in an account from April, 1234, evidences the stricter and more general observation of the ritual laws.[30]

In Palestine, a ritual bath is mentioned as connected with a synagogue building in Ramle in a document written shortly after the severe earthquake of 1034, and also in a letter to a Nagid, most probably with regard to Jerusalem.[31]

The buildings around the synagogue were either erected or acquired by the community, or—and this was more common—donated to it as a pious foundation. The rent from these houses represented one of the synagogue's main sources of income. To be sure, by the end of the twelfth century, the Jewish community of Old Cairo owned property in many parts of the city outside the synagogue compound.

2. *Life in the Synagogue*

In accordance with the purpose of this book and the character of the sources used for its writing, I do not intend here to describe the very elaborate synagogue service with its extremely rich liturgy, as it presents itself to us through the literary treasures of the Cairo Geniza. My aim is limited to defining the place occupied by the synagogue in the life of its members and thus to offer a basis of comparison for a similar sociographic study with regard to other religious groups of the time.

The very character of the synagogue was an object of controversy among the Jewish religious scholars. On the one hand, it was "the House of God" (Psalm 55:15), the "little sanctuary" (Ezekiel 11:16), the Temple of Jerusalem in miniature, and strong words were used against those who called the synagogue "the House of the People" (an allusion to Jeremiah 39:8). On the other hand, the messianic spirit, always alive during the Jewish Middle Ages, objected to any attempt at replacing the lost Temple even temporarily, and the militant iconoclastic tendency of Jewish religion was uneasy with regard to the veneration of any material objects as symbols of the presence of God. One Karaite scholar went so far as to decry the worshipful reverence shown to the holy ark and the Torah scrolls as outright idolatry.

For the popular religion, as evidenced in the Geniza papers, the synagogue was a house of meeting both with God and with one's fellowmen. When the holy ark was opened and the Torah scrolls were exposed to the eyes of the worshiper, he felt himself transported to the presence of God. In a time of great danger, a man tells us in a Geniza letter, he went to the synagogue, opened the ark, and rolled himself on the floor beneath it, showing in this way his utmost contrition and humiliation before God and his need for heavenly intervention. He was saved and "both Jews and Muslims were happy about this and congratulated me. It was a glorious day because God had shown mercy upon us all. He had heard my prayer and had noticed my fasting and how I rolled myself beneath the holy ark." [1]

The oath on the Bible, in our courts a mere formality, was in those days regarded as an almost physical citation of God as witness and was, therefore, administered in the synagogue in front of the open ark and Torah scrolls. These ceremonial trappings were believed to be so essential that we find a query addressed to Maimonides whether an oath on a codex of the Bible (and not before a scroll) was legally binding.[2] In short, the synagogue was revered as a "sanctuary" of God and called thus. To be sure, nowhere in the Geniza records is a synagogue designated as "temple," a modern innovation that would have been regarded by the Jews of that period as blasphemy.[3]

At the same time the synagogue served so many cultural and communal purposes that its character as a house of worship became blurred. Unlike the mosque, where, in prayer, all present turned toward Mecca, that is, to God, the members of the congregation in the synagogue sat along the walls or before them facing one another, thus always being conscious of their fellowmen. Abraham Maimonides, the pietist reformer (1186–1237), tried to change the arrangements of sitting in the synagogue to resemble those prevailing in the mosque and to do away with the comfortable cushions and reclining pillows inconsistent with the duties of "a slave in the presence of his master." [4] He was not successful. In all the genuinely oriental Jewish communities the sitting arrangements remain to this very day just as they were in the Geniza period. To be sure, during the prayer to be recited standing, all worshipers in the synagogue turn their faces toward the holy ark. In Islam, too, there were many complaints that the mosque served too many secular purposes, so much so that the prophet Muhammad was credited with having said: "At the end of the days, people will enter the mosques and sit in them in circles, speaking about worldly things and loving this world. Do not join their circles, for God has no use for them." [5] Still, for reasons explained below, the difference between Jewish and Muslim worship was marked and caused much heart-searching for pious Jews.

On workdays, Jewish services were held three times daily. The Muslims pray five times. Their prayer, however, is incomparably shorter than the Jewish, and although Islam, too, prefers attendance at public service to private prayer, the synagogue was far more insistent in this respect. In a letter from Messina, Sicily, which had at that time only a small Jewish community, a traveler passing through that town writes to his father that it was impossible to live there since only one service was held in the local synagogue during a working day.[6]

On Mondays and Thursdays, when a Torah scroll was taken out and a section of the weekly lection read in public, attendance seems to have been general. There are many references in the Geniza papers to happenings during or after the services on Monday and Thursday. A scholar from Byzantium or western Europe, on return to his country, promises his Egyptian benefactor that he would arrange for prayers to be held for the latter's welfare in the synagogues on Mondays and Thursdays in all the congregations of the land of Edom (i.e., "the Roman empire").[7] A similar promise is mentioned as carried out in a letter from Ramle, Palestine, to Old Cairo. The writer had returned from a journey to Acre and Tyre and asserts that he said prayers for his benefactor on these days (while the ark stood open) and praised his munificence toward him and others.[8] When a man had a portentous dream (Moses and A[aron] sitting in judgment —the document is fragmentary), he repeated the dream on a Monday and a Thursday in the synagogue of the Palestinians, most probably in order to evoke penitence.[9] In order to force a guest from Jerusalem to retract an accusation made against him, a worshiper in the synagogue of the Palestinians in Old Cairo swore during a Thursday morning service "by the Torah scroll, by all his possessions, and by the head of the sultan" that he would not allow the guest to leave the city before he had given him satisfaction. To be sure, in the letter reporting this incident, it is described as an act of exceptional impudence.[10] Appeals to the congregation assembled during these morning services were common, and court sessions were held regularly after them. One document characteristically speaks of a settlement reached between a man from Baghdad and another from Damascus and an oath given by the latter in the synagogue of the Palestinians in Old Cairo "after the prayer." The oath was administered according to the written instructions of the Gaon of Jerusalem, which had arrived shortly before and were known to the members of the congregation present.[11]

As to the Sabbath, Saadya Gaon writes in his prayer book: "For about half a day we stay in the synagogue, devoting ourselves to prayer and to the reading of the Torah and expounding the subjects related to each Sabbath" (i.e., the contents of the weekly lections from the Scriptures).[12] Even in a provincial town, this practice must have been common, according to the letters concerning communal strife in al-Maḥalla referred to below (subsection B, 2, n. 17). On Sabbath and holy days four services were held; the readings from the Scriptures took up a long time, the more so as they were translated verse by verse into Aramaic, a language that had been the international means of communication throughout southwestern Asia before the Islamic conquest. By the time of the Geniza period, Aramaic had become obsolete and even scholars were less familiar with it than with Hebrew. Still, the old custom of reading the translation into that idiom was retained, and even boys were trained to recite the "Targūm."[13] Most likely they did it with the same breathtaking speed as the boys in some old-fashioned Yemenite synagogues in Jerusalem still do.

After the morning service and before the reading of the Scriptures (not after it, as was customary in later times), was delivered a sermon, more exactly a *derāsh,* a combination of sermon, lecture, and disputation.[14] Moreover, in the time left free by the services, another derāsh would be read, either by a guest lecturer for the general public, to be attended by people from various synagogues, or by a scholar for a select group, to which special invitations, calligraphically written, were sent to the notables of the community. According to one letter such a lecture plus disputation lasted through all the daylight hours of the Sabbath. The writer, who apparently had attended it, was a fruiterer.[15]

When the Nagid held a derāsh, it seems to have been customary not to interrupt him with questions and objections, for we have a letter to a Nagid politely disputing a quotation used in his sermon on the preceding Saturday. The writer, incidentally, was lucky in not having brought up his arguments in public; for he quotes a wrong source, gives a faulty text, and tries an awkward explanation of a non-existent difficulty. According to the letter, the preacher's topic was that even the greatest talmudic scholar, Rabbi Aqiba, was a sinner in his youth.[16] Sabbaths and holidays were used for study courses in general (see chap. vi, sec. 6, below).

The most time-consuming portion of the service in those days was the *piyyūṭ,* the poetical pieces inserted at liberty into the official prayer. The word is derived from Greek *poet(es)* and is pre-Islamic. In Arabic these poetical pieces are called *ḥizāna,* because it was this part of the service in which the *ḥazzān,* or cantor, the professional singer, had to prove his mettle. The biblical exhortation "Sing unto the Lord a new song" (Psalm 98:1), echoed in the talmudic injunction "Everyone is obliged to say something new in his prayer every day," was still taken seriously in the Geniza period, which had been preceded by five hundred years of exuberant production of liturgical poetry. Tens of thousands (perhaps over a hundred thousand) of leaves covered with religious poems have been found in the Geniza, testifying to the stupendous output of the more famous liturgical poets of old as well as to the large number of authors, often entirely unknown otherwise, who were active in this field.[17]

This wide diffusion and use of the piyyūṭ in the synagogue service poses a problem. The Hebrew language of these poems is extremely elaborate and involved so that the poems cannot be understood properly without a good knowledge of rabbinical lore and law and a complete mastery of the text of the Bible. Even a modern scholar, equipped with dictionaries and reference books of all kinds, is sometimes at a loss to understand their correct meaning. Thus, one wonders for whom these creations were destined, particularly since they usually consisted of a circle of poems whose full recitation required hours. It must have been the melodies with which the piyyūṭ was sung which formed its main attraction for the congregation at large and made the long hours in synagogue enjoyable and edifying. Both familiar tunes and new melodies were heard with pleasure. The former is indicated by the fact that we often find passages from older pieces inserted into the manuscripts of later creations—no doubt because they had been familiar and cherished songs. The latter is proved by the many references to guest cantors from foreign countries and their appearances found in the Geniza papers. The notation of Hebrew synagogue poetry in Lombardic neumes by the Norman proselyte Obadiah is a case in point.[18]

The renegade Samuel the Maghrebi, who embraced Islam in 1163, found it necessary to explain to his Muslim readers this musical aspect of the synagogue service which was so utterly strange to them (but had a fairly exact counterpart in the liturgy of the Eastern churches):

When the Persians (who had ruled over Iraq and the adjacent countries prior to the advent of Islam) prohibited Jewish prayer, the Jews invented poems into which they inserted passages from the official prayers, then composed for them many melodies, which they chanted in the synagogues. When the Persians rebuked them for acting against the prohibition of public prayer the Jews retorted: we do not pray, we only make music.[19]

This pseudohistorical explanation of the origin of the piyyūṭ was not an invention of the learned renegade. It was a commonplace in the arguments of the many generations of Jewish scholars in the centuries preceding him who wished to eliminate this popular element from the service and tried to discredit its very raison d'être. They were not successful. Their failure is proved not only by the enormous amount of liturgical poems actually found, but also by direct references to their recital in the Geniza letters.[20]

Naturally, we hear also about the actions of the opponents. In an exceedingly eloquent, but somewhat ridiculous, letter overflowing with Bible quotations, a certain group—no doubt in a provincial town—complains about their communal leaders who had abolished the time-honored chanting of the various insertions on Sabbaths, holidays, and weekdays. The group had received affirmative opinions from renowned scholars and even a rescript from the sultan approving their position. But the local potentates had remained adamant in their decision to do away with these accretions to the official liturgy. Now the group admonishes the addressee, a renowned physician and confidant of the sultan, to be as courageous as Queen Esther (quoting the Book of Esther 4:16) and to approach the ruler with a request to enable them to have a service according to the customs of their forefathers.[21]

In the light of this letter we understand Moses Maimonides' leniency with regard to the insertion of poetical passages into the established text of the liturgy. Asked about them by a cantor, newly appointed to a place where these additions were chanted, the sage, in his usual wisdom, replied that they were indeed highly improper, but their recitation was preferable to the communal strife that would inevitably erupt as soon as the newcomer would try to abolish them. This decision, as well as the letter summarized, show how enamored those worshipers must have been of those poetical pieces—or at least of their traditional tunes. (I understand them completely. Having grown up in western Germany, where, at the beginning of the twentieth century, those songs from the seventh were still chanted, I can never fully enjoy a synagogue service on a holiday night in the United

States or in Israel, where, perhaps rightly, the songs have been discarded. To me it is like being in a room with walls bare of pictures.)[22]

The popularity of the piyyūṭ should not be attributed solely to the musical element, as important as it might have been. Otherwise, we would not find the cantors competing with one another so eagerly to find (or produce) ever new texts, as shown in chapter vi, section 10, below. Even at the end of the classical Geniza period there must have been in any large community a considerable number of persons who were able to understand and to appreciate those difficult poems, and the synagogue, we remember, was not only a house of worship, but also of study; or rather, as often said, study was worship. In addition, it seems to me that the piyyūṭs fulfilled in those days a role comparable with crossword puzzles in our own society. Since almost every line contained a hidden allusion to a Bible verse or a passage of talmudic literature, every new poem must have prompted a vigorous contest to determine the poet's sources and intents. Thus, while the traditional, or newly imported, melodies were a devotional pastime for the many, the effort required for the full understanding of the texts was a mental exercise for the more sophisticated.

The leadership in prayer of a congregation was not confined to one or two persons officiating permanently. Instead, both the recitation of the different sections of the liturgy and the readings from the Scriptures were assigned to members or guests present. Selecting them was the privilege of the muqaddam or of the "head of the synagogue," and was indicative of the social status of those selected. While still Third, the future Gaon Solomon b. Judah reports to his friends in Egypt exactly which parts of the prayers, which sections of the Scriptures, and which sermons were apportioned to each of the three highest dignitaries of the yeshiva of Jerusalem (plus one prominent layman) during the entire eighteen festive days of autumn. How even the poorest of the poor would jealously guard his rights in these matters may be seen from a document certifying that a certain young "Levi" was called up in Jerusalem to read a part of the Scripture lection, when no other local or foreign "Levi" was present. This rather comical testimony was given to him "so that he might not be put to shame."[23]

In a beautifully written letter some members of the synagogue of the Palestinians in Fustat beseech the Gaon Maṣlīaḥ to invite a certain blind man to chant (in response to the cantor) "The Song" (of Moses [Exodus 15], recited on the seventh day of Passover), since he was a man of good family, blind, extremely poor, and also endowed with an excellent memory. At least, he should serve as "Third" (singer alternating with the cantor). Such an honor, we might imagine, kept the old, blind pauper happy for a year.[24]

The honor of leading the congregation in a section of the service, for example, reading a lection from the Prophets on a certain Sabbath or holiday, could be bestowed for lifetime and even become hereditary through generations. In a query, possibly sent from an expanding community, Moses Maimonides was asked whether such hereditary honors were lawful since "the Torah is no heirloom" (Sayings of the Fathers 2:12), that is, everyone should be honored according to the knowledge and merits he himself acquired. Maimonides' answer is characteristic. If the persons designated to replace the hereditary readers were more learned or Godfearing, their claims should be heeded. Otherwise, the principle of heredity had precedence, since it was conducive to the preservation of peace.[25]

As an exceptional honor, a distinguished guest was entrusted with assigning the sections of the Scripture lections to the persons to be called up to recite them.[26] Complaints about high-handed procedures in these matters on the part of the synagogue presidents were common. Everyone was called up by his honorific title or titles. When one was omitted, an official complaint was filed with the highest Jewish authority.[27]

Reference has already been made to public prayers for benefactors, recited during the most solemn part of the service, when the Torah scrolls were taken out. It was, of course, an occasion for intense rivalry in social prestige. As the preserved copies of such prayers show, those patrons took no chances, but saw to it that the text of the prayer was written down in advance to make sure that all their titles and merits were set down properly and their specific wishes from God backed by communal supplication. Five texts, referring to the same person, a representative of merchants living around 1200, are particularly instructive. In them, the five titles borne by the person thus honored: "Pride of the Kohens," "Delight of the Nobles," "Trustee of the Merchants," "Eye of the Congregation," "Light of Israel and Judah," are enumerated in the proper order; his munificence toward the poor, scholars, synagogues, and colleges is likewise duly praised; in addition to the usual prayer for a long and happy life and other earthly and otherworldly blessings, one text contains the wish that the representative of the merchants might soon be united with his sister's son (whom he probably had sent on a business tour), whereas others end with blessings for his brother.[28] In these late pieces the language (Hebrew, of course) is stereotyped. One from the early eleventh century, however, is rich and original in expression and also more substantial in content: it tells how much the various donors actually had contributed.[29]

Another opportunity for displaying one's social status in public was the prayer for the dead, for a man's standing was conditioned by the length and quality of his pedigree. The titles and merits of one's forefathers were mentioned in the prayer, up to seven or more generations back, particularly when they had achieved the virtues of piety, generosity, or learning. The very large number of memorial lists preserved in the Geniza testifies to the wide diffusion of this socio-religious custom.[30]

The prayer over the dead was called either by the ancient Aramaic term *dukhrān,* derived from its traditional opening, "To the blessed memory of those who rest in peace," or by the more popular Arabic term *tarḥīm* (taken from the beginning of another—Hebrew—form of the prayer: "May God have mercy upon the soul of . . . "). It was usually followed by a prayer over the person whose ancestors were eulogized (and, we may assume, had made a contribution). The student of Arab antiquities is reminded somewhat of the pre-Islamic contests of boasting of one's ancestors arranged at the Ka'ba, the sanctuary of Mecca.[31]

According to a letter addressed to Moses Maimonides, it was customary in Alexandria and other places for the coffin of a deceased to be brought into the courtyard of the synagogue early in the morning; after the termination of the service the community and the dignitaries would come out of the prayer hall, attend the recitation of the dirges by the various cantors, and then accompany the dead to his last rest. Maimonides objects to this custom in the strongest terms: the synagogue was a house of worship of God, not of mourning for men. Only in the most exceptional case of the death of a very great divine was such a procedure permissible (meaning that the assembly was in honor of the divine, not of the dead man). His answer implies also that the custom was not in vogue in Fustat, nor have I found it attested in any Geniza document. In Fustat, they recited dirges in the synagogue during the seven days of mourning. Maimonides tolerated this custom only on the strength of the legal fiction that at the time of the erection of that building it had been stipulated that a section of it might serve as a place of mourning, a legal fiction for which there was a precedent in the Talmud. The Muslims, it should be noted, carry the bier into the main hall of a mosque, where a special prayer is said over the dead before the funeral.[32]

Wedding ceremonies, as far as I can judge from the Geniza records and literary sources contemporary with them, were never held in a synagogue. Nor were they in a mosque or, as I learn from Professor Aziz Atiya, in a medieval Coptic church.[33]

The Jewish, like the Muslim and Christian, religious service had also a political aspect, inasmuch as it contained a prayer for the ruler and for the Jewish ecumenical and territorial authorities. Whenever there was a rivalry between leaders, the community had to take sides. Prayers for the ruler were said only on special occasions, it seems, especially at the most solemn service of the Jewish liturgical year: the one held on the evening preceding the Day of Atonement. This custom still prevails today in some Oriental communities. Such a prayer, said for the Fatimid caliph al-Āmir (d. 1131) is translated in *Mediterranean People*.[34]

In addition to the public prayer for the communal authorities it was customary for readers and preachers to preface their performance with a symbolic request of permission by the Gaon or Nagid in office (see p. 20, above). Even the reading of the Aramaic translation of the Pentateuch and the Prophets was introduced in this way. The Geniza has preserved a preamble referring to so late a Nagid as David, the grandson of Maimonides (1237-1300). Since Aramaic was no longer generally understood, the preamble was written in Hebrew and in quite elegant Hebrew at that. The reader takes permission first from God, second from the Torah, third from all the saints and scholars, and finally, as the chief of the latter, from the Nagid, whose titles are, of course, enumerated. At the end the wish is expressed that the Nagid be restored to health. Most probably this addition was the reason the preamble was written down and not merely recited from memory.[35]

Whenever a difference of opinion about liturgy, leadership in prayer, or any other question led to communal strife, the dissenting group would refrain from "going down to," that is, attending, the synagogue, not so much for the sake of demonstrating, as out of religious scruples. For it was regarded as unlawful to say a prayer when led by an unworthy person. An Oxford manuscript contains a very detailed query in this respect showing that the writer was as disquieted by the thought of attending synagogue as by that of staying away from it, since communal prayer was regarded to be so much more meritorious than one said at home. An extensive and beautifully written letter of a Gaon of Jerusalem, addressed to Fustat, castigates nonattendance of public prayer as a grave transgression, whatever the reasons.[36] When a worshiper who was assigned a part of the reading of the lection was suspected of improper conduct by other members of the congregation, he was prevented by them from ascending the reader's platform. A detailed witness to such an occurrence is preserved with regard to a small town of the Egyptian delta.[37]

Exactly the same situation prevailed in Islam. Once, when the great al-Ḥajjāj, later viceroy of Iraq, was sent by the caliph together with another ambassador to a rebel prince, he refused to take part in the public prayer. According to him it was an act of impiety to pray behind one breaking up the unity of Islam. His colleague did participate, explaining that he preferred congregational to private prayer under all circumstances.[38] When the people of Qayrawān, Tunisia, refused any longer to acknowledge the suzerainty of the Fatimid caliph and of the religious sect headed by him, they stayed away from the service, but would come furtively to the mosque saying: "God, you are our witness," meaning that they were prepared to join public prayer, but were unable to do so for religious and political reasons.[39]

Since everything done by or for the "Holy Congregation" was hallowed with a religious connotation, the synagogue was also the proper place for attending to communal affairs. The letters of the ecumenical or territorial authorities or of other communities, near and far, were read out, discussed, and acted upon; resolutions proposed by the elders or by an individual leader were acclaimed or rejected; bans were pronounced and public chastisements, such as stripes, were administered; collections were solicited, vows for donations made, and reports about public finances or other matters rendered during or immediately after the service or between the prayers. In our day, public appeals are normally inaugurated by mammoth dinners. In those times, when dire calamities called for concerted efforts, an opposite method was adopted. A public fast was announced, the shops were closed, and everyone was bound to be present at the synagogue service, where he would also vow his share.[40]

In short, all matters of public concern, described above in section B, 1, were normally transacted in the synagogue, in conformity with age-old, even pre-Christian usage *(synagogue,* and its Hebrew equivalent, *bēth kenēseth,* after all, do not mean anything but "house of assembly"), and the Muslim house of worship, the mosque, was its counterpart.[41] Special invitations to meet in the synagogue for deliberations on public affairs have been found in the Geniza. One, which also contains best wishes for the Hanukkah festival, must have been sent to the member of another congregation since it assumed that the addressee would normally not attend that synagogue. The aim of the meeting was indeed "to unite the community, speed up concord, and bring together the separated" (Hebrew rhymed prose).[42]

In Ramle, Palestine, a letter mentions, around 1030, "the meetinghouse in the market of the Jews," *majlis sūq al-Yahūd,* which must have been of sizable dimensions, for the writer of the letter, the Gaon Solomon b. Judah, says that the whole community led by its notables was gathered there, demanding that he pronounce a ban (which he was reluctant to do). It was to bans that widest publicity was usually given.[43] The Ramle meetinghouse should not be regarded as a synagogue, but rather as an equivalent of the classical basilica, regularly found in the central markets of Hellenistic and Roman cities, serving as courtrooms and public halls. This hall in Ramle is also referred to in ULC Or 1080 J 45 (see A, 1, n. 36 below). But I have found no other such examples.

Karaite synagogues and Rabbanite private places of prayer are also referred to in the Geniza records by the term "majlis" (lit., place where one sits down), and not by the common Arabic word for synagogue (or church): *kanīs* or *kanīsa* (derived, of course, from the Hebrew term through Aramaic). Since all Karaite places of worship were erected after the advent of Islam, the noncommittal term "hall" was preferred in order to avoid a conflict with Islamic law which prohibited the erection of new churches and synagogues.[44]

While the formation of secessionist congregations was vehemently opposed, small, private places of worship must have been common and were tolerated because of their transitory character. A prominent physician kept a private synagogue probably because his patients were mostly government officials and other high-standing persons, whom he usually had to visit early in the morning. It would have been impossible for him to do so had he attended the public service which naturally was of longer duration. (Breakfast could be taken only after the service.) A scholarly India trader who had been away in the East for over two decades and had brought back from there native in-laws perhaps felt more comfortable keeping a little private synagogue for a certain period of transition. (He kept the place for at least three years. Later on we find him in another town.) In the first case, we read, the persons participating in the service in the doctor's house vowed a donation for a poor man; in the second, an in-law from India contributed to a public appeal, proving that small temporary places of prayer did not interfere with the regular activities of the community.[45]

The pious Nagid Abraham Maimonides also prayed at home, keeping a kind of pietist conventicle, since he was unable to impose his protracted prayer exercises on the community. Prayer assemblies in private homes were permitted for weddings or periods of mourning—

but without Torah scrolls, which remained the privilege of the communal places of prayer.[46]

One of the most characteristic features of later Jewish life was the foundation of synagogues named after the countries or cities of their original members. In the early seventeenth century (1603) there were in Istanbul, Turkey, approximately five thousand taxpayers (male adults), affiliated with about forty different synagogues. Besides the Karaites, there were only two groups who conducted communal affairs, especially representation before government: the Romaniotes, the ancient Rūm, the original Jewish inhabitants of the Ottoman empire (who were called thus, because at that time, over 150 years after the conquest of Constantinople by the Turks, they still spoke Greek, and not Turkish), and the Sepharadim, refugees from Spain or their descendants, who spoke a Spanish vernacular, but many of whom had lived for many years, or even several generations, in other countries. Unlike the Palestinians and Babylonians of the Geniza period, the Romaniotes and Sepharadim had no central synagogues, but were dispersed in many houses of worship, two synagogues sometimes named after the same place of origin. Names such as "the big Salonika," "the small Salonika," "the big Sicily," "the small Sicily" (alongside of which there was also a "Messina," a town in Sicily) betray the degree of atomization.[47]

In the Geniza we frequently read about foreigners operating as compact groups in a synagogue (occasionally as troublemakers), persons from Hebron in Ascalon, from Gaza in Hebron, from Tiberias in Acre (all in Palestine), from Aleppo, Syria, in al-Maḥalla, Egypt, and Maghrebis, of course, everywhere. But these groups never formed congregations with permanent buildings, either because they were not numerous and prosperous enough, or—and this seems to be the main reason—because the local rites were not as yet so differentiated and their liturgy so rigid as in later times.[48]

The excessive length of the service, the reading by laymen of texts often difficult and to be chanted according to fixed rules, the personal rivalries and public dissensions permitted and encouraged by the procedures described, and, in general, the fact that the synagogue served also as courtroom and clubhouse where the members spent most of the time left free by the bazaar or the workshop—all must have seriously impaired the character of the synagogue as house of worship. Those people, as repeatedly emphasized in this chapter, certainly felt strongly that God himself was present in his House, a notion fortified by sermons to this effect and based on biblical quotations such as Exodus 20:24 ("Wherever my name is mentioned I shall come to you and bless you") or Psalm 82:1 ("God stands in midst of God's assembly").[49] But the flesh is weak. Lack of decorum is decried by Moses Maimonides in his responsa and by his son Abraham in his "Complete Guide of the Pious."[60]

The censures by the two religious leaders are confirmed by the Geniza documents, to be sure, mostly those referring to localities in the Egyptian Rīf. A stern rescript by the Nagid Mevōrākh to the community of Malīj mentions a brawl in a local synagogue on a Saturday which had led to the cessation of the morning service.[51] In an almost humorous letter to a dignitary in the capital he is requested to urge the same Nagid to restrain an inveterate troublemaker or to ban him altogether from the synagogue.[52] From the late Middle Ages we have an Arabic document showing that a Nagid had indeed gone so far as to prohibit a member, a physician, from entering the synagogue. But the physician applied to the authorities, and the Nagid had to retract.[53] A letter from Ramle from September, 1052, reports a fistfight in the synagogue between pilgrims from Tyre and Tiberias on the Day of Atonement so fierce that it became necessary to call in the police. Although the fight, as described in the letter, was occasioned by entirely personal matters, the rather childish writer believed that this incident induced the two rivaling Gaons, the Babylonian nāsī Daniel b. Azarya, and the Palestinian Joseph ha-Kohen b. Solomon, to make peace with each other. Joseph contented himself with the office of president of the High Court, and during the whole week of the Feast of Tabernacles (which follows the Day of Atonement) the two appeared together during the festive assemblies on the Mount of Olives (east of Jerusalem). "Never did we have more beautiful holidays."[54]

Since the synagogue court served as a meeting place, it could occasionally become the scene of unpleasant encounters. A deposition made by two scholars in their own beautiful and painstaking handwritings and attested by a notary reports to the Nagid (Samuel b. Hananya) about a row and subsequent assault on a physician "between the sukka and the gate of the synagogue of the Iraqians" in Fustat.[55]

As a contribution to the psychology of religion, namely the observation that a devotional attitude and indulgence in human passion may easily alternate, I see fit to report here a scene I witnessed in Israel in the early 1950's in a congregation of immigrants from a very primitive region. I should like to note that the occasion was the night of the Feast of Purim, on which the intake of alcohol is not only permitted, but even recommended. Clearly, many of the congregants had not waited for the feast to avail themselves of the license. Still, the scene was one of complete reverence and dignity. Most, but not all, of those present sat on the floor having before them little stools on which they put prayerbooks and the texts of the Book of Esther. I was also much pleased with the quality of the reading done (of course, all by laymen). Had I left in the middle of the service for another place of prayer (as I had intended to do), I could have had only praise for those simple people. Suddenly, however, everything changed. One man at the end of the room remarked in a loud voice that the reader of the scroll had made a mistake. Immediately a man from the other end retorted in an even louder voice that this was not true. In a matter of seconds pandemonium reigned. Everyone shouted together, stools and chairs flew through the air, often splintering to pieces upon hitting the ground. Fortunately, the leader of one faction made a sign to his men to leave the room. Immediately, the other faction followed (outside the womenfolk, obviously prepared for such emergencies on a Purim night, had already summoned the police). Only the required quorum remained (myself the mandatory tenth) and the reader quietly completed the service. But the place was a shambles.

To revert to Geniza times: The congregation assembled in the synagogue served as the highest juridical authority. Persons, women included, who did not get satisfaction of their claims by regular legal procedure could, in extreme cases, interrupt and even stop the service until their complaint was heard by the whole community. This important institution of Jewish law is discussed in chapter vii, section B, 1, below.

Individuals afflicted by particular hardship were also permitted to address the community assembled in prayer after having been authorized to do so by the appropriate official. It was customary for the applicant to appear in the synagogue in person so as to make his appeal more effective. When a girl was "bought back" from a Crusader in Palestine for a particularly high sum, for which a friend stood security, her brother had to take her with him to Egypt in order to present her to the congregations that were solicited for the collection of the ransom. (Perhaps she was beautiful—which would explain the exorbitant ransom—and the man who put up the money for it expected that some young man would cast an eye on her and offer the sum required as her bridal gift, an occurrence that actually happened—only 350 years later, as proved by a marriage contract made on December 28, 1511.)[56] We have the text of a similar appeal, also written for a woman ransomed from her Crusader captors. It is illustrative of life in the synagogue during the Geniza period in more than one respect:

"Thus says the Lord: Do justice and deeds of charity,[57] *for my salvation is near to come and my charity to be revealed"* [Isaiah 56:1]. *"Blessed are those who do justice and deeds of charity at all times"* [Psalm 106:3].

I inform hereby the holy congregation—may God enhance its splendor—that I am a woman *who was taken captive in the Land of Israel.*[58] I arrived here this week from Sunbāṭ and have no proper clothing, no blanket and no sleeping carpet. With me is a little boy *and I have no means of sustenance.* I beseech now God, the exalted, and beseech the congregation—*may you be blessed*—to do with me what is proper to be done *with any wayfarer. The Holy one—may he be praised—may repay you many times and be your help* so that you shall never be driven from your homes.[59] *And may he bring the Redeemer in your days, Amen.*[60]

CHAPTER VI

Education and the Professional Class

1. PRELIMINARY CONSIDERATIONS

In our civilization, people study in order to acquire knowledge. In the society reflected in the Geniza records, study had an additional function: it was an act of devotion, it was worship. To give as much time as possible to the reading and discussion of holy texts was religiously meritorious, and the reputation of being versed in them was a mark of honor, coveted not only by members of the professional class, but by any respectable citizen. And no one could aspire after communal leadership without being distinguished by a certain degree of erudition.

This popular attitude toward learning and scholarship inculcated by the biblical commandment, "This book of the Torah shall never depart out of your mouth, but you shall study it day and night" (Joshua 1:8, incorporated in the daily prayer), had a salutary effect on the whole process of education. Parents everywhere were bound by religious injunctions and the pressure of society to send their children to school, at least for a number of years. The community made strenuous efforts to provide education for orphans and the children of the poor. Adults tried to devote at least a fraction of their spare time to the regular study of the sources of their religion. The maintenance of the higher seats of learning was a concern for all; donations for them were solicited and collected in countries far away, as when the Jews of Spain and North Africa contributed regularly to the upkeep of the academies in Baghdad, or those of southern Italy supported the scholars of Jerusalem. Honorific titles from those institutions of learning were eagerly sought after. They were by no means awarded indiscriminately. It is noteworthy that, as far as we know, during the classical Geniza period, the title *ḥāvēr,* or member of the yeshiva, was bestowed only on persons renowned for some measure of learning.

In view of this state of affairs it is easy to understand why in those days there was no rigid distinction between scholars and persons in economic vocations. A learned merchant could easily become a full-time judge or teacher, while religious functionaries would sometimes do business or even engage in some manual occupation. Nevertheless, although the demarcation lines were fluid, there existed a class of professionals serving as judges, notaries, teachers, cantors, or active in various other capacities. These "servants of the community," as they were called, received salaries and other emoluments from public and private funds, but their position was often precarious owing to the institutional weaknesses or the vicissitudes of fortune of the organizations they served.

Secular education was the preserve of the higher classes. It was of two entirely different types: the scientific-philosophical and the literary-administrative. The first prepared for the medical profession, the second for government service. Only the former consisted of a well-organized and long-established course of studies (which originated in pre-Islamic times) and was acquired not only through private tuition and reading, but partly also in public institutions attached to the hospitals. The training of the government official, the *kātib* (lit., scribe), comprised Arabic calligraphy, language and some literature, and probably also the study of some of the encyclopedias and handbooks of administration, written for the use of the scribes. It was an art or technique rather than a science, and, although it sometimes led to high social positions, it lacked the prestige that the study of philosophy, medicine, and related subjects conveyed. The Arabic term *ḥakīm* (learned) was the word commonly used for "physician," but, at the same time, it designated a man of philosophical erudition in general.

It was characteristic of the period under discussion that religious and legal erudition was often combined with philosophic and scientific training. The most famous examples are the great Spanish philosopher Ibn Rushd (Averroes, 1126–1198), who served as chief qadi, or Muslim judge, in Córdoba, Spain, and his contemporary Moses Maimonides (1135–1204), born in the same city, but spending most of his life in Egypt, whose compendium on Jewish religious law was a masterpiece of the same high caliber as his philosophical work, and who also wrote books on medicine. The Geniza proves that this combination of religious and secular scholarship was by no means exceptional.

On the other hand, only rarely do we find in our documents a kātib, or government official, renowned also as a religious scholar. The illustrious example of Samuel ha-Nagid of Granada (993–1056), who was a vizier and general, a prolific poet and litterateur, and at the same time a most competent author on Jewish religious law, has no counterpart in the East.

In general we have to keep in mind that the cultural climate varied very much from one country to another. Of all the countries represented in the Geniza papers, Egypt, their place of origin, was the least favorable for the pursuit of scholarly studies. Had a Geniza been found in Córdoba or Qayrawān, the standards of education discernible in it certainly would have been much different from what they appear in the Cairo Geniza. Immigrant scholars to Egypt by far surpassed the indigenous crop in both quality and number. It is precisely for this reason, however, that the general level of culture in the Mediterranean basin is perhaps more evident from the Cairo Geniza than it would have been from a hoard of manuscripts found in a more creative, but less cosmopolitan, center than the capital of Egypt.

Owing to its religious character, education in medieval times was more closely connected than other domains of social life with the specific tenets, ritual, and literature of each community. In this chapter, an attempt has been made to eliminate, as far as possible, the specifically Jewish aspects of education. It lies in the very nature of the subject that such an attempt can be only partly successful. It is hoped, however, that the details given here for one educational system prevailing in Mediterranean countries during the High Middle Ages will be useful for the study of education in that time and area in general.[1]

2. ELEMENTARY STAGE

While we know comparatively little about the elementary schools of northern Europe during the eleventh and twelfth centuries, there are many references to them in the Geniza records. When children are mentioned in letters, it is normally in connection with their studies. "Your children are well and go to school every day and to synagogue on Saturday," writes a man in Alexandria to a relative away on travel.[1] A boy in Libya writes to his uncle sojourning in

Egypt: "I am writing you this letter with my own hand [not every child who went to school acquired the art of calligraphy (see below)]. My brother Nabāt still attends school; he is now thirteen. You mentioned in your letter that your boys studied the Sacred Law and Arabic and Hebrew calligraphy. We thanked God for this." [2] In a business letter, a merchant abroad asks his correspondent in Old Cairo to see to it that his boy does not interrupt his studies; if the need arises, his friend was to advance the school fees.[3] There are several instances of fathers on travel giving instructions to their wives or other relatives with regard to the proper education of their children, or complaining bitterly about a wife "letting the boy miss the school and play in the streets." The writer sends his brother 15 dirhems for the teacher and a fine piece of clothing for the boy so that he should feel well in school from which he should not absent himself for a moment.[4]

School fees were a regular item in family budgets, even modest ones. A contract of partnership contains the proviso that wheat and wine—the basic victuals—were to be acquired by the investor with the money accruing from the common business, while rent and school fees were to be paid by him separately.[5] A woman wishing to prove in court that her husband had no claims on her, because he did not behave as the father of a family, argued that he never paid the school fees for their boys (she had done so with her own earnings). The family was so poor that they had allegedly not been able to light a candle on workdays, or even on holidays.[6] In a settlement a wife confirms to her husband that he had paid the expenses for food, drink, clothing, and living quarters of his three children, as well as for their education.[7] The schooling of orphans and poor children was one of the main concerns of the community (see sec. 4, below).

Elementary education, we see, was universal to a very remarkable degree, but its standards seem to have been rather poor. The reason for this is to be sought in faulty educational theories. First, despite many warm words about children in talmudic literature, childhood in general was regarded as a state of imperfection; to occupy oneself with such lowly creatures as minors was almost degradation. Second —and this notion infested higher studies as well—it was believed that knowing a text by heart must precede its understanding; as childhood was at all events only a preparatory stage, the pupil wasted most of his time memorizing. The practice had another purpose. In ancient times, when the sacred texts were only imperfectly rendered in writing, their minute memorizing by children was the only means of preserving their exact reading and cantillation. This notion is the original import of the talmudic saying, so often repeated today: "The world exists solely through the breath of the schoolchildren."[8] By the time of the Geniza records, however, refined methods of noting the pronunciation and cantillation of the biblical text had been developed, so that there was no longer any need to safeguard its preservation by memorizing. Nevertheless, the old and redundant system was continued in many Oriental countries, as we know, right down to the twentieth century.

The main aim of the school was the preparation of its pupils for taking an active part in the synagogue service. In this respect, it fulfilled a function similar to that of the Song School of contemporary northern Europe, in which church chant was the most prominent part of the curriculum. To be sure, the requirements of the synagogue service in those days were very high. The Five Books of Moses (the Pentateuch) were read in their entirety from a sacred scroll, which was written in the ancient fashion without vowels and signs for cantillation.[9] A man called up to read a section had to know it more or less by heart. Similarly, each member wishing to participate had to be fluent in the readings from the Prophets as well as in Aramaic translations, the *Targūm,* of the Prophets, the Pentateuch, and some other books of the Bible. A boy chanting the Targūm "on the Torah," that is, translating into Aramaic the Hebrew lection read by an adult verse by verse, was the pride of his parents. A long business letter sent from Cairo to a merchant on a trip to India contains also this remark: "Your boy Faraj now reads the Targūm accompanying the lections—as I guaranteed you he would." [10]

This passage from a twelfth-century letter reminds me of a complaint by an illiterate Yemenite woman, bitterly criticizing (in her Arabic vernacular, of course) the modern education to which her children were exposed in Israel. "What do you teach in your schools," she said to me, "stories, children's songs, and the like. With us in Yemen, a boy of ten stands up in synagogue and reads the Targūm." Clearly, her idea of education was that only very difficult subjects were worthy of being taught in a school. (We perhaps err a little in the opposite direction.)

Some clarification of this problem of the reading of the Targūm seems to be appropriate since it is apt to throw light on the whole process of schoolteaching in the Middle Ages. In ancient times, when Aramaic was the spoken vernacular, it was a wonderful event for a boy "to stand up in synagogue" and to provide an explanatory translation of the biblical text just read by an adult member of the congregation. It proved that he had understood the Hebrew original and was able to clearly expound it before an adult audience. The custom must have been a most efficient means of initiating a youngster into the society of the grownup. When, however, Aramaic became extinct, the procedure became meaningless, and the text had to be memorized by rote (in addition, of course, to Hebrew, which also had to be acquired in school), undoubtedly a heavy burden which only brighter boys were able to bear. In the Eastern churches, where Syriac and Coptic, the liturgical languages, also became obsolete during the High Middle Ages, comparable educational difficulties must have existed. Similarly, classical Arabic, the language of the Koran, the holy book of Islam, was not the language spoken by a Muslim boy whose vernacular was Middle Arabic. Classical Arabic and its intricate grammar had to be learned in school "just like mathematics," as Ibn Khaldūn, the Tunisian philosopher of history, remarks pointedly (writing in 1377). The position of Latin in western Europe was similar, although the Catholic service does not require participation of the laity to the same degree as do the Muslim and the Jewish, where, as remarked before, study also was worship.

The poetical insertions into the official text of the synagogue liturgy, whose correct chanting must have been difficult even for adults (see chap. v, sec. D, 2, above), were studied in school.[11] The regular prayers, however, although very much extended and involved, are nowhere mentioned as a school subject. The boys obviously were expected to grasp texts by listening and responding while regularly attending synagogue with their fathers. In Oriental rites, it should be noted, virtually the whole liturgy is chanted aloud (and not read mostly in silence, as was customary in Europe).

Christian elementary education in the East was very much like the Jewish. A catholicus, or head of the Nestorian church, reported that the boys learned the Pentateuch, the Prophets, the Psalms, and the liturgy in school, but, when they reached the New Testament, they left school. Understandably, the catholicus changed the order of the texts to be learned to better suit the specific needs of Christian education. But it was the texts used in the church service which were the exclusive object of study.[12] As is well known, the Muslim elementary school, the *kuttāb,* is similarly devoted to the memorizing of the Koran. It is worthy of note that the Geniza papers use the word kuttāb also with reference to Jewish schools.

There was one bright side to this rather unsatisfactory picture of medieval elementary education. The boys had a good incentive for learning, for they could use immediately the scanty knowledge acquired in school. During the weekend, a father would check the progress of his boy ("so that my heart should be happy," as we read in one letter)[13] and, if the result was satisfactory, he would proudly ascend with him the anbōl, or elevated platform in the center of the synagogue, at the next service, where the boy would chant the section of the weekly lection apportioned to his father, or the Targūm, its Aramaic translation.[14] Certain parts of the liturgy were reserved to be sung by a boy.[15] Sometimes a boy would be honored with the chanting of the whole Scripture portion of a holiday, such as the reading of the Book of Esther—no small feat. For such an honor, a large donation had to be made to the congregation. The Geniza has preserved a lovely story from a little town in Lower Egypt, where a mother, with the help of her daughter, bought this honor for her boy for the price of 40 dirhems, whereas the father obviously had second thoughts about such use of so much money.[16]

The syllabus of the elementary school was not confined to religious subjects everywhere. A well-known ruling of Hay Gaon (d. 1038) reads: "It is permitted to teach Arabic calligraphy and arithmetic in the synagogue[17] together with the Sacred Law. Non-Jewish children may also study in the synagogue for the sake of good relationship with the neighbors, although this is not desirable." Since gentile children could hardly have been expected to memorize Hebrew religious texts, secular subjects must have taken up considerable time in the schools, in respect to which the legal opinion quoted was given. Incidentally, the caliph al-Mutawakkil prohibited in 850 the admission of non-Muslim children to Muslim schools or their teaching by Muslim private tutors. Similar prohibitions appear in Arabic literature both before and after that time, so that in actual life confessional segregation certainly was not strictly adhered to.[18]

References to the study of Arabic calligraphy by children are frequent, but those on the teaching of arithmetic are scarce. In one, a fragment in the hand of Ḥalfōn b. Manasse ha-Levi (1100–1139), a widow makes an agreement with an "elder," perhaps an old merchant and not a professional teacher, to instruct her boy in Arabic calligraphy and arithmetic. In calligraphy, the aim to be reached was that the boy be able to take down a dictation without mistakes in spelling, in arithmetic that he master more complicated accounts with the aid of the abacus (the primitive calculating instrument still used by our children) and the "tens," referring presumably to more complicated accounts. For successful teaching the instructor's remuneration would be 2 dinars.[19]

The general reticence of the Geniza documents on the teaching of arithmetic at the elementary stage is probably to be explained by the fact that computing was learned without the use of textbooks. This conclusion can be drawn from the accounts found in the Geniza, where addition and subtraction of long series of sums are seemingly done without any help of writing. It must be remarked that the Hebrew and Coptic numerals, which are used exclusively in our papers, do not lend themselves easily to arithmetical operations in writing. We are usually oblivious of the fact that although the Arabic numerals had been in use in scientific works since early Islamic times, the merchants and other people engaged in economic life in the Arab world continued to use the entirely impractical Coptic (i.e., originally Greek) signs for numbers right down to modern times. The practical use of the Arab numerals was taken over by the Arabs from the Europeans.

The exercise books found in the Geniza show that, with respect to methods employed in elementary schools, the beginning of reading was taught by the tedious analytic method of learning the individual letters (and many other symbols used in Hebrew) and their various combinations. There must have been some teachers, however, who, like modern educators, "taught reading without the alphabet," that is, began with complete words and short sentences. We know this from a learned opinion, given by the renowned Spanish Jewish scholar, Isaac b. Samuel, who served as judge in Old Cairo around 1100. The scholarly judge of course condemned this innovation, which was soon forgotten.[20]

The teachers had other means for making the children's first year at school more cheerful: playful occupations were used as a help to study. The teacher would draw huge and elaborate calligraphic outlines of the letters and the children would fill them in with red, brown, green, and other colors; or the children would draw in various colors the outlines of letters written artistically by the teacher. The same method was followed with the writing of the combination of letters or of verses or passages from the Scriptures and moral sayings. The covers of the exercise books would have decorative drawings, such as eight intertwined snakes having heads of fishes or birds. Ornaments in different colors, for example, the six-cornered star of David (which at that time was not a specifically Jewish emblem) or a candelabrum with seven arms (which was) would embellish the inside. It seems that the children were sometimes even allowed to give free rein to their imagination (or did so without permission). On one page of an exercise book we find alongside shaky, childish letters a crude drawing of the sun and a boat on the Nile.[21]

Medieval ideas about the art of writing differed very much from our own and need some explanation. Every schoolboy had to do exercises which consisted of writing the letters of the alphabet for which purpose he used a wooden board. These exercises were not an end in themselves, but solely a means to learn reading. Once the pupils had mastered the reading, the art of writing was not further pursued in the regular elementary school. Therefore, we find in the Geniza hundreds of signatures on documents not in the cursive script used in day-to-day writing, but in the monumental ductus common in books, and mostly in very shaky and awkward shapes. These were the signatures of artisans and shopkeepers of low standing, who had not gone beyond the elementary stage of schooling.[22] It is also not surprising that a query was submitted to Maimonides about persons signing documents that they were unable to read. Documents were normally written in the cursive script which these persons had not learned. Only at a higher stage of schooling was the art of writing taught systematically.[23]

Four types of students were trained in calligraphy: future government officials, physicians, religious scholars, and merchants. Thus, the art of writing—not of reading, which was far more widespread—was the distinctive mark of a person belonging to the professional or higher classes.

Once I asked a Yemenite informant, a craftsman, but very learned in traditional Jewish studies, to write down for me a word of his Arabic vernacular which I was unable to grasp phonetically. To my amazement I discovered that this man who had put me to shame more than once with his knowledge of Jewish ritual law and cabala, did not know how to write, but drew the letters slowly and insecurely like a child. When he became aware of the expression of astonishment in my face he said contemptuously: "I am not a business clerk."

Not every Jewish merchant of the Geniza period, even one engaged in overseas trade, was versed in Arabic calligraphy. The writer of a letter in good Arabic style and orderly Hebrew characters asks his correspondent not to use Arabic script (as in previous letters) since he did not know it and had to trouble friends to read to him the letters received and then would sometimes forget what he had heard.[24] An important Muslim trader and shipowner did not know how to read or to write at all.[25] We should not jump to the conclusion, though, that in letters written by a person different from the sender the latter was illiterate. At home, bigger merchants employed one or several clerks; in their travels they would ask a friend with a good hand to do the job. We frequently find a calligraphic letter sent from abroad concluded by personal greetings of the copyist to the addressee or followed by a postscript in the sender's own, impatient script (which, sometimes, makes very difficult reading indeed).

We can form some idea of the courses in "Arabic and Hebrew calligraphy" from the material actually found in the Geniza. The numerous fragments of copies of correspondence indicate that the boys were trained in copying model letters. The artistic products of Arabic litterateurs, although not entirely absent from the Geniza, cannot ordinarily have served as models, since we do not find their example followed in the countless letters actually preserved. Rather, the teachers must have adopted a method still practiced at the beginning of this century in Baghdad (and which, with certain improvements, is even used here today in schools of commerce): a teacher would ask merchants of good standing or private persons to furnish him with discarded letters which then were used by his pupils as material for their exercises in reading and writing. And who knows: perhaps a large percentage of the business and private letters we hold in our hands today found their way into the Geniza of the Palestinian synagogue because they had been used as models by schoolboys who had studied them in a room quite nearby.[26]

The legal deeds on the backs of which we find all manner of writings in childish hands, such as verses of poetry or proverbial sayings, most probably served a similar purpose. Most Geniza letters are written in a good and firm style and include many traditional phrases, also pointing to the fact that the art of letter writing was acquired through systematic study.

Each country had its own brand of calligraphy and epistolary style. Letters from Spain are written almost entirely in classical and very ornate Arabic,[27] but in extremely cursive Hebrew characters that make difficult reading. In Tunisia, Egypt, and Syria a straightforward standard Arabic was used for the most part, and the writing was far more similar to the type used in books, although marked differences in detail are to be noted among these three regions. In Yemen again, the Arabic was more flowery, although not classical, while the Hebrew script it was written in was, as a rule, almost ornamental. Similar differences can be observed among the various periods documented in the Geniza papers.

The letters written in Arabic script generally show a fairly good style, while the Hebrew preambles and the many epistles composed in Hebrew usually betray full mastery of the literary language. In order to attain such standards, the writers had to study the grammar and something of the literature of the two languages, demonstrating that the term "Arabic and Hebrew script," mentioned in the Geniza letters as a subject studied by boys, comprised much more than mere calligraphy.

Education in general, and elementary education in particular, was faced with the problem of the relatively high price of books, all handwritten in those days, of course. In well-to-do houses a newborn child would already be presented with a copy of the Bible.[28] In various colophons (postscripts to manuscripts) it is stated that the manuscript was written or bought for boys. Tender attachment to the recipient is sometimes apparent in those notes on the concluding page of a manuscript (whose acquisition, we should remember, required a very considerable expenditure). The notes prove that love between parents and children is strongest where both are committed to a love greater than themselves.[29] I like this colophon:

> This copy of the Hagiographa [the third part of the Old Testament] was bought by Joseph b. Daniel with the choicest of his money, to be studied by his two sons, Manṣūr and Eli, the brothers brotherly united in the striving for knowledge.[30] May God grant them to study the Bible and the Mishnah, and may he grant their father Joseph to rejoice in their happiness with study and in the joy of their day of wedding. And may he let him see their children and children's children study the Torah, so that there should be fulfilled through them what is written "This book of the Torah shall never depart out of your mouth . . ." [Joshua 1:8].[31]

Private teachers provided their pupils with books; books were indeed the teachers' "hoes and ploughshares," as Maimonides observed in a learned opinion.[32] Donations of Bible codices were made to synagogues for the use of orphans.[33] Still, there were not enough books to meet the requirements. Therefore, the medieval pedagogues resorted to an ingenious expedient. They taught their pupils to read a text upside down and from the sides, so that four and more children could easily use one and the same book.[34] In the Yemenite Jewish community, where medieval conditions often prevailed until the middle of the twentieth century, one frequently meets persons who read a text turned upside down with the same fluency as right side up.

Life in school is illustrated in a number of Geniza letters, both those exchanged between parents and teachers and occasional references in others. In honor of the subject taught, the Bible, the boys had to be dressed seemly. This detail is repeatedly emphasized, for instance in this passage from a letter sent in September, 1127, from Damascus to the writer's brother who had traveled to Old Cairo: "Your boy Eli is happy with himself and makes happy the heart of others. He wishes now to be sent to school [kuttāb]. In case you are not back in time, please send some appropriate clothing for his body and cover for his head." (A turban was an indispensable part of a well-dressed person's apparel. Only the lowest of the low would have contented himself with a skullcap.) [35]

As everywhere in the world, boys were sometimes naughty. A teacher writes to a father that his little one had shown great eagerness in study from the day he had entered school, but that another boy (the scoundrel's name is registered, of course) broke the son's wooden writing board with the connivance of the whole class (who obviously disliked the newcomer's zeal).[36] Other disciplinary problems are referred to below. In a letter written in Arabic characters (so that the boy carrying the message would not be able to read it), a teacher informs a parent that his son Mūsā (Moses), after having missed school for a number of days, entered class while he, the teacher, was occupied with another boy. Having been assigned silent reading Mūsā finished quickly, and, when asked to repeat, swore he would never read a text more than once—and had run off. But, the teacher's complaint ends, only by repeating the biblical text four or five times could one know it by heart (which, we remember, was the aim of instruction).[37] The purport of this and other letters not summarized here was of course that the home should take care of the punishment that the school was unwilling or unable to inflict. On the other hand, a father sending his two boys to school asks the teacher not to spank the elder one for being late; he had studied Arabic at home and it had taken more time than anticipated; the father asks the teacher not to spank the little one because he was not expected to go to school alone and had to wait for his elder brother.[38]

With the exception of the religious holidays vacations seem not to have been customary. But it is evident from a number of passages that parents took their children with them when they traveled to attend family events or simply to visit relatives. A sister married in a village invites her brother for a month and adds: "The children, too, will have it better with me here than with you there in the kuttāb." [39]

Our sources do not show how far the elementary school acquainted its pupils not only with the text of the sacred books, but also with their contents and general purport. In any event, this was not the basic duty of the teacher. The religious and moral education and the higher forms of instruction in general were left to the initiative of the home. The biblical commandment that makes parents responsible for the religious education of their children (Deuteronomy 6:7; the text is included in the daily morning and evening prayers) was taken literally. The father, and in his absence other relatives, took care of the young until they were able to attend an institute of higher learning or to join the community as members taking full share in its activities. Against this background, we appreciate the following remark in a letter of a traveling scholarly person to his wife: "Pay special attention to Eli [the youngest boy in the house, it seems], to his food, clothing, and study. Let him stay overnight with his uncle, so that the latter may teach him more than he gets from the teacher, and do not give him a poor education." Obviously, education was regarded as poor if parents were satisfied with what their child received in the elementary school.[40]

3. EDUCATION OF GIRLS. WOMEN TEACHERS

The Geniza papers indicate that women, unmarried girls included, attended synagogue regularly.[1] They were confined to a separate compartment, however, which prevented them from taking an active part in the service. Since the practical aim of elementary education was preparation for participating in the synagogue service, it was natural that girls, as a rule, were not sent to school. In various letters addressed to women it is implied that the recipients could not read and had to rely on male relatives or acquaintances to ascertain their contents. When a woman says in a letter, "I am writing to you," it does not necessarily mean that she did so with her own hand. Where the handwriting of the copyist is known to us it is evident that the letter was dictated.[2]

It is in conformity with the general character of the period under discussion and the position of women in the society described in this book that the education of girls was by no means entirely neglected. In an interesting letter, in which a teacher describes his difficulties with a particularly unruly boy, we read that the boy's sister also attended the school.[3] A learned opinion of Maimonides written in his own hand (and preserved in the British Museum; its photograph is available on a postcard) deals with a class composed entirely of girls. The teacher was blind, and, according to the query addressed to Maimonides, the girls refused to study with anyone except him.[4] In a letter to the Nagid, or head of the Jews of Egypt, a woman entrusted with the supervision of orphan girls suggests placing two of them with a woman who would instruct them in female arts like embroidery, while a private instructor would come to the house to teach them the prayers, "so that they should not grow up like wild animals and not even know 'Hear Israel' [Deuteronomy 6:4–9, the central piece of the daily prayers]." [5]

If such care was taken with orphans, it is natural that the higher classes paid even more attention to the education of girls. Samuel, the Maghrebi, reports in his autobiography, that his mother was one of three sisters from Basra, Iraq, who were deeply versed in Jewish studies and proficient also in Hebrew calligraphy—a noteworthy accomplishment for nonprofessional people in those days.[6] The Jewish community in another Iraqian town, Daqūq (today inhabited mostly by Kurds and called Ṭāwūq) was headed by Azarya "son of the female copyist." He was praised by the Hebrew poet Judah al-Ḥarīzī for his noble descent and character as well as his munificence.[7] In a beautiful and correctly written Bible codex from Yemen, the copyist, Miriam, the daughter of the famous scribe Benayah, asks for indulgence with regard to any shortcomings, as she was at the time suckling a baby.[8] The daughter of Samuel b. Eli, the Gaon, or head of the Jewish academy in Baghdad during the years 1164–1193, was so learned that she was able to teach her father's students not only the Bible, but also the Talmud.[9] (Samuel had no son and was succeeded by the husband of his learned daughter. It was common practice among Yemenites who had no son to instruct a daughter in higher Jewish subjects. Was this for the benefit of the girl or to fulfill the commandment: you shall teach your children?) A Geniza document contains this dirge of a father on his daughter who had died as a mature matron, but whom he had taught while she was a girl: "When I remember how intelligent, how knowledgeable, how graceful of diction you had been. . . . Would I could listen to you again while I taught you the Bible or quested you in its knowledge by heart, 'let me see your face, let me hear your voice' [Song of Solomon 2:14]." [10] Examples of women as scholars and calligraphers are known from contemporary Muslim sources.[11]

Of particular interest is a letter by a Jewish woman who was seriously ill and expected to die soon (she had had dreams telling her so). As her only wish she enjoins her sister to see to it that her younger daughter receives a proper education, although she was well aware that the expenses for this would severely tax the family's strained finances. The letter was written by the woman herself (as is stated in it) and mentions her late mother, a pious devotee. Devotion required a knowledge of the Scriptures. Jewish (and Muslim) pietism were not opposed to study, but were an incentive for it.[12]

Under these circumstances it is not astonishing that we occasionally find references to women teachers, mostly in lists of persons in receipt of emoluments or alms from the community. In most cases, the term *mu'allima,* woman teacher, probably designated a teacher of embroidery and other female arts.[13] We possess, though, a most detailed legal opinion by Maimonides describing the vicissitudes of a woman who took over the Bible school of her brother ("for she had a knowledge of the Bible") and trained her two sons to become her assistants.[14] Maimonides also remarks that the Bible teaching of women was not worth much, illustrating that women as instructors must have been a common phenomenon. When we find, in a slightly earlier period, two teachers called "the son of the mu'allima," it is reasonable to assume they were two sons following the profession of their mother.[15] In the letter about the quarreling siblings referred to above, a woman acts as a teacher in the kuttāb of a relative, most probably her brother or husband. When a male and female teacher from Damietta appear together in a list of needy, they very likely were relatives who had jointly kept a school in their hometown, but, for one reason or another, had been forced to leave.[16]

In many cases it was the mother, and not the father, who looked after the proper education and schooling of their children. In volume III, chapter ix, an attempt is made to define the women's place in the spiritual life of the Geniza period with more precision.

4. ORGANIZATION OF ELEMENTARY EDUCATION. ECONOMIC AND SOCIAL POSITION OF TEACHERS

Schools in the modern sense of the word, that is, institutions comprising a number of teachers and classes of pupils, differentiated according to age and subjects, were unknown to the society described in this book. Each teacher represented an institution in himself, although he was frequently assisted by a relative; a son by his old father, a brother by his sister, or a mother by her two sons.[1] As in any other economic activity, a teacher would occasionally conclude a partnership with a colleague, or would be assisted by a "young man," that is, an employee.[2]

The teaching took place in three different types of localities: in the synagogue (as in the mosque or the church), wherefore schoolboys in those times were called "synagogue children"; [3] in the house of the teacher—mostly, it seems, a place rented for the purpose; in well-to-do families, in the home of the parents. Again there were differences between larger and smaller communities. The latter had to see to it that they had a teacher at all. Therefore, they contracted with a teacher, promising him a minimum weekly salary, a promise not always kept.[4]

In the larger cities, free competition prevailed among teachers, but synagogue buildings were given only to persons approved by the community.[5] Furthermore, the community maintained special teachers for orphans and the poor, or paid the fees for them. Only persons of trust were appointed as "teacher of the orphans." It must have been a position of honor, or we would not find persons adding this epithet to their signatures on documents. "Teachers of the orphans" are mentioned in records from Old Cairo, Jerusalem, Damascus, and Baghdad. In Baghdad, Johannes-Obadiah, the Norman proselyte from southern Italy, received his first instruction in Hebrew and the Five Books of Moses in a class of orphans.[6]

All references to "teachers of orphans" are from the eleventh or early twelfth century, while payments by the community of school fees for individual orphans or poor children become exceedingly common by the end of the twelfth century. In Appendix A, section 36 (dated 1184), one official alone pays school fees to four different teachers. It would not be in accordance with the spirit of the age to assume that this change was the result of greater pedagogical insight into the fact that the segregation of underprivileged children was disadvantageous for them. Financial considerations, namely the discovery that the keeping of separate classes was more expensive, or the shrinking of the size of the communities, or both, were responsible for the development discernible in the relevant Geniza documents.

Competition among teachers was keen. The valiant woman teacher about whom Maimonides was queried (sec. 3, above) declared in court that she was unable to leave her school (as her husband had demanded) even temporarily, although her two boys assisted her, for teaching was not like any other work; if neglected for even one day, it was lost, for the parents would immediately send their children to another teacher. (This remark, by the way, reveals the eagerness of parents in those days to educate their children, for the need of supervision, which prompts so many parents in our own times to send their children regularly to school, did not exist then, as the womenfolk stayed at home most of the time anyway.) Complaints about competition by rival teachers are found in some Geniza letters; particularly impressive is one in which the writer alleges that his rival induced the judge charged with the administration of the estate of orphans to influence some mothers to transfer their boys from the plaintiff's school to his own.[7]

Precisely in view of this tense situation were teachers careful not to trespass on the prerogatives of their colleagues. In reply to a letter of the judge of Minyat Ziftā, who had asked him to take the place of a foreigner intending to return to his country, a teacher from the little town of Damīra writes that he would come only upon receipt of a written invitation of the community confirming that the incumbent was definitely leaving and that they unanimously wished him "to take care of their children." [8]

This competition also had salutary effects, as it was apt to improve the quality of teaching. Most likely, in larger cities, a certain scholastic gradation existed among the various schools. When we find in a list of communal expenses that an orphan was transferred after a few months from one kuttāb to another, it is perhaps correct to assume that his progress in the first prompted the move—at least, that was the procedure in the larger towns of Yemen, where conditions similar to those of the Geniza period prevailed until the mass exodus of the Jews in 1949–1950.[9] Even a wretched little community, like Qalyūb (see n. 4), appreciated the quality of its teacher. When the authorities in the capital intended to replace him by another religious functionary, the ten representatives of the small community signing the document categorically refused to accept any teacher other than the old one, "because of the debt of gratitude which our children owe him for their education."[10]

The average tuition fee, as several official documents tell us, was half a dirhem per pupil per week, when the community bore the cost. Three brothers attending one school were granted a reduction.[11] When provincial towns, like al-Maḥalla in Lower Egypt, promised to pay its teacher 20 dirhems a week, it was probably done under the supposition that around forty boys would attend his school.[12] In the house of a well-to-do merchant, when the private teacher threatened to quit, his salary was raised from 10 to 15 dirhems per week, or 1-½ dinars per month. (In those years, as often, the ratio of gold and silver coins was one to forty.) Thus, he received for private tuition as much as he would have for the teaching of thirty children in a kuttāb.[13] In addition to the fees, "extras" were vowed by the communities, and presents were given to the teachers on holidays, for example, on Hanukkah, the Feast of the Lights, which coincides approximately with Christmas. A private teacher would receive such presents also from the grandmother of his pupil, for she (and not the mother) was the lady of the house.[14]

Fees were normally paid on Thursday and in the family budget were therefore called "The School Thursday." That day was chosen in order to enable the teacher to buy the provisions for the Sabbath (which began on Friday late in the afternoon) on Thursday night, or, in the case of Muslims, for Friday. We have to keep in mind that it was the husband, and not the housewife, who did the shopping.[15]

Sometimes the community was tardy in paying, and we read once about school fees paid after the death of the teacher. Complaints of teachers about extreme poverty are not absent from the Geniza papers. After the holiday vacations, when no classes were held and no fees collected, a teacher asks for a loan of wheat, or its equivalent in cash, as he had nothing to eat.[16] Even a prominent teacher, known to us from many documents, in one of which he states that he taught "the sons of the great," had to ask for an advance, once after having spent all his savings on doctors and medications during an illness, and once after having paid the poll tax.[17] Particularly distressing is a letter written in a good hand and pleasant style, in which a teacher implores the addressee to enable him to buy a medicine and two ounces of sugar for his ill infant child, while he assures him that he and his wife had no money for even a pound of bread.[18]

These examples of poverty are partly to be explained by the fact that, as far as we are able to judge from the very rich documentation in the Geniza records, teachers in Egypt at that time were to a large extent foreigners: refugees, driven out of their homeland by war or persecution, or others who had lost their livelihood through some catastrophe affecting them personally. It is natural that it took some time for the displaced persons to find a suitable appointment; natural, too, for the communities employing them to exploit their indigence.[19] We find foreigners as teachers not only in the large cities of Egypt, but also in the smaller towns. They came from all over the Mediterranean basin: France, Spain, Sicily, Morocco, Algeria, Tunisia, Tripolitania (Libya), Syria, and even Mosul, and in various instances the circumstances that forced them to leave their countries are told.[20] Naturally, Palestine contributed the largest number of refugee teachers, for it was the home of Hebrew learning, it was nearest to Egypt, and, above all, it suffered from incessant warfare and devastation all throughout the Geniza period.

In general, however, teaching was regarded as a comparatively sure and independent source of income, and the records that express or exemplify this fact are more numerous in the Geniza papers than the complaints registered. Thus, a scholar, a Palestinian refugee who served as teacher in a little town in Egypt, refused to take on additional duties in order to avoid conflicts with the local community leader, who was also a Palestinian. In explaining his situation, he says: "I confine myself to the teaching of the boys in order to remain independent of anyone." [21] A court scribe and teacher from a prominent family in Alexandria which had provided the local community with physicians and judges for about two hundred years writes to a friend: "It is only by the teaching of boys that we have bread to eat." [22] With regard to several teachers we possess legal documents or other records showing that they had been able to give considerable loans, or that they left sizable sums to relatives, or that they had possessed a slave girl or part of a house.[23] The Geniza has even preserved the story of a physician in a small place who undertook the teaching of schoolchildren in addition to his medical work, as happened when a local teacher, a Palestinian, had to betake himself to Cairo to pay his poll tax, for aliens had to pay theirs to a central office and not in the town where they were resident. The physician became so enthusiastic, not about his pedagogical success, but about the additional income accruing to him from teaching, that he did not let the children go back to their former teacher when the Palestinian returned from the capital. The document containing the rather ridiculous story is a complaint about the doctor's encroachment.[24]

As only persons with a good handwriting could become teachers, normally, it is natural that some of them served also as scribes, either to private persons, or to courts, or as copyists of books.[25] Some teachers, as the Geniza shows, were accomplished calligraphers.[26] The profession of copyist was connected with that of bookseller, and we find a number of teachers working in that field.[27] Another profession easily combined with teaching was that of the cantor, or singer who led the community in prayer.[28] It is perhaps worthwhile noting that in medieval times the English term "cantor" denoted the elementary teacher in the Song School, which was connected with the church.[29]

Although schoolteachers were not necessarily scholarly persons, there appear quite a number of them in the Geniza who were called *talmīd,* that is, scholar, and even ḥavēr, which corresponds to a doctor of law. The vicissitudes of fate, which forced persons of higher education to work in elementary schools, may have been partly the cause, but it certainly served to enhance the prestige of the teaching profession. In general, the teacher in the Geniza period seems to have enjoyed higher esteem than in late Roman times, when he was ridiculed by the popular pantomime as a stupid ignoramus. This notion was carried over into early Islam, where the imbecile schoolmaster remained the standing object of ridicule and scorn. So much so, indeed, that some learned Muslim lawyers ruled that a schoolmaster's testimony in court should be regarded as being worth only half that of a man (namely, like that of a woman, who, according to Muslim—and other medieval—notions was officially regarded as a creature of limited intelligence). The great viceroy of Iraq, al-Ḥajjāj (d. June, 714), was discredited and satirized for having served in his youth as a teacher. The tenth-century Muslim geographer Ibn Ḥawqal describes the people of Palermo, Sicily, as feebleminded because they held their schoolmasters in high regard.[30] Contempt for the teachers of children remained alive in Egypt until the very end of the Middle Ages, to judge from the stories of *The Arabian Nights* especially devoted to this subject.[31]

The Geniza documents demonstrate that the situation within the Jewish community differed considerably. Fathers addressing teachers do so respectfully, and not as employers talking to their employees; the communal officials, from the Nagid downward, do the same; and the letters emanating from the teachers themselves, as a rule, betray not only a good knowledge of Arabic and Hebrew, but also a certain degree of general culture. In 1237, when the government asked a delegation of ten representatives of the Jewish community in Egypt to testify to the proper election of David, the grandson of Maimonides, as Nagid, a schoolteacher, known to us from other sources, was among them.[32]

The safest indication of the comparatively high social position of the teacher in the Geniza society is the fact that in many instances persons signing a document add after the names of their fathers the word *ha-melammēd* (the teacher, Heb.).[33] No one would have done so had this occupation not been regarded as a title of honor. Nor would anyone have addressed Ephraim, "the distinguished member of the academy" and leader of the Jews of Fustat during the first half of the eleventh century, as "son of the melammēd Shemarya," had this not been a status symbol to a certain degree.[34] It is not impossible that precisely because the general standard of culture was not very high among the Egyptian Jews during the Geniza period, the schoolteacher, by his very profession a man of some erudition, occupied a higher social position there than in other, more scholarly, Jewish communities.

5. VOCATIONAL TRAINING

It was generally accepted that elementary education was to be complemented by some training in a trade or profession.[1] As a son usually followed his father's vocation, the training could often be given by the father himself. Otherwise, a parent had to bear the expenses of this additional stage of his son's education. Vocational schools, as far as we know, did not exist in those days. Instead, there were renowned craftsmen who undertook the training of the boys and were paid for it. As in other agreements concerning work, such arrangements with master artisans were made orally; at least a written one has not been found so far in the Geniza, although there are references to them. In a marriage contract with a divorcee, written 1110 in Minyat Ziftā, the bridegroom promises to feed and clothe the son of his future wife and to let him learn a craft. (He also undertook not to inflict on him corporal punishment or even to hurt him with words.)[2] A settlement between a husband and his wife, made in Old Cairo in 1244, obligates the father to provide his two sons with clothing, while the mother has to pay for the board of the smaller boy for ten years and for the board and poll tax of the elder for two years, as well as for his training in the art of silversmithing.[3]

Merchants, especially overseas traders, are forced by the very nature of their business to use written records. Consequently, we also learn more about initiation into commerce than with regard to manual work. There were different ways to train a novice in business. The most common practice was perhaps to send him to a renowned firm as "servant," that is, employee. Twice we hear of sons of first-ranking families in Tunisia apprenticing in prominent business houses of Old Cairo.[4] In two other instances such relationships were suggested or established between the members of the same family residing in the Maghreb and Egypt, respectively. In the midst of a long business letter from al-Mahdiyya, Tunisia, addressed, in spring, 1064, to the writer's sister's son, the following passage occurs: "I have a boy who is beginning to mature. If you think it is all right, consult the old man [the addressee's father and the writer's brother-in-law] whether I might send him to you next year so that he may stand before you [i.e., be your "servant" and apprentice]. The decision lies of course with the old man. He is a boy according to your taste!"[5]

A father from Palermo, Sicily, who had already entrusted his son to the care of a relative in Old Cairo, the great Ibn 'Awkal, who happened to be his mother's brother (and who had patently neglected this duty as he did with so many other honorary duties that he had taken upon himself) writes this (in an unfortunately much-damaged text): "Do not leave Joseph without your secure guidance. . . . Do not let him go around with [hole in the manuscript]. . . . He is with you. My son is your son. My pride is your pride. Oh God! Oh God! You know the boy. This is his first travel abroad. . . ." [6] The young man was called "pupil" and he referred to his former master as "teacher," even after having advanced to becoming his partner. The relationship itself was called "education." [7]

The relationship could develop into a strong allegiance, lasting a lifetime. In a letter from Sicily, sent in, or around, 1064, the writer reports that he was afraid of traveling with his merchandise to Egypt, as the enemy (the Normans) had captured and burned many ships enroute to the Levant; another merchant, however, who owed him thanks for his "education," undertook to transport the goods of his former master to Egypt, while he sent his own consignments, which he had already loaded on a ship going to Tunisia, with a third party.[8]

Frequently a father would train his son in independence by having business friends send modest quantities of goods to the young man who would deal in them "for the sake of learning." [9] Finally, as overseas business was done mostly by way of partnerships, fathers in different countries would agree to let their boys do business of moderate size jointly, until they would become experienced merchants.[10]

6. ADULT EDUCATION

Adult education is a modern term and carries with it the connotation of something exceptional: normally, we adults are satisfied with sending our children to school, while we regard ourselves free from the obligation of pursuing formal studies, except for professional purposes. The attitude of the society described in this book was approximately the opposite of our own. The elementary school was considered merely as a preparatory stage, and certainly was so in practice. Study, that is, the regular, habitual reading and expounding of the Bible and other sacred texts, was a duty incumbent on everyone and therefore could never be regarded as completed. The house of worship was also a house of learning, and the weekly and seasonal days of rest and prayer were devoted in the main to study. Particular care was taken to keep the synagogue illuminated during the night so that everyone who cared could study as long as he liked. In the introduction to an epistle of the Jewish community of Alexandria to that of Fustat the members of the latter are praised for studying throughout the night until daybreak.[1]

Since this attitude toward learning was general, the Geniza records refer to it only in exceptional circumstances. Once, there was communal strife in the provincial town of al-Maḥalla, and the dayyān Joseph, the spiritual leader of the community, had to leave the place. Several documents deal with this event. In one, a complaint is made that the study of the sacred books, as it had been pursued in that town in regular courses, as well as on Saturdays and holidays, was interrupted. In another it is said that, because of the absence of the spiritual leader, most people were sitting in the streets or in the shade of the sycamores on Saturdays and holidays instead of listening to the words of the sacred law in the synagogues.[2] Conversely, a scholar newly arrived in the same town (about a hundred years later) praised the people's regular attendance of the synagogue service, "their love of the Torah and its teachers." [3] A letter from Alexandria, which expresses deep gratitude of the community for the appointment of an inspired teacher and "judge," mentions that, prior to his arrival, some people had intended to move to Old Cairo because of the lack of spiritual guidance.[4] A young merchant in Old Cairo, describing his prolonged illness to his father, who was away on a business trip to India, adds that he still studies every evening with a scholar.[5]

This passage in a letter from al-Mahdiyya, Tunisia, in which the elder brother of Abū Zikrī Judah Ibn Sighmār congratulates him on the occasion of the birth of his firstborn, is particularly telling. After many good wishes and numerous details about commercial and communal affairs, he continues: "You wrote that you had gone over the Bible a second time and knew it, and, furthermore, that you studied the Mishnah and the Talmud. You made me extremely happy with this. It really is the crowning of your success and happiness . . . but the study of Arabic calligraphy should not be neglected." [6] When a young physician announced his intention to marry soon a relative of his correspondent, the latter answered that marrying a girl of a good family was certainly reasonable, but the study of the sacred law was even more meritorious. The young doctor was bidden to participate, together with his brother, who also was a physician, in the courses given by the local "judge." [7]

The frequency of the weekday courses is not indicated in our sources. One document on the subject (around 1240) mentions that, in the absence of his father, who had to hide for political reasons, the son of a judge in Old Cairo gave public classes, in addition to Saturday, on Sunday and Wednesday nights. The reason for the preference of these times is easily understood. Monday and Thursday were the "holy weekdays" in both Judaism and Islam (see chap. vii, sec. B, 3, below). Therefore, the nights preceding them were devoted to study. In Fatimid times, about two hundred years before this incident, the chief missionary of the Ismā'īlī sect (to which the Fatimids belonged) held his meetings with the scholars of the "House of Learning," the Fatimid school of propaganda, on Monday and Thursday.[8]

In addition to formal lectures read by scholars there were regular and certainly shorter readings of texts connected with the daily service, a conclusion drawn from a letter by a husband away on travel who tries to impress on his wife that only knowledge acquired in tender age and continuously enlarged throughout life secured a man an honored position in society. She had suggested taking a younger boy out of school, it seems because the teacher was too strict. The father warmly defends the teacher and encloses a letter to him with the request to pay special attention to the boy who was of course to remain in the kuttāb. As to two elder boys, with whose previous education the writer was clearly unsatisfied, he asks his wife to have them attend the synagogue service every morning and evening, "so that study may become habitual with them [lit., so that the Torah should be fixed in their hearts]," suggesting that at the time and place concerned, it was customary—as known from many other communities in later times—to conclude or precede the daily service by a short course of study, or at least, the reading by the community of several passages from a sacred, legal, or edificatory text.[9]

An avidly sought-after opportunity for adult study was to attend lectures, sermons, or disputations by visiting scholars (see sec. 9, below).

In view of the technicalities involved, no details can be given here of the exact content of adult courses or lectures. It should be said that adults had the same difficulties in obtaining books as did schoolchildren. When a group in Tinnīs, a town in Lower Egypt renowned for its linen industry, asked a friend in Old Cairo to provide them with certain books, the latter had to reply that he was unable to supply them, but sent others, specified in his letter, and advised his friends to study these, until he was able to find the books desired.[10]

Adult study was not confined to courses given in public. A scholar who had seen hard times reports that he had found favor, love, and honor in the house of a Maecenas, where he gave a study course every Saturday. Ten persons attended, which meant that the courses were concluded with congregational prayer (so that the master of the house did not need to betake himself to the synagogue in the afternoon; he also bought books copied by the scholar).[11]

In a short (and incomplete) memo of judge Elijah b. Zechariah to a notable it is stated that both the addressee and his father wished to take a refresher course in some biblical books, but felt somewhat embarrassed to frequent the writer's house for the purpose. The judge adds that there was no need to since he was prepared to come to their house.[12]

The attainments of laymen must sometimes have been impressive. We are able to recognize their achievements in several business letters that have been preserved, on the reverse side of which the recipients—merchants whose handwriting is well known to us—discuss theoretical problems or actual cases to be decided according to the sacred law. Their discussions are on a high level and do not differ in character from legal opinions written by a scholar.[13] These instances should not be regarded as exceptional. Many letters contain quotations from the Bible, and sometimes also from postbiblical literature, which are by no means mundane, and the poetical proems frequently preceding letters are seldom confined to conventional phrases. Thus, the general standard of adult education, or rather of the regular study by middle-class adults, cannot have been low. It seems that the studies of laymen and of professionals differed in quantity rather than in essence.

7. HIGHER STUDIES: ORGANIZATION

Jewish higher education in the High Middle Ages was distinguished by particular traits of organization, subject matter, and method. A clear distinction must be made between the yeshivas of Palestine and Iraq, which were age-old, ecumenical institutions with semilegislative prerogatives, and newly created ephemeral local schools, mostly centered on the persons of a founder and his immediate successors. Because of their importance as central authorities, the yeshivas of Baghdad and Jerusalem are treated also in the chapters on communal organization and jurisdiction (particularly chap. v, sec. A, 1).

Since the inception of the study of the Cairo Geniza some seventy-five years ago, Jewish scholarship has concentrated on the material it yields for the history of the yeshivas. Since most of the relevant texts are in Hebrew or Aramaic, or, when in Arabic, are easily recognizable as pertaining to the yeshivas because of the names or terms occurring in them, it stands to reason that by now the harvest to be gathered from a perusal of the Geniza is nearing completion. Nevertheless, a comprehensive, critical, and systematic description of these great institutions, which would also take into account contemporary Muslim and Christian higher learning, is still due. Naturally, the difficulties are considerable. The sources are perforce incomplete and sometimes ambiguous. Many changes, often recognizable in their effect rather than in their process, occurred during the centuries. Under these circumstances any attempt to present a coherent and concise, albeit elementary, outline of higher Jewish education in the Geniza period, as done in this and the following sections, necessarily exposes itself to criticism. I prefer such a risk to leaving this most important aspect of Jewish communal life without treatment.[1]

The term "academy," generally used for the Jewish houses of learning in Iraq and Palestine, is inadequate. The yeshiva was originally not an educational institution, at least not for young students.[2] It may well be that *yeshiva* is but a Hebrew version of Greek Sanhedrin *(synhedrion),* frequently mentioned in the New Testament, where it is translated as "council." Literally, it denotes a place where people sit together, namely, scholars who expound the Bible and the sacred law (actually or allegedly contained in it), issue authoritative rulings concerning the interpretation and application of the law, and decide legal and religious questions submitted to them. The yeshiva thus united the functions of an academy, a parliament, and a supreme court. To be sure, the members of the yeshiva never regarded themselves as law*makers,* for "the Law is God's" (Deuteronomy 1:17), but by deciding questions of public import by majority vote, they actually served as a legislative body. In the Geniza period, the yeshiva still preserved much of its original character and, in official documents, was called "The Great Sanhedrin." As stated, in most periods three yeshivas existed side by side, one in Palestine and two in Iraq. The yeshiva of Palestine was also called *ḥavūra,* The Corporation, or *ḥavūrat ha-ṣedeq,* The Righteous Corporation (a term reminiscent of the Dead Sea Scrolls), scholars qualified to interpret and to administer the sacred law and themselves living according to its strictest standards.[3]

The yeshiva originated in Hellenistic times, so that at the beginning of the Geniza period, it had behind it a history of more than a thousand years. The learned opinions on civil and ritual law, as well as the expositions of the Bible developed in these houses of learning, were collected around the conclusion of the second century of the Christian era and promulgated in an official corpus, called the

Mishnah. The subjects contained in the Mishnah and other works from the Mishnaic period were elaborated and discussed in the schools of Palestine and Babylonia (today Iraq) for another two to three centuries. Finally, the material accumulated was assembled in two comprehensive collections, the Palestinian Talmud and the Babylonian Talmud.[4] The Talmud, a term sometimes used to include the Mishnah as well, became the authoritative source of Jewish religion and law and formed the main object of study in the Jewish schools. A similar development took place independently in Islam. There too, at a certain juncture, the then existing literature on sacred law was canonized, "the door of free reasoning became closed," and all a scholar was allowed to do was to interpret the old sources, so as to adapt them to the needs of later developments.

The overwhelming authority of the Talmud may be partly explained by the decline of the yeshivas at the time of its conclusion (approximately 400 in Palestine and 500 in Iraq). Palestine, then under Byzantine rule, was afflicted with terrible oppression and persecution. Iraq, which during the same period formed part of the Persian empire, also suffered from great instability. The subsequent Muslim conquest, although granting relief in certain respects, was a devastating shock at first for the sedentary population, a shock that took centuries to heal. Thus there was a prolonged eclipse of the schools. When they recovered at the beginning of the eighth century, there existed no literary work able to compete with the massive volume of the Talmud, which represented the accumulated wisdom of the yeshivas during their most fertile periods. Moreover, the pervading spirit of Near Eastern and European civilization at that time was in favor of authoritative compendiums that were regarded as containing in final form the entire content of a certain field of knowledge. This tendency prevailed in secular sciences, such as medicine, not less than in religious studies.

There are fairly detailed descriptions of the yeshivas of Iraq, dating from the tenth and the twelfth centuries, and responsa emanating from them have been preserved by the thousands. The membership of the yeshiva was limited to seventy, as was the Sanhedrin a thousand years before; there was, however, no limitation to the number of scholars attached to it. The students were called "sons of a master," or "sons of the house of their master," for, unlike the scholars, they needed the guidance and supervision of a teacher. The majority of the members and scholars did not live on the campus, but served as community officials, or were even engaged in a trade or profession. Twice a year, however, at the end of the summer and the end of the winter, there was a month of common study, when everyone was required to attend. The Gaon, or head of the academy, would announce which section of the Talmud should be studied by the participants during the intervening months, while at the *kalla,* as the month of study was called, the sections were expounded under his personal leadership. While teaching, the Gaon was assisted by "interpreters" *(meturgeman* or *turgeman,* an ancient Near Eastern word, which has found its way into English in the form of *dragoman).* Originally, turgemans were mere broadcasters who carried the words of the master to a large audience; in the Geniza period they relayed to the Gaon the questions raised by the audience, insofar as they themselves were unable to supply the answers and conveyed the explanations to the questioners. A German Jewish traveler recounts with amazement that the Gaon Samuel b. Eli (in office 1164-1193) expounded at one time several sections of the Talmud to an audience of two thousand participants, each section being transmitted by a different turgeman. Muslim higher studies had similar arrangements, and A. S. Tritton, in his book on Muslim education in the Middle Ages, expresses the belief that the Jewish institution served as a model to the Muslim.[5]

At the spring kalla, the many questions addressed to the yeshiva from all over the world were discussed by the assembled scholars. Thus the answers could be sent with the mail or the merchants who set out from Baghdad immediately after Passover (Easter). As repeatedly emphasized, in Jewish juridical practice, these responsa fulfilled the same task as do decisions of superior courts in present-day legal life.[6]

In accordance with the triple role of the yeshiva as high court, educational establishment, and legislative body, it was led by a committee of three, consisting of the Gaon, the *āv,* or "father," that is, president of the court, who served as the deputy head of the yeshiva, and the scribe. The last was in charge of the responsible task of formulating the answers to the queries addressed to the yeshiva, and some Gaons groomed their sons by appointing them to this office. As a rule, in addition to the Gaon, only the president of the court appears regularly in the letters in which greetings are extended from the staff of the yeshiva. He was the second in command (as he was in the centuries preceding the Christian era) and normally replaced the Gaon after his death.

Besides the Gaon and the two assistant dignitaries, the yeshiva was led by scholars styled *rōsh ha-seder,* or head of the row, each of whom was in charge of one of the "rows" (originally seven), in which the members of the academy had their fixed seats in order of precedence.

According to the intensity and success of their participation in the activities of the yeshiva, as well as the availability of seats, the members were promoted or demoted and their emoluments increased or decreased. When, during the period described in this book, Jewish houses of learning sprang up all over the Mediterranean basin, their heads often bore this title of rōsh ha-seder. Various other dignitaries of the Babylonian yeshivas appear in the letters of their heads, especially the *allūf,* or "distinguished member," a title also borne by some prominent alumni in Fustat, Qayrawān, and other cities of the West.[7]

Only persons occupying a seat "in the rows" were supposed to take the floor during learned disputations. Other scholars and the students participated as auditors. They studied in institutions attached to the yeshiva, called *midrāsh.* (This abbreviated term is more common in the Geniza period than the older *bēth ha-midrāsh,* lit., a place where the Scriptures were expounded, but used in the general sense of a school of higher studies.) It stands to reason that there exists some connection between the word for the Muslim houses of learning, *madrasa,* and this term. In the letters of the Gaons the heads of these midrāshim appear regularly after the heads of the rows. They are followed by the scholars reading courses for the broader public, and the latter by the "group leaders." We do not yet know what the latter designation means, but since it also appears in a house of learning even in the small town of Oria in southern Italy, these "groups" must have been a common feature.[8]

The lowest grade of teachers in the yeshiva was the *tannā'īm* (lit., "repetitors," those who make repeat), persons who knew the text of sections of the Mishnah or the Talmud with their correct cantillations by heart and who trained students to memorize them by rote. Cantillation, reciting a text in a singing manner with clear indication of short and long intervals, was of highest practical importance. For, unlike the biblical text, the Mishnah and Talmud texts at that time carried neither punctuation marks nor vowel signs. Therefore, both the pronunciation of the individual words and the correct division of a sentence into its various components depended entirely on the oral tradition, the preservation of which was much helped by the singsong accompanying the recitation. As a rule the repetitors were not learned men; often, blind boys with a good memory were educated to do the job. Even a great scholar, though, had occasion to seek the help of these walking texts for ascertaining the correct reading of a difficult passage.

The Yemenites, who have retained the ancient institution of the tannā'īm down to the twentieth century, possess a sound knowledge of the correct pronunciation of the talmudic texts, especially of the Mishnah, a tradition lost to the European Jews. It is very significant indeed that as early as the twelfth century the German Jewish traveler referred to above mentions the cantillation in use in the yeshiva of Baghdad as something noteworthy.[9]

The Palestinian yeshiva, or Righteous Corporation, was smaller and of less importance in the period under discussion than the Iraqian Jewish schools. It was governed by a board of seven, headed, like the Iraqian yeshivas, by the Gaon and the president of the court. The other members were called Third, Fourth, Fifth, and so on, who, at the death or resignation of their superiors, moved up in strict order of precedence. Therefore, we find in the Geniza papers a person once styled Sixth and later Fourth, or another being first Fourth and then Third; or a scholar, first appearing as Fourth, finally advancing to the post of Gaon, or head of the school. Sometimes, a dignitary died before he had opportunity to be promoted; his title, let us say the Sixth, would then be used by his descendants as a family name. Important documents were signed by the Gaon, the president of the court, and the Third,[10] while, at public appearances, the Third sat at the Gaon's left, and the president at his right.[11]

We see that the Palestinian yeshiva, like the Iraqian, was administered by an executive committee of three, which tallies with the fact that a Jewish court was normally composed of three persons. Only in one exceptional incident, a settlement after internal strife, in which the president of the court had laid claim to the position of the Gaon, do we hear of an executive committee of five. According to that settlement, made in October, 1042, the president of the court and the Fourth, also acting as judge, resided in Ramle, then the administrative capital of Palestine, while the Gaon had his seat in Jerusalem, where, as we know from other sources, the educational establishment connected with the yeshiva was located.[12] The Gaon, Solomon b. Judah, was very old at that time, and, as we know from his own letters, physically and spiritually weakened. The Gaon normally had overriding authority also in juridical matters. When he was younger, Solomon b. Judah himself exercised it freely. In a letter to his son Abraham (who temporarily sojourned in Egypt) he writes that he spent most of his time in Ramle sitting as judge, doing so "at the request of the community" and "at the demand of the parties." The office of the president of the court was a delegated authority, not an independent position. Naturally, the actual working of this office, like that of any other in the world, depended on the strength of the personage occupying it.[13]

The semiannual months of study, the most characteristic feature of the Babylonian yeshivas, had no equivalent in Palestine. The reason for this fundamental difference lies in economic and social conditions. During the eighth through the tenth centuries, the period in which the Jewish ecumenical seats of learning prospered most, Iraq and Iran were among the richest countries of the world. They contained a very large Jewish population, which was able to maintain hundreds and even thousands of scholars as community officials or as part-time students. In Palestine, the scholars, as a rule, devoted all their time to study and prayer, living either on donations sent from all over the world to the yeshiva or to them personally, or on savings made before their retirement. Thus, in Palestine, there was no need for seasonal gatherings. The many "fellows of the academy," who lived in Egypt, Syria, and other countries of the Mediterranean, had opportunity to meet during the holy pilgrimage to Jerusalem, which took place during the autumn festivals and which culminated in the great assembly held on the Mount of Olives during the Feast of Tabernacles. This assembly decided religious and communal issues and was a counterpart to the spring month of study in Babylonia, when the questions addressed to the yeshivas were discussed by the participants.

After the conquest of Jerusalem by the Seljuks in 1071 and long before the advent of the Crusaders, the Palestinian yeshiva moved to Tyre, then the most flourishing seaport on the Lebanese coast. The leading scholar of the Shāfiʿīs, then the Muslim school of law most prominent in Jerusalem, did the same, and perhaps there was some connection between the two moves.[14] After a temporary sojourn in Damascus and other places, the Palestinian yeshiva was transferred to Old Cairo in 1127, where it continued to exist for most of the twelfth century, until it was replaced by the school that gathered around the towering personality of Maimonides (d. 1204). Another branch had its seat for some time in Damascus. Maimonides' descendants through five generations to the middle of the fourteenth century combined the office of the head of the Egyptian Jews with that of the head of a school, in line with contemporary Muslim usage. In the If he did so at all, he assumed his father's post only after his seniors in rank had preceded him in office.[15]
yeshivas proper, with rare exceptions, a son did not follow his father.

In accordance with the medieval phenomenon of the "wandering scholars," popular in both the Christian and Islamic worlds, the yeshivas of Iraq attracted students from many countries, even those outside the orbit of Arabic speech, such as France, Italy, and Byzantium.[16] It is natural that only a fraction of those who desired to pursue higher studies had the means and courage to embark on the long journey. Therefore, local schools of higher learning began to appear wherever a large Jewish community was formed. These schools mostly gathered around an outstanding teacher. The Geniza occasionally informs us about the circumstances surrounding their foundation or about schools whose existence had not been known at all, among them the midrāsh of Old Cairo.

Because of the propinquity of the Palestinian academy, which for its maintenance relied heavily on the Jewish communities of Egypt, there was no strong incentive to have a separate house of higher learning in Fustat. But in the last third of the tenth century, when an eclipse in the fortunes of the Palestinian yeshiva coincided with the prominence in Egypt of a great scholar of Iraqian training, Shemarya b. Elhanan (whose father had already been active there), a midrāsh, or college, was formed in Fustat by him. This development may have been connected with the advent of the Fatimids and the fact that at that time Egypt had become the center of a great empire, as well as the fountainhead of intensive, thoroughly organized religious propaganda on behalf of the Isma'īlīs, the ruling sect. We should keep in mind that, at the same time and place, a former Jew from Iraq, Ya'qūb (Jacob) Ibn Killis, convert to Islam and Fatimid vizier, personally presided over the establishment of the nucleus of what was later to become the famed Muslim University of al-Azhar. Shemarya's son and successor, Elhanan, reports that before al-Ḥākim's persecutions, his college had been in receipt of a government grant and he himself raised funds in Damascus and Acre, presumably, as surmised above, (p. 29), in the congregations adhering to the Babylonian rite. Elhanan was an ambitious man, and, as a critical writer recounts, had his lectures broadcast by a scholar specifically appointed for the task, a custom, we remember, prevailing in the yeshivas. Bans were pronounced against him by several authorities, presumably because of his usurpation of such prerogatives of the higher institutions, and when he appeared at one of the yearly assemblies on the Mount of Olives, he was expelled. He recanted immediately and recognized the authority of the Jerusalem yeshiva.[17] In any event, his school was *not* a yeshiva, and he himself refers to it in his letters solely with the terms midrāsh or bēth midrāsh, a college for students.[18]

"Students," to be sure, does not necessarily mean undergraduates.

By the injunctions of their religions, Jews (like Muslims) were lifetime students, and the dividing lines between adult education and higher studies were fluid. It was natural, therefore, to find a son and his father studying together in the same midrāsh,[19] or for a prominent physician to be styled "main speaker and prince of the midrāsh," no doubt because he often took the floor in the learned discussions following or interrupting a lecture.[20]

The ecumenical yeshivas were not always happy with the establishment of a local midrāsh. The letter critical of Elhanan b. Shemarya cited above emphasizes that it was not so much the impartment of theoretical knowledge as the living tradition of the yeshiva which was essential for the formation of a future scholar. By this he meant the discussions and ways of reasoning by which its members arrived at their learned opinions and its judges at their legal decisions.[21]

Material considerations were also involved. In one of his early letters Sherira Gaon (in office 967-1006), the father of Hay, decried the dangerous competition of the local colleges at a time when the Baghdad yeshivas were faced with financial disaster. "How can you believe," he writes, "that you will remain intact and that your schools will not suffer while the yeshiva goes to pieces? We are your heads, as it is written: 'Your heads—your tribes' [Deuteronomy 29:9] [a pun: there are no tribes where there are no heads]. How can a body remain intact when the head is sick! The body goes after the head." And the Gaon goes so far as to apply to the yeshiva the words of the Prophet Haggai (1:9) said with reference to the Temple of Jerusalem which the Jews, faced with economic difficulties after their return from Babylonia, were loath to complete: "My house lies in ruins while you busy yourselves each with his own house."[22]

It would be erroneous, however, to assume, as has so often been done, that the rise of the local midrāshim automatically meant the ruin of the ecumenical yeshivas. The opposite is true. In no time did Jewish learning flourish more in Qayrawān and other cities of Tunisia then during the first half of the eleventh century when the great Nissīm b. Jacob (d. 1062) developed in Qayrawān the midrāsh of his father[23] and his older contemporary and compatriot Hananel b. Hushiel wrote there the first comprehensive commentary on the Talmud (which still adorns any printed standard edition of that classic).[24] Yet from no period do we know of so many responsa going from Baghdad to Tunisia and of such rich donations sent from there to the yeshivas of Iraq and Palestine as from the first decades of that century. The intimate knowledge of the leading personalities of the yeshivas and the warm interest taken in their well being and other affairs displayed in the letters from Qayrawān seem to indicate that their writers once had passed fruitful years of study in those seats of learning.[25]

The decline and final dissolution of the ecumenical yeshivas were the result of local developments, which no support from afar, financial or spiritual, could permanently remedy. As early as 985, that is, at the very time when Sherira Gaon wrote the letters summarized above, Baghdad was described by so keen an observer as the Muslim traveler al-Muqaddasī as a city living on its past. There were ups and downs, but Iraq and western Iran, which in early Islamic times had harbored the majority of the Jewish people, continuously decayed from the tenth century until the Mongol invasions of the thirteenth finally put an end to their preponderance in the Islamic and Jewish worlds. Palestine, similarly tormented by incessant warfare, raids, and misgovernment from the later part of the tenth century, also became utterly unfit to serve as a spiritual center, until the yeshiva had to go into exile and dispersed. It was not lack of support by the Jewish communities of the diaspora which brought about the eclipse of the yeshivas, but their gradual disappearance that necessitated the development of local seats of learning.

The local schools, it seems, held their courses mostly in the synagogues, although not necessarily in the main hall, as proved by the story of the large mat ordered for the midrāsh of Elhanan b. Shemarya (see n. 18). Similarly, in Islam, down to and including the tenth century, teachers were regularly reported to have had their "circles" in the mosques. In a letter of appointment of a synagogue beadle in Old Cairo, the most important duty imposed on him was regular and adequate lighting of the synagogue, in order to enable the scholars to study during the night. This, too, has its parallels in Islam. In a query addressed to Maimonides from a city situated north of Jerusalem (such as Damascus or Aleppo), reference is made to a college building separate from the synagogue. The mention of the attendance of the midrāsh in Old Cairo (see nn. 19-20, 30), may point in the same direction.[26]

The maintenance of the schools, as well as the rights acquired by the degrees conferred by them, are closely connected with community life in general and are treated in chapter v, above.

Before leaving this topic, it should be noted that any dayyān, or local spiritual leader, would give courses in the Talmud, at that time the subject of higher studies (see next section), if he found qualified ters.[27] Even from Palmyra, situated in the heart of the Syrian desert, students. There are many references to this fact in the Geniza let-a president of the court who held his appointment from the exilarch and from the "gates of the yeshivas of the Diaspora" (i.e., Iraq), reports that scholars from Aleppo (a five days' march from Palmyra) and even two from Christian countries studied the Mishnah and Talmud with him. The dayyān had a good reputation, and the community in the then (around 1020) still flourishing caravan city certainly took pride in maintaining some resident scholars studying with their rabbi.[28]

Finally, because of the existence of many scholarly persons without any official status, there was plenty of opportunity for private study. A learned merchant would return in the evening to his store, and, whoever wished to would assemble there and "read" with him.[29] This occupation was in lieu of other night entertainments such as storytelling and music, also reported in the Geniza (no belly dancers found there yet). We even read about a young man who had just married into a Fustat family and who, in addition to attending the local midrāsh, "studied" regularly in private with a learned relative.[30]

The organization of the Jewish houses of learning should be studied in comparison with their contemporary Christian and Muslim counterparts. Betweeen Muslim higher studies—which up till approximately A.D. 1000 lacked all form of organization, each teacher by himself representing a school—and the authoritative Christian organization of study within the framework of the Church and the monastic orders, Jewish learning, with its collegial arrangements, somehow held the middle. Despite mutual influences effective in different historical periods, each system, it seems, developed essentially along its own lines. A more detailed comparative study promises interesting results.

8. HIGHER STUDIES: SYLLABUS AND METHODS

A Jewish scholar from Iraq, writing in Egypt around the middle of the twelfth century, described the various stages of study approximately as follows: If we disregard uneducated persons, people can be classified in three categories: the broad masses, scholars, and doctors. The masses have learned the written and the oral law, namely, the Five Books of Moses and Saadya's prayerbook (which comprised also the religious injunctions connected with prayer and the keeping of the Sabbath and the holidays); the scholars have studied, in addition to the Pentateuch, the other sections of the Bible, as well as the "ordinances," that is, codified law (the work the writer recommends for the purpose is of enormous length); the doctor is at the highest level, a man who has also made himself familiar with the Mishnah, the Talmud, and their commentaries.[1]

The description cited certainly fails to do justice to a far more variegated reality, but brings out in clear relief the essentials of the syllabus of Jewish higher studies in those times. A scholar was a man who had studied the whole Bible, in particular the books of the Prophets and the hagiographic books along with the aids necessary for a proper understanding of their language and purport. In addition, he had to know the religious and civil law. The scholar was able to deliver a sermon, to write a highly literary epistle, and to serve as an assistant judge. A doctor of the law, usually a man bearing the title "member of the academy," had studied the sources of the law and the learned literature expounding them and was therefore entitled to write a legal opinion on a question addressed to him. Only persons possessing this qualification were appointed to the posts of judges and spiritual leaders in larger communities.

We are in a position to know these courses of study in detail owing not only to the voluminous mass of books and fragments of books from this period actually found in the Geniza, but also to the many book lists preserved, which give an idea of the libraries of individual persons and the studies they presumably pursued. From all this material emerge the following facts:

The study of the Hebrew Bible, together with its commentaries, its translations in Aramaic and Arabic (which also served as commentaries), its homiletic expositions, and the special treatises devoted to it, formed the most important constituent of the general curriculum of any educated man. With it was closely connected the study of the Hebrew language, its grammar and lexicography, and its practical application in writing letters and poems. Many fragments of translations into Arabic of the Bible, commentaries, and treatises give the impression of being notes of students and teachers rather than finished literary products.

In this respect, there was a marked difference between the countries represented in the Cairo Geniza and those of central Europe, especially at the turn of the century from the twelfth to the thirteenth. Just as the Christian scholars in Europe began to neglect the study of the Bible because of their preoccupation with scholasticism, so, among European Jews, did the Bible, and, with it, the Hebrew language, cease to be a subject of higher education when it became confined to the Talmud and cognate disciplines. It is most characteristic that in as early a period as the last third of the twelfth century, the German Jewish traveler referred to earlier (see sec. 7, n. 5) should have expressed his astonishment at the expert knowledge of the Bible and the exact pronunciation of Hebrew displayed by even the common people everywhere in Eastern countries.

The second prerequisite of a scholarly person was a knowledge of religious and civil law—simple, positive law, to be sure, not familiarity with its ancient sources and intricate niceties. Maimonides' famous code was not a "first," as is often erroneously assumed, but the crowning termination of a long line of development, which had begun four hundred years before him, in the eighth century, that is, at the same time that the Muslim scholars tried to codify their own sacred law (or perhaps even a little earlier). During the tenth and eleventh centuries it became the fashion for Gaons, or heads of the Jewish academies, to write monographs on special aspects of Jewish law. For the most part these monographs were written in Arabic and used Muslim legal terms. The outspoken didactic character of the monographs gives the impression that they were originally composed as lectures to undergraduate students, each course term being devoted to one or several special topics. Only a small fraction of these lecture courses was devoted to religious ritual, such as liturgy and ritual slaughtering, whereas the vast majority dealt with civil law, subjects such as legal formularies, sale, gift, preemption, inheritance, money orders, court procedure, the duties of the judges, and similar topics.

This emphasis on civil law had its good reasons. In the period under discussion, Jewish legal practice still insisted on the ancient principle of collegial courts. Even the smallest matters, as we see in the Geniza documents, were attended to by three judges. This could be achieved only if there existed a considerable supply of laymen reasonably familiar with civil law. It was to these future puisne judges that the lecture courses for everyday law were directed.

In this respect, too, there was a fundamental difference between the countries of the Geniza area and those of central Europe. In the latter, the Jewish communities, at least from the twelfth century, had only limited legal autonomy. Therefore, the course of higher studies contained not much of applied civil law. The French Jewish scholars, many of whom emigrated to the Levant shortly after 1200, were often more learned talmudists than their Eastern colleagues, but, because of their lack of practical training, made poor judges.[2]

In Eastern countries, too, opinion was divided as to whether the study of handbooks of the sacred law was sufficient preparation for its correct application. The controversies about Maimonides' famous Code of Law is the best indication of this state of affairs. A Geniza document, preceding the publication of Maimonides' code by many years, serves to illustrate. When a new muqaddam was appointed to the provincial town of al-Maḥalla, he examined the ritual slaughterer and when he found him merely to have studied a handbook on the subject, disqualified him and relieved him of his post, but promised to teach him the relevant sections of the Talmud.[3] Similarly, a learned Yemenite living in Egypt vehemently attacked Abraham, Maimonides' son and successor, for his failure to quote the talmudic sources in his public lectures.[4] The general trend in the East, however, was to base the first stage of higher studies on codified law. Only the select few, those who prepared themselves for the posts of judge and spiritual leader, made extensive studies of the Talmud and the literature that accrued around it. In Yemen this system of study prevailed until the termination of the Jewish settlement in that country.

A similar controversy raged concerning the upper stage of higher studies. Since the conclusion and canonization of the Talmud, both the practice and theory of Jewish sacred law had undergone changes. These changes were largely embodied in the responsa, or learned opinions, issued by the yeshivas of Babylonia and, to a smaller degree, of Palestine. Collections of these opinions appear regularly in the Geniza booklists and, as their titles show, were arranged according to different principles. Either they would bear a general designation, such as "Correspondence with the Academies," or indicate the towns to which the learned opinions were sent, such as "Answers given to," or "Questions asked by the Scholars of Sijilmāsa [Morocco]," or "Qayrawān [Tunisia];" or expressly stated would be the names of the scholars submitting queries or those of the heads of the academies replying to them, or both. Later, arrangements according to subject matter became the standard practice. Sometimes, an answer would run the length of a whole book.[5]

Wherever feasible, learned opinions were based on detailed discussions of the relevant passages in the Talmudic literature, which were usually quoted in full. There thus arose the question whether a scholar dealing with a problem of the sacred law was bound to consult the ancient sources, or whether it was permitted, or even preferable, to base one's decision on a responsum of the heads of the academies, which in any case would quote the pertinent source material. Ibn Migash, the leading Spanish Jewish scholar of the twelfth century (d. 1141), decided in favor of the second alternative, especially for persons whose command of the unwieldy mass of talmudic literature was doubtful.[6] By chance, the correspondence about the controversy which seems to have led to Ibn Migash's famous ruling has been found in the Geniza. During frequent visits to Spain, the

Cairene India trader Ḥalfōn b. Nethanel ha-Levi conversed with the savants of that country about topics of law, theology, and poetry. Once, one of them, whom he had referred to a responsum of the Gaons, retorted in an unusually impolite letter that legal matters could be decided only by recourse to the primary sources found in the Talmud. He would prove it by submitting the matter to the Rāv, meaning Ibn Migash.[7] The writer does not give the impression of being a particularly competent scholar, which would explain Ibn Migash's ruling that it was safer to rely on the considered opinion of a late authority than to follow one's own lights in the interpretation of ancient sources often difficult to understand. Anyhow, Ibn Migash's decision must have reflected the general trend of opinion in his time. Otherwise, the book lists in the Geniza would not contain collections of responsa as frequently as copies of the Talmud itself. Clearly, the responsa formed a major subject of the upper stage of higher studies.

In educational methods, learning by rote the exact wording and cantillation of an ancient text was regarded as a prerequisite for its proper interpretation in higher studies, as it was in the elementary school. To us who make practically no use of learning by heart in higher education this attitude seems strange, but it was based on old tradition and regarded as the only sound method.[8] How deep-rooted such pedagogical convictions are was brought home to me while visiting a school of Moroccan Jews in Jerusalem which had a good reputation. To my amazement the boys recited by heart long passages from the Talmud—complicated legal discussions in a mixture of Aramaic and Hebrew—without knowing a single word of the content (enhancing the excellence of the performance in the eyes of their teacher). When he perceived that the visitor seemed to be less enthusiastic, he was astonished and asked: "Does your honor not know that trying to reason and to interpret a text before knowing it by heart is damaging to the brain?"

Anyone who visited the Muslim University of al-Azhar in Cairo a few decades ago remembers a courtyard full of students running about memorizing texts. How far they understood the contents, I do not know. One whom I asked was perplexed at the very question. But one should not generalize.

According to a letter of Sherira Gaon, the interpretation of texts was done by the students preparing questions at home which they were to ask the teacher in class. When the students failed to compose appropriate questions, the teacher would suggest some himself.[9] The great institution of the responsa was mainly a continuation of study after the young scholar had left the yeshiva, for the major part of the responsa preserved are answers to theoretical questions arising from the scrutiny of classical texts. The head of the yeshiva would evaluate the questions received from abroad in accordance with the acumen displayed in them and mark the progress made. The correspondence with the yeshiva of individual scholars or those of a city represents a continuous dialogue that includes references to previous letters, sometimes also to those of other scholars forwarded by the writers.[10]

Dictation by the teacher or his "interpreter" was the normal procedure in the Muslim madrasa, but, as far as we know, not in the Jewish schools of higher learning. There the students kept a personal diary, called by the ancient Hebrew term *megillat setārīm,* or "secret scroll," in which they recorded whatever seemed worth noting. When they themselves became masters some would continue to note their solutions of problems or answers to questions addressed to them or any other scholarly matter worthy of record. It is reported of several outstanding men, including Maimonides and his son Abraham, that they kept scientific diaries of this type. The most famous case is *the* Megillat Setārīm, the Secret Scroll, of Nissīm b. Jacob of Qayrawān, which was published during his lifetime and which became a classic, quoted and discussed by scores of medieval authors. Since the master had written down the notes at random (or rather in the sequence he had studied the topics, it was necessary to provide them with a "key" indexing them according to subject matter. One such key has indeed been found in the Geniza.[11] The notes were written partly in Hebrew (particularly those discussing classical texts) and partly in Arabic (mostly answers to actual questions or observations on popular usages and cognate matters). Interestingly, as proved by various Geniza finds, the Secret Scroll was published in two separate parts, one in Arabic and one in Hebrew. The Hebrew section, I assume, was prepared for readers in Europe who could not read Arabic.[12]

Although the most prominent contributions to Jewish theology and philosophy happened to be made by scholars heading yeshivas, these subjects seem not to have formed part of the regular syllabus of the establishments for Jewish higher studies. They belonged rather to the domain of secular education. Obviously, it was believed that only persons who prepared themselves for the medical profession and therefore became familiar with Greek science, stood in need of philosophic and theological studies. They were exposed to the onslaught of another world of thought and for this reason needed protection by proper training in the right philosophy and theology.

For an overall appreciation of the educational system described, see chapter x.

9. SCHOLARS, JUDGES, PREACHERS

Professional scholars normally served the community in one capacity or another. In principle, however, it was not public service that distinguished them and made them eligible for emoluments from the communal chest and gifts from private persons, but the very fact that they devoted time to study which others would use for worldly gain. It was for this reason that the community regarded it a sacred duty to contribute to their upkeep. The legal definition of a town, as opposed to a village, in Jewish law is that it was a place that had at least ten *baṭlānīm,* "persons who do not work," which means, who renounce or reduce their profitable occupations for the benefit of study and the service of the community.[1] In the Geniza papers, such persons were designated as students of the sacred law, *benē Torah,* literally, "the sons of the Torah." [2]

The general designation comprised very different grades of scholarship and was applied to occupations varying widely in character and social standing. The donation of an orchard for the benē Torah in Damascus, described in *Med. Soc.,* I, 122, was made to them "for not working, but devoting their time to study." [3] A list of students of the sacred law from the last quarter of the eleventh century enumerates twenty-nine in Fustat and fourteen in (New) Cairo. Of this total of forty-three persons, one was called the *rayyis,* or head of the Jews in the Fatimid empire (who had his seat in Cairo), another called *rabbēnū,* "our master," meaning the leading scholar and religious authority in the twin city, two judges, five "members" of the yeshiva, three rāvs, or "masters," at least six cantors, one teacher, and five beadles. A permanently disabled man and one blind man are also listed, while details for some persons mentioned only by name are known to us from other Geniza documents. Many physically handicapped appear in the rolls of indigents who were maintained by the community; here, however, the two men are listed as learned people with special privileges.[4]

Some details in this list call for comment. The degree that normally entitled a person to spiritual leadership in a Jewish community in Geniza times was that of ḥāvēr, or member of the yeshiva of Jerusalem, or an equivalent degree from one of the two yeshivas of Iraq, or both. The term *rabbī* or *rāv,* "master," which in Europe became the usual title of a Jewish spiritual leader, at that time designated in the East a prominent scholar, whose legal opinions were regarded as authoritative, like that of a *muftī* in Islam. In our list, the title is attached to the names of persons from France, Tunisia, and Damascus, respectively.[5] The strange fact that in this list and in another, contemporary one only one teacher is mentioned does not mean that the many other teachers in the twin city—some of whom are known to us by name from that time—were ignoramuses, but that teaching was a full-time, remunerative occupation, wherefore those practicing it did not qualify as students of the sacred law in the sense defined. The one teacher listed most probably taught orphaned and poor children and therefore received his fees from the communal chest.

Despite the frequency of occurrence in the Geniza records of the title ḥāvēr, or member of the academy, not a single certificate testifying its conferment has thus far been found among them. The reason for this is, no doubt, the fact that such a license was a source of pride not only for its bearer, but also for his descendants, and was therefore jealously guarded and never discarded and thrown into the Geniza. But everything carefully preserved and treasured in private homes has been lost. Only papers that sooner or later were regarded by their proprietors as being without value have come down to us. Yet we are able to form an idea about the contents of such certificates, since references to them are found in other Geniza documents. The act of the bestowal of the degree was designated by the biblical phrase "laying hand upon the disciple" (Numbers 27:18), which symbolized the transfer of the spirit from the initiated to the uninitiated (cf. Numbers 11:17, "I shall take of the spirit which is upon you and shall put it upon them"). The certificate itself was issued in the name of the yeshiva, as was old usage, or, in the Babylonian yeshivas, by both the secular head, the exilarch, and the schools, similar to what had become the final procedure in Palestine eight hundred years earlier.[6] The fellows who formed the early universities of Europe also issued corporate licenses, but this was never done, it seems, in the Muslim houses of learning. There, it was invariably the individual teacher who gave "the permission" to make use of what had been studied under his guidance.[7] In the local Jewish schools, outside the yeshiva, it was the head who conferred the degree.[8]

Since the study of the sacred law was a lifetime duty, the students often did not remain in the yeshiva until the attainment of membership, but frequently, or perhaps mostly, reached the status later in life. This practice was also in accordance with the basic character of the yeshiva as a legislative and juridical body. The main right conferred on the new member was the license to issue authoritative legal opinions and to act as a judge. As a rule, only persons of mature age would qualify for such tasks.

The license to teach publicly was closely connected with that of issuing legal opinions, for the interpretation of the sacred law was tantamount to deciding questions arising from its study. Consequently, a learned schoolmaster was allowed to teach the *text* of the Mishnah, but was prevented from expounding it, unless he received permission to do so by the local judge, that is, a scholar holding a degree and appointed to an official position.[9]

A scholar wishing to establish a school of his own and to read public lectures aided by a (me)turgeman, or broadcaster, as was customary in the yeshivas, needed special permission. This fact is evident from as late a document as the license issued for the purpose by the Babylonian Gaon Samuel b. Eli for his son-in-law who was about to take charge of the large community of Aleppo in summer, 1191.[10] The disapproval of Elhanan b. Shemaryah's seemingly unauthorized appointment of a broadcaster, referred to above (p. 202), points in the same direction.

Actual advancement to membership in the academy was preceded by a period of probation, during which a person was sometimes given the title "fellow designate" or "candidate." If the person never obtained full membership, the title "candidate" would become the family name of his descendants. (This is somehow reminiscent of the "B.A. Failure," which appeared on the visiting cards of some Indian intellectuals in pre-independence days.) [11]

Before conferring the degree, the yeshiva considered not only the scholastic attainments of the aspirant, but also his capacity to get along well with people, particularly appropriate in the case of persons who received the title later in life after having been engaged in public service. In a letter to the Palestinian congregation in Alexandria, discussed before in another connection,[12] the Gaon Solomon b. Judah expressed his astonishment and grief that there should have been complaints about the harsh ways of their spiritual leader. The man had been made member of the academy, an honor reached neither by his father, nor his grandfather, who also had served that congregation, precisely because he had been described as a gentle and unpretentious person (besides his attainments in scholarship, of course, which are also lauded). In the same letter, the Gaon politely, but firmly, refused to grant the title to the local cantor, although the latter's claim was supported by the leading Jewish scholar in Old

Cairo. In general, the Gaon explained, the title was not given by him personally, but by the governing body of the yeshiva as a whole.

As we have seen, a large city harbored many fellows of the academy. Therefore, it was found desirable to distinguish the leading scholar or scholars by specific titles, usually conferred on them at the solemn assembly on the Mount of Olives in Jerusalem on the seventh day of the Feast of Tabernacles.[13] In his later days Nahray b. Nissīm, the scholarly merchant-banker, attained the title "senior of the academy," with which he was often addressed (instead of his name).[14] A member of the academy who also acted as the communal leader in a large city was honored with the title "eminent member," which, within the yeshiva itself, was given to an outstanding scholar when there was no vacancy for him on the board of seven heading the institution. Since a very large proportion of the official correspondence preserved in the Geniza was addressed to "eminent members," it has been assumed that the yeshiva was lavish in conferring the honor. A more attentive examination of the material concerned shows that this was not so. As far as Fustat and Cairo are concerned, only five dignitaries, each of whom led the Jewish community for prolonged periods, have been found bearing that title during the years 1030–1112.[15] In a highly official public document from Fustat referring to the years 1127–1129, the communal leader is repeatedly called *rabbēnū ha-me'ulle,* "our master, the eminent" (with omission of his name), indicating that only one scholar in the city bore that title.[16] Similarly, an "eminent member" stood at the head of the Jewish community in the greatest port city of Lebanon in those days, Tyre, another in that of Palestine, Ascalon; a third one in Baniyas, the frontier fortress that protected the sources of the Jordan. This community (like that of Old Cairo) consisted of a Palestinian and a Babylonian congregation, the latter probably having emigrated to Baniyas from Tarsus in Asia Minor, when this town was taken by the Byzantines.[17] The controversial judge of al-Maḥalla, referred to above, also an "eminent member," was certainly a Palestinian.[18] One or two other instances of that title occur whose date and place have not yet been identified.[19] In the list of dignitaries and notables, Appendix C, section 26, four persons are called "eminent member," but these were the two chief judges of Fustat, that of Cairo, and one styled "Ibn al-Sullamī, head of the ḥavērīm, the ḥāsīd (pious)," probably the leader of a pietist brotherhood.[20] The title remained rare to the end.[21]

The honorary epithet "scholar" (*talmīd,* an abbreviation of *talmīd ḥakhāmīm,* "disciple of the sages"), which originally designated learned persons who were not fellows of the academy, was extremely rare during the eleventh century. Only in the thirteenth century, when titles had become cheap, does it appear frequently in the Geniza records.[22]

The Jerusalem academy conferred a few other titles on distinguished members, but to discuss them here would lead us too far afield and, as the Geniza shows, only a small minority of the members of the academy were so honored. The Babylonian academies had their own system of titles. We have already learned of the most important of them: "the head of the seder." [23] In comparison with those given by the Jerusalem yeshiva they are scarce, which may have its simple explanation in the fact that the Geniza was a depository of writings attached to the synagogue of the Palestinians.

Trying now to describe the various occupations of the scholars, we are puzzled by the fact that one official often carried out tasks normally connected with another office, while, vice versa, persons bearing different designations would fulfill the same function. This phenomenon is typical for medieval times in general. In the Geniza, however, where life is disclosed to us in minute details, this diversity is particularly manifest. Moreover, the offices and their designations did not remain unchanged during the period represented in the Geniza records. During the eleventh century the system was remarkably fluid, the twelfth had a more institutional character, while the rapid decline of Egyptian Jewry during the thirteenth century again necessitated changes. Therefore, the short survey of the occupations of the scholars given below is a mere outline, and cannot do full justice to a far more variegated reality.

In the early years of the Geniza period, the spiritual leader of a Jewish community often had no particular designation at all. He was referred to as "the member of the academy assigned to such and such a town." [24] Later on, his most common title was "dayyān," or judge, as presiding over a court handling cases of civil law was the most conspicuous and authoritative aspect of his office. One should bear in mind, however, that the Hebrew term also covers decisions in the field of ritual law and even theology.

As we shall see, the courts, as a rule, sat only twice a week. Only marriage contracts and divorces were normally dealt with outside the regular court sessions. The dayyān could therefore devote most of his time to study and teaching, regarded as his main duty. "Study," that is, learning in company with other scholars, "should not be interrupted even for one hour," is a quotation from a letter of the very prominent judge Baruch b. Isaac of Aleppo, who was active around

1100. When he himself was kept busy with communal affairs (about which we learn from a number of his other letters), he had his young son substitute for him in the local house of learning.[25] Some Geniza papers seem to indicate that students and scholars attended court sessions as part of their course of study.

Sermons and public lectures were by no means the exclusive domain of the "judge," but formed a regular part of his routine work. The large number of books on homiletics, found in the library of the "deputy" judge of Sunbāṭ (Lower Egypt) in 1150, proves that even in a little town preaching required careful preparation.[26] Moreover, the dayyān was expected to speak at happy family events and at funerals, a task sometimes felt as onerous by him as occasionally by his modern colleagues.[27]

The judge was also in charge of the social services of the community. He had to take care of the orphans and widows, the poor and the sick, foreigners and captives and other persons in trouble. In this respect, a profound change is to be observed during the Geniza period. Until the middle of the twelfth century, these services were entrusted by the community to laymen, with the judge acting as supervisor and coordinator; by the end of the century we find him administering them in person and managing the funds connected with them. This change was certainly attributable to the influence of the model of the Muslim qadi, and also to the intrinsically institutional character of the later period.[28]

Finally, the dayyān was a community leader and represented his flock before the local and central officials of the government and before the territorial and ecumenical authorities of the Jews. As such he had to deal with legal cases that transcended his powers and with administrative matters of all descriptions; and as such he was affected by the vicissitudes befalling government officials and the Jewish authorities, in other words, he was involved in politics—a state of affairs that some enjoyed and others detested.

Scholars of repute were approached with requests to give legal opinions on questions of civil and ritual law and, to a lesser degree, of religious belief and ethics. Maimonides wrote innumerable responsa while both in and (perhaps even more) out of office. A Spanish rabbi, who served as justice in Old Cairo about a hundred years before Maimonides, was asked such questions by scholars from a country as far away as Yemen (which, to be sure, was in close contact with Egypt owing to the India trade).[29] Still a hundred years earlier, a scholar from Spain living in Egypt wrote learned answers to questions submitted to him from various quarters.[30] The Geniza has preserved queries addressed to the Tunisian Nahray, who was sometimes regarded as the leading Jewish scholar in the Egyptian capital (in one case the questioner was the dayyān of Alexandria), to the Aleppan Yehiel b. Eliakim, who was prominent there a hundred and twenty years later, and to the latter's contemporary Anatoli of Marseilles, who was judge in Alexandria.[31] A learned judge in Palermo, Sicily, and the head of a school in al-Qayrawān, Tunisia, gave expert opinions in a legal case occurring in Egypt.[32] It was not the provenance, habitat, or official position of a scholar, but his reputation that conveyed on him religious authority.

In view of the manifold aspects of the office of dayyān or ḥāvēr, it is to be expected that some should have preferred to specialize in one field or another, as is evident from the details provided in the Geniza for individuals bearing these titles. Mere study (which always included the readiness to lead courses for adults) was regarded as a sufficient means for a livelihood, even in provincial towns.[33]

A post that particularly lent itself to specialization was that of the preacher.[34] While the sermons connected with the regular synagogue service were usually given by the local judge or judges, there were many occasions for visiting scholars or professional itinerant preachers to appear before an enlarged audience composed of the members of more than one congregation. Visiting preachers sometimes represented a strong moral force, similar to that demonstrated by their contemporary Christian and Muslim counterparts.[35] When Abraham Maimonides was asked to excommunicate a preacher from Baghdad, who was active in Damascus and had there condemned the writings of his great father, he refused to do so, because the man "by his discourses drew the hearts to the fear and service of God and awoke sinners to repentance." [36] Several Geniza papers show us itinerant preachers clashing with the local divines. A preacher from Basra, Iraq, once agitated against the leader of the Jewish community in Old Cairo and against the heads of the Jerusalem academy, who had appointed and later confirmed him in his office. The militant Basrian was excommunicated by the head of the academy for his actions. The pastoral letter announcing this decision was addressed to a small town in Lower Egypt, which shows that the preacher had not disdained to extend his visits even to communities of very limited size.[37] In a complaint sent by members of the two Jewish congregations of Alexandria to the Nagid, the writers sided with the visiting preacher (also an Iraqian) against the local judge, who had left demonstratively in midst of the sermon, because he was critical of the visitor's interpretation of the Holy Scriptures.[38]

The same document also gives us an idea of the emoluments paid one itinerant preacher. For two appearances, made during the autumn holidays, he received 10 dinars and 1 dinar for expenses—a handsome sum, which a schoolmaster could make in about half a year of laborious work. The preacher's pay tallies with a report from the little Egyptian town Ṣahrajt, where a scholar who stayed only one regular Sabbath for one sermon, made 7 quarter dinars and 100 dirhems, a total of about 4-½ dinars.[39] When a young scholar from a provincial town was given the honor to read a discourse before the two congregations of Old Cairo, he obviously received no remuneration, for in a letter to his wife, which contained a report about the lecture, he boasted of his success (regretting that she was not there to witness it); had he obtained, in addition to applause, also an honorarium, he would scarcely have failed to mention it as well.[40]

A successful public lecture by a guest speaker, then as today, required careful preparation. Various Geniza letters illustrate this fact. One, puzzling at first sight, may suffice. Eli b. Amram, the spiritual leader of the Palestinian congregation of Fustat during the third quarter of the eleventh century, writes to the head of the other congregation that he intended to invite a distinguished ḥāvēr visiting the city to "beautify" the synagogue on the following Saturday by "a word of the Torah" and he asks the addressee—confirming what was already conveyed to him orally—to chair the affair. In reply to his letter he expects a definite answer so that he may go ahead in making the necessary arrangements. The astonishing feature of this highly elaborate letter is that it was written at all, for the offices (and homes) of the two dignitaries could not have been more than a few hundred yards apart. No doubt, the letter was sent, and a written answer was expected, in order to make the joint venture strictly official.[41]

The lecturers themselves took no chances and sent out personal invitations to notables and divines (who do not always seem to have been eager to attend). Three such invitations, very different in style and tone, have been found by me thus far. In addition to the two mentioned before (see n. 42), which are written in flowery Hebrew, inviting the addressee together with his sons, there is one in Arabic in which the preacher describes himself as coming from a distant country and being different from the usual crop of wandering scholars ("to be different" seems not to be an invention of modern advertising). The invitation, addressed to the parnās of the Cairene (not Fustat) community, is formulated in the most urgent terms, suggesting that the size of the audience depended on whether that influential man would decide to attend or not.[42]

It is natural that the pulpit was sometimes occupied by an unworthy person. In an unusually harsh letter, the Nagid Joshua b. Abraham (1310–1355), the great-great-grandson of Maimonides, scolds the community of Old Cairo for having an ignoramus as preacher, who, like a parrot, pronounced speeches on the mysteries of religion which he himself did not understand. In this Joshua echoed the views of his illustrious ancestor, who denounced popular preachers who took the Scriptures and the sayings of the ancient sages literally and, by thus misrepresenting them, brought religion into disrepute.[43] In several instances, cantors served also as preachers, and since, in the late centuries of decay, a preacher would also take over the tasks of a dayyān, an outsider could get the impression that Jewish congregations were led by cantors, as does the Muslim antiquarian al-Qalqashandī (d. 1418) who tells us so in his description of the institutions of the Egyptian Jewish community.[44]

10. CANTORS AND OTHER RELIGIOUS FUNCTIONARIES

Second in importance to the office of the dayyān and, like it, abounding in many facets, was that of the cantor, or ḥazzān, who led the community in prayer, but fulfilled many other tasks as well. We are not concerned here with the history of the word, which goes back to remotest antiquity, nor with the development of the institution in pre-Geniza times, but solely with its various aspects as they are reflected in the Geniza records themselves. The extraordinary position of the cantor in the High Middle Ages finds its explanation in the spiritual situation of the time. Life was dominated by religion and had become very austere. Therefore, the adornments of life itself had to take refuge in the places of worship. It was there that music and poetry found unlimited scope for realization. Unlike the brief Muslim prayer, the Jewish service, like its Christian counterpart, was extended in length even on workdays, let alone on Sabbaths, holidays, and special occasions. The official service was freely expanded and interspersed with poetical accretions, often the work of a local ḥazzān or poet. The texts of the liturgy were chanted by different participants, or responsively by two or more singers, each of whom strived to show his musical talents. Jewish (and Muslim) sacred law provided that every knowledgeable layman was fit to lead a community in prayer, but the Geniza papers show that even small communities had a professional cantor, and often more than one.[1] Five or six cantors or more at a time were not exceptional in the Egyptian capital during the eleventh and twelfth centuries, and two queries addressed to Maimonides prove that several cantors officiated simultaneously during a Sabbath service.[2]

The qualifications required for this office were rather high, at least for the standards of those days, and it took long to attain them. In a contract dated 1040, a cantor in a little town undertakes to teach his art in evening lessons, promising whenever requested to spend the nights in the house of his pupil. The course was to last three full years and penalties were stipulated for both sides if the course was interrupted before its completion.[3] Normally, cantors were prepared for their future task in childhood.[4]

The cantor's equipment was both literary and musical. He had to be competent in the reading of the Bible sections used during the service together with their proper cantillation, in the liturgy of the whole year with its melodies, and in the many religious injunctions connected with both. Of course we should bear in mind that in those days the liturgy was still in a very fluid state. While being transferred from one place to another, or even with a change of superiors, a cantor had to adapt himself to a new prayerbook.[5] The text of the Bible and its cantillation was not yet as rigidly fixed as it is in our printed editions. In as late a period as the beginning of the thirteenth century a cantor in Alexandria asks a colleague in Old Cairo to look up the *Tāj,* the "Crown," as the model codex preserved in that city was called, in order to ascertain the exact reading and cantillation of a passage. As a matter of fact, the cantillation indicated in that letter is different from that found in all our printed bibles.[6] In the same period and in the capital itself, a reading approved by the Nagid Abraham Maimonides was contested by a scholar from Yemen.[7] We can well understand how careful a ḥazzān had to be in the preparation of his lections in order not to expose himself to criticism or even to ridicule.

The correct interpretation of the biblical text as provided by the Arabic translation of Saadya Gaon seems also to have belonged to the equipment of a better cantor. In praise of the nephew of Abu 'l-Majd, his colleague in Fustat, the Alexandrian cantor Judah b. Aaron of the famous al-ʿAmmānī family, notes that the boy read with him every week the relevant lection in Arabic translation, thus preparing himself properly for the service of the community.[8]

A more prominent cantor was also expected to be able to compose appropriate poetical additions to the service (which included songs for weddings and other family feasts, as well as eulogies for the dead), all in Hebrew—and an elaborate Hebrew at that. For Arabic, although freely used even in expounding the Bible or sacred Jewish law, was never admitted to the synagogue service (or to family events, all of which had a religious character). In many liturgical compositions found in the Geniza the author designates himself as a ḥazzān or is known as one from other sources.[9] Religious poetry itself, we remember, became to be known in this period as *ḥizāna* in Arabic or *ḥazzānūth* in Hebrew.

Since the gift or the erudition needed for the composition of poems was not everyone's share, a cantor eager to satisfy the avidity of his congregation for ever new experiences had to do so by selecting appropriate pieces from the diwans, or collections, of famous poets, or by receiving appropriate material from friends, or by abstracting creations heard from colleagues. "I have left Damascus," we read in a letter, "and intend to devote myself to the calling of a cantor. For this purpose, I have borrowed the diwans of Solomon the Little (the famous Ibn Gabirol) and of Judah ha-Levi—may their memory be blessed—and made excerpts from them for my use." [10] An old cantor orders a liturgical poem for which he indicates the biblical verses with which he wished each stanza to be concluded, but asks that the finished product should reach him well ahead of the holiday, for his memory was no longer as good as it used to be and it would take him some time to memorize the poem. (Several other passages indicate that the poems were recited by heart.) [11] Piyyūṭs for the New Year were sent to a cantor in Fustat by "his son," meaning probably a younger colleague.[12]

A letter written in Alexandria on February 4, 1214, contains interesting information of how the writer obtained material for the addressee, a cantor in Old Cairo, who wrote poetry himself, of which one long piece is preserved. The following passage from this letter is particularly illustrative: "I am happy that the penitential poem has been received by you. However, the other one gives me great trouble. May God help me to get hold of it. While my uncle chanted it during the vigils, I observed that it began with the words. . . .[13] But he never sings it on a weekday, when it might be written down, only on a Saturday or the Night of the Sacrifice of Isaac,[14] when one is not allowed to write. By your good life, I have sent for it as far as Marseilles." We have here a Hebrew liturgical poem, available in France, so cherished by those who had heard it in Alexandria, that a cantor in Old Cairo who already knew of it was eager to obtain a copy, but the colleague in Alexandria reserved the exclusive privilege to its use for himself.[15]

Above and beyond his intellectual and musical talents it was the cantor's religiosity and moral conduct that counted. He was the "messenger" who represented his congregation before God, and "a man is judged according to his representative." These talmudic notions were fully alive in the Geniza period, to judge from repeated references. This draft of a resolution recommending a cantor for permanent appointment is particularly telling. After stating that the man had been tried out on Sabbaths, workdays, and holidays (in this sequence) and had been found conforming to all the established requirements by the humility and beauty of his reading and the exactness of his rendering the sacred texts, the draft recommends him because of his "love of God, his religiosity, piety and virtuousness, his pleasant manners, his eagerness to seek knowledge and excellence, and because he was loved by the people for his unblemished conduct, as was known to everyone." [16]

The accounts and other documents assembled in appendixes A and B contain many details about the emoluments of cantors, and not seldom do they head the lists of recipients. Since a main, if not the major source of their income was derived from conducting services at weddings, funerals, and other family events, however, it is difficult to generalize about their economic position. From the mass of material preserved the differences in status seem to have been many. There were well-to-do ḥazzānīm, and others who were wretchedly poor, and again others whose fortunes seem to have been amazingly unstable. The cantor and scribe Hillel b. Eli (see sec. 11, n. 17; below) from whose hand we have a number of personal letters, exemplifies the ups and downs in a cantor's life. He was in service for a prolonged period (at least from 1066 to 1108) and some letters show him enjoying an honored position. But others convey a different impression, one, in particular, in which he complains of neglect by the community (quoting Isaiah 65:1) and of being afraid of the tax collector, proving that he had fallen on bad times.[17]

Like modern virtuosos, cantors traveled from one town or country to another to demonstrate their art and to pocket the collections made for them as their reward. A fledgling cantor writes to his mother in Fustat that she should not worry about him; he had just led a congregation at Shubrā and sung at a wedding in Damsīs, and in both cases "God had sent" him a quarter dinar.[18] Private persons would show their enthusiasm for a cantor by dropping into his hand a number of silver pieces, discreetly wrapped in paper. In Old Cairo one could find cantors from all over the world, including Christian Europe, Spain, and Persia. Foreign cantors appear regularly in the lists of receivers of emoluments from the community.[19]

The cantors of the Geniza period had another trait in common with opera singers of later times. Not few of them manifested a certain predilection for the bottle. A query addressed to Maimonides complains of a group of intoxicated cantors, who, while singing on the platform in honor of a boy reading the lection from the Prophets, filled the synagogue with giggles and raucous shouts. Another query describes a scandal that occurred for a similar reason.[20] In the letter to the cantor who was so eager to get hold of the penitential poem from France, quoted above, we read the following laconic remark: "You mentioned in your letter that your illness was due to drinking. An oath not to take any wine is certainly a good idea. In any case, I should rather recommend that you do not take too much of it." [21]

Since the synagogue singers were so large and motley a crowd, it is understandable that the more serious members of the profession wished to be distinguished from their less well qualified colleagues. A fair number of cantors bore the title "expert" or "certified" and a few were even members of the academy or were otherwise described as scholars.[22] The senior cantor was officially called "the great," not only in large cities like Baghdad or Fustat, but also in a provincial town in Egypt.[23] We also find the title "cantor with tenure" (App. A, sec. 155), as opposed to those of minor stature or peregrinators. The cantor of the private synagogue of the Nagid was called *ḥazzān al-majlis,* "the cantor of the audience hall," to be distinguished from *ḥazzān ha-keneseth,* "the cantor of the synagogue," a designation that had a quite different meaning in ancient times.[24] Cantors were occasionally given honorary epithets, similar in form to those borne by the members of the Jerusalem yeshiva. Such titles were conferred by a Nagid or any other Jewish authority and also by a local community.

The cantors, as we have seen, were busy travelers, and since they were trained in making public announcements, they were used as official envoys both by the yeshivas and the Nagid.[25] On their travels, some, or perhaps many of them engaged in commerce, for travelers in those days normally acted also as carriers of goods.[26]

Finally, there was a vast field of activities for cantors, which is perhaps even more conspicuous in the Geniza records than it was in life: as a liturgical writer, the cantor was required to be a linguist; no wonder then that he was often entrusted with the formulation of legal deeds and court records. Countless such documents, written and co-signed by cantors, have come down to us from the eleventh through the thirteenth centuries.[27] This position of court clerk led to many other kinds of employment. Cantors served as puisne judges and were charged with such minor juridical functions as visits to the houses of women who had trouble in their married life. There, the ḥazzān would either take down a declaration, which would later be used in court, or receive a power of attorney, or he would try to restore marital peace or deliver a bill of divorce. It is almost unnecessary to say that he also served as a matchmaker.[28] In particular it was his duty to formulate and to read out in the synagogue public announcements, including the delicate—and sometimes even dangerous—task of pronouncing the excommunication of a person, a purpose for which solemnly styled formularies were used.[29] Furthermore, he assisted the dayyān and the laymen charged with the social services of the community in their operations, for example, collecting funds for the ransom of captives or seeing to it that a blind man properly received the share allotted to him from the public chest.[30] Many lists connected with these works of charity are written in the hands of cantors well known to us, and some cantors acted during many years as administrators of public property and as treasurers.[31] No wonder, then, that in one document (App. B, sec. 15) a cantor is described as being in charge of the social services and the prayer (in that order). Finally, in smaller places and in the absence of a dayyān or ḥāvēr, the ḥazzān fulfilled the functions of an all round spiritual and communal leader and was installed or recognized as one by the central authorities.[32] A man wishing to emphasize his loyalty to the Jewish authorities therefore writes: "I never disobey a court [i.e., judge], and not even a cantor in a village." [33]

In Geniza records dated between 1126 and 1226, as well as in a number of undated documents, there appear persons designated as *meshōrēr,* a Hebrew term meaning either singer, chorister, or poet. The first meaning is very likely intended, although the word is used twice to mean poet in a letter written in winter, 1140–41, and the Arabic *shāʿir,* poet, also is attached to some names occurring in the Geniza papers. Details about the function of choristers have thus far not turned up and, unlike the *murahhiṭ,* the writer or singer of liturgical poetry, no meshōrēr is listed as receiver of emoluments from the community.[34]

In Geniza documents from the fourteenth century the family name Sōmēkh begins to appear. In Baghdad (where a prominent and ramified Jewish family has borne this name from the nineteenth century) the word still designates an assistant cantor who accompanies and complements the main cantor on Sabbaths and holidays. It would be interesting to know where this institution, which is known also from later, European, Jewries, took its origin.[35]

A whole group of community officials was occupied with the implementation of the Jewish dietary laws. This venerable relic from the days of the Temple service requires some explanation. Any partaking of food was regarded as a communion with God, the giver of life, and was therefore preceded by a benediction and followed by grace. The preparation of animal food, which, according to the biblical account, man was allowed to eat only after Noah had used it as an offering, was regulated by minute injunctions, in many ways reminiscent of the ritual observed at sacrifices in the Temple of Jerusalem. The animal had to be killed in a specific, expert way with a razor-edged knife and a benediction had to be pronounced during the operation, as was the case, incidentally, in Islam. Then the carcass, and in particular the lungs, had to be examined carefully and a large number of greasy substances, minutely specified, had to be removed from various parts of the body together with "the sinew of the hip" (Genesis 33:33). Finally, the meat had to be guarded from being contaminated or mixed with other meat, until it reached the consumer.

Thus, three persons were engaged in this process: the shohet (in the Geniza mostly referred to with Arabic terms), the slaughterer, who performed the ritual killing and also examined the body of the dead animal; the "picker," who identified and pulled out the impure sinews and other taboo parts; and the guard, who watched over the meat.[36] The slaughterer, whose task was regarded as bearing extreme responsibility and who also supervised his minor colleagues, was appointed by the community, but in larger cities he is never listed as drawing a remuneration from the public chest, for there he was paid by his customers, the butchers or other private persons. On the other hand, the "pickers" and guards appear regularly in lists; sometimes four guards are listed at a time, for a guard also had to watch over the milking of goats and cows and the preparation of cheese, processes for which ritual purity was also prescribed.[37]

The office of the religious slaughterer required manual dexterity, but, even more, theoretical knowledge bordering on scholarship. Even familiarity with the relevant sections of the Talmud was regarded as obligatory, at least by some, a subject, we remember, that did not belong to the regular "B.A." curriculum of Jewish studies in those days.[38] Moreover, a shohet had to be a trustworthy person of good conduct and acceptable to the community. A letter of appointment makes mention of these three qualifications: religiosity, good conduct, and scholarship.[39] In a document, written in January, 1160, a man described as both slaughterer and cantor undertakes to attend to his calling punctually, and only in the abattoir, to be nice to people, and particularly not to argue and quarrel with them even when teased or mocked at in the presence of gentiles or others (this clause certainly was occasioned by some unpleasant incident), and, finally, to do also the "picking," a task often done by a specialist.[40] Despite the acknowledged right of a son to succeed to his father's office, the son of one shohet was disqualified even for the minor post of guard, because he did not enjoy the confidence of the community. An incompetent shohet in Damascus was reprimanded and demoted: he was permitted to handle only poultry, not cattle. A negligent "examiner" in (New) Cairo retained his post solely by a special act of indulgence, but had to repent and to accept flogging in public, "to give God what is due to him." [41]

It lies in the nature of such age-old ritual matters that divergent usages and "schools" developed with regard to them. In western Europe (and of course also in America), most or all Orthodox Jews do not consume meat from the hindquarter of an animal, and, therefore, they have no need for the complicated procedures of "picking" alluded to above. The socioeconomic background for this practice is, of course, that in those countries there is no difficulty in disposing of the forbidden meat with gentile butchers. In Yemen, where, until their exodus in 1949–1950, the Jews lived in separate villages and quarters where they were surrounded by a sect of Muslims with even stricter taboos, who would not even drink a cup of coffee touched by a non-Muslim, the hindquarters had to be used, and, therefore the art of "picking" was as common there as in Egypt at the time of the Geniza documents. This is an elementary example of such differences, but there were others, more sophisticated ones, which might appear as minutiae to the outsider, but were of supreme concern to the observant. Matters that were perfectly harmless according to one school or "rite," *minhāg,* were absolutely taboo in another. In a detailed and most illuminating (but poorly preserved) letter by a Palestinian Gaon, he exonerates two slaughterers in Fustat who had been disqualified in the strongest terms by his predecessor: after examining their case it became evident that they were conscientious and learned persons (they were also cantors), but followed a rite different from that of their accuser. In another letter a Gaon emphasizes that he must confirm in office all shohets and supervisors.[42]

The philosophically minded apostate Samuel, the Maghrebi, describes with ridicule and scorn how a Jewish scholar, upon arriving among his coreligionists in a distant locality, would first of all refrain from partaking of their meat so that he would be regarded by them as particularly strict and learned and ended up, after much dissension, as their leader whose rite they adopted. Samuel's unusually long diatribe on this subject suggests that the overemphasis on ritual taboos might have alienated from their religion not few Jewish intellectuals in a century when philosophical and scientific studies were commonplace among them. Not everyone had the singular mind of a Maimonides who combined most rigorous ritualism with highest intellectualism.[43]

The administrative and financial aspects of the shohet's calling are illustrated by a number of Geniza documents from the eleventh through the thirteenth centuries. The oldest known to me thus far is of a more technical nature specifying the conditions imposed on the shohets licensed by the Palestinian congregation in Fustat (signed by six with room left for a seventh).[44] In a "statute" made around 1025, Ḥusayn, alias Japheth, the cantor, son of the cantor David, receives the post of ritual slaughterer and examiner, previously held by his late father, in two abattoirs "one near the Bath of the Mice and one on the Great Market." Half the weekly income belonged to him, the other half was to be put aside until a decision was reached about its use by Joshiah, the Gaon of Jerusalem, Ephraim (b. Shemarya, called here "expert lay judge," and not "member of the academy"), the leader of the congregation, and six other notables specified by name. The agreement, as signed by the appointee, was read out to the plenum of the community. The fact that after the death of the father new, and not even definitive, financial conditions were stipulated shows that the shohet's income, like any other lucrative occupation in that competitive society, depended on agreements rather than on fixed usages.[45]

In the weekly accounts carried through a whole year, described in *Med. Soc.*, Vol. I (App. D, sec. 58), a shohet pays 7 dirhems every week to an official or other person designated by the community and returns to it also the sums that it had spent for his poll tax (ca. 1180).[46] From a detailed account written about fifty years later we learn that the same system still prevailed, namely, that the shohets made payments to different officials including the Nagid (for distribution to the poor), but we learn something about their income, too. For every animal killed they received 2 dirhems—a sum large enough to purchase 2 pounds of meat. (This item invariably appears on the expenditure side every week. Only once a shohet spent 2-¼ dirhems for meat, I assume because he had a guest. A pound of meat, at that time, cost 1-¼ dirhems, but it is clear that the shohets received a slight reduction. It is interesting to note that these killers of animals permitted themselves to eat meat at most at two meals during a week, a pound being a reasonable minimum for a family of medium size.

These two meals were no doubt consumed on Friday night and Saturday. (Many years ago, a Kurdish Jew explained to me: "We eat meat only on the Sabbath, not on weekdays when we work. Meat makes lazy.") Of the two officials referred to in the document, one did slaughtering as a sideline, dispatching two to four animals per week, the other accounted for eleven to fourteen. The animals must have been sheep, for mutton, and not beef, was the common and most favored fare. The reference could not have been to beef, for then the quantities slaughtered would have been far too large for the then (ca. 1230) very much reduced Jewish community of Fustat.[47]

The offices of cantor and ritual slaughterer were often combined, which was reasonable since both required a certain degree of scholarship and both were by their very nature part-time jobs. A number of examples have occurred in the preceding paragraphs and others could easily be added.[48] The combination shohet-schoolmaster was rare, for the simple reason that the schoolmaster was occupied all day long with his pupils. In smaller places which were unable to maintain more than one, or, at most, two communal officials, such combinations (including the cantor) were more frequent. Yemenite village boys of this century remembered with delight the respites afforded them by the chickens demanding the attention of their teacher.[49]

The most colorful community official was the beadle, or "servant" of the synagogue. Since his office required qualities rather than qualifications, its description has been included in the section on communal life (chap. v, sec. B, 2, above). It should be noted, though, that in various documents beadles are listed as students of the sacred law, and we have details on some who seem to have had a share of learning and were so honored.[50]

11. SCRIBES AND COPYISTS

"A scholar should learn how to write." This amazing item in the list of accomplishments required of a scholar in the Talmud[1] is to be understood in the light of medieval conditions and ideas about the subject. While the knowledge of reading was fairly common, writing was an art acquired just by persons who had a special reason to do so, mostly, as we have seen (see sec. 2, above), those who prepared themselves for the profession of clerk, copyist, scholar, teacher, physician, and merchant. In Europe, too, diplomatic writing formed a part of the university curriculum during the twelfth and thirteenth centuries.[2]

Good penmanship comprised the creation of regular and pleasing forms of the letters, an aesthetic arrangement of the writing on the page, exactness in copying, and the avoidance of errors necessitating deletions and corrections. Naturally, there were differences in attainment, not only among individuals, but also among classes of people. While doctors and merchants, and sometimes also teachers, were satisfied with modest results, professional scribes and scholars often displayed regularity and accuracy, as well as a perfect, individual style (which, however, does not always mean easy reading for us).

Many persons, particularly judges, were accomplished scribes and gained a part or the whole of their livelihood by this art, without being so designated. Of the famous Fāḍil al-Baysānī, the sultan Saladin's chief qadi and counselor, it was reported that no one in his generation equaled him in the beauty of his handwriting, and in as late a source as *The Arabian Nights* a Muslim judge asserts that he obtained his high position through his art of penmanship.[3] A minor Muslim judge "copied daily ten folios before going to his court. For this, he was paid 10 dirhems and on this he lived."[4] A number of the most distinguished Jewish judges of the Geniza period also served as court clerks, which can be proved by the fact that many of the documents that are unquestionably in their handwriting are signed not by them, but by colleagues.[5] On the other hand, there were judges who were excellent calligraphers but still did not engage in this profession, as we know from the dozens of documents simply signed by them over a span of thirty or more years, with only two or three written entirely in their hands, done obviously when no court clerk was available.[6] Teachers and cantors often served as scribes, as described above in the sections devoted to these callings.

The scribes proper were of three types: the government clerks, who were designated by the Arabic term *kātib* and who were, of course, trained mainly in Arabic script, although some of them excelled in Hebrew calligraphy as well;[7] the all-around Hebrew scribe, who usually knew a smattering of classical Arabic and who could serve as a court clerk, a writer of business and private correspondence, or as a copyist of books, or in some or all of these capacities together; he was referred to by the general term *sōfēr,* a Hebrew word still common as a family name (as witness the name listed in telephone books of any large city in the United States or England; spelled also Soffer, Sopher, and the like); finally, the copyist proper, who was called *nāsikh,* an Arabic term, applied in particular to experts in the copying of Bible texts, which was a rather diffused occupation, taken up occasionally even by a woman. The copyists were specialists. Solomon, the son of judge Samuel b. Saadya ha-Levi, of whose hand many documents have been preserved, is called in a court record "the skilled scribe [Ezra 7:6], a master in his art, whose Torah [i.e., learnedness] is his craft," but not a single document written by him is known to me.[8]

Unfortunately, the word "kātib" designated any government official, from the head of a department, or a secretary of state, down to the most subordinate amanuensis. It is discussed in chapter vii, which is devoted to government service in general. The sōfēr was intrinsically a student of the sacred law and therefore had claim on the support of the community and the contributions of pious individuals. In the Geniza records we see scribes being in receipt of both.[9] He was customarily paid for his services. The fees seemed to vary with the circumstances and the financial capacity of the parties concerned. In a letter written in Old Cairo around 1065 to Eli b. Amram, "excellent member of the academy," but acting also as a court scribe, his junior colleague specifies the fees received in his absence: "A marriage contract [names provided]—6 dirhems; another marriage contract—4 dirhems; the third one [of a husband who took his divorcée back]—3 dirhems; a bill of divorce—2 "black" dirhems, sold for 1 good dirhem; a power of attorney given to a man traveling to Spain, where he was to receive a bill of divorce from a husband living there for his wife who had remained in Egypt—no fees asked for."[10] (A bill of divorce, or *get* [pronounced like English *get*], was a strictly formal document, confined at that time to about ninety words, whereas a marriage contract, which usually contained a trousseau list, could easily be six and more times as long. The difference in length does not mean that getting a divorce was less expensive than concluding a marriage.)

In order to give an idea of the fees paid for commercial documents, an example from the same time, but from Palermo, Sicily, reveals that for the writing of a deed of partnership in a consignment of pepper worth 608 quarter dinars, 1 quarter dinar, then worth approximately 9 silver dirhems, was paid.[11]

The cases cited represent remunerations for scribal services pure and simple. The fees were higher when legal action was involved. For making out a deed for the sale of a house worth 60 dinars a Muslim notary received 1 dinar in 1088. There is little doubt that this included prerequisites for the five Muslim professional "witnesses" (*'udūl*) who signed together with him and possibly also for one or two lower government officials.[12]

A similar situation must be assumed when a husband traveling in Cyprus (the man who was so outraged about his wife's negligence with regard to the schooling of their boy [p. 174, above]) writes to his brother: "Have Abū 'Imrān [a communal official called Moses] write for me a bill of divorce by the month of Ṣafar, year 31, for half a dinar. Do not delay, please." A *get* is invariably dated according to a Jewish month and year. When the writer uses here a Muslim date (corresponding to Oct.-Nov., 1136), he means to say that by the time he returned from his business trip the legal procedures should be completed and the *get* ready for delivery. Thus we understand why the fee offered by him for a bill of divorce was half a dinar, about twenty times as much as the one mentioned in the letter of the scribe from Old Cairo.[13]

In the letter just referred to, the scribe sends half the sums received to his superior. This seems to indicate that the clerks divided the fees among themselves irrespective of who did the actual writing. Normally, at least two scribes were attached to a court and also served as its assistant members. Even in the small Jewish community of Damietta, the Mediterranean port, two persons calling themselves scriveners signed a document in A.D. 989.[14] From the still smaller town of Sunbāṭ in Lower Egypt, two documents from the year 1149, both calligraphic and well formulated, were written and signed alternatively by two different scribes, one of whom is also called "deputy," that is, deputy judge.[15] In a large community, like the one in Old Cairo, there must always have been one chief court clerk, as the material covering about 240 years (1026-1266) indicates, for in each generation the number of documents drawn up by one individual outnumbers by far those of the other scribes connected with the same court. The most prolific scrivener of Geniza records, from whose hand literally hundreds of fragments or complete pieces have been preserved, was Ḥalfōn ha-Levi b. Manasse Ibn al-Qaṭā'if (dated documents, 1100-1138). He also copied, in Hebrew characters, an Arab commonplace book by a tenth-century Muslim author, the original of which has not yet been found.[16] Second to him with respect to mass of material preserved was his father-in-law Hillel b. Eli, sometimes referred to as the cantor from Baghdad (dated documents, 1066-1108). The latter had an interesting personality, which cannot be said of the former. We are able to form a judgment about them, since private correspondence, both from and about them, has also been preserved.[17]

The art of the medieval scribe, as evidenced in the Geniza records, deserves detailed study, but can be sketched here only in bare outline. The writing material, the papyrus, so typical for Egypt, is entirely unknown in the period covered in this book, and only a few pieces on papyrus in Hebrew characters have been preserved in the

Geniza from preceding centuries. Linen as writing material has turned up thus far only in documents written in India or on the India route. The practice of the Muslim scribes in Egypt (during the thirteenth and fourteenth centuries) of writing marriage contracts on linen seems not to have been imitated by their Jewish colleagues.[18] Vellum and parchment were copiously used (see *Med. Soc.* I, 112), and also, although very rarely, reddish-brown leather. In documents on parchment the four edges were not trimmed evenly, but the natural curves were left especially on the right and lower edges. The long and irregularly shaped blank spaces of parchment this practice created were trimmed off after the document had served its purpose and were used for drafts or copies, sometimes written in tiny letters.[19]

The main writing material was paper, which is preserved in the Geniza in many different types, colors, and shapes. Anyone interested in the history of this prime means of communication will be richly rewarded by a study of the Geniza finds.[20] In general, the paper was good and suitable for preserving the ink well (better than vellum); otherwise, these documents would have been unreadable after they had become disused, neglected, and stacked away in a lumber room, where they lay for nine hundred years or so. People must have been sensitive in this matter because a writer using paper of poor quality apologizes by saying that he was unable to find better.[21]

Paper was traded in different sizes, sometimes referred to in our records (as "cuts," *qaṭʿ*, or *taqṭī*) and as may be concluded from the uniform size of a great many court records belonging to one period. Mostly, the scribes cut the paper to size according to their needs. It is remarkable how dexterous they were in gauging exactly the length of a document or of a letter. Usually only a very small part of the page was left blank. The more experienced a scribe was, the better use he made of the space at his disposal. Clearly, this was a matter of taste and not simply of thrift. Blank space was regarded as an offense to the eye—except where it was intentional.[22]

In letters, including official correspondence, more often than not, the margins were neatly filled with writing, not, as we do, in scribbling afterthoughts, but, after having finished a page, the writer continued on the right margin from the bottom to the top,[23] very often also on the top itself, from right to left (in the direction of the Hebrew and Arabic scripts) and only then turned overleaf to the completion of his text. In documents, narrow margins were preferred. Comparatively little space was left between lines and in some letters none; on the other hand the spaces were sometimes three or four times as high as the writing.[24] In both cases, the page gives the impression of an artistic creation, comparable with a carpet or a piece of cloth with a pattern.

A document was usually written on only one piece of paper in order to prevent fraudulent insertions or omissions, and it often necessitated the use of long strips of paper. When two, three, or four leaves of paper had to be glued together, the copyist endeavored—and almost invariably succeeded—in arranging his lines in such a way that one line covered the edge separating the two leaves so that the upper part of the letters appeared on the first leaf and the lower on the second. Sometimes, he would also write the word *emeth,* or "truth," or a similar expression, or his name on the margin across the join of the sheets and would note at the end the number of sheets and lines.[25] Owing to these precautions, the different leaves, if separated, could easily be identified as parts of one larger unit. Unfortunately, in most cases when several sheets were pasted together they were indeed separated from one another with the result that we have only a part of the letter or document concerned.[26]

Discarded paper was reused, especially for documents, but not rarely for letters.[27] This practice causes many headaches. The page of a manuscript bearing the library mark is referred to as recto, or first page. A librarian, however, cannot be expected to do the work of a specialist, and, therefore, in many cases the reverse side was in fact the first page, that is, the one used originally. Moreover, in reusing a sheet the writer would cut it according to his needs; often in the process the date and other valuable elements of the original document were lost. It cannot be emphasized enough that wherever the two pages of a manuscript do not contain a consecutive text or two different texts complete in themselves, their relationship in time, place, and subject matter can be established only by careful study of the inner evidence. Many strange bedfellows have been found together on one Geniza sheet.

Ink, usually, was not made by the scribe, but bought from a specialist. "I am sending you an ink container," writes a scribe from Ṣahrajt in Lower Egypt to a friend in Old Cairo. "Please have someone buy me ink of the first quality for a dirhem, fill the container, kindly seal it with wax and send it over with the donkey driver, for the ink which Faraj bought for me on the day I left Old Cairo cannot be used."[28] Even in a letter to his superior in the capital a local deputy judge would urgently ask for ink in a postscript written in small letters obliquely on the top of his first page.[29] Some scribes prepared or, as they expressed it, "cooked," their ink themselves.[30] A wide variety of types of ink was available, as may be seen on a sheet of paper that contains texts written by different persons in different places, such as the declarations of allegiance to a head of the Jewish academy of Jerusalem made by the community officials in various little towns in Upper Galilee around the middle of the eleventh century. In each place the ink had a different color.[31] Mostly a viscous and intensely black ink was used. Another that now appears brown is also rather common.

Unlike the preparation of ink, the proper cutting of the pen was an intrinsic part of the scribal art. Its thickness and the resulting shape of the letters had to conform to the size of the paper, and the harmony reached in this respect (by scribes of whose work we have a sufficient number of different specimens) is often apt to evoke our admiration. Only seldom, when the scribe realized that he would otherwise be unable to finish a document on one page or a long business letter on two pages, would he exchange a fine pen for the formerly used heavy one.[32] Not every reed would do for a good pen. Reeds growing in the lake of Maryūṭ near Alexandria were particularly sought after. "As to the reeds of Maryūṭ," writes a fellow of the academy, an excellent calligrapher, to a revered scholar in Old Cairo, "they are still fresh and cannot be cut until the month of Av (July-August). I shall send for the reeds and cut them myself into pens and send them to you."[33]

The subject of the various scripts displayed in the Geniza documents requires a discussion of Hebrew palaeography, which falls outside the scope of this book. Two remarks may suffice. An Arab scholar of the tenth century compared the art of the scribe with that of the musician, who weighs the different musical movements, sometimes mixing the heavy movement with the light, sometimes following other procedures, but always displaying a fine degree of sensitivity.[34] It is a most appropriate comparison. The medieval scribe's creations are often music to the eye for he was an artist not less than a scholar. The combination of the callings of cantor and scribe noted in subsection 10, above, might also have had its reason in the fact that both aimed at beauty. The court clerk and "cantor from Baghdad" Hillel b. Eli bore the title "Joy of all Hearts," presumably because of his beautiful voice and his perfect rendition of the synagogal liturgy. The many creations of his pen left by him still give pleasure to our eyes.[35]

Second, on the basis of the material provided by the Geniza, I have come to the conclusion that the origin of Hebrew calligraphy, and indeed of Hebrew cursive script in general, is to be sought in the Jewish academies of Babylonia (Iraq). While the Palestinian schools and their dependencies used the ancient quadrangular script, which does not lend itself to quick writing, even in letters and court records, the Babylonian schools developed a very beautiful cursive, which spread to and became accepted in most Jewish communities together with the legal opinions and other writings emanating from them. Tunisia, an important seat of Jewish learning dependent on the Babylonian schools, was the second home of this cursive, which finally replaced the old quadrangular script everywhere in daily use. In Palestine and Syria, a distinctive, sharp-angled script resembling a compromise between the new cursive and the old quadrangular evolved during the eleventh century. In Spain, more than anywhere else, the Hebrew (as well as the Latin) cursive acquired a flowing appearance reminiscent of Arabic script. If my assumption is correct, the origin of the Hebrew cursive in the Babylonian academies would present a parallel to the role of the European universities in the development of writing.

The language and style of the Geniza scribes can be studied conveniently, since the more prominent ones have left us both documents and letters written in their hands. Four different worlds have blended in their modes of expression. They combine the exactness and terseness of the jurists with the matter-of-factness apparent in the correspondence of businessmen, and they were the disciples of the great masters of synagogal poetry (an art cultivated also by some scribes),[36] and, at the same time, heirs to the vast tradition of Arabic artistic letter writing. Naturally, the performance varied widely in proportion to the talents and the erudition of the individual scribes, as well as according to subject matter and the circumstances. In some types of documents, such as powers of attorney and releases, the content is drowned in a flood of legal verbiage.[37] In general, however, the legal deeds are comparatively short and remarkably free of involved formulations. The case, as a rule, is stated clearly and completely. In letters written by experts, the introduction, or rather the introductions—for there are often two, one in Hebrew, and one in Arabic—are mostly prolix and extended and often embellished by lines in rhymed prose and sometimes even in verses (these embellishments are invariably in Hebrew). The subject matter itself, however, is usually brought forward in a straight and concise way, except when politeness prevented the writer from being too outspoken, as with requests or refusals, or when the topic itself, such as a formal letter of thanks, required nothing but artistic variations of one theme.

For shorter documents, including marriage contracts for people of lower station, rough drafts were normally not made. Paper, after all, was expensive. The scribe jotted down the main facts, including lists of the trousseau or the estate in cases of marriages or claims of inheritance, and then proceeded to make the clean copy. This procedure is evident both from many such notes and lists preserved, as well as from the fact that many documents show additions between the lines which were not only omissions by the scribes, but the clients' afterthoughts and qualifications. All such additions are carefully noted again at the end even of the most modest court record.

Longer and more important documents were carefully drafted. The clean copy, however, was not always confided to a simple amanuensis. For "the writing is like the countenance of the writer": the man in charge of a case was expected to write the relevant document in his own hand. In connection with a delicate problem of the rehabilitation of an excommunicated synagogue official, the Gaon Solomon b. Judah of Jerusalem was asked by the Jewish community of Old Cairo to write them a letter in his own hand. Many letters written by him have indeed come down to us.[38] In an equally delicate matter the Gaon Maṣlī'aḥ writes an official letter in his own hand, leaving an inch of space between each line.[39] Both these two Gaons were accomplished calligraphers. But we find communal leaders writing elaborate documents who by no means excelled in penmanship. A long query addressed in 1058 to the Gaon of Jerusalem by Eli b. Amram, the then head of the Palestinians in Fustat, although made out with painstaking care, betrays an unpleasant, hybrid style, mixing his traditional square script with the Babylonian cursive without achieving a satisfactory synthesis. At the same time, a secretary of his writes a contract on the same matter in a most beautiful cursive. It was the personality of the copyist, rather than his handwriting, which apparently was sought in important documents.[40]

Better scribes rarely made mistakes. I have copied thousands of their creations, but never matched them in this respect. When they wrote a word or an expression twice, especially at the beginning of a new line (a more frequent error than any other), unlike ourselves, they deleted the first item, not the second.

There was, however, one aspect in the work of these medieval scribes which appears to us to be a drawback, whereas they must have regarded it more a virtue: an astonishing degree of inconsistency, or, as they perhaps would have put it, an outspoken predilection for variety. In legal documents and whenever we have to be exact we are wont to call a thing by one and the same word. They obviously felt the opposite urge. Even in a highly formal statement, such as the validation of a document written in Zawīlat al-Mahdiyya, Tunisia,

1047, by the court of Fustat, the simple notion "they said" is sometimes expressed by two different Hebrew words.[41] In a document from Damietta, Egypt, dated 1106, the town itself is called once by its Arabic and once by its Hebrew name, the technical term "the era of creation," is expressed by two different Hebrew words in two successive lines, and numbers are written once in numerals and once in words.[42]

The predilection for variety is confusing, especially in names. Both the Arabic and Hebrew parts of the name of a person consisted of various constituents. The scribes, using this possibility for variation, would introduce a person by one name and later refer to him by another, not mentioned before. An Abu 'l-Faraj mentioned at the beginning of a document appears later as Joshua, a Japheth as Ḥasan (969), an 'Imrān as 'Umayra (before 1038), a Solomon as Salmān (1049), an 'Allūn as Eli (1057), an Azhar as Yā'īr (1072), and a Bū Najm as Hillel (1207).[43] These Arabic-Hebrew equivalents were hardly stereotyped: the most common equivalent of Abu 'l-Faraj was not Joshua, but Yeshū'ā, and the Hebrew name Solomon was rendered in Arabic by Salāma or Sulaymān or even Tamīm (which was believed to express the meaning of the Hebrew name). Variation was therefore conducive to ambiguity.[44] Even the prominent judge and scholar Nathan b. Samuel would not hesitate to call a person, in a calligraphic document drawn up in his hand, in one line Abu 'l-Ṭayyib (lit., the father of T.) and in the next Ṭayyib, although this creates the impression that he was referring first to the father and then to the son.[45]

The inconsistency in spelling, even of the best scribes, is equally noteworthy. Even a scribe of the caliber of Hillel b. Eli would spell the same word in two adjacent lines in two different ways.[46] The attitude of the Geniza scribes toward wording and spelling deserves a special study, which would perhaps throw light also on cognate problems in the tradition of literary texts.

The copyists constituted a class by themselves, although judges, teachers, and cantors also copied books. It is strange that the work of the copyist which required both knowledge and skill was one of the worst-paid occupations, for the civilization of the period was decidedly bookish, and books were a much sought after article even in commerce. Most of the time, the scribe was merely a wage earner. As in other agreements on work, the material, that is, the vellum or the paper, was furnished by the employer. Unlike other piecework, however, it must have been customary to remunerate the scribe partly in advance, or, as stated in one letter, to make him a "gift" against the promise to copy the book ordered. At least, this custom is presupposed in the records dealing with this matter found thus far.

The letter just referred to, which is written on vellum in a good hand, deserves some attention. A bibliophile from Byzantium had ordered the diwan, or collection of poems, of "Solomon the Little," the Spanish Hebrew poet Ibn Gabirol, from a scribe in a provincial town in Egypt.[47] The addressee, Peraḥya, is almost certainly identical with a scribe from Mazara, Sicily, of the same name who has left us a vivid description of his travel from his hometown to Messina in 1154, which was the first lap of his journey to Egypt.[48] There he became the son-in-law, and later on the successor of the judge of al-Maḥalla. In that letter reference is made to a book he copied on order; actual specimens of that book written in his hand have been preserved in the Geniza. Here, in the letter of the Byzantine bibliophile, he is addressed with the deference due a learned man, but he is asked to return the paper provided, if he had not yet begun the work, for he had not been in touch for a long time. The writer wanted also to take back three quires given to another copyist, a cantor, whether used or not. There is, however, no demand to return "the gift made for the copying of the diwan."

In a document from the first half of the eleventh century, the copying of the eight books of the Prophets (the second section of the Hebrew Bible) is remunerated in the following way. At the outset the scribe received two gold dinars as well as some silver coins and a garment valued at another dinar. Most probably, he needed the gold for his poll tax and the garment because he had no other proper clothing. The work itself had to be done under the supervision of the employer for a payment of 1 dirhem a day—half the average obtained by an unskilled laborer. No work—no payment.[49]

For copying on vellum the Arabic translation of the Five Books of Moses, the Pentateuch, a scribe in al-Maḥalla (different from the two just mentioned, but living approximately at the same time) stipulated a wage of 3 dinars, of which he received half a dinar in advance. After having completed a third of the work, he granted a discount of half a dinar, so that he was left with a total of 2½ dinars—and that for work that, according to him, was almost as complicated as copying and voweling the text of the Bible.[50]

Realizing how difficult it was to make a living copying books one is surprised to read in a letter of a scribe from a small town that he had written a beautiful Pentateuch which had no peer except the one he had written for the addressee, and which he wished to present to the Nagid as a gift. He had "tired his heart and kept awake his eye" to complete the codex and now asked his correspondent to deliver it in person. The story behind this, I assume, was that the Nagid had seen the first copy and expressed his admiration. Etiquette required that he get a copy as a gift, while a return present worth a few dinars could be confidently expected. The letter (preserved in three fragments) displays an excellent hand.[51]

For work requiring special skills, the usually low tariffs would not do. An ancient model codex of the whole Bible, which had been written, it seems, in the ninth century and was the property of the synagogue of the Palestinians in Old Cairo, needed to be restored at the beginning of the thirteenth century. Three experts were invited for the task, but declared themselves unable to carry it out, for "the resurrection of the dead is more difficult than bringing a human being into existence." Finally, a fourth scribe undertook the restoration of sixty particularly bad leaves, for which he asked a compensation of 1 dirhem per leaf. This demand, as stated in the document, was far more than expected. We remember that a Muslim judge of that period received a dirhem for the copying of a folio.[52]

When a scribe was sufficiently well off, he would work independently, providing himself all the materials, including the covers and the book clasps. We find this, for example, in a contract written in December, 1021, where a payment of 25 dinars is agreed upon for a copy of the second and third sections of the Hebrew Bible, to be made after the model of the first section previously done by the scribe for the same proprietor. He was paid an advance of 2 dinars by the banker Salāma b. Sa'īd, alias Solomon b. Saadya Ibn Ṣaghīr. The same price of 25 dinars for a Bible codex is mentioned in a letter to Nahray b. Nissīm.[53]

As proved by the example of the three copyists from al-Maḥalla, the manufacture of books was not confined to the large cities. One letter also stresses that the town had a professional bookbinder.[54] A scribe of high quality living in a little Egyptian town is referred to in *Med. Soc.*, I, 51, and the work of another from the same locality (Ṣahrajt) is preserved in a manuscript of the Bodleian Library, Oxford.[55] In Palestine, Jerusalem was, of course, the ideal place for the copying of books and many letters from there refer to this occupation. We read also about a scribe who chose al-Jūsh (the ancient Gischala, today al-Jīsh, Heb. Gush Halav) in Upper Galilee as his seat.[56] An important center for book production was Tunisia, and not only for religious, but for scientific, books as well.

The scribes seem to have transmitted their art to their descendants even more frequently than was the rule in other occupations. In the colophons of books it is not uncommon to find the copyist mentioning his forefathers up to the seventh or eighth generation.[57] Sometimes when we have a sufficient number of writings in the hands of a father, a son, and a grandson we are able to trace the tradition in the writing style.[58] It was not so much the blood relationship that counted, but the power of actual tradition. In a negative way, we can observe in the family of Moses Maimonides that the handwritings of his son, grandson, and other descendants differ very much from his own, certainly because each of them learned the art of writing not from his father, but from teachers using the style of their own time. But Maimonides (at his best) and his brother David have an almost identical handwriting, certainly because they learned in the same school. Of the two most prolific scribes of the Geniza known to us, Ḥalfōn ben Manasse's early style is very similar to the late style of his father-in-law, Hillel b. Eli, undoubtedly because he either studied with him or was trained in the same tradition. Even more illustrative is the following: an attestation by the court of the Iraqian community of Old Cairo, written in 1044, is so similar in script to that of the circulars of the Jewish academy of Baghdad issued 120 or more years later that one would be inclined to attribute them to the same school, had the documents not been dated. It was of course the strength of the "university tradition," referred to here repeatedly, which accounts for this impression.[59]

In these days of the study of the Dead Sea Scrolls, when scholars draw far-reaching conclusions on the dates of documents from paleographic evidence, the ways of the medieval scribes, who have left us mountains of dated manuscripts in the Geniza, may serve as a lesson worthy of attention. Even two drafts of the same matter, written on the same day by the same scribe, one a short outline, and the other a full rough copy, show some differences in the forms of the letters. Not only "the heart of a man is like deep water" (Proverbs 20:5), but also his hand.[60]

12. MEDICAL PROFESSION

The physicians of our time are certainly better equipped to preserve and to restore the health of their patients than were their medieval colleagues, but cannot compare with them so far as the latter's unique role of spiritual leadership and honored social position is concerned. The medieval doctors of the Mediterranean area were the torchbearers of secular erudition, the professional expounders of philosophy and the sciences. While the lawyers studied and applied the sacred laws of their religions and denominations, and therefore were limited in outlook by their very profession, the physicians were the disciples of the Greeks, and as heirs to a universal tradition formed a spiritual brotherhood that transcended the barriers of religion, language, and countries.

Their noble calling as exponents of the sciences would perhaps not have sufficed to bestow upon the medical profession the halo of social prestige it enjoyed in the period studied in this book. For the main concern of man in those days was religion, and consequently it was excellence in this field which was honored most. The physician had another feather in his cap. Almost any doctor of distinction was also a member of the entourage of a caliph, a sultan, a vizier, a general, or a governor. He shared the glory of the great of his world without being involved in their crimes and their hateful ways of oppression.

Why did medieval rulers, many of whom were soldiers with only scant education, care to attract so many physicians to their courts? The answer is that even those rough soldiers could not escape the spirit of their age. In those times, an immense belief in books, in ancient books in particular, prevailed, and it was the doctors who knew the books. The more doctors around, the more knowledge was available, and the better the prospects for its successful use.

This strong belief in the efficacy of the ancient sciences was not confined to the upper classes. Private correspondence preserved in the Geniza abounds in references to medical advice sought and often paid for with one's last penny. It would be entirely fallacious to attribute this to human nature in general and to the truism that "all that a man has he gives for his life" (Job 2:4). In Yemen, at the beginning of the twentieth century, there was not a single physician in the whole country (with the exception of one or two European doctors residing temporarily in the capital). In the Geniza papers we find a Jewish doctor, and often more than one, in many a little town or a large village and occasionally Christian and Muslim colleagues are mentioned as well. The prescriptions preserved indicate that even for humdrum cases of constipation or of the loosening of the bowels a doctor was consulted. It was the general outlook of a highly bookish age with its deep veneration for scientific attainments which entrenched the position of the medical art in popular conscience. In the thirteenth century, when the orthodox reaction ousted philosophy from most of the countries of Islam, the sciences, and in the course of time medicine too, fell into disrepute, until it reached total eclipse, which was not overcome until modern times.

In Europe, too, the thirteenth century was a period of clerical ascendancy. There, however, philosophy survived as the maidservant of theology. In the course of the centuries the buxom maid outstripped the fading mistress, and medicine, together with other sciences, progressed with mighty strides, albeit against heavy odds. During our eleventh and twelfth centuries, however, there was no appreciable difference between the northern and southern shores of the Mediterranean. As the Geniza shows, a doctor from Egypt could practice his art freely in Byzantium,[1] and as early as the tenth century we find a physician at the head of the Jewish community of Bari in southern Italy, a town famous for its religious scholars.[2] A contemporary and compatriot of this physician, the famous Shabbetay Donnolo of Oria, has left a Hebrew treatise on mixtures and potions (based on Greek, not Arab, tradition), perhaps the earliest extant medical work from Christian western Europe.[3] The medical schools of Salerno, near Naples, and Montpellier, southern France, were largely, if not mainly, secular institutions, and before the eleventh century was over the writings of the major authors on medicine in Arabic were known there in Latin translations. The reception of Greek science through the medium of Arabic transmission was so rapid and smooth because the Greek tradition had never become entirely extinct around the Mediterranean basin. Still, the study and practice of medicine penetrated Islamic civilization more than the Christian countries of Europe during the tenth through the twelfth centuries.

If medicine was a prominent constituent of Islamic civilization during its creative period in general, it was absolutely paramount in the life of the so-called protected communities, the Christians and the Jews. An often-quoted statement of a Muslim visitor to Egypt in the forties of the thirteenth century tells us that most of the (prominent) Christians and Jews of that country were either government officials or physicians.[4] A handbook for the market police, written shortly after that time, scolds the Muslims because many a town had no physician except members of the protected minorities.[5] Four and a half centuries earlier, around 790, the following examples for lucrative occupations of non-Muslims are given in an Islamic legal text: bankers, clothiers, landowners, big merchants, and practicing physicians.[6] During the first 150 years of medical writing in Arabic, the authors were almost exclusively Christians, some also Jewish, and later on, the share of these two communities in the output of Arabic books on medicine was out of all proportion to their numbers or their other contributions to Arabic literature, except of course in the sciences. The secular leaders of the very important Christian community of Iraq under the Abbasids were doctors, and the same was true, as we shall presently see, for the Jews in Egypt under the Fatimids and their successors.

The very first Fatimid caliph to rule Egypt and the neighboring countries, al-Mu'izz, had a Jewish physician, Moses b. Elazar, whose marvelous concoctions had wrought wonders while he was still in Tunisia, that is, before 969.[7] Moses, like Donnolo, was a native of Oria, but was carried off in 925 by Muslim raiders from Tunisia when they sacked that south Italian city. At Qayrawān he became a disciple of the famous medical writer and court physician Isaac Israeli.[8] Moses' writings, among them one on pharmacopoeia, dedicated to al-Mu'izz, seem to be lost, but some of his lengthy prescriptions were transmitted in the books of others. Having served two of al-Mu'izz' predecessors back in Tunisia, Moses became one of the most influential personages at the new Fatimid court of Cairo, and his position of physician in attendance was inherited by two of his sons and a grandson.[9] A great-grandson, also called Moses, was "physician to the exalted Majesty," namely of a descendant of al-Mu'izz, and at the same time "chief of the Jewish community." These titles are found in a document from May, 1038, which states that the synagogue in the newly founded capital Cairo, like all other houses of Jewish worship, were under the jurisdiction of the court physician. Moreover, we learn the interesting facts that it had been so for over forty years and that the synagogue building was surrounded on three sides by houses belonging to the doctor, his father, and his grandfather, respectively. The document, which is preserved in the archives of the Jewish community of Cairo (not in the Geniza, as sometimes stated), cannot be an original from the Fatimid chancellery, as it pretends, for its Arabic is too faulty for that claim. But there is no reason to cast doubt on the historicity of the minor details reported here.[10]

Partly contemporary with this family of court physicians and community leaders was another one about which we have considerable material in the Geniza. The father, Isaac b. Furāt, perished, it seems, in a court intrigue. His son, Abraham, served the government while his father was still alive as head of the dysentery department in the hospital of Ramle, Palestine, where he was asked by Solomon b. Judah, the Gaon of Jerusalem, once to intervene with the Muslim chief justice of Palestine, once to make a request to the governor, and once to act in inner-Jewish affairs.[11] After his transfer to Cairo, he continued to be "a shield and protector" for his coreligionists and even their Muslim friends for a long time.[12]

During the second half of the eleventh century and the beginning of the twelfth a still more important family of court physicians was at the head of the Jewish community of the Fatimid empire. Its most prominent member was the Nagid Abu 'l-Faḍl Mevōrākh b. Saadya. In a letter written in or after 1067, his brother and predecessor Judah appears for the first time as "Nagid," which, later on, became the official Hebrew title of the heads of the Jewish community in Egypt.[13] The father of the two also had been a physician, and is always so designated in the signature of his elder son, and their learned mother must have been an influential woman, since in an elegy on her death it was said that in her wisdom she succeeded in appeasing the wrath of the king.[14] Mevōrākh was succeeded by his eldest son Moses, also a physician.

The first Nagid known to have borne this title in his capacity of head of a Jewish territorial community was a medical man: Abraham b. Nathan, better known under his Arabic name Ibn 'Aṭā', who served two rulers of Tunisia as court physician (see chap. v, sec. A, 2, above).

In the middle of the twelfth century, the leader of Egyptian Jewry and one who loomed large in the Geniza (being second only to Mevōrākh) was the physician Samuel b. Hananya, well known from Arabic sources under the name Abū Manṣūr (in office 1140–1159).[15] When the caliph ordered him to liquidate the rebellious crown prince by poison, both wisdom and the Hippocratic oath induced him to disobey the caliph's order. The Christian doctor who carried it out was executed shortly after having done his duty. Samuel's father and elder brother also had been doctors. In his capacity as ra'īs al-Yahūd, he was succeeded by the court physician of the last Fatimid caliphs Hibat Allah Nethanel (both the Arabic and the Hebrew names mean "a gift of God") b. Moses ha-Levi.[16] Finally, the usurper Zuṭṭa, who used the general upheaval at the termination of Fatimid rule to make himself head of the community, also claimed to be a learned physician.[17]

Soon afterward, Maimonides became the central figure of the Jewish community in Egypt and its dependencies. His descendants continued to head it for over two hundred years. Maimonides and his son Abraham were of course renowned physicians and it can be safely assumed that his grandson, the Nagid David, embraced the same profession, since a famous handbook of pharmacology quotes a prescription of Maimonides as transmitted through him.[18] The latter's great-grandson, the last Nagid of Maimonides' family, David II. b. Joshua (latest known document dated 1409), was also a physician.[19]

Thus we see that an almost unbroken succession of medical men represented both the actual and official leadership of the Jews of Egypt and the adjacent countries during the whole of the High Middle Ages and far beyond.

It is almost unnecessary to stress that the same situation prevailed in the local communities. We find physicians in charge of local affairs in Tripoli, Lebanon, Ramle, Palestine, Alexandria, and various other towns in Egypt.[20] Regarding the doctor and "head of the congregation" in Bari referred to above (p. 242), we read the interesting detail that once, upon learning that a messenger from Spain had been robbed by brigands, he ascended his horse and pursued the culprits "with his men." The scene of a physician carrying out police duties is more characteristic of tenth-century Italy than of the contemporary, somewhat more tightly organized Fatimid empire.

The survey of the physicians serving as community leaders given above also reveals another aspect of the medical profession in the Middle Ages: the prevalence of families of doctors. Many other examples could be adduced from the Geniza records, especially the lists of contributors, where, for instance, in one list, three or more physicians belonging to the same family live in one house, and the same is noted of two oculists, father and son (App. C, sec. 55, cols. 3, 6). Two more examples: The doctor and judge Aaron b. Yeshūʿā Ibn al-ʿAmmānī of Alexandria, famous in Hebrew literature owing to the beautiful poems devoted to him by the Spanish Hebrew poet Judah ha-Levi (who visited Alexandria in 1140), had two grandsons and two great-grandsons who were doctors, and it is more than likely that at least one of his five sons pursued the same profession. His father and great-great-grandfather Aaron, the founder of the al-ʿAmmānī family in Egypt, also were physicians, so that the medical tradition remained alive in the family for at least eight generations.[21]

In a document dated 1378, the father, uncle, grandfather, and great-grandfather of the young lady Shams ("Sun") are designated as doctors, a fact recorded as a mere title of honor and without any connection with the subject matter of the document (the sale by the girl of a part of a house belonging to her).[22] Needless to say, in the Christian and Muslim communities the same system prevailed. The renowned Bukhtīshū family of Christian doctors of Baghdad can be traced through two and a half centuries and this is only one, although the most illustrious, example of a general phenomenon.[23] And a mere glance at Ibn Abī Uṣaybiʿa's priceless *History of the*

Physicians suffices to show that many Muslim doctors were only following in the footsteps of their fathers. The famous Platearius family of Salerno exemplifies the same situation for the northern shore of the Mediterranean.[24]

It has been stressed in *Med. Soc.*, I, 80, that the adoption of the father's vocation was not as common during the Geniza period as one is inclined to assume for the Middle Ages. The same was true for the medical profession. Even where no decline in social status was involved, a son would often choose a career different from that of his father. Still, families of doctors, as the Geniza proves, were more frequently found in those times than in our modern society, from which they are not absent, as everyone knows.

A physician is called in the Geniza records either *ṭabīb,* the technical term for physician, or *ḥakīm,* "doctor of the sciences," or both, that is, he is referred to as "the illustrious doctor so-and-so, the physician."[25] A third term, *mutaṭabbib,* "medical practitioner," is also common, but is not used in the pejorative sense of a man without general philosophical erudition, for we find that highly respected representatives of the profession such as Abraham b. Isaac b. Furāt, are also addressed in this way.[26] The irritating passion for variety, observed in the writings of the Geniza in general, was operative here too. It is noteworthy that the Hebrew term *rōfē* is very frequently found, as occupations are not normally expressed in Hebrew words. The Hebrew title appears often in signatures on documents as well as in memorial lists, in both of which, as a rule, only a dignity connected with religion or the service of the community is noted. No doubt the halo of spirituality surrounding the medical profession accounts for this usage.[27]

Even a young doctor would be referred to as rayyis, or chief.[28] Whether or not the persons concerned actually were, or had been, chief physicians of a department in a hospital could not be ascertained. An aspirant to the medical profession, who had not yet received permission to exercise it independently, was called *mu'allim,* properly translated as "master." We read in a letter of an oculist to his assistant, who was also his relative: "I heard that Menahem has already been licensed, while you are still only a mu'allim." The letter itself shows that the oculist was rather helpless without his knowledgeable assistant, who had quit his service.[29]

During the entire Geniza period, doctors bore honorific titles specific to their calling. At the beginning, titles were confined to the more prominent members of the profession such as "the physician of the exalted Majesty," referred to above, who bore the title "The

Sound." Later on certain titles became very common, especially three of them: "The Sound," "The Successful," and "The Accomplished."[30] Since it was customary to refer to a more prominent person not by his name, but by his title, for example: "best regards to The Accomplished," the identity of the physician referred to is often doubtful. In addition to these common titles there were others, more elaborate ones, such as "The Sun of the Doctors." The person thus honored was addressed with that title even in a short note of a few lines.[31] Some of these presumptuous titles such as "The Crown" or "The Glory of the Physicians" were in Hebrew. Their bearers were no doubt addressed thus in the synagogue when called up to read a section of the Bible, to recite a part of the liturgy, or to make a contribution to a public appeal. Since the heads of the Jewish community were mostly doctors, it was presumably they who conferred those Hebrew titles.[32]

As to the study of medicine, we must beware of applying modern notions to medieval conditions, particularly in the Islamic world with its individualistic approach to higher studies. In order to work independently as a physician one needed a license granted not by a university or a scientific corporation, which did not exist, but by a prominent physician, who was authorized by the government, normally, it seems, by the chief of the market police, sometimes also by the caliph in person.[33]

The ways in which the theoretical knowledge and practical skill needed for the exercise of the profession were acquired varied widely. We learn this from the biographies of physicians, which have been handed down to us by the hundreds in the Arabic books devoted to this subject. It is perhaps illuminating to contrast the first steps of one court physician, as they are described to us by Ibn Abī Uṣaybi'a, with those of another physician, related in two Geniza letters, written by him as a young man. In the first case, the father, also a doctor in the service of a caliph, paid his son a few dirhems every day and had him bleed patients outside the door of his office, until he acquired great dexterity in this technique. Once, when a courtier needed bleeding, the young man was invited to do the job in the presence of the caliph—at the suggestion of his father, of course. He acquitted himself so gracefully that he was immediately admitted to the royal entourage, in which he remained all his lifetime.[34]

The second case concerns the leader of the Jewish community, Hibat Allah-Nethanel, already mentioned. Although later in life he combined the office of a court physician with that of the head of the rabbinical college in Old Cairo, as a young man he must have passed too much time in the company of the "Bird of the Devils" and other members of the jeunesse dorée of his native city. His father, who was a doctor, bribed him with the very large sum of 25 dinars never to leave his house, not even for a visit to the public bathhouse, and to devote his time entirely to the study of medicine, language (i.e., classical Arabic and Hebrew), Talmud, and theology—in short, all an accomplished Jewish physician and scholar had to know. The letters sent by the young man during his confinement show that serious scientific interest had been aroused in him, although he complained bitterly about his separation from his boon companions.[35]

The reading of public lectures to medical students seems not to have been common practice. Where this was done, the biographers made a special point of it. Ibn Jumay', the Jewish physician in attendance to Saladin, "held general meetings for all those who practised under him the art of medicine."[36] To be sure, Ibn Jumay' was regarded as the greatest medical authority of his century in Egypt and was an enthusiastic teacher. Normally one or several students would get what we would call private tutoring from a physician of established fame and would also practice under his or another's supervision, the two aspects of study not always being combined. From a most instructive letter, addressed by the father of such a student to Maimonides, we may conclude that it was not always easy to find the opportunity to study and practice under the guidance of a famous physician. The writer of the letter stresses that he dared to apply to the illustrious doctor and judge only because he had heard that Maimonides' nephew, who had worked under him thus far, now practiced elsewhere. The writer also promised to pay Maimonides a higher honorarium than the former apprentice.[37]

As the example of Maimonides' nephew and the biographies of many doctors indicate, a student would change over from one mentor to another. A large part of the curriculum was covered by private study, which meant mainly memorizing the classics of medicine. One famous Egyptian doctor even opined that studying from books was preferable to working under the supervision of teachers.[38] This opinion, however, was not generally accepted.

The course of medical studies followed can be reconstructed, as far as the Geniza is concerned, from the inventories of doctors' libraries, as well as from actual remnants of medical books preserved. In accordance with the character of this study, which is based on documentary Geniza material, we have to confine ourselves to the first source of information. When a doctor died without leaving a relative who had a claim on and interest in his library, it was sold at public auction. Since the library of a Jewish doctor usually consisted of two parts, one Hebrew and the other Arabic, the auctions were held at two different meetings, gentiles taking a prominent part in the Arabic sale. In a number of cases, only the lists with regard to the Hebrew section have been preserved, not surprising since the lists of Arabic books were usually written in Arabic characters and were therefore not put away in the Geniza.[39] In one example the lists concerning the two auctions, held on two subsequent Tuesdays in the year 1223, have come down to us.[40] In another, that for the Arabic books alone, has been preserved. They were also auctioned on two subsequent Tuesdays, November 13 and 20, 1190.[41] Medical books also appear in various other lists.

The main impression to be gathered from these lists is the absolute preponderance of books of old and established authority. As D. H. Baneth, the judicious editor of the list from November, 1190, has pointed out, the latest authors mentioned in it died around 120 years before the proprietor of that excellent library, which was by no means a commonplace one but contained many books of both Greek and Arabic medical writers which have not been traced thus far. The Arabic translations of works of the Greeks, including above all Hippocrates (fifth century B.C.) and Galen (second century A.D.), were of paramount authority. Studying medicine meant in the first place memorizing selected writings of Hippocrates and even more of Galen. At least 33 out of the 102 volumes sold from the 1190 library contained works by Galen. The serious sudent would not be content with the compendiums and summaries of Galen's work, prepared in the academy of Alexandria in pre-Islamic times, but would study the original writings of the master together with their pre-Islamic and Islamic commentaries, as well as the later Greek authors and the renowned doctors of the Islamic period. Nor should we assume that all students of medicine in the Middle Ages were as exclusively devoted to classical books as was the doctor whose library was auctioned in 1190. The library auctioned in Old Cairo on March 7, 1223, comprised works of the Spanish Muslim Averroes, who died in 1198 and had been a contemporary of the proprietor of the 1190 library. In the 1223 inventory too, Galen far outstripped all other authors, to be followed by Hippocrates and then by al-Rāzī (d. 925), certainly one of the most original representatives of Islamic medicine.

In order to complete his medical education a young doctor would seek work in a hospital. It must have been rather difficult to attain this goal, to judge from the following details contained in a letter sent to a young "doctor" studying in Cairo, who strove to get an appointment in a hospital in his native city, Alexandria. His cousin writes from Alexandria:

> I advise you to obtain letters of recommendation to the wālī (chief of police), to the qadi, to "the Successful" [most probably the famous Ibn Jumayʿ],[42] to Ben Tammām and Ben Ṣadaqa [two well-known physicians, the first Jewish, the second a Samaritan]. This would not be bad, for Ben Tammām is today the superintendent. Whenever anyone comes here and declares that he wants "to read" medicine with them, they reply that the reading has to be done in Cairo and, likewise, that the *tazkiya* [certificate of good conduct] has to be obtained there. Do not worry about anything except that certificate. If you get it, you have everything you need.[43]

The writer had sent two other letters to the capital in order to promote his cousin (who also was his brother-in-law), one to a person in the hospital in which the latter worked, and one to his *ustādh,* or personal mentor. He intended to write a third letter regarding this matter, but was not sure whether the person concerned, a famous doctor, was fluent in the Hebrew cursive (which was used by Jews for writing letters in the Arabic language) and asked his cousin to find out first.[44]

A police certificate of good conduct was required for the exercise of the medical profession in general, not only for work in a hospital. In a fragment addressed to a judge in which a man describes the utter penury of his family, he writes: "So-and-so [name not preserved] cannot work because of the tazkiya. No one is permitted to practice medicine either in Fustat or [in Cairo?] without a certificate of good conduct." The two letters seem to imply that the certificate was secured not so much by good conduct as by appropriate connections and presumably also gifts to the officials handling the matter.[45]

Both the literary sources and the Geniza records suggest that it was the more prominent physicians who worked in the hospitals. Abraham Maimonides mentions in a letter written in October, 1235, when he was at the height of his career as Nagid, that he was unable to attend the wedding celebration of a beloved disciple because it was his turn at the hospital on that particular night and, for special reasons, did not want to ask for a substitute. The father of the unhappy student of medicine referred to above was a prominent scholar whose fame had reached both Spain and Iraq. At the same time, he was a doctor in a hospital, who, as his son writes, used to leave his home very early in the morning—even before the termination of the early morning service—and to come back from the hospital only shortly before noon.[46]

In classical Arabic a hospital was called by the Persian word *bīmāristān* ("place for the sick"), for the institution came to the Arabs from Iran, where it had been developed by physicians of Greek erudition. In the Geniza—where it is written in Hebrew characters—the word is always abbreviated to *māristān* or *maristān,* as in less formal contemporary writings and in spoken Arabic today. We know very little, if anything, of the Fatimid caliphs' interest in this charity. Perhaps they were too religious to try to take out of God's hand the care of human health, although they themselves were surrounded by physicians. Their successors, the Ayyubids, brought with them to Egypt the Mesopotamian tradition that expected a ruler to endow or to maintain a hospital, a tradition so magnificently followed by Nūr al-Dīn Zengi, their former overlord. (His hospital, erected in Damascus shortly after 1154, continued to operate until 1899, and its building is still good enough to harbor a school.) In Fustat, the Geniza papers invariably refer to *the* hospital, even in a deposition in court where exactness is required, as if only one had existed there in Fatimid times ("While passing by the hospital I saw . . . "). This hospital, like those in Iraq and Syria and those in Cairo known from the Mamluk period, probably was divided into different wards, where fever, eye diseases, surgical cases, dysentery, and so on, were treated separately, for even for Ramle, Palestine, we have an eleventh-century Geniza letter addressed to "the head of the dysentery ward."[47]

While the Geniza makes repeated references to Jewish doctors working in hospitals, it never mentions Jewish patients availing themselves of this service. Most probably they refrained from doing so on account of the dietary laws. In those days, people would not agree to transgress the injunctions of their religion, even if recommended for health's sake. A famous example of the attitude was Saladin, who refused to take wine, although one of his Jewish physicians had prescribed it as a remedy against colic.[48]

In serious cases, the house of the doctor served as a substitute for a hospital to patients who could afford it, or who were his friends. In a report on the death of a girl in Alexandria, sent to her grandparents in Fustat, her father describes how she stayed in the house of the physician, who sent her home ("borne in a basket by a porter") only when he recognized that her case was hopeless.[49] Several references indicate that the prominent judge Nathan b. Samuel, the "Diadem" (dated documents 1122-1153, App. D, sec. 18) kept a private hospice for sick and old people, but nowhere in the many Geniza papers related to him is there a hint that he was also a physician. I am inclined indeed to assume that he was not, for in addition to being judge, he acted as the scribe of the yeshiva and the court, a job that must have kept him fully occupied as indicated by the numerous records in his hand still extant. Perhaps the little institution was run by his wife, a woman known otherwise as rich and charitable. In a strong note to a prominent member of the community the judge writes: "In my house are several patients gravely ill who need medical potions and other things. Please send whatever cash is available from the balance [of a collection or a sum promised]. The matter is urgent."[50] An item in a list of indigent in receipt of loaves of bread from the community refers to a sick man "in the house of R. Nathan." This item corresponds exactly to one in another list of receivers of loaves, about a hundred years older: "An acquaintance of Shū'a—in the house of the physician."[51] An old woman turned over to R. Nathan her money (17 dinars) and other belongings on condition that he maintain her until her death and bear her burial expenses. And a day before he died a man not related made a deathbed declaration in Nathan's house.[52]

Sick, homeless foreigners would stay in a synagogue or even in a school, and pious foundations were established for the purchase of medicines for the poor.[53] A physician was expected to treat needy persons without remuneration, as assumed in certain sayings ascribed to Hippocrates. We actually find in the Geniza a Christian army surgeon treating a Jewish woman who had suffered injuries in an accident without taking an honorarium (as the letter reporting it emphasizes).[54]

Persons applying to a civic leader who happened to be a physician would seize the opportunity also to seek medical advice. In an autograph letter, Maimonides gives instructions to a community official in administrative matters, but also takes care of his health. Maimonides had previously prescribed a milk cure, wherefore the official had hired a cow in order to have a steady supply of fresh milk. Satisfied by the patient's report that he had recovered from his illness, Maimonides now advises him to discontinue the hire of the cow and to take only one glass of milk in the morning and another in the evening.

A student of philosophy who had read the first part of Maimonides' newly published *Guide for the Perplexed,* asks the author some questions in connection with his new book, but at the same time consulted him about some dietetic problems. Maimonides, who (as he writes) was himself of very poor health at that time, patiently gives the desired advice.[55]

The Nagid David II b. Joshua, a descendant of Maimonides and a physician like his ancestor, was approached by a woman whose husband had neglected her and their children, being attracted by Sufism, the then very strong mystical movement of Islam. After having requested the Nagid to take steps against her husband and to bring him back into the fold of Judaism and to his duties to his family, she asks also for a medicine for her child who had a sore ear. On the margin of her petition the Nagid wrote: "This very night"—no doubt an instruction to a secretary or assistant to send the required medicine immediately.[56]

In a postscript to a short letter of thanks for expressions of sympathy on the occasion of a bereavement a physician writes a prescription for the growing of hair on a spot of the skin where none would grow (a disgrace in an age when a fine beard was the pride of a man). His correspondent, it seems, had used the opportunity for complaining of more than one ailment, for the doctor writes: "This prescription is only for the growing of the hair." Incidentally, he started writing the prescription in Arabic characters, but continued in Hebrew, presumably because he remembered that his correspondent was not very well versed in the former.[57]

A doctor's office was called *dukkān,* like any other open store in the bazaar. It must have been common practice for two physicians to have a joint office. In one letter reference is made to two joint dukkāns.[58] In the store of a *sharābī,* or seller of potions, there worked a Christian doctor, who wrote out prescriptions while people from the street looked on. A sign above the store publicized the physician's practice.[59] An inventory preserved gives us an idea of the appearance of a doctor's dispensary. It was full of bottles, glasses, boxes, pots, and cauldrons, all in colors, white, black, green, yellow, and blue; there were scales and a mortar and other implements to indicate that the doctor prepared the medicaments himself.[60] As we know from literary sources, even famous physicians did this. On the other hand, numerous prescriptions have been preserved in the Geniza which undoubtedly are instructions given to a pharmacist.

These prescriptions have to be examined by experts in the history of medicine. The layman is impressed by two of their aspects. First, their extremely composite character. Twenty and more ingredients in one medicament seem to have been commonplace. The knowledge of medical plants, inherited from the Greeks and then expanded widely through the influx of Indian, Persian, and local elements, comprised about three thousand items according to an Arabic handbook of commerce written about 1150.[61] In the prescriptions and business and other letters found in the Geniza, about 120 medical plants and other ingredients have been counted, of which about 40 are particularly common. A scrutiny of the Geniza material would thus reveal what was used most in medical practice in those days.

Second, we are moved by the expressions of piety which are rarely absent from a prescription. It would be superscribed with the words: "To be taken with God's blessing" or with the Muslim formula "In the name of the Merciful, the Compassionate," and end almost invariably with remarks such as "It will help, if God will," or "Thanks are due to God alone." Sometimes the name of the patient or the illness is mentioned at the beginning. Even the Jewish doctors seem to have been accustomed to writing prescriptions in Arabic letters. For the benefit of a patient or his relatives who were not fluent in the Arabic script, they were transcribed into Hebrew, as we know from a letter in which the request is made expressly[62] as well as from the fact that at least two of the prescriptions preserved in Hebrew characters were written not by the physician, but by scribes whose handwriting is known to us. In one, the name of the prescribing physician was written by the scribe on the reverse side.[63]

A doctor's day began very early in the morning, as we have already learned with regard to his hospital service. A private doctor, too, even if his clientele consisted of the "great" of the town, left his house at early dawn, when the stars were still visible. In a letter addressed to Maimonides, the writer worries that he is unable to say his morning prayers at the prescribed time.[64] The prescriptions, too, say repeatedly that they should be taken at dawn, while sometimes we hear that the physician should be present while the patient takes his medicine.

On the frequency of a doctor's visits, we find in a letter from Tinnīs, Lower Egypt, that a certain patient who was strong enough to write or to dictate fifty lines and made reference to three other letters sent by him, mentions that his physician came to see him every day. His illness, however, must have been rather serious, since in the letter he asks God to spare him for his little children.[65] In the event of a grave illness, even for a person of limited means, a consultation of several experts was arranged (for instance, in Ramle, Palestine; reported by the patient after recovery).[66] A physician from Fustat mentions in a letter that he traveled in order to visit a patient in a village.[67]

On the other hand, it must have been common practice for doctors to prescribe without seeing the patient at all. The illness would be described to them and they were expected to cure by sending instructions. A short Geniza letter contains thanks for the forwarding of a prescription from one physician and a request for a prescription from another, both for the writer's wife. Her condition is elaborately described for the purpose, and a physician today reading the translation of the letter in *Mediterranean People* will perhaps be able to diagnose the nature of the woman's disease. From a later letter we learn that she recovered.[68]

In a letter from Alexandria to a prominent merchant in Old Cairo he is asked to take (not: "a description from the Song of Songs," as the English translation of the edited text has, but:) a prescription from the Prince of the Princes, who is none other than the Nagid and court physician Mevōrākh. The son of the writer suffered "from a dryness which appeared on his body, in particular boils and dry patches extending from his hip to his feet."[69] We do not know, whether the receiver of this letter acted upon the request, or whether the court physician saw fit to prescribe on the base of such a flimsy statement. But we have a reminder for this request in another letter and learn from a third that the young man for whom the medicine had been requested had died.[70]

In a letter from Old Cairo to a smaller town we read the following: "I received a note from your brother in which he complained that his eyes were in a very bad state and asked for medicaments. I went to the oculists [in the plural], informed them about his complaints, and they prescribed ointments and powders which I sent to him. However, the doctors said to me that the medicines would be of no avail, as long as he continued to work in sunlight, which his profession forces him to do."[71]

The oculists, including women so designated,[72] were the specialists most frequently referred to in the Geniza records. The *kallām,* or *Wundarzt* (a physician treating wounds), as differentiated from the surgeon, appears in several papers, but the word seems not to be listed in any Arabic dictionary.[73] Surgeons are rarely mentioned, which tallies with the fact that only a few of the many Jewish doctors known to us from Arabic literary sources specialized in this field.[74] But the *quḍāʿī,* the healer of *quḍāʿ,* or stomach trouble, is found from the eleventh through the thirteenth centuries. This term, too, seems not to be registered in the dictionaries—but is known as a Muslim family name.[75] Artificial teeth are referred to, but not dentists, for the treatment of the teeth, as Franz Rosenthal has shown in his painstaking study of the subject, was left to the general practitioner.[76] The phlebotomists, experts in bloodletting, did not belong to the medical profession proper, but were required to have theoretical knowledge in addition to technical skill.[77] Only in the fourteenth century do we find a barber dabbling in the treatment of sickness (ear trouble of a child).[78] Professional veterinarians were also regularly employed during the Geniza period, and one was President of the Jewish congregation in Minyat Ziftā.[79] For the healing of a dislocation suffered by a donkey carrying building materials a veterinarian received 1/4 dinar, not a small sum, considering that a donkey could be had for 2 dinars.[80]

The data regarding doctors' fees culled thus far from the Geniza are too sporadic to permit general conclusions. The fees range from 3 dirhems a week for the treatment of a sore eye[81] to a thousand dinars, promised to a Jewish physician in Tripoli, Libya, for the successful healing of the sultan of Gabes, Tunisia. Of this sum, he was to receive 100 dinars before he even left his own house. The physician, who obviously understood the nature of the illness from the description given, was so little eager to attempt a cure that he offered to the bedouin rulers of Tripoli a bribe of 50 dinars if they allowed him to ignore the sultan's summons. They insisted, however, that he treat the sultan, and, in their rough bedouin manner, threw all the Jewish notables of the town into prison and held them there until he would comply. Finally the doctor, a father of four sons, set out on his perilous expedition, but, fortunately for him, the sultan died before he arrived.[82]

Between the two extremes described we find an honorarium of 4 dinars demanded by a Muslim physician for the treatment of a Jewish girl who was affected by dropsy, and of 1 dinar paid monthly by a Muslim family to its Jewish doctor, about which the latter reports this detail: "By chance, I befriended a man from Damascus who introduced me to the family of Sayf al-Islām. I entered their house and treated them, whereupon they fixed for me a payment of 1 dinar every month."[83]

In a petition to an Ayyubid sultan the physician Makārim b. Isḥāq asks for a lifetime appointment in the hospital of (New) Cairo with the usual salary of 3 dinars per month. Two of the personal physicians of the sultan (mentioned by name) were able to testify to the excellence of the applicant's qualifications. The name, Makārim b. Isḥāq, might have been borne by a Muslim, Christian, or Jew. But since a Jewish physician with exactly the same name has left another document in the Geniza (see below), the author of the petition is probably identical with him. The Muslim writers on the history of medicine provide some data on the salaries of physicians, but mostly of the famous ones and those who had gained the special favor of the rulers. The Geniza petition to the sultan contains the valuable information that the standard monthly salary of a physician in the hospital of

Cairo (presumably the one founded by Saladin) was 3 dinars around 1240, at least during a certain period and for a certain type of physician. To be sure, at noontime the physicians left the hospital for home and were free to attend to their private practice. An appointment to the hospital was perhaps sought for reasons of prestige.[84]

A famous story in *The Arabian Nights* suggests that an advance payment of a 1/4 dinar for a single visit was regarded as very high. The humorous story relates that a Jewish doctor, when told by his Sudanese maidservant that a patient waiting downstairs was prepared to pay that sum, became so excited that he sped down the staircase without taking a lamp (it was nighttime) and in the darkness ran the patient over and killed him (or, rather, believed he had killed him).[85]

The British Museum contains an interesting contract made before a Muslim notary, in which the proprietor of a Nubian slave promises to pay to the Jewish physician Makārim b. Isḥāq b. Makārim (see above) an honorarium for the successful treatment of the slave's left eye (June, 1245)—how much is not said. The fee perhaps depended on the degree of satisfaction of the contractor. The idea that payment should be made to a physician only after successful treatment is as old as the Codex Hammurabi (paragraphs 215 ff.), and presumably much older.[86]

It seems that the physicians were renowned for being greedy. A doctor, who was also a muqaddam, or head of a congregation, and a native of Jerusalem (both capacities associated with the task of collecting funds), writes jokingly to a friend: "Although I am a doctor, a president, and from Jerusalem, so that all the reasons for being exacting are combined in me, I am not of this type, as far as you are concerned."[87]

Many of the doctors appearing in the Geniza documents were influential and affluent people. There were, however, others who possessed only modest means or who were poor. Legal documents, such as wills or marriage contracts referring to doctors, or lists of contributions to public appeals reveal their financial status, or it is stated expressly in letters.[88] Competition was keen. A physician from Qalyūb (about 12 miles north of Old Cairo), who had opened an office in the capital, writes to his wife that the response of the public had been excellent, but that the enmity of the other members of the profession was so strong that he could not dare to interrupt his work even for one day to come out and examine her sore eyes.[89] Competition was waged also in the form most congenial to Islamic civilization: in satiric verses. For example, Ibn Shū'a, a prominent Jewish court physician, oculist, and surgeon, and at the same time a guitar player and witty poet, wrote biting verses against his famous colleague Ibn Jumay', who was also the object of poetical invective by others.[90]

It was not regarded as incompatible with the dignity of the profession for a physician to engage in business as a sideline. Mention was made in *Med. Soc.*, I, 92, of Maimonides' advice to a disciple to gain his livelihood by commerce and the teaching of medicine. In the same letter, Maimonides promises the disciple to set up accounts for him with an India merchant. A letter addressed to Maimonides from his brother David, when the latter was en route to India, shows that the great master was well versed in business affairs.[91] Some documents on sugar factories show that physicians not only had a share in them, but also participated in their operation.[92] The son and grandson of a prominent eleventh-century physician were representatives of the merchants in Old Cairo, and in one document he, too, appears as a commercial wakīl.[93] In particular it seems that the doctors, who were bibliophiles because of their profession, sometimes dabbled in the book trade, as illustrated by various examples: a notebook containing, alongside medical prescriptions, many entries with regard to the trading and lending of books;[94] a letter to a physician (also a communal leader), away with the army, reporting the prices of books, both Hebrew and Arabic, which he had left at his departure to be offered for sale;[95] and, most interesting of all, a letter in the beautiful hand of the physician and judge Aaron b. Yeshū'ā Ibn al-'Ammānī of Alexandria, inquiring of the perfumer Abū Sa'īd of Fustat about seven volumes, all on parchment, which he had sent to him—a biblical commentary, a volume on the creations of a tenth-century Hebrew poet, three volumes containing Dioscorides, that is, an Arabic translation of the famous Greek pharmaceutical handbook, and, finally, two volumes on Jewish law. The wide diversity of the subjects of these books shows that they were destined for sale.[96] But the busybody of Minyat Ziftā, the physician and muqaddam whom we have met even as a substitute schoolteacher, definitely was an exceptional case and the times showed signs of decline.[97]

The Muslim historians of medicine have transmitted a considerable number of Arabic poems and selected couplets written by famous, or not so famous, medical men, Muslim, Christian, and Jewish, and it is not surprising that some of it, holographed by its author, has found its way also into the Geniza. I was particularly impressed by these expressions of homesickness which conclude a long poem (lost, of course), written by a physician from Alexandria who practiced in Qūṣ, the desert-port on the Nile deep in the south of Upper Egypt.

He had copied the poem in calligraphic Hebrew characters and equally calligraphic Arabic vowel signs, and, obviously convinced of the significance of his creation, added a long colophon, providing dates according to the Muslim and two Jewish eras (spring, 1253):

Yearning has not left me any endurance, but visits me day and night.
My endurance is dead, entombed deep in the bottom of a grave.
The boats of my longing have thrown anchor on the shores of yearning.

In good Arab fashion he provides his creation with a linguistic commentary, explaining words that might have been unfamiliar to uninitiated contemporaries.[98]

Hebrew poems by physicians are to be found in the Geniza in far greater numbers. Many of the poetical creations of the Alexandrian physician and judge Aaron Ibn al-ʿAmmānī retrieved from the Geniza have been edited.[99] With one exception, a fragment, all these works are liturgical and betray a strong, almost impetuous religious feeling. Their mere literary merits, as far as I am entitled to judge, seem to be limited. Judah ha-Levi, the Hebrew poet laureate, praised Aaron as a great physician, who successfully fought the angel of death, bringing back to life patients already given up, also as an encyclopedic scholar, a powerful judge, an indefatigable teacher, and a man of munificence, but, if I am not mistaken, is silent about his poetical gifts.[100] Twice, when Aaron presented him with poems requiring, according to the refined manners of that period, reciprocation in kind, ha-Levi jokingly replied in a few couplets that he was unable to do so because he regarded himself unworthy of competing with the writer. I take this as a polite way for the Spanish poet to try to avoid a poetical contest in which the Alexandrian physician could but emerge with little distinction.[101]

It is to be expected that the motifs of illness and healing recur frequently in the creations of Ibn alʿAmmānī, the physician. In one liturgical poem, all thirteen couplets conclude with the word "the patient," meaning Israel, as the editor, J. Schirmann, rightly observes.[102] In another poem, however, recently edited by A. Scheiber of Budapest, persons physically sick seem to be meant, subsuming with them, of course, God's eternal patients, the Jewish community:[103]

Ye sick, praise in our tongue[104]
And do come back to our God.
He makes us ill, He gives us health,

"For He strikes and heals" (Hosea 6:1).
We know, You can do everything,
You heal without medicine or nutriment,
You still our pains, when we suffer,
You healer of all our ailments.
"For He strikes . . ."
Heal our diseases, oh Great Physician,
And let our trespasses be forgiven,
For your bounty is hoped for
By all your hosts all the days of their service.[105]
"For he strikes . . ."

Judah ha-Levi himself, as is well known, practiced medicine while in his native Spain, treating the "great" of his city and, as he wrote jokingly to a friend in Narbonne, France, working not only day and night, but also when it was neither day nor night.[106] On Friday morning, when he did not make rounds to patients, his office was crowded with people, as we read in a holograph, hastily written on such a morning.[107] (One of the two laureate Hebrew poets of the twentieth century was also a medical man, but his practice was not as lucrative as that of his Spanish predecessor.)[108] Judah ha-Levi, as we know from various Geniza letters and some allusions in his poems, was well-off, and, as usual with prominent physicians, served also as a communal leader.[109] But, wise man that he was, he had a low opinion of the medical art of his time. In the same letter to Narbonne, he speaks about "this nonsense of medicine" and, with a pun on Jeremiah 51:9, he writes, alluding to the big city in which he practiced: "We healed [meaning: treated] Babylon, but she was not healed." While taking a medical potion, concocted by himself, he prayed:[110]

My God, heal me, and I shall be healed.
Be not angry with me, lest I be destroyed.
My drugs and potions are in Your hand, whether good
Or bad, whether strong or weak.
You choose for me, not I.[111]
You alone know the evil and the fair.
Not on my art of healing I rely.
Only for Your healing do I watch.

The combination of secular with religious scholarship, and accordingly, that of the profession of the physician with the office of the judge or of the head of the Jewish community was not uncommon in the period under consideration and was even characteristic of it. Still the physicians not known as religious scholars by far outnumber those who were. The secular vein in the culture of the period must therefore have been of considerable strength.

For physicians in the army and the navy see chapter vii, section C, 2, below. The next section on druggists and pharmacists is also pertinent.[112]

13. DRUGGISTS, PHARMACISTS, PERFUMERS, PREPARERS OF POTIONS

One need not delve deeply into the writings of the Cairo Geniza in order to discover that a great many of them refer to the professions connected with the processing and sale of drugs, spices, perfumes, and potions for medical and culinary use. The occupations of *'aṭṭār* (from which English "attar of roses"), usually translated as perfumer or druggist, and that of *sharābī* (from the same root as English sherbet), preparer and seller of potions, are among those occurring most commonly in the Geniza.[1] The *ṣaydalānī,* also *ṣaydanī,* pharmacist, apothecary, belongs to the same group, and there were specialists, such as the *safūfī,* or preparer of medical powders.[2]

Out of ten persons whose occupations are mentioned in a list of contributors (App. C, sec. 18), four are described as druggists (around 1095). In the contemporary list C 19, four other druggists and two apothecaries make their appearance. In the collection for wheat for the poor, C 33, made in summer 1178, two 'aṭṭārs belonged to the upper class of contributors, two to the middle, and three to the lower. We should remember, however, that then as today a good drugstore served as a landmark in a neighborhood (often used as an address in a letter), and, therefore, its proprietor was usually referred to not by his profession, but by his name, often the first only, or even a nickname. This explains, at least partly, the strange fact that in C 40, out of 21 occupations mentioned, there were four 'aṭṭārs and four sharābīs, but in the contemporary list C 39 only one out of 105, and in C 46, also closely contemporary, none out of 127 persons or firms listed. There is no doubt that a scrutiny of the relevant Geniza material would reveal that a number of persons mentioned in the last two lists (C 39 and 46) belonged to the professions discussed here, while the 'aṭṭārs and sharābīs occurring in the first (C 40) were probably not prominent members of the community and were therefore identified by their profession.

In the study of the economic and legal aspects of commercial and industrial partnerships undertaken in *Med. Soc.,* volume I, drugstores and pharmacies figure in no fewer than seven documents, more than any other occupation.[3] These contracts originated in the eleventh through the thirteenth centuries and ranged from a large undertaking, into which six hundred gold pieces were invested in 1095, to a modest store worth 620 dirhems in 1228.[4] The enormous variety of situations reflected in those documents is also a testimony to the wide diffusion of those occupations.

In volume I of this book the general nature of medieval partnerships was studied, so that specific contracts on stores of drugs and spices were postponed for discussion here. There are many such documents, two from the first quarter of the year 1126 alone. In one, Banīn (possibly, but not necessarily, identical with the next one mentioned) dissolves his partnership in the perfumery, *dukkān al-'iṭr,* which he shared with Abū 'Alī Ezekiel (a brother of the renowned India trader Ḥalfōn b. Nethanel ha-Levi) in a house belonging to a Muslim in Gizeh, the suburb of Cairo. Banīn, at that time, was probably of limited means, for he promises to pay to his partner a residual debt of 20 dirhems in ten installments.[5] In the second document, the 'aṭṭār Abu 'l-Munā Jacob b. David ha-parnās receives for his business of *ṣinā'at al-iṭr,* or "art of perfumery," a loan of 57 dinars as a *muḍāraba,* or commenda, from various capitalists through the mediation of the banker Solomon b. Ḥayyīm, the "Seventh" (the same, by the way, who, forty-one years earlier, in March, 1085, had granted a loan to the Rabbanite Jews of Jerusalem [App. A, sec. 13]).[6] A partnership in half a hundredweight of opium is noteworthy.[7] In those days and places, no prohibition or limitation of the sale of this drug and similar ones existed. All that concerned the market police was the protection of the pocketbook of the customer, namely, watching that the precious material not be adulterated with cheaper substitutes.[8]

Legal documents and letters relating to members of the professions treated in this section are legion. Properly collected and studied they would shed much light on those professions themselves. A few examples: An 'aṭṭār rents a ground floor and a mezzanine for eight years, making renovations worth 40 dinars, the equivalent of eight annual rents of 5 dinars. The house concerned was situated in (New) Cairo, but the detailed document was written on July 27, 1150, in Fustat, at that time still the spiritual capital of the Jews of Egypt.[9] Another perfumer rents part of a communal building for a period of at least four years in order to use it for reservoirs for rose water (1180–1184) (see App. A, sec. 102). In a Muslim document from October, 1334, a Jewish 'aṭṭār pays to a lady (presumably Muslim) 28 dirhems as his monthly rent for his store.[10] In an earlier Muslim document a Jewish apothecary buys one-quarter of a house, of which he already possessed three-quarters, from three Christian ladies. The price of that quarter was 70 dinars, a total value of about 28,000 dollars, for which sum one could have in those days a mansion. On the reverse side of the document the buyer presents the newly acquired part to a son of a daughter of his and assigns some other shares to some other beneficiaries.[11] A sharābī sells to an 'aṭṭār before a Jewish court one-eighth of a house, which he shared in common with Christians and a fellow Jew (1179).[12] A complete, but old, and partly neglected house, bordering on one Christian and two Muslim properties, was acquired by a Jewish 'aṭṭār in December, 1088, before a Muslim notary.[13] Loans were given and received by 'aṭṭārs and sharābīs.[14] Estates were left by and for them.[15] Some of them were parties to the sales of menials and maidservants discussed in *Med. Soc.*, I, 130–147. Noteworthy in particular is that of an Indian slave, the only such case (*ibid.*, p. 133). Of the many papers on family life about them I should like to draw attention to one, but very elaborate document: the engagement of the son of a perfumer with a girl from a prominent family of India traders.[16]

The center of the drugs and perfumes business in Fustat (also in Alexandria) was the Square of the Perfumers, Murabba'at al-'Aṭṭārīn, often abbreviated to al-Murabba'a (although there were many other squares in Fustat) or al-Aṭṭārīn. There, the wholesalers had their seat. But it has already been pointed out (*Med. Soc.*, I, 150) that because of the costliness of many of the commodities carried by them, the wholesale perfumers often acted also as retailers. I noted at random six other bazaars as harboring Jewish druggists, mainly retailers, as the relevant documents prove. One had his store in the "Lane [called also: Bazaar] of the Lamps," a prestigious neighborhood at the corner of the Great (today: 'Amr) Mosque and seat of the Muslim aristocracy. The place derived its name from the custom of the Muslim nobles to keep lamps burning all night at the entrances to their houses; it served in general as a bazaar for books, precious manuscripts, and objects d'art made of ebony and glass.[17] Another 'aṭṭār, contemporary with the first, was located just around the corner, in the Market of the Berbers, which, by the way, derived its name not from the Berbers who entered Egypt with the Fatimids, but from others, arriving there at the very dawn of Muslim history. He appears in an account together with two others, one in the Great Bazaar and another in the Wardān Market, a Jewish neighborhood, where at least one other contemporary 'aṭṭār had his seat.[18] The Lane of the Makers of Copper Canisters had an 'aṭṭār and the Street of the Blacksmiths a sharābī.[19]

It is perhaps no exaggeration to say that about a third of the Geniza letters that have a more detailed address (in addition to name and city) are directed to the Square of the Perfumers. If the synagogue was first in importance as a social center of the community, the Square was second. The very extensive, but much confused, notes about the place in literary sources indicate that it underwent many structural changes through the centuries, to be expected in a lively business center. A letter to Ephraim b. Shemarya, the communal leader from the first half of the eleventh century so often mentioned in this book, is addressed to the *Old* Square of the Perfumers. And a letter to "the physician of the Murabba'a," whatever this may mean, is directed to the Maṣṣāṣa, a neighborhood adjoining what the literary sources call District, *khuṭṭ*, of the Perfumers. Both that neighborhood and the Square bordered on the Fortress of the Candles, the original seat of the Christian and Jewish populations of the city, which also harbored the two main synagogues.[20]

The professions of pharmacists and druggists, as pointed out in a handbook of market police, required much study and experience.[21] Whether or not the 'aṭṭār to whom the Alexandrian physician and judge Ibn al-'Ammānī sent three volumes of Dioscorides wished to acquire them for himself we do not know. But the Geniza has preserved the inventory of the estate of a sharābī containing two hundred bound volumes and an unspecified number of loose books—a very large private library for those days, when all books were written by hand.[22] In any event, a druggist was required to be acquainted with the current handbooks of medicaments, such as the famous *Dustūr Bīmāristānī,* "Hospital Handbook" by the Jewish (Karaite) physician Ibn Abi 'l-Bayān, defined by his disciple, the Muslim historian of medicine Ibn Abī Uṣaybi'a, as "comprising the compound medicaments generally prepared in the hospitals of Egypt, Syria and Iraq *and in the stores of the apothecaries.*" At the age of seventy-five, this physician still lectured on medicine in Saladin's hospital in Cairo in 1236, where Ibn Abī Uṣaybi'a heard him, the same hospital, we remember, in which the Nagid Abraham Maimonides worked at that time—so warmly described by his younger colleague, the Muslim historian.[23]

Ibn Abi 'l-Bayān's book was short (which perhaps explains its popularity), but the author claimed that it contained all the medicaments commonly prescribed. This claim was strongly contested by a Jewish druggist, known as Abu 'l-Munā al-Kohen al-'Aṭṭār, who, in the year 1259–60 wrote "for his own use and that of his son" a far larger handbook of medicaments, based not only on books, but also on his own observations.[24] Kohen's book became even more popular and was printed in Egypt several times between 1870 and 1940, because it served as guide to the traditional druggists of that country well into the middle of the twentieth century. I should perhaps add that, according to Dr. Max Meyerhof, who spent almost all his working life in Egypt, in modern times no longer did a single Jew or Christian have a store on the bazaar of drugs of Cairo. They had left these outmoded ways of healing to members of the majority group.[25]

The prominence of the Jews in the professions of druggists and pharmacists during the High Middle Ages—which is paralleled by their equally strong representation in the fields of medicine on the one hand, and in that of the international trade in spices and drugs on the other—calls for comment. There is no reason to assume that it represented the continuation of a pre-Islamic tradition. When a saying in the Talmud extolls the profession of the *bassām,* which is the exact Hebrew equivalent of Arabic 'aṭṭār, as the most desirable of all, this had, as the context referring to the craft of the tanner shows, a specific reason of secondary importance. It simply meant to say that it was pleasanter to live in an atmosphere of sweet smells than to suffer all one's life the stench produced by the tanner's work (as it was in those days; I spare the reader a description).[26] When we read that a certain clan in Jerusalem knew how to compound the incense used in the Temple, but did not teach this art to anyone else, it does not testify to any particular Jewish eminence in this profession. The keeping of professional secrets by a specific group, clan, or firm is also ubiquitous and commonplace today.[27] The remarkable tendency of Arabic-speaking Jews of the High Middle Ages to embrace the professions of druggists and pharmacists must have had its source in contemporary developments.

Tentatively, I offer this explanation: In the wake of the revival of the Greek sciences in Islam on the one hand and the efflorescence of the trade with India and the Far East on the other, medicine and pharmaceutics witnessed an unprecedented exuberance. They were almost new professions. It is a law of economic history that minority groups have a chance of being successful in occupations not yet monopolized by the more privileged classes of the society. The Jews, who in pre-Islamic times had been predominantly peasants, were largely dispossessed in early Islam—just as were many other sections of the farming population—and driven into the new cities that rose everywhere. The comparatively new field of pharmaceutics, like those of the silk industry and trade (see *Med. Soc.*, I, 104), offered promising opportunities for the underprivileged.

A subsidiary element might have been at work. The profession of the druggist, as we have seen, was a bookish one. The use of handbooks was officially prescribed and actually practiced. And there was the great Dioscorides and other learned compilations on the subject. Jewish religion, too, as it developed in post-talmudic times, had become very bookish. One could not be a good Jew without regularly studying the Holy Scriptures and the postbiblical sources of Jewish law and rite. Thus there existed also a certain mental disposition for the profession of the 'aṭṭār. But I am not so sure about this point. For in Islam there prevailed a similar situation, at least in theory.

The orders, accounts, bills, and letters preserved indicate that the stores of the druggists differed widely not only in size, but also with regard to the commodities they stocked, and indeed by their whole character. Since it is impossible, at the present stage of research, to present a comprehensive account of the profession, a number of documents apt to illustrate its various aspects are presented here.[28]

A court record tells about a case where a physician prescribed in the store of a seller of potions. I have the impression that indeed many, if not most, of the prescriptions in Hebrew characters preserved in the Geniza were written by druggists according to the instructions of physicians who then added, in Arabic script, the name of the patient, sometimes also a pious wish, by way of confirmation. In some cases we may even be able to identify the handwriting of the druggists who wrote the prescription.[29]

I present here the full text of a prescription that I assume was written by a pharmacist and confirmed by a physician. It is short and composed mostly of ingredients that were rather humdrum in those days, appearing frequently in prescriptions, accounts, and international business correspondence. The identification of these drugs is greatly facilitated by a pharmaceutical glossary written by Moses Maimonides. When the sage of Córdoba moved from the west of the Mediterranean to the east, he, like many other physicians of the Islamic world who were great travelers, became strongly aware of the fact that the same drugs had different names, often three or four, in different parts of the world and sometimes even in the same place. Maimonides' glossary was edited with an excellent commentary (in

French) by the German-Jewish physician Max Meyerhof, which is an indispensable guide for anyone interested in this field.[30]

A Medical Prescription

Take with God's blessing:

Kabul[31] and Indian [namely: myrobalan, a widely used medicine for intestine troubles]—1 ounce of each [37½ grams, 12 dirhems; see below];

Beleric[32] [also a myrobalan, but of inferior quality] and emblic[33] [Indian gooseberry, also a myrobalan, and like the first two, still commonly used in the East]—1 dirhem of each [3½ grams or 48 grains];

Mecca senna[34] [a purgative, as in modern medicine] and Cretian dodder of thyme[35]—1 ounce;

Lavandula[36] and Syro-Palestinian oxtongue[37]—5 dirhems of each.

Armenian stone[38] and lapis lazuli stone—3 dirhems of each.

Red raisins and globular raisins—half a pound of each [a pound=12 ounces], to be pounded separately, not together with the medicaments listed.

Add to the medicaments 3 ounces of sugar, take half a pound of julep[39] for soaking the whole of it, and knead it well.

To be used in doses of 10 dirhems during 3 consecutive days.

As appetizer[40] take rose sherbet,[41] or rose water, or rose oil, or wine.

God willing [the medicine will help].

For strengthening [its effect] take deodar[42] and [or] scammony[43]. [In beautiful Arabic characters:] For the Karamiyya.[44]

We can form an idea of the appearance of a druggist's store when we read how a partnership in one was dissolved (March 29, 1229). Most of the pots, boxes, and bottles were allotted to each of the two partners piece against piece, and, likewise, all the stock was divided into two equal parts, but there is no description of what the items were. Before this was done, however, one of the partners bought a large number of the items for himself, which are noted together with their prices.[45]

The most costly item was a cupboard with its base, worth 110 silver pieces, a high price, but natural in a country with little wood like Egypt. Next comes a settee, certainly for the convenience of the customers, costing 28 dirhems.[46] Alfa mats, serving the same purpose, are also listed. Besides various types of scales and weights,[47] most of the items were vessels of different materials, forms, and colors, in which the medicaments and drugs were kept, as well as half a dozen copper pipes and some mortars.[48]

Only in a few instances are the contents of these pots, bottles, flasks, and so on indicated: grape juice flavored with mint; syrup of honey and vinegar, flavored with pomegranates, a most popular medicine in those days; liquorice jam; "lamb's tongue," translation of a Greek word designating the seed of the plane tree, which was used as an astringent;[49] cassia—extremely frequent in the Geniza papers—a mild laxative made from the pulp of a sweetish plant that grows in the Sudan and in India; and, finally, *rībās,* from which Persian-Arabic word the botanical name and the English *ribes* are derived, a valuable medicine, as the pot containing it was evaluated at 3 dirhems and as is evident also from other Geniza documents.[50]

The bills of druggists, especially those of wholesalers addressed to retailers, are another excellent illustration of the nature and scope of their activities. Of particular value is a bill covering two consignments, one of fifty-four, and another of thirty-four items, because in its first section weights and prices are indicated throughout (in the second, all the weights, but not all the prices). The drugs listed are known from other sources, but the interesting point in the bill is, of course, that they all were carried simultaneously by one retailer.[51]

A list of debts of three retailers to one druggist wholesaler is a post mortem, drawn up by a puisne judge when the dead druggist's store was taken over by another man. The items, as far as specified, were mostly of the usual type, such as many pots with Kabul myrobalan (see the prescription, above) or syrup of honey and vinegar. The wholesaler carried also apothecary's scales and other store implements. One consignment, unfortunately characterized solely as "a number of drugs," was confiscated by the market police, and we are left in the dark as to why. A separate court action certainly would have to decide who would bear the loss.[52]

The junior judge signing two depositions on the reverse side of the document is known from several documents from the 1140's, including a court validation issued by him. He was a nephew of the noble and renowned judge Abraham b. Shema'ya (App. D, sec. 11) and himself an 'aṭṭār, as we know from a letter of his brother-in-law, an India trader, addressed to him. Thus, he was well equipped to deal with the dead druggist's affairs. Like other 'aṭṭārs already mentioned, he was a bibliophile, who bought books and had others, rare ones, copied for himself on order.[53]

Another judge, but this time, a very important one, Samuel b. Saadya ha-Levi, a member of Maimonides' rabbinical court and author of countless court records written between 1165 and 1203, must have been an 'aṭṭār in his earlier days. For pages from an account book of a perfumer, written in his unmistakable handwriting, cannot represent a court action like the document discussed in the preceding paragraphs, for it contains personal remarks, such as "I received," nor can it be a clean copy written for someone else, because it is written in different directions and comprises additions and deletions. Thus, we must assume that Samuel was a perfumer (just as Maimonides was a physician), perhaps leaving his store in the hands of a son when he assumed the judgeship as his main occupation. We remember that the busy merchant-banker Nahray b. Nissīm acted in his later days as judge, drawing a salary from the community of Old Cairo.[54]

The accounts themselves, although incompletely preserved, are of considerable interest. Both the customers and commodities delivered were of varied types. In the period covered (it seems, a week) a house of mourning ordered costly items for fumigation and perfuming, such as odoriferous wood, camphor, and sprinklers, namely for the sprinkling of rose oil on guests. At the end, the total of 256-¾ dirhems was converted into 6-5/12 dinars, both certainly not in cash, but in orders of payment, the former deposited with, and the latter issued by a banker.[55]

Bills for individual households are necessarily less instructive for our knowledge of the druggist profession and more suited as an illustration of daily life in general. I confine myself to one, particularly well-preserved example. We remember that small change was rare in those days. Transactions were made mostly in silver or gold, or, preferably, by orders of payment and charge account. In the case before us, the customer had a previous credit of 50 dirhems, probably from a transfer or order of payment, and paid now 1 gold piece worth 36-½ dirhems. The bill sent to him, together with the commodities ordered, included also a previous consignment and totaled 91 dirhems. The small balance of $91 - (50 + 36 - \frac{1}{2}) = 4\text{-}\frac{1}{2}$ dirhems was to be paid to the messenger.

The first part of the bill, referring to the previous consignment, contains both quantities and prices:

Saffron	1 ounce	9½	dirhems
Pepper	2 pounds	7	"
Caraway	2 pounds	3	"
Chinese wood (cinnamon)	¼ mann (ca. ½ pound)	2¾	"
Mastic	2 ounces	1	"
Nutmeg	(no quantity)	1½	"
Ginger	½ pound	2½	"

The second part of the bill, accompanying the goods sent gives only the prices (certainly because the householder had indicated the weights on his order). In addition to many drugs and spices, like anise, cannabis (hemp), coriander,[56] cumin, fennel, sesame, natron, salt, and raisins, were included household goods, such as three different types of sieves, two large baskets (of the broad type borne on the head), knives, cups, earthenware, and a sponge.[57]

Pepper was used in those days in far larger quantities than today, since it performed largely the function of our refrigerators in keeping meats fresh. Peppering their wines was very popular, too. Cannabis (our notorious marijuana) and similar drugs were widely used in medicine. In submitting his personal expenses to his firm in 1045, fifty-one years before his death, Nahray b. Nissīm included repeatedly the costly item "opium." Had this been a personal luxury and not a medical prescription, he could hardly have charged the firm with this expenditure.[58]

Orders of druggists are of different types. One, sent from Alexandria or Rosetta to Fustat, contains, as one would expect in a letter sent from a seaport, wholesale items imported from or destined for foreign countries, as well as drugs needed by the sender for local consumers.[59] An important order, edited by Albert Dietrich in a special study, actually a complete book, was sent from Aden in southwest Arabia to the capital of Egypt and reflects international trade in drugs rather than the profession of druggist. At the time of the publication, the learned author could not have known those circumstances, revealed subsequently by many letters related to the India trade in general and to the sender of that order in particular. The Adenese merchant had entrusted a business friend traveling to Fustat with 14 pounds of cardamom, an Oriental spice much used to this day, and asked him to order for him Western drugs from two perfumers, personal acquaintances of his. The drugs ordered are arranged in two sections, one containing those items the writer knew to be available, and one listing those of which he was not sure. He purposely does not indicate quantities or prices, leaving the choice to the experience and trustworthiness of his correspondents, who would buy in accordance with the fluctuating market situation.[60]

Letters from the small towns of the Egyptian Rīf frequently contain orders that reveal their writers to be 'aṭṭārs. One, in whose hand I have noted three such letters, also had scholarly interests, not unusual among the men of his profession. The order specified below was accompanied by a copy of three religious liturgies, two of which he asked the addressee to show to his "brother," that is, friend, in the city, who should correct them and send them back in time to be recited in the synagogue on a forthcoming day of fasting. The "brother" should also write him a letter in his own hand so that he, the 'aṭṭār, might "inhale his fragrance." Here is the order.[61]

I am sending you with the bearer of this letter 15 dirhems. Please buy for me
1¼ pounds of emblic ["Indian gooseberry," see above], approximately[62] for 4¼ dirhems or less
2½ pounds of deep-red rose water, approximately ¾ d.
A *fuqqā'a* (bottle of potions)[63], approximately ½ d. or less
1 pound eye powder, well made, on special order,[64] approximately 2 d. or less
1 pound antimony, approximately 3¼ or 3½ d. or less
2½ pounds cosmetic cream, approximately 2¼ d. or less.

In conclusion, I wish to consider orders to a sharābī, or seller of potions, a profession so closely related to those of druggist and pharmacist. As we now know, the better household had what we would call a charge account: a child or a servant was sent to a store with a slip indicating the commodities and quantities desired and often also the date (month and year, not day). After a number of such slips had accumulated the store would send them back with the account.[65] Thirty orders, sent by the prominent India trader Abū Zikrī Kohen to two different sharābīs, contained these items: [66]

	Number of times ordered	Minimum ounces	Maximum pounds
Rose water with lemon	6	2	1
Rose water	1		½
Rose preserve[67]	3	1–3	
Lemon juice	5	2	1
Lemon preserve	3	1–3	
'Aqīd [curds, coagulated milk][68]	6	1–2	
Oxymel [honey with vinegar]	2		½–1
Oxymel potion	2		
Same flavored with pomegranate	1	2	
Apple juice	2	2–3	
Pomegranate juice	1		¼
Sorrel potion	1	2	
Plain potion[69]	1	2	

Despite its close connection with the medical art, the profession of the druggist was strictly separated from it, at least as far as the testimony of the Geniza goes. In the extremely rare cases where we find a man called "X. b. X, the physician, the 'aṭṭār" or "X. b. X., the bloodletter, the 'aṭṭār," the first profession attached to the name was that of the father and served as family name, but by no means indicates that the person concerned exercised the two professions.[70] Reference has been made repeatedly to a physician practicing in a sharābī's store. But it was the physician, not the sharābī, who was responsible for the prescriptions.

CHAPTER VII

Interfaith Relations, Communal Autonomy, and Government Control

A. INTERFAITH RELATIONS

1. *Group Consciousness and Discrimination*

Interfaith relations in the Middle Ages should not be compared with those in our own times. Owing to the religious character of medieval society, the religious minorities formed a state within the state, by law as well as in fact. The group consciousness of the members of the various religions was similar to that of modern nations. The adherents of another faith were not necessarily enemies, but certainly foreigners. The contrast went even deeper. Since each of the three monotheistic religions claimed to be the sole possessor of the full truth, the very existence of other religions was a challenge or even an offense.

In view of these facts, the modern term "discrimination" can be applied to the Middle Ages only in a qualified sense. When an alien today is treated differently from a citizen, for example, if he is not permitted to be gainfully employed, he is not being discriminated against, but is so treated because he does not share the financial and other responsibilities of citizens or permanent residents. Similarly, Christians and Jews under Islam regarded it as natural, albeit burdensome, that certain restrictions were imposed on them by the Muslim community in the midst of which they lived, but to which they did not belong. They, too, discriminated against Muslims. Thus, as a rule, they would certainly not feel themselves obliged to provide for the poor of the Muslims or to ransom their captives.

On the other hand, the minority groups lived in closest proximity to the majority and were bound up with it by the same economy and by being subjects of the same government. They shared similar burdens and were exposed to a similar fate. This made the situation complicated and markedly different from the mutual relationships of the members of modern nations. The Muslim, Christian, and Jewish communities each formed a nation, *umma,* in itself, but in every country they shared a homeland, *waṭan,* in common. Both concepts were of highest practical and emotional significance, as the Geniza letters show. While it was natural, however, to be treated differently as a member of another religion, it was revolting to be discriminated against as a permanent resident of the same country.

This dichotomy in the relationship of a medieval minority group toward the surrounding majority is beautifully expressed in this passage from a letter of the Jewish judge of Barqa (eastern Libya), written in Alexandria. He had intended to make the pilgrimage to the Holy City, but, as usual, the ways in Palestine were unsafe, the winter was cold, and our judge was clearly homesick. Traveling conditions could not have been too bad at that time, for the addressee, who lived in Old Cairo, was indeed setting out for Jerusalem. In view of this, the writer felt somehow apologetic, explaining at length (in a letter sent a short time before the one containing the passage translated below) why his return to Barqa was urgently needed. Before leaving Alexandria for the West he wrote again. After extending greetings to various dignitaries in Jerusalem whom the addressee was supposed to meet and settling some business matters (for the judge, as was usual with pilgrims, had also done some trading on his way), he continues: "On this very day a big caravan is setting out for Barqa under the command of Ibn Shibl. I have booked in it for myself and for my goods at the price of 3 dinars, and have already paid the fare. Most of the travelers are Barqīs. They have promised me to be considerate with regard to the watering places and the keeping of the Sabbath and similar matters. For in the whole caravan there is not a single Jew besides myself. Notwithstanding, I confide in God that everything will work out fine according to his will." Besides demonstrating his confidence in God it was clearly the fact that he traveled in the company of compatriots who gave the lonely Jew the feeling that he was safe.[1]

Since the Geniza documents consist mostly of transactions or correspondence between Jews it is natural that interfaith relations should occupy in them a less conspicuous place than they did in actual life. We should also take heed not to attribute too much to the comparative scarcity of complaints about vexations or persecutions. Let us imagine the letters we wrote during or shortly after World War II scrutinized by a historian nine hundred years hence. Will they give an adequate idea, let alone a detailed picture, of the atrocities committed during that period? Still, since the restrictions and cases of persecution known to us from literary sources are well illustrated by the Geniza, while on the other hand, it is rich in details about close cooperation between the various religious groups, its testimony should be accepted in general as a true mirror of the real situation. In other words, despite the limitations pointed out, the Geniza documents form a rich source of information on interfaith relations and cognate phenomena.

There is no need to recapitulate the legal and actual position of the non-Muslims in the countries of Islam or of the Jews in medieval Europe, known to us from books on law and historical accounts. These subjects have been treated in competent and easily accessible works.[2] Only where the Geniza records significantly confirm or qualify the results of previous research are their contents presented here.

"He is a Christian and I am a Jew—he is not my companion, *ṣāḥibī*." With this argument, repeated twice in the same letter, a Tunisian, writing from an Egyptian town, wishes to make it clear that he was not responsible for the misbehavior of his Christian business friend. "The Bible has said: never trust gentiles," writes a Jewish merchant from Aden, South Arabia, after some bad experience with a Muslim. The saying is not found in the Bible, although Psalm 144:8 "Whose mouth speaks lies and whose handshake is falsehood" was understood in this sense in the Middle Ages. But that maxim must have been quite common, for I heard it as late as 1949, while visiting the South Arabian port.[3]

It would be definitely wrong to see in such utterances any specifically Jewish exclusiveness. Exactly the same maxim is used by Muslims with regard to Jews ("Do not trust a Jew, even forty years after his conversion to Islam").[4] As soon as Muhammad's prophetic message became an institutionalized denomination, he began to enjoin the Muslims not to have Christians and Jews as friends and to avoid their company. Similar injunctions, or even decrees to the same effect, were issued by the highest Christian authorities. Such an attitude is unavoidable in any religion, party, or race which regards itself as following the right path to the exclusion of others. For as soon as people of different allegiance mix closely, they discover that the invisible republic of decent men stretches beyond the barriers of religion, party, and race, a discovery incompatible with the claim of absolute superiority of one particular group. The astonishing fact about the Geniza is that quotations like the two given are so rare. As a matter of fact, thus far I have not come across any others of the same type, and nowhere else are Christians or Muslims as a group cursed or even spoken of detractively. This, however, should not induce us to assume that the spirit of aloofness and superiority was absent or even weak in that period. All we are allowed to conclude from the testimony of the Geniza is that it was not as high pitched and morbidly fanatical as in the later Middle Ages.

Group consciousness made itself felt in many direct and indirect ways. Spiritual life centered entirely on religion (in contrast with scientific studies, which were interdenominational, but confined to limited circles). Economic and legal transactions were made as far as possible within the religious group. Many business letters and legal documents reflect this situation. Whenever a commodity was ordered from overseas or out of town with no business friend available for supervising its transport, the letter would state whether it should be carried by Jews only, or by trustworthy gentiles as well. "I am not quiet when I send it with a Muslim; perhaps I shall find a Jew," writes a man from Minyat Ziftā, apologizing that he had not yet dispatched a piece of fabric, woven by one of the women of his household and promised to a relative in the capital. "I made four copies of this letter, in order to give them to coreligionists traveling in different boats, but the third copy I gave to the proprietor of the Ibn al-Qaddār, for no Jew traveled in that ship." Thus we read in a letter from Alexandria, addressed to Ibn 'Awkal in Fustat. But a merchant newly installed in the capital of Egypt asks his correspondent in Alexandria to give his address to everyone "Jew or Muslim." The absence of "Christians" here means only that they were not active in the branches cultivated by the writer.[5]

Any power of attorney (and there is no type of documents, except marriage contracts, so common in the Geniza as this) indicates whether the attorney is allowed to approach a non-Jewish court in addition or in lieu of the Jewish. Hopes and good wishes, as well as apprehensions, are normally concerned with the religious community. A remark like the following: "May God spare Israel [i.e., the Jews] from the plague ravaging in your parts," made in a letter dated 1217, should not be taken as typical, for in such a context our letters would more regularly say *al-nās,* "the population," or a similar phrase.[6] Whenever we read, however, about an uprising or a war, fears would be expressed in the first place for the Jewish communities affected, presumably because long experience had shown that Jews were the first to suffer wherever peace was broken.[7] Similarly, in the Annals of the Orthodox Coptic church "God's people" would not refer to all those who believe in God, or even to all Christians, but quite specifically to the Copts of Monophysitic persuasion.[8]

Intermarriage of course was proscribed by both the Church and the Synagogue, while Islam permitted a Muslim to marry a Christian woman or a Jewess. No such occurrence, however, is reported or referred to in our documents. The second Fatimid caliph of Egypt, al-ʿAzīz (975-996), had, among others, a Christian wife, but in such cases the female partner normally accepted the religion of the husband. Because of his dietary laws, a Muslim would not partake of a meal in a Christian family, nor a Jew anywhere outside his community. One should also bear in mind that in a Christian or Jewish house even a casual visitor would be offered a glass of wine, while at least the Muslim middle class would shun such an open display of disregard for the prohibitions of their religion.

In view of this far-reaching segregation it is not astonishing that the Geniza letters contain practically no reference to the spiritual life of non-Jewish communities. A simple man visiting Tyre, Lebanon, at the time of its occupation by the Crusaders, adds in Hebrew to his letter written in Arabic: "The Christians here pray in open places." In contrast with Old Cairo, which was full of churches, but where the Christian service had to be held behind closed doors, the public ceremonies of the Crusaders aroused the astonishment of the visitor from the Egyptian capital, just as their splendor, displayed in the same town, impressed a famous Muslim traveler a few years later.[9] The Geniza letters contain many references to the Muslim feasts and month of fast, but only with regard to their impact on economic life. Hindu business friends are mentioned with much warmth and are called "brothers," but nowhere do we find any remark about Hindu religion, whose complete difference from everything known to them could not have escaped those merchants from Mediterranean countries. Only at the end of the Middle Ages, when Islam invaded Judaism in the form of Islamic mysticism, which exercised a deep influence on the weakened and decimated Jewish community, is the reaction to this movement echoed by the Geniza just as the opposition to it is found in Judeo-Arabic literature.[10]

Unlike Europe, where the Jews formed a single and exceedingly small group within a foreign environment, in Islam the detrimental effects of segregation were mitigated by the existence of two minority groups, which, during the Geniza period, were still sizable and influential even on the conduct of the state. The biblical term for gentile, *goy,* assumed disparaging overtones in Europe, while the Geniza, except in legal texts, does not have a word for "non-Jew" at all.[11] In the Geniza, the term "goy," as a rule, designates a Muslim, while Christians are called by the biblical word *'ārēl,* "uncircumcised," but with no detractive connotation whatsoever. In the same document a writer would use indiscriminately 'ārēl and *naṣrānī* (the Arabic term) for Christians, and goy and *muslim* for Muslims. Of a dead Muslim one would write "the goy, may God have mercy upon him," just as one would express himself with regard to a coreligionist.[12]

Still "anti-Semitism," that is, hostility directed specifically against the Jewish community, was not entirely absent from medieval Islam, as has been assumed.[13] Its existence is best proved by the fact that the Geniza letters have a special word for it and, most significantly, one not found in the Bible or in talmudic literature (nor registered in any Hebrew dictionary), but one much used and obviously coined in the Geniza period. It is *sin'ūth,* "hatred," a Jew-baiter being called *sōnē,* "a hater."[14] It should be noted that the phenomenon is nowhere referred to as general; it is mentioned throughout in connection with certain groups, towns, or persons. Oddly enough, the only religious group described as "haters" are the Isma'īlīs, a sect usually believed to have been sophisticated with regard to differences in religion. The Jewish person connected with them was one Ibn al-Salamī, a family name derived probably from Salamiyya, the famous center of Isma'īlī propaganda in northern Syria.[15] Another town in northern Syria, al-Ma'arra, the home of the Arab poet and humanist Abu 'l-'Alā' (died 1058), was notorious for its sin'ūth; with reference to this dubious reputation, a merchant is congratulated on escaping from it unscathed.[16] In a business letter from Fez, Morocco, to Almeria, Spain, a son writes to his father: " 'Anti-Semitism' in this country is such that, in comparison with it, life in Almeria is salvation. May God in His mercy grant me a safe departure." He mentions, however, incidentally friendly personal relations with Muslims (thus, without specifying names) and a lot of business done in the inhospitable country, as well as his intention to proceed to Marrākesh, then (around 1100) the capital.[17]

Particularly frequent are the references to anti-Semitism in Alexandria (while none has been found thus far with regard to Old or

New Cairo). One is reminded of the constant tensions between Jews and pagans in Alexandria during the first centuries of Roman rule, although outbursts like the "pogroms" of A.D. 38 and 88 have no counterpart in Islamic times.[18] Around the middle of the eleventh century we already read about "the oppression by bandits and the rulers of this city."[19] At approximately the same time a merchant, known to us from many letters as a sober and steady person, writes that despite urgent business, he had been unable to leave the house for the bazaar for three days, for the terror was great and if anyone wanted to take advantage of the absence of the head of the family he could do so unpunished.[20] At the turn of the century there was a threat that the ancient practice of turning the estates of foreigners who died in Egypt over to the juridical authorities of their respective communities would be discontinued. A writer discussing this matter emphasizes that "the people of Alexandria" are not like those of Cairo. If they were allowed to lay their hands on Jewish property, nothing would remain of it.[21] In the same period a Jewish scholar traveling to Alexandria stops over for a week in al-Fuwwa (the terminal of the waterway connecting that city with the Nile), asking his brother in the capital to secure for him a letter of recommendation to the Muslim chief judge of Alexandria, "for you know only too well the anti-Semitism of the population of that city."[22]

An occurrence characteristic of this situation is vividly described in a Geniza letter. A Jewish notable bearing the title "the elder (or head) of the congregations," namely, of the Palestinian and Babylonian congregations of Alexandria, was falsely accused of having had an affair with a girl of dubious reputation in a caravanserai. When the girl denied it, the accusers, members of the secret police, urged her to tell the qadi that the Jew had taken her by force and then paid her; otherwise she would be led on a donkey through the city and then burned. Soon a crowd of about a thousand people gathered and dragged the notable before the qadi. The latter examined the would-be witnesses one by one separately, and found out that their testimony was false. "However," the letter continues, "the secret police[23] forced the qadi to give judgment against his own conviction, and now sin'ūth has been let loose in an unprecedented manner. Kindly send a letter to the qadi so that his heart will be strengthened in his favorable attitude toward the Jews, as it had been before. Otherwise, they will perish; for anti-Semitism is continuously taking on new forms and everyone in the town has become a police inspector[24] over the Jews in the worst way of sin'ūth." The letter concludes with the request that the addressee assist the umma, "the nation," that is, the Jewish community, using either his influential position or money to get the notable out of prison.[25]

The precarious situations facing the Jews of Alexandria from time to time found their expression also in official documents. A memorandum by the Jewish community of that city addressed to the Nagid Samuel b. Hananya (1140-1159) described the state of lawlessness to which it was exposed because of the high-handed and fraudulent practices of the officials of the poll tax. Even the honor of the women was not safe from the impudence of those oppressors.[26] This statement—the like of which has been found thus far in the Geniza only with reference to Alexandria—is paralleled by a contemporary poem which complained that Christian officials ruled over the bodies of Muslim women.[27] But while the latter insinuation was perhaps false and intended only to inflame the masses against those officials, the former statement gives the impression of being based on facts. For a similar complaint is found in an important, but incompletely preserved memorandum, submitted by the Alexandrian community to the Nagid Mevōrākh b. Saadya. At that time, it seems, the Muslim population, too, suffered by the lawlessness rampant in the city.[28]

The criminal doings of the Alexandrian poll tax collectors were finally stopped, as we learn from another report about sin'ūth in that city, referring briefly to reforms in the poll tax administration, but describing at length new troubles in the city. The letter credits with the success not the Nagid Samuel, but one Abu 'l-Makārim, most probably identical with a prominent Jewish kātib, or government official, active during that period.[29] Again the situation was scandalous, the mob laying hands on Jewish persons, and every lowbred scamp sticking out his tongue and insulting. There must have occurred something similar to the affair of the "elder of the congregations" described above, for the writer emphasizes that intervention was needed for the public welfare and not only for the particular person concerned. The addressee is requested to secure a letter from the above mentioned Abu 'l-Makārim to the Muslim chief judge of Alexandria, one by another Jewish government official to the *faqīh,* or expert on Muslim law, in the same city, and a third to the chief of the police, in case he remained in office. Otherwise, the new chief should be properly "briefed," before leaving the capital.[30]

By chance, perhaps, the only references to unfriendly relations between the rank and file of Jews and Christians in Islamic countries are also from Alexandria. "Apply to the Church" must have been a standing phrase among the Jews of that city in the meaning "turn for help to one from whom you cannot expect any." Thus an angry schoolteacher addressing his brother, an Alexandrian merchant sojourning in Old Cairo, exclaims: "These days no Jew does one a favor; it is as if one went for help to a church."[31] An Alexandrian notable writing to a friend complains about a common Christian acquaintance who intrigued against him and who caused him harm year after year: "As if I personally had killed Jesus, for otherwise there is no reason for him to nourish that enmity against me."[32]

It is natural that in court intrigues the contesting parties should sometimes be arrayed along denominational lines. The Geniza has preserved a lengthy and highly interesting Hebrew letter of a government official to the Jewish community in Constantinople describing his own falling into disgrace and the rise of a Christian director of revenue. After the death of the Nagid Mevōrākh (in March, 1112) the influential position of that official became a menace to Egyptian Jewry, and four Jewish notables tried to bring about his downfall by making him suspect of connections with the Franks. Jacob Mann takes this letter as an indication of the Christian and Jewish communities "waging bitter war against each other."[33]

This generalization is not warranted by our sources. Even the worst of all the Coptic administrators, a finance minister known as "The Monk" (executed in 1129), whose exactions are depicted in some Geniza documents as a great catastrophe, can by no means be regarded as an exponent of Christian prejudice against Jews. The Muslims and his own community, at that, suffered equally from his rapacious rule; and, besides, newly identified Geniza fragments show that he had two Jewish associates who helped him to plunder their coreligionists.[34] We have met with a similar type of cooperation, this time a beneficial one, when the vizier Ibn Killis, a Jewish convert to Islam, administered the newly founded Fatimid empire of the East with the help of a Christian finance director in charge of Egypt and a Jew in charge of Syria.[35] In short, single occurrences of interfaith strife should never be taken as indicative of a general state of continuous tension, as long as such an assumption is not supported by sufficient evidence.

The position of the Jews (and Christians) in Jerusalem, about which we have many Geniza letters, some still unpublished, is also to be regarded as a special case. In the first place, with regard to the terrible visitation of Bedouin rule during the twenties of the eleventh century, it is expressly stated that the Muslims were suffering similar privations. One letter stresses that nothing comparable had occurred since the conquest of the country by the Arabs, which shows that

Muslim rule was regarded up till that time as orderly. One source even mentions that, in ancient times, "kings and governors" included the Jewish poor, when they distributed food and clothing to the needy of the Holy City. In general, we have to keep in mind the resentment of the Muslims, summarized in a famous dictum by the geographer Muqaddasi, himself a native of the Holy City, that Jerusalem was the most beautiful of all cities, but its beauty was marred by the Christians and Jews having there the upper hand. Since the non-Muslim communities consisted largely of foreigners, they were exposed to heavy financial impositions which were the more burdensome, as opportunities for remunerative occupations were scarce. The repeated reference to the prohibition of the use by the Jews of the Shiloah spring south of Jerusalem as a ritual bath should by no means be compared with similar restrictions inspired by twentieth-century racism. When the Jews returned to Jerusalem after the Arab conquest they settled in the southern part of the city, partly because of the propinquity of that spring. With the growth of the city and the increasing use of the spring for drinking purposes, however, the ancient privilege was withdrawn.[36]

The prohibition of ritual slaughter, imposed occasionally on the Jews of Jerusalem, Old Cairo, and Acre (the latter during its occupation by the Crusaders) is also to be regarded partly as a withdrawal of a privilege rather than an act of discrimination. Ritual slaughter entailed either the maintenance of special slaughterhouses (as in Old Cairo) or the reserving of a separate section in the bazaar where the animals were killed (as in Jerusalem). One can understand that the market police were not always willing to grant this special privilege. Moreover, even the Muslims, who themselves observe a form of ritual slaughter, sometimes resented the strictness with which the Jews refused to eat any but "kosher" meat, but continued to sell them what they regarded as prohibited. In the very oldest collection of questions addressed to a Muslim religious scholar, the following query is submitted to him: a Muslim family employing a Jewish wet nurse has the animals consumed in the house killed by a Jewish ritual slaughterer in order to enable her to partake of the common meals. Is this correct? Answer: X. (a well-known Muslim authority) has said: I prefer to perform myself the religious slaughter needed for my household.[37]

It has often been said that it was incorrect to speak about "anti-Semitism" in the Islamic world, since the Arabs, the originators of Islam, were Semites themselves. This is a mere misunderstanding of the history of the term. The word "Semitic" was coined by a German scholar at the end of the eighteenth century for purely linguistic purposes, namely to designate a group of cognate languages, such as Hebrew, Arabic, and Ethiopic. To assume that the peoples belonging to this linguistic group are of one racial stock is tantamount to the assertion that an educated Afro-American, who speaks exactly the same English as his white classmate, shares with him the same racial origin. In the wake of the blood and race romanticism of the nineteenth century, the idea of a Semitic race was invented and cultivated in particular in order to emphasize the inalterable otherness and alien character of the Jews living in Europe. Hence the term "anti-Semitism." We have used it here solely for convenience' sake, in order to differentiate animosity against Jews from the discrimination practiced by Islam against non-Muslims in general. Our scrutiny of the Geniza material has proved the existence of "anti-Semitism" in the time and the area considered here, but it appears to have been local and sporadic, rather than general and endemic.

It is not difficult to explain this phenomenon. To be sure, the Jews of the Geniza period did not form or belong to any specific social, economic, or occupational group, but, owing to the strict observation of the Sabbath and the dietary laws, they were distinguished markedly and constantly from their environment. On the other hand, both in number and in power they fell far behind the numerous and partly very affluent Christian denominations. Therefore it is not surprising that the Jewish communities should have served occasionally as the targets of exploitation and even of assaults. For human nature, a mixture of pugnacity and cowardice, is always prone to attack where the risks involved seem negligible. In particular in times of general tribulation a small minority is in danger of becoming the scapegoat of a desperate population. When flourishing Tunisia was laid waste by the Bedouin hordes occupying it in the fifties of the eleventh century, the Jews, on top of being visited by the same catastrophe as their fellow countrymen, were, in one city, menaced by the latter with extermination, the pretext for this threat not being stated.[38] In a time of famine in Egypt, a letter reports from a provincial town that the Jewish houses were plundered every Saturday and its inhabitants threatened as being in possession of hidden stores of foodstuff, while, in reality, they suffered the same or more terrible privations as the rest of the population.[39] Such references, however, are exceptional. As a rule, Christians and Jews suffered alike under the discriminations imposed on them by Islam. In the case of the great persecution under al-Ḥākim, so often referred to in this book, we learn from the Geniza that it was first directed against the Christians alone and only at a later juncture were the Jews affected as well.

Mention has been made before of the restrictions to which the Christian and Jewish houses of worship were subjected. In the decades following the al-Ḥākim disturbances, the restoration of old synagogues and the building of a new one (in a town where its predecessor had been converted into a mosque) are referred to without assuming opposition on the side of the government.[40] When in the eleven nineties a new synagogue had to be built in Hebron, Palestine, because the old one was in a ruinous state, the Muslim judge declared that al-Malik al-Afḍal, the actual ruler of the Fatimid empire (to which southern Palestine then belonged) would never allow such a violation of Muslim law. The problem was solved by the synagogue being built on a plot bought from the judge, while the latter was satisfied with the explanation that it was not actually a synagogue, but a home.[41]

In face of this legal situation one wonders what the Christians and Jews did when their congregations increased considerably owing to the influx of coreligionists or otherwise. The purchase, in 882, of the Church of St. Michael in Fustat by the Jewish newcomers from Iraq and its conversion into the synagogue of the Iraqians is a case in point. About this occurrence we know solely from literary sources. The Geniza documents, besides the cases of rebuilding of synagogues just mentioned, report only the renting of modest buildings for their use as assembly halls. One example, a rather curious one, may be summarized here: a building belonging to the government was leased to the Jewish community to serve them as a house of worship. The letter reporting this fact adds that as long as the director of finance of the town was a Muslim, the rent was low, for that pious man, as is expressly stated, did not want to be exacting with regard to a place of prayer. When the Muslim died and was succeeded by a Jew, the rent was immediately doubled. The writer, with all deference toward that overzealous official, who certainly was an important personage in the town, asks the addressee to intervene: the poor were in greater need of that money than the government.[42]

Worship of the non-Muslim denominations under Islam had to be inconspicuous and was required to be confined to the church and synagogue buildings. Only one exception, a privilege referred to in numerous published and unpublished Geniza letters, is known from this period as regards Jewish religion: the yearly procession through Jerusalem and up to the Mount of Olives which took place on the seventh day of the autumnal Feast of Tabernacles. "All the pilgrims circumambulate the gates of the Temple area and recite the communal prayer and then proceed singing up to the Mount of Olives and line up there viewing the Temple, all this with no interference." This privilege, as the source just quoted emphasizes, was not given gratuitously. It was secured every year by heavy payments "to the rulers of the city and its young men."[43]

The Christians enjoyed similar privileges, especially in the good olden times, the tenth and the eleventh centuries. One must bear in mind that some of the Christian holidays were essentially revivals of ancient Near Eastern popular festivities, and often the whole Muslim population, including the courts of the caliphs and governors, participated in full—despite the protests of their religious scholars. In Fustat, in particular, it was the night of Epiphany which was famous all over the Muslim world for its entertainments, like carnivals in certain places today. We know much about these popular feasts from Muslim sources, but no reference has been found thus far in the Geniza, although, for instance, the Christian feast of the visit to the prison of Joseph in Gizeh, the suburb of Cairo, could as easily have been shared by Jews as it was by Muslims.[44]

There was one type of religious ceremony which neither Christians nor Jews could avoid displaying in public: accompanying the dead to their last rest. Funeral processions formed the target for molestations and attacks by the mob and restrictions on the side of the authorities. Around 1123, a Fatimid vizier decreed that Jewish (and presumably also Christian) funerals should be held only during nighttime, shortly before daybreak. Since we have from the same period a charter given to the Christians of Iraq that their ways of interring their dead would be respected (dated 1138), we may assume that this malady of molesting the burials of non-Muslims was rampant. It is attested by the Geniza also for Jerusalem and Ramle, then the capital of Palestine. The wording of the Iraqian charter might have been intended to grant protection from still another insult directed against the dead of the non-Muslims: the destruction of, or the prohibition to erect, tombstones and memorial monuments. The Fatimid vizier just alluded to tried to implement both. He was, however, too short a time in office for doing lasting harm and there are so many references in the Geniza to sumptuous and resounding burials (wailing women and so forth), as well as to the erection of tombstones, that the restrictions and humiliations should be regarded as intermittent rather than permanent.[45]

The most conspicuous aspect of discrimination against non-

Muslims was the obligation to be distinguished from Muslims by their wearing apparel. They were forced to wear a badge of a certain color, a particular type of belt or of headgear, and, in general, to be content with modest clothing as befitting a subject population. Countless references to this imposition are found in Arabic literary sources. The Geniza proves, however, that during the Fatimid and early Ayyubid periods practice must have differed widely from theory. Perhaps no subject is referred to in it so frequently as clothing, but nowhere do we meet in these periods any allusion to a specific Jewish attire. On the contrary, there is much indirect evidence that there was none. A Jewish girl who had an affair with a Christian doctor was regarded by her fellow Jews as being Muslim, which could not have been possible if her clothing marked her as a Jewess. Nor can we assume that the young lady disguised herself purposely, for such an important detail could not have been omitted in a legal document, in particular as her accusers were Muslims.[46] A young Jew, a newcomer to Alexandria, was employed there in a Muslim workshop, until it was discovered that he was a Jew (presumably because he was unable to explain his continued absence from work on Sabbaths), whereupon he was dismissed. Here again it is impossible to suppose that he had exchanged his particularly Jewish attire for Muslim clothing; in the first place, he would have mentioned such a ruse to his elder brother to whom his letter was directed. Second, he would certainly not have escaped punishment, after his real identity was established.[47] In an Arabic source we read that the Jewish physician of the Tunisian Sultan Mu'izz (1016-1062) wore no distinctive mark and was taken by a Muslim judge and courtier for a Muslim.[48] Even more telling than these details, significant as they are, is the custom of describing bearers of letters or carriers of goods as Muslims or Christians, as the case might be. If anyone was immediately recognizable by his clothing, it is difficult to see why such designations were necessary.[49]

The bizarre edict on the attire of Christians and Jews promulgated by the caliph al-Ḥākim in a spasmodic fit of religious zeal (or political expediency) proves only that no such discrimination had been customary before.[50] Nor can that edict have been in force for a long time, since it has left no traces in the Geniza, unlike the caliph's action against the synagogues, which is referred to in numerous documents. Likewise, in 1121, when the Seljuk sultan of Baghdad needed some cash, he had the grand idea of renewing the laws about the distinctive dress of the nonbelievers, embellished by some special harassments. The Muslim historians, as usual, report the event laconically:

"In that year, the non-Muslims were asked to wear their distinctive signs: the affair ended in their paying four thousand dinars to the Caliph and twenty thousand to the Sultan. The Jālūt [i.e., the Ra's al-Jālūt, the head of the Jewish Diaspora] was brought into the imperial presence. He guaranteed the above-mentioned sums and collected them."[51] Since the Christian population of Baghdad was at least as important as the Jewish, one misses here the catholicus, or head of the Nestorian church (who also represented the other Christian denominations). But Muslim historians never tried to be exact when dealing with non-Muslims. Another historian, writing about a similar decree issued in Baghdad thirty years earlier, makes mention only of the Christians.[52]

The harassments of 1121 are described fully in two Geniza sources. One, the autobiography of the Norman proselyte Johannes-Obadiah, gives the following details about the molestations in Baghdad:

[The vizier] decreed that they should wear two yellow badges, one on the headgear and one on the neck. Furthermore each Jew should have hanging on his neck a piece of lead weighing one dirhem [3.125 grams approximately], on which the word *dhimmī* ["non-Muslim"] was engraved. He also should wear a belt around his waist. On the women two distinctive signs were imposed. They should wear one red and one black shoe and have a small brass bell on their necks or shoes in order to distinguish them from Muslim women. The vizier appointed brutal Muslim men to supervise the Jewish males and brutal Muslim women to watch over the females and to harm them with curses and humiliations. The Muslims were mocking the Jews, and the mob and their youngsters were beating them up in all the streets of Baghdad.

After having been softened up in this way, the non-Muslims were of course prepared to pay the exorbitant sums demanded from them.[53]

Another Geniza document, a report about a messianic movement among the Jews of Baghdad originating in the fall of 1120, mentions that the ladies in particular resented the grotesque and humiliating ordinance with regard to the distinctive attire to be worn by them and that the upper-class people were also forced to adopt it.[54] It should be noted that the same technique of extorting money was applied against the Muslim population. In 1121, we learn, the merchants were ordered to pay henceforth one-third of their net profit to the Sultan. There was much lamentation over this crushing tax. After some time it was abolished on condition that the merchants pay the Sultan five thousand dinars as a sign of gratitude for his magnanimity.[55]

In Egypt, too, we find between 1130 and the end of Fatimid rule in 1171 occasional attempts to renew the restrictions about the clothing of the non-Muslims. These attempts, however, recorded by the Arabic historians, were ephemeral and are not echoed in the Geniza papers. Only at the very end of the Ayyubid period, we read the following passage in a letter from Old Cairo: "On that day, a herald of the Sultan cried out in the morning and in the evening that the property and life of any Jew or Christian walking in the streets at day or nighttime without a distinctive mark or belt are forfeited." The much-mutilated continuation of the passage seems to say that a similar proclamation had been made a week before and that it was caused by a scholar, perhaps a Muslim scholar, addressing—whom, is not preserved. The casual way in which this matter is reported after many other details mentioned in the letter seems to indicate that in this late period the wearing of distinctive marks by non-Muslims was already generally accepted and the stern warning was addressed only to a few transgressors, presumably of the upper class.[56]

Next to the specific attire it was the poll tax incumbent on Christians and Jews which emphasized their inferior position. More than anything else it was the poll tax that brought the non-Muslim man on the street into unpleasant contact with the executive organs of the Muslim government; therefore it is treated below in the subsection devoted to it. There the often-repeated prohibition to employ Christians and Jews in government service is discussed, a law that in the Fatimid and early Ayyubid periods was honored in the breach rather than by implementation. The Geniza likewise contains no allusion to the poisonous propaganda against the treatment of Muslim patients by Christian and Jewish physicians. On the contrary, as we have seen, the Geniza frequently mentions Jewish physicians as serving Muslim rulers or working in Muslim hospitals. It cannot have been different with the lower classes, as is proved by the large number of Jewish physicians in provincial towns, where they could not have found a livelihood, if they had to rely exclusively, or even mainly, on the small Jewish communities. The Jewish physician who served as family doctor to the house of a man called "The Sword of Islam" is a case in point.[57]

Aside from the regulations concerning government service and physicians, Islam left to the religious minorities freedom in the choice and exercise of occupations. In this respect, the position of the Jews in Muslim countries differed markedly from that of their brethren in Europe during the late Middle Ages which for them lasted in many parts of that continent well down to the end of the nineteenth century. The forced restriction of the Jews in Europe to a few base or hateful occupations left on them a stigma, not entirely eradicated even today. There was no such a thing under Islam. Economic discrimination against non-Muslims was exercised in ancient Islam, when, in imitation of a Byzantine law, they had to pay a double rate of customs duties. This was a heavy imposition, since in those days custom duties were paid not only at frontiers of countries, but at the entrance to any major city. This law, however, was certainly no longer applied in Fatimid times. It was revived by Saladin and must then have been enforced for some time, for several references to it from the Ayyubid period are found in the Geniza. Thus, a young doctor is advised not to travel from Egypt to Syria, "for, as a Jew, you will have to pay thirty silver pieces as customs duties." Another letter, from a provincial town, states that it was impossible to travel at that time to Old or to New Cairo because of the customs. The Geniza also shows, however, that Saladin himself repealed that decree, which thus had no lasting detrimental effect on the economic or social position of the non-Muslims.[58]

In conclusion we may say that the position of the Christians and Jews under Islam during the period and within the area considered here was both safeguarded and precarious. Islamic law protected their life, property, and freedom and, with certain restrictions, granted them also the right to exercise their religion. On the other hand, it demanded from them segregation and subservience, conditions that under a weak or wicked government could and did lead to situations bordering on lawlessness and even to outright persecutions. During the eleventh, twelfth, and early thirteenth centuries, the sound principles of Islamic law were more conspicuous than its dark sides, at least in Egypt. This was in conformity with the general character of the period, in which the predominance of a flourishing middle class and a brisk international trade made for free intercourse between the various sections of the population and for a certain reasonableness in behavior.

2. *Interfaith Symbiosis and Cooperation*

The massive and reliable testimony of the Geniza documents proves that Muslims, Christians, and Jews lived in closest proximity to one another, to a far higher degree than could have been assumed on the basis of our literary sources. The Geniza reveals a situation very similar to that prevailing today in the United States: there were many neighborhoods predominantly Jewish, but hardly any that were exclusively so.

Jewish "quarters" are very rarely mentioned. Thus far, only three instances have been noted in our documents: for Qayrawān, the capital of the country known today as Tunisia (middle of eleventh century), for al-Maḥalla al-Kubrā, an important town in the Nile Delta (in a document dated 1202) and for Mosul in present-day Iraq.[1] The Jewish "Place" in Mosul is called in a letter dated May 16, 1237, by the same designation that is already used in the oldest report about the conquest of that city by the Arabs six hundred years earlier.[2] That letter, however, which describes the devastations wrought by an earthquake, specifies almost exclusively houses outside the "Place," and it seems that at least two out of the nine houses referred to belonged to Muslims.

We have no deeds for Mosul. Therefore we cannot say whether Muslims or Christians lived in the Jewish "Place" there. In the very document, however, from which we learn about the existence of a Jewish quarter in al-Maḥalla, Egypt, the property situated in it is described as bordering on the house of a Christian. Conversely, another document from the same town, dated 1144, deals with a Jewish house in a neighborhood different from the Jewish quarter.[3] As for Qayrawān, two of three Jewish properties whose description has been preserved bordered on Muslim houses.[4] Thus we see that references to Jewish quarters are by no means indicative of anything comparable with a ghetto.

Our main material comes of course from Old Cairo. There was no Jewish quarter in that city, but the bulk of the Jewish population was concentrated in a few neighborhoods, situated within, and bordering on, the old Roman fortress that formed the nucleus of Muslim Fustat. Jewish houses were also found in other parts of the city, including some fashionable ones, and one deed deals with a mansion that had once belonged to the famous vizier Ibn Killis. As far as our documents indicate boundaries, we see that even in the Jewish neighborhoods, at least half the houses had gentile neighbors. Without doing any special research in this matter, I have noted eight cases of Jewish living quarters bordering on Christian property, seven on Muslim, and five both on Christian and Muslim properties. The preponderance of Christians is to be explained by the fact that Christians and Jews had lived in the Roman fortified city before the advent of Islam and remained concentrated in their old quarters in order to enjoy the propinquity of their ancient and highly revered houses of worship. The instances of Muslims and Christians renting houses or apartments from Jews in Old Cairo or vice versa are too common to be counted. A case from Alexandria, 1132: a Jew rented a house from a Christian, which bordered on both Christian and Jewish properties.[5]

The closeness of Jewish and gentile living quarters is well illustrated in this passage from a letter of a scholar complaining to a prominent notable how he was snubbed by the latter's son-in-law. "When I came to his house he shut the door to my face; I stood at the gate like a dog . . . [Proverbs 26:11], and, while his gentile neighbors were looking on, I stood there and stood, knocking the ring, with him hearing me, but paying no attention."[6]

The Lane of the Jews in Old Cairo represented only a very small fraction of the Jewish settlement in that city. It began near the ancient gateway of the Roman fortress, from beneath the Muʿallaqa church (still in existence) and ran along the synagogues of the Babylonians and the Palestinians. Most probably it received its name when the church St. Michael, which was later converted into the synagogue of the Babylonians, was acquired, together with other Christian property, by the Jews, who thus expanded into a preponderantly Christian neighborhood. It is significant that thus far only two deeds making mention of this lane have been found.[7]

Similarly, we would be entirely mistaken if we assumed that the Little Market of the Jews, mentioned by Muslim historians describing Old Cairo, was the main scene of Jewish economic activities in the city. As a matter of fact, it does not appear in any Geniza document and was probably called thus by Muslims because of a Jewish slaughterhouse situated on it. The Jews, like their fellow citizens of other religions, were active in many bazaars, markets, and squares, each called after a specific commodity or craft and referred to in dozens of Geniza documents. In Palestine the situation was different. The Market of the Jews in Tiberias (which had been the capital of Jewish Palestine in the early Middle Ages) is given as address in a letter and mentioned in a document from September, 1034, which contains the important detail that the property that formed the object of the contract was situated "on its western colonnade." The Market of the Jews in Ramle is repeatedly referred to. These markets were a source of income for the Jewish authorities, both from the ritual slaughtering that was done there and the payments received from the proprietors of the stores. A Muslim source notes a Jews' market in Qayrawān, then the capital of what is known today as

Tunisia, but no mention of it has been found in the Geniza, which is noteworthy, considering the countless references in the Geniza to that city.[8]

The close interfaith relations prevailing in Old Cairo are evidenced by the fact that houses and shops were held in partnership by members of different religious communities. In five cases noted thus far in the Geniza the partners were Christians, in three others, Muslims. The dates of the documents referred to as far as preserved range from 1148 to 1234. One document, an incomplete deed in Arabic script, in which a Christian sells his share to his Jewish partner before a Muslim court, and another in which three Christian ladies do the same, originated in the eleventh century at latest. With regard to Jerusalem, too, we read about a house or compound, in which some rooms belonged to a Muslim and others to a Jew (around 1040). In Minyat Ziftā a house was held in partnership by "the son of the Rav" and a qadi, while the properties surrounding it were partly Jewish and partly Muslim.[9]

In houses in which, as it often happened, the various apartments were not entirely separated from one another, for instance, when all parties had to use the same well, it was difficult for Jews to live together with Muslims. For Muslim custom secludes the female members of the family in a separate section, a custom never accepted by the Jews. Since living quarters shared in common thus caused so much inconvenience to Jewish women, added to which was apprehension of Muslim overbearing and the possible desecration of the Sabbath, the Jewish authorities promulgated a statute forbidding the sale or rent of parts of houses to Muslims. Private persons, too, tried to protect their womenfolk from such inconvenience. When a notable had given a house as a gift to two brothers on condition that a certain woman should be permitted to live there, he stipulated a fine of 50 dinars on the recipients if they sold the house to a Muslim during her lifetime (April, 1156). A woman who had donated part of a house to the poor and a small house adjacent to it to her housekeeper stipulated that the small house should never be sold to Muslims, since this would be a nuisance for the poor (Feb.–March, 1117). Such restrictions naturally had an adverse effect on the price of Jewish property. A query addressed to Maimonides alleges that it reduced the price to one-third of the real value. Maimonides insists repeatedly on the strict observance of the statute, even in case of property belonging to orphans, permitting an exception solely in years of famine.[10]

Another responsum by Maimonides is illustrative of the situation. Minor orphans lived together with their mother in a house owned in partnership with a Christian. The latter converted to Islam—a change that made the sharing of the premises precarious—and, in general, the neighborhood became dangerous (as the relevant letter states). Maimonides rules that the part of the house belonging to the orphans may be sold, although such property normally was not touched until the orphans came of age and were able to dispose of it themselves.[11]

Economic considerations, however, were stronger than those that prompted the issue of the statute mentioned above. Queries similar to those submitted to Maimonides were sent to his son, the Nagid Abraham. In a letter addressed to the latter's grandson and namesake we read that in a provincial town, most probably al-Maḥalla, it was forbidden under the penalty of excommunication to sell houses situated in the Jewish quarter to a Muslim, but the prohibition was not observed. Even more telling is the fact that the charitable foundations belonging to the Jewish community found themselves forced from time to time to rent rooms and apartments to Muslims and Christians. Many such cases are registered in official documents dated 1058 through 1234. Non-Jewish tenants were so common that in an account from spring, 1218, a Christian acted as collector of the rents. When, however, a house opposite the women's entrance to the Iraqi synagogue was once rented to a Muslim, a strong protest was launched.[12]

On the Islamic side, no restrictions with regard to the freedom of choosing their domicile were imposed in our period on non-Muslims. This is attested both by literary sources and the Geniza papers. It was only the fanatical sect of the Almoravids of Morocco which created a ghetto, while a similar decree ascribed to the Fatimid caliph al-Ḥākim with regard to New Cairo was either invented by a later scholar, or, in any case, was ephemeral. The visitors in our day to the horrible mellahs, or Jewish quarters, of Morocco, are reminded that these places are characteristic of the later Middle Ages and not of the period described by us, which, for western North Africa, however, had come to an end one hundred and twenty years earlier than in the Muslim East.[13]

Interfaith cooperation in economic matters was even closer than the propinquity of the living quarters of the various religious communities. There is of course no need to adduce examples for Jews doing business with Muslims and Christians, both local and foreign. Nor is it necessary to emphasize that among their customers were Muslim religious scholars, for in both religions judges and other professionals frequently were active in business and, conversely, business men often were learned. It is perhaps interesting to note that a

Jewish merchant writes to his Muslim business friend a letter in Hebrew characters, asking a Jewish acquaintance to read it out to him (its language was of course Arabic). As is well known, the biographers of the Prophet Muhammad tell us that one of his secretaries learned the Hebrew alphabet in order to be able to read the letters of the Jews addressed to his master and to answer them in the same script. When, as the Geniza shows, Jews would write to their Muslim acquaintances in Hebrew in the eleventh century, when Arabic script was as widely diffused as the Latin, there is no wonder, that such things happened in the seventh, when Arabic script was hardly developed.[14]

It is significant that we find commercial partnerships between Jews, Christians, and Muslims, and again even with qadis. Some Muslim law schools prohibited such connections or attached certain strings on them. In the eleventh century, from which most of the business papers preserved in the Geniza come, no such restrictions are discernible. We find straight partnerships mentioned in them, as when a Tunisian merchant sojourning in Sicily writes in or around 1064: "All my dealings in olive oil [they amounted to the enormous sum of five thousand dinars] are made not on my personal account, but in partnership with Muslims and Jews [in this order], inhabitants of Palermo." In the same letter he refers two more times to his Muslim partners.[15] The archive of Nahray b. Nissīm teaches us that such partnerships constituted a joint undertaking lasting for years and were not merely an ephemeral relationship.[16]

The most common form of partnership was the commenda, in which one party supplied the capital or the goods and the other did the actual business. Many such connections were formed between Muslims and Jews, sometimes the former and sometimes the latter providing the capital. According to some Islamic law schools one of these two business connections or both are undesirable or prohibited. But the Geniza provides examples for each during the eleventh through the thirteenth centuries, and a query addressed to a Muslim scholar of the fourteenth century (answered of course in the negative with regard to both relationships) proves that even in those late and bigoted times such cooperation between the followers of different religions must not have been uncommon. In a letter written in or around 1141 the writer mentions a commenda worth 30 dinars received from a Muslim judge in a provincial town, while one in the amount of 100 dinars was given by a Jewish merchant of Old Cairo to a Muslim in Alexandria, made out, as is stated, before a Muslim court. Two Jews and one Muslim provided the money for a Jewish trader who imported flax from the Sharqiyya province to Alexandria around 1100.[17]

In many cases Muslims acted as business agents, wakīl, for Jews and vice versa. A Jewish scholar confides his goods to the warehouse and agency of "our master, the illustrious qadi Abu 'l-Ṭāhir Ibn Rajā'," as the relevant document, issued in Fustat, 1097 by a rabbinical court, styles him. Tunisian Muslims had their consignments handled in Egypt by a Jewish compatriot Nahray b. Nissīm, traveling to that country in 1046. Still earlier in the eleventh century we find one Muhammad as the permanent representative in Alexandria of Ibn 'Awkal, the prominent Jewish merchant and public figure. Under these conditions it is not surprising to find a Jewish merchant banker in close relation first with a Muslim and then, years later, with his son.[18]

Often our documents do not indicate whether the business connection between Muslim or Christians and Jews was that of a simple partnership, a commenda, a power of attorney, or another arrangement. This is true in particular of the many instances in which commodities belonging to members of one religious community were transported by those of another. A Jewish merchant who was murdered on his way from Egypt to Yemen had carried with him numerous goods belonging to Muslims and others in Tunisia. Another Jew transports copper entrusted to him by a Muslim from Qayrawān via Alexandria to Old Cairo. In one single letter a Jewish merchant, writing from Qayrawān, mentions by name four Muslims traveling in a caravan to Egypt and carrying for him different consignments of clothing and purses of gold. In another Geniza letter the addressee is asked to hand over shipments destined for the writer to a certain Muslim and only if the latter could not be reached, to a Jew called by name. Similarly, two scholarly Jewish merchants from Qayrawān, living in Egypt, entrust their shipments to the slave (and business agent) of a Muslim judge of their native city. At a time when non-Muslims had to pay special customs duties, an India traveler on his way home is advised by his brother in Alexandria to dispatch all his goods with Muslims in order to save the oppressive imposition.[19]

In short, business in those days had to rely largely on personal confidence and was therefore concentrated within a family, a clan, a close knit circle of friends, or a religious community far more than it is in our own times. The Geniza records prove, however, that relations of mutual trust and cooperation between members of different denominations were by no means exceptional. The following passage from a letter of recommendation for two Muslim merchants, who, it seems, were traveling from the West to Egypt for the first time in their lives, is illustrative of the prevailing mood and situation:

> The main reason for the writing of this letter is a recommendation for its bearers, two distinguished, decent, and highly trustworthy persons. If you agree, please send with them consignments belonging to you and to your friends. They asked me to request you to take care of them and to guard their interests. Sell what they carry with them and assist them in their purchases, even if you have to leave your own business for one or two days. I would like them to come back here full of thanks for you, having accomplished their purpose to their satisfaction. If available, send goods with them; they are trustworthy persons. By acting thus you will strengthen my reputation and give me reason to be grateful to you.

The repeated request to confide shipments to the Muslim business friends had the double aim of making their journey more profitable and of enhancing their prestige as trustworthy merchants.[20]

Partnerships in workshops between Jews and gentiles were perhaps not less common than those in commercial undertakings, although we hear of them less for the simple reason that craftsmen had little opportunity to write letters finding their way into the Geniza. Such an arrangement made it possible for the Jew to keep the shop open on Sabbath. The following query addressed to Maimonides is instructive in various respects: "What does our master say with regard to partners in a workshop, some being Jews and some Muslims, exercising the same craft. The partners have agreed between themselves that the [gains made on] Friday should go to the Jews and those made on Saturday to the Muslims. The implements of the workshop are held in partnership; the crafts exercised are in one case goldsmithing, in another the making of glass." Maimonides rules that the arrangement was legal, as long as the Jewish craftsmen did not partake in any profit made on the Sabbath. As is well known, the Muslim Friday is not a day of rest. Should we assume that some Muslim craftsmen of the twelfth century were already as wise as their colleagues of the twentieth century in taking over the idea of a day of rest prevailing in the sister religions? Muqaddasi, the famous Muslim traveler of the tenth century reports indeed that the markets of Fustat were closed on Fridays. But it is not sure whether this observation refers to a general and permanent usage or rather to some special season or occurrence.[21]

Employment, from the point of view of Jewish law, was different. One was not permitted to derive any profit from the work done by a gentile employee on Sabbath. A carpenter who had his Muslim workers making doors on a Saturday was threatened with flogging and was forced to discontinue the practice.[22] Still, the employment of gentiles by Jews, as well as the opposite, must have been common. We read about a Jewish silk-weaver in whose shop Muslims, a Jew, and a Jewish convert to Islam worked together.[23] A Christian doctor and a Jew were employed in a store of potions belonging to a person bearing a name common in the three religious communities.[24] In view of such a situation it seems natural that a rabbinical court, which had to assess the value of the implements and the stock of a workshop for purple dyeing, invited for the purpose both the Jewish and the Muslim colleagues of the deceased proprietor.[25] On the other hand we have had the case of a Jewish weaver from Sicily who got work with a Muslim employer on the day of his arrival in Alexandria, but was dismissed when it was found out that he was a Jew.[26]

In *Med. Soc.*, I, 254, reference was made to the mutual financial help of Muslim and Jewish craftsmen. One case was that of a Jewish *ka'kī* (translated there inaccurately as "baker of cakes"; it should have been "bagels," but at the time of the writing of that volume I shunned such parochial words). A Muslim baker of bread had lent him money which he paid back as stipulated. By an almost comical coincidence, at a recent visit to the University Library, Cambridge, England, I came across another loan taken by the same Jewish baker of bagels, this time from a Muslim miller, exactly a month before he paid back the other debt (which is attested in a document preserved in the Freer Gallery, Washington).[27]

Were there double standards of business ethics, depending on whether dealings were made with members of one's own community or with others? Maimonides, in his law code, strictly forbids such an attitude, and the Geniza documents contain hardly anything indicative of its existence. A recently discovered autograph responsum of Maimonides answers a query concerning the son of a broker who had absconded with goods belonging to Muslims and Jews and later secretly returned to his father the stuff belonging to the latter, but not that of the former. This, however, should not be taken as a case of double standard. The fugitive did not act out of pangs of conscience, but was afraid of the Jewish merchants, who could more easily find out his whereabouts than the Muslims.[28] The opposite, namely the particular care taken with the consignments of gentile business friends, points perhaps to a slight awareness of a specific responsibility.[29] In general, however, no such difference is discernible and should not be expected in a society in which, as we have seen, business connections among the members of the three denominations were so frequent and cordial.

One wonders whether the proximity of living quarters and close economic cooperation led to some social intercourse between the adherents of the various faiths. As the following examples show it was not altogether absent. After Nahray b. Nissīm had lived in a provincial town for some time, a friend writes to him from there: "the *'āmil* [director of finance] and the qadi every day inquire with me about your well being"; a Muslim scribe and a fourth Muslim also send him regards.[30] In a letter from Alexandria, written in, or around 1030, the writer promises to arrange a certain affair on the following day, when he would visit a Muslim friend to congratulate him on his holiday. Such visits thus must have been a matter of routine. It should be remarked, however, that both the sender of that letter and his Muslim acquaintance were Tunisians.[31] In Palestine we find a Gaon requesting an influential Jewish court physician to act on behalf of a Muslim official, who was harassed by a new governor. The Gaon himself had been asked for this favor by a Muslim notable with whom he was on good terms.[32]

Particularly noteworthy are the friendly relations between the religious scholars and dignitaries of the various denominations. Throughout the Geniza letters and in the queries addressed to Maimonides and his son Abraham and their answers the Muslim judges and jurisprudents are referred to in terms of reverence and rarely without a eulogy wishing them temporal or spiritual success or both.[33] Naturally, these niceties would be omitted when a case of taking bribes or accepting false witnesses was reported. The friendship between Hay Gaon, the head of the yeshiva of Baghdad, and the catholicus, the head of the Nestorian church, based on common scientific interests, has been noted before.[34] Of particular interest is a Geniza document, dated March 24, 1182, showing Moses Maimonides, Ibn Sanā' al-Mulk, qadi of Cairo and a famous poet (1155–1211), and a number of other Jewish and Muslim intellectuals as being closely connected with each other.[35] At about the same time we find a similar relationship in Alexandria. The leading Muslim jurisprudent in the city informed his Jewish colleague, a dayyān, of a secret accusation brought against him before the government by some notables of the Jewish community.[36] The spiritual leader of the Jewish community in a smaller town asks the Nagid Mevōrākh to use his influence with the authorities for "the bearer of this letter, the *ghulām* [which could mean: son, slave, or servant] of my lord, the qadi Thiqat al-Dawla

('The Trusted of the Dynasty'), may God make his honored position permanent." No doubt, he was referring to the local Muslim judge.[37] Thus we see that friendly relations between the intellectuals of different faiths were not confined to persons of secular education.

Yet, one is left with the impression that the participation of Muslims in the joyful or mournful events of the Jewish community are reported in the Geniza as something extraordinary, exceptional rather than normal. A (very fragmentary) letter of thanks praises a scholar who had passed a certain time, it seems, during the High Holidays, in a provincial town. His presence highly enhanced the prestige, *jāh,* of the Jewish community "and both Jews and Muslims were happy with him." [38] A description of a particularly festive reading of the Esther scroll, in which over eight hundred adult males, both Rabbanites and Karaites, took part, concludes by emphasizing that Muslims, too, had been present. (Haman, the villain of the Esther story, is denounced as exceedingly wicked also in the holy book of Islam).[39] We have read above how "Jews and Muslims" were happy about the escape of the writer from danger and congratulated him on that miraculous event.[40]

Looking back on the testimony of the Geniza documents with regard to interfaith relations we find that the religious concepts of superiority and seclusion—which should not be rated solely as negative—were counteracted by economic and social conditions that made for a more tolerant attitude. Therefore the picture obtained was not at all simple and uniform. Nor was this antagonism between the zeal for one's own religion and humane broadmindedness only a social phenomenon. It was a split that went right through the personality of some of the best minds of the age.

3. *Converts and Proselytes*

Minorities living amidst a huge majority are prone to be partly absorbed by it. The Jews of the Geniza period were no exception to this rule. First, there were forced conversions. It is true that orthodox Islam objects in principle to compelling the "people of the Book" to abdicate their faith. But practice did not always follow theory, and there were sects that did not acknowledge even the principle of freedom of religion.

Two severe persecutions, marked by forceful conversion to Islam, occurred in the period dealt with in this book. The first was the work of the paranoiac Fatimid caliph al-Ḥākim. As in the case of the destruction of the houses of worship, repeatedly referred to earlier, his decrees seem to have been directed primarily against the Christians. For in 1012, according to our sources the fifth year of the measures taken against the Christians, he was still praised in a Hebrew "Scroll" as a just ruler. Later, however, the Jews were affected as well. We read in a letter preserved in the Geniza about Jews who had been forced to adopt Islam and others who preferred death or who emigrated to Byzantium, Yemen, or other countries. That persecution, however, vehement as it was, lasted for only a short period, for in documents dated 1016 we already see the rabbinical court of Old Cairo doing normal business, and in any case the forced converts were allowed to return to their respective religions before the caliph's death in 1121.[1]

The experience gained under al-Ḥākim probably guided the behavior of the Jews under the far more dangerous and long lasting persecution by the Muslim sect of the Almohads in North Africa and Spain.[2] The victory of this bellicose denomination was accompanied by the wholesale slaughter of Christians, Jews, and dissenting Muslims. Very many Jews, given the choice between the sword and Islam, abandoned their religion, and, as a Geniza letter emphasizes, the leader of the community in Sijilmāsa, the important caravan city in Morocco, was the first to do so. Most probably he regarded that terrible avalanche as a passing visitation, for which the sacrifice of so many lives seemed unreasonable. If he indeed thought so, he was mistaken. The Almohads came to stay for many years, so that there developed a phenomenon of Muslim crypto-Jews very much similar to that of the Marranos in Christian Spain of later centuries: their conversion to Islam did not protect them against ceaseless vexations and sometimes even outright destruction.[3]

Aside from these two persecutions, which have to be regarded as exceptional, no particular pressure to adopt Islam was exercised on the minorities during the Fatimid and Ayyubid periods although they were encouraged to do so. Nor were the disabilities to which they were exposed so burdensome as to cause mass conversions. There is, however, some evidence in the Geniza that there were individual cases of persons from all ranks of the society who, for whatever reason, found it more convenient to join the ruling religion. The Geniza word for apostasy to Islam is *pāsha'*, literally, "to renounce one's allegiance" (cf. I Kings 12:19), from which a Judeo-Arabic word *afsha'* was formed. Neither the verb nor the nouns for "renegade" and "apostasy" derived from it are registered in this sense in any Hebrew dictionary.[4] They occur regularly in our documents, though. A letter from Alexandria, written about 1060, reports the conversion to Islam of the cantor of the Jewish community of Palermo, the capital of Sicily, and describes the stir caused by this step. Its reasons, however, are not revealed, nor do the many letters from Sicily which the Geniza has preserved from that period indicate any particular circumstances that could have formed its background. A Maghrebi who had suffered much from the impositions and false accusations of some Jewish leaders in Alexandria confesses (around 1085) that he had been on the verge of embracing Islam. He fasted eight days, three even during the nights, in order to atone for such a sinful intention.[5] In litigations about inheritance, converts to Islam appear repeatedly as contestants; one such document is dated 1157.[6]

Persons living in a foreign country and thus anyhow uprooted from their habitual environment, were particularly exposed to the lure of the ruling religion. Maimonides, in one of his responsa, calls such occurrences commonplace, and in a query to his son, the Nagid Abraham, we have the strange case of a traveler giving his wife a provisional bill of divorce to be effective in case he adopted Islam while abroad.[7] An occurrence of a somewhat different character illustrates this situation. A Jew, but not his wife, had embraced Islam. (A Muslim, we remember, is permitted to be married to a Jewess or Christian). After a year, when he was about to go abroad, she demanded a divorce, but he refused, arguing that he intended to be away for only a short period. When ten years had passed, and he had never written home from India, where he stayed, his wife applied for a divorce. She wanted to marry another man, for the times were hard and she was unable to support herself. The query, written in Arabic characters, was addressed to a Muslim jurisconsult, but, since she was Jewish, the latter turned the case over to a Jewish court, as may be concluded from the Hebrew writings on the reverse side of the document, which prove that it had found its way back into Jewish hands.[8] In general, it is understandable that a person changing his religion would prefer to move to another town or country, and several such instances can be traced in the Geniza.[9]

On the other hand, we do find renegades maintaining close relations with their former coreligionists. In the case of high dignitaries, where conversion was a matter mostly of expediency, it is perhaps not astonishing, as evident from the life story of the Fatimid vizier Ibn Killis.[10] A similar situation, however, prevailed in the lower classes as well. We have read about a Jewish silk-weaver employing a Jewish convert to Islam. "A red-haired renegade" is referred to in a letter as conveying a message from a relative. We hear even about a couple of converts who wanted to have their son circumcised in the Jewish way.[11]

Nowhere is a curse attached to the mention of renegades and, with one exception discussed below, no derogatory remarks are made about them, not even about that dayyān of Sijilmāsa who led his congregation into Islam during the Almohad persecution. As the Geniza proves, cases of conversion were not very common in that period. In the many lists of receivers of alms discussed in Appendix B only once is the wife of a renegade noted.[12] Uncouth country people, when receiving no satisfaction in a Jewish court, would threaten with conversion to Islam.[13] A Jewish judge in Egypt refrained from pronouncing a ban over a person who had been excommunicated in Spain because he was afraid he would apostatize if treated too harshly by the Jewish authorities of the country to which he had emigrated.[14]

Love, the most common incentive for changing one's religion nowadays, does not seem to have played an even remotely similar role in the Geniza period. We have a document about an affair between a Christian physician and a Jewish girl. But, as usual, we do not know the end of it.[15] In one of the most famous stories of *The Arabian Nights* a rich Christian youth falls in love with a mature Jewish woman of perfect beauty and superior intelligence. After some introductory moves, they meet every day and play chess together, but she invariably defeats him until he loses all his property to her. (In those days they played chess for money.) Finally, after many vicissitudes, they marry, not without having changed first their religion, of course, to Islam; otherwise, the Muslim audience would not have enjoyed the story. (This was also in conformity with the legal situation, but the narrator does not pay the slightest attention to law, whether moral or statutory.) Fortunately, the woman's husband was one of those Jewish India traders who tarried on their travels for years. When he came home, full of yearning for his beautiful wife, he was quickly disposed of.[16]

Three prominent Jews embraced Islam around the middle of the twelfth century: Isaac, the son of the famous (Abraham) Ibn Ezra, and a poet in his own right; his teacher, Abu 'l-Barakāt Hibat Allah (Nethanel, "Gift of God") Awḥad al-Zamān ("The Unique") al-Baghdādī, one of the most original thinkers of the Islamic Middle Ages; and Samuel, the Maghrebi, to whom reference has been made before. The stories of these conversions lie outside the scope of this book, geographically, since they occurred in Iraq and Iran, and materially, since we learn about them not from the documents of the Cairo Geniza, but from literary sources. But the first of the three, Isaac b. Abraham Ibn Ezra, has indeed left his mark in the Geniza records. From them we learn the interesting fact that he was not only the son of a great Jewish author, but also the son-in-law of another: none less than the poet laureate Judah ha-Levi, whom he accompanied on his pilgrimage from Spain to the Holy Land in 1140—that is, as far as Egypt, where their ways parted. Isaac proceeded to Baghdad, where he studied under "The Unique." A poem of his, dedicated to his master's philosophical commentary on the book of Ecclesiastes (Kohelet), completed in 1143, is extant. Isaac returned later to the Jewish faith, claiming in his poems that his conversion to Islam had been a fake. From the same poems it appears, however, that it had not been made under duress, or in the ardors of a love affair (as a learned student of medieval Hebrew poetry is inclined to read there between the lines). Since apostasy from Islam was punishable by death (see below), Isaac had to travel for his second change of religion to a Christian country, but he soon fell ill. His father, who in those years roamed about France, England, and Italy, rushed to his sickbed, but was unable to save him.[17]

The Geniza has preserved a letter sent from Egypt in 1139 by the India trader Ḥalfōn b. Nethanel to Isaac Ibn Ezra while the latter was still in Spain. Although Isaac was then a very young man, twenty-five years old at most, Ḥalfōn addresses him in a way that betrays both intimacy and esteem.[18] Two letters written by Isaac himself show him to be a rather strange person. The letters are partly in cryptic language, and in one passage he uses Coptic numerals in order to express Hebrew characters denoting Arabic words. Not enough with this, he employs also a secret code. The Spanish youth and the seasoned India traveler did some business together, but shared to an even larger extent common literary interests.[19]

Samuel the Maghrebi became a militant Muslim, and his book against his former coreligionists served as a main source for later anti-Jewish Muslim polemics. But Abu 'l-Barakāt "The Unique" adopted Islam only very late in life and possibly under duress (different versions are given for his decision: wounded pride, death of the mother of a sultan whom he had treated, fear of death when captured in a battle); his daughters remained Jewish. Since the Gaon Samuel b. Eli of Baghdad quotes him in his polemic with Maimonides, Abu 'l-Barakāt's apostasy seemingly was not taken very seriously by his former coreligionists.[20]

With the catastrophic worsening of the legal and actual position of non-Muslims in the late Middle Ages, mass conversion to Islam became an epidemic.[21]

As for the opposite phenomenon, the adoption of the Jewish religion by Muslims, the legal situation has first to be considered. According to Islamic law, any Muslim renouncing his religion faced the death penalty.[22] As is natural, those non-Muslims who persuaded or aided him exposed themselves to the same punishment. Such an occurrence is vividly described in two Geniza letters written by one Abū Naṣr on May 11, 1141, in Alexandria. They refer to the Spanish Hebrew poet Judah ha-Levi who was then on his way to the Holy Land. In Alexandria there lived at that time a convert to Islam called Ibn-Baṣrī (family name derived from Basra in southern Iraq), whose brother in Spain had handed over to Judah ha-Levi's fellow traveler an order of payment for him in the amount of thirty gold pieces. Whether on the request of Ibn al-Baṣrī's Spanish brother, or out of his own initiative, the poet tried to persuade the renegade to travel with him to Palestine, then in Christian hands, where he could return to Judaism without incurring danger. The renegade, however, denounced ha-Levi, who had to appear successively before the head of the secret police, the governor, and the qadi of the city. Had he not been well known and highly respected from a prior and prolonged visit to Alexandria—the writer of the letters remarks—his life would have been forfeited. As it was, the anger of the mob became directed against Ibn al-Baṣrī for giving so much trouble to a distinguished visitor, and he was almost killed.[23]

Despite the enormous danger involved, there were sporadic cases of Muslims attracted by Judaism, and, as two letters of Maimonides addressed to such converts show, they were educated persons deeply interested in religious questions. We learn also that the converts had to leave their country, otherwise they would have exposed themselves to certain death. In another letter, Maimonides rules that religious propaganda (he uses the phrase "to draw people to our religion") should be made amongst Christians, not among Muslims. His reasons, however, were theological, not practical: Since the Christians accepted the text of the Old Testament as the unadulterated word of God, it was possible to argue with them about its interpretation; there was no such means of understanding with the Muslims, since they took the distortions found in their Koran as genuine revelation.[24]

Maimonides' favorable attitude toward proselytizing is echoed in the Geniza documents, in which converts to Judaism are mentioned far more frequently than Jews adopting Islam. Most of the converts to Judaism were Christians, in particular from Rūm, that is, Byzantium and western Europe. Foreign proselytes removed to the countries of Islam for reasons of safety are referred to in a number of instances. A report from Alexandria, written around 1200, mentions "the proselyte Jew from Trapani, Sicily" who had arrived from there in a boat a few days before.[25] "The proselyte and his slave girl Mubāraka" who received, at a distribution of wheat made around 1107, so much more than the other beneficiaries, were listed under the heading of persons coming from Europe.[26] When we find in 1121 a Jew "from the land of the Romans" and a proselyte as partners in a three-story house in al-Maḥalla, Lower Egypt, we can take it for granted that both had emigrated together, when or after the Christian embraced the Jewish faith.[27] The son of a proselyte called 'lyvyr (Oliver?) was influential, or at least active, in Cairo around 1090. Thus his father probably had come to Egypt a few decades earlier.[28] The story of Johannes-Obadiah, the Norman seeker of God, and those of other more prominent converts from Christian Europe will occupy us later on.

Since conversion to Judaism was as dangerous in Christian countries as it was under Islam, it is natural that there existed a strong opposition to any attempt of making proselytes. The Geniza has preserved the draft of a letter in which the most terrible curses are hurled against those who opposed missionary activities. The text is somewhat of a puzzle. For it is written on the same leaf and in the same hand in which, on the reverse side, an India traveler lists his expenditure on customs duties on his way to East Africa and copies (or jots down from memory) the formulary for the manumission of a slave. Since the letter was intended to be sent to a European country (as is stated), while the writer promises on his side to divulge the names of "the criminals who prevent salvation" in all countries "from Spain to the isles of India," it was presumably written by a religious scholar who learned about the opposition to proselytizing while on an extended business trip.[29]

We have no express information about local Christians converting to Judaism, although the considerable number of converts and the fact that so many of them were brought to provincial towns make such an assumption probable. The proselyte woman whose letter to a Nagid is rendered at the end of this subsection could hardly have been anything else but a Christian. It should be noted that conversion from Christianity to Judaism and vice versa was prohibited under Islam which permitted no change except to the ruling religion. Still, a Christian source tells us of a Jew who knew how to speak Coptic (which shows that he had lived in an exclusively Christian environment) and adopted the Christian faith in the latter half of the twelfth century.[30]

In six documents, at least, reference is made to a proselyte known under the Arabic kunya, or by-name, Abu 'l-Khayr, ("Mr. Good") and in one he is quite active, taking out a Torah scroll from the Holy Ark and proclaiming a ban on an adversary. In others, he makes sizable contributions to public appeals. But the fact that he bore an Arabic name does not preclude that he had originally been a European Christian who after his conversion and emigration to Egypt was called thus. A Byzantine Jewish glassmaker, also mentioned in one of the documents referred to, likewise bears an Arabic kunya. It is also not excluded that "Mr. Good" was one of the names applied to proselytes (like the name Mubārak, "the blessed one"), and that the documents mentioning a proselyte Abu 'l-Khayr may actually refer to two or more different persons.[31]

Proselytes appear frequently in the lists of indigents in receipt of bread, wheat, or clothing. This is natural, since, as a rule, they had to leave their domicile and so lost whatever income they had. They are either mentioned in a general way, such as "the proselyte woman," or with their names or descriptions, such as "Abraham the proselyte" or "[the wife of] the proselyte who is a gravedigger." [32] To be sure, sometimes the epithet "the proselyte" is given simply as a means of identification. Thus we have the marriage contract of Mubāraka ("the blessed one") the proselyte, "daughter of Abraham," whose trousseau amounted to the considerable sum of 93 dinars, and a reference to such a contract of the son-in-law of a convert to Judaism.[33]

Private charity, too, took care of proselytes, and many relevant instances could be adduced from the Geniza.[34] Of particular interest in this respect is a letter of a former cleric from Europe who expressed his gratitude to a lady for providing him with bread to his taste and gave her instructions how to prepare more.[35] Norman Golb of Chicago recognized [36] that this letter is in the same hand and style as two other important fragments, one recently edited by Alexander Scheiber of Budapest, written by a high-standing and learned proselyte in which he bitterly complains of being neglected by the two Rabbanite communities of Old Cairo,[37] and another, published many years ago by Simha Assaf, containing the story of his conversion. The story ends indeed with the remark that after his escape from prison the convert found himself entirely without means, having chosen a life of "begging bread." [38]

Not all proselytes, however, were poor. Reference has been made already to the liberality of one (or two) "Mr. Good, the proselyte." In a deathbed declaration made in the year 1085, a man with the same name was in charge of the testator's property, a task entrusted normally to well-established persons. He might have been identical with still another Abu 'l-Khayr *al-gēr* (the proselyte, Heb.) who during one public collection, arranged at approximately the same time, donated a higher sum than any other contributor.[39] Even more impressive is a letter mentioning a request submitted to a proselyte called Abraham to permit the writer to accompany him on a business trip to Ceuta (Sabta, Morocco, at present a Spanish possession). This "Abraham" must have been a successful trader, possibly of Italian origin, for the Italians used to do much business with that North African port.[40]

It must have been common practice to direct the proselytes out of the capital city to the provincial towns. We had an example with regard to al-Maḥalla and another in which a muqaddam in a small place declared himself incompetent to deal with a case involving a male and a female proselyte. From the little town Malīj in the Nile Delta two instances, and quite significant ones, are illustrated by Geniza letters. In the first, a letter to a Nagid, three proselytes express their gratitude to all the members of the local congregation and in particular its leaders (mentioned by name), but complain about a certain tanner who excused himself with what he had allegedly done for them for not contributing to any communal funds. Whether that person did or did not share in the burdens of the community, they, the proselytes, did not want to be involved. They were called Asher, Issachar, and Dan, respectively, and since these were strange names for proselytes, we are perhaps right in assuming that there must have been no small number of conversions at that time with the more common names having been given to others.[41]

The second letter from Malīj, also addressed to a Nagid, reports that the pious proselyte Joseph had arrived in the town and was honored by the writer and the whole congregation, "as was obligatory for all Israel." Joseph was not a poor man. He had left one volume of the Five Books of Moses with a dignitary and another with the Nagid himself and wanted to have them back, together with the receipts for his poll tax which he had paid in the capital. Similarly, a proselyte directed by the dayyān of Cairo to faraway Qūṣ in Upper Egypt was a man of means and carried goods with him. A local merchant undertook to sell them, since the newcomer had to hide on the very day of his arrival, but paid him their price in advance. Persons traveling with the proselyte, who also was called Mubārak, "the blessed one" (see above), testified that during the long travel from Cairo to Qūṣ he had passed his days in prayer and fasting, taking some food only before daybreak. He did not regard it as permissible to eat bread bought on the market (i.e., not baked by Jews), but carried bread around with him which he had received in private homes. Clearly the letter wants to emphasize the particular piety of the proselyte, who was far more scrupulous in religious observance than ordinary Jews.[42]

The diversion of proselytes from the main cities had its good reason. A Christian converted to Judaism was not always safe there from molestation. This is strikingly evidenced by a letter of recommendation addressed, it seems, to Shemarya b. Elhanan, the leader of the Egyptian Jews around 1000. The bearer of the letter was a Christian from a noble family who, after his conversion to Judaism, had fled to Damascus and from there to Jerusalem. In both cities, as the writer, a Spanish Jew, emphasizes, the convert was exposed to insults and threats on the part of the local Christians, who were backed by their powerful coreligionists in government service. The Spanish Jew had met the proselyte both in Damascus and Jerusalem and now asks Shemarya to take care of him after his arrival in Old Cairo. It is noteworthy that Egypt was regarded to be a safer place for a Christian convert to Judaism than Syria or Palestine.[43]

A similar case is reported in a letter written over two hundred years later. The muqaddam of Bilbays, that important caravan station on the route from Palestine to Cairo, informs his superior, the judge Elijah b. Zechariah in Fustat, that a scholar called Ibn al-Maqdisī ("the man from Jerusalem") had arrived from Gaza and that he wished to detain him in Bilbays for two months in order to study with him a talmudic treatise dealing with marriage laws (two months were thus regarded by the muqaddam as sufficient for that task). The Palestinian scholar was accompanied by "Ibn Ḥallāb (lit. son of the milker), the proselyte." The way in which the proselyte is referred to shows that some previous correspondence must have been conducted on his behalf between Jerusalem, Fustat, and Bilbays, presumably in order to find out whether it was safe and expedient to remove him from Palestine to Egypt. His family name does not necessarily imply that he was of low extraction.[44]

The most impressive Geniza document on proselytism is the Hebrew "autobiography" of the Norman cleric Johannes-Obadiah, in which he describes the circumstances under which he embraced Judaism, the dangers to which he was exposed in his country after his conversion, as well as his extended travels among the Jewish communities under Islam and the messianic movements that he encountered there. His apostasy was no doubt due to a certain crisis in the church of southern Italy, where the Norman nobleman was born and educated. For he reports that Andreas, the archbishop of the city of Bari, as well as others had adopted Judaism before him. He describes his conversion as the consequence of a dream he had in his youth when he was still in his father's house. He saw himself officiating in the church when he was addressed by a man standing at the altar, who recited the following verse from the book of Joel: "The sun shall be turned into darkness and the moon into blood, before the great and terrible day of the Lord will come" (2:31 in the Authorized Version; 3:4 in the Hebrew text). Johannes-Obadiah, writing in Hebrew at least twenty years after this event, still quotes the words of this verse in Latin (written in Hebrew characters!), as he had heard them at that decisive hour, so mighty was the impression made on him by their very sound. They are indeed the key to the understanding of the whole problem of conversion to Judaism. It was the feeling, so common in the Middle Ages, that the end of the physical world was near and the Day of Judgment at hand which set people thinking. This sentiment caused some seekers of God to adopt Judaism, the original and therefore regarded by them as the true form of monotheism.[45]

Thus the conversion to Judaism of Johannes-Obadiah was essentially an inner-Christian affair. The same is to be said of the cleric whose Hebrew letters have been referred to above. He reports that "after having circumcised himself" and beginning to observe "the holidays of God, as they are written in the Torah," as well as the Sabbaths, he wrote fourteen pamphlets[46] in which he assembled all "the questions and arguments" that had induced him to change his religion. He submitted his book to his archbishop with the request to refute him. In his naïve belief he adds that if the church dignitary had only taken the trouble to read the book, he and his fellow clerics would certainly have been convinced and would have followed the writer's example. In order to fortify this claim he enclosed six of the fourteen pamphlets (presumably translated from Latin or Greek into Hebrew). God, however, had ordained not to enlighten the heart of the church dignitary. Our writer was put into prison and threatened with execution or banishment to an island where he would die, if he did not repent. Fortunately, one of the prison guards had a nightly apparition that induced him to provide for the prisoner's escape, letting him down from a window with a rope.[47]

Astonishingly, the Geniza has preserved a similar case of conversion to Judaism without interference from an Egyptian village. An elderly woman had begun to observe the Jewish holidays and Sabbaths (about which she had certainly learned from the Bible [see the cleric's story in the preceding paragraph]) and waited for an opportunity to convert formally. She was told (by whom is not preserved) that she should go up to Atfīḥ, a center of flax growing which harbored a Jewish community, where she would find what her heart desired.[48] The Jews told her, however, that they were not competent to accept her conversion and that she had to apply to the Nagid. She did as advised, and here is her application, as far as extant:

> . . . Your illustrious Excellency. . . . I do not desecrate any holiday or Sabbath. . . . [and wish] to die in the Jewish religion [which I hope to embrace] during your splendorous days. . . . They said to me: Go up to Atfīḥ; there are Jews; they will proselyte you.[49] Thus, your maidservant traveled to Atfīḥ, went to the Jews[50] and made an appeal to the community.[51] They replied: We cannot act except upon the written instruction of the Nagid. Therefore, your maidservant comes to your auspicious gate and throws herself on God and on you, entreating you by your faith in God[52] not to dash my hopes. For I have nowhere to turn, except to the gate of God and yours. Do not leave me in the lurch. For I would not have undertaken this travel had I not been confident about this matter. It is not for a dinar or a dirhem that I have taken the trouble to move to a foreign place. . . .[53]

The concluding sentence deserves attention. Since the prospect of being maintained by Jewish charity was a strong inducement for conversion to Judaism, this old woman proudly declared that she did not seek membership in the community of Israel for material gain.

Those who, like this woman or the merchant whose piety was probed on the long journey to Qūṣ, converted out of religious motives naturally were the most valuable acquisitions for the Jewish community. Cases in point are Johannes-Obadiah and that other Obadiah, a pious man of Muslim origin to whom Maimonides addressed his famous epistle(s). Johannes' autobiographic "scroll" is a unique creation in medieval Hebrew literature. Although its author learned Hebrew in the Arab East, his scroll has a decidedly European touch (as does also the religious poem that bears his name in acrostic; medieval Latin versification shines clearly through the Hebrew words).[54] In addition to its literary merits the scroll has religious significance: the writer debunks, and not without humor, the false messianic claims that he encountered in some Jewish communities of the East. His searching mind, which had moved him to forsake the faith of his forefathers, was not blunted by his enthusiasm for the new religion he had embraced.

At an early stage of my Geniza studies, when I was surprised and impressed by the frequency of conversion to Judaism testified by documentary evidence, I promised the publication of a special study on the subject.[55] I have not yet carried out this intention—fortunately, for new material is cropping up all the time and the entire question needs to be studied in a wider context. The section of the literary Geniza texts which has already provided the most valuable document on proselytism, the Obadiah scroll, should be searched for pieces of a similar character. I should not be surprised at all, if for instance, the six pamphlets attached to the letter of the disputation-hungry cleric, analyzed above,[56] were to turn up one day amidst a package of unidentified theological texts. Moreover, the question of change of religion cannot be separated from the more general problem of the ever-changing religious situation in each community. In those days, people pondered much about God and had many "questions." Sectarianism, such as pietist conventicles of different types, were one answer; conversion was another.

B. COMMUNAL JURISDICTION

1. *The Judiciary*

Nothing is so characteristic of the position of the non-Muslim minorities under classical Islam as their judicial organization. On the one hand, their judiciary derived its authority and executive power to a notable degree from the Muslim government; criminal jurisdiction, and in particular, capital punishment were, as a rule, prerogatives of the state; and any member of the minority groups was free to apply to a Muslim judge instead of to the courts of his own denomination. Yet, the wide range of cases brought before the rabbinical courts (as proved by the evidence of the Geniza), as well as the marked divergence of the Jewish judiciary, law, and procedures from the Muslim ones are illustrative of the high degree of autonomy and individual life enjoyed by the minorities in the period under study.

In the first place, it was the wide range of legal matters connected directly with religion, such as marriage, divorce, inheritance, and the status of slavery and freedom, which was the natural domain of the denominational courts. In addition, there were many good reasons that would induce a Jew or a Christian to seek justice within his own community. Religious law encompassed the gamut of economic and social life. Therefore the pious, who preferred to be judged according to his religion rather than another law, had no need to apply to the court of the state. Practical considerations were probably even more compelling. Litigation before a Jewish court was inexpensive, no payments being required except a remuneration for the scribe who made out the relevant documents. Application to a state authority involved, in addition to fees, tips to underlings and often also costly bribes to those higher up. The members of the Jewish courts were, as a rule, personally known to the parties either from the synagogue or otherwise, and, in any case were regarded by them as people of their own kind. Finally, since the Jewish court was composed of three or more members, litigants themselves frequently had experience of the bench, which naturally made them more inclined to entrust their cause to an authority and a procedure with which they were familiar.

Finally, the express injunctions of his religion and the pressure of his social group were apt to force a Christian or a Jew to apply to the denominational rather than to the Muslim court. Every reader of the New Testament is familiar with these fulminating words of the apostle Paul addressed to the Corinthians (I, 6:1–4): "When one of you has a grievance against a brother, does he dare go to law before the unrighteous instead of the saints? Do you not know that the saints will judge the world? And if the world is to be judged by you, are you incompetent to try trivial cases? If then you have such cases, why do you lay them before those who are least esteemed by the Church?" This attitude (which reveals Paul's background as a former Jewish divine) remained basic in the Church and in the Synagogue throughout the ages. It is echoed in many Geniza documents, as shown in the concluding section of this chapter.

The Muslim and Jewish judiciaries differed widely as to their origin and nature. The Muslim qadi was originally the delegate of the caliph or the provincial governor, and, like the latter and the caliph himself, never shared his authority with anyone else. He was free to consult the doctors of law or experts in any other matter, but the decision rested with him alone.[1] His duties and prerogatives were not only judicial, but largely administrative. The estates of orphans and other property entrusted to the courts were in his hands. He often combined with his office highly lucrative positions of power, such as that of the controller of the revenue of a district or that of the superintendent of a port (see sec. C, 1, c, below).

Jewish law was based on the assumption that "none may judge alone save One," namely God; at least three men should be convened as a court, in order to avoid errors and miscarriage of justice. In talmudic times, and perhaps under the influence of later Roman judicial organization, where the delegate of the provincial governor had a position similar to that held subsequently by the qadi in Islam, it became a recognized principle that a person accepted by the community or authorized by the Jewish high court may judge alone. But even such a "generally accepted or authorized judge" was enjoined not to make use of this privilege (which infringed on God's uniqueness), but to associate others with himself. Maimonides incorporates this principle in his Code of Law and, as we see from hundreds and hundreds of Geniza documents, it was adhered to throughout in practice.[2]

In the extremely rare cases in which we find a record signed by only one dayyān, it is a draft, as indicated by the word "greetings" attached to it (namely, greetings to the scribe who was to make out a proper copy).[3]

As a rule, the court records found in the Geniza bear three and very often more than three signatures and, as the names known to us or the form of the signatures show, wherever feasible, persons with learning were co-opted as associate judges. The complicated settlement of spring, 1092, discussed in *Med. Soc.*, I, 260, is signed by ten persons, all possessed of a good hand. In addition, two judges signed the court validation. Both principles, specifically, to have as many judges on the bench as possible and, whenever available, to choose learned persons for the purpose, are also laid down in Maimonides' Code.[4]

In most records it is not indicated who acted as the president of the court, nor are we in a position to know this, for even in a provincial town two or more legal experts were often active at one and the same time. Particularly instructive in this respect is a dossier of eleven sessions of the rabbinical court of Old Cairo held in the course of 1097–1098, and dealing with one case of litigation where the same judges appear again and again, but sign in different sequences.[5] In the gaonic period of the Geniza, that is, the major part of the eleventh century, it seems to have been customary for some presidents of the courts to sign last.[6] This tallies with the fact that in the records preserved from the courts of the Gaons themselves, the highest juridical authority, the signatures of the latter appear regularly at the end. In reply to a query referring to this matter, the Gaon Solomon b. Judah says expressly: "According to the ceremonial of the Palestinian yeshiva those who sign first are the lowest in rank, those who sign last are the highest." [7]

Technically speaking, the court records, as a rule, are not judgments, but "testimonies" to depositions by one or more parties or witnesses, or to agreements made by, or forced upon, the parties. Since, according to Jewish law, two persons were sufficient as witnesses, we occasionally find only two signatures affixed to a document; sometimes such a document would contain the remark: "We, two out of three, sign herewith," which means to say that during the procedures themselves three "judges" were present.[8] No substantial differences can be observed between records whose signatories characterize themselves as "witnesses" and those signed by a court. Even in the former case the final decision is sometimes introduced by the phrase "we were of the opinion," a term designating an action by a judge.[9]

Thus, the main characteristic of the Jewish judiciary was a court composed largely of laymen, who frequently supplanted one another. Naturally, in an orderly and developed society, no judicial organization is complete without expert judges appointed for lifetime or at least for some prolonged period. This was the case also in the society represented in the Geniza records. The professional judge was called dayyān. His course of study and many-sided tasks as muqaddam, or executive head, of a local community, as well as his emoluments, are studied in other parts of this book. It now remains for us to define with more precision his role in the administration of justice.[10]

First, a vexatious point of terminology has to be cleared up. Many records open with the phrase: "We, the court, and those [or: the elders and the like] who sign with us." In a document dated December 18, 1027, the reference is no doubt to a court composed of three scholars, mentioned by name, and assisted by the elders.[11] In most cases, however, the term "court" (Heb. *bēth dīn*, "house of justice") does not refer to a judicial assembly of three or more persons, but designates a professional judge confirmed or appointed by an ecumenical or territorial authority and presiding over a court. Often the appointing authority would be mentioned in the introductory sentence of a record. In the capital of Egypt there were three such judges, two in Old Cairo (one for each of the two Rabbanite congregations) and one in New Cairo. The former often sat together, the latter (because of the distance) joined them only in particularly important cases. The word "court," as in English, could thus designate a single judge, so the word was used also in the plural in order to refer to two or more professional judges forming one court. "My lords, the courts" was a deferential form of addressing the two chief judges of the Jewish community of Old Cairo.[12]

With the exception of Old Cairo and Ramle, the administrative capital and commercial center of Palestine, any city had only one officially recognized Jewish judge.[13] Thus we would read in the Geniza letters about "the" judge of Sijilmāsa, Morocco, of Barqa, Libya, of "Sicily" (i.e., Palermo), or of Alexandria.[14] In a city like Alexandria several Jewish professional judges were active at a time. But only the chief justice was styled "the court," whereas he would refer to the others as "my colleagues, the judges," dayyānīm.[15] Similarly, in a provincial capital, such as Damietta, there would be one person of distinction addressed by his superior, the Gaon of Jerusalem, as "court," two others as "judge," and still two others referred to simply as "our master," or "Mr." [16]

The title "court" is an abbreviation of "president of the court," or rather reflects the usage of calling the head of an institution by its name. Thus, Arabic *mathība* does not only mean yeshiva, but also "Gaon, head of a yeshiva"; Aramaic *bē rabbānān,* "house of higher learning" designates also its head. In Arabic documents a similar custom can be observed, but the Jewish usage might be pre-Islamic.[17]

The main prerogative of an officially appointed judge was the right to interpret the law authoritatively. This does not imply that his rulings were irrevocable. Even a decision of a Gaon or Nagid could be contested by another scholar. As a rule, however, the community over which he had jurisdiction was bound to accept his interpretation of the law and its application to any given case. Likewise, once approached by a party, the opponents could not demand to be judged by another court, while, in principle, the choice of a court was a matter of agreement. In short, "the appointed judge has in his district the same authority as the high court of the yeshiva has over all Israel." [18]

Another irritating aspect of judicial terminology in the Geniza records is the frequent occurrence of the biblical word for judge or leader, *shōfēṭ,* especially during the tenth and eleventh centuries.[19] What was its relationship to the other terms just discussed, "court" and dayyān? It seems to me that the biblical word was revived to serve as Hebrew equivalent of Arabic *ḥākim,* the general term for a person invested with juridical authority, whether religious or secular. The talmudic title "dayyān" carried with it the connotation of a scholar versed in all aspects of rabbinical law and lore, including the ritual and theology. Thus, it could not be applied to a person who, although not unfamiliar with Jewish learning, was mainly a community leader and judge in cases of civil and family law. Such a person is clumsily described in an ancient document as "one who occupies himself with the affairs of the community and considers their cases of litigation." [20] The biblical *"shōfēṭ"* was a conveniently short title for such a person of authority, but, like Arabic *"ḥākim,"* designated also full-fledged professional judges holding official appointments. The latter usage is attested for the tenth and the first half of the eleventh centuries with regard to Damascus, Ramle, Alexandria, and Old Cairo, as well as Sijilmāsa, Morocco. Consequently, the biblical term designates also the Muslim qadi—sometimes in the middle of a document or letter written entirely in Arabic.[21]

A shōfēṭ who was not a professional judge or a scholar, would be in charge of a community in a smaller town.[22] We find, however, at least three families of shōfēṭs also in Old Cairo (shōfēṭs, whose son, brother, and grandson, respectively, held the same office) and a lane was named after one of them.[23] The widely dispersed Jews of Yemen were led for a lengthy period by shōfēṭs residing in San'a, then, as today, the capital of the country.[24] During the twelfth century the title fell into disuse. It was a time of growing religious consciousness, which was not favorable to the idea of a secular judge. As our documents show, laymen continued to sit on the rabbinical courts after 1200, but we no longer hear about the office of shōfēṭ. To be sure, the Arabic term "ḥākim" as a designation for Jewish judges, which appears in a document written as early as around 1010, is used regularly in the queries addressed to Maimonides (1204), as well as in his replies.[25]

Muslim influence is clearly evident in another term for judge, *nā'ib,* "deputy." The Muslim qadi, as stated, was originally a delegate of the caliph or of the provincial governor. He had no authority by himself. Thus we have in Islam the curious situation of the qadi who dispensed the heavenly revealed law, to which caliphs and governors, like any other Muslim, owed absolute obedience, who in his turn had no independent position, but was subordinate to the state. The term considered here seems not to have developed out of this relationship, but rather reflects the concept that all judges in the caliph's empire were only delegates and representatives of the chief justice at the imperial court. During the heyday of the caliphate the letter of appointment, say, of the chief judge of Egypt (which was then but a province of the Abbasid empire) would state that he was installed to represent his superior (who had his seat in Baghdad) in the country of the Nile.

The Geniza records reveal that a similar situation prevailed in the Jewish community. Originally, the local judges were appointed by, and were deputies of, the head of the yeshiva, the Gaon, or rather of the president of its high court. Around 1065, when the highest religious authority of the Jews in the Fatimid empire passed from the Palestinian gaonate to the Egyptian Nagid, the latter, or rather the three Jewish judges of the Egyptian capital, made, or approved, the appointments of the local judges. These judges, as their letters show, brought doubtful cases to the knowledge of their superiors or asked the latter to come and deal with them in person.[26] The designation "deputy" was therefore quite appropriate. In a circular to all the Jewish congregations outside Cairo, the address has *nuwwāb*, "deputies," while the text itself is directed to the "judges," *dayyānīn*.[27] It should be noted, that the term "deputy" makes its appearance in the Geniza only at the time of Mevōrākh (ca. 1079–1112), in whom we have seen the real founder of the office of Nagid, whereas for the "representative" of the Gaon, in the very rare cases when an Arabic word was used at all, the more religious term *khalīfa* was applied.[28] The local judges are referred to as deputies of the Nagid and not, as a rule, of the chief judges in Old Cairo, and the latter themselves are sometimes styled thus.[29] It stands to reason, therefore, that not only the word, but also the very idea, namely the derivation of judical power from a semisecular authority, was taken over from the Islamic environment.

As with the Muslim word for judge, the Muslim term "deputy" was translated into biblical Hebrew. As such, Hebrew *mishne* could designate the president of the high court of a yeshiva, who was but a deputy of its head, the Gaon, or of any other judge, Jewish or even Muslim.[30]

Besides nomenclature, the Jewish judge had little in common with his Muslim colleague. In the period under study, the office of the qadi was a very lucrative one. It was customary to purchase the office for high sums. Unlike medieval France, however, where similar practices prevailed, the judgeship was not acquired for life. After having paid for his office, the qadi could be dismissed after a few years or even a few days of service. During the period of four hundred years terminated by the end of the Fatimid caliphate (in 1171), the average time of office of a qadi in the Egyptian capital was five years, and only sixteen out of eighty served until their deaths. The others were discharged often under humiliating circumstances.[31]

In contradistinction, the documents signed by Jewish judges in the capital of Egypt during the years 965–1265 show an amazing degree of continuity. The average time of a judge's office seems to have been twenty-five years, while the signatures of some appear for over forty years (see App. D). We have to keep in mind that the preservation of dated Geniza records and the preservation of dates on records (they are often effaced or torn away) are entirely fortuitous, so that the actual time of tenure of a dayyān might have been considerably longer than that indicated by the documents signed by him. Moreover, in many cases we have definite proof of a judge having been in office beyond the dates provided by documents signed by them (see App. D, *passim*).

As far as our present knowledge goes, none of the Jewish chief judges of Old (and New) Cairo was ever dismissed by a Gaon or Nagid during the period alluded to. We find occasionally that a dayyān did not get along well with his flock and actually left his post; in Alexandria we have complaints about dayyāns during three centuries (although no report about actual dismissals has been found thus far). These complaints are concerned mostly with the dayyān's strictness and overbearing manner, or, on the other hand, with his leniency toward the common people. Charges of bribery or other misconduct are extremely rare. An Old Cairene court record from April, 1085, reports that a divorced woman intruded into the house of her former husband, and, when brought to court, insulted the judges "shouting: 'you have taken bribes and brought about that divorce; that house is my house' and saying other highly improper things." More serious is an unfortunately much mutilated letter of a Palestinian Gaon (early eleventh century), in which he deplores the miscarriage of justice by his deputy in Ramle and concludes with the remark that the elders of Ramle had adoped and put in writing a resolution to the effect that the dignitary concerned would be entitled to act solely as an assistant judge on a court presided over by the Gaon.[32]

One of those parasitic nāsīs, while serving as judge in Alexandria for a short time, is accused in a letter of having taken bribes (from both litigants) and of appropriating books and carpets belonging to the synagogue. Although these details are reported in a rather matter-of-fact fashion, one should keep in mind that the writer was the physician and communal leader Abū Zikrī, son of the judge Elijah, who suggests to his father to take the nāsī's place. Similarly, the accusation that the Palestinian Gaon Solomon b. Judah "sold the properties of the community" is found in the letter of a partisan of his rival Nathan b. Abraham. In view of the mass of information available from the Geniza for about three hundred years, the almost complete absence of complaints must be regarded as an eloquent testimony of generally decent standards of behavior.[33]

Arabic sources present a somewhat different picture of the Muslim judiciary. Whether we read the woeful writings of the great Islamic theologian and teacher of ethics, al-Ghazālī (d. 1111), or the humorous stories and anecdotes of *The Arabian Nights,* or the history books containing biographies of the qadis, everywhere we are confronted with endless charges of venality, embezzlement, and recklessness. Nor are the Geniza documents silent on this point. Attention, however, is drawn to a recently published Islamic history by the eminent French historian Claude Cahen, who warns us not to take these charges too seriously. According to him, the institution of the qadi was one of the most durable of Islamic civilization. The Geniza, too, is not devoid of laudatory remarks about qadis.[34]

The contrast between the Jewish and Islamic judiciaries should not be ascribed to any substantial difference in the levels of morality of the two societies, but, rather, to the entirely different nature of the two offices. The qadi held a position of power, and power tends to corrupt; the dayyān owed his authority to his scholarship and acumen, qualities the exercise of which is mostly harmless and beneficial. The Muslim judge, as we have seen, was an autocrat who gave his decisions alone, the Jewish judge was the member of a court of three, a circumstance that naturally acted as a restraint on high-handed practices.

Moreover, as has been shown, during most of the classical Geniza period the administration of the estates of orphans and of other property committed to the courts was in the hands of laymen called "trustees of the court." This, too, had a beneficial effect on the propriety of public administration. This otherwise healthy separation of the judiciary from administration was, of course, no complete safeguard against irregularities. Thus, we read in a letter to the Nagid Mevōrākh that the social service officers of the congregation of the Iraqians in Old Cairo had embezzled up to 200 dinars from the estates of the orphans and that the judge, a weak person, had connived with them. This accusation, made in a personal letter, might have been exaggerated or perhaps entirely unfounded. But, while discussing a case of inheritance brought before him, the Gaon Solomon b. Judah remarks that without having received any outside information, by mere scrutiny of the evidence, he had come to the conclusion that "those worthy trustees are not trustworthy at all" (with a pun on the Hebrew title of the office). No human institution, however perfect, can entirely eliminate human wickedness.[35]

A vigorous element of continuity was the frequency of cases in which judges were assisted and succeeded by their sons. Appendix D shows six such examples for the Egyptian capital, and three similar cases with regard to shōfēṭs were noted above. Moreover, many of the forefathers of the dayyāns had held high or highest office in the yeshivas of Jerusalem or Baghdad or in other cities outside Egypt. Three or four successive generations of judges, even of chief judges, were by no means an exceptional phenomenon. We find such occurrences in (New) Cairo, Alexandria, al-Mahdiyya, which replaced Qayrawān, as the capital of Tunisia, and in Gabes, an important town in the same country. Similarly, in smaller localities, like Ascalon, Palestine, Barqa, Libya, or in Egyptian provincial towns, we find father, son, and even grandson each following the other as the local dayyān.[36]

It should be noted that a similar phenomenon is to be observed in the contemporary Muslim society. The student of Fatimid history is immediately reminded of the dynasty of qadis founded by the great al-Nuʿmān, who had served four Fatimid caliphs in Tunisia in this capacity, accompanying al-Muʿizz to Egypt, and whose two sons served as chief justices in Egypt after him. Another illuminating case is that of the Banū Jamāʿa, a dynasty of Shāfiʿī jurists, who were active as qadis in Jerusalem, Damascus, and Cairo, just as members of the families of the Gaons and presidents of the courts of the Palestinian yeshiva presided over Jewish courts in those cities.[37]

On the other hand, the Geniza proves that there was a continuous healthy influx of fresh blood; at least half the more important Jewish judges in this period were not succeeded by their sons. For example, both positive and negative evidence seems to show that none of the five sons of Aaron Ibn al-ʿAmmānī, the most prominent Jewish judge of Alexandria during the twelfth century, functioned as dayyān in that city after their father's death. His great-grandson is known from many documents written or signed between 1207 and 1243. He was, however, a notary and puisne judge, not a "court." Occasionally, a grandson would succeed in obtaining his grandfather's rank. The system of succession to the dignity of Gaon and the hereditary aspects of public office in general are discussed in chapter v, sections A, 1, and B, 2, respectively.[38]

The office of notary was not developed much as a separate institution in the Jewish society of those days, at least not to the degree found in Islam. The wide knowledge not only of law, but also of languages (Hebrew, Aramaic, Arabic) required for the job, as well as the necessity of bringing most of the cases before a court anyhow were not favorable to the creation of a special profession. A good many of the legal documents from Old Cairo, dated between 1005 and 1135, as far as they were not made out by judges, were written by six successive and partly contemporary court scribes who also served as assistant judges and most of whom were cantors.[39] The records and deeds dated between approximately 1135 and 1265 were written mostly by professional judges, perhaps because the general knowledge of diplomatics had declined somewhat.

In the more tightly organized Mamluk state it perhaps became customary that a Jewish notary versed in Arabic should keep the Muslim authorities informed of all the happenings of legal import within the Jewish community. A note, dated September, 1278, contains the announcement of the death of a woman on the day it occurred together with information about her legal heir. The note was written by "Bu 'l-Faḍl, son of the Rabbanite al-Maskīl (a Hebrew title normally borne by a judge) in absence of Ma'ānī." I take this as meaning that Ma'ānī was the notary who usually made such announcements and that during his absence a son of the judge did the job. A declaration in Arabic characters details the gift of a property made to a Jewish woman. At the bottom we read: "Witnessed by 'Alī b. Sa'd Allah, the Jew," accompanied by the flourish used in Hebrew and Arabic documents to set apart the signature of the scribe from the text. In both Jewish and Islamic law one person never could be a sufficient formal witness. Thus the word "witnessed" appearing at the bottom of the declaration can mean only "confirmed by the notary." In Islam, the notary is called *shāhid,* witness, or 'adl, "trustworthy (witness)."[40]

Any transaction, including a marriage agreement, required only two witnesses. Therefore the parties needed no more than to go to a notary's office, *dukkān,* and make there the symbolic act of purchase which validated legal transactions, whereupon the notary drew up the relevant documents, signed them, and had someone else sign in addition to himself. The second signature usually betrays a man not fluent in writing. The notary would keep a diary in which he entered the main facts of each transaction, as well as the name of the witness who signed with him.[41] In comparison with the many hundreds of court records signed by three or more, deeds made out by notaries are comparatively rare. Even in small matters, the notary would state that the agreement had to be confirmed by the court so that an official record could be made out, and we would find a debt of 60 dinars contracted in the office of a notary, but confirmed three months later before a court.[42] Naturally, court clerks or a young judge during the lifetime of his father, the chief judge, would also serve as a notary.[43]

The strength of the Jewish court, the plurality of its judges, was also its weakness. Since everyone was busy with his own affairs, it was difficult to assemble a representative court, and procrastination ensued. Two documents of Fustat, from December, 1016, and December, 1027, respectively, and containing a similar story, are most telling in this respect. The first, unfortunately incomplete, court record relates that a merchant from Palermo, Sicily, had complained to the police that he had already waited a full month for a Jewish court to deal with his case, whereupon the head of the police apprehended the Jewish judge for a night. In the second, complete, document, a merchant from Spain was accused of having obtained from the caliphal court a rescript to the *qāʾid* or commander (as the governor of the capital was styled then) to see him righted. The defendant explained that all he wanted was to be judged by a Jewish court, but that one of the three members of the court who were to judge him (after having heard his case in a previous session), had excused himself with being busy "and other reasons." It was resolved that if the three judges mentioned would not take up the matter during the following two weeks, each party was free to apply to a government court.[44]

Under these circumstances it is not surprising to find in a fragment containing court records persons appearing on one page as parties and on another as representatives of the court. In a fragment from summer, 1032, which comprises only two short records and the beginning of a third, two such cases recur. In the many remnants of court records from the years 1097–1099, such instances are commonplace.[45]

During the second part of the eleventh century, when Egypt benefited by a large influx of emigrants and refugees from Palestine and Tunisia, we no longer hear such complaints, at least for the capital. In contradistinction, we see a large number of qualified scholars acting as judges at one and the same time. This also became necessary since most of these men were engaged in business and had to disqualify themselves when one of the parties involved was connected with them in one way or another.[46]

Courts consisting solely of laymen appear in the Geniza documents at all times and in many different localities and they deal with a wide variety of matters. In the gaonic period they seem to have been confirmed in their office by the Gaons.[47] A few examples may suffice to illustrate their activities. A litigation between heirs was settled by them in Damietta, Egypt, in 989. Powers of attorney, albeit in vastly different cases, were made out before the elders of Baniyas, Palestine, in 1056 and before a similar court in Zawīlat al-Mahdiyya, Tunisia, in 1074. A reconciliation after prolonged marital strife was accomplished by the "upright elders" on the eve of the Day of Atonement 1120 in Old Cairo, and in the same city a settlement of a case of inheritance was made through a similar board shortly before 1203. As the wording of the documents concerned shows (the two older ones are in excellent Hebrew), these "elders" were assisted by scribes in full command of the traditional legal parlance.[48]

Of particular interest is a document from Old Cairo, dated 1178, that is, at a time when that city was adorned by the presence of Maimonides and a number of other brilliant doctors of Jewish law. The complainant recounts that he had applied to the rabbinical court, but was given no satisfaction. Thereupon he turned to a session of "the upright elders," where the settlement described in the record was made. The facts reported easily explain why the rabbinical court was of no avail. A man, before setting out on a business trip to Aden, South Arabia, had sold a certain quantity of wine. After his departure, the wine was proved to be of an inferior quality. The seller's father was brought by the buyer to the court, or as the document says: "to the law," which could not do a thing, since a father is not responsible for the commercial transactions of a grown-up son. The elders, however, in accordance with the principles of decent business, had him pay, dividing the indemnity into several installments. The reverse side of the fragment shows that everything was paid to the last penny. It is noteworthy that the document was written by a high-standing member of the rabbinical court.[49]

The elders were but representatives of the community, which, in principle, was the supreme judge. The biblical concept "the people shall judge" (Numbers 35:24) was still very much alive. We have already seen how a Nagid addresses a congregation, women included, while writing to the local judge about a law case. Similarly, "the elders and the congregation" speak together while reporting to the Nagid how a dispute was ended by agreement.[50] A woman seeking a settlement with her husband in Fayyūm, the Egyptian oasis, in 1008, appears "before the Children of Israel."[51] A young man in Alexandria, who was persuaded by a mischief-maker to claim from his widowed mother an alleged inheritance, was reprimanded "before the *qāhāl*."[52] No wonder that the caliphal rescript of December, 1027, mentioned above, orders "to assemble the Jews" for settling the case of the merchant from Spain. It was well known in the high quarters that the congregation as a whole, or at least a plurality of judges, administered justice according to Jewish custom.[53]

Against this background, an institution of medieval Jewish law which has been much discussed, but about whose working in the period studied here little had been known, becomes understandable and meaningful: the right of a complainant who felt himself treated unjustly to interrupt public prayer, or to prevent its being held altogether, until his case was heard. It was an appeal to the highest authority, just as a man would throw oneself before the horse of a caliph or a governor in order to draw attention to a wrong done to him. The technical term for the procedure was "to call the Jews [or: Israel] for help."[54] When the Torah scroll was taken out, the complainant would stand up on the reader's platform and detain the reading of the Torah in order to bring his case before the congregation first.[55] In one letter we even read that the writer intended to lock the Torah shrine altogether until his opponent was brought to court.[56] Female "callers for help" are also referred to. It is, however, hardly imaginable (although not entirely excluded) that a woman would enter the men's section and address the persons assembled there. Since the Geniza has preserved eloquently styled and beautifully written appeals to the community by women, it stands to reason that, as a rule, a woman did not address the congregation herself, but her complaint was read out by her representative, the scribe, or someone else. It was perhaps customary for the complainant to appear in the front of the women's gallery while her plea was read out beneath.[57]

In order to convey to the reader an impression of this strange procedure, the text of an appeal to the community is translated here in full. Two orphan girls appeal against two older, married, sisters (perhaps from another mother), in the absence of their natural protectors, their two brothers.[58]

By doing justice all the offspring of Israel will find glory with the Lord [Isaiah 45:25].[59]

The orphans of Dōsā (may God have mercy upon him).

In the name of the merciful and gracious God [Exodus 34:6].[60]

We appeal to God, and to you, men of Israel! Do not forsake us! You use to pronounce a ban on the *Mount of Olives* on anyone who takes his heritage in *a Muslim* court.[61] (But what can I do?) I am an orphan girl confined to the house and have a sister who is a mere babe. Yesterday, the two married sisters came and put their hands on the house and drove us out. We have two brothers, but they are absent. Thus, we, two orphan girls, confined to the house, have no one to assist us except the Lord of the Worlds and Israel, and their judges. The sin committed against us adheres to everyone who hears this appeal and does not secure for all of us a decision according to the law of inheritance of the Torah. Do not forsake us!

God can be trusted that he will not orphan any child of yours.[62] Seize the opportunity for doing a good work by giving us satisfaction according to the law of the Torah. *And peace over all Israel!*

The swiftness with which the case of the two orphan girls was brought before the community only one day after the occurrence that prompted the complaint is noteworthy.

In response to such an appeal, the complainant would be promised that his case would be heard by the court on such and such a day, or, if the content of his complaint was that false accusations had been made against him, his declaration would be heeded and included in a statement witnessed by some of those present.[63] The interruption of the public service could also assume a different form: when a person called up to read a part of the weekly section was regarded by others as having done something illegal or immoral, they would bar him from leading the congregation in prayer. About such an occurrence a statement, properly witnessed, would be made out as well, destined, of course, to be followed by an action in court.[64]

One may wonder whether the Jewish society of the Geniza period possessed an institution similar to that of the Muslim muftī, or jurisconsult, who wrote legal opinions and rulings without acting as a judge himself.[65] The *jus respondendi,* the privilege to answer legal questions addressed to him, was the prerogative of a member of the yeshiva or of a judge appointed as "court." Since *responsa,* the Hebrew word for these answers, is an equivalent of the Latin, there may be some connection between Roman and rabbinic judicial organization in this matter. As the wording of many responsa shows, the Jewish scholars cannot have been unfamiliar with the *fatwā*s (the word is derived from the same root as muftī) of their Muslim colleagues. Here we are concerned solely with the question of whether there is any indication in the Geniza records of jurisconsults who were not judges. It seems that this was indeed the case.

Nahray b. Nissīm, the man from whose archive several hundreds of letters and accounts written by him or addressed to him have come down to us, was styled "Master" (rāv) and "the senior member of the yeshiva." Requests from him for a fatwā (called thus in one letter) have been preserved and there are references to others.[66] But not a single court record written or signed by him has been found. He signed, together with many others, the marriage contract of a friend in 1050 and gave witness together with the same person thirty years later, in 1080. A power of attorney was assigned to him in 1055—as was done with any respectable citizen—and a letter of his was produced in court in 1075.[67] Nowhere, however, is there any indication that the "great Rāv" functioned as a judge. Similarly, Nahray had a teacher who had emigrated, like Nahray himself, from Tunisia to Egypt. This scholar is referred to in numerous letters from the second half of the eleventh century as "the Rāv," and Nahray refused to write responsa as long as this man was alive. But this rāv, too, nowhere appears as a judge. It should be also noted that Maimonides, who lived for about forty years in the Egyptian capital (ca. 1165-1204), has not left a single court record signed by him in the Geniza, while many other writings of his, and in particular responsa, were among the treasures of that ancient hoard of manuscripts.

In a number of Geniza documents Maimonides is called "the *master (rabbān)* of all Israel" and even more commonly "the great rāv," which, with Arabic nomenclature, could be properly rendered as "grand muftī."[68] The ancient title: "the court," or "the judge for all Israel," did not fit him. He was a jurisconsult—about 460 of his responsa have been preserved—combining with this capacity the office of the "head of the Jews" during certain periods. The three scholars just mentioned, Nahray, the Rāv, and Maimonides, were all from the Muslim West, and it seems that there, as also in western Europe, the rabbinate trod paths different from those of the East.[69]

Maimonides' son Abraham, although following in his father's footsteps, betrays signs of assimilation to the eastern tradition. He was a prolific writer of responsa, but, as the Geniza shows, also sat in court settling even minor litigations and revising in his own hand records drafted by his colleagues or adjuncts.[70] Similarly, Nissīm, the son of Nahray, although like his father referred to as rāv, "master," and not as judge, signed and even wrote court records.[71] Thus it seems that the divorce of the office of the jurisconsult from that of the judge was characteristic of the Jewish communities west of Egypt, but was occasionally imported to that country, where, as a rule, the learned doctor of law was also expected to act as a judge. Was this differentiation due to internal Jewish developments, or to the influence of the environment, or to both. This question is better left to subsequent research.

The preceding survey has revealed that in the Jewish communities represented in the Geniza records, law was administered by a wide variety of authorities. The survey is by no means complete. This much, however, is evident from it: in the face of such rich documentation we are not permitted to make generalizations not warranted by our sources. Thus, Jacob Mann, the pioneer of historical Geniza research, ventured to maintain that the Egyptian Nagid had under him a supreme court comparable with that of his predecessors, the Palestinian Gaons, and that the president of this court bore the title dayyān al-Yahūd, "the judge of the Jews." As a scrutiny of his quotations (which could be augmented) shows, all refer to the same person, the judge Elijah b. Zechariah, who lived at the beginning of the thirteenth century, and the title was probably merely a designation, since it is found only in the addresses of letters sent to him. In any case, we do not encounter such a title, let alone an office of the character alleged, in any document during the whole of the Fatimid and Ayyubid periods. As we have seen, each of the three congregations of the Egyptian capital had its own chief justice appointed by the Nagid. Throughout the thirteenth century there were still several learned Jewish judges in Old Cairo at a time, and Elijah b. Zechariah was not the most prominent among them. It may be that by the fourteenth century, when Old Cairo had dwindled almost to insignificance and the Egyptian Jewish community as a whole had shrunk very much, the Nagid, when appearing before the government, was accompanied only by one judge, styled by the Muslim historians dayyān al-Yahūd. A late Geniza document in Arabic characters seems indeed to confirm such an assumption. But here, as in the case of the office of the Nagid himself, we should be on our guard not to attribute to the Fatimid and Ayyubid periods what was in fact a far later development. During "classical" Geniza times, the Jewish judiciary was fluid and variegated, a true mirror of the society whose law it administered.[72]

2. *The Law*

Reviewing the vast legal material embedded in the Geniza records one gets the impression that it was not so much the contents of the law applied as the authority administering it which gave the parties the feeling that they were judged according to "the Law of the Torah." Documents related to family life, such as marriage contracts, bills of divorce, and deeds of manumission (which qualified the freed slave to marry a Jewish mate) usually stated that they were made according to "the Law of Moses and Israel," or "of Moses and the Jews," or even "of the Jews" alone.[1] Even this time-honored formula contains an element of customary law. Moreover, contracts of all descriptions, including marriage contracts, often conclude with the statement that they were as valid and sound as any such contracts "instituted by our sages and in use in the world."[2] In some eleventh-century marriage contracts it is even stated that they are properly executed and binding both "according to the statutes of our sages and the laws [invariably the Greek loan word *nomos* is used] of the state," or "the gentiles."[3] These formulas are in the Aramaic language and certainly originated in pre-Islamic times. Some documents conclude, like Byzantine legal deeds, with the Greek word *akolythos,* "no objection," "without impediments," a usage found even in Egyptian provincial towns.[4]

"Freedom of contract," the right of the parties to choose the conditions that met their needs best, was the most conspicuous aspect of the law speaking to us through the Geniza records. This right applies in the first place to commerce, as when the Jewish courts dealt most frequently with the "partnership according to the gentiles," that is, the Muslim brand of the commenda, or the "bills of exchange," called *suftaja.* "It is true," writes a Gaon in reply to a query, "that our sages have said that one should not send bills of exchange, but we see that people actually use them; therefore, we admit them in court, since otherwise commerce would come to a standstill, and give judgment exactly in accordance with the law of the merchants."[5]

The marriage contracts, as well as other settlements made with regard to family life, also betray an amazing latitude of provisions and variety of usages. The principle of rabbinical law "any stipulation made with regard to financial matters is valid" supplied ample possibilities for satisfying the demands of the highly developed society living on the shores of the Mediterranean basin during the period of the eleventh through the thirteenth centuries.[6]

On the other hand, as soon as the Law, that is, the strict religious law, called also "the preserve of God," was administered, harsh or strange decisions, to be expected in a legal system going back to remote antiquity, could not always be avoided. The Law applies in particular to such institutions as the levirate marriage, as well as to certain other aspects of family law and the law of inheritance which had their origin in an intrinsically agricultural society. The sabbatical year, that is, the provision that every seventh year all debts were automatically annulled, unless protected by a specific deposition in court by the creditor, seems to have been revived in Egypt by Maimonides, for the relevant Geniza documents come mostly from the beginning of the thirteenth century. In economic matters, the situation was different. After the experts had given their opinions as to the legal position according to the religious law (and sometimes, as we shall see, divergent opinions), the parties knew what they could expect from a judgment and tried to come to an agreement as favorable as possible to each side. As a last means of pressure, one party would threaten to apply to a Muslim court. As far as we are able to judge, the settlements reached were, as a rule, fair and reasonable.

It mattered little that Jewish law required certain symbolic formalities in order to validate legal transactions. According to Islamic law, mere oral offer and acceptance were sufficient for making a contract binding. No doubt with an eye on the law of the cognate religion, Maimonides opens the *Book of Acquisition* in his Code of Law with the following words: "Title to an object is not acquired by oral agreement alone, even if witnesses testify to that agreement." Then he goes on to explain in sixty-six, sometimes lengthy, paragraphs, the various ways in which each type of movable and immovable object may be acquired.[7] The reader of Maimonides' Code who is not familiar with the practice of the courts, as manifested in the Geniza records, will conclude that Jewish, like ancient Roman, law, was a peasants' law, utterly unfit for the exigencies of a highly mercantile economy. The sixty-six paragraphs, however, become obsolete by paragraph five of chapter five of the *Book of Acquisition,* which reads:

> Real estate, slaves, cattle, and other movable [i.e., everything] may be acquired by symbolic barter. This act is called *qinyān* [lit., purchase]. The fundamental principle of this mode of acquisition is that the transferee should give the transferrer an article of however small a value and say to him, "Acquire this article in exchange for the yard or the wine or the cattle or the slave that you sold me for as much and so much." If this is done, then the moment the vendor lifts the article and takes possession of it, the vendee acquires title to the land or the mentioned movables, though he has not drawn them or paid their price, and neither party may retract.

In practice, a kerchief, or a similar small object was handed over by one party to the other and then immediately returned as a gift. From the Hebrew word *qinyān,* the Judeo-Arabic verbs *qanā,* "to acquire a right," and *aqnā,* "to confer a right," found in most Geniza deeds, are derived.

Intangible rights, such as a power of attorney, were conveyed by a symbolic act called "transfer adjunct" (namely, to the transfer of land) *qinyān aggāv.* Different forms of this symbolic act are represented in the Geniza records, from the old, but rare formula of "giving" the threshold of the entrance to one's house, to the commonplace phrase of giving four square cubits of the soil of the Holy Land, in which each Jew was supposed to have a share. Such symbolic formulas should not be mistaken as actual conveyances of land, as has been done even by a competent student of the Geniza. Moreover, I am not so sure that the symbolic act itself was always performed. When five representatives of the Great Synagogue in Alexandria, namely the Palestinian, acknowledged the receipt of a donation for the erection of the holy ark to the traveler who delivered it, they wrote: "We made the symbolic purchase *from ourselves*." What else could this mean than simply: "We declare herewith in a legally binding form"? The document is signed by four other persons.[8]

Criminal cases and punishments are confined in the Geniza almost entirely to transgressions in the sphere of religion or of community life. A religious slaughterer who was careless in the exercise of his duties was flogged and forced to make public confession in 1028—punishments described in the document as lenient.[9] A carpenter who let his gentile employees work on Saturday was to be flogged according to some scholars, while others wanted him to be fined and excommunicated as well.[10] When a man declared in a public statement that he was prepared to suffer the death penalty if it was proved that he had cursed the head of the Jerusalem yeshiva, we are certainly not allowed to conclude that such punishment was ever inflicted by the Jewish community on an offending member during the Geniza period.[11] We read about a Jewish official, a cantor, in Alexandria retrieving a theft, but nothing is said about the punishment of the thief. With one exception, no reference has been found thus far to the apprehension of a culprit by a Jewish authority.[12]

It is particularly noteworthy that sexual offenses are nowhere dealt with in the court records of the Geniza. There is occasional talk about persons suspected of having had illicit relations, but the question raised with regard to them is always whether they are allowed to marry each other (forbidden by Jewish law), not how they should be punished. In one court record a Jewish girl is charged by two Muslims with being too intimate with a Christian physician. The document is written, as usual, in Hebrew characters, but the signatures of the three Jewish "witnesses" are in Arabic, suggesting perhaps that the case was finally to be brought before a Muslim judge (to whom the text of the accusation would be read out by his Jewish colleague.)[13] Of a man with abnormal sexual behavior it is said in one letter that he should be expelled from the town (as was done with prostitutes). But no expulsion could be carried out without the assistance of a state authority.[14]

Fines stipulated in contracts for the case of breach were extremely common. It is therefore strange that we hear next to nothing about payments imposed by a court as a punishment. We just noted the case of the carpenter who was accused of having desecrated the Sabbath and for whose punishment some scholars suggested, *inter alia,* a fine. A statute promulgated in Acre, Palestine, around 1230, lays down the principle that any penalty imposed on a person for disrespectful behavior against a communal leader should never be paid to the latter, but go to the poor or to a synagogue.[15] In general, it seems, fines imposed by a Jewish authority were regarded as unlawful, or, at least, as an irregular means of punishment.

On the other hand, bans in various degrees of gravity, as well as excommunication, were an accepted form of castigation, acknowledged by the Muslim authorities. I am not dealing here with the "conditional ban," or "ban in general terms," which was a means of legal procedure, to be discussed in the next subsection. Here, I am referring to ban or excommunication as a way of chastisement intended to force a party to comply with the decision of a court or the ruling of an authority. A few examples illustrate its application.

A Nagid had arranged a settlement between an insolvent debtor and his creditors, according to which he would pay them a part of what was due them. Despite the solemn promise given to this effect by the debtor, he did not pay, whereupon the procedure of excommunication was instituted against him, which, however, at the time of the relevant document, had not yet become effective.[16] When it became known in Aden, South Arabia, that a merchant from Baghdad living in India intended to abscond to Ceylon in order to evade the fulfillment of his financial commitments, a conditional letter of excommunication was sent by the rabbinical court of Aden to one of its representatives in India to be used in case the Baghdadi carried out his plan. The addressee was admonished to use utmost circumspection and secrecy so that the contents of the letter would be made known only in case things had turned for the worse.[17]

A woman who had brought her brother before a Muslim court using falsified documents was threatened with excommunication, but the threat was not carried out for a long time, although attempts to bring about a reconciliation had failed.[18] The Geniza has also preserved a request from a Gaon of Jerusalem to excommunicate a woman who claimed from her brother a part of her father's estate (to which she had no right according to Jewish law) in the court of the Muslim high justice.[19] Another Gaon of Jerusalem, appointing sixteen notables as a panel of assistant judges and community officials, rules that anyone trespassing on the privileges of these people should be brought to court and, if found guilty, could be excommunicated by him in Jerusalem, with the notification of any other community where the culprit happened to be.[20]

A ban could be used also against a recalcitrant party who refused to respond to a summons of the court. A holograph of Elhanan b.

Shemarya threatens in this way a person who had repeatedly dodged such a call.[21] The husband of a woman who was accused of having frightened the wife of another by necromancy and bone-rattling was similarly warned. (The couples lived in Malīj, but were ordered to come to Fustat.) But instead of the ominous word "ban" a milder phrase was used: "If he tarries, action will be taken against him according to the law of Moses, the son of Amram."[22] A summons was regarded as binding only when delivered by an official representative of the court, not by a mere errand boy.[23]

As in the Christian churches, ban and counterban or mutual excommunication were favorite weapons in communal strife and were used even by private persons.[24] When the nāsi David tried to become the head of the Jews in the Fatimid empire, as his powerful and learned father Daniel b. Azarya had been, and temporarily succeeded in ousting the Nagid Mevōrākh, he proclaimed a *ḥerem,* or ban, against spiritual leaders who recognized the authority of the Nagid by praying for him during the public service. But this was a delicate matter, and in one document such a ban was indeed temporarily revoked by him: Nahray b. Nissīm, who during this period of turmoil was in charge of both the Iraqian and Palestinian communities of Fustat was asked by the nāsī to instruct the cantors in the two synagogues not to read out the ban on the ḥāvēr of Tinnīs which had already been handed over to them for promulgation.[25]

Excommunication meant that no person of Jewish faith was allowed to have any dealings with the punished, to talk or to shake hands with him, let alone give him food or shelter or do business with him.[26] The man so banned was not admitted to the synagogue service, nor granted burial in death. In addition, the most horrible of curses were pronounced against him, of which the Geniza has preserved some quite strong examples.[27] Thus, the merely spiritual aspects of excommunication were commensurate in harshness with its practical consequences.

A person under ban would normally try to "clean himself" by acceding to the settlement or judgment originally refused by him, or would seek a new agreement. As a rule, only the authority that had pronounced the ban was supposed to revoke it. Therefore, we find that a man who had been excommunicated in a provincial town was advised by the court in Fustat to travel to that place and to clear his case there. Moreover, a time limit was set to him for this purpose, after the lapse of which he would have to pay a fine ("to the poor") in Fustat in addition to the satisfaction to be given by him to any one who had a claim against him in that provincial town. It is perhaps noteworthy that the penitent appeared in the court of Fustat "on the morning after the Day of Atonement." The respite given him amounted to fifty days.[28]

Sometimes, a person under ban would try to escape to a place where his case was unknown, or where he could tell stories that he had already redressed the wrongs that had been the cause of his punishment. To judge from a report on such an occurrence, it must have been rather difficult to succeed with this stratagem since inquiries made by the local authorities would soon reveal the truth. A man who had been put under ban in Fustat, Cairo, and at the holy shrine of Dammūh because he had taken a second wife arrived in Qūṣ in Upper Egypt with his "real" wife and a baby daughter, telling the people that he had already divorced the new one and consequently been released from the ban. A number of persons believed what he said and received him in their houses—a grave sin since no official notification of the release had reached the south Egyptian town. The letter, which deals also with other communal matters, inquires of the authorities in the capital and asks for instructions.[29] In principle, a local community or even a single scholar (normally in concert with two other persons forming a court) was entitled to proclaim a ban.[30] In order to be effective, however, the ban had to be general, covering, as far as possible, all Jewish communities. Therefore, as a rule, an excommunication was effected by a Gaon or Nagid, or confirmed by him if it was first promulgated in a place over which he had no jurisdiction.[31] During the classic Geniza period, the authorities were reluctant to make use of this stern disciplinary measure and slow in putting it into effect. The various degrees of reprimand and ban, known to Jewish legal theory, are represented in the Geniza records, although the distinction between them is by no means always clear or consistent. All in all, this important instrument of medieval law deserves new scrutiny in the light of the Geniza, preferably in conjunction with the parallel institutions of the Coptic and other Oriental churches.[32]

In conclusion, the reader is reminded that law in those days was personal and not territorial. A Jew, whether he happened to be in Granada, Spain, in Jerusalem, or in some port on the Malabar coast of India, was judged according to the same law. The same applies to Christians of the same denomination and to Muslims adhering to the same "school." Local custom and tradition accounted for some shades of difference, but these, as a rule, were small. This legal unity was a great convenience to the widely traveled Jewish middle class and contributed much to its stability and inner coherence. As we shall presently see, the court procedure itself presupposed lively international traffic.

3. *Procedures*

Naturally, procedures differed according to the character of a case and the authority before which it was brought. Yet some general trends are clearly discernible throughout.

The court records preserved in the Geniza are of three main types. The first is concerned with fact-finding, consisting of depositions made by the parties, questions addressed to them by the presiding judge or the opposing party, or both, and the answers given to these questions, as well as the evidence provided to substantiate the claims.[1] Formal judgments, quoting the legal sources and detailing the reasons for the decision made, are almost entirely lacking.[2] Instead, a litigation is concluded (often, as stated, after long proceedings) by a declaration of one or both parties, fortified by the "symbolic purchase," discussed above. Such a declaration is either an "acquittal," in which the parties release each other from any further obligation, after the conditions specified in the document have been, or will have been, fulfilled,[3] or an "acknowledgment," in which one party declares to owe such and such a sum or another obligation to the other. Normally the terms of the payment or of the fulfillment of the obligation are also specified.[4]

It would be entirely wrong to assume that the courts acted merely as boards of arbitration, without having recourse to statutory law. Many hundreds of responsa, or legal opinions, have been preserved from this period which indicate that conflicts in economic life not less than family matters, were decided according to rabbinical law, handled by legal experts. How, then, is the almost total absence of judgments from the Geniza records to be explained?

There can be little doubt that this apparent deficiency was a mere matter of form and procedure. Interpreting or applying the law of the Torah in a wrong way was regarded as a very grave sin. "May God preserve me from the sin of judgment," that is, of handing down a wrong judgment, was a phrase even used in the conclusion of a legal opinion.[5] "A judge who does not render an absolutely true judgment causes the Divine Presence to depart from Israel. If he unlawfully expropriates money from one and gives it to another, God will exact his life from him."[6] These and similar warnings of the ancients, reproduced by Maimonides in his code, were taken literally in medieval times. Therefore, in order not to expose themselves to such jeopardy, the judges refrained altogether from giving formal judgments, a procedure expressly recommended by the Shulhan Arukh, the authoritative Jewish book of laws (sixteenth century).[7] The Geniza has preserved a tenth-century query concerning a judge who accepted his appointment only on condition that he should never be obliged "to give formal judgments in cases which he would decide."[8] The Muslim judges adopted a similar attitude.

In view of these religious scruples, the decisions of the courts were given the form of declarations of the parties. Rather than stating that the court sentenced a person to make such and such a payment, the minutes would contain an "acknowledgment" by that person that he owed this sum to the other party. Instead of an acquittal by a court, a party thus freed from an obligation would receive a "release" from the claimant. But the user of the Geniza records should not be misled by this legal formality. In the cases of real settlements outside the court our documents would state that "upright elders," or "peace-loving persons" or simply "those present" intervened and brought about an agreement through arbitration or persuasion. The countless "releases" and acknowledgments that do not contain such remarks have to be regarded as results of judicial decisions.

How were these decisions reached? In our own time—and the same was already the case in later Roman juridical practice—each party employs an attorney who presents the facts and interprets the law so as to appear as favorably as possible to his client. Attorneys of this type were next to unknown in the courts depicted by the Geniza. As a rule litigants were represented by attorneys only when they were absent or unable to attend a court meeting in person. Such attorneys, as a rule, were not professional lawyers, although of course, for this task one preferred prominent and scholarly persons well versed in business matters (and therefore often known to us through other Geniza papers). Litigations between persons living in different localities were so common that powers of attorney constitute the type of document found most frequently in the Geniza. The appearance in court of a party together with an attorney was so exceptional, however, that Maimonides was asked whether such a procedure was legal altogether. Maimonides answers in the affirmative, but gives the other party the right to disqualify the attorney if he found him disconcerting, and to demand to have dealings only with his adversary.[9] Thus far, only one court record (dated Dec., 1027) has been found in which an adult male person appears together with his attorney and in which the latter does the speaking.[10] This was perhaps an exceptional case, for the attorney here is referred to not with the regular term for legal representative, wakīl, but is designated as *waṣiyy,* which, in addition to meaning "executor," "guardian," is a general word for "mandatory." The attorney in question signed many Geniza documents and was probably a professional notary.[11] In one, unfortunately incomplete, document, the attorney receives one gold piece as remuneration, but most probably he represented an absent party.[12]

Under these circumstances, there was no room for the development of forensic eloquence. The absence of this type of rhetoric, noted with regard to Muslim literature, is felt also in the Geniza records.[13] Still, many court depositions rendered in our papers are impressive in their lucidity and force, and some, such as those (from the years 1038 and 1041-1042) translated in *Mediterranean People,* are not devoid of eloquence, perhaps a natural propensity of the Mediterranean atmosphere.[14] We have to keep in mind, of course, that according to both Maimonides' code and an express reference in a Geniza document, the presiding judge would recapitulate the statements made by the parties, the recapitulation being taken down verbatim by a clerk or the beadle of the court. Thus the clear and concise wording of most of the court records preserved in the Geniza might reflect professional skill rather than natural gifts.[15]

Very often the judges found that the litigants said things that had no actual bearing on the subject matter of the dispute. In such a case our records would contain the remark: "Many statements were made which to report would lead far afield. The upshot of all that was the following."[16] In smaller matters the presiding judge himself would take notes and, as is human, sometimes failed to do so. The Geniza has preserved a note by a judge to a colleague stating that he had forgotten the exact date and some of the conditions of a settlement made before them; overleaf, the desired data are provided.[17]

As to evidence, statements of witness were often submitted in writing. The handwriting of the witnesses on the original document had to be validated by a court (local or other) so that it could be used everywhere. The validation was often executed in the same session in which the original deposition had been made. The judge would write both the minutes and the validation. The witnesses would sign the minutes, while the judge and his adjuncts would sign the validation.[18]

The Jewish courts in the countries stretching from Spain to India seem to have known one another's signatures. We see also in the Geniza that samples of such signatures were kept in the archives. In smaller places, either the validation of the local court was attested by another and more generally known authority, or the judge accepting the validation stated expressly that he recognized the handwriting of his colleague residing in a foreign country.[19]

Two adult witnesses were required by Jewish law. A party who believed that for a lawsuit over only one gold piece one witness was sufficient learned to his dismay that he was mistaken.[20] In practice, frequently five, six, and more witnesses signed a testimony. In such cases, only two signatures required attestation by a court, although in many documents all the signatures, sometimes seven at a time, were validated as genuine. No fixed procedure seems to have prevailed in this matter.[21]

In the extremely frequent cases where testimonies had not been validated by a court, each signature had to be attested by two witnesses. Owing to the lively traffic in the Mediterranean there was no difficulty in finding in Old Cairo or Alexandria witnesses for the handwriting of persons living in the West (see *Med. Soc.,* I, 69). The very custom of letting as many persons as possible testify with regard to an occurrence or a legal transaction probably had its origin at least partly in the endeavor to make subsequent validation easier, since, as we have seen, any two signatures to a testimony were sufficient for its validation.[22]

Documents were widely admitted as evidence. "This letter of mine is your proof in court" writes one eleventh-century merchant to another advising him to dispose of goods costing a large amount of money.[23] This remark is echoed in a responsum by Hay Gaon of Baghdad, sent to the Jewish scholars of Gabes, Tunisia, in 1015, which states that the letters of the merchants in which they give instructions to their correspondents are to be accepted as evidence like depositions in court.[24] In actual court records we indeed see letters produced and used as statements of parties.[25] Account books of merchants were also admitted in court as proof, and were quoted as such in the records.[26] Islamic law, too, although opposed in principle to the acceptance of written testimony, softened its attitude in this matter through the centuries.[27]

Circumstantial evidence, *amāra,* literally, "a sign," is involved five times in a letter dealing with a case brought before the Maimonid Nagid Joshua b. Abraham II (1310-1355), and the details substantiating it are indicated. Thus far, that term has not yet been found in earlier records.[28]

Depositions in court were not made under oath, as is customary today. The allegations made by the litigants sometimes differed so much from one another that they appear to be trial balloons rather than attempts to report facts.[29] No wonder that occasionally the payments finally agreed upon are in no relation whatsoever to the sums first claimed.[30]

There was no formal pleading in the Jewish (or Muslim) courts of the Geniza period, since the office of the attorney in the Roman or modern sense of the word was almost entirely unknown. The function of the attorney was fulfilled to a certain extent by the legal opinions given in writing, the responsa of the experts. The normal procedure of a legal case of some importance would thus be as follows:

First the court would try to verify the facts and to define as exactly as possible the legal position. For this purpose, the judges would hear the depositions and arguments of the parties, examine the witnesses, and study the documents submitted to them. In one case, the dossier of which has been preserved almost completely, this procedure required nine sessions held in the course of ten months. Then the parties, and if he saw fit, also the presiding judge, would present the case, as it had been formulated in court, to one or more legal experts. The latter would not always answer. Thus we read in one letter that Nahray b. Nissīm, "the most illustrious member of the academy," refused to give his opinion in writing, most probably because his old master was still alive and sojourning in the same city, and Jewish etiquette required that a scholar give no legal opinion of his own as long as his teacher was around. The writer of that letter was so sure that Nahray's opinion would be heeded by the court, however, that he asked the addressee to find out his opinion by approaching him personally.[31]

The answer of the legal expert would not decide the case automatically. In one letter the writer expresses his alarm over the fact that the Nagid Abraham Maimonides had sent his responsum to a judge Elijah (b. Zechariah) with instructions and the latter had taken no action as yet.[32] About two hundred years earlier, around 1030, a man, writing from Egypt, reports having secured responsa from Rabbi Hananel (the famous author) of Qayrawān, Tunisia, and from Maṣlīaḥ, the Jewish chief judge of Palermo, Sicily, both being in his favor, but still the case was pending and, one gets the impression, was not developing to the writer's satisfaction.[33] Around 1140, Ezekiel b. Nathanel complains to his brother, the India trader Ḥalfōn, that his case had struck a snag because the four scholars on the bench were of divided opinion. Two opined according to Hay, the Gaon of Baghdad (d. 1038), and two according to the RIF, Rabbi Isaac of Fez, Morocco (d. 1103). The former opinion would be in the writer's favor, wherefore one of the scholars sharing it suggested he obtain responsa written in the same vein by Joseph Ibn Migash, the contemporary chief rabbi of the Jews of Spain (d. 1141). No doubt, these responsa had been secured by the addressee during one of his business trips to that country, trips we know about through other Geniza letters. He certainly had informed his brother about their contents; now the court wanted to see the originals.[34]

After receipt of the opinions of the legal experts, a settlement outside court would be attempted first. Throughout our records, several arbiters, never a single one, are referred to, and, as with the composition of a court, a large number of arbiters was considered more conducive to equity than a small one. In a little town in the Nile Delta we find nine persons mentioned by name acting as a board of arbitration with a circuit judge sent from the capital presiding. The circuit judge was advised by his superior to attempt a decision by law only if arbitration failed.[35] Many lawsuits mentioned in the Geniza were settled by such agreements. In one letter we even find a complaint about judges "unwilling to make decisions, trying only to reach a settlement." [36]

If the parties did not come to an agreement, the court would often not hand down a judgment immediately, but would first make sure to have the support of its superiors, one or more of the three chief judges in the capital, or if the latter themselves were dealing with a lawsuit, of the Gaon or Nagid who had appointed them. Many queries preserved by the Geniza or in the collections of responsa are just such veiled feelers. Modern scholars have wondered about queries that contained questions to which Jewish law gave simple and clear-cut answers. They were consequently inclined to believe that those asking them were mediocre scholars. This is a misunderstanding of the procedure. The judge submitting the question was not in doubt about the answer, as can be seen from the way he presented the matter, but he wanted to have a ruling from above in order to fortify his own position. Therefore, we frequently find in the answers the cryptic remark: "If the case is indeed as stated in the query, the law is such and such."

The parties, too, after having failed to reach a settlement, would apply to the high court of the yeshiva or, later, to that in the Egyptian capital and, in particular, to the Nagid, whereupon those approached would instruct the local court how to deal with the case. The strange procedure of applying to a higher authority before the lower court had made its decision corresponds somehow to the procedure of appeal, which, although not unknown, was not the established and organized course of action it is in modern law. Proceeding from the higher to the lower judicial authorities has occupied us while discussing the office of the Nagid and we come back to it again in describing the working of the Muslim courts.

A decision according to the Law often required an oath. This aspect of medieval juridical procedure is entirely unfamiliar to the modern reader. An oath in court today is a mere formality. In medieval times it was a matter of life and death. For swearing meant troubling God to be present as witness, and "the Lord does not hold him guiltless that takes His name in vain," the third of the Ten Commandments (Exodus 20:7). In order to impress the person obliged to give an oath, the ceremony was held in the synagogue. A Torah scroll was removed from the ark and clad in black; the communal bier and the ceremonial trumpet, the shōfār, were brought in to remind those present of death and the last Judgment, and then the oath had to be given "in the name of God and the Ten Commandments." In a document from Syracuse, Sicily, we read that the party giving the oath was even obliged to read the Ten Commandments aloud from the Torah scroll opened before him. A woman, too, would make a sworn declaration in the section of the synagogue reserved for males and keep a Torah scroll in her hands while doing so.[37] These paraphernalia were believed to be so essential that Maimonides was asked whether an oath on a mere codex of the Bible was valid at all.[38] A merchant would risk his reputation, even if the oath given by him was true. A false oath was regarded not only as a great sin, disqualifying the guilty from serving in future as a witness, but was also a disgrace and even a calamity for the community at large. Therefore, we find in numerous Geniza records that even when everything was ready for the oath, some well-meaning elders would intervene and arrange at last for a settlement.[39]

From the various types of statutory oath fixed by biblical and talmudic law is to be distinguished the procedural "ban in general terms," *ḥerem setām*; it is normally listed in the Geniza records together with the former, when one party releases another of all obligations. The "ban in general terms" served as a kind of lie detector, inasmuch as a ban and the most awesome curses were pronounced on anyone who evaded an obligation defined in the pronouncement, as well as on anyone else who was able to testify about the whereabouts of that person or his obligation and ability to pay. The ḥerem was of two forms, the first being promulgated in the presence of the person accused of evading an obligation. The accused was obliged to answer "Amen," that is, he took upon himself the curses and the ban in case the accusation was true. The second form was used when the whereabouts of the accused were not known. Since people were very mobile in those days, the ban had to be pronounced in different localities and countries, in particular on holidays when it was customary to assemble in the main synagogues.

The wording of this ban had to be of utmost precision in order not to leave loopholes by which the accused could escape responsibility. In a Hebrew letter, sent from Palestine to the capital of Egypt with the request to pronounce such a ḥerem in the latter country, the writer, the Gaon Solomon b. Judah, gives the text of the ban in Arabic, to make sure that all details were understood and noticed by everyone attending the promulgation. There are other texts of this type, albeit interspersed with many Hebrew words. The procedure is well illustrated in the following passage from the letter of a community official in Jerusalem who was asked from Old Cairo to pronounce the "ban in general terms" for a merchant in Egypt called Ibn al-Ḥijāziyya ("the son of the woman from Ḥijāz." In those days, Jews still lived in northern Arabia): "I have already informed you in one of my previous letters that in all the provincial towns and in Jerusalem on the Hosanna day [the seventh day of the Feast of Tabernacles] I excommunicated everyone who owed a dinar or a dirhem or merchandise or the fulfillment of a contract to Ibn al-Ḥijāziyya, or had taken receipts or money orders belonging to them [thus!], or denounced them to a governmental authority, or who caused them any other harm. I shall renew this pronouncement on every holiday." [40]

An interesting combination of procedural ban and statutory oath is found in a holograph ruling by the Nagid Abraham Maimonides. A man suspecting the trustworthiness of another had first to attend a ban in general terms on anyone suspecting that person of being prepared to swear falsely, whereupon the latter was to proceed with giving the required oath.[41]

Many, if not most, court records conclude with the declaration that the parties had not made a secret deposition in another court which would impair the validity of the undertakings forming the object of the record concerned. Such secret depositions, called *mōdaʿ*, have indeed been found in the Geniza. In one case a qadi, who was also the proprietor of a dār wakāla, was involved; in another, denunciation was alleged; in a third and fourth, agreement under duress was given as a reason. All four claimants were notables. A fifth relevant document is rather curious: the front page contains the draft of a deed of manumission for a minor slave girl; on the reverse side, the husband alleges that he had been forced by his wife by illegal means to grant the manumission. Pity we do not know the end of the story (if it had one). The modern reader may find this procedure strange and even repugnant. But in a period of weak state control such a procedure could serve as an effective measure against high-handed persons. A case about which we have a full report may illustrate its working. A man who did not find satisfaction in the Jewish local court of Minyat Ziftā agreed to a settlement in the district court in Alexandria, where he received 10 dinars. Before doing so, he deposited a mōdaʿ in another court nullifying that settlement by a declaration that it would be made under duress. He then submitted both the mōdaʿ and the settlement to the Jewish high court in Fustat, which approved the mōdaʿ and instructed the judge Abraham b. Shabbetay in Minyat Ziftā accordingly. Confronted with this new situation, the tarrying debtor ceded to the pressure of "upright, pious, and peace-loving" elders and agreed to pay an additional 6 dinars.[42]

The handing down of a judgment did not always mark the end of a lawsuit. Its execution, even with the aid of the state authorities, as we shall see, sometimes caused great trouble. If the losing party was a notable of high standing, the court tried to give him opportunity to save face by satisfying his opponent before promulgation of the verdict.[43] The last resort against a recalcitrant party was excommunication (see the preceding section).

In accordance with ancient Palestinian custom, the Jewish courts in Egypt held their sessions on Mondays and Thursdays. This is attested by hundreds of records, even for the congregation of the Iraqians in Old Cairo.[44] The original reason for this arrangement was the fact that these two days were market days in Palestine; the peasants brought their products to the towns and settled their legal affairs on those occasions. The synagogue seized the opportunity for the instruction of the masses and fixed readings from the Five Books of Moses for these days, which thus became "the holy weekdays," honored by the pious by the abstention from food.

Islam adopted this custom and made fasting on Mondays and Thursdays particularly meritorious.[45] Dispensing justice on these days must also have been regarded as a work of piety in Islam. Thus we find the Fatimid caliph Ḥāfiẓ (1131–1149) holding his levees on Mondays and Thursdays, and the famous Saladin is reported to have done the same, holding public audiences on these days, in which he received and settled complaints. According to *The Arabian Nights,* the merchants of Cairo made payments on Mondays and Thursdays because the notaries and money changers were available in the bazaars on those days.[46]

There was a practical reason for retaining Mondays and Thursdays for the sessions of the Jewish courts. Since everyone came to synagogue on those days in order to listen to the obligatory readings from the Torah, it was easy to give a case the publicity needed and to find enough persons ready to serve as witnesses or adjunct judges. When the Palestinian yeshiva moved to Cairo, its high court held its meetings on Wednesdays and Fridays, presumably in order to give the judges of the twin cities the opportunity to sit together in more important cases, as we indeed see in the documents preserved.[47]

The judges did not remain idle during the rest of the week. Marriages and divorces were not confined to fixed weekdays. On Tuesday, as we have seen, auctions of estates had to be supervised.[48] Other business, such as the making or checking of inventories of estates, was also attended to on that day.[49] Regular sessions of the court on days other than Monday or Thursday were rare, however, and sometimes a special reason for the change is recognizable in the contents of the court record.[50] Whether the same custom prevailed in the countries west of Egypt is doubtful.[51]

In at least the larger cities, the courts kept archives or made other provisions to preserve the minutes of the transactions. This is evident from various facts. Persons who wished to substantiate claims or who had lost documents applied to courts and received from them the desired material.[52] Most of the documents preserved are leaves from record books, as proved by the the fact that reports about entirely different cases are written on one and the same leaf and sometimes even on one page. Finally, dossiers of complete lawsuits have been found which bear a superscription or docket indicating their contents.

The largest preserved fragment of a record book is contained in the Firkovitch collection in Leningrad. It consists of twenty-eight consecutive folios comprising sixty-six items, all but one (the last) written by the judge Mevōrākh b. Nathan during the months of April through August, 1156. The official character of such a record book emerges from the fact that the signatures are originals throughout, and not copies. On the other hand we find in this particular specimen also a medical prescription, indicating that the border line between public and private papers was not too sharply drawn at that time.[53]

A similar impression is created when we meet cases where documents are obtained from the widow, sons, and even more remote heirs of judges and Gaons. This seems to prove that, at least in the cases concerned, the documents were kept not in an archive in a synagogue but, rather, in the home of the official concerned (perhaps because it was regarded as safer and more conducive to privacy).[54] The books of formularies, which were such important instruments for the application of the law and are for us such an invaluable source for its knowledge, grew out of copies of actual documents preserved in those primitive but precious archives.[55] We are also able to reconstruct the books of forms from which the scribes of the Geniza copied, especially in the case of court clerks such as Hillel b. Eli (1066–1108) and Ḥalfōn ha-Levi b. Manasse (1100–1138) from whose hands a great number of records have come down.[56] Clearly, different legal usages and variant scribal traditions are reflected in the Geniza. As late as 1250, the Book of Documents (*sheṭārōt*), or formulary, of Hay Gaon (d. 1038) was still studied in Egypt, but even the documents written at the end of the eleventh century by no means conform with the formulations prescribed by Hay.[57]

Of particular interest is a badly damaged piece of vellum bearing entries by the hands of two scribes separated in time by about half a century. On the main part certain specific conditions of a marriage contract are written in the bold hand of Abraham b. Aaron, and entirely in Aramaic. On the head of the page a few lines, in the smallish and elegant script of Halfōn b. Manasse, are addressed to his Nagid, summarizing some of those stipulations in the Arabic language and asking permission to include them in a marriage contract. Ḥalfōn, by submitting the ancient formula to the Nagid, obviously wished to emphasize that the conditions in question were in accordance with ancient local custom. The interesting point is that Abraham himself wrote his documents in Arabic, which everyone understood, and not in Aramaic, which had become obsolete. The conditions were specific, but by no means exceptional: (1) The young couple will live with his wife's parents (and not the husband's, as usual; marriage in those parts and times was patrilocal); (2) he is not permitted to move to another town, except if she wishes so; (3) money earned by her through work will be her personal property (and not go to the common pool, as was the rule); (4) he is not permitted to acquire a maidservant except with her consent and must dismiss her as soon as she demands.[58]

In short, the study of the legal records of the Cairo Geniza is a very rewarding and promising field of research. How fascinating are the results that may be expected may be seen in the Ph.D. dissertation of

Milton Friedman on the (ancient and deterrently fragmentary) marriage contracts according to Palestinian customary law. Concepts and formulations that had thus far been known only from passing quotations in the Talmud (often regarded as merely hypothetical), or from Dead Sea Scrolls, or even from the Aramaic archives of Elephantine (fifth century B.C.) are now proved as having formed a living tradition right down to the eleventh century. The relationship of the law and the procedures revealed by the Geniza records to the economic and social conditions of the period, as well as to the contemporary Islamic and Christian laws and procedures, should form a similarly attractive object of study.[59]

C. THE STATE

1. *The Government and Its Servants*

a. RULERS AND THEIR ENTOURAGES

As is well known, and shown below in greater detail, non-Muslim minorities during the Fatimid and most of the Ayyubid periods, were represented in the entourage of the rulers and the administration of the state in numbers out of all proportion to their sizes. Thus one would expect that the Geniza, a repository of writings originating in one of these minority groups, contained particularly rich information about the court and the machinery of the government. This, however, is not the case. The reason for the deficiency is to be sought mainly in the fact that the courtiers and government officials, as well as the richer merchants connected with the court, lived in Cairo, the newly founded residence, while the Geniza was attached to a synagogue in Fustat, or Old Cairo, the former capital of Islamic Egypt.

This state of affairs is illustrated by many Geniza records. A woman, writing from the capital to her brother, reports among other gossip that a high official was fired from his post by the vizier al-Ma'mūn (1121–1125) and was asked to leave Cairo and to take up his domicile in Fustat.[1] Presumably that man, like other well-to-do Jews, possessed houses in both cities, but preferred to live at the seat of the government. An India traveler, recommending to his brother two distinguished business friends from Morocco, who were returning from the Orient in 1134, admonishes him to receive them well and to put them up—not in Fustat, but in Cairo.[2] The Jewish court physicians who served three generations of Fatimid caliphs and viziers during the eleventh century all lived in the new city, as we know either from letters addressed to them or from express evidence.

The same applies to the Nagid and court physician Mevōrākh, who devoted so much of his time to the affairs of his community. Only during the month of the autumn holidays did he reside in Old Cairo and, as we may assume, it was then that he received the numerous petitions and letters that we still find in the Geniza.[3] The Jewish upper class in general is represented in the Geniza by such requests for help or expressions of gratitude or by poems addressed to their members as well as by references to them in other letters. Only very few private letters emanating from their own pens have been preserved.

There may have been other reasons for this deficiency. Although quite a number of persons belonging to the higher Jewish society of those days seem to have been good Hebrew scholars, they might have used the Arabic script and not the Hebrew cursive for their private correspondence. Thus there was no reason to confide their letters to the Geniza. In a letter written at the beginning of the thirteenth century we find the following remark with regard to an illustrious physician: "I do not know whether our lord 'The Successful' is fluent in [the] Hebrew [cursive] so that I could write to him. Please find out and let me know." [4]

Moreover, some of the more prominent Jewish families of the Geniza period, such as the Tustaris, belonged to the Karaite persuasion and therefore had no opportunity to deposit their writings in a Rabbanite synagogue. For all these reasons, it is only in exceptional cases that we find an "inside story" of the Jewish upper class, as well as of the court and the administration with which they were connected. What we mostly have is seen from outside and from below. It is the government as reflected in the mind of those who had little, if any, direct contact with it, the middle and lower classes.

On the other hand, the few "inside stories" preserved are colorful and highly instructive. The eccentric oculist and surgeon of the sultan al-Malik al-'Azīz (Saladin's son; ruled 1193–1198) describes to his parents how he reacted upon hearing tidings of the death of his younger brother. In the middle of the street he threw off all his clothes except his underwear, ran home, and put ashes on his head and face "from all the ovens in the house." Immediately, the whole entourage of the sultan turned up to express their sympathy and to persuade the mourner to show more moderation in his grief. First came all the court physicians, three even accompanied by their wives (although the oculist himself seems to have been unmarried.) They were followed by the chief commander of the guards and the sultan's *faqīh,* or house chaplain. After the faqīh had reported the physician's predicament to the sultan, the latter sent two high-standing officers to convey to him the following message. "The sultan has delegated us to express to you his sympathy and to say to you the following: accept the death of your brother in the same way as I accepted the death of my own brother al-Malik al-Amjad. Our beloved ones are trusts confided to us, which their proprietor may take back any time. What can one do against this?" The delegates implored the writer by the sultan's life to change his attitude, whereupon he consented to wash his face, but not to interrupt his fast, which he continued until the noon of the following day. In conclusion, the writer describes the subsequent visits of the courtiers, but the rather poor response of the Jewish community.[5]

In another letter, the same oculist, writing from Jerusalem, reports that his masters, al-Malik al-ʿAzīz and al-Malik al-Muʿaẓẓam (the latter's nephew), were laying siege to Damascus and that he was unable to get through to them to ask for a leave. Although ill himself, he visited the sultan's palace every other day, obviously to treat the families and the retinue of the two princes mentioned.[6]

When a libel was brought before the sultan al-Malik al-ʿĀdil (Saladin's brother, 1198–1218) against the Nagid Abraham Maimonides, who also happened to be a court physician, the sultan in person handed the document to his faithful servant. This version of the story, as a letter written by one of the Nagid's adversaries asserts, was the one promulgated by some of the Nagid's followers. The truth, according to the writer, was that a clerk devoted to the Nagid managed to remove it. The contents of the accusation and its treatment by the court occupy us later.[7]

From a report to a high-standing government official often referred to in the Geniza papers, we learn that even a lawsuit to be decided by the sultan in person (Saladin, or perhaps his son al-Malik al-ʿAzīz) required dispensing of substantial bribes, specified in the letter. The opposing party was more lavish and "money answers all things" (Ecclesiastes 10:19). The comforting aspect of this report is the writer's assurance that the addressee would eventually succeed, since the law, Muslim law of course, was clearly on his side.[8]

The early Fatimid period is reflected in a letter of congratulation to a physician transferred from a hospital in Ramle, Palestine, to the personal service of the vizier in Cairo, who bestowed on him a robe of honor and gave him a munificent allowance.[9] Less enthusiastic, or rather outspokenly critical, was a notable writing to his brother who had joined the service of the family of Nāṣir al-Dawla, the commander of the Turkish troops, who, around 1065, was the actual ruler of

Egypt. According to the writer, the costly gifts made by these rapacious generals to their entourage were a disgrace rather than a blessing, and carousing with them was damaging to the body and to the soul alike.[10] The Jews helping "the Monk," the Coptic minister of finance, who ravaged Egypt in the eleven twenties, were condemned in even stronger terms.[11]

The intrigues between higher government officials are well illustrated by a letter of "the president of the court of all Israel" in Jerusalem, addressed between 1057 and 1062 to an overseer of the caliph's mint in Cairo. It concerned an official of the *dār al-ṣarf,* the caliphal exchange, who, after being married in the Egyptian capital in 1050, allegedly intended to marry again in Ascalon, Palestine. This was not only against the standards accepted at that time by Jewish religion, but was disapproved, albeit for quite different reasons, also by the government. The president of the court admonishes the addressee not to use these allegations, which according to the best of his knowledge were untrue, in order to secure the downfall of that official, but, on the contrary, to exert his influence to stop any machinations against the latter. The precarious position of government servants in general is illustrated more than once in the course of this chapter.[12]

Turning now to the popular concept of government as culled from the Geniza papers, we realize that a bottomless chasm divided the rulers from the ruled. The former were half-gods with standards of morals and conduct differing from all that was regarded as decent or even permissible by the common people. The picture of most of the Fatimid rulers of Egypt, as left to us by the Muslim historians, is one of incompetence, debauchery, abject intrigue, and sadistic cruelty. Nowhere in the countless letters preserved in the Geniza do we find an allusion to this state of affairs or any word of disapproval of criticism. Rulers are mentioned in connection with acts of justice or favors granted by them, or when their armies were, or were expected to be, victorious in battle. The opposite, states of oppression and lawlessness, as well as military or economic disasters, are never attributed to the government, but are accepted as a decree of God, or simply as a fact. For, as a geniza letter has it, "the hearts of the kings are like water courses in the hand of God which he might divert into whatever direction he will [Proverbs 21:1]."[13] The breakdown of public order or oppressive measures by the government were regarded as natural phenomena like famines and earthquakes. At most, a minister or other high official was blamed, and this, it seems, only after he had fallen into disgrace—which proved his guilt. Only the lower officials, with whom the people were in daily contact, would be fully exposed in their depravity. For with regard to them the writers could hope that the influence of the Jewish notables was sufficient to bring about their dismissal or at least to stop their misconduct.

It is instructive to consider briefly the role of the viceroy al-Malik al-Afḍal (1094–1121), who is referred to in the Geniza papers more frequently than any other man in power. Both the Muslim historians and the writers of the letters preserved in the Geniza are unanimous in praising him. Still, according to our taste, he could hardly be called the model of a ruler. At his death, he left a harem of eight hundred concubines, of whom fifty were favorites. Once, when he saw one of his slave girls looking out the window, he immediately had her beheaded. The historian who reports this fact to us does not mention it with horror, but with admiration, meaning that al-Afḍal was a he-man who jealously demanded exclusive attention. In corroboration, verses to this effect, recited by the viceroy when the head of the executed girl was presented to him, are quoted,

> While I looked at her, she looked at her shadow—
> But I am too proud a man to share attention with anyone.
> I am a jealous man; were the moon like myself,
> He would not tolerate the company of the stars.[14]

Moreover, the historians cannot find words enough to describe the fabulous riches, the gigantic treasures of nonsensical rarities amassed by the mighty man. Again, this is taken as a sign of his prowess and outstanding ability. No one asks at what price such riches were brought together. We, who know from the Geniza how the common people lived at that time, are aware of the fact that such extravagance could be bought only by keeping millions in misery.

Still, al-Malik al-Afḍal is extolled in the Geniza letters in the most glowing terms. In part, this may have owed to the efficiency of Fatimid propaganda. In part, we have to pay attention to the fact reported by the Muslim historians, that his rule, like that of his father before him, was particularly beneficial for the merchants, and, naturally, most of the letters preserved originated in the middle class engaged in commerce.[15] Even so, it must have been the general character of their rule which earned al-Afḍal and any other deserving ruler of his time the gratitude of their subjects. Government in those days was not concerned with the welfare of its subjects. It had to provide only two things, seemingly so obvious, but so rarely to be had: security and justice. Occasionally, we find in letters the remark that, at the writer's place, security and peace prevailed.[16] Such remarks have to be understood as meaning that those gifts were exceptional. Similarly, rulers are glorified because justice flourished in their day or they are reminded in petitions addressed to them that it was inconsistent with their good name that injustice should prevail under their rule. Al-Malik al-Afḍal is praised repeatedly for his justice. In addition, like other popular sovereigns, he seems to have been accessible to humble petitioners, even from the countryside.[17]

A story about al-Afḍal and a Jew, recounted by a Muslim source, is particularly noteworthy. When the viceroy laid siege to Alexandria, which then was held by Nizār, the eldest or one of the elder sons of the late caliph who had been chosen as successor by the Isma'īlī hierarchy, a rich Jew in that city was conspicuous in denouncing and cursing al-Afḍal who had passed over the legitimate successor and put on the throne the youngest of seven brothers, a mere youth of eighteen. But the city was taken and the Jew was brought before al-Afḍal, who scolded him and ordered him to be executed. The Jew pleaded for his life and promised to pay the viceroy five thousand dinars if he pardoned him. Al-Afḍal set him free without taking a penny from him, "lest people should say I killed him in order to take his money." [18] Presumably it was not only the opportunity for a noble gesture which recommended clemency in this case. What the Jew stood for was legitimacy, and al-Afḍal, who bore the title Shāhinshāh, King of Kings, and had just succeeded his own father as viceroy of the Fatimid empire, was perhaps not unsusceptible to devotion to such a cause.

The minority groups, and perhaps the common people in general, seem to have been loyalist by conviction: a stable though oppressive government was preferable to disorder and turmoil. The person of the ruler was sacrosanct. One swore by the king's life or head, as one swore by one's religion or by the Torah, and one would even mention the Torah and "the King" in one breath while making a public declaration in the synagogue.[19] Swearing falsely while using "the King's" name was a crime deserving heavy punishment.[20] Even in private letters, the name of the ruler would be invariably accompanied by good wishes, such as "may God give him victory and make his days perennial," and not only in Arabic, but also in Hebrew, as when the phrase "may his Rock [God] preserve him" is attached to the name of the caliph al-Ḥākim in one letter and to that of a provincial governor in another (where, by the way, he is described as having done harm to a Jewish scholar).[21] The caliph of Baghdad is honored by the apparition of the prophet Elijah as was a pious woman visionary at the same time, of course in order to ward off some danger threatening the Jewish community.[22] Those in power were regarded as somehow being in some special relationship with God.[23]

Communal prayers for the rulers first appear in Jewish textbooks of liturgy at the beginning of the fourteenth century.[24] In the Geniza, however, we already find the text of such a prayer two hundred years earlier, in the years 1127–1131, and, as many words in it are given in abbreviations, the custom must have been in vogue for a considerable time. It seems that even then, as still habitual in many Oriental Jewish communities today, the prayer was said at the most solemn moment of the Jewish liturgical year, during the opening of the evening prayer ushering in the Day of Atonement.[25] In addition to these regular demonstrations of loyalty, special prayers were held on particular occasions or Hebrew poems were recited in honor of the ruler. Thus the Gaon, or head of the Palestinian academy, arranged for solemn prayers of thanks in Ramle and Jerusalem when the Fatimid caliph and his vizier acquitted the leader of the Jewish community in Old Cairo from false accusations leveled against him. The justice of "the king" and his adviser was extolled and supplications for his success in peace and war were recited. When an attack of the Seljuk Turcomans on Cairo was repulsed (by gold, rather than by sword), an enormous Hebrew poem was dedicated to the caliph al-Mustanṣir by Solomon ha-Kohen, the son of Joseph, the president of the court of the Jerusalem yeshiva, on January 23, 1077.[26] A prayer for a sick sultan said by Muslim, Christian, and Jewish schoolboys in common, albeit in three different groups, is known to me only from literary sources and only with regard to a period preceding the time of the Geniza records.[27]

The entourage of the rulers, the *aṣḥāb al-khila'*, "the bearers of robes of honor," are frequently mentioned in the Geniza, but normally only in letters addressed to them or to their friends with requests for intercession or expressions of gratitude for help given. The term occurs in a letter to a prominent personage containing an appeal to tackle the bearer's problem with the aid of "those honored with robes." [28] The honor of receiving robes from the government in a special ceremony was not confined to the upper crust of officialdom, but was granted even to government agents or physicians as a recognition of good service.[29] It is not always possible to define according to references in the Geniza the exact position or rank of the persons addressed or referred to. Thus when Abū Sa'd Abraham Tustarī, who before his assassination in November, 1047, wielded power in the Fatimid government tantamount to actual rule, is called *mishne la-melekh* (Heb.), "deputy of the King," viceroy, the epithet was not very far from the truth since some Muslim writers give him the title vizier.[30] But the same Hebrew epithet is attached to the name of the Nagid Mevōrākh, who was al-Malik al-Afḍal's physician and, according to the Geniza, also his counselor "from the days of his youth," and in addition, occupied himself with the affairs of the government. It is not unlikely that Mevōrākh (called in Arabic Abu 'l-Faḍl) held in al-Afḍal's administration a position not reflected in Arabic historiography, which is rather scanty with reports about the inner affairs of Egypt in this period.[31]

In all letters, addressed to an official or court notable the wish is expressed that he should find favor in the eyes of the ruler, the viceroy, and all others in position of power, and sometimes even the ladies of the court. Letters written in Arabic use the same word for "favor" as that applied to a favorite concubine; in Hebrew, the corresponding phrase, so familiar from the Book of Esther (2:17; 5:2, 8; 7:3) is applied.[32] The mysterious gift of being acceptable appears to have been the main equipment of the courtier. Moreover, the protection of Heaven is usually implored against all those who envy the addressee and intrigue against him. The phrasing of such wishes gives the impression that the writer does not speak in general terms, but refers to specific situations laden with danger. There is no need to remind of the downfall and assassination of the "vizier" Abū Sa'd Tustarī in 1047, and the same fate of Joseph b. Samuel of Granada in 1066, events fully reflected in the Geniza. But even where positions of power were not lost in such a brutal way, royal disfavor frequently seems to have terminated the role of high Jewish dignitaries who combined the leadership of their community with the service of the ruler. This has been assumed with regard to Jacob b. Amram, the Nagid of the Jews of Tunisia around 1060 and may well have been the case with Samuel b. Hananya, the Nagid in Egypt (1140–1159); for his two sons are repeatedly called his successors designate, but we never hear of anyone of them having obtained an office within the Jewish community. A poem praising Samuel's son and successor designate, presumably when he assumed the post of physician-in-attendance to a lady of the caliph's household, says this: "He has become a son to the royal house, like Moses to the daughter of Pharaoh." But he must have fallen into disfavor and so lost his qualification of future Nagid.[33] The sudden discontinuation of references in documents to the Gaon Sar Shalom ha-Levi as highest authority of the Egyptian Jews in 1171 and to Maimonides in 1177 might have had similar reasons. Maimonides himself speaks eloquently and in a way suggesting personal experience about the treacherous character of court positions that were often terminated by the liquidation of the incumbent.[34]

The ups and downs of court life and the irrational ways of the rulers were accepted as unavoidable as fate. We have a lengthy letter in Hebrew written by a man who claimed to have been in charge of al-Malik al-Afḍal's "granaries, fields, villages, treasures, and stores of food, drink, and clothing." The writer must have been a European Jew, as evident from the way he spells Arabic names. After describing how he successfully withstood all the intrigues and calumnies of his adversaries, he remarks: "Then came the fateful day," and, without giving any explanation, he describes how he lost his position, was robbed of all his property, put into prison, and tortured, while his children "were removed from him," which possibly means that they had to flee the country.[35] In a long Hebrew poem, one Solomon is congratulated on being elevated, like a second Joseph, from prison to the rank of the "deputy of the King" and "Scribe." Even most prominent people would tremble before him, when he shouted at them and he used (of course) his prominent position to feed the poor and to do other works of mercy.[36]

When one high official was dismissed, all those appointed or approved by him faced the same fate. The situation was not dissimilar to that of a change in party rule in a present-day state or municipal corporation. Thus, under al-Malik al-Kāmil when the governor of Alexandria fell into disfavor, a Davidite nāsī who was a physician (and presumably in attendance to that governor) lost his position as head of the Jewish community in that city, as well as the government stipend given to him in this capacity. Moreover, his misconduct as judge and community leader was laid bare.[37]

As we have already seen, the family of an official who lost his office was affected as well. The Geniza has preserved a huge circular urging all Jewish communities to assist a man whose father had been in the service of the king of Granada, but fell into disgrace, whereupon his son had to leave the country.[38] In general, the family was held responsible for the misconduct of any of its members who were in the government service or had other connections with it. Therefore, as soon as a government official or any other person who had had dealings with the government died, all his belongings were confiscated and held under seal until his conduct was cleared. This was a much dreaded procedure, affecting, it seems, also people of the lower ranks of the society.[39]

Many a prince, especially from the house of Saladin, experienced humiliating vicissitudes and the total or partial loss of power. It is natural that a ruler thus affected appreciated the loyalty even of a member of a minority group. This is vividly brought home in a Geniza letter referring to Saladin's grand-nephew al-Malik al-Nāṣir Da'ūd ("the victorious King David"), in which he is assured of the writer's long-standing and unfailing loyalty. Nāṣir is called in the letter "the sultan, may God make his victories glorious," but we certainly do not err much in our assumption that the letter was written at a time when he had already lost most of his possessions. Kings and commoners were brought nearer to each other through the ups and downs of fortune.[40]

The downfall of high government officials, especially those belonging to the minority groups, was so taken for granted that it was reported by historians even if it did not take place in fact. The most conspicuous instance is that of the Jewish chief secretary of Damascus, Manasse b. Ibrāhīm Ibn al-Qazzāz, who had been appointed by the caliph al-'Azīz (d. 996) at the recommendation of the Christian vizier 'Īsā (Arabic for Jesus) b. Nestorius. Ibn Taghribirdī, a late but prominent historian, reports that both fell into disfavor with al-'Azīz and were crucified on his order. But 'Isā suffered such a fate only after having been reappointed by al-'Azīz' mad successor al-Ḥākim, and Ibn al-Qazzāz died peacefully, as is evident from a Hebrew poem dedicated to his son.[41] His granddaughter refers in a legal deed to her share in his palace in Tyre, which would have been confiscated had he been executed.[42] Long after his death his time was remembered as one of tranquillity and amical relations between Muslims and Jews.[43]

b. GOVERNMENT OFFICIALS AND AGENTS. TAX-FARMERS

The administration of the Muslim state was run only in part by officials, that is, by employees receiving a fixed salary and other emoluments. To a large extent, the regular business of the state was carried out by agents and farmers of revenue. Thus it seems that most persons working in the royal mints and in the "house of exchange," dār al-ṣarf, which supervised the payments in cash made to the government, were paid by the job, rather than by the month, while tax-farming affected practically all departments of the government. I consider the three groups of employees, agents, and tax-farmers together, differentiating among them only as far as is warranted by our source material.

There was no strict dividing line between the executive on the one hand and the judiciary and security service on the other. The qadi, or judge, the *wālī,* or head of the local police, and the *muḥtasib,* the superintendent of the market, all had important administrative functions. For reasons of expediency I treat the last group separately.

Government service was called either *'amal,* "work," a term going back to the ancient Near East, or *khidma,* "service," which is also of pre-Islamic origin. Thus a letter from al-Mahdiyya, Tunisia, written shortly after 1057, speaks of "our coreligionists in the administration (*'amal*) of the King of Granada," while a document from Old Cairo, dated 1140, in order to express the idea "the government gives him no post" uses the word khidma. These examples could easily be multiplied. Letters in Hebrew most appropriately use the biblical term "those who do the work of the King" (Esther 9:3 and elsewhere) a phrase borrowed from the administration of the ancient Persian empire, which served as model also for the Arabs.[1]

The usual designation for a government officer was *kātib,* scribe, equally applied to the head of a department in the central government and to a humble clerk in a provincial town. Thus, the "Secretary of the State," Abu 'l-Barakāt Judah ha-Kohen, who in letters addressed or referring to him, is accorded the epithet "the great prince," "the Mordecai of his time," and a dozen other grand Hebrew titles, was officially only a kātib, the same as "the scribe from Tinnīs," for whom a document containing fifty-two closely written lines was made out in 1088 regarding a debt of half a gold piece. Even a little boy who happened to be born into a family of government servants would bear the proud name Zayn al-Kuttāb, "The Ornament of the Scribes" (the one referred to in the Geniza happened to be a grandson of the "Secretary of the State" just mentioned), and girls from such families would not infrequently be called Sitt al-Kuttāb, "The Queen of the Scribes," although it is not quite certain whether they actually learned how to write.[2]

The exact position of a kātib in the hierarchy of officialdom would be defined by the honorary titles and epithets conferred on him by his superiors. The Geniza contains a plethora of them. Lower officials had to be satisfied with an honorific epithet such as "The Sound," bestowed also on physicians.[3] Those higher up were honored with one or more titles lauding the services they rendered to the state. Thus the Abu 'l-Barakāt mentioned above bore at least two such titles: Thiqat al-Mulk, "Trusted [Official] of the State," and 'Amīd al-Dawla, "Support of the Government." The first title was received by him first and is rather common. In a contract dated December, 1175, and in a letter sent to him when his sons were still very young he is referred to by this title.[4] In a letter addressed to Abu 'l-Barakāt's elder son (also a "scribe" who bore the title Sa'd al-Mulk, "A Blessing for the Government") concerning his boy "The Ornament of the Scribes" just mentioned, the old man is called "The Support of the Government," abbreviated to "The Support." [5] A notable was referred to not by his name, but by the title he received last.

A similar promotion was awarded about eighty years earlier to the banker and administrator Abu 'l-Munajjā Solomon, well known also from Arabic sources as the constructor of a famous canal bearing his name in the eastern Nile Delta. It was begun in January, 1113, and took a full six years to complete. The viceroy al-Malik al-Afḍal was very angry that the new waterway was named after its constructor rather than after him, and he put Abu 'l-Munajjā into prison. Abu 'l-Munajjā managed to obtain a Koran: he copied it and signed his work: "Written by Abu 'l-Munajjā, the Jew" and sent it to the bazaar of the books in Alexandria, where it caused an uproar. Asked about the purpose of his undertaking, he declared that he wanted to be liberated from prison by death. Al-Afḍal, however, understood and set him free; he was again employed in government service, as alluded to in a poem dedicated to him. Clearly the man who had brought relief and prosperity to such a large stretch of land had already become a legendary figure in his lifetime. Thus it was told that a poisonous snake was hidden in the room in which he was confined but was fed by him with milk whenever it came out with the effect that it did him no harm.[6]

The references to Abu 'l-Munajjā in the Geniza are of a more prosaic nature. In a document dated 1098, we learn he lived in Damietta not far from the scene of his later activities and transferred money from Old Cairo to Syria.[7] Here he bears the title Thiqat al-Mulk. After distinguishing himself further in the service of the state, he was called Saniyyu 'l-Dawla wa-Amīnuha, "Exalted by the Government and Trusted By It." [8] The title Thiqat al-Mulk was borne also by the chief qadi of the Fatimid empire under al-Afḍal,[9] and the second, Amin al-Dawla, was even more distinguished, since its first bearer was Ibn 'Ammār, the actual ruler of Egypt in the early years of the caliph al-Ḥākim.[10] It seems strange that under the same ruler a Jewish official should be given a title that was borne by the highest Muslim dignitary and by which the latter was commonly known. Thus the assumption that titles had become cheap and were given indiscriminately, although basically true, must somehow be qualified. It seems rather that in each department, or with each type of official, the various titles carried with them a certain rank or at least prestige specific to that particular section of the bureaucracy. This would explain why we find an advancement from Thiqat al-Mulk to another appellation in two cases, separated from each other by so many years, and why a Jewish administrative officer could bear the same title as a contemporary chief qadi. A comprehensive study of the rich data in Muslim and Christian sources, as compared with the copious instances of titles referred to in the Geniza, would probably yield more clarity on this subject, which is paralleled in Byzantine bureaucracy and ceremonials.[11]

Examples have already been offered for the well-known fact that the Muslim government kept tight control over the financial affairs of its officials, or rather regarded the riches amassed by them as its own, often culminating in wholesale confiscation or at least sequestration of the estates they left. The Geniza shows that the government interested itself in the family life of its employees as well. A Sicilian Jew, who had married a wife in Damascus, was about to get a government post in Cairo. He was told, however, that he would not obtain the appointment unless his wife followed him to the Egyptian capital (but she refused). He then approached the rabbinical court with the request to be permitted to marry a local woman on condition that he deposit with the court the indemnity due his first wife in case of a divorce. The record reporting the granting of this request emphasizes that this policy of the government was well known to the judges. We have already had a similar case, where a high official of the caliphal exchange of Cairo suspected of having married a woman in Ascalon, Palestine, was in danger of losing his post. The reason for this principle is obvious: when the official's family lived in another country, the government did not have a firm hold on him; if he fled, there was no one to be taken as hostage.[12]

Exact statements about salaries and emoluments are rare in the Geniza, rarer even than those about commercial profits, and the reason for this reticence is the same in both cases: one was reluctant to confide these delicate details to paper. We read about salaries only in a specific case, for instance, when a person unacceptable to both the writer and the addressee of a letter was appointed to a post that they would have preferred to see occupied by one of their own faction. Thus in a report to a high official in Saladin's time (ca. 1180) the writer mentions with regret that X. was made *mushārif,* or controller, of the revenue of a town, and was promised 180 dinars and 100 waybas (about 2,500 pounds) of wheat per year. As usual, the emoluments consisted of both cash and kind. A mushārif of a village received, at approximately the same time, 1-½ dinars per month, or 18 a year, exactly one-tenth of the salary just mentioned.[13]

Arrears in the payment of salaries seem to have been common, and even higher officials had difficulty in getting them on time. In one letter the addressee is asked to approach no less a man than the Nagid with the request to induce Abu 'l-Munajjā to give orders to pay the writer the accumulated arrears.[14] When one official asked another to substitute for him he would give instructions to transfer his salary to his colleague for the time of his absence.[15]

Lower officials who were in direct contact with the public, such as the messengers of the tax collectors, official money changers, customs officers, controllers of weight, gatekeepers, and port clerks, apparently did not receive any fixed salary from the office employing them. Instead they were remunerated with a small gratuity for each service rendered by the persons concerned. References to such payments abound in all reports of expenses, whether communal or commercial.[16]

We read, too, about persons working in the mint of the caliph in partnership and for *fā'ida,* "profit," that is, they were paid by the piece and were not in receipt of regular emoluments.[17] Whether the same held true for the Jewish official called "director of the mint" is not evident from the references found thus far. As he is called "director of the mint and agent appointed by the government" in one legal document, it is likely that he, too, was paid by the job.[18] The Muslim official who was in charge of the mint and who bore the title "director of coinage" is repeatedly referred to in one source as "the farmer of the revenue from the mint," that is, he, too, was an employee with no fixed salary.[19]

We have to keep in mind that even a post like that of the head of the police would sometimes be farmed out, that is, the aspirant would promise to pay the government a fixed sum every year and then indemnify himself by imposing heavy fines on whatever culprits he could lay his hands on. A letter referring to such an arrangement emphasizes that persons committing even a slight offense (such as a Jew—not a Muslim—getting drunk) would "perish," since fines constituted the personal income of the wālī.[20]

In general, the farming of revenue of all descriptions pervaded from top to bottom the system of administration and economy of the time. The regular term for tax-farmer was *ḍāmin,* literally, the one who stands security (occasionally also *mutaqabbil).* The word was used not only in relation to public revenue, but also for leasing property from a private person or from a community like a Jewish congregation or for collecting rents for them, as well as in the literal meaning of standing security for a person's poll tax or any other financial obligation.[21] The term *nā'ib,* "deputy," which we have already met as designating a judge, could also refer to a tax-farmer, for, as we shall see, it was common practice for the bigger ḍāmins to sublease their rights to minor substitutes.[22]

Research on the subject becomes even more complicated by the fact that, as a rule, a farmer of revenue is called simply "al-ḍāmin" without any further definition, and only the context of the document or a reference to the same person in another Geniza record enables us to determine with more precision the nature and extent of his contract.[23] On the other hand, references to this institution are so numerous in the Geniza that a systematic search for them is able to provide important source material for this interesting aspect of medieval administration.

Trying now to classify the different types of tax-farming, we find that most farmers of revenue are mentioned with the name of a locality attached to them. Fourteen examples of such references are given in a note.[24] Where a village or a small town is concerned, it is perhaps reasonable to assume that the ḍāmin collected all the various dues payable by that place, although this assumption is by no means certain. It was common practice "to travel to a locality in the Rīf [the Egyptian countryside] and to farm its revenue," or for a woman from Old Cairo "to join her husband, who was the ḍāmin of a place in the Rīf."[25] The father of a profligate son was afraid that bad people would induce the youth to stand security for a village in the Rīf. "You will eat and drink and your father will pay," that is, the income from the revenue would serve the boy as a regular source of income, while the old man would be held responsible by the government.[26]

Where a larger provincial town or the capital itself is mentioned as the domain of a tax-farmer, the reference is no doubt to only one specific type of fiscal income. Thus, 335 dinars as *'ibra,* or yearly assessment, for a provincial capital like al-Maḥalla, can represent only a fraction of the taxes to be collected there. Most probably it was the tax on silk-weaving and dyeing, the farming of which was so popular among Jews.[27] In a letter concerning (New) Cairo, the context clearly implies that it was this tax of which the *ḍāmin al-qāhira* mentioned was in charge.[28] Even in a small place like Atfīḥ, otherwise known as a center of flaxgrowing, the ḍāmin, as the continuation of the document proves, was concerned only with taxes on silk work, and for an equally small locality, Qalyūb, this is said expressly. A statute forbidding women to dye silk at home without notifying the ḍāmin takes it for granted that the term referred to the farmer of the silk tax. There are other examples below. Since the Jews were so conspicuous in the silk industry, they were best qualified to take care of the taxes levied on it.[29]

The dues on dyeing and selling silk constituted only part of the revenue "from the market" in general. We have already had the case of "the judge of the Jews" in Manbij, a town in Syria, who was also *al-ḍāmin lil-sūq*, the tax-farmer of the bazaar of that locality. Naturally, this office was not very popular. We read, for example, in a letter with regard to another Jewish scholar: "God forbid that he should farm the market, as has been rumored, a task affecting so many coreligionists."[30] When a merchant received a payment, "the master of the market, namely the tax-farmers [thus, in the plural]" would sequester it until any claims on dues from former transactions were satisfied.[31] In at least one case, the tax-farming of a locality (without further definition) refers to that of its market. On the other hand, there were such specialized items as *ḍāmin birsīm al-iskandariyya*, "farmer of the taxes on the lands sown with Egyptian clover in the district of Alexandria," illustrating that provision of the city with vital fodder for riding beasts was the concern of a separate branch of the administration.[32]

An important field of activity for tax-farmers was the revenue from the sale of houses or parts of houses. A request to stop the machinations of an overreaching ḍāmin dealing with this revenue reveals many interesting details.[33] In the many deeds concerning the transfer of immobile property this tax is referred to only in specific instances.

Finally, the collection of customs duties was also farmed out. The Geniza refers to this fact with regard to the Nile ports of Old and New Cairo and to the busy seaport of 'Aydhāb on the coast of East Africa. The Muslim traveler Ibn Jubayr reports the same for the Palestinian harbor city Acre, which, at the time of his visit, was in Christian hands. Still, it seems doubtful that this usage was general and permanent during the period discussed in this book. Otherwise one would expect to find more references to it in the numerous letters and accounts regarding persons and goods passing through customs stations.[34]

It should be noted that in some localities the poll tax incumbent on non-Muslims was also farmed out. Thus in a letter from a village the writer complains that he was unable to come to the capital since the ḍāmin issuing receipts of the poll tax had not yet arrived (and without such a certificate one was not permitted to travel). Similarly a Muslim tax-farmer is mentioned in a query submitted to Maimonides as being in charge of the jāliya, and a Jewish *ḍāmin al-jawālī* is referred to in a letter addressed to Isaac b. Samuel, the Spaniard (ca. 1100).[35] It seems, however, that the collection of the poll tax in smaller places formed a part of the type of tax-farming discussed first, that which comprised all the payments due from one area. In his brilliant analysis of an Ayyubid source concerning the revenue from the Fayyūm district, Claude Cahen shows that the jāliya was included in the general estimate of the revenue from that district.[36]

A *ḍamān,* or appointment as tax-farmer, was obtained either from a local revenue office, or from a dignitary to whom a certain revenue was allocated, or from the central government. A man writing from a small town in or around 1096 claims to have received one of his appointments from the father and predecessor of al-Malik al-Afḍal.[37] Similarly, a document made out in Damietta in 1106, states that the farmer of the tax on dyeing and selling silk in that district held this privilege by a rescript from the sovereign.[38] The revenue from al-Maṭariyya (Heliopolis) was leased from an amir called in a fourteenth-century letter Malik al-Umarā', "The King of the Amirs."[39] In general, the *dīwān,* the government office concerned with the tax in question, or its director, *'āmil,* or controller, mush(ā)rif, is referred to as granting the ḍamān.

Competition was keen, and a ḍāmin had to work hard both to procure and to retain his post. The officials of the relevant departments, local and central, had to be won over for the applicant's case and the same applied to the local police and its head in the capital. For without the help of the police the tax-farmer was lost. No one would pay him. Although the amount to be guaranteed by the tax-farmer (also called ḍamān) and the term of his office were fixed in the patent of his appointment, it must have been common practice to force him to pay more as soon as a higher bid was made by someone else. In a later century, when public mores had sunk to a low level, outbidding a fellow tax-farmer had become a rampant social evil and was punished with excommunication.

The tax-farmer was usually a capitalist who stood security for a larger district and subleased his rights to a host of substitutes who did the actual collection of the taxes or practiced monopoly in the area allotted to them. In a contract dated 1138, a ḍāmin grants to another the license for selling and dyeing silk in a certain quarter of Old Cairo against 18 dinars per month (not a small sum) for the duration of his own tenure of office. The capitalist promises not to accept any higher offer and not to discontinue the lease for any other reason. In case of default he would pay the lessee a fine of 100 dinars. He would use his influence on the head of the police to help his substitute against any one evading the payment of the dues. The substitute was entitled to open as many stores in his area as he wished and to undertake the dyeing of silk himself, if he preferred to do so. The main ḍāmin reserved for himself certain rights such as employing Muslim women to act as his agents in the quarter concerned (seven are mentioned by name and their women partners are referred to). The contract contains a number of other stipulations which prove that much experience had been accumulated in this field of administration and economy. Among other things we learn that the tax-farmer was entitled to make out a warrant of arrest and to send policemen to carry it out.[40] Two partners with equal rights and duties farmed out three localities in a south Egyptian district in June, 1156. But the government patent was granted to only one of the two.[41]

In the document of 1106 referred to above, the farmer of the dues from dyeing and selling silk in the district of Damietta subleases his rights regarding a small town to three partners for the duration of one year against a payment of 2 dinars per month.[42] Conversely, two capitalists who had farmed out *munfalit al-Fayyūm,* the arrears (or rather the taxes evaded) in the Fayyūm district, take as collector a silent partner who was registered only in a Jewish court but not with the government. The two main tax-farmers made substantial profits, but cheated their partner of his share. The letter that has come down to us was written under extremely dire circumstances in prison, to which he was confined because he was unable to meet his obligations.[43]

In general, tax-farming was a hazardous undertaking, and references to severe losses are not infrequent.[44] We read bitter complaints about the government offices and their arbitrary and ruthless ways with the ḍāmins.[45] In a document dated 1147, a tax-farmer takes over from two others promising to pay their debts to the government, which they had been unable to do.[46] Such debts were not always a sign of poverty. The last leaf of an inventory of an estate notes a debt of 125 dinars on tax-farming, but registers purses with gold and silver coins, vessels made of the same metals, promissory notes, and many other assets far exceeding a thousand dinars.[47] The Muslim historians tell us the story of a prominent Jewish tax-farmer of Basra, Iraq. He was the confidant of Niẓām al-Mulk, the famous vizier (d. 1092), and so influential that all Basra, with the sole exception of the qadi, turned out at the funeral of his wife. When the Seljuk sultan Malik Shāh had him executed in the course of an intrigue, maneuvered by

Niẓām al-Mulk's enemies, the great vizier refused to appear before the sultan for three days and took up his duties only after Malik Shāh had expressed regret about what he had done. This did not hinder him, however, from appropriating a hundred thousand dinars from the Jew's estate. The same amount, together with a hundred horses, had to be delivered by the new tax-farmer of Basra every year. With a few exceptions, sums of such magnitude do not occur in the Geniza records.[48]

Tax-farming was rampant in the Roman and Persian empires and, as the New Testament and talmudic literature eloquently testify, weighed heavily on the population. It seems to me, however, that the system of tax-farming in Fatimid and Ayyubid times, as we are able to know it through the Cairo Geniza documents, was somewhat different. Although pernicious in more than one way, it fitted well into the general framework of the economy and society of the Geniza period. Most of the ḍāmins belonged to the middle class, and, being themselves merchants and industrialists, possessed knowledge and understanding of the problems they encountered while collecting taxes. They wielded little power and therefore could not become very oppressive. Complaints about overbearing tax-farmers are rare. In addition to the one concerning the tax on the transfer of houses mentioned above, only few others have been found thus far, one, for instance, in which the ḍāmin is accused of having sold the complainant's fruit trees and "marked" his date palms (presumably for the same purpose).[49] In another, "the dyers in Qalyūb" complain that they perish because of the high cost of the wheat, little work, and the heavy ḍamān.[50] The standards of tax-farming depended to a certain extent on the efficacy and code of morals of the judiciary and the security forces.

c. JUDICIARY AND POLICE

Next to the nominal and actual rulers and their viziers, and more even than the generals, the attention of historians has been captured by the qadis, the "judges" of Islam. Literally thousands of biographies of qadis, arranged according to the cities or countries over which they presided, or according to the years in which they died, have been preserved, and much is to be found about them in other branches of Islamic literature. Under these circumstances one wonders whether the Geniza letters, which had no reason to refer to them except occasionally, could contribute anything to a subject so richly documented elsewhere. It seems, though, that those passing remarks, precisely because of their ephemeral and unintentional character, are apt to throw some interesting sidelights on that important and often misunderstood institution.

In trying to describe the office of the Jewish judge, I was repeatedly induced to compare it with that of the Muslim qadi, which is so different from it, although the two offices did not develop entirely without mutual contacts. There is further opportunity to refer to the Muslim judiciary while discussing the interplay of Jewish and Muslim laws. Here some incidental information provided by the Geniza is reviewed.

The most impressive aspect of Muslim juridical organization, as evidenced in our records, is its strict centralization. The lower courts investigated but were loath to decide matters before making sure of the opinion of their superiors. A qadi in Qūṣ, a town near the southern border of Egypt, wanted to have the *tawqīʿ qāḍi ʾl-quḍāt,* the instructions of the chief qadi of Cairo, signed by him in a case of inheritance of middle-class Jews. For this purpose, the party concerned had to send a messenger to the capital, an expensive trip that required over two months of travel alone.[1] Even the powerful qadi of Alexandria decided about the disposal of the goods of a drowned silk merchant only after having received a *tawqīʿ ʿālī,* a rescript from the caliph's court.[2] Two disputes that had come before the qadi of Jerusalem, one concerning the Jewish community of the city and another regarding a house shared by a Muslim and a Jewish notable in common, were expected to be settled by the chief qadi of Ramle, then the capital of Palestine. The tenor of the two letters dealing with these cases shows that this was the regular course of action.[3] The following incident is particularly characteristic. A prominent merchant, who had dealings with many others, was found drowned. Before his death he had acknowledged in the Jewish high court that he owed 400 dinars to the writer of the letter telling us about the occurrence. The writer wished now that the witnesses testifying to the dead man's avowal should be heard by the qadi who dealt with the latter's assets and liabilities. This appears to be merely a matter of procedure. Still, a rescript by the sovereign (al-Malik al-Afḍal) was needed for the action, and the writer most emphatically asks the addressee to secure for him the desired document.[4] A similar system of procedure was in vogue in the Jewish juridical organization of those days. Instead of deciding a case and then allowing for an appeal, the lower courts deferred their judgments until they received proper instructions and backing from the central authorities.

This weakness of the lower courts had a twofold corollary. On the one hand, people applied, or threatened to apply, directly to the chief qadi.[5] On the other hand, high dignitaries and other influential notables exercised pressure on the court, the chief justices, and the legal experts in order to obtain instructions favorable to their clients. The Geniza has preserved numerous letters in which persons engaged in lawsuits make requests to such an effect or allude otherwise to this state of affairs. This mode of trying to influence the judges is reflected in our records far more frequently than outright bribery (perhaps because the latter did not require expression in writing). Bribes to the higher judiciary, such as the qadi who had his seat "in the Palace," were not paid directly, but to a go-between and were a heavy imposition on the parties.[6] Lower judges were content with as little as 10 dirhems, very likely a kind of fixed fee known to every one.[7] Middle Easterners familiar with practices that still prevailed during the first half of the twentieth century will find nothing strange in such arrangements.

A qadi in a big city like Alexandria had doorkeepers and a bodyguard of armed slaves whom he would also send to apprehend persons against whom charges were made.[8] Otherwise, however, his executive power was limited. The police were by no means automatically at his disposal. Giving judgment was one thing, implementing it quite another. The divorce of the juridical from the executive authorities is beautifully illustrated in a story about a case of inheritance in the little town of Rafaḥ in southern Palestine. The local Jewish judge had referred the case to the Gaon of Jerusalem, as usual, and the latter had sent in his decision. The losing party vilified the judge and applied to the qadi, who upheld the decision made by the Jewish authorities. Not content with this, the losing side, which had meanwhile taken possession of a part or the whole of the estate, turned to the governor, who in the early Fatimid period was called *qā'id,* or commander, as he had been in North Africa, from where the Fatimids had come. But the qā'id confirmed the rulings of the Gaon and the qadi. Full of joy, the Gaon held a public prayer in Jerusalem in which he paid high tribute to the justice of the Muslim authorities as well as to the local Jewish judge. But the affair was not yet concluded. The object of contention was not returned to those recognized by all as the legal heirs. At that juncture, the Gaon, in the document telling us the story, put the losing party under ban until he complied with the judgments handed down. We do not know whether this device was more successful than the decisions made before.[9]

In general, the chief qadis of the larger cities loom in the Geniza as powerful persons whose authority was paramount so that one sometimes gets the impression that they were the actual rulers of their area. In a time of tension among the various sections of the population in Alexandria, a traveler on his way to that city tries to secure a letter of recommendation to the Muslim chief judge—and not to the governor or head of the police.[10] Likewise, a traveler from France asks to be granted a rescript from the viceroy al-Malik al-Afḍal to the qadi of Damietta, then the second largest port of Egypt, first for protection during his stay in that city and second in order to be commended by that judge to the captain and sailors of the boat on which he would continue his travel.[11] For the qadi in a maritime city often served also as *nāẓir,* or superintendent of the port. The father of Saladin's chief justice held such a double appointment in Ascalon, then the main port in southern Palestine.[12] The Geniza, in addition to the case of the qadi of Damietta just mentioned, tells the same of his contemporary, al-Makīn, the chief judge of Alexandria, who died in 1134 after serving in office for many years.[13] No wonder, then, that we often find in the Geniza qadis as shipowners, especially those of the Lebanese ports Tyre and Tripoli, owners not only of coastal craft, but of the largest ships plying the Mediterranean during the eleventh century, each carrying five hundred passengers. In pre-Islamic times, the head of the Christian church in Alexandria, the patriarch, played a similar economic role.[14] It may be that such combinations of religious and legal authority and economic power represented an old tradition going back perhaps to the ancient Phoenicians and Carthaginians.

The Alexandrian judge al-Makīn, who, by the way, was the one whose protection was sought by the uneasy traveler from France referred to above, had his finger also in another pie. In addition to his substantial duties as judge about which we read repeatedly in the Geniza records, he was mushārif, or controller of the office of revenue. As such he was approached by a representative of the Nagid, or Head of the Jews, with a request to free one-quarter of his crops, which he needed for his household. (Normally, no one was permitted to make use of the products of his fields before his accounts with the government's director of revenue were settled.)[15]

Most frequently we find qadis engaged in mercantile undertakings and, in particular, as proprietors of a *dār wakāla,* a combination of storehouse and bourse (see Med. Soc., vol. I, chap. iii, sec. C). A wakīl, as explained there, was originally and essentially the legal and commercial representative of foreign merchants. Qadis, who were themselves charged with the dispensation of justice, were the representatives most sought after by foreigners. The same qadi of Tyre whom we have met as shipowner, possessed also a storehouse in which among many other wares he kept precious Persian silk brocade before it was shipped to the West. In behalf of the merchants who stored with him their goods awaiting transport he ruled that they were not obliged to pay certain taxes (or customs) they had evaded unless they sold locally.[16] From a document dated 1097 we learn that Jews sent their merchandise from Syria to the warehouse of "our lord, the illustrious qadi Abu 'l-Ṭāhir b. Rajā' " in Old Cairo although a prominent Jewish representative of merchants was active in the city at that time. The same qadi's dār wakāla is referred to as a bourse, where inter alia mercury was traded, and there are other references to qadis as representatives of merchants.[17]

Next to the qadi, the faqīh, or Muslim doctor of law, is frequently referred to in the Geniza records, where he appears in two different capacities. At the lower level, he acts as a notary making out legal documents, or as puisne judge, who settles minor business such as the approval of the appointment of an attorney.[18] On the higher level, he is a very influential legal expert whose opinion is sought, for instance, with regard to the amount of the poll tax, and who, in a meeting with other jurists, may take precedence even over the qadi (in Alexandria!).[19] Faqīhs are repeatedly mentioned as belonging to the entourage of the rulers and as traveling in their company.[20]

The term "muftī" for a Muslim jurisconsult, so common in Mamlūk times, is surprisingly rare in the records of the classical Geniza period, although the word "fatwā," legal opinion, and its derivatives are frequently used, and even a Jewish dignitary is referred to with the title "muftī."[21]

One of the most characteristic institutions of Muslim legal procedure was that of the officially certified witnesses of good reputation, the *'udūl,* or "the just," as they were called for short. Originally such certificates were issued so that a testimony could not be contested because of alleged blemishes adhering to the witness' character. By the fourth century of Islam, these 'udūl had become a fixed institution, serving as assessors witnessing the court procedures, as well as notaries. In the Geniza, the two meanings of the term, the original and the institutional, are equally alive. A Hebrew "Scroll," or poetical story, praised the caliph al-Ḥākim, among other things for appointing as night watchmen only "faithful witnesses" (Isaiah 8:2), that is, 'udūl, or persons of certified good reputation.[22] On the other hand, in the descriptions of the session of a Muslim court in Alexandria, 1143, the judge is assisted by two "just witnesses" and by the scribes of the government office in which the session was held, and we meet a similar pair of 'udūl witnessing an oath given by a Jewish woman before a Muslim judge.[23] When Jews make a contract before "four just witnesses," the reference is to a Muslim notary and his assistants.[24] The facts attested to in such a way were usually accepted by a Jewish court as true, although complaints or reports that the 'udūl gave false witness are not lacking.[25]

Turning now to the security forces, some notes about terminology are unavoidable. The classical word for police, *shurṭa,* is almost absent from the Geniza records. It was retained as designation for the office and guardhouse of the police in Old Cairo. The honorary title *ṣāḥib al-shurṭa,* "head of the police," was borne by a number of Spanish Jewish notables, but was unknown in the East. As name of an office it is extremely rare.[26] Both expressions were relics from more ancient times. With that craving for euphemistic terms so characteristic of this period, the police building, although containing gruesome prisons, was called *ma'ūna,* "help," while the security forces themselves were divided into a number of specialized groups.[27]

The head of the police was called *wālī,* literally, "governor," but its occurrence in numerous Geniza records leaves no doubt about the meaning of their use of the term.[28] The wālī is found in big cities like Cairo and Alexandria, in provincial towns, and even in a mere village.[29] In cities like Alexandria, Ramle, or Jerusalem, as a rule, the government was represented by an amir; in smaller places the wālī was also the head of the civil government. Therefore, in view of that dichotomy of judiciary and executive power, whenever one had a lawsuit or was in any other predicament that could lead to an intervention of the authorities, one applied to both the wālī and the qadi, or, if the person concerned was of lower social standing, he would ask a friend to ask another friend, still higher up, to approach the two for him.[30] A fine paid by a community was collected both by the wālī and the nā'ib, or "deputy" (as a judge other than the chief qadi was called). The former took five hundred silver dirhems as a "requisition," the latter two hundred, characterized in the document concerned as "bribe." For those who paid these amounts, it presumably made little difference what the items were called.[31]

One tried to be on good terms with the custodian of order. When a new wālī was appointed in a townlet of the Rīf, a fruiterer living there was alerted by his brother in the capital that the new wālī was a relative of his predecessor and prepared to carry on his vendettas. It would be good if "a gift of honor would reach him soon." In a detailed description of a brawl in a small town the attacking party is accused by the other of having arranged matters with the wālī beforehand to look the other way.[32] When the Spanish Jewish poet Judah ha-Levi visited Alexandria, a notable of that city was eager to have him as guest for Friday night, an honor that the poet generally refused to grant in order to avert unpleasant rivalries. The undaunted host induced his friend, the chief of police, to send a message to the distinguished visitor, however, whereupon the poet accepted the invitation. Whether this behind-the-scenes report is true, or represents only the gossip of Alexandria in fall, 1140, is hard to say. In any case, the poet did well to heed the wālī, for when he returned to that city in spring, 1141, he experienced a quite unpleasant encounter with the police.[33]

Another very important security officer was the muḥtasib, or superintendent of the market. His duties were manifold and ranged from the supervision of commerce and industry to enforcement of the religious law (which partly concerned the non-Muslims as well) and the infliction of corporal punishment. Detailed books on this interesting office began to be published toward the end of the twelfth century. Since a letter from Alexandria, written around 1140, says: "Everyone in the city behaves as if he were a muḥtasib set over us," it must have been common by that time. Still, it should be emphasized that, with one important exception (a case from the thirteenth century), discussed below, the writers of the Geniza records are very reticent with regard to this office, all the more remarkable, since most of them deal with economic and legal matters and thus had good reason to make mention of the muḥtasib, if his presence made itself felt in the bazaars. The dearth of material in the Geniza records with regard to the muḥtasib is matched by the same scarcity in the literary sources of the Fatimid period. One later historian states indeed that in Fatimid times, the office was often united in one person with that of the chief of police. Thus it seems that the prominence of the muḥtasib under the Ayyubid and subsequent regimes was due to Mesopotamian influence on Egypt and Syria. For in Iraq this office had a long history behind it.[34]

Each urban area, compound, or quarter had its own police inspector, called *ṣāḥib al-rub'*, the supervisor of the quarter. He and his patrolmen were the first to appear on the scene when public order was disturbed.[35] He also had other functions, for instance, to assemble the inhabitants of his quarter and to lead them to meet a ruler at his solemn entry into the city.[36] The ṣāḥib rub' appears frequently in the accounts of the Jewish community, for he received monetary presents at the time of the Jewish and Muslim holidays, as well as on special occasions. In a document from the year 1041, he received 5 dirhems for Pentecost (in early summer) and 7 for the autumn holidays, but in April, 1234 (for Passover), only 2. In 1247 he was given two silver pieces "for assembling the Jews." Similar amounts are mentioned in other records. The document of 1247 notes also that he had lived in a house belonging to the Jewish community (and had left without paying rent). All this points to the fact that, despite his title, his rank was rather low. Naturally, everyone tried to be on good terms with him. In one document we find "the supervisors of the quarters" acting as a kind of advisory council to the superintendent of the market (see below).[37]

The police force itself consisted of different contingents. The one most frequently mentioned is the patrolmen, the all-purpose police. We find them under the command of the police inspectors, or carrying out orders given by qadis, customs officers, collectors of the poll tax, and the director of the mint. In the last case, they were accompanied by mounted police, because in order to search for counterfeit money, they were required to encircle a complete neighborhood. In two instances, the patrolmen appear in groups of five.[38]

Another common member of the security force was the raqqāṣ, "runner." In modern Arabic the word means "dancer," but in the Geniza period it designated an unskilled laborer and an errand boy for any government office, especially one who had the task of summoning or arresting a person. In one document, the "runners" are identified with the patrolmen. Normally they were attached to the wālī, or head of the police.[39]

The executive arm of the poll tax office was the *ḥushshār,* "ralliers," who summoned the non-Muslims to the offices where they had to pay their taxes. The ḥushshār are often referred to, and it is evident that they were not concerned with the actual collection of the taxes, but formed a kind of auxiliary police whose task it was to let no one escape from fulfilling his duty.[40]

The royal mint was protected by a guard. Elsewhere in the Geniza the term for guard is used for combat soldier. Thus this vital institution was obviously protected by members of the regular army.[41]

Of particular interest is an armed force, called *aḥdāth,* "young men," mentioned in the Geniza with regard to Jerusalem and Aleppo, and perhaps also to Sfax, Tunisia. From three letters sent from Jerusalem around 1040, it is evident that the Jewish inhabitants of that city paid a special contribution toward the upkeep of this militia. Most probably the same was done by the Christians. For Lambert of Hersfeld, in his description of the Christian pilgrimage to the Holy Land of 1064–1065, speaks of "a guard of light armed youth," which accompanied the pilgrims from Ramle (then the capital of Palestine) to Jerusalem. No reference to these aḥdāth, has been found in the Geniza with regard to Egypt.[42]

Finally, there were the "messengers" of the chief of the secret police and his "spies," plain-clothesmen to all intents and purposes. Patrolmen, "runners," and "ralliers" certainly did not wear uniforms, but by one way or another were recognized, whereas the detectives and informers remained, or wished to remain, unidentified. We have already met the secret police of Alexandria in the case of the notable who was accused of having had an affair with a woman of ill repute and in the account of the adventures of the poet Judah ha-Levi in that city. We find them also in Old Cairo, Palermo, Sicily, and Fez, Morocco. In the two cities mentioned last, they also served the customs offices.[43]

As with government offices in general, there was no clear-cut and fixed division of duties among the various branches of the judiciary and the security force. Thus we find, for example, in Damietta, the office of the chief of police dealing with cases of inheritance, normally the prerogative of the qadis.[44] It was therefore natural that people were sometimes at a loss to whom to apply. In a detailed but lamentably incomplete report from Alexandria, an emissary of a Jewish authority describes how he wanted to have someone corporally punished for an offense against religion. After sketching the contents of his charge, he continues:

I did not know to whom to submit it, to the qadi or to the wālī. Finally, it occurred to me to send it secretly to the muḥtasib, the superintendent of the market, emphasizing that a light punishment was sufficient. The latter sent his messengers to summon the supervisors of the quarters, who advised him to bring the accused before the wālī. The wālī decided that he should be flogged and pilloried, a decision that was carried out after the messengers of the muḥtasib had brought the man into the presence of the wālī. The public asked that he be put into prison as well. The messengers dragged him around the whole Qamra [a predominantly Jewish quarter], and cried out that he had vilified the [Jewish] religion.

The report concludes by saying that the chief of police was prepared to bring the case before "the great wālī," the superintendent of police in the capital, which was done only in exceptional cases. The writer emphasizes with satisfaction that his appeal to the Muslim authorities was heeded, although he was not known personally either to the muḥtasib or the wālī.[45]

The punishment most frequently mentioned in the Geniza, and

no doubt forming also a major, if not the main, source of income for the police, was the so-called *tarsīm,* "the dues for guardsmen." Originally, it meant that a person would be confined to his house and a guard would be posted before it, for which the accused had to pay. Thus, in a letter from Ramle, Palestine, written early in the eleventh century, the son of the president of the Jewish high court describes how the governor scolded his father for having arranged a funeral of a beadle with more pomp than the Muslim authorities had permitted. After nightfall, the governor sent guards, for whom 5 dinars per day had to be paid (the confinement was lifted after twenty-four hours).[46] In most cases the term designates a warrant sent to anyone who owed a tax to the government or a debt to a private person, whereupon he had to pay a certain sum for each day on which he "remained under tarsīm." Thus a physician in Alexandria, whose brother, also a physician, had traveled to Old Cairo without having paid his poll tax (or having forgotten to send the receipts back), was put under tarsīm until he would pay the poll tax for that brother. After two days of refusing to do so, he was confined to prison. One day and one night there taught him better and he paid.[47] We read about another person remaining ten days under tarsīm, a third losing the considerable sum of 13 dinars in this way, and a fourth who was freed from it only after a change in the government.[48] In order to obtain such a warrant against his debtors, a merchant needed the intervention of the representative of the merchants in the capital.[49]

Imprisonment in those days did not mean simply denial of freedom. It was a far more cruel punishment. First, the prisoner was in danger of dying from starvation in the event no one looked after him. For the prison authorities did not feel themselves obliged to feed him. Thus, a poor woman whose husband was in prison because he was unable to pay the poll tax, asks in a letter for bread which she needed to bring to him.[50] A Muslim convert to Christianity who was thrown into prison was on the point of dying because his family refused to take care of him. The story goes that he was finally rescued by a Christian saint.[51]

Imprisonment, like any other service of the government officials, had to be paid for. If the prisoner defaulted or was unable to pay, he was cruelly maltreated. "I am afraid to leave my hiding, lest the poll tax collector finds me and puts me into prison, where I shall die, since I possess nothing with which to save my soul," writes a man who had lost everything when all his goods were jettisoned from the ship in which he traveled. A mother from Alexandria, pleading with the Jewish authorities in Old Cairo to work for the release of her son from prison, remarks that he has to pay the jailer every day several dirhems, a luxury she cannot afford.[52] Even a person apprehended for only one night had to remunerate the prison guard for his uninvited hospitality.[53] A report about imprisonment is usually accompanied by a remark about how much it cost. It should be noted that in medieval England the same features prevailed, namely the obligations of the prisoner to provide himself with food and to pay for his imprisonment.[54]

Corporal chastisement and torture were applied even in cases of insolvent debtors. In addition to being flogged and beaten, the prisoner was put into the stocks, his joints wrenched, he would be chained with a nose ring like a bull, needles would be driven beneath his fingernails and into other sensitive parts of his body, and there is repeated mention of another instrument of torture (with a Persian name) not yet identified with certainty. Persons facing jail for any reason, for example, nonpayment of the poll tax, expected to be unable to survive torture and life in prison in general.[55]

Prisoners were allowed to receive the visits of their relatives and friends, or at least to see and to talk to them as the visitors stood outside. Where this privilege was denied, it was expressly stated.[56] They were also allowed to send letters out of prison, some of which we still have, and since in one such letter a complaint is made against a particularly wicked jailer who cursed and beat the writer without reason, we may assume that in some places at least the authorities in charge did not tolerate excessive cruelty. Jews were given certain facilities to keep their Sabbath, and similar consideration no doubt was extended to the adherents of other creeds. In pre-1950 Yemen, then a traditionally Muslim country, Jews were let out of jail altogether on Saturday if someone stood security for them.[57]

Thus far, in all the Geniza documents and letters, not a single report of or even reference to an execution has been found. When one reads the Muslim historians of the period one gets the impression that most public figures of consequence ended their lives by being put to death by their superiors or by being assassinated by foes. In the middle and upper lower classes represented in the Geniza an entirely different climate of morality prevailed, and crimes punished by the death penalty were next to unknown. Moreover, it seems that in contrast with the barbarity and cruelty rampant in the Middle Ages in general, the judiciary and police of the Fatimid and Ayyubid periods were comparatively lenient and civilized.

d. NON-MUSLIM GOVERNMENT OFFICIALS

After having mustered the ranks of Muslim government and administration as they were eyed by the Geniza people, it remains to ascertain how the representatives of the non-Muslims, the Geniza people themselves, fit into that general frame.

It has often been emphasized that the Fatimid period was the golden age of government officials coming from the minorities. The same was true for the subsequent Ayyubid period.[1] The "government servants," together with the judges, who also have to be regarded to some extent as government officials, formed the cream of Jewish society.[2] Both in number and power the Christian government servants far outstripped the Jewish—a fact fully evidenced in the Geniza records. Still, Jews frequently attained positions of powerful influence, as illustrated in the following often quoted verses of a malicious Egyptian poet:

> The Jews of our time have attained the goal of their aspirations:
> The honors are theirs and so are the riches. Counsellors and kings are taken from their midst.
> Egyptians! I advise you, become Jews, for Heaven itself has turned Jewish.[3]

The last verse contains a pun. Venus and Jupiter, the propitious stars, were both called *sa'd,* "good fortune," and Abū Sa'd, we remember, was the name of that powerful Jewish courtier who met a violent death in November, 1047.

We should view this preponderance of non-Muslims in government service in its proper historical perspective. Office may have given power and wealth to some, but it did not grant precedence over the members of the ruling religion. A ceremonial of the Fatimid court from the year 1122 shows that at a reception of the caliph all the Muslim officials and even the notables of Old and New Cairo came first, while the end of the long procession was formed by the patriarch with the Christian officials and the Jewish officials led by "the head of the Jews" (the Nagid).[4]

It seems to me that the generous admission of non-Muslims to government service in the Fatimid and Ayyubid periods and the violent opposition to them and their actual ousting in later times is to be attributed not only to a change from a more tolerant to a fanatical religious atmosphere, but to a large extent also to socioeconomic conditions in general. Long before the tenth century, the Muslims had attained the same standards of educational and professional prerequisites for administrative work as their non-Muslim compatriots. Why, then, did they leave the field of government service so much to the latter? Obviously because in the free economy prevailing at that time business and industry offered more lucrative and less dangerous opportunities than the often humiliating and mostly precarious service of the sultans. We have indeed seen that big business was largely in Muslim hands. From the thirteenth century on, however, when the economy became increasingly monopolized by the state, the clamoring Muslim candidates for government posts became ever stronger, and the members of the minority groups had to give way. Fanatical religious propaganda then formed an effective superstructure for this socioeconomic pressure.

In short, it was the unattractiveness of government service which made it available to non-Muslims at a time when plenty of other outlets for economic activity were open to Muslims. This explains why the mints in most Muslim states remained largely a domain of the Jews even in later periods. Daily work with hot melted metals in a hot climate must have been extremely unpleasant under the primitive working conditions of those days—and just good enough for Jews. In addition, no other branch of government work was so exposed to the temptation of fraud and embezzlement as the manufacture of coins. Jews, the least protected minority, were by their very status the most faithful servants of the state, for they knew only too well that in case of discovery of any impropriety no one would shield them from punishment.

Finally, we have to keep in mind that Muslim writers often exaggerated grossly in speaking about the non-Muslims' share in government. The verses quoted are one case in point. As late as the forties of the thirteenth century a visitor to Egypt from the Muslim West reports that most of the Christians and Jews in that country were officials working in the revenue offices and physicians.[5] As far as the Jews are concerned, the Geniza enables us to check that statement. The medical profession did indeed form an unproportionately large section of the community. We may also assume that persons styled *ṣayrafī,* or money changers, were at least partly attached to some government office. But *kātib*s, officials proper, definitely formed a small group.[6] Even if we account for this by the assumption that most of them lived in New Cairo and not in Fustat, where the Geniza chamber was situated, a survey of the occupations generally exercised by Jews in that period certainly would not corroborate the assertion made by that Muslim visitor to Egypt. As a traveler he had many dealings with customs and other government offices and was astonished to find there far more Christians and Jews than he was accustomed to in his home country. We should not take such remarks too literally, although it is generally true that in the Fatimid and Ayyubid periods the non-Muslim minorities were conspicuous among the servants of the state.

Trying now to specify the various branches of administration in which persons represented in the Geniza were active, we are up against our imperfect knowledge of the nomenclature and administrative practice of those times—and this despite the rich literature about the subject produced by the Muslims. Thus we find in Cairo in December, 1236, a highly praised Kohen, bearing the title Nafīs al-Dawla, "Priceless [Servant] of the Government," and described as the deputy of a qadi. Now it goes without saying that a Jew could not become a deputy judge in Islam. Thus we must assume that that qadi, in addition to or instead of his substantial duties, headed a government department where the Nafīs, as he is referred to for short in other Geniza documents, acted as his substitute.[7]

Around 1140, a person bearing the title ʿAmīd al-Dawla, "Support of the Government," was in charge of a dār wakāla, a warehouse and bourse, and the same is reported for the year 1203 with regard to one Amīn al-Dawla, "Trusted [Servant] of the Government."[8] This could mean that these persons were public servants who used their high position for running a profitable dār wakāla; or such a dār wakāla itself was a semiofficial institution, as is indeed suggested by some Islamic sources.[9] Only in exceptional cases is the department over which an official presided expressly stated, as when a calligraphic personal letter is addressed to the tax office, or when a *ṣāḥib dār al-ṭirāz,* head of the government embroidery workshop in Damietta, called Jalāl al-Dawla, "Splendor of the Government," receives a loan of 50 dinars in a document from the thirteenth century, unfortunately undated.[10] As a rule, the kātibs are referred to by their names and titles, not by the office they held, which was known to all concerned.

The uppermost stratum of officialdom was formed by the courtiers who had direct access to the caliphs and sultans, or, where these did not exercise the highest power, to the actual rulers, whatever titles they chose to bear. To this group belonged above all the court physicians, about whom we hear so much in the Geniza, and some of whom, such as the Nagids Mevōrākh and Samuel b. Hananya served, according to the same source, also as counsellors. These physicians bore titles similar to those of government officials. A Jew called Ibn Abi 'l-Dimm, "The Son of the One Whose Pet Was a Cat," was head of the chancellery of the caliph al-Āmir (1101–1130). Despite the rarity of the name and the chronological coincidence it is doubtful that he was identical with a physician bearing the same name in a Geniza document.[11] The famous Abū Sa'd was vizier to the mother of the caliph al-Mustanṣir who ruled for her minor son, wherefore he, and not the vizier of the caliph, exercised the highest power in the state. The Geniza, as remarked before, calls him simply viceroy.[12] Of a similar type was the man who claimed to be the administrator of al-Malik al-Afḍal's fabulous treasures and possessions. In order to be able to hold high office, however, Jews as a rule had to convert to Islam, as proved by the examples of Jacob Ibn Killis and of Abū Sa'd's own son, who was given an important position after his father's assassination but attained the vizierate only after his conversion.[13]

A less conspicuous but still important position was occupied by those officials who controlled the revenue of the state in one capacity or another. Throughout, the Geniza refers to two different types of such officials, sometimes confused in the literary sources: the mushārif or mushrif, controller of revenue, and the 'āmil, director of the revenue office. The two acting together, with the mushārif mentioned first, fixed the amount of the yearly payments to be made to the government by tax-farmers.[14] The control of the revenue of a large district such as that of Alexandria was a powerful position. We have learned from a Geniza letter that it was once held by the famous qadi al-Makīn, and a literary source shows that even a former vizier did not regard it beneath his dignity to occupy it.[15] Abu 'l-Munajjā, the Jew, the digger of the canal named after him, was mushārif of the equally rich Damietta province.[16] In one Geniza letter a person boasts of having received by a rescript from the caliph ishrāf al-Rīf the control of the Egyptian countryside, which makes him so bold that he defies the orders of the Nagid. No doubt, the appointment referred only to a certain district.[17]

As in the case of "kātib," the term "mushārif" was applied to the controller of both a whole province and a little village. Therefore we are not astonished to find that such a post was sought even for a young good-for-nothing aged twenty-two years. In some places, the synonymous term *nāẓir,* "overseer," was used instead of "mushārif." A striking description of the doings in a revenue office in the capital with its host of officials from the minority groups is contained in the letter translated in *Mediterranean People.*[18]

The controller of revenue was entitled to issue a warrant of arrest and to send raqqāṣin, "runners," to carry out his order. We remember that even a tax-farmer had this right.[19]

The duties and authority of an 'āmil, director of revenue, are illustrated by the following instances. In Jerusalem around 1060 that post was occupied by a Karaite Jew, which, by the way, may partly explain the powerful position of that sect in the Holy City. When he was replaced by a Christian, we read in a letter sent from Jerusalem to a notable in Old Cairo: "I learned today that Ben 'Allūn [the Karaite] was dismissed from his post of 'āmil of Jerusalem . . . and that Ben Ma'mar, the Christian, has been appointed. If it seems right to you, please approach 'the prince of the community' [a court physician] who should obtain a letter from X. [a high dignitary] to Ben Ma'mar advising him to be considerate toward our coreligionists with regard to taxes and other matters." This shows that an 'āmil had a say not only in fixing the amount of taxes, but "in other matters" as well. To be sure, the word should never be translated as "governor." The governor of Jerusalem was an "amir." [20]

On the other hand, we find 'āmils in small towns of Egypt where they were befriended by the Tunisian merchants who went there to buy flax. For flax, the staple crop of Egypt those days, was a government preserve and could not be bought except with a permit from the local 'āmil.[21] Again, like the mushārif, the director of revenue of a whole province was also called " 'āmil," as was the one in charge of the Buḥayra district to whom the young good-for-nothing referred to above (through the intercession of his grandmother, the widow of another 'āmil) applied for a post. Finally, of course, the director of revenue dealt also with the collection of the poll tax, whereas in a big city, like Alexandria, this branch of revenue was in the hands of a special 'āmil. In an account of expenditure from the eleventh century a significant item is called: gift to the attendants of the director of revenue.[22]

A more comprehensive designation that comprised the two offices just discussed, as well as the customs stations, was the *ṣāḥib al-dīwān,* "director of the government office." He is mentioned as fixing the amount of rents to be paid for houses owed by the government or the amount of the purchase tax for mules and camels. Even a private person who had farmed out the revenue from a customs house was addressed in this way.[23]

The monetary system of that time necessitated a host of money changers, bankers, and accountants to cope with the collection of the taxes and the accounting of expenditures. Such persons were either outright employees, when they bore the title *jahbadh al-dīwān,* government cashier, or were more or less loosely connected with the administration.[24] As with the terms "kātib" (official) and "mushārif" (controller), the word "jahbadh" could designate both a powerful minister of finance and a wretched money changer who could hardly make a living. These full- or part-time servants of the government are discussed in *Med. Soc.,* I, 248–250.

Since the Jews were avid travelers, it is not surprising that some of them occupied government posts connected with seafaring. We find Jews as superintendents of the ports of Alexandria, Egypt, and of Denia, Spain, and as "controllers" of ships, who were in charge of the passengers and their goods. Like other government officials, the latter were permitted to do business on their own account while on travel and could not be sued during the time they were actually in service. On the other hand, merchants were reluctant to make use of them as agents, precisely because of their connection with the government.[25]

Although it may seem odd at first, the Geniza proves that Jews served as police. Persons working in the shurṭa (the guardhouse of Old Cairo) or as a *ḥāshir,* "rallier," or as nightwatchmen, or as members of the secret police appear in our documents at different times. Jews are repeatedly called raqqāṣ, "runner," which had various meanings. But when, in an argument, a person threatens to become a raqqāṣ, it is most likely that he meant enlisting in the auxiliary police. Since the "ralliers," "runners," and plainclothesmen assisted the authorities in the collection of taxes and customs dues, the surveillance of minority groups was facilitated by employing for these tasks persons from their own midst.[26]

The army was composed of foreign contingents, such as Berbers, Turks, Negroes, and some Bedouin levies, and, as a rule, did not admit members of the local sedentary population, whether non-Muslim or Muslim. In two letters from Alexandria, when a desperate father asks his friends in Old Cairo to help him find his son who had run away to the army, we may safely assume that the young man expected to be employed as purveyor or clerk, not as a soldier. For he carried with him goods, and the unhappy father did not preclude the possibility that the adventurous youth had traveled as far as Yemen.[27] A *kātib al-ʿarab,* chief clerk of a contingent of Bedouins, is described in one letter as a particularly influential and reliable person, and a Karaite family, famous for its copyists of Hebrew books, had as patronymic the same appellation, proving that such an appointment was regarded as a distinction.[28]

There was one army service that must have been rather popular among the minority groups: the "medical corps." We have already made mention of a Christian army surgeon. Letters to and from Jewish physicians serving with the army or navy are by no means rare. A letter dated 1137 of an Egyptian doctor who had settled in Byzantium mentions that he had previously written from the army camp in Jaffa, Palestine.[29] A physician of the navy (or rather of the battleship, *usṭūl)* has left us his accounts for the year 1139.[30] Abū Zikrī, the elder son of the judge Elijah b. Zechariah, so often mentioned in the Geniza, served around 1220 in the army of the Ayyubid prince al-Mu'aẓẓam. He must have been quite influential, since in one letter he promised to procure for his old father a pension from the sultan al-Kāmil; still, he could not get away from the army whenever he wished.[31] A similar and far stronger complaint is made by another army doctor who had first to cure a Mamluk who resided on his fief in an out-of-the-way Egyptian village and then to report back to his amir and supervise his taking medicine, with the result that he was unable to attend the confinement of his own wife.[32] Of particular interest is a long letter to an important physician who was away with the army while his son-in-law, the writer of the letter, collected his salary, which was obviously paid in the capital. He reports on the manifold affairs regarding which the old man had written to him and to his friends. The son-in-law again and again expresses his astonishment that the busy doctor found leisure to think about all these public, private, and business affairs, and so do we. Needless to say, the doctor also sent prescriptions for indisposed members of the family.[33] The great Abu 'l-Barakāt, "The Unique," also served for some time as army physician.[34]

While the sedentary population, and in particular the non-Muslims, were thus exempt from military service, there were other impositions, partly permanent and partly temporary, which often made life very hard.

2. *The Poll Tax and Other Impositions*

There is no subject of Islamic social history on which I had to modify my views so radically in passing from literary to documentary sources, namely, from the study of Muslim books to that of the records of the Cairo Geniza, as the jizya, or jāliya, the poll tax to be paid by non-Muslims. It was, of course, evident that the tax represented a discrimination and was intended, according to the traditional interpretation of the Koran's own words, to emphasize the inferior status of nonbelievers. It seemed, however, that from the economic point of view it did not represent a heavy imposition, since it was on a sliding scale, originally of 1, 2, and 4 dinars, and thus adjusted to the financial capacity of the taxpayer.[1]

This impression proved to be entirely fallacious, for it did not take into consideration the immense extent of poverty and privation experienced by the masses, and in particular their way of living from hand to mouth, their persistent lack of cash, which turned the "season of the tax" into one of horror, dread, and misery. The provisions of ancient Islamic law which exempted the indigent, the invalids, and the old were no longer observed in the Geniza period and had also been discarded in theory by the Shāfiʿi school of law that prevailed in Egypt. It is precisely persons of such descriptions about whose plight we read so much in our records. The payment of the poll tax was item number one in the budget of families with modest income, such as teachers or laborers. For a man could clothe himself inexpensively, he could eat at starvation level, as perhaps a very large section of the population did. But he could not escape the tax-gatherer—at least not for long. If he was caught, he was beaten and suffered other corporal punishment, *ʿuqūba,* and was thrown into prison, where, because of starvation and maltreatment, he faced death.

A few passages selected at random from a mass of pertinent Geniza letters serve as initial illustrations. A schoolmaster from Qalyūb, a small town north of Cairo, who also earned some money by copying books, complains to a relative in the capital around 1225: "This place does not provide me with the poll tax or clothing, and, as to food, the fees suffice only for me alone. For they amount only to 5 dirhems a week and I need three-quarters of a dirhem a day at least. Thus my income is not enough even for having a robe laundered. . . . The Nagid promised me a year ago that he would take care of the jāliya. But the year has passed and I have not received anything from him. I am now perplexed and pondering where to turn and where to flee." He sends four books copied by himself, hoping, somewhat faintly, that the proceeds would resolve his predicament. Even of the teacher Solomon, the son of the judge Elijah b. Zechariah, we have two letters with requests for money for the payment of the poll tax.[2]

An old, half-blind refugee from Ceuta, Morocco, in a letter written in his own hand (as he emphasizes), asks a countryman for a few pounds of flour in order to keep body and soul together, but this only after other friends had helped him with the poll tax. Before becoming disabled by failing eyesight, he had worked as a silversmith, but his beautiful handwriting, his good Arabic and Hebrew style, and his copious Bible quotations show him also to be a man of learning.[3]

The writer of the following letter, too, must have seen better days, for he speaks to the addressee, a person of high standing, almost as an equal. After only a few introductory phrases, he continues:

> My present state is marked by illness, infirmity, want and excessive fear, since I am sought by the controller of revenue, who is hard upon me and writes out warrants of arrest, sending "runners" to track me down. I am afraid they will find out my hiding place. If I fall into their hands, I shall die under their chastisement or will have to go to prison and die there. Now I take my refuge with God and with you—may God save you from all misery—please ask Shams al-Dīn [the director of revenue in the capital] to write a letter to al-Maḥalla that they should register us as *absent,* for every one says: your only salvation is to be registered as absent. Furthermore, if God ordains that some money will come together for my jāliya, it should be said that it is for the fugitives (al-hāribīn), for it is not myself alone, but my sons as well, for whom I am held responsible.[4]

The last sentence shows that, in a previous letter, the addressee had been asked to arrange a collection for securing the writer's jāliya, an extremely common occurrence. As an example, translated here is the main part of an autograph letter by Moses Maimonides, written by the master with particular care: "Kindly assist the bearer of this letter, Isaac of Der'a [a town in Morocco], for he is an acquaintance of mine. Ask the ḥāvēr [the local spiritual leader] to make the community care for him, so that he will get the money for his poll tax in your place. He has to pay two jāliyas, one for himself and one for his son. If possible, enable him to pay the tax in your town, Minyat Ziftā. For he is a newcomer and thus far has not paid anywhere. He is now on his way to Damietta on an errand important for me. On his way back, action should be taken for him according to your means." [5] The letter implies that the foreigner was not yet registered anywhere and recommends that he should become listed as a permanent resident neither in the capital, nor in the city of Damietta, but in the provincial town Minyat Ziftā, where the rates of the tax presumably were lower or where the collectors were less rigorous.

Trying now to define in detail who was bound to pay the poll tax, or for whom it had to be paid, the illustrative passages quoted above are sufficient to prove that poverty, old age, and illness did not provide an excuse for exemption. A person was regarded as taxable long before he was capable of making a livelihood. In a settlement between a husband and his wife, dated 1244, the latter undertakes to provide full board for their elder son, to let him learn the craft of silversmithing, and to pay his poll tax for two years.[6] From a query submitted to Abraham Maimonides we learn that the guardians of an orphaned minor had to pay the jāliya for fully ten years before the latter was declared by a Jewish court a major and competent to take care of his property. In a letter addressed to Moses Maimonides a person is accused of having neglected his duties as pater familias, since he had never paid the poll tax and school fees (in this sequence!) for his two boys, one of whom was seventeen and the other thirteen at the time of the complaint.[7] From a document written around 1095 it seems that the jāliya was due from the age of nine.[8]

Whether death canceled arrears in poll tax due was a moot point among Muslim doctors of law. In the Geniza period it went without saying that it had to be borne by the legal heirs. Therefore we find provisions for the payment of such debts in deathbed declarations. Particularly moving is one made on a Sabbath (when no financial arrangements are allowed), the day before the person concerned died, in which a provision is made for a payment of 2 dinars due for the jāliya (dated 1142).[9] A responsum of Maimonides shows that even in the case of a very poor widow no exemption was made from this rule.[10]

The members of a family were held responsible for each other's poll tax. A silk-weaver fled from Old Cairo and went as far south as Aswan (now famous for its dam), since bearing such a burden for his father and three brothers was too much for him. We learn this from a letter of one of the brothers assuring him that all members of the family had paid—not without the father having spent one night in prison—and that he could now safely return.[11] Cases of persons who had to account for a brother or for sons have been quoted before. The same applied to brothers-in-law.[12] The poll tax was due also on travelers to distant countries to be paid for them back home. We learn about a merchant who sojourned in India nine years and finally died there that his brother had fulfilled this duty for the whole period—a fact mentioned in the document concerned as in no way extraordinary. In a similar case, where a brother had disappeared in Syria, the demand was contested (whether successfully, we do not know), because, during his absence, the traveler had not charged his brother with the payment of his poll tax.[13] In a letter from Alexandria, a brother away in India is politely reminded to send something for his jāliya, since his father was spending money for this purpose all the time.[14] At his arrival in Alexandria after an absence of four years of which he had been kept back in Constantinople by illness for two and a half years and had suffered also shipwreck, a merchant asks his relatives in Old Cairo to tell the tax collector about his misfortunes with a request to register him as a newcomer (in order to save four years' tax). "Promise him half a dinar or a dinar and remind him that I am Joseph who had his store beneath the Mu'allaqa church." [15]

Persons traveling within the realm of Islam, and indeed anyone leaving his domicile even for a short period, had to carry with him a *barā'a,* acquittance, showing that he had absolved himself for the current year. In a smaller locality when the taxgatherer had not arrived in time, no one could set out on a journey, since it was dangerous to do so without a barā'a. A scholar from Ascalon, Palestine, writing a letter of recommendation for a colleague from Damascus who traveled to Egypt emphasizes that the latter was in possession of a certificate issued by the poll tax office (and not merely by an individual tax-gatherer). Even so he asks the addressee to see to it that the Egyptian authorities should not "interpret" the certificate in a way that would enable them to squeeze an additional amount from his friend.[16] It was a common occurrence that Nile boats were not allowed to depart or were even turned back by the police because one of the passengers was unable to produce his jāliya receipt.[17]

Since everyone paid where he was registered as resident, one would expect that a traveler would not be held liable to contribute to the jāliya of the locality where he sojourned temporarily. The Geniza shows, however, that the tax collectors found ways to have foreigners too pay under one pretext or another. The letter regarding the scholar from Damascus just mentioned, as well as the stories of the merchants from Sicily and Tunisia sketched earlier, are cases in point.[18] Even while setting out from one town of Egypt to another, a traveler would provide himself with a letter of recommendation to an influential personality asking him for protection against overreaching tax collectors. A letter written in Arabic characters to a notable in Fustat by his brother traveling in the Rīf contains this story: The muqaddam of the little town of Damīra paid his poll tax in the provincial capital al-Maḥalla. While staying in Fustat for a year he paid there as nonresident and received a proper Barā'a. When he returned to Damīra, however, the authorities did not honor the receipt and asked him to pay a second time. It was regarded necessary to obtain a caliphal rescript for the redress of this oppressive act.[18]

It was not only the government officials and tax-farmers whose rapacity was dreaded. The leaders of the local denominational communities who had a say in the assessment also contributed to the plight of the "newcomers." A passage from a letter of a Tunisian merchant writing from Alexandria is very instructive in this respect:

> I wish to tell you what happened to me with regard to the poll tax since your departure from here. There are many in this city who have arrived prior to myself, but were not treated the way I experienced. Every day they molest me and summon me to the court, asking me to pay the jāliya in full. They want to register me as a resident, whereas my father, as you know, was only a "newcomer." What they impose on me, is remitted to others, who do not allow themselves to be molested—you know whom I mean. The benefit which I derived from your intervention for me is that I have to pay this year almost 2 dinars. I would not have minded, if others had been treated in the same way. The tax-gatherers (ḥushshār, "ralliers") and the director of the jāliya are not to be blamed; all this is entirely the work of the Jews!

The role of the local communities in the collection of the poll tax is discussed presently.[19]

When did a person cease to be a newcomer, *ṭāri'*, and obtain the status of a permanent resident, *qāṭin?* Owing to the astonishing mobility of the Mediterranean middle class of those days, this question caused many headaches both to the administration and to the persons affected. As we have already seen in the example of the Egyptian merchant who was immobilized by illness in Constantinople, much depended on the goodwill of the individual official (and the amount of the bribe offered to him). In general, however, it appears from the Geniza records that it was not easy to change one's status. An eleventh-century Tunisian merchant and scholar who, after having lived in Egypt for years, spent some time later on in Byzantium and finally settled in the Holy Land, writes: "I intend to pass the winter in Jerusalem, for I have learned about the [bad] Nile [which meant famine for Egypt to where the writer expected to travel]. Furthermore, I am registered in the revenue office *(kharāj)* of Old Cairo as resident. Originally they registered me as a newcomer, but when my stay in the country extended, I became a *qāṭin*. By now, I have been away from Egypt for ten years and this is my eleventh." Since the writer wished to pay the poll tax incumbent on a resident where he actually lived, namely in Palestine, he preferred not to return to Egypt, where he still was registered as such.[20]

Because of the large number of Syro-Palestinians living all over Egypt, a special office was created for them in the capital, where they had to appear every year in person for the payment of their jāliya. The occurrences described in *Med. Soc., I,* 63, show the inconvenience caused by this arrangement to the individuals concerned. It was perhaps an Ayyubid innovation. No direct reference to the "Syro-Palestinian jāliya" has been found thus far in the Geniza with regard to the Fatimid period.[21]

Were there any exemptions from the duty to pay the poll tax? The ancient idea that those who dedicate themselves to the service of God should be free from the service of men was realized in the Jewish community by its bearing of the tax burden for its scholarly officials. It was an internal arrangement. The Muslim authorities had nothing to do with it. There are, however, two reports in the Geniza, from the eleventh and the twelfth centuries, respectively, claiming that certain Jews in Baghdad were granted exemption from the poll tax. It is stated in one that they should not publicize this special favor; in the other, that the beneficiaries themselves declined to accept it, because the tax protected their life and property (as is indeed the official Muslim theory). Those reports are semilegendary and although they may contain a grain of truth, lack the details to make them significant.[22]

A few cases of exemption from the poll tax occur in Geniza letters related to Egypt. A distinguished traveler from France acknowledges gratefully his having been freed from the *zimiya,* a term he explained by a Hebrew word for capitation, as well as from other impositions, by a special rescript of the viceroy (al-Malik al-Afḍal).[23] A man who had lost his riches and served as a minor community official earning 1-¼ dirhems a day ("which is really not a salary") informs the Nagid Samuel (1140–1159) of his intention to settle definitely in a village near Minyat Ziftā belonging to one Nāṣir al-Din, whose inhabitants did not pay the jāliya. Another destitute person writes that he had been offered a government post in Alexandria, "where he would not be held for the poll tax." Whatever this expression may mean, the last two cases do not represent a real exemption, but rather payment rendered in the form of a service, which, to be sure, was salvation for persons without cash.[24]

The strangest case of an exemption from the poll tax is that of the poet Yākhīn, who had settled in al-Maḥalla but fled from there when the superintendent of revenue "harassed him" by demanding from him the poll tax. The letter supposes that Yākhīn was entitled to tax exemption because he was a Khaybarī, a Jew from a north Arabian clan that asserted it had received special privileges from the Prophet of Islam. A forged document to this effect has found its way into the Geniza and is preserved in extended form in the popular literature of the Jews of Yemen under the title "The Letter of Protection

Granted by the Prophet." References to persons called Ibn al-Khaybarī are found in various Geniza documents of the eleventh century. But no express testimony that any tax collector did honor the Khaybarīs' claim has turned up thus far. And it seems to me that a distinction should be made between Jews who really emigrated from north Arabia and were called Ḥijāzīs and the Khaybarīs, who probably came to the West via Iraq and had no real connection with their region of origin, the oasis of Khaybar.[25]

The Geniza proves that the data given by the Muslim handbooks of administration on the amounts of the poll tax, although hardly reflecting the realities in full, are basically correct. Ibn Mammātī (a Christian convert to Islam, d. 1209) notes as the highest yearly rate 4-1/6 dinars. This is exactly the sum paid by a physician according to a document dated 1182.[26] As lowest grade he gives "1 plus ⅓ and ¼ dinars and 2 ḥabbas," that is, 1-⅝ dinars. We find this amount in the Geniza repeatedly for Saladin's time, but also 120 years earlier, when a Tunisian merchant in Old Cairo paid the poll tax for a Jewish packer who worked in the flax-growing center of Būṣīr, but who as a foreigner most probably had to deliver his jāliya in the capital.[27] According to the "Scroll" of the Norman proselyte Obadiah, in Baghdad, around 1100 the three classes of non-Muslims paid 1-½, 2-½, and 4-½ dinars, respectively.[28]

In practice, these rates were adjusted in conformity with local conditions. A passage from a letter, written in Alexandria in May, 1141, is instructive in this respect: "Rayḥān [a freedman or slave of the caliph or the vizier] promised the Jews and the Christians to obtain for them a properly ratified rescript vouching that the rates of the jizya would remain as they are at present and that no one would have the right to ask them for more. The rates should be the same as those fixed by the qadi al-Makīn [the well-known judge of Alexandria, who died in 1134])." [29] At approximately the same time there were complaints about gross misuse and embezzlement of the proceeds of the poll tax in that city. In a later letter the same writer alludes to both, namely, the attempt to raise the rates and the malpractices of its collection, when he says: "It was X. [an influential personage in Old Cairo] who saved the Jews from the jizya and the ways of its collection." [30]

It seems to me that such adjustments represented not only increases in the rates (as when the caliph al-Ḥākim doubled the poll tax for some time),[31] but occasionally also alleviations made with regard to the poverty of the affected population. A large section of the Jewish community of Alexandria consisted of people with low income, as proved by the Geniza for three centuries. It may well be that the qadi al-Makīn reduced the rates to some extent. When we find that both foreigners and persons native in Egypt registered for the jāliya not in the cities where they lived, but in smaller towns, we may safely assume that this practice was advantageous, most probably because of lower rates. Unfortunately, it is not possible for the time being to answer this question with the aid of the many details about actual payments given in the Geniza records, for these amounts may either include fines for arrears, or, on the contrary, represent only installments.

A few examples may suffice to illustrate this complex situation. A local Egyptian Jew, registered in a small town, who was momentarily out of cash, asks for a loan of 2 dinars for the payment of the current year's jāliya. As security he provides three books: a compendium of medicine, valued at 50 silver dirhems, the *Maqāmāt* of Ḥarīrī (a famous work of Arabic belles lettres), worth 13 dirhems, and a book of rabbinical law, whose price is not indicated. He promises to return the loan in a month's time. The three books combined betray the writer as an educated medical practitioner who would be expected to pay at least the rate for medium income, officially $2\frac{1}{12}$ dinars in Egypt. Thus we could assume that the amount of 2 dinars mentioned in the letter represents a reduced rate. The writer also remarks, however, that most of the year had already passed, which means that he had to pay arrears. Consequently, either the rate for medium income in that little town was considerably below 2 dinars, or the physician paid the jāliya for the poor, which is unlikely. Since the letter is from the late Ayyubid period, for which a flat rate of 2 dinars is attested in literary sources, this rate might have been in effect here, too. The same rate is found in two other Geniza documents from the 1230's.[32]

Similarly, when a religious slaughterer paid 1-¾ dinars around 1180, it may represent either a substantially reduced medium rate or a slighty raised minimum. Arrears could not be assumed in this case, because the person worked on the market and the accounts of his payments to the community for every week of the year have been preserved. Thus he could not escape the tax collectors.[33]

In the financial report of a parnās, or social officer, in Old Cairo for the last month of the Muslim year coinciding with April–May, 1182, we find the following items: "jāliya for X: 13 dirhems, balance of the jāliya for Y: 11-½ dirhems." Since we are here near the "closing of the accounts" (see below), it stands to reason that the first item, like the second, represents only a last installment.[34] But there is no complete certainty in the matter, particularly since similar sums are mentioned elsewhere as payments for the jāliya.[35]

The vital question of whether special rates existed for individual, meritorious cases cannot yet be decided with the material at our disposal. On the one hand we find many requests addressed to notables to use their influence on the tax officials with regard to a certain person or local community.[36] On the other hand, one wonders whether so much hardship could have existed had the granting of alleviations been common practice.

There are repeated references to fines for arrears. These were actually payments to the "ralliers" sent to summon the non-Muslims to the tax office. A man who was 30 dirhems in arrears had to pay one silver piece, *fiḍḍa,* every week. Another one writes that he gave the ḥushshār 4 dirhems at a time (perhaps four "ralliers" appeared together). Moreover, his house was offered for sale by auction.[37]

The extortion of payments of the poll tax in advance is thus far known from Geniza records only for Palestine and for the second quarter of the eleventh century, a period of anarchy and misrule. According to one report, payment was asked a full five months before the Muslim New Year on which it was due.[38]

It has often been asserted that the jāliya was collected by the non-Muslim communities and their official heads. This assumption is refuted by the evidence of the Geniza records which show that each individual was contacted by the state authorities directly and had to find the means for payment himself. A person lacking the required cash would sell or pawn his clothes or take from his wife's marriage portion, which he was not allowed to touch, or even appropriate material given to her for processing, such as raw silk that she was supposed to unravel.[39] If such supplementary sources were unavailable he would ask for an advance or a loan, and, if that was not forthcoming either, he would request of a person known for his munificence to contribute something himself and to introduce him to others.[40]

In addition to the references given, three more examples illustrate a subject so profusely represented in the Geniza records. A letter by a Jewish judge from Old Cairo recommends to a physician and scholar living in the provincial town of al-Maḥalla a young cantor, whose father had pursued the same profession: "When the bearer of this letter learned that the time of the collection of the poll tax was nearing, he sought rescue by traveling to the Rīf [the countryside] and appealing to the beneficence of God and of Israel. Before all others he is turning to the gate of God and your gate that you yourself should do for him all that is in your power and, moreover, help him by using your influential position. He is a fine young man, aspiring to noble goals, religious and devout and deserving of all the good you will do for him." A religious functionary in Bilbays, another provincial town, writes to his superior in Old Cairo: "What holds me back here is the hope to get the money for the poll tax for me and my son. Otherwise, I would have left the place, since one cannot really make a living here." Despite the reference to his son, the man must have been comparatively young, for he asks the addressee's permission to come to the capital to continue his studies with him. When a ḥazzān asks a benefactor to give him money for the poll tax, as he had done for two hundred others, he no doubt grossly exaggerates, but the very assertion proves how heavily this tax weighed on an impoverished subject population.[41]

When all efforts to obtain the sums due for the jāliya failed, the insolvent taxpayer went into hiding, an expedient very often encountered in the Geniza. One letter remarks: "This week the people experienced hardships because of the jāliya and we all were hiding in the houses." [42] This means of escape had many drawbacks, though. First of all, as we have seen, the fugitive's male relatives were held responsible for him. Second, he was unable to earn a livelihood, especially if his income was derived from a workshop or a store. When a person in such a predicament writes that his wife and children had died of hunger because he was in hiding and unable to maintain them, he meant it literally, not figuratively. Finally, such a person often owed money also to private creditors who would track him down even without the aid of the state police.[43]

Imprisonment, the routine punishment for failure to pay the poll tax, was not always confined to such short terms as those mentioned. We read about a cantor who had been in jail for two months because he had found no one to pay for him and was not set free despite a serious illness.[44]

In view of the Geniza evidence presented, which could easily be expanded, it is impossible to maintain that the local or territorial non-Muslim communities were in charge of the collection of the poll tax of their members and automatically took care of them in this respect. Still, the denominational units played an important role with regard to this branch of public revenue. First, direct and indirect references in the Geniza records prove that both the local muqaddams and the Nagid were consulted by the state authorities when they assessed the financial capacity of the taxpayers, and it goes without saying that the same must have been so with the Christian local and territorial leaders. The total amount to be levied in one area, like other items of the budget, was fixed in advance (otherwise it could not be farmed out), and explains why the Jewish authorities were so eager to register foreigners, who sojourned in a city even for a short while, as residents.[45] Moreover, although, in Egypt at least, the Jewish local leaders were not held responsible for the total amount of the poll tax to be raised—we do not read even about threats in this respect—they themselves regarded the payment of the jāliya for the poor as a holy obligation and a pious deed comparable with the highly meritorious ransoming of the captives. For the organization of this charity see above (chap. v, sec. C).

It is evident from many Geniza records that during long periods and in many places the assistance of the indigent taxpayer was not handled by the community, but was left to the vagaries of private philanthropy, as repeatedly illustrated. Conversely, there were times when a local non-Muslim community was charged with a global poll tax or, where its leaders saw themselves coerced, to take into their own hands a yearly collection, at least for a section of the community. When, owing to the dismal economic and security situation in eleventh-century Jerusalem, the population fluctuated spasmodically, a fixed sum was made mandatory on the Jewish community, and its leaders were held responsible for its payment, as we may conclude from desperate appeals for help to brethren in the Egyptian capital. "A heavy poll tax is imposed on us in a lump; but we are few, and unable to pay even a fraction of it. Every year we take loans [from Muslims] for interest so that the pilgrims to the Holy City should not be molested with warrants of arrest for nonpayment of the tax."[46] One letter from Jerusalem sent around 1040 is an appeal for a collection toward the repayment of such a loan incurred by the community together with the arrears due from previous years.[47]

A somewhat similar but still different situation is reflected in orders given by the Nagid Abraham Maimonides to his treasurer (and, by the way, written in his own hand): "Please pay immediately eighty-one dirhems to the qadi Shams al-Dīn [the director of revenue in Old Cairo] in order to close the account for the balance of the jāliya for the year 614." The Muslim year in question ended on March 29, 1218, and the paper is dated April 22. "Send thirty-five dirhems to the illustrious elder The Trusted to be taken from the revenue of the houses belonging to the community. This is the balance due for the Jewish poll tax of [New] Cairo to the government revenue office, for which The Trusted stood security with the consent of the community. Please rush. The claims of the revenue office suffer no delay." Even for a balance due, the sums mentioned are insignificant. Therefore we are certainly right in assuming that the Nagid took care solely of the jāliya incumbent on the poor. Since the community paid for them anyhow, they were not approached by the tax collectors individually. This assumption is corroborated by a third order of the Nagid, found in the same batch of papers (but written in Arabic characters) dealing with the ground rent paid for the poor living inside the old Roman fortress of Fustat.[48]

In the orders just mentioned the department in charge of the poll tax is referred to in a general way as "the government office." But it is evident from many records that this task was assigned to a group of special officials, one called 'āmil, who took care of the administrative side, while the technicalities accompanying cash payments were handled by a government cashier, who was styled *jahbadh al-jawālī* down to the twelfth century, whereas later on the general designation for banker or money changer, *ṣayrafī,* was used instead.[49] In case of irregularities the chief of police and even the governor of a city were approached. This was done in Alexandria, around 1140, when the 'āmil, with the connivance of the cashier, issued receipts to the taxpayers but left their names "open," that is, as still owing the tax in the government records in order to extort from them two payments, one for the state treasurer and one to be pocketed by himself and his accomplices. As the document shows, the local authorities approached had good intentions but their efforts were of no avail and an appeal was lodged with the central government.[50]

The express testimony of the Geniza letters to the severe hardship caused by the jāliya is confirmed by implicit evidence of the Arabic papyri. In his painstaking study quoted in note 1, A. Grohmann comes to the conclusion that the numerous data about arrears and installments in the payment of the jāliya indicate the straitened circumstances in which the large mass of taxpayers usually found itself. The papyri discussed by Grohmann refer to Christians.

In general it has to be emphasized that the subject of the poll tax occupies far more space in the Geniza records than one would anticipate. A very considerable section of the non-Muslim population must have been unable to pay it and often suffered humiliation and privation on its account. Whereas, in the higher circles, the prospects of appointment to leading government posts acted as an inducement for embracing Islam, the mass conversions in the lower classes might well have been caused in part by the intolerable burden of the poll tax.

Taxes and government impositions connected with economic activities have been treated in *Med. Soc.*, volume I, chapters ii and iii. Impositions on special occasions are referred to in the Geniza records, but as a rule we cannot make head or tail of them since the writers presuppose that the addressee has knowledge of the pertinent facts. Thus, one letter describes most vividly a requisition, *muṣādara*, carried out against a whole town, in which Muslims, Christians, Samaritans, and Jews were all affected, with the latter suffering even more than the other communities. All the clothing and the provisions of wheat and wine hoarded in the house of the writer's uncle were plundered; even the rope of the well was taken away. The authority ordering the requisition is circumspectly referred to as the biblical "Haman the wicked" so that we are left in the dark as to his identity.[51] When, in a letter from Alexandria, dated October 21, 1219, we read about a "voluntary contribution" of 6,000 dinars collected from "the people of the city," the date makes it evident that it was a war effort in connection with the attack of the Crusaders on Damietta, taken by them a few weeks later. "The people of Alexandria" must mean the whole population, for a letter written about 1195 tells about the share in a weekly tribute to be paid by the Jewish community (*milla*, as called here) which, although amounting to only 7 dinars, was regarded as a heavy burden on the decimated and impoverished community.[52]

Finally, in war and peace alike there were occasions when the civil population was summoned to do corvée, enforced and unpaid labor for the government or for whomsoever was in power. "The markets are closed and no one is to be seen in the streets, for anyone making an appearance is taken to digging trenches," says one letter referring to a state of war in other passages.[53] Nowhere is there an allusion to the special singling out of non-Muslim minorities for such duties. On the contrary, a query addressed to Maimonides refers to a generally accepted custom that Jews were not forced "to dig trenches and to pull down walls" on Sabbaths and holidays. This tallies with the report of a German traveler who visited Cairo after Acre had been taken by the Mamluks in 1291 and reports that the prisoners were forced to work on buildings, but the Jews were given freedom to observe their Sabbath.[54] It is natural that local people tried to devolve such unpleasant duties on foreigners. A group of workmen who were newcomers to a provincial town complain: "We were dragged to the corvées, beaten with sticks and told: you do the work for the sultan." The same group asserts that the old-timers did not permit them to exercise their crafts.[55]

Besides the corvée, common all over the Middle East to the beginning of the twentieth century, the Geniza refers to another form of enforced labor about which we are less well informed: the mandatory recruitment of skilled artisans for government workshops. The plight of one such man is told in *Med. Soc.*, I, 82. I suspect that the many persons described as (government) employees without further definition were craftsmen working for the government.[56]

Next to the poll tax the appropriation of estates by the government caused constant concern to the people speaking to us through the Geniza records. This affliction was by no means confined to the religious minorities, as we know only too well from Muslim literature. But the Christians and Jews had to fight to preserve the right to have their cases of inheritance treated according to their own law and before their own courts. Although practice varied widely in different places and times, it seems that during the Fatimid period this right was generally recognized, although it had to be reinforced from time to time by caliphal rescripts. Al-Malik al-Afḍal, whose reputedly beneficial regime has been referred to so often in this book, was credited with stopping the illegal appropriation of estates by the government.[57] While this applied to the population as a whole, the Geniza reveals that measures were taken under his reign to safeguard the specific rights of non-Muslims as well. His court physician, the Nagid Mevōrākh, obtained from him an order reemphasizing the exclusive rights of Jewish authorities to deal with the estates of alien Jews who had died in the country. When, after Mevōrākh's death and in the wake of some dispute among the dead foreigner's acquaintances, the Alexandrian qadi's Office of Estates appropriated the property left, recourse was immediately sought with the central government in the capital. On that occasion we hear that only a short time before the Christians in Alexandria, as well as those in Upper Egypt, Tinnīs, and Damietta, had received rescripts confirming that no government office was to interfere with estates of persons of their denomination. This remark, written around 1115, proves that there had been many such attempts and that each region had to fight separately to have its rights reconfirmed.[58] This question must be studied in the general context of the interplay of laws and authorities to be observed in the Geniza records.

D. COMMUNAL AUTONOMY AND GOVERNMENT CONTROL

1. *The Interplay of Laws*

The fight of the Christian and Jewish communities for the right to apply their own laws of inheritance had its good reasons. In certain cases, Muslim law gave the government opportunity to lay claims on a part or all of the estate, and, in addition, opened the door for arbitrary and unscrupulous practices. A few examples selected from the relevant Geniza records illustrate the complex situation.

According to Muslim law, a woman is worth half a man. Therefore, a daughter can never inherit more than half her father's estate. If no other heirs are extant the other half falls to the government. According to Jewish law, an only daughter inherited the entire estate of her father. No wonder the Muslim authorities were eager to apply their own law. In addition, they would not investigate too deeply whether other heirs existed or whether the possessions left actually belonged to the intestate or not. In view of all this, any interference by the Office of Estates was dreaded as harmful.

In 1058, an Egyptian Jewish merchant entrusted a business friend returning to his native Sicily with a large consignment of Oriental spices, drugs, and other goods. The agent died on the high sea, and the ship arrived in Tripoli, Libya, instead of Sicily. The Jewish authorities in Tripoli sequestered everything carried by the deceased in order to guard the rights of his widow and only daughter back in Sicily. The very fact that "the Jewish court and elders" were able to take possession of the goods of the foreigner proves that in those days the right of the non-Muslim communities to deal with the estates of their coreligionists was still recognized in principle. The Egyptian merchant tried to get his shipment back, but the Jewish authorities in Tripoli refused to return it except on the basis of a full-fledged lawsuit between the merchant and the representatives of the widow and the orphan, a protracted affair. In order to protect their countryman, the rabbinical court in Old Cairo turned to the Jewish high court in Jerusalem. The reasoning of the Cairene court was the following: Any delay in the return of the goods of the Egyptian Jewish merchant might lead to their confiscation by the Muslim government of Tripoli who would use the pretext either that they belonged to a foreigner (and would not care to inquire whether they really had been his property) or that the heir was a female (who had claim on only half the estate of her father). Since the original of the letter has been found in the Geniza together with a draft concerning the same matter, it is likely that the Jewish court of Tripoli had accepted the reasoning of its Cairene colleagues before the latter had opportunity to dispatch the appeal to Jerusalem.[1]

The practice of Muslim governments to seize a part of an inheritance when only female heirs were left is attested to by the Geniza for the late tenth, or early eleventh, century. This happened to the estate of the freedman Bundār, about which a detailed, but much mutilated document has been preserved.[2] Around 1200, Maimonides mentions in one of his responsa as a well-known fact that the Office of Estates in the locality concerned used to confiscate one-half the property left when an only daughter was the heir.[3]

A particularly interesting case, which illustrates also the interplay of government and communal jurisdiction, is described in a Geniza document dated 1231. A woman had left a daughter and a sister. According to Muslim law the former was entitled to one-half, the latter to one-sixth, making a total of two-thirds of the estate. Accordingly, the government appropriated one-third of a house the dead woman had possessed. In actuality, she had been the proprietor of two houses. During her lifetime, in order to restrict government seizure of her estate to the possible minimum, she had given her sister the other house as a gift. In the 1231 document, the sister declares in a Jewish court that she laid no claim on the estate handled by the government office, since she had received her share before.[4]

By their very nature, most cases of succession are complicated. Since it was taken for granted that the government would appropriate a part of the estate when there were only female heirs, and since the Muslim authorities did not want to be bothered too much with the intricacies of administrative practice superimposed on Jewish law, we read about agreements on flat sums between the two authorities. According to Jewish law a widow was not an heir, but was entitled to an indemnity fixed in her marriage contract, which was regarded as a debt and, as such, had precedence over the claims of the heirs. Some Geniza documents show that this principle was recognized by the Office of Estates. In an agreement on a flat sum between the latter and "the elders of the [Jewish] community," dated 1203, the balance left to the survivors by the state was presumably the share of the only daughter, which was approximately equal to that of the state, and the widow's indemnity, which was considerably higher.[5]

We find private persons, too, engaged in high-handed practices against orphans. In an unfortunately much damaged petition to a

Jewish notable, a representative of two female heirs reports that two ruins belonging to the women's estate were appropriated during the period of their minority by an oppressive Muslim, who had converted one of the ruins into a stable for horses of the sultan's cavalry. As usual, the case was complicated. Their mother, who had no right to do so, had sold those ruins to a Jew before they were taken by the Muslim. The very fact that the sisters, now grown up, expected to obtain their right shows that the Muslim state—we are in early Ayyubid times—respected law when there was someone ready and able to fight for it.[6]

It was not only in cases of females as sole heirs that the interference of the government Office of Estates was dreaded. It was the same with male heirs, and even where there was no discrepancy at all between Jewish and Muslim law. An heir who informs his correspondent that no one, the government included, had any claim on his inheritance, adds resignedly that, as his case stood, there was only the question whether the government would take one-half or three-eighths.[7] An old man, who was supported by his nephew out of the estate of his late brother, lost this support when the nephew died and the family of the deceased was not prepared to continue the help. But the old man was afraid of invoking the help of the government. When the heir was a son, a brother had no legal claims according to both Muslim and Jewish law. Still, it was assumed that, if approached, the Office of Estates would intervene and use the opportunity to appropriate a lion's share of the remaining estate. The letter is addressed to the judge Elijah b. Zechariah, requesting him to submit the matter to the Nagid Abraham Maimonides for redress; otherwise, it would finally reach the Muslim authorities.[8] Around 1040, a merchant from Tunisia applies to the head of the Jewish community in Old Cairo to look after the goods of a countryman of his, on which the qadi of Tyre, Lebanon, had laid his hand. We have already met that qadi as the proprietor of a large ship, a warehouse, and a bourse. Thus, it is not clear whether the man had acted in his capacity as Muslim judge or as representative of the merchants.[9]

The confiscation by the state of the goods of a merchant who had died in a foreign country was in itself a conflict of laws. According to the concept that law was personal and not territorial, the very notion of a foreigner did not apply to the sphere of the law of personal status. All the local authorities had to do was to let the representatives of the denomination to which the dead man belonged deal with his estate. This principle was indeed recognized and reinforced by rescripts granted Jews and Christians under al-Malik al-Afḍal. A legal opinion given by Muslim experts of law in the time of Saladin emphasizes again the exclusive right of the non-Muslim communities to handle their members' estates.[10] In 1143, still under Fatimid rule, the goods of a silk merchant which had been salvaged when he was drowned near Alexandria were turned over to the Jewish authorities by the Office of Estates in that city for the benefit of his legal heirs. The document states, however, that this was done only after a caliphal rescript had been issued in that matter. While this procedure was in conformity with the centralization of the Muslim judiciary, it also indicated that although the rights of the non-Muslim communities in matters of inheritance were respected in principle, their actual implementation required the intervention of the highest quarters.[11] With the progressive deterioration of the legal status of the non-Muslim minorities (and that of Islamic justice in general), estates were confiscated simply when the legal heirs happened not to be present at the time of a person's demise.[12]

The direct interference of Muslim authorities in the legal matters of non-Muslims, with the exception of the field of inheritance, is less felt in the Geniza records than the opposite process: the application to government courts by Jews. The vast material on the subject can be grouped under three different heads. First, persons approached a government court when the law applied there was more advantageous to them. Second, for litigants unsuccessful in a lawsuit in the Jewish court, the government served as a kind of court of appeal; or vice versa, when the opposite party refused to appear before the Jewish court, government was approached with the request to force him to do so. Finally, deeds were made out at a government court (or, concurrently there and before a Jewish authority) in order to safeguard their legality and to have them as an instrument of proof should litigation at a government court ensue.

The first point is best illustrated by examples from the field of succession. The Muslim and Jewish laws of inheritance differed not only with respect to females as sole heirs, but in many other points as well. This contrast owed to their entirely different origins. Israelite law, like the Roman and Germanic, grew in a peasants' society, which is eager to hold an estate together in an agricultural unit large enough to sustain a family. For this reason, laws of inheritance give the firstborn preferential treatment, a trait unknown to Muslim law. On the other hand, the ancient Arabs were Bedouins and merchants whose possessions were flocks, goods, and cash, which, unlike land, lent themselves easily to division. Moreover, an inheritance was regarded as a kind of spoil in the distribution of which numerous members of a clan participated. Thus Muslim law granted many persons excluded by Jewish law a share in the succession. It was natural that in such cases Jews tried to take advantage of the privileges offered to them by the law of Islam. For example, if a son and a daughter were the heirs, according to the ancient Jewish peasants' law the son took the whole estate, normally the father's farm, but he was under the obligation to provide his sister with a marriage portion. In Islam, according to the principle that a female was worth half a male, the brother received two-thirds of the estate and the sister one-third. To forestall a conflict between his children arising from the discrepancy in coexistent laws, a Jewish father would will two-thirds of his property to his son and one-third to his daughter, or provide the latter with a house and other parts of her marriage portion early in life. Similarly, Jewish courts would compensate sisters, or the families of sisters, with an appropriate share in order to avoid the interference of government agencies.[13] These precautionary measures must have been successful, for cases of a sister claiming a share in an inheritage from her brother in a Muslim court are extremely rare.[14] One must bear in mind that lawsuits of a sister against a brother were almost unheard of in this period, since he was regarded as her natural protector against her husband.

When a father "sells" to his firstborn one-half a house, but wills to two others one-quarter each, it is evident that the "sale" was a formality intended to safeguard the rights of the firstborn and to deprive the others of the possibility of claiming equal shares in a Muslim court.[15] When Jewish authorities allot a small part of the estate of a man whose only heir was a daughter to the son of his paternal uncle, they no doubt acted so because Muslim law granted the nephew this right.[16] A protracted lawsuit between a father and his son over the latter's inheritance from his mother, grandmother, and great-grandmother was argued before a Muslim qadi, but was finally settled in a Jewish court on December 31, 1100. Naturally, we read in the Geniza records only about cases connected in some way or another with Jewish courts.[17]

To be accurate, the protracted lawsuit was originally an appeal to Muslim authorities against the decisions of a Jewish court. Such appeals were made even in family matters, normally the prerogative of the denominational judiciary. In Maimonides' times, when a Kohen was refused by Jewish authorities the permission to marry a divorcee (prohibited by Jewish law) he contracted the marriage in a Muslim court. A similar occurrence is told in an earlier Geniza letter.[18] Conversely, in 1042, a Jewish judge and ḥazzān in Alexandria had to testify before a qadi that there were no objections to the marriage of a certain woman who had been denounced as being legally bound to another man.[19] When a settlement was reached in 1052 between a husband and his former wife concerning the maintenance and education of their five-year-old boy, the divorcee promised not to trouble the contracting partner with appeals to a Muslim court or to the government and was menaced with excommunication if she did.[20] Another divorcee who laid claim to the house in which her former husband lived threatened "to meet the sultan" in this matter, which could mean (the document is dated 1085) that she intended to apply directly to the viceroy Badr al-Jamālī in one of his public audiences when he was accessible even to persons of low rank.[21] There is no need for references to appeals to Muslim judges in commercial matters.[22]

Non-Muslims appeared and argued in Muslim courts in person or were represented by a Muslim attorney.[23] In exceptional circumstances, Jewish witnesses were admitted in matters affecting Jewish parties.[24]

In the great majority of cases mentioned in the Geniza, Jews made use of the Muslim judiciary not for litigation, but for the concluding of contracts. Even the Jewish community chest stipulated in an agreement made with a tenant in 1156 that a contract of lease should be written *fi 'l-muslimīn,* before a Muslim authority.[25] The Geniza record mostly represents a settlement in which one party hands over to the other "the document written according to gentile [Muslim] law" granting at the same time some delay in payment or discount, after the other party had fulfilled, or promised to fulfill, the obligations emanating from the new agreement.[26]

It was common practice to make contracts before Muslim and Jewish authorities concurrently. Business partnerships concluded in this way are referred to in a Geniza document written in Alexandria in 1077 and in a query submitted to Maimonides about a hundred years later.[27] Both the contraction of a debt in Alexandria and its settlement in Old Cairo were arranged before the two authorities in 1129.[28] A man who had married his slave girl adopted her two daughters and made them his sole heirs in Jewish and Muslim courts.[29] The transfer of houses was made almost regularly in this way and many documents to this effect have been preserved.

A settlement made in the Egyptian town of Bilbays in 1239 is particularly illustrative of the practices described. A man had contracted a debt in both Jewish and Muslim courts and given a house as security. When, after four years, he was unable to pay, he was forced by the Muslim court to renounce the house. But before the Jewish court, an agreement was reached giving the debtor the right to buy the house back in the course of twelve years. When an Arabic *ḥujja,* or legal document, containing all the details of a case is attached to a Jewish record merely summarizing its upshot, it stands to reason that the Jewish court was approached solely out of religious scruples. Similarly, when a contract presupposing hidden interest is made between two Jews and a Muslim before a rabbinical court in Alexandria, it was probably done to give the transaction additional force.[30]

In principle, Christian and Jewish authorities alike regarded any application to a Muslim court by one of their flock as a religious offense. As we have already seen, this transgression was liable to be punished with excommunication.[31] In quite a number of Geniza records, the contracting parties undertake not to apply to a gentile court. This was done not only in matters of family law and inheritance (documents dated 1052, 1117, and 1055), but also with regard to purely commercial matters (dated 1027, 1052, and 1098). The very fact that such provisions were stipulated in contracts proves, though, how common the practice of turning to the state judiciary had become, and we are not astonished to find a judge newly transferred to al-Maḥalla stating with relief that his flock apply solely to him and never "transgress" to a Muslim court.[32] There are many references to this fact in the responsa of the Gaons and those of Moses and Abraham Maimonides, and its discussion betrays many shades of opinion. The different views on this complicated problem voiced in those sources can be summarized as follows: While, in principle, only the denominational courts had religiously approved competence, it was permitted and even recommendable to apply to the state authorities when the causes of justice and expediency were served by such a step.

The numerous relevant Geniza records are in the same vein. Almost all the powers of attorney made out in Jewish courts allow the appointee to bring the person or persons accused before a gentile court. Letters of attorney were written mostly in extreme cases after all other means had failed. Therefore, it was assumed that only the threat of arraignment by a government authority would bring the recalcitrant debtor to reason. The creditor would deposit his "Arabic legal proofs," that is, documents written by a Muslim notary and witnessed by Muslims, with the Jewish court in deference to Jewish jurisdiction, but received the permission to make use of them in a Muslim court should the opposing party not turn up at the *bēth dīn.*[33] When an Iraqian Gaon gave a decision in 1166 in a case of inheritance occurring in Egypt, he instructed the local court to take recourse to the government if the losing party disobeyed his instructions.[34] Above we read of a similar action taken even in the case of disrespect shown to Jewish religion.[35]

The clause giving the bearer the right to apply to a Muslim court, found in so many letters of attorney, was not entirely for inner consumption. The Muslim authorities on their side did not accept any Jewish case indiscriminately and, as the Geniza shows, there was a good deal of cooperation between the state and the denominational courts. A slave girl, who claimed to be Jewish, was sent by a Muslim judge back to his Jewish colleague.[36] When two parties, after having made a settlement in the Jewish court of Alexandria in 1152, wanted to make a different one before the qadi "according to the noble religion of the Muslims," the qadi sent his messengers first to the rabbinate, where a declaration, properly fortified by the symbolic purchase, was deposited by the parties acknowledging that they annulled their former arrangements.[37] A female heir, who felt herself wronged by a Jewish judge to the advantage of her late father's business partners and who had applied to the qadi of Alexandria, was favorably treated by the qadi, but was directed for a final settlement to the Nagid Mevōrākh in the capital.[38] There is no need to emphasize that such cooperation prevailed particularly in the realm of family law.[39] Sometimes it was apt to cause the Jewish judge twinges of conscience. Should he submit his findings to his Muslim colleague when he knew that this would lead to the imprisonment of one of the parties? [40] From the same query and other sources it seems that a false oath before a Muslim court was not permissible under any circumstances.[41]

The Geniza records also report about gentiles, both Christians and Muslims, making settlements with a Jewish party before a Jewish court, but such cases seem to have been exceptional.[42]

2. *How Much Autonomy?*

A postscript to a letter, sent in 1016–1017 by the representative of the Baghdadian yeshivas in Qayrawān to Ibn 'Awkal, the head of the African diocese (who had his seat in Old Cairo), contains this request: A Jewish merchant from Baghdad had died in Sijilmāsa, Morocco, the other end of the Muslim world. The Jewish authorities there had informed the writer of the possessions left by the deceased in that city. In addition, the traveler had left goods with merchants in Qayrawān. The writer now asks Ibn 'Awkal to request the Jewish authorities in Baghdad either to appoint a legal representative for the heirs or to transmit their names and claims to the Nagid of Tunisia, its chief Jewish judge, and to the elders of Qayrawān, all of whom would then take care of the matter.[1]

This unassuming piece of correspondence enforces the statement made on the first page of this volume, namely, that the non-Muslim communities formed a state not only within a Muslim state, but also beyond its confines. Months of travel separated Baghdad from Qayrawān, and the latter from Sijilmāsa. Several frontiers of mutually hostile countries had to be traversed. Still, the disposal of the deceased's estate is treated here as an entirely Jewish affair. No reference is made to the governments of the countries concerned. Instead, all the Jewish authorities, religious and lay, ecumenical, territorial, and local, are involved. Could there be a more eloquent testimony to the autonomous character of a non-Muslim community within a Muslim state, as revealed by Geniza documents?

Naturally, this is not the whole story. Looking back on the varied material assembled in this volume one turns cautious and feels that it is not easy to discern how much of the communal life described here was the fruit of long-standing tradition and inner strength and how much was due to outside pressures and models. Where pre-Islamic precedents, parallels from Christian countries, or definitely un-Islamic elements prevail, autonomous developments should be assumed. The yeshiva was pre-Islamic, and, even during the heyday of Islam, differed completely from its Islamic counterpart, the madrasa (as far as it could be compared with the yeshiva at all). Therefore, the ecumenical Jewish authority and all that is connected with it, in particular, the diocesan organization of the diaspora, which later gave rise to religious and secular territorial heads, must be regarded as essentially autochthonous. The Jewish local community, with the prominent participation of the laity in all its functions, is age-old and, as far as our present knowledge goes, nothing comparable with it existed in Islam. The works of charity described in this volume had their roots in talmudic ordinances and were matched by those practiced by Jews in Christian countries, although we are less well informed about them since a Geniza has not yet been found in Europe. Jewish education grew organically out of the needs and practices of Jewish religion many centuries prior to the rise of Islam, but was open to Islamic influences because of the close affinity between the two religions. Secular education within the Jewish community was identical with the courses of study in the corresponding social milieus of Muslims and Christians.

The impact of the environment was strongest where the contacts were broadest: in the economic, legal, and political spheres. Ultimately, all power and authority rested with the state. But before the state's influence can be appraised, some preliminary questions must be asked: What was the character of this state? How far was it willing and able to occupy itself with its non-Muslim subjects?

In our days, most inhabitants of the globe live either under totalitarian systems or in welfare states. In one way or another, the personal fortunes of the individual citizen are affected by the state day in and day out. Things being so we are hardly able to envisage a state entirely different from what we are accustomed to. The Muslim state, like most others in the past, was concerned mainly with supplying two precious commodities: security and justice. Not more. The welfare of people—providing them with food, clothing, shelter, medical care, education, and other needs of life—was the concern of God. God devolved his task on human charity, obligatory on everyone, in the first place, of course, on those with power and wealth. The state as such had contact with its subjects only in two respects: it needed their money in order to maintain court, army, administration, and judiciary, and provided them with police and juridical protection—if asked for. The institution of public prosecutor was unknown. Instead, every Muslim was under the obligation "to order people to act properly and to prevent them from acting improperly." This important koranic precept could be and was understood and applied in very different ways by both individuals and whole groups. The Almohads of North Africa coerced Christians and Jews to accept Islam and put to death Muslims who refused to conform with their particular creed. The Fatimids of Egypt were of the opposite type. They excelled in laissez-faire, out of indolence, it seems, rather than conviction. The far-reaching degree of autonomy enjoyed by the Jews (and, of course, the Christians) during their rule has a very simple explanation: their Muslim subjects, too, were left mostly to their own devices.

The data about communal life culled from the Geniza should be understood in the light of this situation. Everyone wishing to exercise authority, the exilarch, the Gaons of Baghdad and Jerusalem, territorial and local leaders, and, of course, the Christian patriarchs and other dignitaries, needed the backing of the state. But it was the person seeking appointment, or his followers, who were eager to obtain such confirmation; the state itself was not particularly interested in providing the dhimmīs, or non-Muslim groups, with a strong organization. The assumption that it was the Muslim state that united the Jewish congregations into local communities shows very little understanding of the nature of both. At the reverse, we see that a caliphal rescript is granted to dissenters,[2] or that petitions are addressed to a Fatimid caliph with the request not to recognize a secessionist juridical authority,[3] or that a public meeting is held condemning a similar attempt.[4] The vacillating attitude of the Fatimid caliphs toward the controversies of the Rabbanites and Karaites in Palestine, granting privileges once to one party and once to another, also betrays little care for the upkeep of peace. Certainly there was no government initiative, for the relevant decrees were given at the request of the interested parties. The same happened during the three years of communal strife resulting from the rivalry between the Palestinian Gaons Solomon b. Judah and Nathan b. Abraham (1038-1041). Once, at the request of one or two of the parties, a high Jewish personage in Cairo, apparently a government official, was appointed to put the affair in order. But he did nothing, and no further action was taken by the central government. After some time, the crisis came to a head anew and the government was approached again by both sides. Finally, the authority of the legitimate Gaon was upheld by the government, but, as the document reveals, the settlement between the parties resulted from the intervention of the Jewish laity.[5]

Since the local community leaders were appointed or confirmed in their position by the Gaon of Jerusalem, they were quasi government officials, and misgivings about them were voiced before the Muslim authorities in the form of complaints over the Gaon who was responsible for them (Solomon b. Judah).[6] Conversely, when, in 1134, the prerogatives of Maṣlīaḥ, the head of the Palestinian yeshiva, who then had his seat in (New) Cairo, were not respected in Aden, his supporters, who happened to pass through that south-Arabian port on their way back from India, threatened to apply to the local Muslim authorities for redress.[7] Confirmation of local leaders by the state is rarely mentioned during the Fatimid period, and then only in the case of dissension. When Abraham (III) b. Nathan (II), originally a high dignitary of the Palestinian yeshiva, met with much opposition while trying to create for himself a position in Egypt, he requested Nahray b. Nissīm to secure for him "government papers."[8]

The position seems to have changed slightly under the Ayyubids. In Saladin's time, a Jewish judge in Alexandria declares having received a letter of appointment from no one except the sultan (meaning: none from a Jewish authority), which he had presented to the governor of the city.[9] It seems that Saladin himself, when he was still vizier of the last Fatimid caliph, appointed a Jewish muqaddam in Minyat Ziftā, who was, however, soon replaced by the local man who had held the position before.[10] A French rabbi, chosen by the Nagid Abraham Maimonides as one of the three Jewish judges of Alexandria, who was incurring difficulties with one of his colleagues wants to have a public confirmation by a "gentile writ."[11] In accordance with this situation Jewish judges received, or expected to receive, a salary or pension from the Ayyubid rulers. But there seems to have been no regularity in this matter.[12]

The dangerous practice of turning to the Muslim government even in controversies of a purely religious nature became rampant in Ayyubid times. The Ayyubids were Kurds and staunch supporters of strict orthodoxy and the preservation of established rites. No wonder that the opponents of innovations in the Jewish cult were confident to have the ear of a similarly minded government. A case in point is the rescript of a sultan in favor of the retaining of the time-honored poetical insertions into the synagogue liturgy, which reformers, for various reasons, wished to abolish, or, at least, to reduce in size.[13] The Geniza has indeed preserved a query written in Arabic characters and addressed to one 'Imād al-Dīn, entitled *muftī dawlat amīr al-Mu'minīn,* "legal expert of the realm of the caliph," containing this question: Jewish prayer on workdays, Sabbaths, and holidays follows ancient patterns and long-established customs. Now certain people want to introduce changes. Are such innovations permissible "in the days of Islam, may God make them permanent"? The expected answer was, of course, that any "innovation" was anathema.[14]

Even more serious was the action taken with the Ayyubid government by the adversaries of the Nagid Abraham Maimonides, using as pretext his pietist reforms. Abraham strove to give the service a strictly devotional character. The members of the congregation should be seated in rows facing the Holy Ark (and not along the walls facing each other, as is still the custom in Oriental synagogues), cushions and pillows should be banned, and, when seated at all, everyone should maintain an upright position. Prosternations and genuflections, as of old, should underline the character of the prayer as "service," and copious ablutions precede them—stressing man's need for inner purification. The text of the liturgy was also to be reformed. The opponents of these measures, led by Abraham Maimonides' political foes, approached the sultan al-Malik al-'Ādil (d. 1218), and the Nagid took pains to explain that his reforms were a matter of personal religion and confined to his private synagogue; he did not use his office in order to exercise pressure on anyone to make changes in his established customs. How aware Abraham was of the dangerous character of such an accusation may be gauged from the fact that he had "the whole community, almost 200 persons" sign an appropriate declaration.[15]

None of Abraham Maimonides' religious reforms went through. But it was not so much the attitude of the government, as the opposition of the Jewish community of Egypt that frustrated his efforts. How little even the Ayyubid government was concerned with the inner affairs of the non-Muslim communities may be decided from the contemporary history of the Coptic church: starting in 1216, the see of the patriarch of Alexandria remained vacant for nineteen years, that is, during most of the time of al-Malik al-Kāmil, one of the most energetic Muslim rulers of Egypt.[16] All in all, I believe, it is fair to say that while the Christians and Jews shared with their Muslim compatriots their language, economy, and most of their social notions and habits, their communal life was left mainly to their own initiative.

APPENDIXES

Author's Note

Appendixes A, B, and C list and describe the main sources on which chapter v, section C, "The Social Services," is based. Items 1–112 of Appendix A and 1–51 of Appendix B were included in my paper "The Social Services of the Jewish Community as Reflected in the Cairo Geniza Records," *JSS*, 26 (1964), 3–22, 67–86, but appear here in greatly enlarged form. Since that article and the lists accompanying it have been copiously used and referred to, I decided not to change the order and numeration of the sources as given there. Material that was excluded from that article either because I regarded it as unsuitable for publication in a periodical or because I found it later in the course of subsequent research is contained in the supplements to these appendixes, which, like the original lists, are arranged in approximately chronological order. Some items were brought to my notice by E. Ashtor, *Zion*, 30 (1965), 151. Appendix C is new, but some of the material listed in it has of course been used in the article on the social services mentioned above.

The sources included in appendixes A, B, and C, as far as their dates could be ascertained exactly or approximately, seem to belong to six different periods:

		Number of documents
I. 1000–1050		
A	1–9, 98, 113–124, 163, 169, 170, 175, 178	27
B	1–10, 52, 55, 56, 57*a–c*, 100, 108	18
C	1–11, 121	12
Total		57
II. 1050–1100		
A	10–16, 111, 171, 179	10
B	12–16, 59, 60, 106, 107	9
C	12–22, 79, 95–97, 115, 119–120, 122–125, 137, 138	24
Total		43
III. 1100–1165		
A	17–24, 99, 106, 108, 125–136, 164, 165, 176–177, 180–182	30
B	17–34, 61–69, 95, 96, 101	30
C	23–30, 80, 81, 93–94, 133–135	15
Total		75

IV. 1165–1200		
A	25–41, 100–104, 112, 137–144, 160, 166, 167, 172	35
B	35–36, 70–73, 102	7
C	31–35, 82–85, 116, 126, 139	12
	Total	54
V. 1200–1266		
A	42–97, 105, 109, 145–157, 183–184	73
B	37–51, 74–90, 97–98, 103–105	37
C	36–62, 66, 86–89, 98, 99, 114, 117, 127–128, 136, 140	40
	Total	150
VI. Later		
A	110, 161, 173–174	4
B	92, 100	2
C	67–78, 100–112, 129–132	29
	Total	35
Number of dated or datable documents		414
Not datable		20
	Grand total	434

Appendix A

DOCUMENTS REGARDING CHARITABLE FOUNDATIONS (MAINLY HOUSES)

(Chap. v, sec. C, 3)

If not otherwise stated, the reference is to the Jewish community of Old Cairo. Documents arranged in approximate chronological order.

1000–1050

1. TS 16.115, ed. S. Assaf, *Tarbiz,* 9 (1938), 206–8*. Deathbed declaration of a woman willing one-third of a house belonging to her to the Babylonian and Palestinian synagogues of Old Cairo in equal shares. Most of the remaining two-thirds went to relatives, one-eighth to a poor girl in order to enable her to marry, and one-twelfth was reserved for the expenditure on the burial of the testator in Jerusalem (1006).

2. Bodl. MS Heb. a 3 (Cat. 2873), f. 37, ed. S. A. Wertheimer, *Ginze Yerushalayim* (Jerusalem), 3 (1902), 15–16; *Sefer ha-Yishuv* (Jerusalem, 1944), pp. 51–52. Deposition in the Jewish court of Tyre, Lebanon, by two brothers to the effect that their father had donated the family home in Aleppo, Syria, to the Great Synagogue in that town (1028).

3. TS Arabic 18(1), f. 35 and TS 20.96 (both fragments form part of one document), ed. S. D. Goitein, *Eretz-Israel* (Jerusalem), 7 (1964), 83–87. The history of the houses in possession of the synagogue of the Palestinians in Old Cairo up to 1039. A fragment of another copy of this priceless document is preserved in ENA 2738, f. 2.

No mention is made of the property referred to in A 1. In the Hebrew translation I took *sm'nh,* l. 14, as *sammāna,* seller of melted butter. Since the word is not preceded by the article I prefer now to take it as a name: *Sumāna,* quail, a female name. For *darbī,* l. 15, read *dhahabī* (so rightly E. Ashtor, *Zion,* 30 [1965], 75 n. 130).

4. TS Arabic Box 18 (1), f. 181: Revenue from houses belonging to the synagogue for the years 1037–1039.

5. Bodl. MS Heb. b 11 (Cat. 2874), f. 5. Verso detailed, but fragmentary,

draft in Arabic characters of a report on rents received by the writer for the community in the Muslim year (4)32 (ended on Aug. 30, 1041) with summaries of previous years. The revenue collected in A.H. 432 was 19 dinars (corresponded to ca. 750 dirhems) and 1,211½ *waraq* dirhems (ll. 4–5). The arrears totaled 916 dirhems (l. 24).

Recto contains calligraphic and most detailed accounts of building operations (35 complete, 7 fragmentary lines) in large Hebrew characters. Last date mentioned: end of Elul (1)351 (Era of the Documents = Aug. 27, 1040). The document certainly was displayed for many months in the synagogue; after it had served its purpose, the reverse side was used by the writer for his draft. The Arabic hand is strong and beautiful (and found, by the way, in some important Geniza fragments of the period) and somehow similar in character to the Hebrew. I assume that both texts were written by the same official.

I analyzed the building accounts in *Eretz-Israel* 7 (1964), 88.

6. TS 20.168. "List of the sums collected by me, the cantor Ben Shekhanya, from the arrears and rents due from the compound of the synagogue of the Palestinians for four months, Jumādā I–Shawwāl 434" (Jan. 16–May 13, 1043). Only the first 32 lines of this document, which was written in huge characters and certainly destined for public display, have been preserved. They contain twenty items for the month preceding Jan. 16, and three, totaling 155½ dirhems, for the four months following. Some tenants owed rent for more remote periods.

7. TS K 15, f. 45. A similar list in the same hand and referring largely to the same parties. Reverse side: expenditures for repairs. The list shows how many parties lived in each house.

8. TS K 25, f. 169. Part of a similar list, but written in a more orderly fashion. Many names identical with A 4, 6, and 7. Also mentions rooms not rented.

9. TS 8 J 13, f. 18. Accounts, in the handwriting of Ben Shekhanya, of repairs in the synagogue and in a house belonging to it not mentioned in the preceding sections (but is in A 118, l. 27, and A 121, l. 7, "the House of the Blue-eyed"). Grapes, costing 1 dinar (dinar is written out in full), were made into wine that was to be used in the synagogue service and which was stored in jugs, an item also listed. Muḥarram (43)6 = Aug., 1044. August was the vintage month in Egypt.

1050–1100

10. TS Misc. Box 8, f. 86. Payments of tenants (among them at least one Muslim) in houses belonging to the community during 1058–1059 (in the clumsy hand of the parnas Eli ha-Kohen b. Yaḥyā-Ḥayyīm [see Index]).

The list refers to apartments, not houses. Thus it is not evident from it whether new estate had been acquired by the community since 1044.

11*a*. Dropsie 392. Letter from Jerusalem, signed by Joseph he-ḥāvēr b.

Solomon Gaon and ten others, inquiring about the revenue from a house in Old Cairo which had been donated to the poor of the Holy City (before 1042, when Joseph already had another title).

11*b*. TS NS J 119. Left half of a calligraphic letter from Jerusalem to Abū Kathīr Ephraim al-ḥāvēr b. Maḥfūẓ (more commonly: Shemarya), the leader of the Palestinian community in Fustat, informing him that neither the dinars from the rent of "The House," nor those pledged in the Egyptian capital on the Feast (of Passover) had arrived. The writer asks now to expedite the remittance so that the poor (*ḍu'afā* [see Dozy, *Supplément,* II, 10*a*]) of the Holy City should get their share on the forthcoming Feast (of Pentecost).

The address is in beautiful Arabic script, it seems by the same scribe who wrote the text in Hebrew characters. The crudely written Arabic family name *al-Bayṭār* (Veterinary, still a common family name among Arab townsmen) found beneath the address is that of the postal agency forwarding the letter (see *Med. Soc.,* I, 292–294).

11*c*. TS 13 J 36, f. 6, ll. 22 ff. References to letters sent to the parnāsīm of Old Cairo regarding money due the Jews living in Jerusalem from the revenue of "the compound of the poor" in the former city (letter of Eli ha-Kohen b. Ezekiel, writing from Ramle, Palestine, to Eli ha-Kohen b. Yaḥyā (see A 10) before 1071, since the head of the yeshiva is referred to as still residing in Jerusalem).

12. BM Or 5566 B, f. 7. Donation of a building adjoining the Great Synagogue of Damascus to the latter. Made before the court of the exilarch David b. Daniel, around 1090. See Mann, II, p. 220.

13. TS 13 J 5, f. 2. Solomon b. Ḥayyīm "the Seventh" (i.e., member of the board of the Jerusalem academy) confirms having received from the parnās Eli b. Yaḥyā 20 dinars as payment of a promissory note given to him by the Rabbanite Jews "still remaining" in Jerusalem against a loan for that amount granted by him to them. The payment was made out of revenue from "the house donated to people living in Jerusalem" in Old Cairo (March 3, 1085).

Partly edited by Mann, I, 192 n. 1, who misunderstood, however, the import of the document. In his text, these corrections must be made: *'nqbḍt,* read: *an qabaḍt,* "that I have received"; *'ly,* read *'lyh*; *khs??,* read *dyn (dayn)*; Israel, read Jerusalem; *bty,* read *khaṭṭī*. The title *ha-talmīd,* the scholar, is omitted after the signature of the witness Joseph b. Samuel.

14. Bodl. MS Heb. d 66 (Cat. 2878), f. 88*. Donation of a house in the Lane of the Synagogue of the Iraqians in Old Cairo, half of which the proprietor had inherited from his mother, having acquired the other half by purchase. The revenue is to be divided in equal shares between the synagogues of the Palestinians and the Iraqians and to be used for their lighting. (Draft in the late style of the handwriting of the scribe Hillel b. Eli, ca. 1095).

15. TS Misc. Box 8, f. 76*. Detailed accounts of expenditure on repairs in

a synagogue and perhaps also other buildings. The cost was covered by payments of a parnās, a collection made by a woman, and two smaller contributions. The major part is listed as "debt on the [item] building [operations]." Ca. 1095 according to the names mentioned.

16. TS K 6, f. 106. Income from buildings of the synagogue compound in Damascus, especially "the new shops erected in the synagogue lane by the servant of the community [beadle] Na'īm b. Benjamin."

1130–1165

17. TS 16.122. Fragment of a huge sheet of parchment, containing a contract of lease and twelve entries, dated 1134 through 1146, of payments of a quarter dinar per year as rent of a house belonging to the Jewish community of Ascalon, Palestine. The payments were made to "the trustworthy elders in charge of public property and communal affairs" *hā-'ōmedīm be-ṣorkhē ha-qāhāl uv-ṣorkhē ha-heqdēsh,* and confirmed by the signature of two judges. The contract itself was signed by the elders. See *Med. Soc.* I, 381, sec. 53.

18. TS 13 J 22, f. 2*, ed. S. D. Goitein, *Sefunot,* 8 (1964), 111–113. The wife of the judge Nathan, "the Diadem of the Scholars," b. Samuel, gives one half of the house that served as her domicile (she possessed others) to her husband and the other half to the community. The latter was given on condition that two virgin slaves, whom she freed at her death, should be permitted to live in that half during their lifetime, provided they adhered to the Jewish faith (the judge Nathan signed documents 1122 through 1154). See *Med. Soc.,* I, 135. A small Muslim minority group in Burma followed a similar method. They bought Chinese children, brought them up in the Muslim faith, and then set them free and had them marry Muslims (see M. Yegar, "The Panthay (Chinese Muslims) [of] Burma," *Journal, Southeast Asian History,* 7 [1966], 74).

19. TS 8 J 11, f. 9. Abū Sa'd b. Ḥātim farms out the revenue from "the compound of the Jerusalemites" (see A 11 and 13) in Old Cairo for 110 dirhems per month (July 16 or 17, 1151).

20. *Ibid.,* verso. Statement that the farmer of revenue named above had spent 209¾ dirhems on repairs and delivered an order of payment to the amount of 230 dinars. Signed by three, including the judge Nathan (see A 18).

21. Bodl. MS Heb. d 68 (Cat. 2836, no. 22), f. 100. Agreement between the community chest and the tenant of a house belonging to it, regulating payments in connection with repairs and additions made by the latter. The document stipulates that a further contract of lease will be made before a Muslim court (Feb., 1156).

22. TS 8 J 33, f. 10*v,* Sec. *a,* ed. S. D. Goitein, *Eretz-Israel,* 7 (1964), 96. The beadle Maḥfūẓ receives 12 dinars, the price of the fruits of an orchard be-

longing to the synagogue of the Palestinians for the year 1161–1162. The round sum proves that the revenue from the orchard was farmed out.

23. *Ibid.,* Sec.*b*. The beadle Maḥfūẓ receives 20 dinars (17 in bankers' notes and 3 in cash) and 200 dirhems from a farmer of revenue from houses belonging to the community. The sum represented the payment for the first quarter of the Muslim year 557 (began on Dec. 21, 1161), but was delivered only in Elul (Aug.–Sept.) 1162.

24. TS Arabic Box 18 (1), f. 155*. Accounts of expenditure on twenty-five houses belonging to the community chest made during the second half of the Muslim year 559 (ended on Nov. 17, 1164). The cost of repairs and maintenance as well as administration amounted to 1,127½ dirhems. The revenue during the same period was 3,683 dirhems. Dated Kislev 14 (Dec. 1) 1164.

In addition to four community officials (a rāv, a Dayyān, a beadle, a parnās), no less than seven lay members dealt with individual properties. The final accounting was made in the presence of the Rayyis al-Yahūd (then Nethanel Gaon b. Moses) "and the elders."

1180–1195

25–36. Twelve monthly and bimonthly accounts of the parnās Abu 'l-Bayān b. Abū Naṣr al-Ḥalabī ("originating from Aleppo"). Revenue from public buildings and expenditures on their maintenance, oil used for the lighting of the synagogues, taxes, and other sundry items, as well as on emoluments of communal officials and on the support of needy people. 1181–1184. With the exception of sec. 26, all accounts are in the handwriting of the judge Samuel ha-Levi b. Saadya. Therefore, "Samuel" without any title refers to him.

These detailed and carefully executed documents are a prime source for our knowledge of the communal finances and services.

Abu 'l-Bayān was in charge of two groups of properties, the first comprising about twenty-one houses, reported upon in A 25, 26, 28, 30, 31, 33, 35, 36, the second represented by few houses but mostly by payments of individuals, listed in A 27, 29, 32, 34. The overlapping of the dates of various documents finds its explanation in the fact that they concern two different sets of communal properties administered by the same official simultaneously.

The average income from the two groups together was 450 dirhems per month. In the following, a few illustrative details are provided.

25. Bodl. MS Heb. f 56 (Cat. 2821, no. 16), f. 43*a–c*. Aug. 14–Oct. 11, 1181.

Revenue from twenty-one houses (many owned by the community only in part) during two months	606¼ dirhems
Balance held by the parnās	26 dirhems
Total	632¼ dirhems

General expenditure	412	dirhems
Collection fees	60	dirhems
Former balance paid back	26	dirhems
Balance remaining	134¼	dirhems

26. *Ibid,* f. 43*c–d*. Oct. 12–Nov. 9, 1181.

Income for one month	308	dirhems
Expenditure	223	dirhems
Collection fees	30	dirhems

Same twenty-one houses and almost exactly the same revenue from each—an indication of a normal economy and orderly administration. ("The apartment Abu 'l-Bayān" is perhaps not one occupied by the parnās in charge, but named after someone else, for it brought 10 dirhems in A 25, l. 11, A 26, l. 10, and again in A 35*v*, l. 5, but in between, A 30, l. 10, sec. 35*v*, l. 6, only 7, obviously because then it was occupied by a smaller family and less completely.)

27. TS 8 J 11, f. 7*d*. March 7–May 4, 1182. None of the houses in this account is identical with those in the two preceding lists.

28. TS Box J 2, f. 63*c–d*. March 8–July 4, 1182. Two bimonthly accounts, partly overlapping with A 27. (March 8, and not 7, because this list is dated according to Muslim months, while the former refers to the Jewish calendar. According to the standard works on the two calendars, there is one day difference between the beginnings of the months in the two systems.)

29. TS 8 J 11, f. 4. March 26–May 23, 1183. Besides distributing 71 dirhems to the poor, ḍu'afā, and making some smaller sundry expenses, the parnās delivered to the beadle Maḥfūẓ, who served at that time as cashier, 40 dirhems loose, and 100, 30, and again 100 in sealed purses.

30. TS K 3, f. 11. May 24–June 22, 1183. Revenue from only eighteen properties (all identical with those listed in A 25) amounting to 205 dirhems.

31. Same, verso. June 23–Aug. 20, 1183.

32. TS 8 J 11, f. 7*a–b*. Aug. 21–Oct. 18, 1183 (beginning lost). This account contains the largest single item of expenditure in A 25–36: 194 + 46 + 200 = 440 dirhems for sending off, *tasfīr,* the family (or: wife, *bayt*) of a late nāsī.

33. TS Box J 2, f. 63*a–b*. July 22–Sept. 18 and Aug. 21–Oct. 18, 1183 (overlapping with A 32).

34. TS K 15, f. 13*b–c*. Oct. 19–Dec. 17, 1183. Among the expenditure: Cash in lieu of clothing for fifteen women (four receive 5 dirhems, three, 4, seven, 3, and one, 2 dirhems). The parnās himself receives under this heading ("as due to him," *'an rasmih fi 'l-kiswa*) 12 dirhems, and in A 35 (Bodl. MS Heb.

f 65, f. 60, l. 3), which refers to another collection but bears almost the same date, 10 dirhems. Another item: "Food for the female prisoner–4, and again –3 dirhems."

35. Bodl. MS Heb. f 56 (Cat. 2821), fs. 59–61. Sept. 19, 1183–Jan. 15, 1184. "The house," or wife of Ben Zabqala, who here receives food for 9 dirhems (Bodl. MS Heb. f 56, f. 59*v*, l. 16) is probably identical with the female prisoner in the preceding section.

36. TS K 15, f. 13*d*. Jan. 16 or 17, March 14–15, 1184. A prominent item in this short account: School fees for poor children paid to four different teachers, altogether 54 dirhems in two months. Since the standard fee for a poor boy in this period was ½ dirhem per week, this parnās paid fees for thirteen or fourteen boys.

37. Bodl. MS Heb. f 56 (Cat. 2821, no. 16), f. 43*d*, sec. 2. Abu 'Sḥāq (Abraham) of Aden pays in advance 100 silver dirhems as rent for the upper floor in a house opposite the synagogue of the Iraqians for twelve lunar months beginning with 1 Adar II (Feb. 22, 1186).

38. Bodl. MS Heb. f 56 (Cat. 2821), f. 48. Income during five months (July 20–Dec. 14, 1186) from the quarter of a house in the Tujīb quarter of Old Cairo, donated by Naẓar, the wife of a dyer, who herself paid rent to the community chest. Total revenue 24¼ dirhems. The expenditure comprises, as usual, repairs, administration, and payments to persons specified.

39. TS NS Box 306, f. 1. "List of the houses being in the possession of the pious foundations, *aḥbās,* of the Jews for the benefit of their poor, according to the details submitted by their administrator." The list, in excellent Arabic script, enumerates twenty-six properties (ten of which were shared by the community with other proprietors) ending with this item: "The house of the Jerusalemites in the Mamṣūṣa quarter," and, after a line left blank: "Only the house mentioned above belonging to the Rabbanite Jews is under the administration of Maḥfūẓ [the beadle, dated documents 1159 through 1188; see A 22, 23, above]."

I assume that "houses" is to be read for "house" and that, at a certain time, Maḥfūẓ was responsible to the government for the payment of the ground tax and other dues for all the houses contained in the list, a copy of which was handed over to the authorities. For this reason the document was made out in Arabic characters.

Only seven of these houses are identical with those listed in A 24, and ten have not yet been found anywhere else.

40. TS K 6, f. 54. "The House in the Mamṣūṣa quarter belonging to the Jerusalemites–may God multiply them." Payments by six parties living in the house. Dated 1192. See A 11, 13, 19, 20, 39.

41. DK XXI*. Agreement made in the presence of Moses Maimonides, the judges and the elders, but not signed, to the effect that Abraham b. Yaḥyā ha-Levi al-Najīb (dated documents 1150–1183) should receive the amount of

1¾ dinars, owed by him for the poll tax, from "the compound of the poor," in exchange for which he was to supervise building operations in a *funduq,* or hospice, belonging to the community.

1210–1250

42. TS K 15, f. 3. Fragment of a list of payments received from the tenants of communal houses. Early thirteenth century. Four items refer to storerooms in the funduq.

43. TS K 15, f. 54. Detailed list of revenues from fifteen houses and of items paid with them. Same script and arrangement as A 42, but far more comprehensive. A comparison with contemporary lists shows that a large number of tenants failed to pay their rents. Unoccupied: 1 house, 3 ground floors, *qā'a,* 2 upper floors, *ṭabaqa,* 4 apartments, *sukn.* The "House of the Glassmaker," containing twelve apartments, one unoccupied and one used as a passage, brought 45 dirhems, as against 78–79 in 1182–1183 (A 27, 29, 45). Total monthly revenue 435½ dirhems. Among the items of expenditure: 23 dirhems for the burial of a man from Qalyūb.

44. BM Or 5566 B, f. 33. Accounts of repairs in houses belonging to the community and in the synagogue of the Palestinians (dated 1215).

45. TS K 15, f. 110. A list of thirty-two houses indicating the revenue derived from them during one month (as can be concluded by a comparison with the sums in other lists). Nine houses appear here for the first time.

The maximum total rent received from a house during one month was the sum of 49 dirhems collected in "the house of Yaḥyā," referred to in other documents as "the house of [Yaḥyā] the glassmaker." In most cases the monthly revenue was considerably smaller. In the house of R. Yeshū'ā, of which the community owned only one-eighth, only 1¼ dirhems were received at the time of that account.

46. TS Box J 1, f. 32. "Expenditure made by R. Yeshū'ā from the revenue by rents during the [Muslim] months of Sha'bān and Ramaḍān." Sundry expenses of the community, mainly for the maintenance of buildings. Various names and details as in previous lists. "Clothing for a woman–4." The rest repairs.

47. TS K 15, f. 21. Fragment of a shorter, similar list with a total revenue of 523 dirhems. The expenses include several deliveries of chickens for the nāsī's retinue and barley for their riding beasts.

48–92. TS K 25, f. 240, secs. 11–38 and 40–56. Fourty-five orders of payment, written in the hand of the Nagid Abraham Maimonides (partly in Hebrew and partly in Arabic characters) and addressed to the cantor Abu 'l-Majd ha-Mēvīn, who served as treasurer. In fourteen cases (and most likely also in all other, unspecified, cases), payment is to be made out of the revenue from the "compound of the poor," in ten others (payments for the education of poor children and for sick people) out of a foundation made by the physician al-Muhadhdhab (see A 94). In one case, a mason is paid for repair of the street running in front of the house of the Jerusalemites (see A 40). All dated orders are from spring and summer, 1218.

93. TS NS J 375. Sundry expenses of the beadle Abu 'l-Ṭāhir for small repairs, cleaning and lighting of the synagogue, doles to government officials, and the like, covered by fifteen months' rent of an apartment belonging to the community (dated 1223). Upper part of an exceptionally calligraphic document.

94. TS Box J 1, f. 47. Draft of accounts of revenues from houses and expenditure made from them during one month. Christians and Muslims are among the tenants, and property is owned in common by them and the Jewish community chest (April 4, 1234).

"The house of the Pious" (see A 144, dated 1201) still brought considerable income and so did "the *waqf* [pious foundation] of Abū Thanā al-Muhadhdhab," who had donated three-quarters of a house belonging to him (A 48 ff., 1218). In the latter place lived the son of *"our deputy* R. Jephthah," a formulation that seems to indicate that this large, but disorderly draft was written by the chief justice Hananel b. Samuel. The numerals are Coptic, as usual in this late period.

95. TS K 6, f. 44. "Obtained [payments of rent] during the month of Muḥarram, corresponding to Sivan 1558" (May–June, 1247). There follow twenty-nine items of payment and one of "loss," all in Coptic numerals. Verso: "Expenditure during the month of Muḥarram. . . ." The revenue was 200½, the expenditure 200¼, including 20 dirhems collection fees. In addition to the usual expenditure on repairs, cleaning, government dues and fines, and payments to individuals: 41 dirhems on wax candles (see B 89, 90, C 55). A valuable document.

CONTRACTS OF LEASE OF PUBLIC PROPERTY, AND RELATED DOCUMENTS

96. TS 13 J 21, f. 31. Conditions imposed on tenants of houses owned by the community (four items preserved).

97. TS 8 J 15, f. 17, ed. S. D. Goitein, *Tarbiz,* 34 (1965), 232–236. A complaint submitted to Moses Maimonides in the hand of Meir b. Hillel b. Ṣādōq Āv (dated documents: 1160–1171). Mr. Isaiah, the administrator *(mutawallī)* of the charitable foundations, leased ruins to persons who rebuilt them and lived in them until they had recovered their expenses. The complainant had rented such a ruin, but had lost the use of the property when Isaiah was dismissed.

98. ULC Add. 3358, ed. Assaf, *Texts,* p. 28*. The members of the Great Synogogue in Ramle, Palestine, lease half a ruin (most probably resulting from the terrible earthquake of Dec., 1033) for twenty years against ½ dinar

per year. At the end of the period the lessee is to be refunded all his expenses, either in cash or by staying in the building until the expenses are recovered (autumn, 1038).

99. TS 16.222*. Lease of a date grove belonging to the community for eight years against a yearly payment of 11 dinars. The lessee was obliged to provide one thousand palm branches every year, to keep the property in good condition and to operate the irrigation wheel with oxen (in the handwriting of Nathan b. Samuel [see sec. 18]).

100. TS 10 J 4, f. 11, ed. Assaf, *Texts,* pp. 158–159*. Draft of a lease of a piece of land with a well with perennial water for thirty years against the payment of 6 dirhems per year. The purpose of the lease was the revival of the land which had fallen into decay. (The lessee is known from documents dated 1181 to 1183.)

101. ULC Or 1080 J 10*. Abu 'l-Bayān the parnās (see A 25–36) leases an apartment in a house of the community to another parnās against a payment of 5 dirhems per month for six months, beginning Aug. 24, 1180.

102. TS 12.487. Prepayment of 6¾ dinars as rent for two years for a part of the tower, *burj,* adjacent to the synagogue of the Iraqians, to be used by the perfumer Abu 'l-Makārim Nādīv as reservoirs for rose water. He had already made another prepayment for another part of the same building. June 26, 1180–June 3, 1182. Verso: same agreement continued until April 14, 1184.

MISCELLANEOUS DOCUMENTS

103. TS 10 J 20, f. 5*v**, ed. S. D. Goitein, *Tarbiz,* 32 (1963), 184–188. Instruction in the handwriting of Maimonides to follow the advice of a *ḥājj* (a pilgrim to Mecca) who had farmed out an orchard belonging to the Jewish community, not to replace him by another lessee and to refrain from changes until he, Maimonides, would be free to attend personally to the affairs of the orchard. The letter also contains some medical advice for the addressee.

Corrections to the edited text, l. 3. For *sth* read *ttm,* and translate: "by which your expenses for rubbish removal will be completely refunded" (correction suggested by D. H. Baneth). L. 5. For *'m'ny* read *'m'rh,* see *ibid.,* p. 299.

104. Same, recto, ed. as above. Part of a calligraphic letter to Maimonides of a person who was in receipt of a pension from the revenue of the Ibn Finḥās (Ben Phineas) house often mentioned in our documents from 1164 (see B 32, l. 59).

105. TS 6 J 1, f. 1. Testimony of a judge and another signatory that an upper floor and a wooden building above it in a house belonging to the community formed a part of a charitable foundation (around 1230).

106. TS 13 J 20, f. 15. In reply to a query from the Gaon (Maṣlīaḥ, 1127–

1139), the writer, Moses b. Ṭōviyāhū ha-Kohen, informs his cousin, the judge Nathan b. Solomon ha-Kohen, that a former tenant had sent with various persons to the *wakīl,* or administrator of the qōdesh, 29 + 14 + 20 dirhems as payments for arrears, still owing 12, and that he had delivered the key to the new tenant, a Karaite. The apartment remained unoccupied for two months, but since the former occupant had been overcharged by 37 dirhems (per month?) for five months, the loss had been made good in advance.

107. TS 13 J 8, f. 25. Will bequeathing one-third of an orchard with a house in the village Ḥammūriyya near Damascus to a board of trustees for the benefit of Jewish scholars who devoted their time to study in that city.

It is interesting to note that in exactly the same neighborhood a piece of land of considerable size was acquired by Ibrāhīm b. Finḥās b. Yūsuf, the Jew, in 922, according to a Muslim document, originally found in the Great Mosque of Damascus and presently preserved in the Museum of Turkish and Muslim Art in Istanbul (see Janine Sourdel-Thomine and Dominique Sourdel, "Trois actes de vente damascains du debut du IVe/Xe siecle," *JESHO,* 8 [1965], 169 n. 3).

108. TS NS J 27*v,* sec. 2. Instruction by the court to charge the community chest with 75 dirhems, the price of 8 waybas (about 215 pounds) wheat due an amir (1143).

109. Bodl. MS Heb. d 68, f. 101 (Cat. 2836, no. 23). Certificate by the Jewish elders of Alexandria that a poor old man of good family was entitled to receive rations of bread from the weekly distributions and the money of his poll tax from the revenue of houses belonging to the community (Jan., 1253).

110. MS (Richard) Gottheil, edited by him in *Mélanges H. Derenbourg* (Paris, 1909), p. 96. The community of Old Cairo informs a Nagid that it had turned over the income from the charitable foundations to Ben al-Ḥazzān, to whom it was indebted and to whom the curtains of the Holy Ark had been given as security (fourteenth or fifteenth century). The editor erroneously took *al-qodesh* as meaning "Jerusalem."

111. TS K 15, f. 87. Accounts for the years 1094–1096 of three tenants (one called Sitt Qawdaf, "Lady Slim") of rooms in a house of the community. Each paid 1/6 dinar per month. There were arrears up to six months. The accounts are written alternately in the awkward hand of the parnās Eli b. Yaḥyā (see A 10) and in the elegant script of the scribe, who wrote B 13, 17, 18.

112. ENA 4011, f. 28. The Kohen Abu 'l-Munajjā, surnamed *al-Zārīz* (Heb., alert, eager), collector for the charitable foundations in (New) Cairo turned in 100 dirhems that were used for the distribution of clothing, and an additional 50 that were spent on another approved charity (dated Cairo, Dec. 30, 1181).

Verso: Incomplete specification of the expenses made from a balance of 70¾ dirhems remaining from a previous month. The statement was approved by the judge Isaac (b. Sāsōn).

FIRST SUPPLEMENT

1035–1045

113. TS 10 J 11, f. 26. "Statement about expenditure made within the synagogue compound in the year 429 (A.H., began on Oct. 14, 1037) by Ḥusayn b. Dā'ūd Ben Shekhanya (i.e., Japheth b. David, the cantor and court clerk, who also wrote the report) and the purple maker Jacob b. Bishr (referred to as parnās in TS 20.96, l. 29 [see A 3])."

Item 1: "Work on the Holy Ark, gypsum—2 dirhems."

Item 2: "Repair of the road, through the keeper of the compound—4."

The main part of the accounts deals with the erection of the "New House."

114. Mosseri L 21*v*. The first 4 lines of a report on comprehensive building operations, four sawyers working on the first day and six on the second. Written by Japheth b. David Ben Shekhanya on the reverse side of a letter by the Babylonian Gaon Samuel b. Ḥofnī, dated 1008, ed. Mann, *Texts,* I, 163-164. For sawyers working on the building lot see *Med. Soc.,* I, 113.

115. TS NS J 230. Fragment of a similar account in the same hand. Parts of 23 defective lines preserved. In the item "workman sifting earth," *raqqāṣ raghbal al-turāb,* the word *raghbal* is a mispronunciation, not a scribal error, for *gharbal.*

116. ULC Or 1081 J 38. Right side of draft entries on repairs and other communal expenses, it seems, also in the hand of Ben Shekhanya. Related to TS 18 J 2, f. 1 (see *Eretz-Israel,* 7 [1964], 87 [see A 3]) .

117. TS Arabic Box 54, f. 45. "List of the payments of outstanding [rents]." Payments from nineteen parties (sixteen persons, three apartments), several identical with those in A 6. Most of the arrears were for four months.

118. TS K 25, f. 208. Revenue from rents (only left side of page) . The account for one (Muslim) month is preserved in its entirety, the preceding and following only in part. All names known from contemporary records.

119. TS NS J 264. Long, but badly damaged page from a record book in the hand of Ben Shekhanya, containing 28 complete or only partially preserved lines of entries on payments of rent, arranged according to months. All parties known otherwise.

120. TS K 25, f. 84*v*. Left lower corner of a calligraphic account on communal income from rents, mostly paid for three months. One apartment unoccupied for two months, another for three. All names known.

Recto a complete, but rather enigmatic account of two weekly collections arranged by two different persons and payments to two Muslims, probably craftsmen engaged in some repairs.

121. TS Misc. Box 8, f. 10. Another small fragment in the hand of Ben

Shekhanya on receipts of rents from persons and apartments in communal buildings. Also part of a list to be displayed publicly.

122. TS Arabic Box 6, f. 3. Lower leaf, originally forming part of a large sheet with calligraphic accounts of building operations (18 lines) and other expenditure made by the writer, Ben Shekhanya, and other communal officials. Very similar to A 5, but differing in width and script. A characteristic item: 4 dirhems from the rent for a shanty, *khuṣṣ,* were used for the government fee for the contract of lease with a mason.

123. TS NS Box 320, f. 15. Accounts of rents, repairs, and gifts related to the synagogue of the Palestinians for Nov., 1043, through Nov., 1044 (in the Verso a document from the year 1048, also written by Ben Shekhanya, but same arrangement and hand as A 7) ; 38 lines, but major part of right side lost.
not connected with recto (draft of marriage settlement).

124. TS 12.23. Extensive report about building operations in same hand, 22 lines visible on one side and the same number on the other, but all mostly destroyed.

1120–1165

125. TS NS J 292*v*. Draft of an account for the year 1119-20 with regard to a house belonging to a female orphan (and another house in the Maṣṣāṣa quarter, which belonged to her in part), written on the reverse side of a letter addressed to the judge Abraham (b. Nathan). As far as preserved, the account enumerates mostly payments made by the tenants for the ground rent, the nightwatchmen, and the keepers of the compounds (gifts made on the occasion of the Nayrūz, or popular New Year feast, or the 'Īd al-kabīr, the Muslim feast of sacrifice).

126. TS NS J 342*v*. As expressly stated (ll. 21-22), this account, also written by the judge Abraham b. Nathan on the reverse side of a letter addressed to a judge (presumably to him), deals with the estate of a female orphan and her two houses, most probably the same orphan referred to in the preceding section. Here the final account of all the revenue from the houses and other assets of the orphan is presented, as was usually done when the orphan came of age and could take over the management of his or her property.

127. TS NS J 318. Fragments of accounts on repairs in the two synagogues of Fustat and in communal houses. The money for the repairs had been advanced by the elder Abū 'Alī, probably a banker. Written by Ḥalfōn b. Manasse during 1127–1139.

128. Bodl. MS Heb. f 56 (Cat. 2821, no. 40), fs. 129–130, ed. E. Ashtor, *Zion,* 30 (1965), 153-156. Long fragment (58 lines) of a report on measures taken with regard to a pious foundation during the time of the *kōmer.* As in other

documents, this Hebrew word translates Ar. *al-rāhib,* "The Monk," the appellation under which the rapacious finance minister Abū Najāḥ is known both in Arabic letters and in the Geniza (active 1127-1129) (see S. D. Goitein, *H. A. R. Gibb Presentation Volume* [Leiden, 1965], p. 271).

As it stands, the text is not coherent, probably because it was copied by a clerk from a disorderly draft. After a line left blank, a seemingly new item starts on f. 129, l. 12, superscribed: "The House of the She-camel" (nickname of a woman; this house is also mentioned in A 24, dated 1164, and 45, ca. 1215). One has the impression, however, that the preceding lines deal with the same building. In f. 129*v,* ll. 10-12, the writer announces that he is going to quote the will of the donator of the house verbatim, but f. 130, l. 1, continues differently.

The donation, dated 1127, was for poor persons *(ḍu'afā* [see A 11 *b* and *B* 65]) to be used either for medicine or for the poll tax for people confined to their homes by illness, *munqaṭi',* or for funeral expenses. In the first place, the revenue from the house should be used to put it into good repair, and a certain amount had accumulated for that purpose. When, however, the Monk confiscated all money on which he could lay his hands, the then administrator of the pious foundations distributed the sum at hand to the poor and had the text of the will changed accordingly.

The edited text needs some slight revision. In f. 129*v,* l. 8, one line has been skipped. It reads: *minhū yuṣraf immā fī sharāb,* "the balance should be used either for medicine."

F. 130*v,* l. 9: *.tmh;* read *ktbh,* "which he wrote."

Ibid., l. 12: read *āmanu* and translate: "This was safer than that the Monk should hear that money was deposited with him." The interpretation of the document should be changed accordingly.

The will was made in favor of both the Rabbanite and Karaite communities, but my surmise (Journal of Jewish Studies, 12 [1961], 153) that it was made before a Karaite court is not borne out by the text, which says only that the head of the Karaites, their muqaddam, possessed a copy of the will.

129. TS 16.63*v,* Sec. A, ed. S.D. Goitein, *Tarbiz,* 34 (1965), 244–247*. Copy of a letter of appointment of R. Isaiah as general administrator of all the property of the Jewish community of Fustat, especially of the houses and apartments belonging to it, as well as the synagogues of Fustat and Dammūh with their furnishings, libraries, and orchards. Spring, 1150. See also A 157. In l. 12 of the edited text read for *wḥynyd?: wa-sadīd,* "his sound administration."

130. ENA 4011, f. 42*v**. Beginnings of two drafts of an agreement between Isaiah, the mutawallī, or administrator of the Compound of the Poor (see A 129) and Mr. Ṣubḥ and his wife concerning the House of the Dyer, 15/24 of which belonged to the community and 9/24 to the couple. The administrator will carry out all the necessary repairs, while the couple renounces all their income from their share and rights to sell or to lease it until the expenses are retrieved.

131*a.* ULC Or 1080 J 126*v.* Fragment of accounts of revenue from houses belonging to the community. Coptic numerals. Bū Sa'd b. Ḥātim, the parnās (see A 19, repeatedly referred to. April, 1151).

131*b*. John Rylands Library, Manchester, Gaster Collection A 859. A similar fragment from Tishri (Sept.–Oct.), 1154.

132. ENA 4011, f. 44. Fragment of three columns of accounts—with a person who had seemingly farmed out the rents of one or several apartment houses, for he owes the community 50 dinars, 10 dinars per month, which is far more than any apartment could cost. The same man had paid during many years (1149–1159) 10 dirhems per year for the ground rent due for ⅛ the house named after Hiba al-Abzārī ("the dealer in seeds"). In A 45, l. 18, which is later than our document, one *quarter* of this house was communal property. The donator Hiba was a party to a legal document in 1151–1152 (TS 8 J 5, f. 15). Thus he might originally have donated ⅛ and later added another ⅛.

133. TS 8 J 33, f. 10. Payments made from different sources to the firnās (parnās) Abu 'l-Makārim for carrying out repairs in a house belonging to the community. Written in the hand of the judge Mevōrākh b. Nathan like A 22 and 23 and signed by the same two witnesses as those two statements.

134. TS 8 J 5, f. 22*v*. Sitt al-Naẓar, daughter of Ḥalfōn, donates a quarter of a house in the Mahra district as waqf to the poor and a sixth to Faḍā'il b. 'Awā'id (who is not described as her relative), the latter's mother and children, and after their death, to the poor. She stipulates that during her lifetime she receives the rent from this sixth.

Also in the hand of the judge Mevōrākh b. Nathan, jotted on the otherwise blank reverse side of a marriage contract written and signed by him on Nov. 29, 1161. It seems that the contract was invalidated immediately after it was written and signed (e.g., by the discovery that one of the witnesses was a relative of the bridegroom or the bride) and the paper then used by the judge for his notes.

This Sitt al-Naẓar is different from Lady Naẓar who also donated a quarter of a house, but whose father's name was 'Abdallah (sec. 38, above).

135. ENA 4011, f. 35*v*. "The collector of the rents from the compound of the Jerusalemites is requested to pay to the children of Hiba, the brother of Abū Isḥāq, the silk worker, 9½ dirhems, which is their share in that compound for the year 1477 [Era of Documents, 1165–1166]." Written and signed by the judge Samuel b. Saadya.

136. TS NS Box 320, f. 32*v*. Exactly the same instruction, written and signed by the same judge for the same sum and the same year with regard to Abū Manṣūr ha-Levi b. Abraham al-Dimashqī (of Damascus).

1181–1200

137. TS Arabic Box 52, f. 247*d*. The farmer of the revenue from the orchard of Dammūh dictates his report on his expenditure for the year 1182–1183 to the judge Samuel b. Saadya. It consists of wages and materials for gardening and the upkeep of buildings, payments to beadles and watchmen, and, in particular, six large payments made to the parnās al-Mēvīn.

138. ENA 4011, f. 62*v*. Details about 1,010 dirhems and other sums received from rents and delivered by the writer to various communal officials.

139. TS Arabic Box 54, f. 15*a**. Important account of expenditure on repairs in a communal building, as proved by the large format and careful execution, obviously destined for public display, and also by the reference to an elder who bore a part of the expenses "on his own choice." See *Med. Soc.,* I, 96 and 415 n. 25, where 15*a* should be read instead of 15 (the *a* belongs to the MS mark). As the architectural details show, the building concerned was an apartment house, not a synagogue.

140. TS NS J 433. Left upper corner of a large-sized, calligraphic account of building operations. Another leaf was pasted on, but is lost.

141. Bodl. MS Heb. c 56, f. 10. Important account of building operations. Al-As'ad had promised to pay rent in advance for two years to the community and had already handed over part of the sum stipulated. The account details how this amount was used.

142. TS K 3, f. 21. Accounts concerning communal buildings during repairs and times of disorders. Several items remain obscure. "During the repairs payment to the police [this is the meaning of *raqqāṣīn* here], the prison guards and the keeper of the compound. . . . Another payment through the elder Hārūn to the prison guards on order of the chief of police." The amir al-Mubāriz receives a fine from the community through the money changer al-As'ad (see A 141), but owes rent for "the ground floor" for 5½ months, 34¼ dirhems per month (see bottom). A settlement, *muṣālaḥa,* was made with the parnās Ibrahīm, "as resolved by the elders," *bi-ra'y al-shuyūkh.* One al-Rashīd remained in arrears for both rents and a fine imposed on him, and a teacher's rent was reduced, *musāmaḥa,* after he had not paid for 4½ months.

143. TS 10 J 28, f. 13. A ground floor, described as the property of the poor of Fustat, is rented to Abu 'l-Surūr for two years at a total rent of 160 dirhems in Oct., 1194. Verso entries showing that the rent was continued until July, 1199, and 2 dinars paid every year (1 dinar=40 dirhems [*Med. Soc.,* I, 382, sec. 59]). The revenue was used for expenses on other buildings and so forth.

144. TS K 15, f. 100*v*. Page from a record book: "List of expenses for repairs in the large apartment owned in common [by the community] with the judge Manasse, occupied by his son, the elder Joseph." The expenses for the first three days, consisting of twenty-four details (materials, wages, lunches for workmen, administration), amounted to 68¼ dirhems. One wonders how items of ⅛ dirhem (gypsum—12¼ ⅛, a bonus—½ ⅛) were paid since no such coins were on the market. The details for the following days are mostly lost.

Recto list of the trousseau of Sitt al-Naba', married to Elazar b. Tobias in March, 1199, and a note about a payment of 2 dinars by Abu 'l-Surūr ha-Levi Ibn al-Zakkār (see A 143).

1200–1240

145. TS Arabic Box 51, f. 144. Upper part of an important report on revenue from communal property. Left column: "Record of the [places] occupied during the month of Muḥarram [5] 98 [began on Oct. 1, 1201]." Details about the open space (see A 39), five houses, and the upper floor of the caravanserai have been preserved. "The House of the Pious, of blessed memory," which brought 40 dirhems per month, cannot have been donated by *the* pious of that period, Abraham b. Abu 'l-Rabī', for he died twenty-two years later.

The right column notes ten apartments in ten different houses as unoccupied during the subsequent month. Here, too, the rent due and not collected is indicated in each case, presumably because the ground tax had to be paid whether premises were occupied or not (see A 149).

146. TS 13 J 8, f. 11*v*. Extensive drafts of accounts on

a) revenue from payments of tenants for rent, ground tax, fees for watchmen, as well as from collections and private donations (e.g., from a *nazīra* [Heb.], or holy woman, giving 6 dirhems for orphans and the same sum for the *heqdēsh*), and

b) expenditure on repairs in the synagogue of the Palestinians and of Dammūh and on gifts to foreigners (from Rūm, Maghreb, Damascus, and others). The Rūmī receives the unusually high amount of 40 dirhems while the item "the poor on Passover" amounts to the astoundingly low sum of 16-½. The only one contributing a dinar (and a light one, at that) is the Rayyis (Abraham Maimonides), who also contributes 30 and then ½ dirhem. (He treated perhaps less affluent patients gratuitously, but asked them to contribute something to charity.)

The elder Abū Isḥāq b. Abu 'l-Rabī', who, together with the Rāṣūy (see C 39) and the writer collected 40 dirhems for two unspecified strangers, is none else than the famous Abraham the Pious, the elder companion of Abraham Maimonides in their endeavors toward pietist reforms (see A 145).

The date is contained in the following note: "Apartment of the scribe Abraham b. Samuel al-Der'ī [from Der'a in Morocco], namely, the ground floor adjacent to the Secret Gate [i.e., women's entrance] of the synagogue of the Palestinians as from Tammuz 17, 1624 [= Aug. 6, 1213]—6 dirhems per month."

147. Bodl. MS Heb. c 50 (no Cat.), f. 14. Repairs in the Ben Phineas house, carried out during the months of October and November, 1215. (The date *qkz* = 127 is to be complemented by *'t* = 1400, making a total of 1527 of the Era of the Documents = 1215. Such abridgments were common at that time. The last letter looks more like *w* than *z*, the two letters being similar. But only in 1215 did the sixth of Marheshvan fall on a Thursday, as stated in the document.)

148. TS Arabic Box 54, f. 61. Accounts for a tenant in a communal house called after R. Manasse (b. Joseph) (see A 144). The apartment was defined by the name of the former occupant, Ibrahīm Ibn al-Shā'ir (The Poet, a

family name). The rent: 15 dirhems per month. During ten months, the tenant had made payments to the cantor Abu 'l-Majd, to a synagogue beadle and—a small one—also to a Christian collector. He had also paid for the repair of door locks, the removal of rubbish, and the keeper of the compound. Out of a total of 150 + 75 dirhems, he still owed 16-¾ dirhems at the end of the year. The account is made here according to the Jewish year, ending in Adar (Feb.–March) 1219.

149. BM Or 5549, f. 6. Three entries:

a) Nonpaying tenants, namely six communal officials, such as the judges R. Anatoli of Marseilles and R. Jephthah, and a "poor woman," who occupies an apartment of the same value as the renowned judge Anatoli. At each apartment, whether paid for or gratuitous, occupied or not, the value is indicated (see A 145).

b) Record of revenue from the "open space" (see A 145) and thirteen buildings for one month, totaling 378 dirhems.

c) Small expenses made from this revenue, such as payments to watchmen (20 dirhems), windowpanes (presumably in the synagogue, 4 dirhems) raisins for (the wine used at) the Havdala ceremony at the termination of the Sabbath.

The collector's fee was only 15 dirhems, less than 5 percent.

150. TS Box J 1, f. 52. Two accounts of revenue specifying either persons or buildings. The first, a report for *jm'y 'l-'wl* (a double misspelling for the Muslim month Jumādā I) is written in calligraphic, very large characters. The second, undated, is crossed out and superscribed *nuqil,* "transferred," namely, to the final monthly account.

Some names identical with A 94, but must be somewhat earlier since the beadle Maḥfūẓ and the cantor Abu 'l-Majd (see A 148) are still active here.

151. ENA 2727, f. 7*a*. Certificate that the elder Aaron, son of Joseph the tanner (*burseqī,* Heb., derived from Greek) had a share, *ḥiṣṣa,* in the "houses," *dūr,* of the Jerusalemites in Fustat, since he was a native of Jerusalem and in straitened circumstances. He renounced his part in any special collections made for the benefit of the poor of Jerusalem.

A small stripe cut out of a record in the hand of Hillel b. Eli (dated documents 1066–1108), but the certificate seems to be from the first half of the thirteenth century, and the teacher Solomon in charge of those houses probably was Solomon the son of judge Elijah.

152. TS NS J 221 (c). Addition in Arabic characters (see B 48). A *lazzām,* or farmer of revenue from agricultural land, leases a vineyard from the community against a weekly payment of 10 dirhems. These terms of payment seem strange in an agricultural contract, where one expects yearly, half-yearly, or, at most, quarterly payments. (In the contract discussed in *Med. Soc.,* I, 119, the whole yearly lease of 6 dinars was to be paid at one specified date.) Since, however, the community was always short of funds in that period (1219), a weekly revenue, even though small, was welcome.

153. TS NS J 189. The elder Abu 'l-Faraj b. Maḥfūẓ (a son of the beadle

mentioned often, who himself served in this capacity [see A 38]) pays the rubbish removers their wages of 30 dirhems in the presence of Amram b. Ḥalfōn ha-Levi, who writes and signs the document. This person signed TS 16.200 with huge, monumental letters in 1225.

1240–1260

154. TS NS Box 320, f. 31. "Obtained [i.e., sums cashed from tenants] during the [Muslim] month Dhu 'l-Qa'da, corresponding to Nisan 1554 [both months began on March 24, 1243]."

Only thirteen names preserved, ten of which are identical with A 95, dated 1247. The only sum preserved (5, in Coptic) is also identical with that paid by the relevant tenant four years later.

155. TS 10 J 11, f. 4*. When Abu 'l-Thanā, the banker, son of Abū Sa'd, known as Ibn Ṭayyib, the cantor with tenure, *qāvū'a,* of the synagogue of the Palestinians wished to rent an apartment in one of the communal houses near the synagogue for the convenience of his father, none was found to be free and none of the occupants could be moved out. Thereupon the banker undertook to rebuild the house of Sitt Ghazāl (often mentioned in the records of 1181–1183), which was situated near the Gate of the Well of the synagogue, on condition that the community provided 200 dirhems in cash ("a small sum"), as well as the timber that was in its possession. After the banker recovered his expenses he would have to pay rent. Dec. 1243. (Written as an entry in a record book, not as a contract, and therefore, not signed.)

156. ENA 3824, f. 1. Expenses made by the beadle Abu 'l-Ṭāhir, March, 1236, through April, 1237, mainly for oil for the synagogue (average for regular month: 16 pounds; for month with holiday: additional 5, 10, 15 pounds) and smaller items, for example, the *faqīh,* a lower Muslim official, receives 3-½ dirhems per year. Repaid by his rent for an apartment in a house belonging to the community and a balance to be made good by the parnās Abraham.

157. TS 16.63*v*, section B+*. The document of spring, 1150 (see A 129) is presented over a hundred years later, in Nisan (March–April) 1252 to the Nagid David b. Abraham, because it was the legal basis for all claims with regard to pious foundations belonging to the community. Explanations are given how the document was transmitted to the writer.

158. TS NS J 305. Short and irregularly written account of repairs in communal houses indicating the persons responsible for the operations.

159. TS Misc. Box 25, f. 38. Four pages of complicated communal accounts. Two officials, called for short Ya'qūb (Jacob) and Badr ("Full Moon," in the Geniza more common as a name of girls) are referred to throughout. Their names appear after other names and are followed by sums, which I take as rents, since the same persons are usually associated with the same sums, rents that were collected by Ya'qūb or Badr. The item "Badr 6 Badr" I understand as meaning that the official lived in a communal

building and collected his own rent. Ya'qūb also received a share in a pesīqā, or collection for community officials, and (twice) in the weekly distribution of food for the poor (which, in his case, was converted into cash). When he gets 3 (dirhems) for a chicken (a high price), 4 fulūs (also meaning dirhems) for the bathhouse, and the same sum for the Friday night dinner, however, these sums were certainly destined for a foreigner whom Ya'qūb had to put up.

Written in big, almost calligraphic characters and perhaps from a place other than Fustat.

160. ENA 3124, f. 13. Accounts, mainly on the administration of communal houses (ground tax, watchmen, keepers of the compounds, repairs in buildings specified by name, and so on) for the year 1170, written in the neat hand of Samuel b. Saadya (A 26). The two pages are cut to book size and are arranged in full lines with all numbers spelled out so that the text gives the impression of being part of a book, not of an account.

161. ENA 1822, f. 68. Fragment of late administrative notes. Reduced prepayment of rent (*'alā sabīl al-ta'jīl*), cost of small repairs, a woman giving 40 (dirhems). The writer (who calls himself thus) lists for twenty months the number 3, and for another sixteen months other small sums, presumably for final settlement.

162. TS Misc. Box 25, f. 129. Rents from women's quarters. A calligraphic list of about forty-five persons accompanied by sums. In the first column the names appear after those of houses, for example, the "House of the Scarfmakers," which is certainly identical with the communal building described in A 25 and 26 (dated 1181) as the "House held in partnership with the son of the Scarfmakers." The second column is headed "The Synagogue [compound], a room of Sālim—5," with which is to be compared verso, col. II, "Room of Sālim, the beadle: his wife and his mother-in-law—6." The numerals thus represent rents, or, rather, the sums owed by the tenants for the apartments occupied. Only in a few cases are the names and sums crossed out with a stroke the head of which represents the Arabic letter *'ayn,* which I take as the last letter of the word *dafa',* "paid."

Sitt Ṣalaf, "Lady Inaccessible," seems to have been deaf not only to improper advances but also to the approaches of the collector of the rent, for only above the first of four payments due by her the remark *ustukhrij,* "got out of her," is written (in another pen and ink). A bride, *bint 'irs,* living in the room al-Yesōd, a room donated by a notable bearing the honorific title "Foundation [of the yeshiva]," paid a ¾ dinar, which was reckoned as 30 dirhems, at the common rate of 1 : 40. The woman, who most probably was not young any more at all, wound up her accounts with the community before moving to her new husband's house. Another woman also paid in gold (verso, col. I, l. 4), but only a quarter dinar.

I pondered long over this document, since, with one, or possibly two exceptions, all persons listed in it are women. In most records referring to communal housing women form the majority, but are not listed as sole tenants. We are in Ayyubid times here, and it may well be that the tendency of stricter supervision of the mores of the population required separate housing for males and females. One is reminded of later Islamic pious foundations described as houses of widows. The official (perhaps a woman herself) reporting in our document clearly was in charge of the communal properties inhabited by women.

163. BM Or 5566 B, f. 29. As a reward for his services as administrator of communal property (here called heqdēsh) Jacob b. Mevassēr is granted, against a rent of 5 dinars per year, the lease of a locality in the Ibn Khabīṣa lane, which served him as a dyeing workshop. The agreement was approved by four parnāsīm and witnessed by the community, a complicated procedure probably made necessary because the synagogue of the Palestinians was situated in the same lane and some people may have objected to having dyeing works so near the sanctuary. Jacob leased the place to another person who sublet it again to a third—all with the approval of the communal authorities. Dec., 1030.

164. Bodl. MS Heb. f 22 (Cat. 2728, no. 5), f. 43, ll. 5–12. Entry in a notary's record book, witnessed by three. The wailing woman Sitt al-Riyāḍ (a poetic name: "Lady Gardens") donates to each of the Karaite and Rabbanite communities 7½ shares (i.e., a total of 15 out of 24) of a house and site belonging to her. Thus, her house must have been in a suburb and not in the urban district of Fustat, the ground of which was government property. Wailing, like funeral services today, was a lucrative business. Around 1160.

165. Bodl. MS Heb. f 22, f. 47, ll. 1–6. Entry in a notary's record book, witnessed by two. The uncle of Bū Sa'īd, "the son of the Jerusalemite," cedes him his share in the revenue from the compound of the Jerusalemites in Fustat. Whether the nephew was not entitled to these doles, or received his uncle's share in addition to his own, is not evident from the laconic entry. Around 1160.

166. Westminster College, Arabica I, f. 49. Four pages of a report on expenditure made by the cantor Abū Sahl for repairs in the Muhra house, mentioned also in A 24 (dated 1164) and A 94 (1234). The report is written in large Arabic characters, presumably for the benefit of a Muslim who had a share in the property.

167. Bodl. MS Heb. f 56 (Cat. 2821, no. 16), f. 52. Note in the hand of the judge Samuel b. Saadya on repairs in the Oil House. Dated 1182.

168. TS Misc. Box 28, f. 52. Fragment of a letter of a schoolmaster who had lived in a communal house near the synagogue for thirteen years paying 12 dirhems per month. He produced a ruling from the Nagid David (1238–1300) saying that the teacher, in principle, was entitled to free lodging, but that a reduced rent of 12 dirhems had been agreed upon. The request made by the writer is not preserved. The letter was perhaps written in Alexandria since the Nagid is referred to as being in office, but not present; also the term "heqdēsh" (and not "qōdesh") is used for communal property.

SECOND SUPPLEMENT

169. ENA 2808, f. 63. Calligraphic account (10 complete, 5 partial lines) in the hand of Japheth b. David Ben Shekhanya on repairs in the *qaṣr* of Ḥammūd; here qaṣr does not mean "castle," as elsewhere in Arabic (both the English and the Arabic are derived from Latin *castrum*), but "hall" or ground floor in a smaller building (see Dozy, *Supplément,* II, 356*b*). The Hall of Ḥammūd also in A 7. Ca. 1040.

170. ULC Or 1080 J 104*v*. Detailed report, in large, clear Arabic script, about work done intermittently by at least seven different masons—normally two working together on one day—and one carpenter during July through November 1045 (see A 9, 123). The report used the reverse side of a letter from Qayrawān written on parchment. One of the masons, Abu 'l-Yumn *al-shammās* (the deacon) certainly was a Christian, and another, called Ja'far, a Muslim. The names of the others could have been borne by Jews. With one exception (a dinar for Ja'far, certainly an advance), neither wages or lunches, nor the nature of the work carried out are indicated. Superscription: "What the laborers of [. . .] have done."

171. ENA 2808, f. 66. A complicated court record in the hand of the judge Abraham b. Nathan Āv of Cairo. The parnās Musāfir had donated to the heqdēsh of that city 5 dinars for the purchase of trunks of fir trees, *shūḥāt*. It had been stipulated that the trunks should be bought in Alexandria, where they were five times cheaper than in Cairo (they were imported from Europe). For this purpose, the money was delivered to the parnās Abū Sa'd, "the Head of the Congregations," who died, however, "under the well-known circumstances," perhaps on his way to Alexandria. The problem now was how to retrieve the 5 dinars. The donor could be identical with Musāfir b. Wahb (= Nathan), the brother of the prominent notable Abraham b. Nathan, the Seventh (not to be confused with his contemporary namesake, the judge mentioned above). Around 1100.

172. ENA 2591, fs. 14, 15. "Record [*tasqī'*, as in A 143, which has the more correct *ṣ*] of the apartments for which rent is being paid." This implies that then, as in A 149, there were also some nonpaying tenants. Page 15*v*, which is blank, was perhaps reserved for them.

The record lists the apartments in geographical order: Synagogue Lane (with the main funduq), the Great Bazaar (with a smaller funduq and "the teacher's place"), Khabīṣa Lane (with Lady Gazelle's house), the Tujīb quarter (with the house of 'Ablā and that of the glassmaker). The total (due): 267½ dirhems.

Col. II on p. 14*v* contains this superscription: "Examination of the cadastre" *(lamsat al-'ibra)*. It was 267½ dirhems per month and 1,337½ for the five months for which the official concerned reported; of these he "obtained" (mustakhraj, as in A 154) 1,075½. 'Ibra is the regular term for the revenue expected from a house, a piece of land, or a whole village. The term "lamsa," literally, "touching" (namely the body of an animal at its purchase), has not yet been found by me in the general sense used here.

The document is important since it shows both the revenue due and that actually received.

173. Firkovitch II, f. 1367. The elders of the Karaite Jews of Cairo lease the right of way through a doorway of the street of the synagogue, *darb al-kanīs,* "may it soon be reopened" (in Hebrew in an otherwise Arabic text), to al-Ṣafī Abu 'l-Maḥāsin b. al-As'ad Abu 'l-Ḥasan for 6 dirhems per year. Tammūz 1613 (Jewish), Shawwāl 701 (Muslim) = June, 1302.

During the persecutions of 1301–1302 the houses of worship of Christians and Jews were closed by the Muslim authorities for about a year until the Byzantine emperor and other Christian monarchs obtained their (partial) reopening (see Strauss, *Mamluks,* I, 86–87).

174. Firkovitch II, f. 1412. Accounts of repairs in a house made a pious foundation for the poor, *ṣa'ālīk,* of the Karaite community. Dated 1433.

Firkovitch, the great collector of manuscripts (*Med. Soc.,* I, 5) was himself a Karaite, which explains his interest in these late documents.

Addition

175. Dropsie 336. Four witnesses testify that one-sixth of a certain house in the Lane of the Poor was a waqf for the two synagogues of Fustat, *waqf 'ala 'l-kanīsatayn.* The heads of the two synagogues, Sahlān b. Abraham (Iraqians) and Ephraim b. Shemarya (Palestinians) sign the court validation. May, 1047.

The Lane of the Poor is repeatedly mentioned. It was a blind alley in the vicinity of the two synagogues.

176. TS 20.3. A woman who lived in a house a part of which had been given to the poor (probably by her) donates an adjacent one-story building to her housekeeper on condition that no additional floor be erected above it and that the house never be sold to Muslims. Both stipulations are aimed at the protection of the poor living in the large house (see chap. vii, A, 2, n. 10). Feb.–March, 1117.

177. TS 20. 87. One Obadiah who owned three-quarters of a house in the Lane of the Poor (see A 175), the remaining quarter of which belonged to the heqdēsh, requested thorough repairs of the whole building, since its ruinous state threatened danger to his little children. On the recommendation of a committee elected by the community, the expenditure for the repairs was approved by the Gaon Maṣlīaḥ. On completion, the accounts were examined by Abu 'l-Faraj Yeshū'ā ha-Talmīd b. Ṣedāqā al-Ramlī, renowned both for his piety and for being an expert in building operations. One-fourth of the expenses, which totaled 24 dinars, had to be borne by the heqdēsh, and since, as usual, it had no cash, Obadiah received a certificate authorizing him to collect the monthly rents of the tenants until the sum owed to him was recovered. July, 1134.

On the reverse side are some entries about rents paid to Obadiah, one being a broker's promissory note, *ruq 'at dalāla,* worth 5¾ dirhems.

178. TS Arabic Box 44, f. 223. Large fragment of accounts detailing revenue from communal property and expenditure on repairs in the synagogue and other buildings. New technical details, for instance, about the *mīḍā'a,* or basin for ablutions, in the synagogue, or, that, in addition to timber from

sycamores, mentioned in other documents, wood from pines and acacias was used here in the building operations. Closely related to sections A 5–9 and, like them, to be dated around 1040.

179. TS Arabic Box 49, f. 166*v,* ll. 16 ff. Query (addressed to the Gaon and nāsī Daniel b. Azarya) about a man who had vowed a donation for the building of a synagogue and later claimed to be unable to keep his promise. At his death, however, he possessed land and other property. His heir was sued for the sum pledged but asserted that he was under no obligation to pay. Ca. 1060.

180. TS Misc. Box 28, f. 79, sec. 12. The elder Japheth b. Jacob wills on deathbed that his share in the rent of a house that he held in partnership with others should be spent in two equal shares, one on bread for the poor and the other on a person specified by name. In the hand of Ḥalfōn b. Manasse (1100–1138).

181. TS Arabic Box 48, f. 42*v*. A man on deathbed gives two houses to two distant relatives, forestalls the possible claims of two other female relatives by assigning them 5 dinars each, and donates to the synagogue of (New) Cairo (they had only one at that time) a codex of the Five Books of Moses and 3 dinars for the purchase of a copper case for a Torah scroll. Ca. 1150.

182. Westminster College, Arab., II, f. 160. Detailed accounts on building operations in a synagogue, here called *kanīsiya,* and other expenses. Of particular interest: costs, in materials and work, of the erection of a gable roof, *gamalūn*. Same script and arrangement as in the account TS Misc. Box 8, f. 66*. The hand seems to be identical with that of the writer of the letter TS 12.581, who reports indeed, l. 15, that he constructed a gable roof on the synagogue of Minyat Ziftā. Ca. 1150.

183. TS Arabic Box 4, f. 7. Four pages of accounts of income from communal houses and stores and of expenses on administration (30 dirhems for the collection of 493 dirhems), repairs, salaries, fees for the teaching of orphans, ground rent, and so forth. Heading: "Record [taṣqī', as is A 143, 172] for the month of Marheshvan." Many items similar to, or identical with, those of A 43, above. Early thirteenth century.

184. TS 13 J 21, f. 25*v*. A man on deathbed charges his executor to buy landed property worth 500 dinars, the proceeds of which to be divided equally between the poor of his town and the family of his paternal uncle. Draft of a query possibly older than the letter written on recto in 1208 (see chap. v, C, 4, n. 59, below).

TYPES OF RECORDS IN APPENDIX A

1. List of communal properties: 39.

2. Donations of houses and other properties to the community (in parentheses, references to such donations): 1, 2, (3), 12, 14, 18, (38), 107, (128), (132), 134, 164, (176), 179–181, 184.

3. Accounts of income from communal properties (rents and payments of farmers of revenue): 4, 6, 10, 16, 17, 19, 20, 22, 23, 42, 45, 111, 117–121, 131, 132, 138, 145, 148, 150, 154, 160, 162, 172.

4. Combined accounts of revenue and expenditure: 5, 7, 8, 25–36, 38, 43, 47, 93–95, 112, 142, 143, 146, 149, 156, 159, 161, 178, 181, 183.

5. Cost of repairs and other building operations: 9, 15, 24, 44, 113–116, 122, 124, 127, 133, 139–141, 144, 147, 158, 166, 167, 169, 170, 174, 177, 182. See also types 4 and 6.

6. Sundry payments made by or to the charitable foundations: 46, 48–92, 108, 110, 112, 123, 137, 153.

7. Agreements between the community and tenants and other documents referring to pious foundations: 21, 37, 41, 96–106, 109, 128–130, 152, 155, 157, 163, 168, 171, 173, 175–177, 179, 180.

8. Documents pertaining to the compound for the Jerusalemites in Fustat: 11, 13, 19, 20, (39), 40, 135, 136, 151, 165.

Appendix B

DOCUMENTS LISTING THE BENEFICIARIES OF THE COMMUNITY CHEST

(Chap. v, sec. C, 4)

1020–1040

1. TS 24.76*. List of 136 households (mostly women with, or without, children, foreigners, disabled and indigent people) receiving approximately 570 loaves of bread. A postscript in Arabic characters states that the whole document was written by Ephraim b. Maḥfūẓ (i.e., Shemarya), the well-known leader of the Jewish community of Old Cairo during most of the first half of the eleventh century. It was witnessed by Isma'īl (i.e., Samuel) b. Ṭalyūn (i.e., Avṭaliyōn), a prominent member of the Palestinian congregation, and two others. Ephraim and Samuel signed many documents together in the years 1026–1029 (see Mann, II, 97–99).

Despite its length (about 14 inches, 40 lines), the leaf represents only the lower part of a longer sheet. With the exception of the beadle and his mother-in-law (12 + 4 loaves, verso, l. 6) and the Shekhanya family (i.e., that of the cantor and court clerk Japheth b. David, 16 loaves, l. 28) no community officials are listed. Others might have been included in the part lost, or our list comprises solely the needy attached to the synagogue of the Palestinians, which, at that early time, might have had only one cantor and one beadle.

At least eight persons are defined as "acquaintance of," *ma'rifa,* and, throughout in an informal way, for example, "acquaintance of Ibrahīm," l. 14 (and exactly the same in B 52, last line); see also ll. 21, 23 (twice), 27, 28, 32, verso, l. 4. Others are characterized as "the relative of," *qarāba,* for example, "the relative of Ibrahīm," l. 22. A porter is described as working, *'ammāl* (as opposed to *baṭṭāl,* out of work), perhaps as an explanation for the low number of loaves assigned to his family.

Alongside foreigners whose provenance is indicated, others, unspecified, are listed, for example, "a foreigner—2 [loaves]," l. 28, "the foreign woman —2," l. 34, "the foreigners—6," l. 35, "a foreigner—1" (the allocation of one loaf was exceptional), verso, l. 8. One wonders how those persons could be identified. In Egypt, together with places frequently occurring in the Geniza, such as Tinnīs, l. 2, Ṣahrajt, l. 22, Damsīs, verso, l. 1, others, rarely mentioned appear here: "the family Faraskūr—8," l. 21, "the son of the woman from Sawāda—4," l. 29, "the woman from Būra and her son—4," l. 31, "the wife of the man from Ghayfa—2," l. 38. Three families or persons were from Palestine, one each from Barqa, the Maghreb, Damascus, Persia, and faraway Tiflis in Georgia ("the son of the Tiflīsī," l. 22; cf. TS K 15, f. 66 [B 5], col. II, l. 11: "the Tiflīsī, the dyer," B 59, l. 30: "Joseph, the Tiflīsī"). The list might well contain many more foreigners, described as acquaintances of local people (see above) or simply referred to by their names.

This important list is analyzed in tables 1 and 2 at the end of this Appendix. See also B 2*a*, 2*b*, 3, 52.

2*a*. TS 20.112. A list similar to the preceding one in the same hand having many names and figures in common with it. Much damaged and effaced. It represents partly the left and partly the lower part of B 52. Together, the two pieces comprise 42 lines. Still, the original manuscript was longer, for there is clearly a scissors cut through the last line. The two parts are discussed together in B 52.

2*b*. ENA 2713, f. 26. Fragment in the same script and arrangement as B 1, 2*a*, 14 + 14 lines, containing the names of 51 households, at least 15 of which are identical with B 1. As far as legible,

17 receive 5 (dirhems), total	85 (dirhems)
17 receive 10 (dirhems), total	170 (dirhems)
9 receive 15 (dirhems), total	135 (dirhems)
4 receive 20 (dirhems), total	80 (dirhems)
1 receive 25 (dirhems), total	25 (dirhems)
1 receive 30 (dirhems), total	30 (dirhems)
49 receive a total of	525 (dirhems)

The basic unit allotted to one person clearly was 5 dirhems, as evident from such items as "the man from Malīj and his mother—10," "the daughter of Nissīm and his mother—10," "the two women from Ramle—10" (see B 29, 100).

In several lists the number 1 or 2 is written after the amounts of 10, 15, 20. The number could hardly mean a simple additional payment (since then the writer would have changed the number 15 to 16 or 17, respectively); it must have had some other meaning (see B 100).

Had the sheet been preserved to the length of the contemporary B 1 (also only a fragment) and the sums distributed on the lost part of approximately the same size, the communal expenditure on this charity (presumably doles for a holiday) would have approximated 1,500 dirhems. Even assuming the lowest value of the dirhem at this period (*Med. Soc.*, I, 371, sec. 8), this sum would correspond to about 37 dinars, twice as much as the distribution of bread in B 24 during one month.

3. TS 20.23*v*. A list similar to the preceding ones, on vellum, the majority of the names legible belonging to community officials and women. The recto contains a legal document (a release) dated 1049. It seems, however, that the list is older than the document. Unlike B 1, the beadles of three synagogues

and at least two cantors are listed here. "The elder from Tiberias," who receives six loaves in B 1, l. 14, appears here again, l. 5, but instead of the man from Damsīs, the recipient is his daughter, l. 12.

1040–1060

4–5. TS K 15, fs. 14 and 66, the latter forming the upper part, and the former the lower part, of one list of about a hundred persons, all male, foreigners, laborers, craftsmen mostly of lower standing, community officials, persons called *ghulām* or *ṣabī,* that is, slave, freedman, or employee, and five others designated as *ḍamīn,* persons for whom security was given. They contribute or are asked to contribute from 1/6 to 3/4 dinar, that is, a partial payment of the poll tax, the community making up the balance. The sums following the names may also indicate the amounts to be paid by the community (see B 58).

The notables whose employees are mentioned (Dōsā, Ibn Sighmār, Ibn 'Awkal [son of the famous Joseph], Bahūdī, Ibn Ḥirbish) were active around 1040.

Foreigners: From Palestine, 5 (Tiberias, 3; Baniyas, 1; Jīsh, 1, the latter also B 9, l. 21); Persia, 2; Tiflīs, 1; Spain, 3; Ṣaqlābī (of Slavic origin), 1. Some names are only partly visible.

6. TS K 15, f. 93. A list of about ninety persons similar to the preceding one. Many names and sums identical with those in it. Three details call for special comment. As in official documents from the Fatimid chancelleries, blank space, three times as wide as the height of the script, is left between the lines. Thus, no doubt, the list was destined for public display.

In one place, col. I, l. 2, the words "from the collection, pesīqā" are added. Certainly a special circumstance, where it was found that the person concerned was unable to pay even the very reduced rate of 1/4 dinar imposed on him.

Verso, col. II, l. 11, Yaḥyā al-Majjānī is listed with 9 qīrāṭs. Yaḥyā b. Mūsā al-Majjānī was a Qayrawānese merchant commuting to Egypt and known from many Geniza documents. It would be hazardous to assume that another person bearing the same rare name (derived from Majjāna, a little town in inland Tunisia) lived in Egypt at that time. It is more probable that the well-known Yaḥyā al-Majjānī was in dire straits that particular year (as we find him in Bodl. MS Heb. a 2 [Cat. 2805], f. 17*, and in other letters of his) and was therefore assisted with the payment of his poll tax. This point needed elucidation because a list containing the name of a well-known merchant is taken prima facie as one of contributors, not of beneficiaries of a reduced poll tax.

Foreigners: From Palestine, 5 (only 1, Sa'd al-Bāniyāsī, identical with those in the preceding section; Acre, 1; Haifa, 1; Tiberias, 1, "the man from Jerusalem who works with Qāsim, the silk-weaver"); Maghreb, 4; Persia, 3 (among them a cantor and one called Mordecai, a name rare at that time in the West, but appropriate in Persia, the scene of the biblical story of Mordecai and Esther); Iraq ('Ukbara), 1; Barqa, 1; Sicily, 1; Spain, 1.

7. TS 13 J 6, f. 20. Fragment of a list similar to the preceding one and in the same hand. Much effaced.

8. TS K 15, f. 96. Eight columns containing more than 180 names, a few of them identical with B 4–5. Many payments of ⅛ dinar.

Foreigners designated as such: from Palestine, 13 (Acre, 3; Ramle, 3; Gaza, 2; Jerusalem, 2; Tiberias, 2; Ascalon, 1); Iraq, 12 (Mosul, 6; Baghdad, 3; Āmid, 1; Āqul, 1; 'Ukbara [different from the one in the preceding section], 1); Syria-Lebanon, 7 (Damascus, 4; Tyre, 2; Aleppo, 1); Rūm (Europe and Byzantium), 3; Sicily, 2; Qayrawān, 1; Barqa, 1; Spain, 1.

The strong influx of foreigners from Asia seems to reflect the reaction of the populace to the Seljuk invasion.

9. TS NS J 191. A calligraphic list of male persons of a description similar to those mentioned in B 4–6 and some identical with those occurring there. With one exception ("he paid ¼ dinar") no amounts are indicated. Ll. 19–20: "Ḥasan the Persian [mentioned also in B 4, verso, col. I, l. 2] pays for his son-in-law Faraj, the teacher from Mosul, for whom Abraham Dustarī stands security." Abraham Dustarī is the usual Hebrew name of the "vizier" Abū Sa'd al-Tustarī. Thus, Abū Naṣr, who stands security for another person (l. 10) might be Abū Sa'd's well-known brother.

10. TS K 15, f. 17. Nine entries on vellum in huge calligraphic letters, such as "two freed women, two persons from Ḥijāz, two from Ṣahrajt [Egypt], the daughter of Misha'el," accompanied by numbers ranging from 1–6. One exceptionally rare name, al-Zayyiq, occurs also in the preceding section.

11. TS NS J 179. About 125 persons, as far as defined, with a few exceptions either craftsmen and laborers or foreigners (many from Palestine and Syria, but none from Iraq or Persia; two Karaites). The script points to the second half of the eleventh century. Since no names could be identified with certainty with those in the preceding sections, however, a considerable interval must be assumed between their respective periods. No numbers.

1060–1100

12. Bodl. MS Heb. c 28 (Cat. 2876), f. 6, ed. Mann, II, 245–246. "Students of the Torah, may God increase their number." A list of scholars, that is, persons having a claim on the community chest, in Old and New Cairo. Many persons are known from other sources. Discussed above, chap. vi, 9, n. 4.

13. TS K 15, f. 70, ed. Mann, II, 247, but needs to be reedited (see *JESHO,* 1 [1958], 180). Payroll of community officials, foreign and needy scholars. In the same hand as B 17, 18.

14. TS Misc. Box 28, f. 42. A list similar to, but shorter than, B 12 and likewise headed by R. Nahray (b. Nissīm), here called Nehōray.

15. Bodl. MS Heb. d 66 (Cat. 2878), f. 62. A longer list of the same type as the one before headed by Sayyidnā al-Nāsī, referring, it seems, to the exilarch David b. Daniel (ca. 1090).

The lower part of the document contains the letter of a man describing himself as *munqaṭi'*, confined by illness to his home (and unable to work), asking a cantor who was also in charge of the social services (*ṣadaqa waṣalāt*) to look after him.

16. TS NS J 288. Left upper corner of a list of persons (receiving emoluments from the community), headed by two judges and including two scholars, three parnāsīm, the beadles of the two synagogues, a woman teacher, and five unspecified others. The rayyis Abū Mufaḍḍal was judge in the capital of Egypt (see TS 16.253, TS 13 J 26, f. 6), but also a merchant who traveled as far as Qūṣ and probably farther afield. It is not surprising, therefore, that he appears also in the list of contributors, see C 18, 19, 119. Compare the case of Nahray b. Nissīm, B 12, 14, and C 14.

Written in the neat hand of the cantor Ḥalfōn b. Manasse Ibn al-Qaṭā'if, who refers to himself modestly as Ibn Qaṭā'if. The widow of Nuṣayr b. Thābit, l. 8, receives clothing from the community in B 25, col. II, l. 2, and appears in a list of indigent people in B 34, col. II, l. 16, and his orphans receive wheat in B 66, col. II, l. 16.

1100–1140

17. TS NS J 41. Distribution of about 430 loaves of bread, weighing 450 pounds, to 104 households on the Friday before the Fast of Av (which fell on Sunday). Heading: "Spent on the Poor, may God, in his mercy, make them rich."

At least seventeen of the persons listed under the heading Rūm (from western Europe and/or Byzantium) in B 19, 21, 23 also appear here, but only three are characterized as such. Only a few persons are described as foreigners and without the indication of their names, for example, "a woman from Sicily—4 [loaves of bread]," col. II, l. 16; "the man from Acre—6," col. I, l. 7; "a newcomer from Baghdad—6," col. III, l. 15; "the man from Ḥijāz—3," col. II, l. 19. For some reason, the compiler of this and the following list refrained from describing persons as foreigners when he knew their names. See also B 13.

18. TS Misc. Box 8, f. 9. List in the same hand, headed "Fourth Friday, 550 Pounds," specifying about 140 households receiving approximately 600 loaves of bread. Most of the names in the preceding section recur in this one, as well as in B 19–24, but from which group it is separated by many different names. In addition to the foreigners mentioned in B 17 there appear here four others from Palestine (a cantor from Ascalon, a Jerusalemite, a shōmēr from Tiberias, "the son of the man from 'Ammān"), one from Lebanon (a cantor from Baalbek [see B 22, verso, col. I, l. 6]), a woman from Barqa, and one from the Maghreb, and an Andalusian with his son. The Ḥijāzī again receives 3 loaves and the newcomer from Baghdad 6, showing that this list must have been very close in time to B 17. There are three additional Iraqis (Baghdad, 1; Raqqa, 2).

19–22. TS K 15, fs. 5, 15, 39, 50, all parts of one booklet; the original order, as shown by the dates, is 5, 39, 15, 50. The beginning is f. 5, left column. Like the title page of a book, it is blank except for the following: "List of the Poor of Old Cairo—may God in his mercy make them rich and help them in his grace and kindness." Inside (i.e., f. 5, right column): "Available 600 [loaves] weighing 600 pounds. Price 3 dinars, which I have received from the Prince of Princes [i.e., the Nagid Mevōrākh]—may he live forever." Here the date is not preserved, but f. 39 is dated Tuesday, Marheshvan 18 (Nov. 5), 1107, continuing: "490 pounds, number [of loaves] 539 from the baker Ma'ālī. Ten [pounds] were added, making a total of 500, namely ten loaves of old bread." F. 15 was written on the Friday of the same week and notes 500 pounds yielding 567 loaves. F. 50 contains the distribution of the following Tuesday again comprising 500 pounds, but only 547 loaves. Most of the 137 to 145 names in the four lists are identical. Fs. 5 and 39 contain special sections superscribed "The Rūm," listing 39 and 42 persons, respectively.

The final addition in f. 50 resulted not in 547, as in the superscription, but in 552, as stated in the postscript, this being the correct sum total of 165 + 217 + 170, the totals noted on the bottoms of the three pages of this account. The distribution on this Tuesday, Nov. 12, 1107, was this:

Number of loaves	Number of households	Total loaves
1	6	6
2	29	58
3	35	105
4	33	132
5	10	50
6	9	54
7	1	7
8	14	112
10	1	10
(Loaves for those transporting the bread and an illegible item)		(18)
	138 + 1	552 loaves

A comparison of this list with B 23 and 24 (see table 1 at the end of this Appendix, last four columns) shows the important fact that the distribution on a Tuesday was exactly the same size as that on a Friday. On the other hand, it is remarkable that even in the course of three days (Nov. 12 to 15) there were so many little changes in the amounts of loaves allocated.

The handwriting is that of Abraham b. Aaron, who also wrote B 23, 24 (see B 24).

23. TS Box J 1, f. 4*. Two similar lists, same scribe and mostly same names as in the preceding documents, one dated Friday, Marheshvan 14. For details see the commentary in *Med. People*.

Has also a special section for Europeans (42 persons).

24. TS Misc. Box 8, f. 25*. "Also spent on them, Friday the 28th, 500

pounds, 555 [later corrected to 559] loaves." Postscript: "Total expenditure on 3,600 pounds of bread during the month of Marheshvan: eighteen dinars," signed by the two parnāsīm 'Ullā b. Joseph ha-Levi and Eli b. Yahya ha-Kohen and the copyist of the document, Abraham, son of the well-known scribe and cantor Aaron ha-Mumhe b. Ephraim.

Students of B 19–24 should keep in mind that the leaves were originally folded so as to form a booklet. Therefore the left of a leaf usually does not represent the direct continuation of the right half, for there were intervening folded leaves. Thus far, lists for only four days: Friday, Marheshvan 14 (Nov. 1, 1107) and the following Tuesday and Friday, and Friday, Marheshvan 28, each consisting of three leaves showing twin columns, have been found in their entirety (except for minor damages).

25. TS K 15, f. 48. Two lists, in two different scripts, the first part, extending from col. I, l. 1, to col. II, l. 14, the second from col. II, l. 15, to col. IV, l. 21, of receivers of clothing, at least half of whom were women. Four names recur in both lists, meaning that two different distributions are recorded here. Only seven names are identical with those in other lists of this and the following groups.

Details about 44 + 37 households preserved, but the leaf, which is folded to form a booklet of four pages, is superscribed "Leaf no. 3," so that the total number of persons listed originally might have been not 81, but three times as many. It is not excluded that this one and B 33 and 64 originally formed one document (see B 33, 64).

Abu 'l-Faraj the parnās in charge of the second distribution (which was made in two steps, col. II, l. 15; col. IV, l. 6), is listed as recipient of a *thawb,* or gown, in the first distribution (col. I, l. 20), where, however, the item is crossed out. This could hardly mean here, as in some other documents, that the garment had already been delivered to him, for about forty items, or half the total contained in this leaf, exhibit the Arabic final *m,* which I take as an abbreviation of *(tasalla)m,* "received" (the same in B 33, 64 and C 41). Thus, the deletion of the parnās' share probably had another reason. Other parnāsīm, mostly outsiders, or their relatives, receive clothing, for example, "the sister of the parnās from Jerusalem," col. I, l. 18, "the firnās of Dami-etta," col. I, l. 31, "the parnās of Crete," col. II, l. 6 (also crossed out), also col. II, l. 1, col. IV, ll. 1 and 5.

Foreigners designated as such: From Palestine, 5 (Jerusalem, Acre, Haifa, Tiberias, Baniyas, the latter a newcomer since his address is given); Aleppo, 2 (1 living in the synagogue, where also a proselyte in receipt of clothing lived); Baghdad, 2; Persia, Tripoli, Crete, Jerba, Maghreb, Qal'a (Algeria), 1 each.

John Rylands Library, Manchester, Gaster Collection, G 21, is a small scrap of paper which looks like a fragment of the lost pages of our document. Three persons, a shōmēr, a woman from Malīj, and an acquaintance of the parnās 'Allūn (latest dated document: 1098) receive a jūkhāniyya.

26. TS K 15, f. 113. In the hand of the scribe who wrote B 13, 17, 18. Distribution of wheat to Europeans, altogether 49 households including households consisting of only one person. First item: "The proselyte—3; his slave girl Mubāraka—½ wayba."

Wheat was measured, not weighed. A wayba was equivalent to approximately 4 gallons. At this distribution a person received an average of ¼ wayba or 1 gallon, and the average household consisted of only two persons. The proselyte, certainly a Christian from Europe, received special consideration perhaps because his eating habits were so different from those of the local population.

17 persons or households received ¼ wayba,	total waybas: 4¼
21 persons or households received ½ wayba,	total waybas: 10½
4 persons or households received ¾ wayba,	total waybas: 3
4 persons or households received 1 wayba,	total waybas: 4
1 person or household received 3 waybas,	total waybas: 3
2 allocations not legible	x
49 persons or households received	total waybas: 24¾ + x

27. TS 13 J 28, f. 10. Mūsā b. Abi 'l-Ḥayy, a prominent merchant, uses the reverse side of a letter received by him and the free space on the first page to jot down the names of the poor in receipt of loaves from the community and the number of loaves due them. Most of the about eighty names are identical with those in B 17–24, 26.

At least twelve persons are described simply as Rūmī.

The list of beneficiaries is preceded by accounts showing the numbers of pounds and loaves distributed by three communal officials and the shares two of them received themselves:

	Pounds	Loaves
Joseph b. Ḥātim	125	144
Joseph b. Ḥātim	36½	43
Joseph b. Ḥātim	26	not indicated
Abū Sa'īd	130	145
Ya'qūb	87½	97
Ya'qūb	50	54
Personally	4	not indicated
Abū Sa'īd	62	not indicated
Personally	13	not indicated
Total pounds	534	Price 128½ (dirhems)

Since 40 dirhems had approximately the value of 1 dinar at that time (*Med. Soc.,* I 376, secs. 45–47), the price of the bread as given here is more or less identical with that in B 19, 24.

Mūsā b. Abi 'l-Ḥayy, the writer of this elaborate statement, which thus must have been written around 1107, already appears as a party in a mercantile undertaking forty years earlier (ENA 4020, f. 16, dated 1068), and some letters addressed to him and others sent by him preserved in the Geniza might even precede that date. Abū Sa'īd, one of the officials entrusted with the distribution of the loaves, is probably identical with the cantor and court clerk Abū Sa'īd Ḥalfōn b. Manasse (dated documents 1100–1138).

28. TS K 3, f. 34. A more complete list (about 110 names, almost all of them mentioned in the previous sections) in the same difficult script. Mūsā obviously served as head parnās in those years.

29. TS K 15, f. 97. List of persons in receipt of 5 or 10 (dirhems) or of a felt cloth, with a postscript signed by Isaac b. Samuel, the Spaniard (dated documents 1095–1127), another judge (signing a deed in 1099), and the scribe Hillel b. Eli (1066–1108) to the effect that the list, which had been compiled by the elders, needed further study.

10 persons each receive a felt cloth
22 persons each receive 5 dirhems (including two women from Hebron, Palestine, who receive 10 together)
4 persons each receive 10 dirhems

It is clear that the monetary compensation granted to one person was 5 dirhems, as it had been about seventy-five years before (see B 2*b*).

A woman and her brother get 12 *dinars;* this cannot be a donation, but certainly was a debt the community owed them. The list is not complete. The total of 580 dirhems preceding the remark and signature of the judges cannot be related to the individual items.

30. John Rylands Library, Manchester, Gaster Collection A 923. Fragment (18 items) of a list that apparently formed a draft for a distribution of clothing. Some names are identical with the preceding list.

31. TS K 15, f. 102. List of about 85 households. About a dozen names are identical with B 22 (f. 50), but the wide divergence of the main part of the list from the others indicates that a number of years must have intervened between it and the rest of this group. On the reserve side room was left for the Europeans. Instead, there is a note: "The Europeans cannot be counted."

The note and the exceptionally large and calligraphic script (similar to, but not identical with, that of Ḥalfōn b. Manasse [see B 32] induce me to assume that our list was prepared to form the basis for the allocation of communal assistance. I take the numerals that are squeezed in between the lines as the numbers of the members of each household and the entries that bear no numbers as households consisting of only one person. At the beginning, in ll. 3 and 6, the clerk wrote the numeral 1, then decided to leave it out when a household had no more than one member. For other such lists noting the size of families, see B 74, 76. Poor families were always small, for a boy in such a family was expected to be an independent breadwinner by the age of ten.

27 names are without numbers, total assumed	27	persons
2 names are followed by 1, total assumed	2	persons
13 names are followed by 2, total assumed	26	persons
18 names are followed by 3, total assumed	54	persons
14 names are followed by 4, total assumed	56	persons
10 names are followed by 5, total assumed	50	persons
1 name is followed by 6, total assumed	6	persons
85 households with an assumed total of	221	persons

32. BM Or 5566 C, fs. 9–10, ed. and well analyzed in Braslavsky, *Our Country,* pp. 75–83, facsimile facing p. 97. Ninety-three households in receipt of about 250 (loaves, not money). In the late style of the handwriting of the scribe Ḥalfōn b. Manasse (see B 27).

Foreigners: From Palestine, 11 (4 families from Hebron, perhaps expelled in 1119–1120, when the Christian clerics became interested in the tombs of the Patriarchs there, 2 from Jerusalem; 1 each from Acre, Baniyas, Caesarea, Jīsh [misspelled *jshy*], Mā'ūn [Transjordan]; Asia Minor, 1; Syria, 4 (Damascus, Aleppo, Ma'arra, Tripoli); Malatia (see below), Ḥijāz, 2 (1 a Levi); Spain, 1. The list is headed by an anonymous described as *ben ṭōvīm* (Heb.), a man from a good family, and concluded by "the orphans in the cantor's house," with which B 52, end, should be compared.

The numbers of loaves assigned to each household are indicated by Hebrew numerals written to the left of the names, but in four cases by strokes. Since such strokes appear in several instances also on the right side, sometimes identical with the numeral and sometimes representing half of it, I assume that these indicate the loaves already distributed.

				Total loaves
3	households	received	1 loaf	3
59	households	received	2 loaves	118
13[a]	households	received	3 loaves	39
4[b]	households	received	3 loaves	12
5	households	received	4 loaves	20
4	households	received	5 loaves	20
2[c]	households	received	6 loaves	12
1	household	received	8 loaves	8
2	households	received	10 loaves	20
92	households	received		252 loaves

[a] Three of these households consisted of two or more persons.
[b] Indicated by strokes.
[c] One of these: the drivers of the mules (who distributed the loaves).

The recipients of 5 or more loaves were communal officials and their ilk. Even numbers of loaves: 69, uneven: 24. See page 128, above.

Some suggestions for corrections in the edited text and its translation:

F. 9, l. 4. Malaṭī does not refer to the island of Malta, but to the town Malatia in Asia Minor, today Malatya in Turkey.

Ibid., l. 5. *Raqīqī,* read: *ruqūqī,* maker of parchment, a person frequently mentioned in the lists of this period.

Ibid., l. 9. *yadayhā* refers to the preceding line. The proselyte woman receives her share through the woman of Tyre (the two probably arrived in Fustat together).

F. 9*v,* l. 1. *Snywn* is without doubt not an Arabic word, but a Romance name. Snywn, the Rūmī, also appears in B 33. He might be identical with Snywr (Senior?), mentioned in B 26, or the Rūmī Smywn (with *m*), who receives, however, in B 17, col. II, l. 18, and B 18, col. III, l. 5, *four* loaves, while our Snywn gets only *two*. S. M. Stern, in his letter to me of Feb. 23, 1961, suggested that the name was an abbreviation of *bon(um) signum*, "good augury," with the first element omitted, but has not yet found the Italian original of such a name.

Ibid., l. 59. House Phineas. The MS has: House *Ben* Phineas. This little detail is not without importance. For the House Ben Phineas appears in at least fifteen dated documents between 1164 and 1214, but our document antedates 1164 by about 40 years.

Ibid., l. 69. ?, read: *jayyid al-qiṭ'a*, "of good cut", a byname.

Ibid., l. 70. ?, read: *al-qashāshī*, "dealer in secondhand clothes."

Ibid., l. 71. ?, read: *muḥimm*, "affected by fits of fever."

33. TS NS J 293. "List of the Clothes for the Poor, 1451 of the Documents" (A.D. 1139–1140). Four fragments altogether, three of which being in the hand of the scribe of B 25, part one. They are headed by the parnās Abū 'Alī Ibn Baruch, receiving a *muqaddar*, and the *shōmēr* Abu 'l-Surūr allotted a *shuqqa*; all the remaining forty whose names are preserved get a *jūkhāniyya*. In the fourth fragment (which was attached to one of the others by a thread), in the hand of the second part of B 25, a piece of clothing of the sari type, called *fūṭa*, is given to fifteen persons.

It should be on record that I did not find these fragments all together; I assembled them while starting to arrange the New Series in the Taylor Schechter Collection of the University Library Cambridge (see *Med. Soc.*, I, 4). The type, form, and state of preservation of the paper and the arrangement of the script on it leave little doubt, however, that they form parts of one document. See also B 25.

Of the total of 57 items, 35 refer to male persons, 22 to females; thus, women are not in the majority, as a first superficial glance might induce one to believe.

34. TS K 15, f. 85. About sixty needy persons, some identical with those in B 33. One section of the list is superscribed "In the Tujīb" (a quarter of Old Cairo). No numerals or other indications of the charity involved. Like B 31 written in very large characters, but in poor script and with bad spelling. A work list like B 31.

1160–1190

35. TS K 15, f. 30. "Specification of the Distribution of Wheat," upper section of partly effaced list; about forty names preserved, among them that of Maimonides' sister-in-law, the widow of David b. Maymōn who perished in the Indian Sea. She received "a quarter and an eighth" of a wayba, obviously a quarter for herself and an eighth for her infant daughter (see B 26). At least five persons are characterized as *shāmī* (from Palestine, or from Damascus); otherwise no persons from outside Egypt.

36. TS 8 J 5, f. 14. Distribution of money and clothing, superscribed "The Rest through Abu 'l-Bayān" (the parnās [see A 25–36]). Since this heading is

not followed by a sum, it does not represent the balance of an account, but indicates that one or more preceding distributions were carried out by other officials.

In the handwriting of the judge Samuel b. Saadya (see *ibid.*) who wrote on the margin an item of another type dated Tishri (Sept.–Oct.), 1183.

Nine persons receive 5 (dirhems), eight, 3, and one, 2, altogether eighteen recipients, all women except for three, two of whom are characterized as foreigners. Umm Maʿānī, the widow of al-Daqqī (not Raqqī, as often; Samuel distinguished clearly between *d* and *r*) received first 3 dirhems, then 5. Daqqī may mean producer or seller of fine sugar, or of fine linen, and several other things.

It is noteworthy that the widow of the parnās Zayn here receives alms of 3 dirhems and in A 34 (No., 1183) she receives 5, while her three daughters were well enough off to emancipate their slave girl (and not to sell her) on Jan. 20, 1181 (TS 8 J 12, f. 3).

The strange name *q'lṣ* is Greek *kalos,* beautiful. The father-in-law of the widow concerned is most probably identical with the gravedigger Kalos, spelled *q'lws* (see B 25, col. III, l. 5, and B 66, col. II, l. 21). As a foreigner he was forced to choose this low occupation.

Verso, four distributions of a muqaddar (three to male persons) and four of a jūkhāniyya. Among the recipients a freedwoman and "the orphans" of one household.

In two entries, the items are followed by the name Maḥfūẓ (the beadle in A 22, 23, 39), in the entry of the orphans the items are followed by the name Abu 'l-Faḍl (a parnās). The persons concerned probably were unable to select the clothing themselves, wherefore these communal officials were charged to help them.

1210–1225

37. TS 13 J 8, f. 11*v*. Draft of accounts bearing the date 1213. Sundry revenue and expenditure of the community chest. Discussed in A 146.

38. TS NS J 76. Expenditure of 427½ *bakhāya* dirhems on clothing for communal officials, on payment of a balance due for the distribution of wheat and other items. Superscribed: "Collected 427½. The expenditure entirely in bakhāya" (dirhems bearing the inscription *bkh*). Of the 119 lines there are 16 items preserved. The writer received the price of a *Yūsufī* cloth worth 22½ (ll. 18–19, while the judge Jephthah, the cantor Jedūthūn, the parnās Abraham, and the beadle Abu 'l-Faraj (b. Maḥfūẓ, of the Iraqi synagogue since 1181 [see *Eretz-Israel,* 7 (1965) 96]) each got 45, enough for two such pieces of cloth. For verso see C 87.

39*a*. ENA 2736 (Yedūthūn). Request from the judge Elijah to pay the cantor Yedūthūn the balance from the weekly collection for *mezōnōt* (see p. 544 n. 25), 4 dirhems, as ordered by the Nagid (Abraham Maimonides) "at the funeral" (lit., "the tearing of the garment"), obviously of a poor man, at which the cantor sang the liturgy.

39*b*. TS K 25, f. 240, sec. 38. Order, in the handwriting of Abraham Maimonides, to pay the beadle Ṭāhir 2½ dirhems for participation in a wedding, most likely of an indigent couple.

40. TS K 15, f. 90. Ten weekly payrolls for the second through the tenth weeks and then again for the fourteenth week of the liturgical year, which begins after the autumn holidays. In this account and those in B 41, 42, and 49 the total sum spent on the distribution of loaves is also listed every week.

These important lists are drafts in the hand of Solomon, the son of judge Elijah, presumably in preparation of fuller reports such as those represented in B 41 and 44*b*. Each week is headed by its liturgical name (mostly differing from those used in the synagogue today, but easily recognizable) and the sum put at the disposal of the writer. Often noted, too, are the name of the collector who handed over the money (always *one*), a balance from the preceding week, or arrears due on its account. Then, never in the same order, follow the items actually paid, concluding with the balance remaining or due. Payments to officials (not their total salary, of course, but their share in the weekly collection) remain the same for many weeks: "the cantor—7 [dirhems], [the judge] R. Jephthah—6½, the Cleaner—4, R. Yeshū'ā—3, judge Manasse—2½, the two beadles [namely, Ṭāhir and Maḥāsin]—4 [together]." When we find Maḥāsin once with 2½ dirhems, the reason is that ¼ dirhem went to raisins for the "wine" used during the service, as evident from the item "beadle and raisins—2½" in the eighth week and the payment of 2 dirhems to each beadle in B 44*b* and 48*b*. The weekly expenditure on bread was 29, 30, 30½, 32, 32¾, 33¼ dirhems and similar sums. Compare this with 128½ in B 27 and the amounts in B 19–24. It is possible, however, that there were one or several distributions handled by other communal officials, whose notes have not come down to us (cf. B 27, where we indeed find three distributors).

41. TS Misc. Box 8, f. 100. Similar payroll in the same hand as preceding payrolls for the seventh and eighth weeks of another year. Mostly same names and sums. The entries for the eighth week are in Arabic script. Some payments of arrears from the sixth week are also noted.

This is a full report. The numerals are not defined. In the first 15 lines they represent dirhems, in the remaining 20, loaves of bread. Proof: (*a*) the beadles appear twice, because they receive their cash payment in the first part, their bread in the second. The same in B 44*b*, ll. 1–14 and 15–31. (*b*) The numbers of loaves of the families of the beadles and of some other households are completely, or almost completely, identical with B 47, which is expressly characterized as a distribution of bread on a Friday.

There remains another difficulty. In B 42, l. 20, 150 pounds of bread cost 15 dirhems (their transport ⅜ dirhem), in B 47, bottom (upside down, Coptic numerals), the same amount costs 13-1/3. The total loaves or pounds distributed in this payroll was 126 (see below). Since the standard price in that period seems to have been 10 pounds for 1 dirhem, as we have seen in B 42 and 47, one wonders why during the week covered by this payroll the item "bread" required 32 dirhems. The solution is this. There still were *two* distributions every week, on Tuesdays and Fridays, as had been the practice a hundred and more years before. Our list notes the number of loaves allocated to each household for *one* distribution (habitual in all lists of the poor), but registers the *total* spent on bread during one week (by the distributor concerned).

The comparatively rare occurrence of the item "2 loaves for one person" catches the eye, especially if compared with the lists from the early eleventh and twelfth centuries (see the tables at the end of this Appendix and B 22, above):

1 person receives 1 loaf
5 persons receive 2 loaves
6 persons receive 3 loaves
10[a] persons receive 4 loaves
3[b] persons receive 5 loaves
2[b] persons receive 6 loaves
2 (beadles) receive 8 loaves
1 (beadle) receives 14 loaves

[a] Including the item "4 passing my house," i.e., not regular recipients.

[b] The number 5 beneath Bu'l-Faraj the beadle is crossed out and replaced by 6 behind it.

One again notices the preponderance of even as against uneven numbers of loaves (or pounds) per person. Small children presumably received less than 2 loaves per head (see B 35), and in larger families the total allotted was sometimes reduced.

42. TS K 15, f. 63. Payroll similar to the preceding one, partly in the same hand and noting mostly the same names and sums for the 28th, 29th, and 35th weeks. Cash was given to persons from Ascalon and Mosul and to a Persian devotee, nāzīr (Heb.). In the 29th week space was assigned to salaries, superscribed *al-rusūm,* but the space was left blank.

43. TS K 15, f. 2. Accounts for 64 dirhems received from the collector (called Sulaymān ha-Levi), plus 30 donated by Abraham the Pious (d. 1223) and spent during the 22nd week. The first 30 lines are in the hand of Solomon b. Elijah, the remaining 48 lines in that of another scribe whose ways of accounting were very much different. Expenditure for bread: "54 plus 6 at the end of the day through Abraham Dyer." At the conclusion of the week it had become evident that the allocation had not been sufficient. The total of 60 dirhems is twice as much as the average in B 40–42. These were perhaps later, or this payroll reflects a specific state of emergency, for instance, a low Nile with high prices for wheat.

44*a*. ENA Uncatalogued 89. Fees paid to two teachers for the teaching of orphans and the sons of community officials.

44*b*. *Ibid.,* verso. List of nineteen persons receiving sums of money and others getting loaves of bread. Similar to B 40, 41.

45. JTS Geniza Misc. 21. Payments to the teacher Abū Sḥāq (Abraham) for three boys studying with him during four weeks.

46. TS Misc. Box 8, f. 61. Fragment. Middle part of orderly accounts in the hand of Solomon b. Elijah. In addition to items known from previous accounts, many new ones appear, for example, "myrtles [for the Sukkot Feast]—2½ dirhems; a shoe for the ḥalīṣā [Heb., a ceremony based on Deuteronomy 25:9]—1½; to the Meuzzin [the Muslim cleric who calls people to prayer], who lives near the synagogue of the Palestinians—2; from the Yemenite for Dammūh—6."

47. TS NS J 98. Distribution of 150 pounds of bread, to 39 households. Same hand. A number of names as in B 40, 41, 44*b*, but the system of distribution differed slightly:

8 households received	2	loaves or pounds, total	16
1 household received	2 + 1	loaves or pounds, total	3
1 household received	2 + 2	loaves or pounds, total	4
12 households received	3	loaves or pounds, total	36
1 household received	3 + 1	loaves or pounds, total	4
10 households received	4	loaves or pounds, total	40
3 households received	5	loaves or pounds, total	15
1 household received	6	loaves or pounds, total	6
1 household received	9	loaves or pounds, total	9
1 household received	14	loaves or pounds, total	14
39 households received loaves or pounds totaling			147

The large number of households receiving 3 loaves was clearly attributable to some monetary shortage, when the normal ration of 2 loaves per person could not be maintained, cf., for example, the item "the woman from Būna [Bône in Algiers]—3," while in B 41, she receives 4, no doubt for herself and a relative, such as an old mother or child living with her, or " 'Aṭiyya's house, she and her daughters [i.e., at least 3 persons]—4." The additional allocations were certainly answers to protests.

48. TS NS J 221*. (*a*) Communal accounts, perhaps defective, consisting in payments to specified persons (all in promissory notes), to three officials, for bread, and for the transport of palm branches (for the Sukkot holiday). Sept. 24, 1219, two days before the first Sukkot holiday. (*b*) Complete accounts of revenue and expenditures on Sept. 29, 1219, the eve of the concluding Sukkot holiday (officials, bread, some needy persons).

49. TS NS J 105. Payments to officials and to the families of deceased officials during the sixteenth week. R. Manasse, so frequently mentioned in the previous lists, as well as his colleague R. Daniel, are mentioned here as dead. The collector "Samuel b. Solomon, the partner of R. Ḥalfon" is identical with Bū Manṣūr b. Solomon in B 42, but his description as the partner of another man shows that he must have been comparatively inconspicuous.

Solomon b. Elijah, the writer of the account, paid out the total of 44½ dirhems he had received from the collector. When no money was left for one of the beadles, he had to "transfer" him to another social officer, the Kohen al-Naḥḥāl (Mr. Beekeeper, often mentioned as a donor). Only 16 dirhems was spent for bread, presumably for only one of the two weekly distributions.

1240–1250

50. TS K 15, f. 25. Expenditure for the distribution of bread (100 pounds costing 31½ dirhems [cf. B 41]) and payments to a nāsī, to teachers and other officials during the eleventh week of the liturgical year (Dec., 1241).

51. ULC Or 1080 J 46. Carelessly written and badly preserved accounts from the same period for the thirteenth through the eighteenth weeks. The accounts contain only the liturgical name of the week, that of the collector (changing every week), the sum delivered by him, the amount spent on bread (in the seventeenth week: 28¼ out of 54 dirhems) and the balance. Salaries and so forth were obviously distributed by another official (cf. B 42).

FIRST SUPPLEMENT

1020–1040

52. TS 18 J 2, f. 4. Remains of 28 lines, partly torn and very faded, each containing the names of three or four households in receipt of 2, 4, 6, 8, or more (loaves of bread). Script and arrangement, as well as some unusual names, and in many cases even the numbers of loaves allotted to each household are identical with B 1.

Of the first line, written in Arabic characters, only the beginning "Witnessed by . . ." is preserved. The line corresponds to the end of B 1, where the correctness of the distribution of bread is also testified by various witnesses.

The left ends of ll. 10–28 are torn away, but are preserved in TS 20.112 (B 2*a*), where an additional 14 lines, albeit partially effaced, are to be found. Thus, the two lists, B 1 and 2*a* + 52, the first comprising 40 lines and the second a total of 42, complement each other. Despite the close affinity of the two lists there are also wide discrepancies. The details that are identical appear in an entirely different order. Of the many new items in B 52, note in particular: "*kanīs al-mu'allim,* the synagogue of the teacher—[14, deleted and replaced by] 16," that is, schoolchildren receiving rations of bread in the school.

1040–1080

53. TS NS Box 226, f. 8. Three, much damaged columns, seemingly in the hand of the scribe of C 1, 2, containing about sixty names of male persons. The first four are styled "elder"; among the others: 4 dealers in olive oil, *zayyāt,* 2 dyers, 2 packers, a cook, a gravedigger, a *ghulām,* servant or employee, of the (senior) Tustarī brothers, all people of low professions. The son of the *muqrī,* the professional reader of psalms and other prayers over the dead (col. III, l. 1), might be identical with the son of the *meqōnēn,* the Hebrew name of the same profession, in C 7, col. III, l. 26. Our list, which contains no numbers, was obviously drawn up in connection with the payment of the poll tax.

54. Bodl. MS Heb. c 28 (Cat. 2876), f. 24. Two lists of partly identical persons, the first without, the second with sums, ranging from 1 through 11 dirhems and ¼ dinar. The first list comprises about forty persons, of these some scholars, others people originating from places such as Aleppo, Tyre, Damascus, Ramle, or the Maghreb, or dealing in Syro-Palestinian products such as mint and acorns, or persons in inferior positions, such as the employee (called *ṣāḥib* in the first list and *wakīl* in the second) of Abū Naṣr, or two gatekeepers of 'Imrān of Tyre, or the ghulām of Ibn al-Tahertī. I take these lists, too, as having been prepared for the poll tax, the second indicating perhaps the sums still due (and to be borne by the community, if the persons concerned were unable to pay).

This document may be from Alexandria.

55. TS NS J 420. Fragment of an important similar list, in the hand, it seems, of the judge Yeshū'ā ha-Kohen b. Joseph of Alexandria (dated documents 1028 through after 1062). The time of the list is assured by the names of persons well known from the first half of the eleventh century, such as Musallam b. Mu'ammal (TS 13 J 10, f. 5, l. 2 from bottom), Faraḥ b. Ibrahīm (many letters), Nāmūs (TS 10 J 22, f. 7, l. 20) and Raḥmūn (six persons of this name are known from 1030–1050). The name Ma'ālī Ibn Dihqān is also found in B 32, which is beyond doubt from the twelfth century, but Dihqān (Squire, nobleman of the low gentry, Persian) is a family name found throughout the centuries, and Ma'ālī is a common personal name.

Besides outsiders from Rūm, Damascus, Tyre, Haifa, and Buzā'a (near Aleppo), one is listed as Miṣrī, that is, from Fustat. Most payments are of 10 dirhems, others 15 or 15½, some 5, and for several persons others stand security.

56. BM Or 5566 D, f. 10. List of names each followed by a sum, mostly 1 or 1½, some 2. The references to the ghulām, or factotum, of Ibn 'Awkal (B 4–5, C 8) and to "Colocasia" (nickname derived from the name of a plant similar to taro), whose three sons appear in B 11, l. 8, and verso, l. 16, induce me to put this list not later than the middle of the eleventh century. Its spelling is faulty and its exact nature not immediately evident.

57*a*. ULC Or 1080 J 48. Calligraphic and beautifully styled Hebrew note to the cantor Aaron requesting him to look after the bearer, a man called Shabbat, who "is of the blind and receives his share with them, but claims that they cheat him, for they take from (New) Cairo. He asked me to write to you so that you should examine his affairs in connection with them."

We find repeatedly that the poor from Cairo received assistance in Fustat (e.g., B 75, 76). But it would be odd to assume that "the blind" of Fustat had to walk twice a week the two miles to Cairo to get their shares. The complainant must therefore have been a Cairene who came to a dignitary in Fustat to lodge a claim with him. In most of the longer lists of poor from Fustat one or several blind are mentioned, but their number is smaller than one would expect. Naturally, many persons called simply by name or place of origin could have been blind.

57*b*. TS 8 J 22, f. 14. Note in the same script and style as the preceding one, but in Arabic language, instructing Rabbānā Abraham (i.e., Abraham b. Sahlān, head of the Babylonian congregation of Fustat) to find another source for the immediate payment of 5 dirhems to a poor sick man after Samuel b. Avṭalyōn (see B 1) had erroneously omitted him from a collection arranged for persons of his description.

57*c*. ENA 4011, f. 25. Request from a notable to remit immediately the sum pledged by him for the poll tax of the poor.

These notes and similar ones no doubt emanated from the office of Elhanan b. Shemarya (see S. D. Goitein, "Elhanan b. Shemarya as a Communal Leader," *Joshua Finkel Jubilee Volume* [New York, 1970]).

58. BM Or 5549, f. 8 (Cat. no 1135, sec. VI). "List of the Prisoners—may God help to rescue them."

A fragment, twenty-four names with sums preserved. Those listed were persons imprisoned for nonpayment of the poll tax, and the sums represent the amounts still due (and to be provided by public or private charity). At least three persons, the cantor Sa'dān, l. 1, Ḥasan the Persian, l. 4, and (Yaḥyā) the son of the Tiberian, l. 5, recur in B 4–5 with the same sums. (Mubārak), the son of the female physician, also in B 8 and 59.

59. TS K 15, f. 94. Long, irregularly written, and mostly effaced list of male persons, some of whom are to be found in B 4–5, 8, 57. In many cases were added sums like 1/8, 1/4 (dinars), 5 qīrāṭs; in other instances a well-to-do person, such as the prominent banker Abu 'l-'Alā b. Sha'yā, stands security (col. II, approximately l. 27). The same banker contributes to the general appeal for the payment of the poll tax (C 7, l. 8).

In several places the words "may God have mercy upon him" are added, which indicates that the poll tax had to be paid for persons who had died in debt to the state.

60. TS 10 J 13, f. 1. Letter by Isaac b. Asher Sefaradi to the Head parnās Abu 'l-Faḍl Mevōrākh b. Abraham (dated documents 1049–1090) instructing him to make payments to needy persons, ranging from 1/8 dinar (to a proselyte) to 1/2 dinar (to a flax-worker). It is expressly stated that the sum needed for the flax-worker was for the poll tax.

1100–1150

61. TS NS J 362. Fragment on vellum listing communal officials and needy families in receipt of loaves of bread. Several names and numbers identical with B 18–24. Large, calligraphic script, same style, and perhaps same scribe as in B 19–24. (Because of the difference in the size of the script, the identity of the writer cannot be established with certainty.)

62. BM Or 5542, f. 8. Calligraphic letter of a scholar, presumably on travel, who writes flawless Hebrew and Arabic, asking the cantor Saadya to write down the pesīqā made for him on the day before (a Saturday or holiday, when no notes could be taken) and to be careful not to omit anything.

63. TS NS Box 320, f. 30. "Record of the list of the poor, *thabt jarīdat al-'aniyyīm,* may God help them." First item: "A woman from a good family [no name, of course]"; second: "An acquaintance of R. Isaac [b. Samuel, the Sefaradi]"; third: "Abū Naṣr, son of the ḥāvēr Shālōm," found also in B 16. Most of the three pages torn away; only 36 items preserved. The parchment-maker of B 31, col. II, l. 8, and B 32, l. 5, appears again, but instead of Simḥa the gravedigger (B 22), his orphan. No numbers.

It seems to be in the hand of the scribe of B 13, 17, 18.

64. TS NS Box 321, f. 6. In the hand of the scribe of B 25, part 2, B 33, part 1. Distribution of 23 jūkhāniyyas to thirteen women, seven men, and three persons defined as "acquaintances of" or "the house of." The names of three (e.g., the laborer employed by the beadle and parnās Sālim) are crossed out and nine bear the sign resembling an Arabic final *m* as in B 25 and 33, with which our fragment might once have formed one document.

65. TS Arabic Box 30, f. 67. Two lists in an unusually large cursive script with a postscript in another, small and neat script.

a) The superscription "I[n Your] N[ame]" shows that this is the first list. It is followed by: "Those who have not yet received their share" (and are receiving it now, as is proved by the second list [*b*]). And then comes the list:

Number of households	Number of dirhems received	Total dirhems received
1	1	1
3	2	6
6	3	18
5	4	20
8	5	40
2	6	12
1	7	7
1[a]	8	8
2	10	20
1	Not preserved	x
30 households receive		132 + x dirhems

[a] "The glassmakers from Tyre."

b) "Expended on . . ." (illegible, perhaps referring to the holiday concerned). In five places *dr,* dirhem, is added after the numerals, but dirhems are intended throughout, since the postscript says with regard to fifteen recipients: "To be added to the orders of payments," that is, the persons concerned received their shares not in cash, but in checks. The heading of the postscript actually has *lil-ruqa'ī,* "to the trader of orders of payments," the banker with whom the community used to deal and who was prepared to accept these orders.

The numerals in the postscript are Coptic, but conform with the Hebrew numerals in the main list, as far as preserved:

4 households receive	2 dirhems, total	8
3 households receive	4 dirhems, total	12
3 households receive	5 dirhems, total	15
1 household receives	6 dirhems, total	6
2 households receive	10 dirhems, total	20
1 household receives	12 dirhems, total	12
5 households receive	Not visible	x
19 households receive		73 + x dirhems

A number of characteristic names are identical with those occurring in B 17–24.

Note here specifically: "The water carrier from Baghdad—4; a European [*ifranjī*] who lives in the synagogue—2 [?]; a Byzantine scribe—2; a poor young man [*ḍaʿīf,* A 11(*b*) and 127] who arrived in the evening and whose overcoat, *kisā,* was taken from him as a collateral for 5 dirhems; his name is Abu 'l-Munā, he is sick; Jacob, the Maghrebi—5; Mu'ammala ["the one hoped for"], a widow of good family who never in her life had taken anything from anyone—5; the old man from Jerusalem—10."

The whole seems to be a distribution of money, probably before a holiday, in a time of severe hardship, when the community had not enough means, and about fifty families had to wait for their shares. Even then about one-third received their allocations in orders of payments—and we do not know how much the ruqaʿī charged for converting them into cash.

66. TS Misc. Box 28, f. 184*. List of 103 persons, households, or groups in receipt of ½ through 3 waybas of wheat (see B 26):

6 parties receive	½ wayba,	total 3	waybas
5 parties receive	¾ wayba,	total 3¾	waybas
15 parties receive	1 wayba,	total 15	waybas
5 parties receive	1¼ waybas,	total 6¼	waybas
21 parties receive	1½ waybas,	total 31½	waybas
5 parties receive	1¾ waybas,	total 8¾	waybas
33 parties receive	2 waybas,	total 66	waybas
2 parties receive	2¼ waybas,	total 4½	waybas
2 parties receive	2½ waybas,	total 5	waybas
8 parties receive	3 waybas,	total 24	waybas
1 not clearly visible		x	

103 recipients of a total of 167¾ + x, approx. 170 waybas

Special attention must be paid to these details:

13 items are followed by the remark "died," *halak, -at*
8 items are followed by the remark "he, or she, is doing well," *ya-, taṣlaḥ*
4 items are followed by the remark "absent," *ghāʾib,* or *ghāb*
2 items are followed by the remark "leaving," *musāfir*
1 item is followed by the remark "left," *sāfar*

The remarks about the changes ("died," "absent," and so forth) give the impression that they were written during the execution of the carefully written document and not added as an afterthought.

In view of all this, the nature of the list should be understood thus: Before a comprehensive distribution of wheat was made, the list tabulating the preceding distribution was scrutinized and all major changes, such as cases of death, changes in the economic situation of a family, or its departure, actual or impending, were indicated. This up to date list would be copied by an accomplished scribe and then be submitted to the communal authorities for action. Therefore we find one item followed by this remark: "Note, *ruq'a,* from the rayyis: this man should not receive anything." The reference can be only to the Nagid Samuel b. Hananya, who assumed office in 1140.

At least twenty-eight persons with specific names are also found in one or several of lists B 25 (at least nine), 29, 31, 32, 33 (at least eight), 34 (at least nine). Three persons mentioned in the previous lists are noted here as dead and there are other indications (dependent children instead of parents mentioned) showing that our list is slightly later.

Only seven persons are referred to as foreigners, among them "the divorcée of the Indian." Whether he was really an Indian Jew, or a local merchant who received this by-name because he traveled to India so often (wherefore his wife became impatient and divorced him), I do not dare to decide.

67. TS Box J 1, f. 26*. Exact account of expenses for a distinguished sick foreigner, showing also how these expenses were covered. See the commentary in *Med. People.*

1150–1190

68. Bodl. MS Heb. f 103, f. 41. The blind woman Sitt Ṣāfī receives on Dec. 10, 1159, the 10 dirhems due her for the two months Elul and Tishri (Aug. 16 through Oct. 13). In the hand of the judge Mevōrākh b. Nathan and copiously witnessed.

69. TS Arabic Box 52, f. 248. "David, the nāsī, the crown of the Chosen People, the nāsī of all the Diaspora." (So designates himself the writer, "a scion of the House of David," but certainly not a man of consequence. Maimonides, who arrived in Egypt approximately at the time of the writing of this note, made fun of the highfalutin titles of the "Easterners.") "Please pay to the judge Jacob Kohen the due for the month Tebeth 1476 [ended on Jan. 15, 1165], as is the custom. The farānisa [parnāsīm] shall not delay him under any circumstances. Likewise, the judge Manasse: 60 [i.e., dirhems] to the rāv [i.e., Jacob Kohen] and one dinar to judge Manasse, total 96 [1 dinar = 36 dirhems]. And Peace."

The nāsī was in charge of the revenue from some communal property, part of the proceeds of which formed a source of income for the judges. Jacob b. Joseph ha-Kohen signed documents in 1161 (three, TS 8 J 33, f. 10 *a–c*) and in 1174 (TS Misc. Box 25, f. 25) and is also otherwise known (see *Tarbiz,* 34 [1965], 232).

70. TS NS Box 321, f. 14. "Account of the dirhems of the distribution,

tafriqa." Payments to community officials, for example, Sālim, the parnās and beadle (1161–1170)–7 (or 6), Maḥfūẓ the beadle (1159–1188)–3, the rayyis Abu 'l-Najm–10.

71. (*a*) TS NS Box 324, f. 132, pages *a–c*. "The Clothing, *al-kiswa,* Teveth 1488" (began on Dec. 5, 1176). The last but one numeral of the date is not fully visible, but its reading is ascertained by the many names in common with the lists A 25–36 (1181–1184).

Distribution of about 110 pieces of clothing (40 muqaddar, 49 ordinary, and 15 small jūkhāniyyas, the rest illegible) to community officials and/or their dependents and to needy persons. At the head of the list at least five cantors and three shōmērs. One beadle of Dammūh is listed at the beginning of the list (p *a*, l. 5), another at the end (*c*, l. 6). Almost all the males receive a muqaddar, all but one of the females (p. *b*, l. 2) a jūkhāniyya. Males receiving a muqaddar: p. *a*, l. 8 (written above the line), p. *b*, ll. 1, 6, 18. Various members of the same household each get a piece of clothing: Sālim, the porter, a jūkhāniyya (p. *a*, 1. 8) his wife, a jūkhāniyya (p. *a*, 1. 13); Abu 'l-Majd, the milkman, a muqaddar (p. *a*, l. 16), his son, a small jūkhāniyya (p. *c*, l. 3); Maḥfūẓ, the beadle and his son, each a muqaddar. Still, such occurrences are far rarer than one would expect. The conclusion to be derived from this and related documents: normally, only one member of a household received a new piece of cloth at each distribution.

(*b*) Page *d*. "Dirhems expended." After the first item, "the judges," is left a blank space. Al-Najīb (the parnās) follows with the number 20 after it and l. 12, Abū 'Alī the parnās, with 12. The remainder:

6 receive 3 dirhems
4 receive 4 dirhems
7[a] receive 5 dirhems
2 receive 6 dirhems
2[b] receive 8 dirhems

[a] Among these was "the widow of the man from Tyre; a foreigner."
[b] Among these was "the widow of the man from Haifa."

As other lists show, the cash was given as a partial compensation for clothing. Thus the two parts of the manuscript actually form one record.

72. TS Arabic Box 52, f. 247*a–b*. A list of about sixty-eight persons (among them about thirty-one females) receiving clothing of the same type as in the preceding section; nine community officials or their relatives, ten widows, ten orphans, seven foreigners (not specified, but listed together), one blind, one paralyzed, others defined by their profession, for example, a *nassāja,* a female weaver, perhaps of a specific type. No cash.

In the hand of Samuel b. Saadya, who also wrote f. 247*d*, dated 1183.

73. BM Or 5566 C, f. 1. "The Collector of mezōnōt," money for bread for the poor.

Payments of dirhems to communal officials made by that collector during three weeks. Of the eight persons listed under the second and third weeks, six recur also in the first, which contains fourteen names. The nāsī receives

7 dirhems twice, followed by R. Nissīm with 4 dirhems in the second week, 3 in the third, and 2 in the first.

1200–1240

74. TS NS Box 320, f. 41. A survey of households. A leaf, 8 by 6 inches, folded so as to form four pages, each originally containing data about 33–34 families, a total of about 135, of which about 110 are preserved, many defective. The list is important inasmuch as it mentions the number of persons in each household. It was no doubt prepared in order to form the basis for the weekly distribution of bread to the needy and to community officials. The names of the assistant judge Jephthah, the beadle Ṭāhir, and the cantor Abū Sahl put the list into the beginning of the thirteenth century, preferably after B 47, where Ṭāhir receives 14 loaves, indicating that he still had a large household, whereas here only one child lives with him, and a son of his is listed as a separate family. As far as legible, the composition of the families receiving relief was approximately thus:

	Number of families	Total loaves
Man alone	13	13
Woman alone	17	17
Husband and wife	18	36
Parents with 1 child	9	27
Parents with 2 children	11	44
Parents with 3 children	2	10
Parents with 4 children	1	6
Parents with 5 children	2	14
Parents with more than 2 children (number not preserved)	3	15
One person living with brother	3	6
One person living with sister	3	6
One person living with mother	1	2
One person living with grandmother	1	2
Data legible	84	199

Average size of family of relief recipients: 2.4.

For a realistic appreciation of this breakdown one should keep in mind that most of the persons listed must have been elderly people who either no longer had a family or whose older children (from the age of ten) were seeking their livelihood out of their homes (see B 31).

75. TS 8 J 41, f. 13*v*. A census for the poll tax. A list of male persons with consecutive numbers written above the names. The first complete number visible is 19, but some names are discernible before. Total: 68 households. Outsiders: 7 from Cairo (in a separate appendix, superscribed "The Cairenes" and including the beadle of the synagogue of that city), 3 each from Alexandria and Maḥalla, 1 from Qūṣ in Upper Egypt, 1 Maghrebi, 1

from Damascus. Some are listed together with their descendants, for example, "(52) Abū Ḥayyūn, the old carpenter, and (53) the son of his daughter" (who presumably worked with him).

Those listed were certainly persons for whom the community had to provide the poll tax, either completely or in part.

76. ULC Or 1081 J 50. *Al-Qāhiriyyīn.* List of indigent families from Cairo, an appendix, similar to that attached to the preceding list. First item: "The daughters of Abu 'l-Faraj, the son of the woman from Jerusalem." Then comes, as a superscription, the Coptic number 3, indicating that each of the following five families consisted of three members. The numerals following the names show the gifts made to them. The group superscribed 2 consists of four families. The last is not preserved.

77. TS NS J 251. Accounts on weekly expenditure of a type similar to B 41–43, 49, and also in the hand of Solomon b. Elijah. A clean copy for three weeks, always opening with the amounts collected by *two* persons: first week, two laymen; second, the beadles Ṭāhir and Maḥāsin; third, Ṭahir and the cantor Abu 'l-Majd. Cash was 74 dirhems in the first week, 32½ in the third. The expenses for the first week are given in detail:

Bread for the poor	[a] 16½ dirhems
Salaries	32 dirhems
The Nāzīr (devotee)	1 dirhem
Wine for the service	1 dirhem
Carpenters (Jewish) for repairs in a communal building	6 dirhems
Sundry	6½ dirhems
Total	63, balance 11

[a] Certainly for only *one* of the two weekly distributions.

Here, too, the standard price of bread was 1 dirhem for 10 pounds (see B 40, 41), since in the second week 9 loaves of bread were resold for ⅞ dirhems. In the second week, a loan of 10 dirhems had to be taken from the judge Hananel to cover the expenses for the bread, and in the third another loan from a different source. See also next section.

78. TS NS J 438. Four pages of drafts of communal accounts, all crossed out, usually done after a clean copy was made. Page one is almost entirely identical with the preceding account, and represents the final copy of that page. The other pages are highly interesting for they contain many instructions by the Nagid Abraham Maimonides showing administrative practices in times of severe hardship. For instance, a collection, totaling 30 dirhems had been promised to a young Maghrebi, for which a notable had stood security and paid to the foreigner. When only 17 dirhems came in, the Nagid ordered 13 dirhems taken from a collection for a man from Damīra, Egypt, and turned over to that notable. The situation probably was that the traveler from the Maghreb had to leave, while the man from Damīra could wait, and people who had stood security should get their money back immediately,

otherwise no one would be found in the future to undertake that task about which we read so much in our records.

79. BM Or 5566 C, f. 2. "[Received on account of the] Food for the Poor—101½ [dirhems]." Accounts for one week, headed by 115 pounds of bread costing 33½ dirhems, twice as much as in B 77. A similar situation in B 43. The salaries, however, remained exactly the same. On Friday, the Nagid made special distributions in cash and wheat to a foreign scholar and to the Rūm, here meaning persons from Byzantium, "male and female." After the conquest of Constantinople by the Latins in 1204 and countless other disasters befalling the Byzantine realm, it is not surprising to again find refugees from there in the capital of Egypt. See B 85.

80. TS Misc. Box 25, f. 84. Expenditure for a week. Here 100 pounds of bread and its transportation cost 22½ dirhems. The salaries again as before. When a beadle is listed here with 4 dirhems (instead of 2, as usual), the sum certainly included arrears from the preceding week. Also some entries of personal expenditure made by the official.

81. TS NS J 267. Slip of paper with expenditure for one week. Among the recipients R. Elijah the Rūmī (see B 79). Bread, 18¾ dirhems.

82. ENA 2727, f. 54. Fragment mentioning (the local) judge Elijah and his elder son Abū Zikrī. Communal accounts; sources of revenue: "A [public] Fast—29." "Food for the Poor—39." Among the expenses, besides bread and salaries, payments to a traveler called by name and his *rafīq,* companion (see *Med. Soc.,* I, 348).

83*a*. TS NS J 239*v*. Short list (without numbers) of communal officials and needy persons, mostly women and foreigners, ending with "the strangers in the synagogue." Recto: sums owed to or by the community.

83*b*. Westminster College, Frag. Cairens. 58. List containing rare names women and foreigners. Nineteen persons, among them the two beadles, receive 3 (ounces), or ¼ pound, one woman half a pound, and "my paternal aunt" a pound. Presumably of oil for lighting, perhaps parallel with the (Umm Kifā', Umm Ḥayyūn) identical with the preceding list, also mostly distribution of wax candles to male persons (B 89, 90).

84. TS NS J 245. Small slip containing twenty-two names of indigent persons, mostly women. The first three persons also in sec. B 83*a*.

85. TS 8 J 6, f. 3*v*. "Those who have not received their share" (in the distribution of wheat). Three lists.

I. Parties receiving wheat (6, ½ wayba; 8, 1 wayba; 1, 2 waybas).

II. Twelve parties (of whom at least six are repeated from list I) get sums, mostly of 2½ or 5 (dirhems).

III. Names without any explanation added, some identical with those in the next list. Written on the verso of a power of attorney given in 1216.

The neglected people listed were mostly outsiders, either foreigners (Rūm, [see B 79]; Persia, Jerusalem, Barqa, each 1), or from Egypt itself (Alexandria, al-Maḥalla, Minyat Ghamr, Benhā, Damīra, Dakarnas [the latter also B 71]). A similar list of neglected people, about eighty years later, in B 65.

86. TS NS J 440. List of thirty-two names with Coptic numerals (recipients of loaves of bread), as, for example, "the son of the little Sesame" (a female nickname), found also in B 41, 44, 47. Written in a hand superior to that of Solomon b. Elijah who wrote most of the contemporary lists of this type. When "the Maghrebi scribe" receives 10 loaves, but the water carrier Wafā only 2, the reason was certainly a difference in the size of the two households, but since such discrepancies are found often, the idea also occurs that perhaps a scholar should devote his time to his work and not to the search for a livelihood.

87. TS K 15, f. 49. Payments made on a Thursday. In addition to the usual expenditure for bread, salaries, and extras, the official twice paid ¾ dirhems to a teacher, the weekly tuition for a poor boy (or two brothers) for whom the community paid. School fees were paid on Thursday.

Verso, ll. 1–3, contributions, possibly received on the morning of the same day in the synagogue. Headed by Ibn Jalāl al-Mulk, "the Splendor of the Kingdom," a government official, who contributes also in A 39, 42, 46.

88. TS NS Box 320, f. 33. Irregular notes on communal expenditure, the first section summarized "82½ dirhems besides the poll tax."

89. ULC Or 1081 J 67. "Number of Wax Candles [distributed]—20." List of twenty male persons each receiving a wax candle, presumably for a holiday (the Day of Atonement?) (see also C 55).

Upside down: 5 lines of incomplete accounts for one week. In addition to *al-jum'a,* his weekly salary, a judge receives 7 dirhems.

90. BM Or 5549, f. 7 (Cat. no. 1135, V). Another list of twenty males each receiving a wax candle. No superscription, but all written in large calligraphic letters, and the word *sham'a,* candle, is written out in full after each name. One of the recipients is a beadle, two are described as ghulām, factotum, four are not local people (one shāmī, one Maghrebi). Sulaymān b. Hānī (l. 4) also occurs in the preceding section, and at least four others might be identical, but are called or described differently.

91. TS 6 J 8, f. 4. "May the cantor Abu 'l-Riḍā please arrange a collection for the bearer on Thursday morning in the synagogue, when the Torah is being taken out from the ark, for two chickens and bread. He is poor, old, and sick, and in need of this." Superscribed: "Truth," like an order of payment (see *Med. Soc.,* I, 241).

92. ENA 2763, f. 20. Late list of about thirty recipients of small sums (mostly fractions, type of money not indicated). Characteristic names: 'Abd

al-Karīm, 'Abd al-Dā'im (also in C 70), Nāṣir (see C 71), Naṣr Allāh. Beneath the names on verso:

"The women—3 [the women as separate unit as in A 162]. To the poor of the Iraqian synagogue—1. Due to the rabbi—5."

93. TS Arabic Box 54, f. 52. Communal accounts from the year 1387. Accounts for 20 weeks, seven preceding the Jewish New Year (Sept. 14, 1387), and thirteen following it. Each week starts with the name of the person receiving the money collected and in charge of the payment (the first is called Joseph *syry'qwsy,* which refers not to Syracuse in Sicily, but to Sirāqaws, a pleasure ground for the Mamluk high society, about 11 miles north of Cairo (Ibn Duqmāq V, 49; Popper, *Egypt and Syria,* p. 33). These persons were mostly laymen, but one week the work was done by a cantor, another by the beadle Surūr (see below), and twice by scholars (ḥāvēr). The second item is always the total sum spent, which is sometimes less and sometimes more than the amount received. Through the first 14 weeks the largest item of expenditure is "Amlaj—5." The numbers 7 through 18 immediately follow the word "Amlaj" to mean that in the first week a seventh installment was paid to him, in the second, an eighth, and so forth. *Amlaj* is Arabic for myrobalan, a common tanning and dyeing plant, but is here the name of an official to whom the community made payments in installments. Other items that recur almost every week: the beadles, 2 (once: "according to our means"), a watchman, *ghafīr,* ½. Once: the collector of the poll tax and his messengers, 5. (these were doles, while the weekly installments to Amlaj probably represented payments of the tax itself, perhaps arrears). The beadle Surūr once receives 1 for teaching a boy, and the entry *shālīaḥ,* messenger to the government, once gets 2 and once 1. The weekly account concludes with *ta'akhkhar lahum* or *'alayhim,* balance in favor or to the debit of the community.

Since no payments to cantors and spiritual leaders are noted, they must have received their emoluments from other sources, such as the rents of communal houses. The item "bread for the poor" is also entirely absent.

For the technique of bookkeeping in this late period the very similarly arranged private account TS NS J 227 from the year 1384–1385 should be compared.

94. TS Misc. Box 28, f. 40. Letter to a parnās on vellum and in Hebrew, presumably by a European, asking him to increase the allotment of two loaves of bread, which were not sufficient food, and also to address the community on Saturday on his behalf.

95. Bodl. MS Heb. d 68 (Cat. 2836, no. 29), f. 107. Thābit, the cantor, the son of the astrologer, *munajjim,* requests the Gaon Maṣlīaḥ (in office 1127–1139) in a most calligraphic letter to help him since he and his numerous family had nothing to live on. The reverse side of the letter is blank and does not contain the usual instructions on how to help the applicant.

96. ULC Or 1081 J 61. A request made for the same person who had been in prison for two months because of nonpayment of the poll tax and, in addition, was seriously ill.

Thābit Ibn al-Munajjim appears in the lists of indigents (B 34, 66).

97. Bodl. MS Heb. d 66 (Cat. 2878), f. 59, sec. 3. Commercial accounts for the year 1215 of a silk merchant who served also as parnās. His business correspondent was charged with collecting a yearly pledge for R. Jephthah (see B 79 ff.), wherefore this detail of communal finance appears in the private account of these two merchants. The sums collected are debited to the business correspondent (l. 5), the monthly payments of 4 dirhems to R. Jephthah are credited to him (ll. 24–26; verso, ll. 3–4, 12–14).

98. BM Or 5542, f. 23*. The teacher Abī (!) Sa'īd asks the notable Rāṣūy (see C 39) in the most deferential terms to arrange for the payment of the school fees for the three orphans of a Persian woman living in the communal funduq, or hospice, and for the boy of a Maghrebi carpenter due for a period of four months. He also requests some extra food for wretched little orphan girls entrusted to his care in view of the impending Pentecost holiday. He himself had had meat only eight times since the preceding Pentecost, a whole year. The boys referred to here seem to be identical with those for whom fees were paid in B 44.

99. Westminster College, Arabica I, f. 28*v*. Notes of an official, probably in a small locality, about doles handed out to him on the Passover feast. Part I, Pesīqat Pesaḥ ("The pledges for Passover"), lists six persons, of whom three donate 1 nuqra each, one, 4 waraqs, and two, 2 waraqs. Part II, "What I earned on the Holiday," notes six payments totaling 8½ waraqs and 2 consisting of ½ nuqra each. Part II seems to represent partial payment of the pledges mentioned in Part I.

Compare this with C 68, where on one single day of a feast 115 persons contributed to a pesīqā for a foreigner!

SECOND SUPPLEMENT

100. TS Box J 1, f. 34. Important, but much damaged list of the type of B 2*b*: distribution of sums of 5 dirhems and its multiples (many of 15 or 20, some even of 30), also several of 7½ dirhems. Many names identical with the contemporary lists B 1, 2, 52 (e.g., the rare Ma'shūq, "Beloved," here, ll. 1 and 7 = B 1, l. 35), also some new persons. Here, as in B 2*b*, after the sums assigned, numbers are added, which seem to indicate here the number of persons in each household.

A note: "For transport and the balance of the flour—21" shows that simultaneously with this distribution of money the poor received certain quantities of flour. Ca. 1030.

101. ENA 2591, f. 21*c*. Fragment of list of recipients of bread (twelve out of twenty-two receive 2 loaves each). At least ten persons are identical with those listed in B 23 (in or around 1107).

102. ENA 2591, f. 18. List of weekly emoluments, preceded by the collection made for the purpose. The only document found thus far in which the total sum required for the weekly payments is indicated.

Superscription: "Statement about the revenue from the collection for the weekly payments, *jibāyat al-mujāma'a,* for the week of Nāsō (i.e., the lection of Numbers 4:21–7:89, read mostly in May or June)."

"Our Master"[a]	8 dirhems
The Trustworthy[b]	12 dirhems
3 of the others	10 dirhems
1	6 dirhems
3	5 dirhems
5	4 dirhems

[a] Moses Maimonides.
[b] Title of Maimonides' father-in-law.

Several items are lost. On the reverse side (as the manuscript is bound, it is recto) the Trustworthy and others give additional sums. Still, only 124 dirhems was collected, while another 31 was required.

Besides communal officials (R. Anatoli, 8 dirhems; R. Jephthah, 6; the cantor Abū Sahl, 6; and others) payments to women and for a poll tax are included. R. Anatoli's monthly salary of 52 dirhems, which was covered by income from houses (A 43; see also chap. v, sec. C, 4, end) probably was simultaneous with this weekly emolument, which was paid from a collection.

103. Bodl. MS Heb. e 94, f. 27. A bashful pauper informs the judge R. Elijah, who was in charge of the poor, *yanẓur fī ḥāl al-ʿaniyyīm,* that he had not eaten anything for two days and that he dared to address the judge only because "the knife had reached the bone," in other words, that he was in a state of extreme want.

104. TS Arabic Box 30, f. 163. A man from Alexandria who was forced to flee from that city because he was unable to pay the poll tax for his little boy (which had been imposed on him unlawfully) implores the Nagid Abraham Maimonides for help. He had been unsuccessful in obtaining work, although he was prepared to be content with one silver dirhem per day as wages. Judge Elijah had helped him, but by now he and his boy had not eaten for two days. (In Arabic characters.)

On the reverse side, Abraham Maimonides writes to judge Elijah ordering him to provide the man and his boy with appropriate food for the Sabbath out of the local mezōnōt.

The remaining space was used by the judge for jotting down the names of ten prospective contributors and those of several other persons entitled to some emoluments.

105. Firkovitch II, f. 1415. Abraham Maimonides instructs two notables (names not preserved) to help a needy man "in accordance with your well-known liberality" and to report back to him what action had been taken in that matter. The letter, in Arabic, of course, was dictated, but the Hebrew greetings (including "May redemption be near," an equivalent of the Nagid's signature), as well as the date, are in the hand of Abraham Maimonides. Aug.–Sept., 1213.

106. Dropsie 465. Lower part of a list of male persons, mostly craftsmen or foreigners (for whom poll tax was to be paid); seventeen names on the

left column, two on the right. All names have a horizontal stroke on the left going partly through the name. In six cases, *ṣaḥḥ,* "in order," "paid," is written on the right side. In five other instances, an oblique stroke, which might stand for the Coptic sign for ½, is found on the right side. Perhaps, one day the upper part of this carefully executed list will be recovered.

At least five names are found also in sec. 8, above, two in the next section. Last third of eleventh century.

Foreigners: 2 from Iraq (Baghdad, Āmid); 3, Syria (2 Damascus, 1 Aleppo); 2, Palestine (Gaza, Tiberias); 1, Sicily.

Occupations: 3 porters, 1 packer, 1 night watchman, 1 dyer, 1 soapmaker, 1 mosaicist (*muzawwiq;* mentioned in this sense in an inscription of the al-Aqṣā mosque in Jerusalem, dated 1035. M. van Berchem, *Corpus Inscriptionum Arabicarum,* Section Jérusalem (Cairo, 1920–1922), II, 381–392. Professor M. Rodinson of Paris alerted me on this detail. See *Med. Soc.,* I, 423. Since the ground floor and courtyard in any better house was laid in mosaic, the frequency of this occupation is not astonishing).

Joseph b. Furqān (a rare name) is defined here by his family name Sha'rānī, Mr. Hairy, but in sec. 8, above, by his native city, Damascus.

107. Dropsie 468. Two lists of persons for whom poll tax was to be paid. The first, containing 51 names, is beautifully written, registers each name on a separate line, and provides many additional details. The second list, continuing the first without interval, comprises about 55 items, is in a childish script and horrid spelling, the information given is incomplete, and in many instances only the first name of a person is listed. Many of the 105 or so names are found in secs. 4 through 8, above, especially in secs. 6–8. Late eleventh century.

Foreigners: 2 from Iraq (Baghdad, Mosul); 4, Syria-Lebanon (Damascus, 2 from Tyre, 1, Lādhiqiyya); 4, Palestine (Acre, Haifa, Jaffa, Tiberias); 1, Libya (Barqa); 1, Rūm.

Among the occupations: 3 muqaddams, 2 teachers, 1 cantor, 4 clerks of private persons, referred to as ṣabī, kātib, and ṣāḥib, respectively; a musician (*ālātī*; in sec. 6, col. II, l. 1: Bishr, the stepson of the musician; here: Bishr, the musician; when his mother remarried, she probably stipulated that her husband should teach him his art); an embroiderer (*raqqām,* rare); many from the food industry. These two lists significantly complement secs. 4 through 8 above.

108. TS Arabic Box 40, f. 161. List of names, many rare, of male persons. The document is in Arabic characters, with the exception of the heading, which is in Hebrew: "The progeny blessed by the Lord" (Isaiah 65:23). Several persons are described solely as the sons of, or are listed together with unnamed brothers. The occupations mentioned are low (porter, cook, seller of hazelnuts, roaster of lupines, measurer of grain, etc.) Many foreigners, among them three Palestinians (from Bānyās, Dalāta, Tiberias); Eli ha-Kohen is most probably the poet Eli ha-Kohen b. Ezekiel, who was active in Egypt around 1030.

The heading is euphemistic. It designates poor people, probably requiring assistance for the payment of their poll tax.

109. TS 16.230. Large, but fragmentary list of male persons, many mentioned together with their brothers, sons, one also his workmen, others simply as sons of . . . ("the three sons of . . . , the four boys of . . ."). About seventy names preserved, none identifiable with certainty with persons known from other documents. Perhaps a list of persons unable to pay the poll tax in full from a city other than Fustat. Among the foreigners, besides the common Barqī and Maghrebī, Surūr the Khurasānī and his brother. Surūr, "Joy," is the Arabic equivalent of Hebrew Simḥa and Persian names composed with *shād* (Happiness), borne also by other Jews from Iran during this period.

110. TS Arabic Box 38, f. 95*. "Indigents in Fustat and Cairo: Entirely destitute, to be deferred to next year—150 persons. Others whose state is unknown but from whom not more than 2 dinars can be taken, and this only in installments—150 persons."

A statement headed thus and then specifying groups of persons listed as residents, but originating from Alexandria, the Sharqiyya and Gharbiyya provinces, the Dawāḥī, that is, the villages around the capital (all entirely destitute), and towns such as Ashmūm, Damietta, and Qūṣ. In conclusion, the memo states that the indigents are equally divided between natives of the capital and resident outsiders.

The document is in Arabic characters for it was certainly destined to be submitted to the Muslim authorities.

TYPES OF DOCUMENTS IN APPENDIX B

1. Census.

(*a*) Names without details, headed "List of the Poor," or without superscription: 30, 34, 63, 75 (names numbered consecutively), 83, 84.

(*b*) Work lists noting the size of families or previous distributions: 31, 66, 74, 76.

(*c*) Lists of scholars and officials: 12, 14–16.

2. Payrolls: 13, 39, 69, 70, 73.

3. Payrolls and charities combined: 37–46, 48–51, 77–82, 92, 102.

4. Distribution of bread: 1, 2*a*, 3, 17–24, 27, 28, 32, 39–43, 44*v*, 47–52, 61, 77–81, 86, 87, 101. In Alexandria: A 109, C 53.

5. Distribution of wheat: 26, 35, 66, 85, C 82*a*, (100).

6. Distribution of clothing: 25, 29, (30), 33, 36, 38, 64, 71, 72, (A 112).

7. Distribution of cash (before holidays or in lieu of clothing or wheat): 2*b*, 29, 36, 65, 71*b*, 85, 92, 100, (A 29, 34, 35, 46), C 82*a*. (See also B 57*b*, 68).

8. Poll tax (arrangements for persons unable to pay the tax in full or at all): 4–9, 11, 53–55, 57*c*, 58–60, 75, 88, 93, 96, 106–110. (See also A and C, *passim*).

9. Distribution of wax candles or oil for lighting: 83*b*(?), 89, 90, (A 95, C 55).

10. Documents dealing with individuals: 57, 62, 67, 68, 91, 94–96, 98–99, 103–105, (A 97, 159, 165, 167). See C, Types of Documents, no. 19.

11. Sundry, 10, 37, 39, 46, 56, 97.

BREAD FOR THE POOR

TABLE 1

NUMBER OF LOAVES OF BREAD PER HOUSEHOLD

	App. B, sec. 1 ca. 1026		App. B, sec. 18 ca. 1100		App. B, sec. 23 Nov. 1, 1107		App. B, sec. 24 Nov. 15, 1107	
Number of loaves doled	Number of households	Total loaves	Number of households	Total loaves	Number of households	Total loaves	Number of households	Total loaves
1	3	3	4	4	13	13	6	6
2	51	102	23	46	42	84	26	52
3	5	15	25	75	27	81	33	99
4	32	128	43	172	20	80	27	108
5	1	5	10	50	9	45	11	55
6	19	114	13	78	11	66	14	84
7	1	7	1	7	1	7	1	7
8	14	112	6	48	7	56	13	104
9	—	—	1	9	—	—	—	—
10	1	10	4	40	6	60	1	10
11	—	—	1	11	1	11	—	—
12	3	36	1	12	—	—	—	—
16	1	16	1	16	—	—	—	—
Illegible or omitted by scribe	5	?	8	?	—	—	5	?
Total	136	548+	141	568+ 550 pounds	137	503 500 pounds	137	(525+) 559[a] 500 pounds

[a] Indicated in the source.

TABLE 2

EVEN AND UNEVEN NUMBER OF LOAVES OF BREAD DOLED

Appendix B section	Number of households receiving loaves		
	Even number	Uneven number	Unknown number
1	121	10	5
18	91	42	8
23	86	51	—
24	81	51	5
32	69	24	—
41	20	10	—

TABLE 3

CHANGES IN THE NUMBER OF LOAVES DISTRIBUTED TO EACH HOUSEHOLD MADE BETWEEN FRIDAY, NOVEMBER 1, 1107, AND NOVEMBER 8, 1107

Number of households receiving increased number of loaves	From	To
5	2	3
2	2	4
8	3	4
1	5	6
2	6	8
1	7	9
Number of households receiving reduced number of loaves		
1	4	3
3	10	8
Total changes 23		

A week later, Friday, November 15, ten of the changes made one week before remained in force, three were reduced to their former numbers, namely,

2 households	from 4	to 3
and		
1 household	from 9	to 7,

and one that had been increased from 2 to 3, was again bettered up to 4.

Appendix C

DOCUMENTS OF APPEAL AND LISTS OF CONTRIBUTORS

(Chap. v, sec. C, 1 and 2)

1–11. First half of eleventh century

1. TS Loan 137. Magnificently written list of names, mostly accompanied by sums, 69 lines. Vellum.

The time of the document is defined by several persons mentioned in it and known from dated documents. BRYH (probably to be read *Burayh,* an Arabic diminutive of Barhūn = Abraham, still frequent among village Jews from Yemen) b. Isaac (l. 37) made a settlement with his brother Sa'īd in 1002 (TS 24.11). One BRYH is mentioned in TS 18 J 5, f. 9, dated 1040, as dead. Solomon b. PSh'Ṭ (Arabic *Fashshāṭ,* one who humbugs, boaster, a common name in that period), appearing here (l. 2) together with his brother Isaac, is mentioned in Mosseri A 134, dated 1007 (see J. Mann, *HUCA* 3 [1926], 266), in TS 13 J 1, f. 3, dated 1016, and TS 16.191, written around 1000. Moses b. Ghulayb (l. 39) died in spring, 1026 (TS 18 J 2, f. 16). Sha'yūn b. Isaac, mentioned here (l. 46) together with his elder brother Hillel, signed a document in 1041 (TS 13 J 1, f. 9 [see Mann II, 99]).

In ten cases, two or three brothers, or a father and his son give together—an indication of the frequency of family partnerships in the earlier parts of the eleventh century (see *Med. Soc.,* I, 181).

A complete analysis of the contributions made is impossible since some of the numbers following the names are effaced or partly torn away. Seven names are clearly not accompanied by sums, that is, the persons concerned had not yet made up their minds. Of the rest, eleven give ¼ dinar, some 1/3, others ⅛, one contributes 11 qīrāṭs, or almost half a dinar; most donations are in dirhems: 1, 1½, 2, 2½, 3, 3½, 4, or 5.

2. TS NS Box 320, f. 62. Fragment of a similar list in the same hand and arrangement as sec. 1, in which at least twelve of the twenty-three names preserved recur. Most of the few sums extant are exactly or nearly identical with those listed there.

The average of the sums contributed in silver in the two lists has about half the value of those given in gold.

3. TS 10 J 5, f. 11. Eight persons, headed by Abraham b. Sahlān, the head

of the Iraqian congregation, and Ephraim b. Shemarya, the head of the Palestinians of Fustat, undertake to refund Isma'īl b. Ṭalyūn (i.e., Samuel b. Avṭalyōn) the sum he guaranteed for the ransom of two prisoners, in case it will not be paid.

Dated "Holiday week, *mō'ēd,* [1]333" (either Sept., 1021, or March, 1022). Mann, II, 97, edited only the names of the signatories (and omitted the last one).

It is remarkable that, with the exception of Abraham b. Isaac (C 1, l. 4), none of these notables, whose names occur so frequently in the Geniza documents of the 1020's and later, are among the seventy-seven contributors listed in C 1.

4. TS 13 J 8, f. 14. Report on a joint Karaite-Rabbanite collection made in the capital of Egypt for the Jewish community of Jerusalem which was hard pressed by Muslim moneylenders (*mōzīfīm,* Hebraized Aramaic *yzf*) (cf. *Med. Soc.,* I, 257).

The main contributors were Karaite notables, headed by David b. Isaac, "the Pride of the two denominations" (see chap. v, sec. B, 1, n. 84), who donated 20 dinars, followed by Joseph b. 'Awkal with 15, and the three senior Tustarī brothers (together as one firm) with 10. The total collected in Fustat and Cairo was 133-17/24 dinars, in addition to which the considerable amount needed for the forwarding of the money to Jerusalem was donated by the writer and others. During the week of the writing of the report there arrived 35 dinars from Sicily, and over 200 dinars were on their way from the Maghreb, sent with the Muslim pilgrim caravan (which was regarded as a relatively safe means of overland transport in those days).

Ibn 'Awkal referred to here as Joseph Rōsh Kallā ("Head of the Assembly," a title conferred by the Iraqian yeshivas), appears among the Karaites either because he contributed together with the other prominent merchants and bankers, who were Karaites, or because he had embraced the Karaite persuasion (see *Tarbiz,* 34 [1965], 164. Ephraim ha-Kohen b. Abraham (ll. 12 and 16) was a government official and a Rabbanite judge in (New) Cairo.

5. DK (1), ed. S. D. Goitein, *Epstein Jubilee Volume* (Jerusalem, 1950), pp. 193–201. See C 6.

6. TS 12.374*v, Nahray* 222. Two enigmatic notes, the first extensive, the second short, referring to properties worth millions of dinars, from which contributions had to be made by both Karaites (again mentioned first) and Rabbanites. The notes are written in the same hand on the reverse side of two letters from Jerusalem sent by one person and dealing with the same (private) matter. The addressee is Isaac b. Jacob al-Maqdisī (the Jerusalemite), a merchant known from several business letters, but by no means prominent.

The first note opens as follows:

> 20 Karaites–200 million d[inars. Later the abbreviation is *dīn*].
> All the Karaites–400 million d.
> All the Rabbanites–400 million d.

The two denominations together contribute 160 millions, or one-fifth of their estimated property.

These sums are impossible to believe, since the entire yearly revenue of Egypt during the efficient administration of Ibn Killis (see *Med. Soc.*, I, 33–34) amounted to only 4 million dinars (see Mez, *Renaissance*, chap. 8, p. 122 n. 4). On the other hand, the lists must be realistic, for most of the names mentioned in them are well known. We come down to earth at the end of the longer list, where two persons each pay 10 dinars (the second is Ibn Ṭarsūn, not *wrswn ?,* as printed) and this statement—recurring in the second list—is found: "Ibn Ḥayyīm—500 dinars from the times of [the caliph] al-Ḥākim." The term "million" must stand here for some other sum.

Listed as property for which a tax was to be contributed twice are 200 slave girls. Should this mean that each of the two groups was estimated as harboring this number of maidservants?

I interpret these lists as a preparatory plan for the payment of an extraordinary levy imposed on the Jewish community of the Egyptian capital, probably after the downfall and murder of the "vizier" Abū Sa'd Tustarī and his brother Abū Naṣr. The letters from Jerusalem on the reverse side of which these notes are jotted were written in, or shortly after, 1051, which fits in with the date of the liquidation of the two brothers (see *Med. Soc.*, I, 183). Properties of the two brothers are mentioned in the longer note, and the second note refers to treasures of Abū Sa'd hidden in bathhouses. (I have grouped C 5 and 6 together with C 4 because of the cooperation of Karaites and Rabbanites evident in them. C 4 is about twenty years earlier.)

7. Gottheil-Worrell, XIII, pp. 66–71. "Outstanding Pledges for the Poll Tax. Paid." Contributions had been solicited toward the payment of the poll tax for those who were unable to pay or could contribute only a part of the sums due from them. Our list shows that many had not made good their promises for some time, but finally paid.

Mūsā Ibn al-Majjānī (l. 29) was dead by 1040 (Bodl. MS Heb. a 3 [Cat. 2873], f. 26). On the other hand, a number of other contributors are known as having been active around 1050.

As often in collections for the poll tax of the indigent, most of the payments were low standard averages with only a few being exceptionally large or exceedingly small.

		Total
1	person paid 2 dinars	2
1	person paid 1½ dinars	1½
4	persons paid 1 dinar	4
10	persons paid ½ dinar	5
1	person paid ⅜[a] dinar	⅜
30[b]	persons paid ¼ dinar	7½
8	persons paid ⅛ dinar	1
1	person paid 1/12 dinar	1/12
56	persons paying	21-11/24 dinars

[a] Thus corrected for ¼ dinar.

[b] Including firms consisting of 2 or 3 persons and paying ½ or ¾ dinars.

This sum of about 21½ dinars paid by fifty-six contributors, many of them belonging to the lowest class of taxpayers. Compare this with the ninety poor for whom the Fustat community had paid the poll tax according to ULC Or 1080 J 87 at a time when the operation was not yet completed, and it becomes evident that our list—as stated in the superscription—represents only a fraction of the communal effort for this charity. To be sure, many of the indigents paid part of their tax.

In view of the importance of this ancient list, the edited text and translation are corrected here with the aid of a photostat kindly provided by the Freer Gallery of Art, Washington, through the good services of Professor Richard Ettinghausen. The line number refers to both text and translation:

L. 2, for Bmārīn read Kammādīn. This is the address of the person concerned: "Street of the Mangers or Burnishers" (see Dozy, *Supplément,* II, 488*b,* under *kammād;* the verb is common in the Geniza). The reading Khammārīn, "Street of the wine merchants," is possible, but unlikely, for that street was called Nabbādhīn, a religiously less revolting name. (Wine, called khamr in the Koran, is prohibited in Islam.)

L. 3, for Sudūr read Surūr. Not "Lotus tree" but "Happiness."

L. 4, for Sukkarī read not "sugary," "Suessman," but "Maker or seller of sugar."

L. 7, for Bahwarī read Bahūdī, a well-known family.

L. 10, for "The scribe who [lives in] the house of Lmāṭ" better: "The government official who had his office in the Carpet Bourse" (*lmāṭ* stands for *al-anmāṭ*).

L. 11, for Tirmidhī read Tadmurī, "from Palmyra."

L. 12, for Ibn Abūh read Ibn Akhūh, not "illegitimate" but "nephew."

L. 15, for Rifā read Raffā, not "Harmony" but "darner, mender of clothes."

L. 18, for 'Umrān read 'Imrān, not "Prosperity" but the biblical name Amram in its Arabic form. Same in ll. 32, 33.

L. 20, for Ubzārī read Abzārī, not "from the village of Buzar" but "vendor of seeds."

L. 27, for Majānī read Majjānī, not "Profit" but "from the town of Majjāna [in Tunisia]."

L. 42, for Ṣafīn read Ṣaffayn, not "Hidden Treasure" but "his office is in the Colonnade" (see *Med. Soc.,* I, 194).

L. 44, for 'Assāl read not "sweet as honey" but "maker or seller of honey."

L. 54, for Sidr read Faraḥ. The latter reading is beyond doubt, as proved by the man's kunya: Abu 'l-Surūr, both name and by-name meaning Joy, Happiness.

8. TS 13 J 35, f. 7*v*. A list of nineteen persons, eight of whom are expressly described as *ṣayrafī* (money changer, banker, spelled here *ṣ'rfy*), while others, like Ibn Ezra and Abu'l-Faḍl Ibn Ṣaghīr, belong to famous banking families. Mūsā, the factotum of Ibn 'Awkal (see B 4, 5, 56), is here a ṣayrafī. Lines are drawn over eight names, presumably meaning that these have already been approached and need not be considered any more. The list is written on the draft of a rhymed request for a contribution and in the same hand, which seems to indicate that copies of the request were sent to the persons noted.

May be connected with recto, an eloquent appeal by a learned merchant from Damascus who had lost all his riches.
9–11. Three short, informal lists that seem to be collections made during the service of Monday or Thursday morning. Since change was scarce, the pledges, albeit small, were listed and paid after several of them made by one person had accumulated.

9. TS 16.209*v*. Piece of vellum (fragment of an ancient marriage contract) with a list of names headed by Abraham "The Cherished," *al-sāgūl*. This is an abbreviation, used also in the letter ULC Or 1080 J 265, ll. 6. 16, of the unique title "The most cherished and esteemed of the people of Fustat," borne by the notable Abraham b. Mevassēr (dated documents 1028–1045 [see Mann I, 98–100]) The second item: Abraham al-Tāhertī could stand for any of four cousins from Qayrawān called thus. all of whom frequented Egypt. In letters and accounts they usually are mentioned by their Arabic name Barhūn. A third Abraham, called Ṭaḥṭāḥī, was also probably from Tunisia, since the word *ṭaḥṭāḥa* ("open space," perhaps a place name) is Tunisian.

The contributions:

6 contribute 1 (dirhem ?)
2 contribute 2 (dirhem ?)
2 not indicated
1 not identified

10. TS NS J 400. A list in the same large characters as the preceding section, mentioning everyone by his first name or otherwise in an abbreviated form. "Joseph, the parnās" appears here as in C 9. At the bottom, a line is drawn, followed by the remark: *al-Shāmiyyīn b,* no doubt meaning that this collection was made on a Monday morning (*b* = second day of the week) in the synagogue of the Palestinians (see C 49). The contributions:

7 pledge 2	total 14 (dirhems)
6 pledge 1	total 6
4 pledge ½	total 2
Total 17 pledge	22 (dirhems)

11. TS Box K 15, f. 28. Much effaced list of donors, with one exception all called by their first names. Three appear together "with partner," or as sons of, or simply together with, someone else. The script is similar to, but not identical with, the two former lists. The contributions:

10 pledge ¼ dinar
1 pledge ⅙ dinar
5 pledge ⅛ dinar

---

2 pledge 3 dirhems
1 pledge 2 dirhems

---

19 pledges of at least 22 persons

In l. 11, it seems, the pledge "3 dirhems" was converted to ⅛ dinar, which is slightly more.

12–14. Third quarter of the eleventh century

12. ENA 2727, f. 11, sec. B. List of contributors, pledging 1, 2, or 3 dinars, mostly from the well-known families Ibn Sha'yā, Ibn Ṣaghīr, and Bahūdī, or prominent notables such as Abū Zikrī Ḥayyīm b. ('Ammār) Madīnī (of Palermo) and Abū Zikrī (Yaḥyā) b. Manasse (see C 21). Probably helping the poor with their poll tax (see C 14).

13. TS K 15, f. 109. Much dilapidated parchment bearing lists of weekly revenue and expenditure in the elaborate hand of Aaron, "the expert cantor," son of Ephraim, the scribe" (dated documents: 1058–1066).

Seven persons, one of them called simply *al-qammāḥ,* the wheat merchant (because this was not a common Jewish occupation), are in charge of the collection of pledges. During the first week, they collect on Sunday, 2 dirhems, Monday, 4, Tuesday, 34, Wednesday, 35, a total of 75, reduced by small expenses connected with the collection so that a total of 72 dirhems and 2½ dānaqs (see *Med. Soc.,* I, 359, bottom) remained.

On Thursday payments to four community officials are made, two of whom are mentioned solely by name or title. The two others:

The cantor—5 (dirhems) less 1 dānaq
The ḥāvēr ("member of the Academy")—6 less ½ dānaq

A sum total of 36 dirhems transferred from another leaf certainly was spent on bread for the poor. This list may refer to a community other than Fustat.

14. TS K 15, f. 94*v*. "Roll *(thabat)* of the names of the elders who . . . ," written upside down on the reverse side of a list of payers of incomplete poll taxes (see B 59). The superscription is almost entirely effaced, but the word *jarīda,* "list," mostly used of lists of the poor, is clearly visible in the second line. Thus, it stands to reason that the sixteen elders enumerated had to take care of the poll tax of the persons listed overleaf. The elder Abraham b. Isaac the scholar is listed as thirteenth and Nahray b. Nissīm as last. Since these two personages were very prominent in the Fustat community in the last third of the eleventh century, this list should be dated not later than 1070 (approximately).

15–22. Late eleventh or early twelfth century

15. Bodl. MS Heb. e 94, f. 21. Incomplete and partly defective list of about thirty-three contributions in gold. As far as extant and legible:

3	contributions of 1 dinar
3[a]	contributions of ½ dinar
12	contributions of ¼ dinar
8	contributions of ⅛ dinar
2	contributions of 2 qīrāṭs

[a] two of these are Maghrebis. A third Maghebi, listed above the others, had not yet decided.

The banker Abū Isḥāq b. Ṭibān, one of the few who donates 1 dinar in C 19 and who makes the largest contribution of wheat mentioned anywhere in the Geniza (C 21), gives only 1/8 dinar here.

16–18. Three lists from the end of the eleventh century written by one and the same scribe.

16. TS K 15, f. 106. Complete list of fifty-four contributors, neatly written by the scribe of A 15, B 13, 17, 18, headed by the representative of the merchants Jekuthiel b. Moses, called here, as often, solely by his family name al-Ḥakīm ("The Doctor"). The second donor is "The Pride," that is, Japheth b. Abraham, the Pride of the Community (dated documents 1076–1103). He gives 2 qīrāṭs, worth about 3 dirhems. This proves that all the other sums are dirhems, not dinars, as follows:

10 give 2 dirhems
23 give 1 dirhem
17 give 1/2 dirhem
2 not identified

Two donors are Maghrebis, one is from Aleppo, one from Yemen, and one is called Ibn al-Malaṭī, that is, from Malatia in Asia Minor. Only in one instance do two partners give together and in two, two brothers. The occupations range from locksmith to overseer of the caliphal mint (the "Pride" mentioned above). Above most names a line is drawn (the medieval way of deleting), meaning certainly that payment was made. A similar list from the same period in C 79.

17. TS Misc. Box 8, f. 29. Equally calligraphic as the preceding list, but a defective one with only twenty-six names preserved, many identical with those of C 16. The first two donors, including again the representative of the merchants al-Ḥakīm, give 1/8 dinar, which approximates the value of 5 dirhems; the others:

4 give 5 dirhems
1 gives 4 dirhems
1 gives 3 dirhems
13 give 2 dirhems
2 give 1 dirhem
2 not indicated, 1 not preserved

One of the contributors is *mawlātī*, "my mistress," the scribe's mother or grandmother. In A 15, written by the same scribe, a woman arranges a collection.

18. TS NS J 403. Complete, calligraphic list of twenty-four persons (to be solicited; no amounts), headed by the judge and overseas trader Abu 'l-Mufaḍḍal and the banker Abū Isḥāq b. Ṭībān. Other bankers, a clothier, four perfumers, a government official, a merchant from Yemen (identical with that listed in C 16, where he is called Joseph, while here his kunya Abū Ya'qūb is given), and one Abū Sa'd al-Zaylūsī, from Zaylūsh, Palestine, are also included. Several names recur in C 16, 17, 19.

The honorific by-name Abu 'l-Mufaḍḍal, appearing here and secs. 19 and 119, might refer also to the scholarly merchant Nethanel b. Japheth, a nephew of the Nagids Judah and Mevōrākh b. Saadyah, who bore the same by-name (DK xix, *India Book* 217). He was believed to be very influential with the viceroy al-Malik al-Afḍal (TS 18 J 4, f. 6*v*, l. 8). He signed documents in 1098 (*India Book* 3 and 15) and died in or shortly before 1121; at that time, his second daughter, Sitt al-Kamāl ("Lady Perfection"), was engaged to the judge Abu 'l-Mufaḍḍal (Moses), TS 16.119, l. 26.

19–20. Two contemporary lists of contributions in gold, written in the same hand around 1095.

19. TS Misc. Box 8, f. 102. Important, but partly damaged list of about seventy-five persons, donating mostly fractions of a dinar. Abu 'l-Mufaḍḍal heads this list, too, giving 1 dinar. The highest amount, 2 dinars, is given by Abu 'l-Khayr al-gēr, "Mr. Good, the proselyte," who is hardly identical with a proselyte bearing the same name and donating ¼ dinar in C 7, l. 35. Abū 'Alī, the only other person giving 2 dinars is Japheth b. Abraham, "the Pride" (see C 16).

2	contributions of 2	dinars
7	contributions of 1	dinar
8	contributions of ½	dinar
16	contributions of ¼	dinar
3	contributions of ⅙	dinar
15	contributions of ⅛	dinar
8	contributions of other fractions	
59	total legible contributions	

Some fractions are odd: Col. II, l. 2, Yaḥyā of Fez: ¼ + ⅙ + 1 qīrāṭ + 1 ḥabba = 34/72, almost ½ dinar. The same strange combination in the contribution of Ṣedāqā, the Translator (l. 6). A number of donors refer for payment to their banker (see *Med. Soc.*, I, 246, 461 n. 98).

20. TS NS J 315. List of about thirty-two contributors, mostly identical with those noted in C 19.

With the exception of Abū 'Alī, "the Pride" (see C 16, 19, 21) who donates 1½ (dinars?), and Abu 'l-Ḥusayn al-Ḥalabī, who gives 2 together with his workman, *ṣāni'*, and his partner, the others provide either 1 or ½, or have not yet decided.

21–22. Collections of wheat, made around 1100

21. Bodl. MS Heb. d 79, f. 35. Extensive and valuable, but damaged list of donors of wheat to the poor. It is headed by the banker Ibn Ṭībān (see C 15, 18, 19), who, together with his son, gives a *tillīs*, or sack (weighing approximately 150 pounds [see Grohmann, *Einführung*, p. 164; Hinze, *Masse*, p. 51; *Med. Soc.*, I, 333]). The same quantity was given by Abū 'Alī, "the Pride" (C 20), and the banker Abū Zikrī b. Manasse and his son. Two persons of this name appear in the Geniza documents of the eleventh century, one, whose first name was Judah, presumably the one who contributed ¼

dinar in C 7, l. 25, and a later one, Yaḥyā, who must be intended here and in C 12.

Most of the others give only 1 wayba (about 4 gallons, weighing about 25 pounds), or fractions of it, some others 2 or 4. One person whose name has not been preserved, but who follows immediately after the first three mentioned above, donates 4 irdabbs = 24 waybas. Those who had not yet made up their minds are listed at the end of page one merely by name. On the reverse side persons contributing dirhems, for example, two weavers each 3 dirhems, one giving together with his workman. "The Doctor," the representative of the merchants Jekuthiel (see C 16, 17), donates ⅛ dinar (for which one could buy at that time approximately 1 wayba of wheat).

Written in different scripts, among them that of the writer of C 16. Although a number of contributors are identical with those of the five preceding lists, this might be somewhat later since Ḥalfōn b. Manasse, who was one of the copyists, is known from dated documents only from 1100.

22. TS NS J 444. Much damaged, but valuable fragment of a similar report, containing twenty-six names of contributors of wheat. In at least ten places, both the names and amounts are identical with C 21. But the order of the names is different, there are some new names, and occasionally the amounts differ. The copyist is the same as that of C 16–18 and part of C 21. This collection must have been very close in time to the preceding one.

23–27. Five lists from the 1140's

23. BM Or 5549 (Cat. no. 1135, IV), f. 5*v*. Neat copy of a list of notables, the first two contributing 2 (dinars), twenty others, 1, and a foreigner from Sicily, ½. The first donor, Abu 'l-Makārim b. Nissīm (a grandson of Nahray b. Nissīm), signed a check for 200 dinars around 1145 (TS K 15, f. 91, ll. 12–14). The wife of the second, Amīn al-Dawla, received a payment of 100 dinars from the renowned India traveler Abū Zikrī Kohen in 1140 (TS Arabic Box 30, f. 184*, *Med. Soc.,* I, 241). Abū Zikrī himself also appears among the contributors, inconspicuously listed tenth, but the slip on which the list is written had been neatly cut out of a letter of his (*India Book* 221*a*). The two *mūrids*, or suppliers of metal to the caliphal mint (see *Med. Soc.,* I, 466 n. 2), recur in C 27. In l. 3 the copyist wrote the senseless *'bws byd,* a misreading for *'bw s'yd*. Abū Sa'īd b. Ghulayb also contributes in C 24.

24. TS NS J 422. Lower part of a twin list of contributors, the first with, the second without, sums. Almost all the persons who are noted in the second list had made a contribution according to the first. In five instances the donors reduced their gift to one-half or less, and in one case an original ½ dinar, which was reduced to ¼, was restituted. One of the reducers was *al-'arīf al-shaykh Abū sijill,* "the head of the profession, the elder with a document" (perhaps a nickname for one who boasted having received a caliphal rescript). Abu 'l-Ḥasan al-wazzān, the weigher, who appears also in C 23 and 25, was party to a settlement in 1147 (TS 12.544), and Abu 'l-Barakāt b. al-Lebdī, who traveled to India in 1134–1135, was dead by December, 1146 (*India Book* 20, where the data about him are collected).

The contributions, as far as preserved:

2 give	1	dinar
7 give	½	dinar
9 give	¼	dinar
5 give	⅛	dinar
3 give	2	qīrāṭs
1 give	2	dirhems

The strange fact that so many reduced their contribution is perhaps to be explained by the assumption that while the first collection was going on, it already became known that another one was necessary.

25. TS Arabic Box 6, f. 8. A similar, but smaller fragment of a list of persons donating 1 or 2 (dinars?), or not yet decided.

26. TS NS Box 246, f. 22, ed. N. Alloni, *Sefunot,* 8 (1964), 129–137, superscribed "Titles" *(alqāb).*

This is not a list of donors, but of honorific titles borne by forty-three different persons. The list was certainly jotted down by, or for the use of, a cantor, who had to mention them with their proper designations, when their contributions to public appeals were lauded in the communal prayer. Many of these notables are known from other sources, which enables us to assume 1142 as the approximate date of this important document.

27. TS Arabic Box 54, f. 21. Fragment (middle part) of a list containing the names of eleven prominent persons contributing 1 (dinar). The two purveyors of metal to the mint mentioned in C 23 head the fragment.

28–30. Three items from the 1150's

28. TS 10 K 20, f. 1, ed. Mann, II, 291–292. A booklet with a calendar for three years (Sept. 21, 1153–Sept. 6, 1159) indicating for each year the persons who donated the olive oil for the uninterrupted illumination of a synagogue for one month, a few individuals for two months. For the second and third year the list is completely preserved and shows that nine of the ten persons contributing during the second year did so again during the third.

The list is in the unmistakable hand of the Maghrebi India traveler Abraham (Ibn) Yijū, who returned from India to Aden in 1149 and from there to Old Cairo in 1151 or 1152. "Abū 'Alī, the brother-in-law of Ibn Yijū," who donates in C 29*v,* col. I, l. 1, is referred to here twice as "Abū 'Alī, *my* brother-in-law." This man was probably a Yemenite or an Indian Jew, who had accompanied Abraham Yijū to the Egyptian capital and had become known there as the relative of the scholarly and influential Maghrebi merchant.

The synagogue referred to probably was a private place of prayer for merchants and refugees from the Maghreb. As of the late 1140's, an incessant stream of refugees moved eastward in the wake of the terrible Almohad persecutions, as abundantly proved by the Geniza documents.

Some notes to Mann's edition of the text: The words "Olive oil for the synagogue" are written each year in the form of a superscription. For Ḥashūsh read Ḥashīsh, a family name derived from the drug and known from other Geniza papers. Instead of the senseless Abu 'l-Ḥasan Abū Sa'd, the manuscript twice has the correct Abu 'l-Ḥasan Ibn Abū Sa'd. "Perpetual lamp" (Mann, I, 233) is a mistranslation. It should be "Continuous illumination."

29–30. Two emergency collections for Byzantine Jews captured by Muslim pirates. With the exception of the enigmatic C 5, 6, the sums in these sections are the highest encountered thus far in the Geniza for charity purposes (around 1157).

29. TS 8 J 17, f. 18+. See also Shaked, *Bibliography*, p. 86, and *Med. Soc.*, I, 381, sec. 56. Ten Egyptian provincial towns contribute (together with two notables listed separately) 226⅛ dinars. The copyist of this calligraphic document (four pages), who was also one of the two persons in charge of the collection, was "the distinguished" member of the academy, Abu 'l-Surūr b. Ṭarīf. When he wrote the letter TS 13 J 23, f. 17, he lived in a small town, which would explain why he was entrusted with the collection in the Rīf. In C 26, l. 46, he is counted among the notables of Fustat.

30. TS K 6, f. 149. A collection in the Egyptian capital, made, it seems, for the same purpose as C 29 (see *Med. Soc.*, I, 381, App. D, sec. 57). A booklet reporting collections made during fourteen days, of which four columns, containing details about the first (incomplete), second, thirteenth, and fourteenth (complete) days have been preserved. At the end of each day, the total collected is indicated:

First day	154⅛ dinars	385 waraq dirhems
Second day	44⅝ dinars	280 waraq dirhems
Thirteenth day	76-5/24 dinars	39½ waraq dirhems
Fourteenth day	2½ dinars	—
Total preserved	277-11/24	704½[a]

[a] Sum not preserved; addition mine; actually, the scribe converted some dirhems to dinars.

Since the exchange rate of the waraq dirhem in this document was approximately 1:40 (see *Med. Soc.*, I, 381), the value of the dirhems collected equaled 17.6 dinars, and the total of the four days preserved, 295 dinars. This sum was brought together by seventy-four households, consisting of at least eighty-two breadwinners (plus the contributors mentioned on the lost first leaf [see below]):

First day (partly)	12 households
Second day	39 households
Thirteenth day	18 households
Fourteenth day	5 households
Total	74 households

Two persons donated with their sons, two with their brothers, one with his nephew, one (donating 20 dinars) with his brothers and his paternal uncle, and one item is "Sons of the Foreigner." The sums given:

In gold		In silver	
2 households give	¼ dinar	1 household donates 10	dirhems
2 households give	½ dinar	6 households donate 18½–20	dirhems
18 households give	1 dinar	2 households donate 25	dirhems
2 households give	1¼ dinars	3 households donate 28¾–30¼	dirhems
11 households give	1½ dinars	4 households donate 39–40	dirhems
3 households give	2 dinars	Total households donating in silver	16
1 household gives	2½ dinars		
2 households give	3 dinars		
2 households give	4 dinars		
8 households give	5 dinars	1 household not yet decided	
1 household gives	5 + 5 qīr.	2 households not legible	
2 households give	7½ dinars		
1 household gives	20 dinars		
Total households donating in gold	55	Total households 74	

One person, Munajjā b. Ḥātim, gives 39 dirhems on the first day (col. I, l. 6) and 20 on the second (col. II, l. 23). Similarly, Abu 'l-Munā al-Kohen Ibn Jāzuliyya, who donates 39½ dirhems on the first day (col. I, l. 10), is probably identical with Ibn Jāzuliyya who gives 10 on the thirteenth day (col. III, l. 17). Such double notations prove that the list represents actual payments, not pledges. A further proof of this assumption are sums such as "3 dinars less 1 qīrāṭ" (col. II, l. 7), or "1½ dinars less one ḥabba" (col. II, l. 13). (On the other hand, "Abu 'l-Ma'ālī b. Nu'mān—5 dinars," written twice [col. III, ll. 2–3], is probably a scribal error.)

If we disregard the first day, for which the contributions of only twelve households are preserved, and the fourteenth, when a few stragglers were approached, but take the second and thirteenth days as average, we find the total gold donated on these two days to be 120 dinars; total silver, 320 dirhem (or 8 dinars); total value of two days, 128 dinars; average of one day, 64 dinars; ten days for which the lists have been lost, 640 dinars. Grand total of the collections of the capital and the Rīf:

Actual, C 30	295 dinars
Estimate, C 30	640 dinars
Actual, C 29	226 dinars
Total	1,161 dinars

The ransom for three prisoners amounted to 100 dinars (*Med. Soc.*, I, 329). Money was also needed for the feeding, clothing and transport of the captives. On the other hand, we do not have the lists from Alexandria, where no doubt a collection was also made. Around thirty Byzantine Jews must have been captured causing the emergency drive reflected in C 29, 30. So large a number of Jews traveling together was not common, but not unheard of. *Med. Soc.*, I, 315, notes "36 or 37" Jewish passengers in one ship.

31–35. Last third of the twelfth century

31. TS K 6, f. 177. Two strips of paper, forming three columns (*a, b, c*) and

containing 27 + 28 + 17 = 72 names of persons and firms to be solicited for a public appeal.

The names are arranged according to the business addresses, such as "The Great Bazaar" (*a*, l. 1), "The Surayya" (*a*, l. 13), "Bazaar of the Threads" (*b*, l. 8), "[Street of] the Dyers" (*b*, l. 22) "The Money Assayers" (*c*, l. 10). Four persons are noted together with their brothers, one with his brother-in-law; one firm is called "Sons of." Several groups of persons belonging to the same profession appear together, such as four *musta'mals*, persons employed in a government workshop (all in the Bazaar of the Threads [*b*, ll. 10, 15–17]), three *labbāns*, or dairymen (*a*, ll. 12, 13, 19), three *sabbāks*, metal casters (employed in the mint [*a*, ll. 26, 27, *b*, l. 2]), or three money-assayers (*c*, ll. 12, 14, 16). At least five names of very specific character, such as Durrī, the ghulām of the Nagid (see *Med. Soc.*, I, 133), or Manṣūr of the family of the scarf makers, *maqāni'ī*, are identical with those in C 30, and at least eight recur in C 33.

The cut of the papers proves that the slips had been separated originally, presumably to be given to two different solicitors.

32. Hebrew Union College, Cincinnati, Geniza MS 24. Lower part of a carefully written list of contributors (about thirty-eight names preserved), almost all of whom give 1/3 (dinar ?) Two laborers of a Tabaristan upholstery contribute together. Characteristic names in common with C 31 and 33. At the bottom of each of the four columns the total in Coptic numerals. The scribe, it seems Ephraim b. Meshullam (dated documents 1142–1159), at his best, but in small script.

33. TS K 15, f. 6*. "Collection for wheat, Av 1489 [= July–Aug., 1178], through our masters the judges, may God preserve them." In the hand of Mevōrākh b. Nathan, himself a judge, four pages, containing eight columns.

Group A, superscribed "Wheat," that is, donating wheat in kind, namely:

1 giving 3	waybas, total 3	waybas
10 giving 1	wayba, total 10	waybas
2 giving ½	wayba, total 1	wayba
1 giving ¼	wayba, total ¼	wayba
14 contributors in kind	14¼	waybas

A wayba (about 4 gallons) of wheat cost about 6 dirhems in normal times during the period concerned.

Group B, superscribed "Dirhems," that is, contributing dirhems on two consecutive days. On the first day, as indicated in the list, 65 dirhems were collected. Total 90½. The 45 donors are enumerated in no visible order. Summary:

4 give 5	dirhems, total 20	dirhems
5 give 3	dirhems, total 15	dirhems
2 give 2½	dirhems, total 5	dirhems
16 give 2	dirhems, total 32	dirhems
4 give 1½	dirhems, total 6	dirhems
11 give 1	dirhem, total 11	dirhems
3 give ½	dirhem, total 1½	dirhems
45 give a total of	90½	dirhems

Part C begins on page *c*, col. I, after l. 2 and after a blank space of five lines. It lists the contributors in groups according to the amount donated:

15 households contributing 1½ dirhems each,	total 22½	dirhems
36 households contributing 1 dirhems each,	total 36	dirhems
8 households contributing ½ dirhem each,	total 4	dirhems
1 household contributing ¼ dirhem each,	total ¼	dirhem
60 households contributing a total of	62¾	dirhems

(A note on the margin has 62½, but the first letter might be r = 200, and the note might refer to something else.)

All these were actual payments, not pledges, as proved by the fact that nine donors noted on the first day appear again on the second with an additional gift, for example, Maʿālī b. Nuʿmān (see C 30) gives 1 wayba on the first day (p. *a*, l. 6) and 1½ dirhems on the second (p. *c*, col. I, l. 7). Another proof: the contribution of an order of payment drawn on another person (p. *b*, col. II, ll. 18–19).

In this list, four persons are noted together with their partners, one with his employee, one with his brother-in-law, and one item reads "the shop of" (p. *d*, col. II, l. 5). *Sons* and *brothers* are listed separately, albeit sometimes with very small sums. Reason: these donations were certainly made in connection with the fast of the Ninth of Av. Giving alms on a fast was an act of piety and had an expiating power. Therefore, everyone had to give in person.

Assuming that a wayba cost 6 dirhems (see above) and taking into account that nine persons donated twice, the contributions might be summarized thus:

1 firm gives	18	dirhems
1 firm gives	7½	dirhems
10 firms give	6	dirhems
5 firms give	5	dirhems
7 firms give	3	dirhems
3 firms give	2½	dirhems
19 firms give	2	dirhems
16 firms give	1½	dirhems
38 firms give	1	dirhem
11 firms give	½	dirhem
1 firm gives	¼	dirhem

Total 112 firms consisting at least of 117 persons

Reduced to six main groups:

I.	1 gives	18	dirhems
II.	16 give	5 –7½	dirhems
III.	10 give	2½–3	dirhems
IV.	35 give	1½–2	dirhems
V.	38 give	1	dirhem
VI.	12 give	¼– ½	dirhem

The main groups were not divided entirely according to the professions of the donors. Taking as indicators the two most common professions mentioned, that of the *ʿaṭṭār,* perfumer, and *ṣayrafī,* banker or money changer, this distribution emerges:

2 ʿaṭṭārs each contribute 6 dirhems
2 ʿaṭṭārs each contribute 3 dirhems
3 ʿaṭṭārs each contribute 1 dirhem

1 ṣayrafī contributes	6	dirhems
2 ṣayrafī contribute	5	dirhems
2 ṣayrafī contribute	3	dirhems
2 ṣayrafī contribute	2	dirhems
1 ṣayrafī contributes	1½	dirhems
2 ṣayrafī contribute	1	dirhem
1 ṣayrafī contributes	½	dirhem

34. TS NS J 416. Lower part of a neatly written list of twenty-one persons (to be solicited), each carefully described by his family name or profession or both. At least three persons recur in C 33. With three exceptions (including two names written on the margin), all names are preceded by a stroke, indicating perhaps that the task of soliciting the persons concerned had been assigned.

35. TS 10 J 26, f. 13*v*. Upper part of a fragmentary list, written in the hand of the judge Samuel b. Saadya (see A 26), on the reverse side of a document issued on the authority of Maimonides in spring 1172. The contributions are partly in dinars (¼–2, the latter sum appearing four times), partly in dirhems. Practically all the names recur in contemporary lists, but because of the dilapidated state of the manuscript no general conclusions are possible. Of the sixteen persons whose names are discernible in the left column, four give together with their partners.

36–58. Twenty-three lists from the time of the Nagid Abraham Maimonides (1205–1237).

36. TS 12.419*v*. "Account of the pledges, *pesīqā,* for [the synagogue of] Dammūh." Gives the impression of a supplement (1213–1218).

Eleven payments, five from women, the largest being "From Minyat Ghamr—40," the second largest, 39½, from "Lady Muqbil, a relative of the wife of the physician al-As'ad." She also seems to have headed this drive: "I handed the money over to her." Other contributors: a Maghrebi, a man from Damīra, and "one whom I do not know." Two items of expenditure: locks, *ḍibāb*—5, the (Muslim) preacher, *al-khaṭīb*—10.

Recto, in the same neat hand, a poem on the occasion of the circumcision of the boy of a learned notable. It has this marginal note: "Your servant Ḥalfōn. Please copy this in your exquisite hand. You have already received the paper." This Ḥalfōn (b. Elazar ha-Kohen) is known from many documents signed by him from 1208 through 1222 and others whose dates are not preserved.

There might be some connection between the two pages. The congratulatory poem strangely concludes with a stanza directed against the adversaries of the Nagid (Abraham Maimonides), who is advised to excommunicate them. A report about machinations against the Nagid (TS Arabic Box 51, f. 111+ [see chap. v, sec. A, 2, n. 50]) mentions that, at the time of the crisis, a large gathering was convened, but instead of excommunicating his adversaries, the Nagid threatened with this punishment those who had made pledges for Dammūh, but had not yet paid. Our list might well represent one group of such defaulters. TS 10 J 32, f. 12+, is a circular admonishing the community to contribute toward the upkeep of Dammūh.

37. ENA 2727, f. 15E. Note to the effect that the physician Mukhtār, known as Ibn Ilyās (Elijah), had left his cash and medical books, "all he left," to the synagogue of Dammūh. (He had a son.)

38–46. Nine lists headed by the Nagid Abraham Maimonides or his chief justice Yehiel (earlier period) or Hananel (later period). A tenth and eleventh such list (C 55 and 57) belong to the Nagid's last years. See also C 58 and 80.

38. BM Or 5566 B, f. *33v*. "Addition to [the collection for] the prisoners," *shevūyīm,* written on the reverse side of a communal account from 1215–1216 (see A 44). The Nagid and two others give a dinar, two names are not followed by a sum, one gives ¼, and two give ⅛ dinar.

Most of the "prisoners" were probably not captives of pirates, but persons put in jail because they had not paid the full poll tax (see B 58).

The column is written in large childish quadrangular script.

39. TS K 15, f. 36. List of about 105 prospective contributors, headed by the judge Yehiel b. Eliakim (dated documents, 1213–1233). At least fifteen names recur in C 46. Only the judge, who gives 1 (dinar), the Rāṣūy (a title), who appears second here and in C 40, 46 (see also C 44, 50, 88, A 146*b*, B 98), and another two who pledge ½, have sums attached to their names, but enough space is left between the lines for inserting numbers. About twenty different professions. Some groups, such as the goldsmiths, the money changers, or the vendors of food, are listed together. Only *one* dyer, as against *fourteen* in C 46. This proves, of course, that the list comprises only a fraction of the members of the Rabbanite community of Fustat. Probably here only the more affluent were approached.

40. TS K 15, f. 61. Neatly written list of sixty-seven contributors, headed by "our lord, may his glory be enhanced," that is, the Nagid Abraham Mai-

First list

	2	give	10	total 20
	1	gives	4½	total 4½
	6	give	3½	total 21
	1	gives	3	total 3
	6	give	2½ + ⅓	total 17
	1[a]	gives	2	total 2
	1	gives	1⅓ + ¼	total 1⅓ + ¼
	2	give	1½	total 3
	28	give	1	total 28
	17	give	½	total 8½
	65	give		108 + ⅓ + ¼
Illegible	2			
Total	67			

Second list

1[b]	gives	4	total 4
1[c]	gives	2½ + ⅓	total 2½ + ⅓
2	give	1	total 2
9	give	½	total 4½
Total 13	give		13⅓

[a] "My uncle."

[b] This entry is the Rāṣūy (see C 39) who, in the first list, came right after the Nagid and therefore did not want to give more than the 3½ he had donated, but added on the second day in accordance to his means.

[c] "The office of [the physician] al-Rashīd," which had provided the same sum at the first collection.

monides, who gives 3½ (dinars or dirhems). Another list, superscribed *sh* (= *shēnī* [Heb.], second), of thirteen persons mentioned before and making a second contribution, is attached. At least twelve persons recur in C 46 and at least eight in C 41. There is only one entry called "Sons of . . . ," one "Office of . . . ," and one ". . . and partner."

41. TS K 3, f. 22. List of about fifty contributors, arranged in two groups, the first donating gold, the second silver. At least ten characteristic names recur in C 46.

The first section is arranged in descending order:

The Nagid (Abraham Maimonides) gives	1 dinar
2 persons give	½ dinar
5 persons give	¼ dinar (in one case + 2 Nāṣirī qīrāṭs)
3 persons give	⅛ dinar (in one case + 1 dirhem)

The second section has no visible order, although the scribe tried, unsuccessfully, to group donors of the same sums together:

1 donates	10	dirhems
8 donate	5	dirhems
6 donate	3	dirhems
8 donate	2	dirhems
4 donate	1	dirhem
1 donates	½	dirhem
10 not indicated		

A circle-shaped sign above names in ll. 7, 13, 15, 19, and others, seems to be a final *m*, standing for *(tasalla)m*, "received."

The careful arrangement of the list shows that it was a clean copy, made for public display.

42. TS K 15, f. 74. Small list of pledges, seemingly for a specific occasion (e.g., a sum of 170 dirhems was needed for a traveler); arranged in two sections, separated by a blank space.

First section

4 (including the judge, i.e., Hananel)	give	20	(dirhems)	total	80
4 headed by the Nagid	give	10[a]	(dirhems)	total	40
8	give	5	(dirhems)	total	40

Second section

2	give	3	(dirhems)	total	6
4	give	1	(dirhem)	total	4
					170

[a] Cf. C 45, which lists a payment of 10 dirhems by the Nagid.

Most of the names are known from contemporary lists. Like many documents of this period, the list is in the hand of Solomon, the son of the judge Elijah.

43. TS K 15, f. 88. List in the same hand and arrangement as the preceding one, with thirteen donations in the first group and ten in the second. The contributions:

2 give	10	dirhems
1 gives	5½	dirhems
6 give	5	dirhems
5 give	3	dirhems
4 give	2	dirhems
3 give	1	dirhem
2 illegible		

44. TS NS J 256. Upper part of a twin list in the same hand as the preceding two, seemingly a draft, one list, with, and one mostly without, amounts. The sums donated range from ½ dirhem, given by the son of a bell-maker, to 5½. The Rāṣūy (see C 39) gives 1 Nāṣirī through the judge Yehiel.

45. TS Arabic Box 54, f. 59. Fragment (lower part) in the same hand as the three preceding ones, of a list of cash receipts, arranged according to days and indicating which official collected the sums and to whom they were delivered. In several cases, orders of payment, referred to here as ḥawāla, literally, transfer of debt, were given. Some items are noted as "balance of his vow," or "part of what he owes."

Only the column "Tuesday," headed by the Nagid who gives 10 dirhems (next highest payment: 5), is completely preserved (9 contributions). Besides a ḥawāla of 5, there were 34 dirhems in cash, of which 25 were delivered to the parnās Baqā, while the writer retained 9. The total of one collection, presumably for a week, was 162 dirhems, for which a collector's fee of 6 dirhems was charged, while three other persons, two parnāsīm and a beadle, brought 45 + 19 dirhem + 1 dinar and 45 + 10½ total 119½ dirhems + 1 dinar; also a sum of approximately 160 dirhems, for which a *jibāya*, collection fee, of 6 dirhems was paid.

46. Bodl. MS Heb. c 28 (Cat. 2876), f. 47, ed., with an extensive commentary, by E. Strauss (now: Ashtor), *Zion,* 7 (1942), 140–145. As the date indicates, this edition was made by Strauss-Ashtor at an early stage of his Geniza studies. Most, or all, of the corrections suggested in the following would probably have been made by him, had he published the text at a later date. Out of the same consideration I refrain from discussing his commentary.

A list of 127 persons, households, or firms, headed by the judge Hananel and contributing as follows:

2 give	2	(dirhems?)
1 gives	1½	(dirhems?)
8 give	1	(dirhem?)
2 give	¾	(dirhem?)
2 give	⅝	(dirhem?)
45 give	½	(dirhem?)
2 give	⅜	(dirhem?)
49 give	¼	(dirhem?)

1	gives	⅛ (dirhem?)
13		no amounts
2		not legible
127		

A remarkable aspect of this list is the preponderance in it of the standard small sums of ½ and ¼, 94 cases altogether out of a total of 112 legible amounts; also the fact that most of the notables, too, contented themselves with contributing ½, or 1. (The editor erroneously mistook the sign for ½ as another form of 1; in seventeen entries in his last column—which, actually, is the first (see below), and contains the names of most of the notables—the number 1 is to be replaced by ½, easily verifiable by the total written at the end of the page.) While in many collections the upper class shoulders the main burden (see, e.g., 30, 33, 40), a fact conspicuous especially in appeals to a limited number of persons (e.g., C 23, 24, 41–43), here the bulk of the revenue comes from small contributions, and there is little gradation in scale. List C 32, where practically everyone gives the same small sum, and which is very neatly written with totals at the end of each column, is very much of the same type as our list, but, because of its fragmentary state, cannot contribute much to a comparative study of both. Too, our list is undoubtedly incomplete; since it notes the totals of each column, there must have been the customary final column summarizing the totals.

Tentatively, I take these lists as yearly pledges for the weekly contributions toward feeding the poor and paying the community officials (see C 49). Charity is obligatory on every Jew (as on every Muslim or Christian), and its continuous practice was safeguarded by these pledges, the amounts of which were held to a comparatively low and general level. The innumerable collections for special purposes or on extraordinary occasions gave the more opulent or more liberal members of the community the opportunity to prove their mettle.

Notes on the edited text: The sequence of columns as printed has to be reversed: the first is verso, col. II = *a;* recto, col. I = *b;* recto, col. II = *c;* verso, col. I = *d*. Reason: the scribe folded a leaf so as to form a booklet of four columns. Most (but not all) the Geniza scribes folded their paper so; that it was done here is proved by the state of the leaf and the fact that col. *a* starts with the judge Hananel, followed by the notables, most of whom are known from contemporary documents and who alone contribute sums of 1 or more. For easier identification, however, in the following all references are made to the columns in the sequence in which they are printed by Strauss Ashtor.

The printer omitted the totals at the end of recto, cols. I (10) and II (9). On verso, col. II, there are two sums, one, 23½ (of course, not: 23 1, as printed [see my comment above, about the sign ½]) and another, 22 less a quarter (read *r* = rubāʿī, a quarter, not *d*). The words "less a quarter" seem to be crossed out, but are correct according to my own summation (one numeal is not quite clear).

Recto, col. I

l. 2 *nākhodā* is not a captain, but a shipowner.

l. 14 *al-ṭl* read *al-nīl,* trader in indigo.

l. 21 *shbwy* is Heb. *shāvūy*, captive (and ransomed by the community, a common family name). Same verso, margin.

Recto, col. II

l. 27 *tl'l* read *hl'l*, Hilāl (name).

Verso, col. I

l. 10 *n* . . read *nnw*, Nānū (a children's word with different meanings [cf. British "nanny" for nurse]), a common family name. The person listed here gave a loan to a physician (TS 13 J 6, f. 16).

l. 14 *ṣ'* . *h* read *ṣāgha*, goldsmiths.

l. 26 *mḥ* . . . . read *mutasawwiq*, purveyor.

Verso, col. II

l. 1 *rb'n* ? read *rbnw*, rabbēnū, our master.

l. 9 *'byhm* misprint for *'khyhm*.

l. 10 *karīma* in the Geniza is neither daughter, nor wife, but sister.

margin *b* . . *jy* read *bn n'jy*, Ibn Nājī, perhaps identical with Japheth b. Solomon Ibn Nājī in Bodl. MS Heb. d 66 (Cat. 2878), f. 136, dated 1246.

In col. II, remember that seventeen entries and in the sum total the number 1 is to be read as ½.

47. TS NS J 151. Slightly damaged lists of daily collections. Many names in common with C 41, 46 and other contemporary lists.

Almost all give either 1 or 2 (dirhems), a few even less; only two ṣayrafīs give 5 each, and Abu 'l-'Alā and Abu 'l-Faraj, the sons of al-Nafīs, each 10. On Tuesday the total is summed up in four denominations of money, in copper, waraq (silver of low value), qīrāṭs (fractions of dinars), and nuqra (silver of high value). The lower part of col. III and all of IV are occupied by accounts of expenditure on communal property in the Great Bazaar, written in Arabic characters.

48. TS 8 J 13, f. 14*v*. A neatly written list of contributors of wheat.

4 contributions of 1	wayba		total	4	waybas
1 contribution of 1½	waybas		total	1½	waybas
1 contribution of 3	waybas		total	3	waybas
2 contributions of ½	irdabb (= 3 waybas)		total	6	waybas
1 contribution of 1	irdabb		total	6	waybas
9 contributions			total	20½	waybas

Should we assume that ½ irdabb was packed differently from 3 waybas? The list is written on the reverse side of a letter of condolence addressed to a physician. Perhaps the wheat was given in connection with the mourning rites which required special acts of charity.

49. TS K 15, f. 60*v*. "Collection by R. Baruch during the week 'In the Beginning' " (the first week of the liturgical year). Twenty-seven contributions totaling 36½ (dirhems). With the exception of two scholarly persons, a banker, entitled ḥāvēr, who gives 9, and a goldsmith, styled r(abbi)—the only one in the list besides the collector—who contributes 5 together with his

partner, all the others content themselves with gifts of ½, 1, or at most 1½.

At least eleven persons are identical with those in C 46. Some give the same sum as pledged there, some less (e.g., Makārim, the oculist, pledged ½ dirhem and gives here ¼ + *fulūs,* "some copper coins"). Most paid more, which is easily explained by the scarcity of quarters. Actual payments were made once for several weeks.

The insertion in small letters of "Thursday" between ll. 18 and 19 shows that R. Baruch completed his collection during the synagogue service on Thursday morning. See C 10.

50. BM Or 5566 C, fs. 11 and 12. Four pages of names, largely identical with those in contemporary lists, with contributions of ¼, ½, 1, 1½, 1¾, 2 (dirhems?). Some give together with the laborers of their workshops: Ibn al-Shā'ir (the Son of the Poet, a family name), wa-ṣunnā'h, Sa'īd wa-ṣunnā'h. Altogether about 214 names legible. The Rāṣūy appears again, as sixth in the first column, but with the highest sum.

51. TS NS J 235. Lower part of carefully written list of contributors, practically all of whom appear in the preceding or following sections.

The first 15 donate	2	(dirhems?)
9 donate	1	(dirhem?)
2 donate	½[a]	(dirhem?)
3 no amount indicated		
4 amount not preserved		
Total 33 persons or households		

[a] The sign used is similar to, but not identical with, the usual sign for ½ in accounts with Hebrew numerals.

The collection represented seems to be one made for a special occasion.

52. TS NS Box 320, f. 35. Right upper corner of lucidly written list of contributors, the first thirteen each donating 2 (dirhems?). With one exception, all the names appear in abbreviated form (first name, family name, or title only), wherefore it is apparent that the collection concerned was of minor importance. At least three names are identical with those in C 51.

53. ENA 2727, f. 22. Contributions to a collection of bread for the poor ranging from 100 down to ½ pound. Instead of bread, one gives 3 dirhems. Alexandria?

Most of the contributors of larger amounts are introduced with the title "[my lord] the elder," while most of those giving small ones are simply called by name, such as: "Jacob—½, Ibrahīm Ibn al-Mawāzīnī (maker of scales)—1, the oil-makers—1, the Karaite—½." No consistency, however, was observed in this distinction. The donors of the third and fourth largest amounts (25 and 10 pounds, respectively) receive no title, while others giving only 2 pounds do.

The handwriting of the much-effaced document is of the calligraphic type used in books, which is extremely difficult to locate and date. Tentatively I offer: Alexandria around 1230. Reason: The list is headed by Abū Zikrī, while R. Yeshū'ā is second, even though he donated only 4 pounds. "The ḥāvēr" is also listed. All three—taking Abū Zikrī as the elder son of the judge Elijah, who was a prominent physician in Alexandria—are conspicuous in TS 10 J 16, f. 6, a complaint by the administrator of the *quppā,* or breadbasket of the community, in Alexandria who was threatened with death when he retained certain quantities of wheat in order to meet emergencies in a time of scarcity. The Nagid might have asked that all the relevant lists connected with the breadbasket be submitted to him, one of which would have finally found its way into the Geniza.

54. Dropsie 358. Request from judge Elijah to collect the money for the poll tax owed by one Bu 'l-Makārim at the congratulation reception (wedding) of either Ibn al-Muzaghlil ("The Dazzler") or that of Bu 'l-Barakāt. ENA 3150, f. 7*v* contains a memorial list of the Ibn al-Muzaghlil family, whose first ancestor, Judah, had four sons.

55. TS Misc. Box 8, f. 99. Emergency appeal for the purchase of wax candles both for the synagogue and needy persons (see B 89, 90) and also for some other communal expenses. Written mostly in Arabic characters and with Coptic numerals. Each household is listed with the number of adult male persons (sometimes three generations) and the amount they are expected to contribute. Some brothers, or fathers and sons, appear as one household, others as separate contributors, but following each other. In a factory each person is charged with 3 dirhems—the highest contribution—and the machinery, called *dūlāb,* literally, "the wheel," with 7 dirhems. A tavern, *qā'at al-sharāb,* pays 5½ dirhems (in the second instance, the sum is torn away).

Difficulties were expected since by that time (1235–1236) the community of Fustat had been reduced to "less than 200 [male adult] persons." The list is headed by "Our Master Abraham and his boy" (the Nagid Abraham Maimonides and his son David), then came "Our Master Solomon and his boy (the nāsī Solomon b. Jesse and his son Abū Naṣr Samuel, the latter mentioned, e.g., in TS 20.175), and then "Our Master Samuel and his boy," probably the French rāv, who was Jewish chief justice in Alexandria before moving to Cairo (see TS 10 J 19, f. 14, l. 15). Each of the three pays 2 dirhems, or 1 for each adult male, like all other persons except those engaged in specifically lucrative occupations.

The list, although only a partial one, is the most comprehensive found thus far in the Geniza with regard to this period. Page 1, incompletely preserved, states the purpose of the appeal and the goal ("over 300 dirhems" or "350 dirhems") to be reached. Columns 2–11 contain the actual pledges (with a few exceptions all in Arabic characters) totaling 291 dirhems. Columns 12–14 list the names of the persons who paid (mostly written in large neat Hebrew characters). Column 15 notes the expenditure made from these sums, in particular payments to the banker Munajjā: 30, 20, 15 dirhems and other, smaller sums, as well as some minor items, such as wax, 20, olive oil, 1½, police officials, 2 + 2. Columns 16–17 enumerate thirty-two persons who received wax candles, among them three makers of pastry, three dyers, a fishmonger or fisherman, two from al-Maḥalla, and others, all evidently people in need of help.

The list of pledges names about 65 households, comprising about 135 adult male persons; some 15 names, referring presumably to 30 or so persons are lost. The total of about 165 male adults comes rather close to the "less than 200 persons" referred to above. The balance were paupers who were beneficiaries of, rather than contributors to, the collection. But a few of the 32 receivers of wax candles appear also among the contributors. At least 6 names identical with C 57.

56. TS K 15, f. 32. Fragmentary list of contributions, it seems in the hand of Solomon b. Elijah, details of about twenty-five preserved, five giving 1, eight, ½, two, ⅜, three, ¼. Many names known from slightly earlier lists. The son and the grandson of the Zakī (see C 46, col. I, l. 9), appear here. For Solomon (b. Jesse) see C 55.

57. TS K 15, f. 64. List of about sixty (*bayt*, "houses"), and eight male individuals, each followed by Coptic numerals (⅓ and ¼). About forty-five are crossed out, meaning probably, as usual, that they had paid. The house of "the Rayyis, our lord Abraham" appears between those of the keeper of a tavern (regarded as a rich source of income [see C 55]) and a goldsmith. Six households, presumably of widows, are in the names of women. Mention of the Nagid identifies this list as one of contributors, not of recipients, but its exact nature escapes me. A collection arranged by women to which also a few gentlemen contributed?

58. TS K 3, f. 6. Calligraphic list of fifty-seven persons, of whom

4 are mentioned together with an unnamed brother
6 are mentioned together with an unnamed partner
1 is mentioned together with an unnamed father
1 is mentioned together with an unnamed brother-in-law
1 is mentioned together with unnamed "neighbors"

The fact that persons of the same family or profession are repeatedly mentioned together or persons are described as neighbors of those mentioned before, prove that this list was prepared for solicitation. In thirty-three instances the profession is indicated, but not in the usual way with the article: "So-and-so, the physician," but throughout without it: "Rashīd—physician," as if a stranger, not familiar with the now very reduced community, was supposed to use that list, which might indeed have been the case. A needy traveler might have been authorized to make the rounds and for this purpose the list was prepared for him.

"Dāwūd, the son of the Rayyis," that is, the son of the Nagid Abraham Maimonides, is among the listed. Since he was only sixteen at the death of his father in Dec., 1237, this document might have been written in the course of that year, since the Nagid was already dangerously ill in the spring.

59–66. Eight lists from the time of David b. Abraham, Nagid 1238–1300.

59. Bodl. MS Heb. c 13 (Cat. 2807, no. 5), fs. 6–8. Three long strips of paper with exactly the same measurements (28½ x 5½ cm), each carefully written with the names of twelve persons elaborately described (e.g., "the

elder Abi 'l-Riḍā, the banker, son of Abi 'l-'Izz, the banker"). On each of the three slips one name is crossed out, among them that of the Nagid David.

Most probably persons to be solicited by three notables who divided among themselves the onerous task in exactly equal quantities. Some characteristic names recur in C 50 (dated Dec., 1241), for example, Muḥriz, who might also be identical with Muḥriz b. Ṭāhōr, who signed TS 8 J 5, f. 25, in 1261.

60. TS K 15, f. 107. Long strip of paper, with both head and bottom torn away, containing about twenty-five names (among them four sukkarīs, or sugar makers), contributing ½, 1, or 1¼, partly in waraq, and partly in nuqra (see *Med. Soc.*, I, 388).

61. TS NS J 108. Calligraphic but incomplete, list, it seems in the hand of Immanuel b. Yehiel (ca. 1231–1265) of forty-one contributors, peculiar in the wide differences among the pledges made:

1 contributes	½	(low-value dirhem)
2 contribute	1	(low-value dirhem)
6 contribute	1½	(low-value dirhems)
1 contributes	2	(low-value dirhems)
9 contribute	3	(low-value dirhems)
8 contribute	5	(low-value dirhems)
1 contributes	9	(low-value dirhems)
8 contribute	10	(low-value dirhems)
1 contributes	18	(low-value dirhems)
1 contributes	19½	(low-value dirhems)
2 contribute	20	(low-value dirhems)
1 contributes	28	(low-value dirhems)

All preserved: 41 contributors making 12 different gifts

Persons of the same profession were of very different financial capacity or liberality. Ṣayrafīs: two contributed 3 dirhems, two, 5, but one, 18. The 'aṭṭārs, elsewhere often belonging to the well-to-do, gave here ½ to 3 dirhems. Two partnerships contributed, 20 and 28, the highest sums, another only 3. It is also interesting that a maṭbakh, or sugar factory, appears as a contributor (see C 55).

On the reverse side entries in Arabic characters and Coptic numerals:

Still due (*al-mutabaqqī* [see Dozy, *Supplément* I, 105]):

The Rayyis (the Nagid David) and a ḥawāla (transfer of debt)	30
The Factories (two names)	30

The rest are five pledges of 5 dirhems, and two of 10, and another ḥawāla.

62. TS K 15, f. 43. List in large characters, apparently destined for display, of six persons under the heading "Sunday" and of ten others under the heading "Wednesday"; verso, similar lists in different hands for "Monday" (ten persons), "Thursday" (twelve), "Tuesday" (eleven). These seem to be the names of the collectors of the weekly alms. Only one man, Jacob, the money assayer, served twice.

Abu 'l-'Alā, son of Mufaḍḍal, known as Ibn al-Marāwiḥī, the maker of fans, probably was a brother of Abu 'l-Faraj b. Abū Mufaḍḍal Ibn al-Marāwiḥī mentioned in C 59. Mufaḍḍal Marāwiḥī also in B 75, where he appears in a list of male persons, certainly in connection with the payment of the poll tax.

63. TS K 15, f. 12. A collection, it seems, at a wedding, containing twenty-two names with Coptic numerals. The bridegroom Muwaffaq (read *ḥtn,* not *ḥzn,* l .7 [?] but he should come first) gives ½. Verso, five names are repeated with the same numerals, beginning of a final copy, which eventually was drawn up on another sheet. Some specific names, such as Isaac b. al-Sharaf (i.e., Sharaf al-Dawla, "The Honor of the Government"), also in C 64.

64. TS K 15, f. 62. A list of thirty persons making small contributions as follows: one, 2 (dirhems?), three, 1, seven, ½, thirteen, ⅓, six, ¼. Similar in script and arrangement to the preceding section, but written pleasantly in large characters. Perhaps also a collection at a wedding.

65. TS K 15, f. 16. Pledges made at a wedding. The bridegroom, styled "the elder, the scholar Abu 'l-Bahā" (written in large letters, different from the rest) pledged, *asmā,* ½ dirhem, and so did the others. A fragment.

66. TS NS J 404. Sums promised or paid ranking from ⅛ to 6½, mostly in fractions, wherefore in cases in which exactly 1 or 2 dirhems were given the word *sawā,* "exactly," was added. The mother of the writer gives 2 dirhems, and in three instances the entries consist in balances owed to the contributors. In the hand of the teacher Solomon b. Elijah. Probably representing school fees for needy children.

On the reverse side the scribe noted the prices obtained for four books sold by him, for example, Maimonides' *Guide of the Perplexed,* 30 dirhems, 2 dirhems brokerage. Formal statements on the sale of three of the four books mentioned here are found in Bodl. MS Heb. d 66 (Cat. 2878), f. 119, dated 1229, ed. S. D. Goitein, *Kirjath Sepher,* 44 (1969), 125–126.

67–73. Seven lists from the fourteenth century.

67. TS K 15, f. 58, recto. Neatly written list of twenty-six persons pledging gifts ranging from 5 to 60 (Coptic numerals). The ten most generous donors remain anonymous, the relevant entry being *mattān,* which is the beginning of the biblical verse, "a gift in secret averts anger" (Prov. 21:14), understood as "the anger of God."

Verso, in a different script, hasty entries of donations made over three consecutive weeks (the first is incomplete) and, again in another hand, notes on pledges during a later week. On this page, too, a number of donations are anonymous.

The second week is headed by "the ḥ[āvēr], the Nagid Mūsā," contributing 44 (dirhems). Moses was the eldest son of the Nagid Abraham II b. David b. Abraham I Maimonides. His date of birth (Nov., 1290) was known, but not the fact that he served also as Nagid, which, thus far, is testified only here. He died early (see *Tarbiz,* 34 [1965], 255).

68. Bodl. MS Heb. b 13 (Cat. 2834, no. 36), f. 55. "Collection, *jibāya,* made on the first day of the holiday for the Maghrebi, the Kohen." About 115 contributions, mostly in Coptic numerals. Some of the names are encircled (persons solicited for payment?), others are crossed through (having paid?), a few again are left untouched. The list is headed by the ḥāvēr Obadiah, presumably the great-grandson of Abraham Maimonides bearing that name (b. 1297, d. before 1355). The other names also fit into the fourteenth century, for example, Nāṣir ("helper," three times [see C 71]), Shams ("sun," ll. 4, 27), Faraj Allah ("God has helped," ll. 8, 14). At least ten persons recur in C 69 (dated 1335), while in several cases in the latter document there are listed *sons* of persons mentioned here.

In this collection for a foreigner, many persons from places other than Fustat took part: from Acre and Gaza in Palestine, Aleppo and Damascus in Syria, Barzān (the Kurdish locality that gained fame in our time), from the Maghreb and western Europe(*ifranjī),* and, from Egypt itself, Alexandria and Qūṣ.

69. TS K 15, f. 18. "Pledges on Sabbath *lekh lekhā* of the year 1647," the third week of the Jewish liturgical year, falling in October, 1335. The list is headed by *hd* (= *hadrat,* His Eminence, normally reserved for the Nagid) the judge Samuel ha-Kohen, who contributes 20 (dirhems), far more than anyone else:

1	pledges	20
2	pledge	10
6	pledge	5
1	pledges	3
18	pledge	2
56	pledge	1
2	pledge	½
4	not indicated	
18	illegible	
Total contributors 108		

This dated and extensive list is an important source for our knowledge of the composition of the Fustat community during the first half of the fourteenth century.

70. TS NS J 205. Neatly written list of twenty pledges made during six weeks. One person, ʿAbdallah (Ibn) Barābik, "Tales" (one of his ancestors told fibs or stories), pledged twice. The pledges: one, 20, eight, 30, four, 50, two, 60, one, 100, one, 110, two, 112½. Among the donors only two persons, father and son, were called ḥāvēr, and the grandfather, too, had borne that title.

The reverse side is superscribed: "Received," noting 16 items, among them "220 through the Nagid," "225 anonymous gift," but only 3 contributions from overleaf, among them from ʿAbdallah Tales. One person, "Sulaymān at the gate of the caravanserai, *wakāla,*" who had pledged 30, is listed here as owing 50, certainly from previous weeks. Since two persons are listed as living at the Gate of the Breach, Kharq, of (New) Cairo, the list might refer to that city.

71. TS K 15, f. 34. Calligraphic list of twenty-nine persons (to be solicited), professions ranging from butcher to physician, among them four called Nāṣir (see C 68), including Nāṣir, the son of the judge. Al-Manāshifī, maker of towels, has been found thus far only in C 69 and here.

Verso, hastily jotted and effaced list in Arabic script of about thirty contributors with sums. The names are similar, but not identical, for example, Nāṣir b. al-'Afīf, l. 1, might be identical with Menaḥēm b. al-'Afīf, recto, l. 8. But the Hebrew name Menaḥēm appears also in Arabic script, verso, col. II, l. 3.

72. TS NS J 441. Late list with Coptic numerals, apparently of contributors (photostat momentarily not available).

73. TS 12.573*v*. List of names with sums in two columns written on the reverse side of a deed connected with the sale of a house written in 1378.

74. TS NS J 330. Two columns of interesting names of persons, partly mentioned as neighbors or relatives of others, accompanied by various sums, mostly 6 and 2. Each column is headed by Mr. Sīmān Tōv ("good augury," Heb.). The other half of the leaf is occupied by accounts for the elder Shālōm Ṣughayyir (Mr. Very Small), and verso, by private accounts for the week ending on "Sabbath Nāsō [Scripture lection, Numbers 4:21–7:89], coinciding with the eve of Pentecost." Since all the writing is in the same hand it is not sure that the first two columns represent communal accounts.

75. TS K 15, f. 10. Hastily written list of about forty contributors, eighteen of whom are entitled R(abbī). Another indication of very late origin: the father's name follows that of the son without *b.* (son of), like a family name: Nathan Ephraim, Yeshū'ā Mē'īr. A person named after his native city is introduced either by the article: Abraham al-'Adanī (of Aden), Aaron and Isaac al-Qala'ī, or without it: Shabbethay Qala'ī. Qarsantī is Spanish (for Qalsantī from Calsana in southern Spain. Karsenti is still a common family name among North African Jews). Sinoplī refers to Sinop(e) on the northern coast of Asia Minor. List C 76 has three persons from that city, which is not mentioned in the Geniza before.

The two elders appearing twice at the top of the reverse side, but without numbers, Elimelech Kohen and Eliezer, probably were in charge of the collections for two weeks.

76. TS K 15, f. 86. Two lists and beginning of a third, comprising twenty-five, thirty-two, and four names, respectively, all headed by *hā-r.* (the rabbi) Joseph Israel. The first two lists are in the same hand as C 75 and have many names in common with it.

In the first list all, and in the second most, names are followed by both a large and a small sum, the first obviously being the pledge and the second the first installment of the payment actually made. In addition to new family names, such as Sinoplī (see C 75), very old ones, like Sijilmāsī, are found.

77. TS NS J 424. "List of Donations," *qā'imat al-nedāvā* (Heb.), carefully written, about forty-five names with sums preserved. On the reverse side collections made, one by a layman, one by the ḥ(āvēr) Ibrahīm. Among the contributors are also women, and in several cases both men and women contribute a silver ring instead of cash. In earlier periods such contributions are mentioned in letters, but never in formal lists.

78. TS K 15, f. 82. Highly interesting list from the sixteenth or seventeenth century with about 130 contributors.

FIRST SUPPLEMENT

79. TS Arabic Box 51, f. 140. Calligraphic, but defective, list of contributors, headed by Maḥfūẓ of Tyre, who gives 10 (dirhems?), while most of the others give 1 or 2. The sum after the name of Abū Ya'qūb al-Ḥakīm, the representative of the merchants (see C 16, which is in the same script) is not legible. Around 1095.

80. Bodl. MS Heb. e 94, f. 22. Collection made at a circumcision feast. The *ba'al ha-mīlā*, or father of the boy, gave 1 (presumably: dirhem), a few others did the same, most of the rest contented themselves with ½ or even ¼. Only lower part of list with about thirty-four contributors preserved. Early twelfth century.

81. BM Or 5542, f. 34 (formerly: f. 3). Certificate in the hand of the judge Mevōrākh b. Nathan and signed by two witnesses, stating that the perfumer Abu 'l-Fakhr Saadya b. Abraham, known as Ibn al-Amshāṭī (son of the combmaker), had acted as collector of mezōnōt, or money for bread for the poor, in Dec., 1161.

82–85. Four items referring to the Alexandrian communal leader Nethanel b. Ḥalfōn.

82*a*. AIU (Consistoire, mark of MS not indicated), ed. Israel Lévi, *MGWJ*, 69 (1925), 375–377*. Spring, 1174. Nethanel informs Moses Maimonides (who was then head of the Jews of Egypt for the first time) that the scholar for whom a collection was to be organized according to the addressee's instructions arrived two weeks before Passover, exactly at the time when a drive was under way to provide the poor of the city with wheat and cash for the forthcoming holiday. Although that drive was more successful than it had been for many years, the collection for the foreigner too—as the writer reports with pride—brought 70 dirhems. Naturally, a man sent by such a great scholar as Maimonides was worth 70 dinars, not dirhems. These words should be taken merely as polite phrases: such sums were never collected except for the ransom of captives or the payment of communal debts (which also were "ransoms," since defaulting debtors were imprisoned).

Some necessary emendations of the text will be made in *Med. People*.

82*b*. TS 12. 192, ed. R. Gottheil, *M. Gaster Jubilee Volume* (London,

1936), pp. 173 ff., reedited with facsimile Assaf, *Texts,* pp. 163 ff. Moses Maimonides asks the community of Minyat Ziftā to arrange a collection toward the payment of the poll tax for Isaac Der'a (Morocco), a newcomer to Egypt who owed the tax for two years for himself and his son.

83. TS NS J 384. Nethanel reports to a relative (as whose pupil he describes himself) that a collection (called *ṣīniyya,* lit., "tray") arranged at the wedding of Musallam the embroiderer, brought around 30 dirhems. Since Nethanel was not present the money was handed over to the "Pride of the Cantors," who did not deliver it to the addressee, as usual, but to the writer. Was this a collection for the poor or one for the cantors functioning at weddings? The addressee presumably acted also as a cantor, since the writer most urgently asks him to deliver to the bearer of his letter the *"Raḥamān"* (Heb.), a religious poem beginning with this word (Oh Merciful, like *Kyrie eleison* in the Church). At Muslim weddings it was common custom to collect money on a tray for the musicians active at the celebrations, see, for instance, *The Arabian Nights,* Story of Nūr al-Dīn and Shams al-Dīn, Night no. 21. For payments to cantors on weddings, cf. C 63–65 and B 39b.

84. TS 8 J 16, f. 13. Fragment of a calligraphic letter of a former official of the Alexandrian community. He requests that the "Pride of the Cantors" together with the scholar Nethanel see to it that the pledges made for him on the Day of Atonement, as well as the fees that were still due him from the revenue of the abattoir, be paid now without further delay. That the punctual fulfillment of such obligations was a religious duty need not be proved from the sayings of the Sages, since this maxim is found in the express text of the Bible.

85. TS 13 J 20, f. 28. In a well-worded Hebrew letter to the Cairene notable Obadiah b. Benayahu, Nethanel asks him to help discreetly and instantly a scholarly man from Europe "whom Fate had caught in its net," and who had traveled to Cairo solely because he had heard of the generosity of the addressee's father. The request was urgent since the foreigner wished to be on the high seas by Passover.

On the reverse side a similar letter by the foreigner himself to another notable in the Egyptian capital. Nethanel's letter obviously was returned to the foreigner by the addressee and was then used by him for a draft which, after having been copied, was thrown into the Geniza.

86. TS 8 J 41, f. 1*v*. Much damaged list of names, followed by Coptic numerals. Arranged in two columns (11 lines preserved, 2–4 names in each line of each column), the second column mostly in Arabic characters. 'Ubayd, l. 1, not common as Jewish name, also in B 40, 41, 44, and C 74*v*, l. 7.

87. TS NS J 76*v*. "Still owed by the people." Upper part of a long list of persons who had not yet made good their pledges. In two cases (of 8 dirhems each), the outstanding amount is designated as balance. In all the others obviously the sums accompanying the names represent the total pledged. Written by Solomon b. Elijah; many persons known from contemporary documents (ca. 1220).

3 persons owe	½	dirhem
18 persons owe	1	dirhem
6 persons owe	2	dirhems
2 persons owe	3	dirhems
2 persons owe	5	dirhems
3 persons owe	3	dirhems
4 persons sum not indicated		
5 persons sum not preserved		
43 names visible		

See also B 38.

88. TS NS J 222. A list of ten donors, headed by the Rāṣūy (see C 39), seconded by the Shā'ir (Poet [see C 50]), and followed by other names known from the beginning of the thirteenth century. All but the last give 1, namely, jug (of wine), as proved by the last contribution which consisted of "half a jug." Wine is required at the domestic Passover ceremony "even from the poor" and is provided here in kind to those who had no adequate supply.

89. ULC Or 1081 J 63. Long, but mostly effaced list (two pages) of contributors, headed by "our lord" the Nagid, which could be either Abraham or David Maimonides, followed by Walī al-Dawla, "The Confident of the Government," who appears also in C 55 and 61.

In the first group all give 1 (dinar), in the second all give ½, then come those who donate dirhems. The present verso originally was recto, as proved by the names and amounts. On the reverse side are names known from the times of both Nagids, al-Sa'īd b. Nīsān (C 51 and 60), or Fakhr, the cheese maker, whose will was written in May, 1241 (TS 8 J 6, f. 14*a*).

90. TS NS J 389. A man calling himself the father of the cantor asks a prominent physician to arrange for him a collection, *pesīqat ṣedāqā,* in his private synagogue—and first to give himself. Superscribed and signed with the word Truth, *EMeTH* (see *Med. Soc.,* I, 241), a word that seems to be out of place here. I take it as a refined allusion to the second half of verse 12 of Psalm 85: "Truth springs out of the earth and justice looks down from heaven," the Hebrew word for justice at that time denoting charity.

91. TS 10 J 15, f. 27. Calligraphic request from a Nagid to appoint a man who would make the rounds of "the noble community" and collect money for the clothing of a poor orphan girl who was about to marry. Even a mere jūkhāniyya and a cover, *malḥafa,* would be welcome.

92. ULC Or 1081 J 8*. An old woman whose mantle, *ridā',* was stolen while she was about to wash it in the Nile asks the community in a well-styled address to help her to buy at least a large shawl, *izār.* As long as she had been in good health she had never applied to anyone for help.

93. TS NS J 270, ed. S. D. Goitein, "A Letter from Ascalon during Its Occupation by the Crusaders," *Tarbiz,* 31 (1962), 287–290*. A girl who was bought back from a crusader for an unusually high amount (the document mentions a balance of 60 dinars, almost twice the usual ransom per head [see

Med. Soc., I, 329]) appears in person, accompanied by her brother, before the communities in Egypt, in order to collect her ransom. If she failed to obtain the balance still outstanding she had to return to her captor.

94. ENA Uncatalogued 98, ed. S. D. Goitein, "New Sources on Palestine in Crusaders Days," *Eretz-Israel,* 4 (1956), 149–150. A woman who had been ransomed from Crusaders asks a congregation to provide her and her little boy with clothing, bedding, and food.

95. TS NS Box 31, f. 8*. A woman whose only remaining son had been killed by the Ghuzz (Seljuks), after four other grown-up sons had died, and herself unable to work, munqaṭiʿa, appeals to a community for appropriate clothing for the holidays.

Calligraphically written by Hillel b. Eli (1066–1108).

96. TS NS J 430. Appeal of a blind woman to the head of the congregation and to the congregation itself to provide her with 4 dinars, the fee demanded by a Muslim physician for the treatment of a daughter of hers for dropsy (see *Med. Soc.,* I, 259).

Written, it seems, also by Hillel b. Eli.

97. TS NS J 294. Beautifully written note by Hillel b. Eli, asking the parnās and trustee (Eli b. Yaḥyā) to look after Ṣedāqā b. Nufayʿ and his father who were local people and deserving.

Verso: eight persons donate ¼ (dinar) each, presumably for the needy mentioned on recto (poor hand, but not that of Eli b. Yaḥyā, who also had a peculiar handwriting).

98. ULC Or 1080 J 122. "List of the Collection for the Jerusalemites, Sivan [coinciding with May], 1242." The Pentecost holiday falls in the month of Sivan. (About collections for Jerusalem on holidays see A 11*b*.) Only two contributors are listed. The writer obviously realized that the piece of paper was too small and took another sheet. On the same page, upside down, copy of a (slightly annotated) passage from the Babylonian Talmud (Yevamot 37*a*, ll. 11 ff.), dealing with a man wedding a widow or divorcee within three months after her bereavement or divorce. Verso, business notes.

99. TS 12.543*. A special drive, arranged in Minyat Ziftā from Sept., 1265, through April, 1266, in support of the Jewish community of the Egyptian capital. It brought 1,020¾ dirhems.

100. ENA 1822, f. 76. Three columns of contributors, giving *fiḍḍa,* "silver" (a late equivalent for "dirhem"). Characteristic names: Sōmēkh (assistant cantor, Heb., also in C 70), Furaykh ("Little Chick," twice), Frjlh (also twice, an abbreviation of Faraj Allah, "God has helped" [see C 68]).

101–112. Twelve pastoral letters from the office of the Nagid Joshua b. Abraham II Maimonides (1310–1355), from his seat in (New) Cairo to the decimated and impoverished community of Fustat, asking them to arrange collections: two letters for poor old men, one for a widow and her little boy, three for travelers on their way to Jerusalem, one for a person from Safed, Palestine, and four for the payment of the poll tax; one letter reprimands persons who had not only failed to contribute to a collection for a stranger recommended by the Nagid, but even offended him. The specific needs of Palestine in that period are illustrated by TS 24.63, ed. Mann, II, 329–330, where Jacob, the Poet, b. Isaac b. David, the Maghrebi of Hebron, asks Joshua and the Cairene community to provide him with regular assistance, as was done by a physician in Damascus, who sent him a stipend of 8 dirhems every month; the congregation of Hebron was too poor for being able to maintain its officials, who had to look for income from occasional visitors from abroad.

These and similar letters emanating from Joshua's office (see Goitein, *Education,* p. 134) need further study in comparison with other Geniza material related to this Nagid before their editing can be tried successfully.

113. ULC Or 1080 J 2. "Appendix to the pledges," *al-muta'akhkhar* (same expression in C 38) *min al-pesīqā,* a list of thirty-four names (two unnamed with father and brother, respectively), of which eleven are crossed out.

Only few are accompanied by numbers. The Nagid (Samuel b. Hananya) gives 3 dirhems, the physician Abu 'l-Najm contributes 2 for his father and himself, which he pays by transfer, ḥawāla; three other persons also pay by transfer.

In the hand of Mevōrākh b. Nathan, in his early style. Some names identical with C 30 (ca. 1155). In order to avoid confusion: The glassmaker Abu 'l-Ḥasan, mentioned here, col. II, l. 10, and C 30, col. I, l. 1, might have been the father of Abu 'l-Futūḥ b. Abu 'l-Ḥasan the glassmaker in C 44, p. *d,* col. I, l. 12 (dated 1178), and the latter the father of Abu 'l-Ḥasan the glassmaker in C 46, verso (as printed), col. I, l. 29.

The persons to be solicited are mostly grouped according to their professions, *al-Ṭibb,* the members of the medical profession, forming the largest single group of tardy contributors.

114. PER H 181. List of about forty contributions, ranking from ½ to 22 dirhems, partly arranged according to days. In the midst of col. I a space of about 5 lines (about twelve contributions), destined for one day, is left blank. Cash payments, one by transfer. Headed by Ibn Jalāl al-Mulk, "the Splendor of the Kingdom" (who contributes 20), as in B 87, verso (*q.v.*), and C 42. He, like most of the other donors, appears in several additional lists from the first half of the thirteenth century.

115. Bodl. MS Heb. c 50 (no Cat.), f. 16. A booklet of four pages, listing contributions in dinars or fractions of a dinar. About seventy-two numbers preserved. The list is headed by the Nagid, who pledges 3 dinars, while the others give 2, 1, ½, ¼, ⅛, $\frac{1}{12}$, 1/24 dinars, respectively. A number of the persons listed are known as having lived around 1100; consequently, the Nagid referred to was Mevōrākh. A contribution of 3 dinars by the Nagid Mevōrākh is noted in B 19.

Some groups, such as the dyers, the flax-workers, the Alexandrians, and some individuals had not yet made their pledges. Most of the persons on pp. *a* and *b* are styled "the elder," most of those on pp. *c* and *d* are not.

116. Bodl. MS Heb. f 56 (Cat. 2821, no. 16), f. 52. The leaf containing the note described in A 167 was used as a cover for a booklet with the title "Collection for the Clothing, *jibāyat al-kiswa,* for the year 1497 (= 1186–1187), made by the elder al-Mēvīn." This al-Mēvīn, "The Understanding," was a parnās (also mentioned in A 137, dated 1183) and should not be confounded with the cantor Abu 'l-Majd (A 48–92, dated 1218, and often), who bore the same Hebrew epithet.

Some of the fragmentary lists from this period, such as C 32 or 35, once might have formed part of this booklet.

117. Westminster College, Arabica, I, f. 53. List of forty-five contributors mostly referred to in an abridged and informal way. Some persons with characteristic names (such as 'Alam Ibn al-'Udī, "the Luminary, the son of the dealer in odoriferous wood") appear also in C 55, written around 1235.

118. TS Box J 2, f. 25. Pastoral letter, presumably addressed to the Fustat community. In addition to general admonitions (pray assiduously, do charitable and other good works, dedicate yourself to the religious education of your children), the epistle states specifically that anyone selected by lot to serve as a collector of alms and refusing to act as such, or anyone objecting to participate in the weekly collections for the poor (still called mezōnōt) was liable to be punished with the "heavy ban." The beginning of the letter is lost. Late thirteenth or fourteenth century.

119. ENA 3846, fs. 6–7. "List of the Pesīqā," upper part of three pages containing the names of contributors, headed by Abu 'l-Mufaḍḍal (see B 16, C 18, 19), who pledges ⅛ dinar. The others give dirhems, namely:

1 party gives 3	dirhems
8 parties give 2	dirhems
16 parties give 1	dirhem
4 parties give ½	dirhem
2 (sum not preserved)	

As indicated by the cut of the extant fragment it probably contains less than half the original list. Still, it is remarkable that with the exception of Abu 'l-Mufaḍḍal himself and Abū Ya'qūb al-Ḥakīm ("The Doctor" [see C 16, 17, 79, occurring also in C 19, l. 10, and elsewhere]) none of the thirty-two persons appearing here seems to be mentioned in the contemporary lists C 18, 19.

120. ENA 3738, f. 11*v*. A sheet, large enough to contain on the reverse side a complete business letter (in Arabic characters), cut from the middle of a list of contributors. It is in the hand of the copyist of A 15, B 13, 17, 18, C 16–18. Of the twenty-two names preserved, at least five appear also in C 80, three in C 16, two in C 18, and many are known from other sources. With the exception of the ubiquitous Abū Ya'qūb al-Ḥakīm (see C 119), none of the about seventy-five persons listed in C 19 seems to have contributed here. Pledges: 2, 1, ½, or not yet entered.

Now that we have fifteen lists of contributors from around 1100 (C 15–22, 79–80, 115, 119–120, 124–125), this period, which is well documented in other respects, might serve as a starting point for a study of the methods of solicitation for public funds.

SECOND SUPPLEMENT

121. ENA 2348, f. 1*v*. An almost entirely "egalitarian" list of contributors from the first half of the eleventh century: forty-four persons pledge ½ (dirhem), nine parties, of whom six consist of two or more members, 1, and only one pledges 2 (dirhems). Almost all names appear in abbreviated form: Abū Kathīr is Ephraim b. Shemarya, the leader of the Palestinian congregation of Fustat, Sahlān (b. Abraham), the head of the Babylonians, Hillel *hpns,* that is, ha-parnās (also in A 163). Others are referred to simply by nickname: "Son of the Mule," "The Philosopher." Ca. 1035.

122. TS K 25, f. 161. Nahray (b. Nissīm, who presided many years over the Babylonian congregation in Fustat), is requested, presumably by his Palestinian counterpart, Eli b. Amram, to address, *yukhāṭib,* his flock and to arrange a collection for the family of the cantor Samuel ha-mēvīn (about this title see C 116), so that the cantor could go on travel after the Sabbath as he intended to do. Ca. 1070.

123. ENA 2805, f. 11*b*. A similar request for help to a needy man, addressed to Nahray. Here, the Iraqi congregation is explicitly mentioned. Neither of these items is included in *Nahray*.

124. ENA 2591, f. 1. Sheet, folded so as to form a booklet of four pages. But only one page, headed by the superscription "In Your Name" (which indicates the list started there), contains writing.

List of twenty notables, solicited for a special drive, eight already having made their pledges, ranging from 5 dinars, contributed by a *jahbadh,* to 1 dinar each from two glassmakers and "Mr. Good, the Proselyte" (C 19). Among the others: Ṭībān (see C 15, 18, 19, 21, referring to his son) and Samuel Ben Nahum, the father-in-law of Jekuthiel b. Moses, known as al-Ḥakīm (C 16 and often). Ca. 1090.

125. ENA 2591, f. 9. Short list in monumental cursive, contemporary with C 124, several names being identical,

6 contributing 2	(dinars, it seems)	total	12 dinars
5 contributing 1	(dinar)	total	5 dinars
12 contributing ½	(dinar)	total	6 dinars
Total, indicated in the list			23 dinars

The sum was probably needed for a special and urgent purpose, such as the travel expenses of a foreigner who was about to leave.

126. ENA 2591, fs. 8 (upper part), 11 (lower part). List in large, beautiful Arabic script (perhaps of the judge Samuel b. Saadya ha-Levi?), containing about fifty-five names, followed by a column in Hebrew characters with

about twenty-three names, some identical. Abu 'l-Barakāt *al-mūrid,* the purveyor of gold and silver to the mint (see *Med. Soc.,* I, 267), mentioned in C 33 (dated 1178), and many other individuals known from documents written around 1180 appear here. Only three contributions are indicated.

127. TS Arabic Box 7, f. 13*v*. Two lists of contributors, neatly written (by Solomon b. Elijah?) one above the other. The twelve names in the upper list are repeated in the lower (which has one more), often in abbreviated form (Abu 'l-Majd: Majd, Najīb al-Ma'tūq: Najīb). The contributions, ranging from ½ to 1½ (dirhems) are also almost identical in the two lists. Perhaps a collection for two musicians at a minor family affair. Ca. 1225.

128. ENA 2591, f. 6*v*. "Collection for the Poll Tax," *jibāyat al-jawālī* (for the sixth week of the liturgical year, usually falling in November). As the very small sums show, these were not payments to the government, but contributions toward the poll tax of the poor. Many names identical with C 46. The collection was made on a Thursday (twenty-one persons) and the subsequent Friday (fifteen):

1	contributing 1½	dirhems[a]
13	contributing 1	dirhem
3	contributing ¾	dirhem
12	contributing ½	dirhem
2	contributing ¼	dirhem
5	unclear or not preserved	
36	contributors	

[a] Expressly stated as *waraq*.

All these sums together would not make the total of the yearly poll tax required from one man. Because of the extreme poverty of the population the tax was collected in installments.

129. ENA 2348, fs. 2–5. Seven pages (f. 5*v* is blank) each containing about twenty items, mostly of contributions, in large and widely different sums, certainly paid in copper money. 'Abdallah "Tales" (see C 70) appears here again (f. 3*v*, l. 14), and also another man with the same family name, al-Raḍī Barābik (f. 5, l. 14), an "R. Moses, the brother of the Nagid," another man styled rabbi, two dayyāns, four ḥāvērs, one cantor, one teacher, three religious slaughterers, and two persons called Miṣrī, that is, from Fustat. This list, like C 70, originated in Cairo. Several gifts are anonymous, and one woman gives separately from, and simultaneously with, her husband (f. 4, l. 10). There are only a few details about expenditure, for example, for wine. Fourteenth century or later.

130. ENA 2591, f. 4. Calligraphic list of contributions, thirty-two names preserved, of the type common among Jews at the end of the Middle Ages, such as Naṣr Allāh (twice), 'Abd al-Karīm, Khaḍir, 'Abd al-'Azīz, 'Abd al-Wāḥid.

These names recur in BM Or 10578, a list of 126 contributors with the sums pledged by them, described by me in *JQR,* 51 (1960), 42–43. That list excels in the mass of nicknames, such as Ḥurayfīsh, "little vagabond," (see W. M. Brinner, "The Significance of the Ḥarāfīsh and their Sultan," *JESHO,* 6 (1963), 190–215), Fulayfil, "little peppercorn," (cf. the infamous obscurantist Pfefferkorn, who was active in Germany around 1500), Musaykīn, "little pauper," bazbūz, "nozzle, spout," Shuwayk, "little thorn." Only one of the occupations listed is new: *baḥrī,* probably meaning Nile boatsman. (Somewhat later, there was a corporation of Jewish boatsmen in Istanbul, Turkey.)

131. TS Arabic Box 39, f. 79. List (3 columns), carefully written in Arabic characters, of thirty-four contributions (twenty-seven give ¼, probably of a silver dirhem, seven, ½). Two persons are called "son of the midwife," but are not listed together, two others, also separated from each other, "son of the [female] dressmaker," a third pair, not listed together, *nushādirī,* "dealer in sal ammoniac." The list seems to be a collection at a wedding (for cantors or musicians), when different members of the same families were present. Some persons, like Isaac b. Nīsān, are also in C 64. The name al-Ḥinnāwī, "dealer in henna" (which became famous in our own time), also in C 71, but not necessarily designating the same person.

132. ENA 2808, f. 47. Note of a Nagid to the "noble congregation" of Fustat (same type as described C 101–112), asking them to complete the collection of the pledges made on the Day of Atonement, especially those for a traveler from Europe, *ifranjī,* who was to leave on the morning after the first two days of the Feast of Tabernacles. The interesting fact to be learned from this note is the speediness with which the pledges were collected. There are only four days between the Day of Atonement and the beginning of the Feast of Tabernacles. The letter seems to assume that, say, on the third day of the interval between the two holidays most of the pledges had already come in.

Another interesting point is the Nagid's admonition to think of the poor on the Siyyūm (Heb.), the festive conclusion of the yearly reading of the Pentateuch, which takes place at the end of the autumn holidays.

133. Bodl. MS Heb. b 3 (Cat. 2806), f. 5, ed. D. H. Baneth, *Alexander Marx Jubilee Volume* (New York, 1950), Hebrew part, pp. 86–87. Another example of a collection solicited for a traveler from Europe. He was called Joseph al-Rūmī and had come to the Mediterranean port of Damietta with a letter of recommendation from the Nagid Samuel b. Hananya. The appeal (presumably made on the Day of Atonement) brought 1 dinar worth of dirhems. The traveler boarded a Nile boat on the eve of the Feast of Tabernacles ("at sunset," i.e., when, according to strict custom, the holiday had already begun) and, after having collected the money on the half-holiday immediately following the Feast, and also wares "for the perfumers in Sammanūd," he departed.

Working-day actions, such as traveling or accepting money and merchandise, are not prohibited on a half-holiday (the meaning of *mōʿēd* [ll. 8, 12]), but were avoided by the more scrupulous. The purport of the rather exceptional document seems to be that the foreigner did not really deserve the recommendation of the Nagid.

The amusing side of the matter is that the document itself, according to its date, was written on a half-holiday, which was regarded as highly improper. See S. Assaf, *Mi-sifrūt ha-geōnīm* (Jerusalem, 1933), p. 92, n. 1. (I have found in the Geniza several documents so dated, one bearing the reshūth, or authority, of Maimonides.)

134. Dropsie 464. A hastily written list of 37 contributors whose names are provided in abbreviated form. Perhaps a collection for a singer at a minor family event, such as a circumcision ceremony. Of 37 persons

23 donate	½	dirhem
5 donate	1	dirhem
1 donates	2	dirhems
1 donates	8	dirhems

7 items are not fully legible.

The names of Abu 'l-Faḍl b. Qaṭā'if (TS 16.356) and the cantor Yākhīn senior (mentioned in TS Misc. Box 8, f. 102, sec. 19, above), taken together with the notables Abū 'Alī (Japheth b. Abraham) and Abū Ya'qūb (al-Ḥakīm, "The Doctor") (for both see next sec.), put this list around 1100.

135. Dropsie 466. "Ransom of Captives. A collection for the man from Antiochia."

Written, but not very carefully, by the scribe of A, sec. 15, B, secs. 13, 17, 18, C, secs. 16–18. The list is arranged in four columns and divided into six sections, bearing the dates of the days on which the various collections were made. Around 1100. The manuscript is defective; names, dates, and sums are often incompletely preserved.

The sums contributed were astoundingly small, ranging from 16½ dirhems collected from 5 persons, to 102½ dirhems given by 22 contributors; but several persons, about 10, contributed more than once. Many of the altogether about 70 names preserved are identical with those listed in secs. 16–18, above. The contributions were made mostly in dirhems, but on the second and third days, in qīrāṭs, which is exceptional. Abū 'Alī, that is, Japheth b. Abraham, "The Pride" (see secs. 16, 19–21), gave ½ dinar, converted into 24 dirhems, which is in conformity with the exceptionally low exchange rate of the dirhem in those days (1:48) (see *Med. Soc.*, I, 378–379, secs. 38–44). The highest payment in dirhems was made by Abū Ya'qūb al-Ḥakīm (see sec. 16, and especially sec. 21, above), namely 6 dirhems, then worth ⅛ dinar. Several payments were made through the banker Ṣadaqa al-'Aṭṭār (col. II, ll. 9, 21, 29).

The whole collection must have brought less than 10 dinars, far less than needed for the ransom of a captive. When we remember that Antiochia was taken by the Crusaders in 1096, "the man from Antiochia" might have been ransomed with money provided by a notable, partly to be restituted by the community. Our list might have been drawn up for such a purpose. There are, of course, other possibilities. The Hebrew term "ransom of captives" was applied to many different states of hardship, for instance, a man in prison for failure of paying taxes.

Note: B. Halper, *Descriptive Catalogue of Genizah Fragments in Philadelphia* (Philadelphia, 1924), p. 221, states, on the basis of a note at the end of the first section, that the collector, Abū Manṣūr b. Zaffān, took about 3 percent of the 105 dirhems collected on that day for himself. This is a misunderstanding of the Arabic text. What it says is this: a man called Ibn Abū Sahl (1.5) had donated "a sixth in gold," that is, a sixth of a dinar, then worth 8 dirhems, but he intended to donate only 5; therefore, 3 of the total of 105½ dirhems collected on that day were restituted to him so that a balance of only 102½ dirhems remained.

136. Dropsie 467. List of about 95 prospective contributors, consisting of four columns on recto, and one on verso. Col. I is superscribed Maṣṣāṣiyyīn, that is, people living in the Maṣṣāṣa quarter. Likewise, " 'Aṭṭārīn" in col. III must be understood as an abbreviated form of "Square of the Perfumers," for many persons listed had professions other than 'aṭṭārīn. Col. V: "Physicians," 13 names, mostly known.

Many names in common with secs. 39–47, above. Our list seems to be somewhat earlier: in several of the lists contained in secs. 39–47 "the son of the nākhodā [shipowner]" is registered; here, the "elder, the shipowner."

This is a valuable addition to the 28 items from the time of the Nagid Abraham Maimonides (1205–1237) contained in secs. 36–58, 87–88, 117, 127–128.

137. TS Arabic Box 40, f. 53. List of bankers and money changers and their locations "in front of the house of exchange," "inside its gateway," "within the house of exchange," or indicated by neighborhoods, such as "Mahra quarter," or "Banāna prison (*ḥabs*)." Only one had his seat in Cairo. Followed by a second list, in another hand, of contributions made, mostly of 1 qīrāṭ, sometimes a quarter (dinar), or qīrāṭayn waraq, two qīrāṭs in low value silver, a rare expression.

Characteristic names, such as Abu 'l-'Alā Ibn Sha'ya (Isaiah) Ibn Tadmurī (from Palmyra), Ibn Sim'ān ("Simonson") are identical with those of contributors to the collection C 7, ll. 8, 11, 46, above.

No doubt, an indigent foreign ṣayrafī was given this list and with it made the rounds of the local fellow bankers. A similar case in C 8, above.

138. TS Arabic Box 48, f. 42. Request from Nissīm (b. Nahray b. Nissīm, here referred to as rāv) to obtain from his father and the nāsī (David b. Daniel) letters to the community of al-Maḥalla recommending a collection for the writer be arranged (ca. 1090).

139. TS Arabic Box 39, f. 449. List in large, beautiful Arabic characters containing the names of 31 contributors with Coptic numbers (1, 1½, 1¾, 2, 2½, 3, 4, 4½, 5, 8, 9) but no denominations of coins. Several of the most characteristic names, such as Mufaḍḍal Ibn Nānū, Abu 'l-Ḥusayn Ibn Nufay', Abu 'l-Faḍl the Persian ('Ajamī), are those of the most liberal contributors to the collection C 30, above. Two physicians are listed here and there, one a private practitioner, donating 5 dinars and 5 qīrāṭs there and 4 unspecified coins here, and "the physician of the hospital, "pledging in both cases one coin (in C 30 he is referred to with his honorific title Sadīd).

Arabic was used here no doubt because the originator of the collection was a merchant who was accustomed to corresponding in Arabic rather than in Hebrew script. He also arranged collections in two noted bourses of Fustat (two collections in each bourse), one, the *dār al-Fāḍil,* founded by al-Fāḍil al-Baysānī, originally a Fatimid official, but later chancellor and confidant of Saladin, and *dār al-zaʿfarān* (saffron house), which was adjacent to the house of gems, repeatedly mentioned in this book. (See Casanova, *Reconstruction,* pp. 26 and 231.)

140. TS Arabic Box 46, f. 253. Eloquent circular for a man from Baghdad, written in summer 1229 by Solomon, the son of judge Elijah, in Fustat, and endorsed on verso by the judge Yehiel b. Eliakim from Aleppo (see App. D, sec. 30).

TYPES OF DOCUMENTS IN APPENDIX C

1. Names without sums (persons recognizable as prospective contributors by their titles or occupations, or by being otherwise known: 8, 14, 18, 26, 31, 34, 39, 58, 59, 71, 78, 126, 136.

2. Contributors belonging to different layers of the society, but all donating small sums, mostly ½ to 2 dirhems: 9, 10, 16, 32, 46, 47, 49–52, 55, 56, 60, 80, 113, 117, 119–121.

3. Groups of persons widely differing in amount of contributions (some often paying in gold and others in silver): 1, 2, 15, 17, 19, 30, 33, 35, 40–44, 53, 61, 67, 69, 70, 79, 87–89, 114, 115, 124, 129, 139.

4. Contributors paying in gold (exclusively or mainly): 7, 11, 12, 15, 19, 20, 23, 24, 27.

5. Names with numbers, but money donated undefined and difficult to establish: 25, 32, 57, 71*v*–77, 86, 125.

6. Collections arranged on specific days or during certain weeks: 13, 30, 45, 47, 49, 62, 67–70, 84, 132.

7. Donations toward the poll tax of the indigent: 7, 12, 14, 38, 54, 82*b*, 128.

8. Appeals for the ransom of captives: 3, 29, 30, 135.

9. Special and sundry drives: 4, 5, 6, 99, 117, 122–123, 134, 137.

10. Donors of wheat: 21, 22, 33, 48 (the last at a mourning ritual?).

11. Donors of bread (Alexandria): 53

12. Donors of wine: 88.

13. Donors of lighting oil for a private synagogue: 28.

14. Donors of wax candles for synagogues and the needy: 55 (see App. B).

15. Donors of school fees for poor children (?): 66.

16. Special collection for Jerusalem: 4, 98, 101–112, A 11*b*, 151.

17. Vows for the holy synagogue of Dammūh: 36, 37.

18. Collections at weddings: 54 (poll tax), 63–65, 83 (for the cantors [cf. B 39b]), 127 (?), 131 (?), and on circumcision feast, 80, 134 (?).

19. Collections for one person (mostly foreigners): 8, 54, 58, 68, 82*a*, 82*b*, 85, 90, 97, 101–112, 122, 123, 132, 133, 137, 138, 140; for one woman, 91–96.

20. Peculiarities of late lists: (*a*) anonymous contributors, 67, 70; (*b*) two sums after name, 76; (*c*) silver rings instead of cash, 77.

21. Records from places other than Fustat: 13, 53, 70, 84.

Appendix D

JEWISH JUDGES IN OLD (AND NEW) CAIRO 965-1265

The dates standing alone (not those in parentheses) designate years in and between which a judge signed documents. As a rule, two or three judges served simultaneously.

1. Ephraim he-ḥāvēr (b. Eli b. Ṭarsōn: ca. 965–995). See TS 20.96, ll. 3.8.14⁺, and *Eretz Israel,* 7 (1964), nn. 12–15.

2. Shemarya, "the President of the Court of all Israel," b. Elhanan (ca. 980–1010). Signed document: 1002. For this and undated documents and letters, see *Tarbiz,* 32 (1963), 266–272; Abramson, *Bamerkazim,* pp. 156–173.

3. His son Elhanan b. Shemarya, who assisted and later succeeded his father, d. ca. 1025. See Index.

4. Ephraim he-ḥāvēr b. Shemarya-Maḥfūẓ. 1016–1047 (d. around 1060). He, or his father came from Gaza, Palestine. 1016: TS 13 J 1, f. 3. 1047: Dropsie 336.

5. Samuel he-ḥāvēr, the "Head of the [Palestinian] Congregation," b. Avṭalyōn ha-Kohen, in Arabic: Ismā'īl b. Ṭalyūn. 1016–1041. 1016: same documents as in preceding section. 1041: TS 13 J 1, f. 9⁽⁺⁾.

6. Abraham b. Sahlān, ordained by the yeshivas of Jerusalem and Baghdad and head of the Iraqian community in Old Cairo. Son-in-law of Ephraim Ṭarsōn (sec. D 1). 1017. Died in, or shortly before, 1032. Native Egyptian in the seventh generation (from Sunbāṭ). 1017: TS 16.124. Signed together with nos. 4 and 5. Called Barhūn in the Arabic address of a letter to his son (TS 13 J 25, f. 3).

7. Sahlān b. Abraham, son of no. 6 and bearer of the highest titles from the yeshivas of both Jerusalem and Baghdad, 1034–1049. 1034: TS 8 Ja 2, f. 1, see Mann, II, 102, sec. 4. 1049: TS 16.162. In both he signs as president of the court.

8. Nathan, the excellent ḥāvēr, b. Yeshū'ā ha-Levi. 1040–1050. Signed documents together with nos. 4 and 7 and was prominent under the gaonate of the nāsī Daniel (1051–1063). 1040: Bodl. MS Heb. c 28 (Cat. 2876), f. 30* (in the Catalogue read 1040 for 1041). 1050: TS 20.7, see Mann, II, 245.

9. Eli, the excellent ḥāvēr, son of Amram, the emissary of the yeshiva (of

Jerusalem). 1055–1066, but certainly in office before 1051, the death of the Gaon of Jerusalem, Solomon b. Judah. Cf. Mann, I, 182 n. 1, a reference that is confirmed by several letters in which Eli shows himself an enthusiastic follower of Solomon's rival, the nāsī Daniel. 1055: TS 10 J 26, f. 9. 1066: TS 20.38.

10. Abraham, the judge, son of Isaac, the scholar. 1078–1093. His marriage contract, TS 20.7., dated Jan. 1050 (see D 8), is preserved. He was sometime official in the Exchange *(dār al-ṣarf)*, and many letters refer to his mercantile activities. 1078: TS 13 J 1, f. 18. 1093 (Dec.): TS 13 J 2, f. 3.

11. Solomon ha-Kohen, son of Joseph, president of the High Court of the yeshiva in Jerusalem, and grandson of the Palestinian Gaon Yehōsēf (Joseph), 1077–1098. In Fustat and Cairo. Jan., 1077: TS Loan 174, ed. Julius H. Greenstone, see Shaked, *Bibliography,* p. 159. This is not a legal document, but a long Hebrew poem in honor of the caliph al-Mustanṣir and the viceroy Badr al-Jamālī (see chap. vii, sec. C, 1, n. 26). In TS 24.1, ed. S. Schechter, *JQR,* 13 (1901), 218–221, a mixed Karaite-Rabbanite document, he signs first. Oct., 1098: ULC Add. 3413.

Note: For TS 8 J 4, f. 12*, signed by him, Mann, II, 231, gives the year 1413 = 1102, but the manuscript clearly has twice and in words the date 1403, which is 1092. TS 8 J 4, f. 12, contains only the beginning and the end of the document. The middle and main part is preserved in TS NS J 6*.

12. Abraham, son of Shema'ya he-ḥāvēr and descendant of Shema'ya, the Gaon. 1092–1132. Although he appears in the document of 1092, as well as in others (e.g., TS 16.77), as a member of the court instituted by David b. Daniel, the rival of the Nagid Mevōrākh, he was appointed by Mevōrākh, together with no. 13, to be one of the two "courts" in Old Cairo, and was reappointed by Mevōrākh's son Moses and later (1127) by the Gaon Maṣlīaḥ. 1092: TS 20.31. 1132: Bodl. MS Heb. d 66 (Cat. 2878), f. 7, see Mann I, 270, II, 275. Here he is assisted by seven other judges. including nos. 17 and 19.

Note: Mann, II, 232, quotes PER H 3 (now 31), according to J. Karabacek, *Papyrus Erzherzog Rainer, Füher durch die Ausstellung* (Vienna, 1894), p. 266, as bearing the date Marheshwan 1400, that is, A.D. 1088. That document is signed by nos. 12 and 13 and others. But an inspection of the manuscript reveals that its right-hand side, containing the last two digits of the date is cut off leaving only 14 legible. Some of the other names prove indeed that the manuscript must be at least fifteen years later than 1088.

13. Isaac b. Samuel, the Spaniard, an important scholar and author. 1099–1127. He was in office sometime before 1099. 1099: TS NS J 259. 1127: Bodl. MS Heb. d 65 (Cat. 2877), f. 25. Validation of a document, written and signed by him as president of the court.

14. Abraham, "the Pride of the Judges" and bearer of many other honorific titles, son of Nathan Āv, the president of the High Court (of the Jerusalem yeshiva), in 1096 was still judge in Ramle, Palestine. In (New) Cairo 1098–1114. In 1116 referred to as dead (TS 18 J 1, f. 18 [see Mann, II, 231–232]). 1098: ULC Add. 3416*d, India Book* 18. 1114: TS 8 J 5, f. 1*. Because

of his seniority in the yeshiva, he takes precedence here over his colleagues nos. 12 and 13.

15. Nissīm b. Nahray was called rāv like his more illustrious father, but unlike him was a regular member of the rabbinical court. 1098 to 1115–1116. The court records Bodl. MS Heb. d 66 (Cat. 2878), f. 46, dated 1099, and that of 1115–1116 were written by him. 1098: *India Book* 3 and 11. 1115–1116: ENA 4020, f. 2.

16. Eli ha-Levi, "the Diadem of the Enlightened" (Nezer ha-Maskīlīm), son of Nethanel, presided over the court of the Palestinian yeshiva in (New) Cairo, JNUL, f. 5, ed. S. D. Goitein, *Kirjath Sepher,* 41 (1966), 267–271, Jan., 1133, wherefore next to no documents signed by him have reached the Geniza. Often mentioned in letters to and from his younger brother, the India trader Ḥalfōn b. Nethanel. 112(0)-1133. Eli died in or shortly before 1139. About a hundred years after his death he was still remembered as an important spiritual leader. *India Book* 86, 99, 100, 123, 124, 149; *Tarbiz,* 24 (1955), 148.

17. Nathan ha-Kohen b. Solomon, a Palestinian who intended to return to his country, but wrote and/or signed in Old Cairo at least thirty documents between 1125 and 1150. Besides, many letters addressed to him and some he wrote have been found. Cf. also Mann, II, 366–367. 1125: ENA 4011, f. 56 (formerly 57). 1150 (Dec.): TS 13 J 20, f. 5* (in his handwriting). Latest document in which his signature is preserved: Bodl. MS Heb. c 28 (Cat. 2876), f. 7, dated 1148.

18. Nathan, the "Diadem" *(Nezer),* "Scribe of the yeshiva," son of Samuel he-ḥāvēr. 1128–1153. Seems to have come from the branch of the Jerusalem yeshiva, which then had its seat in Damascus. At least sixty documents written and/or signed by him have been preserved. He was also a poet (see chap. vi, sec. 11, n. 36).

The famous account by Nathan ha-Bavlī of the Iraqian academies (TS Loan 48, ed. I. Friedlaender, *JQR,* 17 [1904–1905], 747–761) is in his handwriting. 1128: TS 16.51. 1153: Bodl. MS Heb. b 11 (Cat. 2874), f. 36; TS 12.569.

An additional part of this account in the hand of Nathan b. Samuel is found in Arabic Box 48, f. 121.

19. Ḥiyyā b. Isaac, son of Isaac, the Spaniard (D 13). 1129–1159. Signs together with nos. 17 and 18, or with one of them, until approximately 1145, then with no. 20 and others. 1129: Bodl. MS Heb. f 56 (Cat. 2821, no. 1*i*), f. 16*v*. 1159: TS 10 J 7, f. 6*b*, col. I. A business transaction of his in TS 18 J 1, f. 9 (dated 1160) (see N. Golb, *JSS,* 20 [1958], 24–25 [needs revision]).

20. Ephraim b. Meshullām. 1142–1159. Signing with nos. 18 and 19, and generally in close contact with the Nagid Samuel b. Hananya. 1142: TS 10 J 17, f. 9. 1159: as in D 19.

21. Jacob ha-Kohen b. Joseph. 1161–1164. Signs with nos. 22 and 23. He seems to have been chief judge under the short gaonate of Nethanel ha-Levi

b. Moses. 1161: Bodl. MS Heb. d 66 (Cat. 2878), f. 77. 1164: Merx, *Paléographie hebraïque,* Pl. III.

Numbers 19–21 are enumerated in Bodl. MS Heb. b 13 (Cat. 2834, no. 22), f. 41, ll. 13–14+ (see chap. v, sec. A, 2, n. 37) as the chief judges in the period immediately preceding that of Maimonides.

22. Mevōrākh b. Nathan, son of no. 18, of whose hand many documents have been preserved. 1150–1181. Mevōrākh's youngest brother Yehōsēf, "the excellent judge," who had a number of other titles, among them "Trustee of the Government" (Amīn al-Mulk), most probably was judge in New Cairo, wherefore no documents signed by him have been preserved (see Mann, I, 227 n. 1).

Maimonides' circular to the congregations of the Egyptian countryside (TS 12.238, ed. Mann, II, 317) was written by our Mevōrākh. The handwriting of a contemporary Mevōrākh b. Nathan, whose father was a melammēd, or schoolteacher, is similar, but inferior, to that of the judge (he wrote, e.g., TS NS J 164, dated 1140).

1150: TS 13 J 1, f. 21. 1181: Westminster College (the former Lewis-Gibson Collection, no. 4), ed. S. Schechter, *JQR,* 19 (1907), 117.

23. Samuel b. Saadya ha-Levi, a member of the court headed by Maimonides and one of the most prolific scribes (see Index). 1165–1203.

1165: TS 13 J 3, f. 12. 1203: Bodl. MS Heb. c 28 (Cat. 2876), f. 54*v,* second entry.

His son Joseph is listed in ENA 1215 as a member of the court of the Nagid Abraham Maimonides (in office 1205–1237). But thus far only one court record written and signed by Joseph ha-Levi b. Samuel during the lifetime of his father has been found (TS 10 J 4, f. 7*, Aug., 1181).

24. Sāsōn b. Meshullām, father of no. 25, was judge in Cairo, wherefore only little of his hand is preserved. His own father, Meshullām b. Manasse he-ḥāvēr, signed TS 13 J 8, f. 15 (date not preserved) together with Isaac b. Samuel the Spaniard (no. 13). 1155. His genealogy in Mann, II, 319. 1155: TS 13 J 34, f. 4. This manuscript formerly had the mark TS 10 J 24, f. 6, cf. Mann, II, 287, sec. (1).

25. Isaac b. Sāsōn, son of no. 24, judge in New Cairo, approved and countersigned a number of Maimonides' decisions. His title: "Head of the Judges" *(Rōsh ha-dayyānīm).* 1167–1198. 1167: TS 20.118. See also A 112 (Cairo, 1181). 1198: TS 13 J 3, f. 16.

26. Menaḥēm b. Isaac b. Sāsōn, judge in New Cairo, son of no. 25. He was famous for his liberality (Mann, I, 247 n. 1, TS 16.286*v,* l. 30* [written Oct., 1219], ENA 2730 [Menaḥēm], where he is described as the support of everyone). A legal opinion written in his own hand is preserved in ENA 2728, f. 9. Succeeded by his son Isaac b. Menaḥēm as *dayyān muvhāq,* or presiding judge, in Cairo (TS 13 J 21, f. 8, ll. 4–6). See chap. v, sec. A, 1, n. 49.

27. Manasse b. Joseph, member of the court headed by Maimonides. 1164–1199. "Retired" in 1219. See chap. v, sec. C, nn. 16, 17, where the references are given.

28. Jephthah b. Jacob, the "deputy judge." 1182–1219. Same references as in preceding section.

29. Elijah b. Zechariah, called in the Arabic addresses of letters to him "the Judge of the Jews." Of Palestinian provenance, but bynamed the Alexandrian, because he had served for many years as a judge in that city, at least from 1204 (TS 16.126). He was in charge of the poor and the orphans, and a great many petitions connected with this office as well as many family letters (also by his two sons, one an army doctor and the other a teacher and bookseller) have been preserved. In Old Cairo, 1222–1236. See *Med. Soc.*, I, xi.

His Alexandrian colleague Anatoli of Marseilles, France, was also judge in Old Cairo for some time (see p. 125, above).

1222: TS 12.664. 1236: TS 8 J 17, f. 6, letter addressed to him in Fustat in his capacity as judge. Latest document signed by him: Dropsie 347, dated 1232, ed. D. W. Amram, in *The Green Bag* (Boston), 13 (1901), 339–343 (see Mann, II, 382, bottom).

30. Yehiel b. Eliakim of Aleppo, "the Splendor of the Judges and Pride of the Scholars," ULC Or 1080 J 67. 1213–1233. Signs together with Elijah (no. 29) and the Nagid Abraham Maimonides. In TS 13 J 8, f. 28. greetings are given to him and to Hananel of D 31 before the Nagid. See also J. Mann, *HUCA*, 3 (1926), 298. 1213: TS 13 J 8, f. 11*v*. 1233: ULC Or 1080 J 11.

31. Hananel, *rāv* and *dayyān,* b. Samuel, chief judge in the later years of the Nagid Abraham and the early period of the latter's son David. 1223–ca. 1249 (the latter date from a letter referring to him). 1223: TS 20.44, ed. E. J. Worman, *JQR,* 20 (1908), 455, 460–463. His full signature in TS 12.62, dated 1224. Ca. 1249: TS 6 J 7, f. 3, ed. S. D. Goitein, *Tarbiz,* 34 (1965), 240–244. His son Samuel signed as judge AIU, VII E 145 (1259).

32. Immanuel b. Yehiel. Many records in his characteristic hand have survived, but mostly in a fragmentary state. Ca. 1231–1279. There is almost no doubt that he was the son of judge Yehiel (no. 30), for the name Yehiel was not common in the East and the handwriting of the two men bears a striking similarity. The fact that the memorial list TS 8 K 22, f. 1, ed. Mann, II, 320, does not mention Immanuel is no proof to the contrary. Yehiel was then still in his beginnings (no honorific titles yet) and Immanuel most probably was born after that list was written.

Ca. 1231: TS 12.55, written under the Nagid Abraham (before 1237) and referring to an incident mentioned in a document dated 1231 (Gottheil-Worrell VIII, p. 41).

1279: Gottheil-Worrell, XI, pp. 58–61. A bill of divorce issued on July 11, 1279. Immanuel signs twice: as witness to the writing of the bill and its delivery.

The list in this Appendix is to be regarded as provisional. It indicates the minimum periods during which each listed person signed court records identified thus far. Judges who are referred to in letters, but of whose juridical activities no record has been preserved, are not included. An example: the highly praised judge of (New) Cairo, Ephraim ha-Kohen he-ḥāvēr b. Abraham, who was in office both under the Gaon Solomon b. Judah (d. 1051) and the latter's successor Daniel b. Azarya (see Mann, II, Index).

Notes

Notes

CHAPTER V: *Communal Organization and Institutions*

INTRODUCTION: *The Functioning of a Medieval Democracy*

[1] For details see chap. vii.

[2] See *Med. Soc.,* I, 66–70.

[3] Claude Cahen, "Mouvements populaires et autonomisme urbain dans l'Asie musulmane du moyen age," *Arabica,* 5–6 (1958–1959). E. Ashtor-Strauss, "L'administration urbaine en Syrie médiévale," *Rivista degli Studi Orientali,* 31 (1956), 74–209, in particular pp. 118 ff. I. M. Lapidus, *Muslim Cities in the Later Middle Ages* (Cambridge, Mass., 1967) (with extensive bibliography).

[4] Samuel b. Hofnī, active 977–1013 (see B. Dinur, *Yisrael ba-Gola,* I, 3 [Tel Aviv, 1961], p. 11).

[5] For a general survey of the subject see S. W. Baron, *The Jewish Community* (Philadelphia, 1942), 3 vols., complemented by Baron, *History of the Jews,* Vol. V, chap. xxiii, "Communal Controls." Louis Finkelstein's classic *Jewish Self-Government in the Middle Ages* (New York, 1924) deals with the Jews in Europe. The same holds true of a recent study by M. P. Golding, "The Juridical Basis of Communal Associations in Mediaeval Rabbinical Legal Thought," *JSS,* 28 (1966), 67–78. See also E. Ashtor, "Some Features of the Jewish Communities in Medieval Egypt," *Zion,* 30 (1965), 61–78, 128–157, and the sources quoted below, secs. A, 2, n. 2; B, 1, n. 1. My paper "Jewish Community Organization in the Light of the Cairo Geniza Documents," read at the third World Congress of Jewish Studies in Jerusalem in 1961 (*Zion,* 26 [1961], 170–179), was a kind of blueprint for this volume and is echoed in the conclusions at the end of chap. vii. For other studies of mine on the subject see secs. A, 2, n. 2; B, 1, n. 1; C, 1, n. 1.

A. ECUMENICAL AND TERRITORIAL AUTHORITIES

1. THE GAON, OR HEAD OF THE ACADEMY, AND THE "HEAD OF THE DIASPORA"

[1] M. Margulies, *The Differences between Babylonian and Palestinian Jews* (Jerusalem, 1938) (in Heb.). This ancient book enumerates fifty-five differences, but does not include, e.g., the important detail about the dowry of a childless woman mentioned here. Many contracts preserved in the Geniza contain this condition and some call it expressly: "according to the custom of the sons of the Land of Israel," e.g., TS 10 J 27, f. 3*a,* dated 1107. It is interesting to note that this specifically "Palestinian" stipulation goes back to neo-Babylonian law (see Z. W. Falk in *Tarbiz,* 37 [1967], 42).

[2] S. D. Goitein, "Congregation versus Community," *JQR,* 44 (1954), 294; Abraham Maimuni, *Responsa,* p. 182 n. 34. In al-Maḥalla there existed more than one synagogue around 1100, as proved by TS 20.125, and in 1282 a case for a Torah

scroll was donated to the synagogue of the Palestinians, obviously in that town, where, in 1929 the scroll was still in existence. See Alfred Yallouz, "Relation d'un voyage d'études à Mehalla el-Kobra, *Bulletin de la Société d'Études Historiques Juives d'Égypte* (Cairo), 1 (1929), 49–52, which contains the full text of the dedicatory inscription. The text provided by J. M. Toledano in *HUCA,* 12/3 (1937–1938), 713, is not the original, but a retranslation into Hebrew from a European language. Two synagogues in Tiberias: Mann, I, p. 167.

Concerning another provincial town of Egypt, which has since disappeared, Tinnīs, the important center of the linen industry, we hear that it was full of both Iraqi and Syro-Palestinian merchants (TS 8 J 18, f. 33, margin [eleventh century]), and that a prayer book of the Iraqi rite was sent there to a group of Kohanim ("priests") (Bodl. MS Heb. d 66 [Cat. 2878] f. 58). Thus, there too, perhaps each of the two rites possessed a house of worship. For Palmyra see Mann, I, 37, n. 1. (Tadmor is the correct reading despite the remark in Mann, II, 341.) E. Ashtor (*Zion,* 30 [1965], 62 n. 7) maintains that even a small place like Minyat Ghamr had two such congregations and adduces TS 18 J 16, f. 4, as proof. No manuscript with such a mark exists, however, and consequently it was impossible to check this assertion.

[3] Main (Palestinian) synagogue in Old Cairo: TS NS Box 323, f. 3, ll. 5, 8; BM Or 5560 A, f. 6, l. 14, ed. Mann, II, 34 (1012); E. J. Worman, *JQR* 20 (1908), 454. Alexandria: TS 13 J 1, f. 7 (see Mann, I, 89 n. 1 [1033]). Ramle: ULC Add. 3358, Assaf, *Texts,* p. 28. Damascus: BM Or 5566 B, f. 6*a* (around 1090) (see Mann, II, 220, last line). Aleppo: Bodl. MS Heb. a 3 (Cat. 2873)+. Since the term "great synagogue" is rendered in our documents not only in Hebrew and in Arabic, but also in Aramaic (Worman, *ibid.*), we may safely assume that this differentiation goes back to the ninth or the beginning of the tenth century at latest.

A record book from Damascus, dated 933, states three times that the marriages registered were contracted "according to the custom of the small synagogue of the Babylonians" (TS 16.181, ed. Assaf, *Texts,* pp. 64-69). This should not be understood as meaning that the Iraqians had two synagogues in Damascus, one large and another small, but that the Babylonian synagogue was called "the small" as opposed to the main synagogue which followed the Palestinian rite (see S. D. Goitein, "Four Ancient Marriage Contracts," *Lĕšonénu,* 30 [1966], 201 n. 6). For the Muslim historians on the synagogues of Damascus see N. Elisséeff, *La description de Damas d' Ibn 'Asākir* (Damascus, 1959), pp. 106–107, 222–223.

[4] Mann, *Texts,* II, sec. i, pp. 1–283, "Ḳaraism in the Near East." Also Mann, II, 400, Index, s.v. "Ḳaraite(s)." Leon Nemoy, *Karaite Anthology: Excerpts from the Early Literature,* trans. Leon Nemoy (New Haven, 1952). Baron, *History of the Jews,* Vol. V, chap. xxvi, "Karaite Schism."

[5] A. Cowley, "Samaritan Dealings with Jews," *JQR,* 16 (1904) 474–484, discussing Bodl. MS Heb. d 66 (Cat. 2878), f. 8*, the record from Damietta, and editing Bodl. MS Heb. b 11 (Cat. 2874), f. 13, and TS 16.26, the letters of the carpenter. The TS shelf mark is not supplied in the article. Sassoon 713*v*, l. 15+ (see *Med. Soc.,* I, 432 n. 24) mentions a high Samaritan government official, Fakhr al-Ṣanā'i, "The most glorious of the Favorites" (1148). He was preceded by Abū Ya 'qūb Ibrāhīm, "the Samaritan," who attained the highest secretarial position under the caliph al-Āmir (who ruled without a vizier), but, as so many other high-standing personalities, found a cruel death (1130) (see Ibn Muyassar, p. 74, l. 14). Two other important Samaritan state officials, father and son, are recorded for the end of the eleventh century in Ramle (see Mann, I, 18).

[6] Khalīfa: PER H 160, l. 8*. "Your synagogue": TS 13 J 26, f. 24, ed. S. D. Goitein, *Eretz-Israel* (Jerusalem), 7 (1964), 88–90.

[7] TS 16.318, l. 12; ed. Mann, *Texts,* I, 139.

[8] TS 13 J 8, f. 2 (1029). Mosseri A 43 (1055), beginning ed. J. Mann, *HUCA*, 3 (1926), 279; TS 13 J 2, f. 19 (1136, a document written in Damietta and validated in Fustat).

[9] Cf. "the Gaons, dead and alive, who invested him," TS 13 J 11, f. 9, l. 9, ed. Mann, II, 119, and chap. vi, sec. 9, n. 11, below.

[10] Bodl. MS Heb. f 34, f. 40*v*, ed. A. Cowley, *JQR*, 18 (1906), 399, 401–402.

[11] Mann, *Texts*, I, 558–567, editing a manuscript in the possession of the late A. Harkavy of Petersburg (Leningrad). The writer of this rebuke to the scholars of Qayrawān was the Gaon Naḥshōn b. Ṣādōq of Sura (in office approximately 871–879, succeeding his father after a waiting period of about fifty years).

[12] S. D. Goitein, "The Qayrawān United Appeal for the Babylonian Yeshivoth," *Zion*, 27 (1962), 156–165, esp. p. 164, ll. 28–29. Also TS 8.265 (see sec. A, 2, n. 10, below).

[13] TS 13 J 19, f. 16*v*, l. 8 (in the course of edition by D. H. Baneth), a highly interesting, but incomplete, letter by the Jerusalem Gaon Solomon b. Judah.

[14] Mann, *Texts*, I, 67 n. 11.

[15] Lane-Poole, *History of Egypt, p. 81.*

[16] The letter has been re-edited in Abramson, *Bamerkazim*, pp. 34–40. For previous editions and discussion see next note.

[17] Like many others, this document has not been preserved in its entirety, but some parts of it have been found and published by various authors. The whole material is discussed in Mann, *Texts*, I, 67–72, from which the references given here are taken. Fragments of another inaugural circular by a Gaon dealing mainly with questions of religious thought, *ibid.*, I, 166–177; see also *ibid.*, p. 154.

[18] Hebrew Union College, Cincinnati, Geniza MS 2, ed. J. Mann, *Hebrew Union College Jubilee Volume* (Cincinnati, 1925), pp. 249–252. The Gaon refers to a similar statement made in the Babylonian Talmud in the time of Persian rule.

[19] The letters are contained in a Paris manuscript, ed. B. M. Levin, *Ginze Kedem* (1925), pp. 14–23, and in TS 16.95. The whole material is discussed in S. D. Goitein, "The Donations of the Jews of Yemen to the Academies of Iraq and Palestine and the School of Maimonides," *Tarbiz*, 31 (1962), 357–370.

[20] In the letters to Yemen and, e.g., in a letter of the Gaon Nehemiah b. Kohen Ṣedeq, dated 962 (Mann, *Texts*, I, 82, l. 24).

[21] See the indexes of Mann and Mann, *Texts*, s.v. *ḥōmesh*. Both the Hebrew and the Arabic term *khums* were used. Mann's explanation of the term (Mann, II, 126 n. 6) is unlikely. The "fixed charge": *ḥoq* (Heb.).

[22] Called *pesīqā*, e.g., Mann, *Texts*, I, 82 (see above, n. 20).

[23] References in my *Tarbiz* article cited in n. 19. Government: TS 13 J 26, f. 16, ll. 12–14, ed. Mann, II, 70. See n .38, below.

[24] Mosseri L 279, ed. Mann, *Hebrew Union College Jubilee Volume* pp. 235–236 (referring to Elhanan b. Shemarya of Old Cairo).

[25] TS 8.265, last line (about edition see sec. A, 2, n. 10, below). The Gaon concerned, Hay, was then in his eighties.

[26] ULC Or 1080 J 106, ll. 15–16. The writer, Solomon b. Judah, was very advanced in age at the time of that letter.

[27] J. Mann's criticism of L. Ginzberg's contention that only the Gaon had the right of responsum in the name of the yeshiva (Mann, *Texts*, I, 559) fails to make this distinction.

[28] The letter contains an instruction to coerce two couples to cede part of an inheritance to an orphan girl (TS 13 J 9, f. 7, dated 1166). At that time the Gaon Nethanel ha-Levi b. Moses was the official head of the Egyptian Jews. The letter is incomplete, but the identity of the issuer is established beyond doubt by a

comparison with TS 13 J 6, f. 3+ (see Shaked, *Bibliography,* p. 117) and TS 13 J 23, f. 7, as well as the motto taken from Psalm 68:21*a,* which served Samuel b. Eli as signature.

[29] TS 12.217, 11. 10–11, 21, ed. Mann, II, 145–146. On the organization of the yeshivas in general see also chap. vi, sec. 7, below.

[30] The technical term for the expulsion of a member: "removal from the gate of the yeshiva" (BM Or 5536 III, nos. 8–9 [during the gaonate of Samuel b. Eli]).

[31] For Spain and Morocco see *Med. Soc.,* I, 53. The Gaon Abraham Qābisī, who was in office around 830, either came himself from Gabes, Tunisia, or his family hailed from there (see J. Mann, *JQR,* 7 [1917], 483–484).

[32] Naṭrōnay: M. Margalioth, *Biographical Dictionary* Tel Aviv, 1950, p. 618. Dōsā: TS 13 J 36, f. 1, 11. 6, 14, ed. S. D. Goitein, *Tarbiz,* 34 (1965), 174 ff. Saadya died in 942 and was succeeded by his son Dōsā in 1013 (Mann, *Texts,* I, 153). About Naḥshōn b. Ṣādōq see above, n. 11.

[33] Mann, I, 185, II, 64–65. In the manuscripts quoted there, only the years, not the months have been preserved. Thus, for 1037 a more exact rendering would be 1036–1037 (but not 1038, as in Mann, I, 185). Gaon designate: TS 20.19, 1. 29. Worman, JQR, 18 (1905), 743, gives the address only, and faultily. The word in Arabic characters after "the Rabbanites" is not *mftkhyn,* but *muqīmīn,* "living in."

[34] The handwriting of Abraham, son of Solomon b. Judah Gaon, is known through the letters TS 10 J 30, f. 14, and ULC Or 1080 J 265, both signed by him. While in Fustat, he also wrote two court records and signed one of them in 1026, both contained in TS 8 J 6, f. 18 (cf. Mann. II, 97–98 [who does not reproduce the records themselves]).

[35] Mosseri L 21, ll. 7–9; BM Or 5338 II, 11. 10–11; both ed. Mann, *Texts,* I, 164, 166.

[36] ULC Or 1080 J 45, 11. 20–26. B. Spuler, *Die Morgenlaendischen Kirchen: Handbuch der Orientalistik,* A VIII, 2 (Leiden, 1961), p. 147. The order of succession in the Palestinian yeshiva, called *netīvōt,* "guidelines," was fixed through "statutes made by the congregations," *kātevū ha-qehillōt taqqānōt* (TS 10 J 32, f. 9, ll. 6–7, verso, ll. 4, 10).

[37] TS Arabic Box 30, f. 278, sec. III, 1.7, IV, 1.6, ed. S. M. Stern *REJ,* 128 (1969), 203–222. Mann, II, 162, 1. 22, 163, ll. 12–13.

[38] TS 24.43, 11. 44–45. The official letter is appropriately called *nishtewān* (Ezra 4:7). Al-Ẓāhir is described as needing "health for his body and peace for his soul (*yishqoṭ*)." This shows that his abnormality, reported by the historians for the end of his rule, was already apparent to his subjects at its beginning. Dropsie 354, ed. S. D. Goitein, *Eretz-Israel.* 10 (1970).

[39] Literature on the exilarchate in Baron, *History of the Jews,* V, 293–297 nn. 2–9. Baron takes perhaps a too sanguine view of the ecumenical importance of the office during the eleventh and subsequent centuries. Latest discussion of the exilarchate in talmudic times in Jacob Neusner, *A History of the Jews in Babylonia* (Leiden, 1968), III, 41–94. See also here, n. 49, below.

[40] TS Loan 40, ed. Mann, *Texts,* I, 182, 11. 9–10, 21; cf. *ibid.,* p. 209 n. 14.

[41] Bodl. MS Heb. f 56 (Cat. 2821, no. 16), f. 17, 1.2, ed. S. D. Goitein, *JQR,* 43 (1952), 73; cf. *ibid.,* p. 68.

[42] *Med. Soc.* I, 396 n. 19. Mann, *Texts,* I, 230–235, esp. p. 233 n. 71.

[43] TS 8.115. It is signed by Eli ha-Kohen b. Yaḥyā and Abraham b. Isaac, the Scholar. About these two men see the indexes of *Med. Soc.,* Vol. I, and of this volume. TS 13 J 2, f. 3 (Dec., 1093), signed by the same and Ezekiel II ha-Kohen he-Ḥāvēr b. Eli he-Ḥāvēr I, cf. *Med. Soc.,* I, 292.

[44] Bodl. MS Heb. c 28 (Cat. 2876), f. 65, a letter by Nathan ha-Kohen b. Mevō-

rākh of Ascalon to Eli ha-Kohen b. Ḥayyīm (= Yaḥyā), cf. *Med. Soc.*, I, 489 n. 5.

[45] G. Makdisi, "Autograph Diary of an Eleventh Century Historian of Baghdad," Part III, *BSOAS*, 19 (1957), text: p. 25, trans.: p. 43. (My attention was drawn to this passage first by a student of mine, Khidr al-Duri, himself a native of Baghdad.) The events of 1058 are reported in Ibn al-Jawzī, *Muntaẓam* (Hyderabad, A.H. 1357–1359), VIII, 190, trans. Dinur, *Yisrael ba-Gola*, I, 1, p. 97 (where, however, the Arabic word translated as "businessmen" means "government officials"). About the first Ibn Faḍlān see sec. A, 2, n. 6, below.

[46] "We, the undersigned merchants arriving in Aden from India and partly also from Egypt, found here a man from Persia, claiming to be a member of the house of David and having the right to assume authority. The local people conceded to him complete jurisdiction over all the synagogues in the country" (TS 20.37 [1134 A.D.], ed. S. D. Goitein, *Sinai*, 16 [1953], 230; *India Book* 87). A *nāsī*, perhaps the same, is found in Aden twenty years later (see E. Strauss, *Zion*, 4 [1939], 230; *India Book* 35). These Geniza documents confirm the report of Benjamin of Tudela (ca. 1173) about two nāsīs, brothers, who divided between themselves the authority over the Jewish communities of Yemen.

[47] See Mann and Mann, *Texts*, Indexes, s.v. "Daniel b. Azarya" and "David b. Daniel." About the former, some interesting new Geniza letters have come to light which show inter alia that Daniel's own brother who had preceded him to Palestine, disapproved of his pushing for the gaonate (TS 13 J 26, f. 18). The pastoral letter referred to is contained in TS 12.239. According to TS NS Box 312, f. 82, ed. Abramson, *Bamerkazim*, p. 33, the combination of nāsī and Gaon already occurred about 180 years before Daniel.

[48] TS 20.116, l. 4 (1088); two other sources: Mann, II, 220, sec. 5 (1089); TS NS Box 320, ff. 27–28 (1092). TS 13 J 19, f. 6, ll. 15–16 (a letter): *rōsh gālūyōth kol yisrā'ēl*. Arabic Box 40, f. 48, contains an eloquent letter of apology by 'Imrān b. Muhājir for disrespectful remarks about the House of David. It is in Arabic language and characters, but addressed in Hebrew to "The Sublime Port" of the nāsī.

[49] A letter about an encounter with the Mongols (Bodl. MS Heb. a 3 [Cat. 2873], f. 24, partially ed. S. D. Goitein, *Levi Della Vida Jubilee Volume* [Rome, 1956], I, 398 ff.) is addressed to him. Full edition, together with TS 20.128, another letter to the same, in S. D. Goitein, "The Nāsīs of Mosul and the Destruction of Their Houses by the Earthquake of 1237," *Braslavi Jubilee Volume* (Tel Aviv, 1970), 486–501. Four other letters to this nāsī (TS 12.352, 12.654, 20.175, and 13 J 21, f. 8) are discussed in the same article. The Mosul nāsīs might have had a pre-Islamic "pre-history"; see M. Beer, "The Exilarchate in Talmudic Times," *Zion*, 28 (1963), 32–33, about exilarchs in Nesibin (today Nusaybin in Turkey), not far from Mosul. See now M. Beer, *The Babylonian Exilarchate in the Arsacid and Sassanian Periods* (Tel Aviv, 1970) (in Heb.). With the exception of TS 20.175, all the letters referred to above are in the same hand, that of a close relative of the nāsī. A sixth letter by the same writer, TS 16.36, describes in moving terms the misery of the Mosul nāsīs arriving in Egypt in close succession, "like the messengers of Job" (Job 1:16–18), and only degrade themselves while seeking to be honored with gifts.

[50] TS NS Box 110, f. 26*; (Professor Shalom Spiegel kindly drew my attention to this document); Mosseri L 199, ed. J. Mann, *HUCA*, 3 (1926), 265, where the prayer for the hard-pressed Palestinian Gaon Joshia (around 1015) contains the wish that he may prevail over his adversaries. A copy of the prayer was sent to him.

[51] An example in A. Butler, *Ancient Coptic Churches* (Oxford, 1884), I, 233.

[52] TS NS Box 320, f .16, 11. 4–5 (in Arabic characters), ed. S. D. Goitein, *Salo W. Baron Jubilee Volume* (New York, 1970). TS NS Box 169, f. 11*v*, ll. 6–9, ed. Abramson, *Bamerkazim*, p. 57. See *ibid.* p. 44, where the addressee is assured that his name and title were solemnly mentioned in the presence of the scholars of the yeshiva and "many thousands of Israel."

[53] Up to the present day the Jewish grace after a festive meal is introduced by the formula: "With the permission of our lords and masters and the permission of my masters." While "my masters" refers to the persons present, "our lords and masters" is nothing but a remnant from ancient times, when the ecumenical and/or territorial authorities were mentioned by name on such an occasion.

[54] INA D-55, f. 10, *India Book* 331*a*.

[55] Thus the recently identified Mangalore document (see preceding note) proves that the exilarch Daniel b. Ḥisday (who confirmed the Egyptian Gaon Nethanel in 1161 [see *Med. Soc.*, I, 396 n. 19]) was already in office in 1132. Hitherto it had been believed that he acceded to office after 1147.

[56] TS 20.37+; TS Arabic Box 48, f. 270, both ed. in S. D. Goitein, "The Jews of Yemen between the Gaonate of Egypt and the Exilarchate of Baghdad," *Sinai*, 16 (1953), 225–237 (see n. 46, above). Since the publication of that article additional material on the controversy has come to light.

[57] TS 16.187*, ed. S. D. Goitein, *I. Goldziher Memorial Volume* (Jerusalem, 1958), II, 49–54, where further sources and literature on the subject. According to TS 12.657, ll. 7–8*, even the government interefered in this matter.

[58] TS 12.39, a document from Minyat Ghamr, dated 1315–1316, with a reshūth for Abraham II b. David, Abraham Maimonides' grandson.

[59] ENA 4020, f. 48, ed. Mann, II, 182, no. 5 (the title is found both on the address and in the exordium, ll. 7–8). When Mann used the manuscript, it did not yet have a mark.

[60] A letter by the Babylonian Gaon Solomon, ed. S. Assaf, *Letters of Samuel b. Eli* (Jerusalem, 1930), pp. 78–82. English summary and important emendations of the text in Mann, *Texts*, I, 212–213.

[61] TS 13 J 16, f. 17; TS 12.17, both ed. Mann, II, 236–238. The writer's hand is intricate, and Mann's rendering needs thorough revision.

[62] See the sources noted in sec. A, 2, n. 7, below.

[63] When Josephus, *Antiquities*, XVIII, ix, 1, reports that the contributions for the Temple of Jerusalem from all over northern Mesopotamia were stored in Nisibis, some sort of diocesan organization must have been in existence at that time.

2. *The Territorial Heads of the Jewish Community. The Nagid*

[1] Mann, *Texts*, I, 394.

[2] Literature on the subject: A. Neubauer, "Origin and Growth of the Nagid Dignity," *JQR*, 8 (1896), 551–555 (the first to make use of the new Geniza material. He lists Paltiel of the Ahimaas Chronicle and his descendants as Nagids). E. N. Adler, "The Installation of the Egyptian Nagid," *JQR*, 9 (1897), 717–720 (a historically feasible interpretation of this document is tried below, n. 36). David Kaufmann, "The Egyptian Nagid," *JQR*, 10 (1898), 161–164 (comments on the fragment published by Adler). R. Gottheil, *JQR*, 19 (1907), 500–501 and 528–532 (publication and translation of passages from Arabic historians about the office of the Ra'īs al-Yahūd, an appendix to his article, "An Eleventh Century Document Concerning a Cairo Synagogue"). Mann and Mann, *Texts*, *passim* (see the indexes), in particular Mann, I, 251–257. D. Neustadt (now Ayalon), "Some Problems Concerning the 'Negidut' in Egypt during the Middle Ages," *Zion*, 4 (1939), 126–149 (destroys the legends [*a*] that the office of Nagid was created by Muslim rulers, [*b*] that Paltiel was the founder of the office. This article has often been quoted, but, it seems, never thoroughly read). D. Neustadt, "On Maimonides' Title of Nagid," *Zion*, 11 (1946), 147–148 (draws attention to the fact that Maimonides is clearly and repeatedly described as Ra'īs al-Yahūd by Muslim writers). Strauss, *Mamluks*, II, 237–245 (the most detailed and thorough treatment of the subject, but unaware of the considerations recommended in this section. H. Z. Hirschberg,

"The Salars and Negidim of Kairawan," *Zion,* 23–24 (1959), 166–173, cf. also *ibid.,* 25 (1960), 62 (seems to assume that the ruler of Tunisia appointed a Nagid in defiance of the Fatimids of Egypt). Hirschberg, *The Jews in North Africa,* II, 440 (Index). Baron, *History of the Jews,* Index to Vols. I–VII, p. 106 s.v. *Negidim* (the word should have been listed also under *Nagid*). Dinur, *Yisrael ba-Gola,* I, 3, 12–19. E. Ashtor in *Zion,* 30 (1965), 141–147. My paper, "The Title and Office of the Nagid: A Reexamination," *JQR,* 53 (1962), 93–119, has been used here, but in a completely revised version.

[3] The original form of the title was *negīd ha-gōlā,* "Prince of the Diaspora," see, e.g., Bodl. MS Heb. a 3 (Cat. 2873), f. 26, l. 16* (dated 1041). Moses b. Mevōrākh bore, among others, four titles in which the word Nagid occurred (TS 18 J 2, f. 13 [dated 1117], partly ed. Mann, II, 249 n. 1, end). The official title of Samuel of Granada was *negīd yisrā'ēl* (ENA 3765, f. 8, ll. 12, 28, ed. J. Mann, *HUCA,* 3 [1926], 286, 287).

[4] Ibn 'Aṭā' 's role of court physician is known from a Muslim source (see H. R. Idris, *Zirides,* pp. 178–179; *idem,* "Deux maîtres de l'école juridique kairouanaise sous les Zirides," *Annales de l'Institut d'Études Orientales,* 13 [1955], 55–56, cf. *Zion,* 27 [1962], 12).

[5] In a letter to Ibn 'Awkal (TS 10 J 9, f. 26, ed. S. D. Goitein, *Tarbiz,* 34 [1965], 166–169), Ibn 'Aṭā' calls himself "Prince of the Diaspora, Ibrāhīm, son of Nathan, Rōsh ha-Qehillōth."

[6] S. D. Goitein, "Who Was the First Nagid?" *Zion,* 27 (1962), 165. Since people wanted to have *new, unusual* honorary epithets, they were assured that the title bestowed was borne (as in the case of "Nagid" here) by persons long dead. See Mann, II, 86, where a dignitary lived in Egypt around 1060 is informed that his new title "Splendor of the Yeshiva" (*Hōd*) was held only once before, namely by the prominent financier Abū 'Alī I Ibn Faḍlān I of Baghdad (whose refusal in 998 to grant a loan to an amir led to a riotous attack on the Jews of that city [see Fischel, *Jews,* p. 33 n. 1]).

[7] S. D. Goitein, "New Sources concerning the Nagids of Qayrawān," *Zion,* 27 (1962), 11–23; *idem,* "The Qayrawan United Appeal for the Babylonian Yeshivoth and the Emergence of the Nagid Abraham Ibn 'Aṭā'," *Zion,* 27 (1962), 156–165.

[8] Bodl. MS Heb. a 3 (Cat. 2873), f. 26, ll. 16, 44*; TS 24.6, ed. J. Mann, *JQR,* n.s., 9 (1918–1919), 175–179. About Jacob b. Amram, see Hirschberg, *The Jews in North Africa,* I, 159–160, 364.

[9] In addition to the sources mentioned or referred to in n. 8: Bodl. MS Heb. a 2 (Cat. 2805), f. 17, ll. 42–45, and margin*.

[10] TS 8.265. Mann, *JQR,* 11 (1920), 454–455, quoted a few lines of this Arabic text, but misread it and did not recognize the word Nagid occurring in it.

[11] TS 16.179, ll. 32–43*. Sicily: Bodl. MS Heb. d 76, f. 59*v,* ll. 5–7. Ayyūb. b. Tamīm (see Idris, *Zīrīdes,* p. 285) is referred to as Ibn al-Na'nā', presumably the name of his mother (Tamīm had over a hundred sons). Zakkār b. 'Ammār, according to his letter TS 16.13, was a representative of merchants in Palermo like his brother Ḥayyīm.

[12] TS 20.24, ed. S. Schechter, *JQR,* 12 (1899–1900), 112–113, re-edited E. Ashtor, *Sefarad,* 24 (1964), 60–63. At the time of Schechter's publication the manuscript had no number.

[13] The history of these two men is exhaustively treated by Ashtor, *Jews in Muslim Spain,* II, 27–117, cf. S. D. Goitein, *Speculum,* 42 (1967), 714–716. The title Nagid was conferred on Joseph B. Samuel by the Palestinian Gaon Daniel b. Azarya; see ENA 3765, f. 8, l. 34, ed. J. Mann, *HUCA,* 3 (1926), 287, where "the new name," on which he is congratulated after the death of his father is none but the one borne before by the latter, while Joseph himself had been ornated with other honorific epithets earlier.

[14] For these three persons, see the Index.

[15] Latest document mentioning Mevōrākh as alive, known to me: TS 24.5. His death on March 30, 1112: Bodl. MS Heb. d 75, f. 13, see n. 37, below. Unpublished TS documents issued under the authority of his son Moses: 24.3 (a marriage contract, dated 1115); 12.164 (almost entirely lost); 8.149, 16.57 (dated 1120); 16.52 (1124). Two letters addressed to him by the cantor Nathan b. Solomon ha-ḥazzān b. Yā'īr: TS 24.55 (partly ed. S. D. Goitein, *Goldziher Memorial Volume* (Jerusalem, 1958), II, Heb. sec., pp. 53–54); TS 8.79.

[16] The official head of the Egyptian Jews referred to in n. 47, below, did not bear the title Nagid.

[17] Details in S. D. Goitein, "The Life of Maimonides in the Light of New Finds from the Cairo Geniza," *Peraqim* (New York), 4 (1966), 29–42 (in Heb.).

[18] TS 13 J 3, f. 22, a document dated Aug., 1213, has many titles, but not that of Nagid. Bodl. MS Heb. b 3 (Cat. 2806), f. 6, dated Dec., 1213–Jan., 1214, TS 13 J 3, f. 25 (April, 1215), and later documents have it. Likewise, a deposition in the court of Alexandria in 1209, rendered "word by word and letter by letter" in Abraham Maimuni, *Responsa*, p. 165, contains no reference to him, while a similar record from the same town, dated 1234, in *Responsa*, p. 178, is made "under the authority of our Nagid Abraham, the Prince of the People of the Lord of Hosts." See also Mann, II, 326–328.

[19] Besides the four well-known Nagids David I, Abraham II, Joshuah, and David II, Moses, Joshuah's elder brother (born 1290 and known to have died young) seems to have been Nagid for some time (see TS Box K 15, f. 58*v*, l. 9: Mūsā al-Nagid).

[20] For Maḍmūn and his sons, see *India Book*, chap. ii and *passim*. About the thirteenth-century Nagid Shemarya b. David, see Mann, II, 338, and *India Book* 309 and 310. The tombstone of 1248 in Eli Subar, "Medieval Jewish Tombstones from Aden," *JQR*, 49 (1959), 305. See S. D. Goitein, "The Nagids of Yemen," *Bō'ī Tēmān* (Tel Aviv), 1967, pp. 15–25 (in Heb.). For the Syro-Palestinian Nagids (second half of the twelfth and early thirteenth centuries), see Mann, I, 257. Mann rightly draws attention to the fact that the later Muslim sources also make mention of a "head of the Jews" in Damascus in Ayyubid times.

[21] R. Gottheil, *JQR*, 19 (1907), 500–501 and 528–532, quoting Faḍl Allah al-'Omari (wrote his *Ta'rīf* in 1340), al-Qalqashandī (d. 1418) and a Paris manuscript.

[22] For more details with regard to the Nagid's jurisdiction over the Karaites and Samaritans, see Strauss, *Mamluks*, II, 238–245.

[23] TS 20.96, ll. 3, 8 and 14+. His name was Ephraim, but his father's name is not yet known.

[24] Thus Shemarya b. Elhanan signed himself, e.g., TS 12.43, ed. S. D. Goitein, *Tarbiz*, 32 (1963), 271, cf. Abramson, *Bamerkazim*, p. 171. For Shemarya and his son Elhanan see the indexes of Mann and Mann, *Texts*, and Abramson, *op. cit.*, pp. 105–179.

[25] Mann, I, 31–32, corrected by himself in *HUCA*, 3 (1926), 258–262.

[26] TS 12.153, partly ed. Mann, II, 341. The title "The elder of the Diaspora" could not be abbreviated to "The elder," since everyone was addressed thus. Therefore, Hay Gaon looked for another title that lent itself to abbreviation more easily and found it in "Nagid." For the title Rōsh ha-Seder, or "head of the scholars," see below, chap. vi, sec. 7, n. 7.

[27] TS 12.153 (see preceding note), which emanated from the Palestinian community. In TS NS J 51, ll. 11–16, the late Elhanan is referred to in a document dated 1027 as having arranged a settlement in Sahrajt.

[28] Acre: TS 13 J 35, f. 2. Damascus: TS 18 J 4, f. 5, ed. Mann, II, 40–41; re-edited Abramson, *Bamerkazim*, pp. 175–179.

[29] The second source quoted in the preceding note, cf. Mann, I, 39.

[30] The document of 1038, ed. R. Gottheil, *JQR*, 19 (1906–1907), cf. above, n. 2, does not come from the Geniza and clearly was worked over and adapted to later

usage. No record issued directly from the Fatimid chancellery could contain such blunders as those manifest in that document.

[31] See above, sec. A, 1, and below, sec. B.

[32] Letters addressed to Ephraim b. Shemarya (active ca. 1015–1050) from the Rīf: TS 8 J 21, f. 6, ed. Mann, II, 109–110 (request for help to pay the poll tax); TS 10 J 22, f. 7 (formerly bearing the mark TS 12.857, cf. Mann, II, 111, from Ṣahrajt, a complicated case of divorce); TS 13 J 13, f. 1 (from Malīj, a widow, appointed by her late husband as executrix, requests delivery of valuables deposited with the great houses of Ibn Sha'yā and Tustarī of Cairo).

[33] TS 13 J 13, f. 2 (letter from Ṣahrajt to Eli b. Amram, Ephraim's successor).

[34] The Gaon Solomon b. Judah writes from Jerusalem to Ephraim b. Shemarya: "I learn that a large group of people wanted to submit to the government—may God preserve it—a complaint accusing me of having appointed an unworthy man (i.e., Ephraim)" (TS 13 J 9, f. 2, l. 15, ed. Mann. II, 120).

[35] When Yeshū'ā ha-Kohen he-ḥāvēr b. Joseph of Alexandria had serious troubles with his congregation, Eli b. Amram, the communal leader of Fustat, was warned by the Gaon and Nāsī Daniel b. Azarya (1051–1062) of Jerusalem in the strongest terms not to interfere, but to leave the matter to him: TS 24.56*v*, l. 32, margin (l. 12). Identification of writer by comparison with Bodl. MS Heb. a 3 (Cat. 2873), f. 17.

[36] About the Karaite allegiance of the Tustarī family, see S. D. Goitein, *JQR*, 45 (1954), 36–38. [Expressly stated in Arabic Box 30, f. 278, see sec. A, 1, n. 37, above.]

[37] The date of Mevōrākh's death: in the letter Bodl. MS Heb. 75 [no Cat.], f. 13, dated May 28, 1112, and reporting that he died on a new moon day coinciding with a Sabbath, which, in that year, occurred only on March 30, 1112. The writer asks the addressee, his father and a "distinguished member" of the academy, "to pray" for the new Nagid, i.e., to accept his leadership. The Nāsī: TS 18 J 4, f. 12, ll. 3–4. For the appreciation of Mevōrākh by later generations see Bodl. MS Heb. b 13 (Cat. 2834, no. 22), f. 41, ll. 10 ff.; ed. Mann, I, 222 n. 2.

[38] This seems to be the correct interpretation of the text edited by E. N. Adler in *JQR* 9 (1897), 717–720, under the title "The Installation of the Egyptian Nagid." See Mann, I, 253, for further literature about the subject. The letter was most probably written by Zuṭṭā, the impostor.

[39] TS 13 J 13, f. 13, sec. 2, addressed to Daniel b. Azarya.

[40] TS K 21, f. 21, a eulogy for a Nagid who succeeded his father. This is a partly rhymed piece from a formulary, based on I Chronicles 29:23 and Psalms 45: 3–5, and not a congratulatory poem (of the type preserved in TS 10 H 3, fs. 11–12, ed. Mann, II, 369–370, written for the inauguration of Moses, the son of Samuel b. Hananya, as Nagid designate).

[41] It was the installation of the Babylonian Gaon Daniel b. Elazar by the caliph al-Nāṣir on May 15, 1209, ed. S. Poznanski, *Babylonische Geonim im nachgaonäischen Zeitalter* (Berlin, 1914), pp. 37–39. Arabic Box 38, f. 93*, a complete letter of appointment of a ra'īs al-yahūd in Damascus was found by me in August, 1970, after this volume was set in type. TS Arabic Box 39, fs. 453 and 452 (in this order), contain a copy of the letter of appointment of a Christian dignitary by the Fatimid viceroy al-Malik al-Afḍal. The Jews obviously were eager to obtain a copy of such a document, since their legal position was similar to that of the Christians. There is indeed some similarity between the two documents.

[42] Westminster College, Frag. Cairens 51. The letter is addressed to Mevōrākh in his capacity as rayyis, but does not call him Nagid, while his late brother Judah is referred to by this title. The same in Bodl. MS Heb. d 66 (Cat. 2878), f. 79*v*, ll. 1–3, Nahray 31, and TS 13 J 23, f. 3, l. 8, Nahray 71.

[43] TS 10 J 16, f. 12*, ed. S. D. Goitein, *Tarbiz*, 34 (1965), 236–240. According to all our sources, David was born in 1222. Strauss, *Mamluks*, I, 118–120, tried to show in great length and with much acumen that the sources erred by ten years and

that David must have been born in 1212. But in a letter dated 1217, addressed to his father Abraham (TS 16.305), the writer expresses the hope that he may be blessed with a son like himself. Thus, the traditional date of David's birth must be retained. E. Ashtor (identical with Strauss), *Zion,* 30 (1965), 142, 146, adduces additional proof for the date 1222, but believes that he had shown this in *Mamluks,* I, while he ascribes the erroneous date of 1212 to someone else. I mention this little detail as a consolation for scholars who are unhappy when they discover that they have misquoted a colleague. Such things may sometimes happen to us with our own writings.

[44] Mann, II, 251. TS Arabic Box 18(1), f. 34.

[45] On (Abū Zikrī Yaḥyā) Zuṭṭā, see S. D. Goitein, *Tarbiz,* 32 (1963), 192, where also the literature on the subject is noted.

[46] Abū (Bū) Sa'd "the Seventh," later advanced to "Sixth," which finally became the name of the family, see S. D. Goitein, *Homenaje a Millás-Vallicrosa* (Barcelona, 1954), I, 709. His name was Moses b. Nethanel ha-Levi, and his son Sar Shalom calls him Gaon (Mann, II, 294, sec. (4)), a claim not yet substantiated by any document. His endeavors to become head of the Jews are described in the fragment TS Arabic Box 54 (formerly: Hirschfeld IV), f. 60, ed. E. Ashtor, *Zion,* 30 (1965), 156–157. (Text, translation, and comment need revision.) As the references to the viziers Riḍwān (spelled also Rūdwān, 1137–1139; killed 1148) and Ibn al-Salar (pronounced also Salār; murdered 1153) show, Abū Sa'd's machinations were directed against the Nagid Samuel b. Hananya, see Lane-Poole, *History of Egypt,* pp. 169, 171. In TS 13 J 13, f. 12, ll. 18–margin, l. 10 (*India Book* 97), he orders books, it seems from Europe, for the man charged with the order traveled on a Pisan ship. Abū Sa'd was a physician and worked in a government hospital, as we know from a letter of his son Nethanel (TS Box K 25, f. 64*, see Goitein, *Education,* p. 202).

[47] Nethanel died after 1184, see chap. vi, sec. 12, n. 16, below. In Bodl. MS Heb. a 3 (Cat. 2873), f. 6, ll. 16–17, he is referred to as living, while as official head of the Egyptian Jews at that time one Saadya, otherwise unknown, is mentioned.

[48] To the data given by Mann, II, 294, Mann, *Texts,* I, 258, D. H. Baneth, *Alexander Marx Jubilee Volume* (New York, 1950), Heb. sec., p. 77 n. 7, add Bodl. MS Heb. b 12 (Cat. 2875), f. 32 (dated 1194) and f 56 (Cat. 2821, no. 16*i*), f. 52*b* (dated 1183). See also the article cited in n. 17, above.

[49] TS 12.822, ed. I. Friedlaender in *Herman Cohen Jubilee Volume* (Berlin, 1912), pp. 257–264.

[50] TS 16.187+* ; TS Arabic Box 51 (formerly Hirschfeld), f. 111, ed. S. D. Goitein, *Homenaje Millás-Vallicrosa* (Barcelona, 1954), I, 717–718.

[51] Mevōrākh: e.g., Westminster College, Frag. Cairens. 50 (dated 1098); Bodl. MS Heb. a 3 (Cat. 2873), f. 2 (a letter of the two chief judges). The nāsī David b. Daniel appointing a *muqaddam* in Ascalon, Palestine: TS 18 J 2, f. 3, and three judges in Old Cairo: 13 J 2, f. 3 (Dec., 1093).

[52] TS 16.57 (dated Dec., 1120).

[53] Bodl. MS Heb. a 3 (Cat. 2873), f. 2*v*, l. 2, *ibid.* c 28 (Cat. 2876), f. 10, l. 9.

[54] Bodl. MS Heb. b 11 (Cat. 2874), f. 9*.

[55] A particularly instructive case of this procedure is contained in TS 10 J 29, f. 5 (a letter from Jerusalem by Eli I ha-Kohen b. Ezekiel I) with regard to Daniel b. Azarya of Jerusalem and his president of the High Court.

[56] "The savior, *mōshī'a* (Heb.), of a people with little power": ULC Or 1081 J 16.

[57] "The Rayyis will send a policeman after you, whereupon I shall submit a petition to the government": ULC 1080 J 112, ll. 12–13. In TS 13 J 18, f. 25*, which is a letter of apprehension issued by the Nagid Samuel b. Hananya to all the communities of the Egyptian countryside in 1143, he asks to send to him a fugitive debtor, if necessary with the help of the *raqqāṣīn al-wālī,* the state police.

For a case of apprehension carried out by a Jewish communal official see p. 84, above.

[58] Sources in *Med. Soc.* I, 411 n. 17.

[59] TS 13 J 20, f. 2.

[60] TS NS J 277*. See *Med. Soc.*, I, 260; also TS 8.183, where Maṣlīaḥ Gaon personally arranges the settlement of a debt.

[61] TS 16.305*v*, 11. 22–23, 29–31. The writer: Judah ha-melammēd b. Aaron al-ʿAmmānī.

[62] Bodl. MS Heb. a 3 (Cat. 2873), f. 2*v*, 11. 5–8*. Ritual matters: e.g., TS 16.296* (the Nagid Joshua taboos the food by the cooks of the bazaars because of their irreligious behavior).

[63] Abraham Maimuni, *Responsa,* p. 191.

[64] The term "widow" in this much used phrase comprised also deserted or neglected women, e.g., TS NS J 262. Cf. also TS 16.134, 1. 12.

[65] TS 13 J 18, f. 3, margin.

[66] Pilgrim and debtor: TS 8 J 17, fs. 13, 27. The poor man from Sunbāṭ: ULC 1081 J 10. In an Arabic letter, TS Arabic Box 39, f. 57, a pauper, *ṣaʿlūk,* threatens to flee from the country and to leave his family of six to the Nagid.

[67] Maimonides: TS 10 J 20, f. 5*v*+*. His son Abraham: TS 10 J 18, f. 15.

[68] Westminster College, Frag. Cairens. 51, 1. 27.

[69] Alexandria: TS 13 J 33 f. 9. Small place (Shaṭṭanawf): ULC Or 1081 J 16.

[70] See *Med. Soc.*, I, 280.

[71] TS 20.145. Cf. *Med. Soc.*, I, 329–330.

[72] Bodl. MS Heb. c 28 (Cat. 2876), f. 60, *India book* 136. Cf. *Med. Soc.*, I, 332.

[73] TS 13 J 24, f. 4. The term used: *mezōnōt.*

[74] TS 16.296*. At that time, a muqaddam was the head of the Jewish community of Old Cairo. For the poll tax see chap. vii, sec. C, 3, above.

[75] TS 13 J 26, f. 19*, and ENA 2743, f. 4, both addressed to Mevōrākh; TS Arabic Box 18 (1), f. 183.

[76] TS 13 J 26, f. 8: Two bowls are sent from Alexandria to the Nagid (Judah) and two mats and one bowl to his brother Mevōrākh. With this may be compared a present consisting of grapes and wax offered to the nāsī Daniel b. ʿAzarya of Jerusalem, ULC Or 1081 J 18, ed. S. D. Goitein, *Eretz-Israel,* 6 (1960), 167. An *ʿarḍī,* a broad shawl (used by some as prayer mantle), worth 60 dirhems: TS NS J 344, 11. 1–5. For presents to the patriarch, see Cl. Cahen, "La Chronique des Ayyoubides," *Bulletin d'Études Orientales de l'Institut Français de Damas,* 15 (1955–1957), 128.

[77] See sec. A, 1, above, and chap. vi, sec. 7, above.

[78] TS 16.179*, cf. *Zion,* 27 (1962), 18–19.

[79] Megillat Evyatar, ed. S. Schechter, *Saadyana* (Cambridge, 1903), p. 91. Megillat Zuṭṭa, ed. A. Neubauer, *JQR,* 8 (1896), 546: "He piled up gold pieces by oppressing the poor." Yearly contributions to the rayyis in return for an appointment: TS 13 J 25, f. 16, ed. S. D. Goitein, *Tarbiz,* 32 (1963), 193; TS NS J 193 (see S. D. Goitein, *Tarbiz,* 34 [1965], 232), in which Mēʾīr b. Hillel b. Ṣādōq is required to pay a yearly contribution of 12 dinars for his appointment as judge.

[80] S. Pines, "Une notice sur les Rech Galuta chez un écrivain arabe du IXe siècle," *REJ,* 100 bis (1936), 71 ff. Baron, *History of the Jews,* V, 12. The officials actually engaged in the ritual killing of animals or writing marriage and other contracts received of course remuneration for their services everywhere (see chap. vii, above).

[81] S. D. Goitein, "Abraham Maimonides and his Pietist Circle," *Jewish Medieval and Renaissance Studies,* ed. A. Altmann (Harvard University Press, 1967), pp. 145–164.

[82] A number of Geniza texts referring to David b. Abraham I, Abraham II b.

David, and Moses b. Abraham II have been edited by me in *Tarbiz,* 34 (1965), 236–256, one, relating to David II, in *JQR,* 44 (1953), 37–49. I have collected around thirty items emanating from the office of Joshua b. Abraham II or related to him. TS 13 J 4, f. 16*, referring to the Nagids Solomon and Yeshū'ā, the sons of Joseph, in 1482, is translated in *Med. People.* Of particular interest is TS Arabic 38, f. 131, see chap. vii, sec. D, above.

B. THE LOCAL COMMUNITY

1. *Its Composition and Organization*

[1] For *ha-qāhāl ha-qādōsh,* or holy congregation, in a Hebrew papyrus see Mann, I, 15 n. 4. For Jerusalem: Bodl. MS Heb. a3 (Cat. 2873), f. 21, ed. Mann, II, 38; Old Cairo: TS NS J 39, TS 13 J 19, f. 15, the latter ed. Mann, II, 198; Alexandria: ULC Or 1080 J 34 (addressed here as *qehal ha-qōdesh*). Towns in Palestine: Mann, II, 201 (Ascalon); S. Assaf, *Gaonica* (Jerusalem, 1933), p. 93 (Tiberias). Townlets in Egypt: Bodl. MS Heb. b 11 (Cat. 2874), f. 9* (Ṣahrajt), TS 13 J 22, f. 15 (Qalyūb). Mastaura in Asia Minor: TS 16.251, l. 2, ed. Mann, II, 93. *'Adat Ēl,* or assembly of God: TS 16.130. In Ar. *al-jamā'a al-muqaddasa,* Maimonides, *Responsa,* I, 47, and often. For *jamā'a,* exceptionally also *ṭā'ifa,* TS 13 J 23, f. 9, and *milla,* TS 20.133, l. 20 (both referring to Alexandria) were used. In Spain, it seems, *jumla* was preferred, *India Book* 101, l. 8; 105, l. 18.

For the history and significance of the term see I. Baer in *Zion,* 15 (1950), 9, 17, 20–22. The subject of this section is treated in my paper, "The Local Jewish Community in the Light of the Cairo Geniza Records," *Journal of Jewish Studies,* 12 (London, dated 1961, appeared July, 1963), 133–158.

[2] See sec. B, 2, above.

[3] Syracuse: Bodl. MS Heb. d 79, f. 36 (in the course of publication by N. Golb). Ṣahrajt: TS 10 J 22, f. 7, l. 13 (*'asīnū mōshāv,* Heb.). This manuscript originally was marked TS 12.857 (see Mann, II, 111). Minyat Ziftā: TS 13 J 16, f. 8. The nāsī addressed was probably Solomon b. Yīshay (chap. v, sec. A, 1, n. 49, above). The writer, the physician Eli b. Nathan, might be identical with the last signatory on TS 13 J 3, f. 20 (spring, 1208), where, however, a finer pen is used.

[4] The oldest marriage contract bearing this wish for the congregation on its superscription noticed by me thus far for the classical Geniza period is dated 1080 (TS 16.330), the latest is dated 1292 (TS 16.76). There are countless examples in between, and it also remained in use in subsequent centuries, e.g., TS 16.112, dated 1534 (communicated to me by Mr. M. Friedman).

[5] Palermo–al-Mahdiyya: TS 24.6+; Tyre-Aleppo: Bodl. MS Heb. a 3 (Cat. 2873), f. 37+; Old Cairo–Qayrawān: ULC Or 1080 J 6. The Gaon Joshiah "to the holy congregations in Shafrīr Miṣrayim [Old Cairo]": TS NS J 92. Another letter to them: TS 10 J 24, f. 9. To both Old Cairo and Alexandria: TS 8.13.

[6] TS 13 J 16, f. 13, ll. 15–16 (Ramle); TS 13 J 34, f. 3, l. 15 (Alexandria), ed. Mann, II, 345. Bodl. MS Heb. b 13 (Cat. 2834, no. 25), f. 44, ed. A. Freimann, *Judah Zlotnik Jubilee Volume* (Jerusalem, 1950), p. 176 (David II). TS 13 J 19, f. 6, ll. 6–7 (al-Maḥalla); Bodl. MS Heb. b 11 (Cat. 2874), f. 9* (Judah b. Saadya).

[7] Lists of groups composing a congregation: e.g., in the first two sources quoted in n. 5 and in TS 13 J 6, f. 6; TS Loan 206; TS 12.153+; TS 16.251, l. 10, ed. Mann, II, 93; ULC Or 1080 J 211 (*India Book* 247); ENA 2804, f. 7; also in the earlier documents discussed by I. Baer in *Zion,* 16 (1950), 20. Government officials, representatives of merchants, and other merchants: TS NS Box 324, f. 104; TS 13 J 14, f. 10, partly ed. Mann, II, 66 (written around 1015). Physicians in the letter of David II, see preceding note. Merchants also in ULC Or 1080 J 211+.

[8] TS 20.104, 1.16.

[9] TS 20. 117*v*, 1. 35, ed. Assaf, *Texts*, p. 161: *wa'adhinat al-jamā'a al-muqaddasa . . . yanūb 'anhum fī murā'āt al-kanīsa al-madhkūra.*

[10] ULC Add. 3358+: *anshē ha-kenēsā.*

[11] Maimonides, *Responsa,* II, 518, and TS 13 J 25, f. 16+.

[12] PER H 93, ed. D. H. Baneth, *Alexander Marx Jubilee Volume* (New York, 1950), Heb. sec., p. 88.

[13] TS 13 J 7, f. 25; Bodl. MS Heb. b 13 (Cat. 2834, no. 22), f. 41+.

[14] TS 12.543* (Minyat Ziftā, 1266).

[15] Cf. also E. Ashtor, "Prolegomena to the Medieval History of Oriental Jews," *JQR,* 50 (1959), 57, repeated in *Zion,* 30 (1965), 64, and Josiah C. Russell, "The Population of Medieval Egypt," *Journal of the American Research Center in Egypt,* 5 (1966), 69–82. While the assumption of the comparative smallness of cities during the High Middle Ages might be true, it is doubtful that the source material at present available warrants the (interesting) conclusions reached by the author. [Despite the published date of the journal, E. Ashtor's study, "The Number of the Jews in Mediaeval Egypt" (part one), *Journal of Jewish Studies* (London), 18 (1967) 9–42, actually appeared in the summer of 1969, when this volume had already been sent to the University of California Press. I am gratified that Ashtor and I arrived at the same results as to our estimate of the Jewish population of Minyat Ziftā (see *ibid.,* p. 34). Ashtor's shelf marks of Geniza manuscripts seemingly not included in the survey provided here: TS 20.8 and Bodl. 2874, f. 69 (*ibid.,* p. 33 nn. 169 and 170) are misprints for TS 20.80 and Bodl. 2876 (see nn. 24, 25, 37, below).]

[16] 1156: PER H 91. 1154: Bodl. MS Heb. b 11 (Cat. 2874, no. 22), f. 23. See n. 19, below.

[17] ULC Add 3341, referring to the judge Moses b. Peraḥyā.

[18] TS 12.543*. See *Med. Soc.,* I, 19.

[19] 1135: TS NS Box 323, f. 7 (a bill of divorce). 1178: ENA 4011, f. 65 (validation of a document written by Shabbetay himself but signed by others). The documents of 1154 and 1156 (see n. 16, above) were also validated by him.

[20] TS 18 J 2, f. 11, 11. 4 ff. The large fragment contains 31 lines of text and 11 in the margin, but the names of the writer and the addressee are not preserved.

[21] TS 12.56*v*, ll. 11–13; *ibid.,* l. 8. Here and in some other documents the name of the town is spelled *munyt zfty,* which indicates that it was pronounced *Munyat Ziftē* (with *u* for *i* and with so-called Imāla). In some documents from the thirteenth century, such as TS NS J 30 (1232) and TS 12.543* (1266), it is called Minyat Ziftā Jawād. The same in a deed of sale of part of a house written by a Muslim notary (TS Arabic Box 53, f. 19).

[22] Baedeker, *Ägypten,* 1928 p. 177.

[23] *Benjamin of Tudela,* ed. Adler, pp. 69, 74.

[24] Flax: TS 13 J 23, f. 16 (a letter from Minyat Ziftā). Indigo: TS 13 J 28, f. 12, bottom. Sesame: TS 20.80, 1. 42, *India Book* 273.

[25] TS 8 J 5, f. 18, *passim;* TS 20.80*v*+, 11. 49–50.

[26] TS 12.581*v*, 1. 8: *'amal al-Rīf,* "five large cubits long."

[27] TS 12.581, 11. 6, 7, 14.

[28] *Med. Soc.,* I, 190. Maimonides, *Responsa,* II, 448–451.

[29] Sugar factories: TS 24.25, 11. 25, 31; TS 8.4, 11. 5, 7, 11 (called here *al-dār al-skryya*). Beverages: TS 12.56, top, end, where a *fuqqā'ī,* or producer of the popular drink *fuqqā',* gambled with the guest of the judge, the writer of that letter.

[30] Letter to the Nagid Samuel b. Hananya in the hand of Shabbetay b. Abraham, composed of the fragment TS 10 J 15, f. 29, directly continued in 10 J 15, f. 32.

[31] "Trusted by the Dynasty," *amīn al-dawla* Sa'd, *'ateret ha-sōferīm* (Heb. title,

"Pride of the Officials"): TS 8.23*v,* l. 6, fragment of letter by Mevōrākh b. Nathan, containing other interesting details about Minyat Ziftā. Physicians, tax-farmers, druggist, and silversmith: TS 12.543* (1266). "The veterinary who takes the Torah scroll from the holy ark in Minyat Ziftā and leads the congregation in prayer," *al-bīṭār alladhī yukhrij sēfer tōrā* (Heb.) *wa-yuṣallī:* TS Arabic Box 54, f. 91, l. 5 (same period). Tannery: TS NS J 30 (1232). Dyer: TS 8 J 5, f. 18*b*, l. 6 (late twelfth century).

[32] TS 12.581, l. 8 and margin.

[33] TS 8 J 17, f. 18+. One or more lists of contributions from other localities in the Rīf might have existed but not come down to us.

[34] TS 12.543* (see n. 18, above).

[35] TS 12.192+.

[36] TS 12.289*, ed. S. D. Goitein, *Tarbiz,* 33 (1965), 189–192.

[37] E.g., PER H 91 (1156): a debt of 183 dinars. Bodl. MS Heb. c 28 (Cat. 2876), f. 69 (written in 1155, signature deferred to 1160, but still unsigned): two houses owned by a woman.

[38] TS 8 J 17, f. 6. The year 196, equivalent to 1236, is referred to in the letter, which is addressed to the renowned judge Elijah, "The Diadem of the Judges," the contemporary of Abraham Maimonides. The era of the Creation is intended, and, as customary in that century, the letters *dtt* = 4800, are omitted. 4996 Creation = A.D. 1236.

[39] Mann, *Texts,* I, 446–447, where the second date is to be corrected according to Louis Ginzberg, *Genizah Studies* (New York, 1929), II, 375, 378.

[40] TS 28.23 (Oct., 1106; a marriage contract). TS 10 J 27, f. 3*a* (June, 1107; contract at engagement). Bodl. MS Heb. c 28 (Cat. 2876), f. 68, l. 5 (Oct., 1125; a memo from Fustat).

[41] TS 12.494 (marriage contract). TS 12.528 (a fragment written and signed by Saadya b. Ṣedāqā). TS 8 J 4, f. 19 (Dec. 24, 1103) seems to contain the upper part of this fragment. Same hand.

[42] Dropsie 339; TS 20.124 (Japheth b. Nissīm marries Sitt al-Dār b. Isaac).

[43] TS 13 J 13, f. 20. The places are noted by Mann, II, 259 n. 7. The circular is concerned with ritual matters (the cleanliness and ritual purity of cheese produced for the forthcoming Passover holiday).

[44] TS 32.8, ed. Mann, II, 257–259. Mann, with the self-assurance of a scholar born in the nineteenth century, "emendates the text" written by the judge and substitutes "wife" for "mother," because he believed that the Nagid's mother, Mevōrākh's wife, had died before her husband. But the dirge edited by Mann, II, 255–257, was written not for Mevōrākh's wife, but for his mother (Moses' grandmother). That woman was also the object of particular praise in a letter from Jerusalem, written a long time before Mevōrākh became the head of the Jewish community of Egypt (TS 13 J 9, f. 3).

[45] TS 12.56. References to gambling are extremely rare. The phrase "lashing with shoes" also in B, 2, n. 30, below.

[46] TS 10 J 10, f. 7. The notable (whose name is not preserved) might be identical with the one addressed in Gottheil-Worrell, II, in the next note. The letter also contains good wishes for the Purim feast (as does that by Shabbetay's father, cited in n. 44). A report about grave troubles with tax collectors in Minyat Ziftā in a letter from the beginning of the thirteenth century: TS 13 J 20, f. 3, ll. 4–7, ed. Mann, II, 301.

[47] Gottheil-Worrell, II, pp. 12–13. Many corrections by Mann, *Texts,* I, 447. Final elucidation by Baneth in *Alexander Marx Jubilee Volume,* pp. 80–84. The quarter referred to in the Arabic address (*ibid.,* p. 83) is *al-Murabba'a,* or Square of the Perfumers (in Fustat); for *al-qāhira* (Cairo) read *balligh tu'jar,* "deliver and God will reward you" (see *Med. Soc.,* I, 284). These words used to be written in an abbreviated style.

The receiver of this letter Judah b. Elazar Kohen is known from many letters, e.g., TS 18 J 4, f. 19, also written by Shabbetay b. Abraham, TS 13 J 33, f. 3 (where he has nine Hebrew titles), and TS 13 J 33, f. 8, trans. Goitein, *Education,* pp. 92–95.

[48] 1175: ULC Add. 3423 (written by him, signed by five others), see *Med. Soc.,* I, 451 n. 64. 1178: above, n. 19.

[49] ULC Or 1080 J 214 (with interesting details about Shabbetay's illness).

[50] Above, n. 30.

[51] ENA 4011, f. 34 (letter of Shabbetay to Zakkay b. Moses, judge of al-Maḥalla). For documents, see nn. 16, 19, 48.

[52] TS Arabic Box 53, f. 19. The house, which bordered on those of three Muslims and one Christian, must have been very sizable.

[53] TS 13 J 4, f. 1 (April, 1226). TS 12.597 (letter by Moses b. Peraḥyā). TS 12.360 (letter to him by the teacher Abu 'l-Majd Uzziel of Damīra).

[54] Bodl. MS Heb. a 3 (Cat. 2873), f. 15, ll. 17–18* (dated 1234).

[55] TS 16.294. The name of the writer is lost.

[56] TS 12.581, ll. 14–16. The perfumer describes the repairs effected by him in the local synagogue. The physician: TS 24.38.

[57] Visiting judge: TS 16.213. Congregation: TS 13 J 16, f. 8, l. 8.

[58] Baedeker, *Ägypten,* 1928, p. 178. The name is repeatedly spelled *ṣhrsht,* e.g., TS 13 J 10, f. 5, TS NS J 35 (see n. 65, below), which shows that it was normally pronounced *Ṣahrajt,* and not *Ṣahragt,* as in the dialect of Cairo.

[59] Dropsie 335, two drafts written in Fustat on March 15, 1041.

[60] TS 13 J 20, f. 13, l. 11, ed. Mann, II, 108–109. A statement to the contrary in the *Catalogue of Hebrew Manuscripts of the Bodleian Library,* II, 374, is based on the misinterpretation of a fragmentary letter. Bodl. MS Heb. c 28 (Cat. 2876), f. 10, l. 8, says that a Nagid, on a holiday, had a cantor of Ṣahrajt lead the community in prayer in one of the two synagogues (of Alexandria).

[61] TS 13 J 20, f. 13+, l. 11 (the *shōfēṭ* [see p. 315, above] does not bear any scholarly title). Bodl. MS Heb. b 11 (Cat. 2874), f. 9* addresses the cantor together with the community of Ṣahrajt (see *Med. Soc.,* I, 249).

[62] ULC Or 1080 J 85, a draft, written in elaborate Hebrew.

[63] Bodl. MS Heb. c 28 (Cat. 2876), f. 5, ed. S. Assaf, *Tarbiz,* 9 (1935), 218. The text is in Hebrew with a sprinkling of Aramaic. None of the mistakes marring the printed edition is in the original. Line 8: *tv,* MS *twv; mmnyh,* MS *mnyh* (Aramaic); l. 9: *k'mry,* MS *m'mry* (which is correct, see l. 10); l. 15: *mwshvyh,* MS *mwshvh.*

[64] TS 13 J 13, f. 2. On the legal document the scribe signs his name in Hebrew (Judah b. Abraham) but uses an Arabic form in his letter (the identity is established by the handwriting). Similarly he addresses the then leader of the Fustat community, commonly known as Eli b. Amram, under the Arabic name 'Allūn b. Ma'mar.

[65] TS NS J 35, partly trans. in Goitein, *Education,* p. 78.

[66] E.g., Qalyūb, three instances in *ibid.,* p. 81.

[67] Capital: Bodl. MS Heb. c 28 (Cat. 2876), f. 5+, l. 7. Abroad: the teacher referred to in n. 65 was from Qal'at Ḥammād in Algeria. Byzantium: TS 13 J 21, f. 17*, ed. S. D. Goitein, *Tarbiz,* 27 (1958), 534, trans. *Speculum,* 39 (1964), 301.

[68] Chap. v, sec. A, 2, n. 27, above. The document containing the settlement arranged by Elhanan b. Shemarya was preserved in Ṣahrajt, not at the court of Fustat.

[69] TS 13 J 10, f. 5. His name was not Abū Sāhir, as in E. J. Worman's *Handlist* in the University Library, Cambridge, but Yōshiyāhū b. Hārūn (Joshiah b. Aaron). He became a member of the academy in 1030–1031 (see TS 12.722, ed. Schechter, *Saadyana,* p. 55, partly cited in Mann, II, 52). Our letter must have been written before 1035, since Abū Kathīr, i.e., Ephraim b. Shemarya, the head of the Pales-

tinian congregation in Fustat, is asked to send the letters promised by him to his son-in-law Joseph, who then lived in Ṣahrajt. This Joseph is known to have died in 1035 (see Mann, I, 94).

[70] Bodl. MS Heb. e 39 (Cat. 2712, no. 23), ff. 125–136: *Azharōt,* or liturgical poems, by Saadya Gaon. The scribe, Shabbāt b. Elazar, signed a document in Fustat in 1040 (Bodl. MS Heb. c 28 [Cat. 2876], f. 30)*.

[71] Above, nn. 3, 62.

[72] TS 13 J 20, f. 13, 11. 12–14+.

[73] Bodl. MS Heb. a 3 (Cat. 2873), f. 28, ed. A. Cowley, *JQR,* 19 (1907), 250–256, cf. Mann, I, 88–89. Ṣahrajt is mentioned together with Damietta and Tinnis, because all three are situated on or near the eastern arm of the Nile.

[74] Maimonides, *Responsa,* II, 624. TS 12.597*v,* 1. 8 (letter of Abraham Maimonides): R. Peraḥyā is muqaddam in Bilbays; he is described in TS 12.654*v,* l. 12, as the most learned judge and most prominent teacher in all Egypt. Forced conversion in 1301: Strauss, *Mamluks,* I, 249, according to Sambari. TS 16.277 is a letter from Bilbays at the time of the Nagid Joshua (1310–1355).

[75] TS 13 J 26, f. 24+.

[76] TS 18 J 4, f. 12; AIU VII A 17, ed. B. Chapira, *Mélanges H. Derenbourg* (Paris, 1909), pp. 125–126, cf. Goitein, Eretz-Israel 7 (1964), Eng. summary, p. 169.

[77] Mann, *Texts,* I, 416 n. 3; Mann, I, 222 n. 2.

[78] A fragment in the ENA Collection, quoted in Mann, *Texts,* I, 455 n. 17, l. 6.

[79] E.g., Mann, I, 118 ff. and 124 ff.

[80] Fines: e.g., TS 12.580, which belongs together with TS 13 J 1, f. 13 (dated 1057); TS 16.79, ed. I. Abrahams, *JQR,* 17 (1905), 426, cf. J. Teicher, *Journal of Jewish Studies,* 1 (1948), 156–158 (the date is not 751, but Nov., 1050). TS 12.129 (date not preserved). House given to the community: Bodl. MS Heb. d 66 (Cat. 2878), f. 88, and n. 83, below. Ramle-Fustat: TS 20.19, address.

[81] Details in sec. C, 1, above.

[82] TS 18 J 2, f. 1 (referring to A.D. 1039): "Due to the Palestinians as their right on one half," analyzed by S. D. Goitein, *Eretz-Israel,* 7 (1964), 87.

[83] Bodl. MS Heb. f. 56 (Cat. 2821, no. 40), f. 129+.

[84] Letter: TS 12.215* (written 1066–1067). Joint collections: App. C secs. 4, 5. "Pride of the two denominations," David b. Isaac: TS 13 J 14, f. 20, l. 12, ed. Mann, 87. The word *pē'ā,* used here (and elsewhere) for denomination, is Hebraized Arabic *fi'a.*

[85] See chap. vii, B, 1.

[86] See chap. v, sec. B, 2.

[87] Guest preachers in Old Cairo and in Alexandria: chap. vi, sec. 9. Special occasion in Damascus, Karaites attending: Mann, II, 172; *Benjamin of Tudela,* ed. Adler, p. 70.

[88] ENA 4020, f. 5, ed. J. Mann, *HUCA,* 3 (1926), 291–292.

[89] TS 13 J 33, f. 9, ll. 5–6*, ULC Or 1080 J 34.

[90] Mann, II, 201. Cf. also *ibid.,* pp. 198–199, 203 (*qehillōt*). The same expression is used with regard to Tyre and al-Mahdiyya, n. 5, above. Alexandria: Mann, *Texts,* I, 368; Mann, II, 91, 344; Ramle: TS 20.19. Constantinople: ULC Add. 3335, ed. A. Neubauer, *JQR,* 9 (1896), 32.

[91] This seems to be the concept underlying I. Baer's admirable study mentioned in n. 1, above. Babylonian honorific titles in Palestine: ENA 4009, ed. Mann, *Texts,* I, 106.

[92] As when a couple of Palestinian scholars left a Babylonian synagogue during the service, when the cantor began to repeat the main prayer aloud, after it had been said by the congregation silently (according to the Palestinian ritual the prayer is said only once) (TS 18 J 4, f. 12, ll. 18–24).

[93] TS 12.388, top, *Nahray* 109.

[94] TS 13 J 9, f. 6, quoted in Mann, I, 224 n. 1 (Samuel b. Nathan writing in 1142).

[95] TS 13 J 14, f. 16* (referring to Yeshūʿā ha-Kohen he-ḥāvēr b. Joseph). See also chap. vi, sec. 9, n. 12.

[96] TS 12.328, partly ed. Mann, II, 345 (written by Solomon b. Judah, not his predecessor, as assumed by Mann).

[97] Hebron: TS Arabic Box 18(2), f. 4, ed. Assaf, *Texts,* p. 46. "The community was consulted," *shāwarū 'l-jamāʿa:* TS 13 J 21, f. 30, l. 12, ed. J. Braslawsky, *Eretz-Israel,* 3 (1954), 208.

[98] TS 12.371*v*, l. 10. Bodl. MS Heb. b 11 (Cat. 2874), f. 9*.

[99] Bodl. MS Heb. d 66 (Cat. 2878), f. 29, l. 7. TS 16.149, end*.

[100] TS 20.104, ll. 33–34.

[101] As n. 13, above.

[102] Mann, I, 15, n. 4.

[103] TS 13 J 30, f. 5*, ed. S. D. Goitein, *Journal of Jewish Studies,* 12 (1961), 156.

[104] 1038: PER H 160*. 1034: ULC Or 1080 J 6. 1208: TS 13 J 3, f. 20. Around 1050: Dropsie 392. 1195: PER H 93+.

[105] ENA 2804, f. 1, partly ed. Mann, II, 115.

[106] TS 10 K 20, f. 2.

[107] J. Wansbrough, "A Judaeo-Arabic Document from Sicily," *BSOAS,* 30 (1967), 305–313.

[108] Alexandria, ca. 1085: TS 13 J 23, f. 3, l. 21+. "Ten," led by two official representatives. 1237: TS 10 J 16, f. 12+*.

[109] TS NS Box 324, f. 17, ll. 11–12.

[110] Maimonides, *Responsa,* II, 519 (a query from the Maghreb). TS 20.104, see n. 144; TS 16.187+. Seven signatories, e.g., TS 8 J 4, fs. 1–2 (in addition to that of the scribe, dated 1027–1028); TS 10 J 5, f. 11 (App. C 3), Mann, II, 97. Ephraim b. Shemarya heads a list of seven notables in TS NS Box 320, f. 26, followed by Eli b. Amram, Eli ha-Kohen, the parnās, and the latter's son Ephraim (written around 1055). It is not sure, however, that this list is complete.

[111] TS 13 J 21, f. 30, ll. 11–12, ed. J. Braslawsky, *Eretz-Israel,* 3 (1958), 208.

[112] TS 12.239. Sent to a town in Syria.

[113] Gaza: PER H 94, ed. Assaf, *Texts,* p. 36 (no. not provided). Palermo: TS 24.6+.

[114] TS 20.96, ll. 26–27+: *wa-aqām al-ḥavēr wal-jamāʿa faránisa,* "the ḥāvēr [spiritual leader] and the community installed social service officers."

[115] E.g., TS 8 J 4, f. 9d (dated 1099); TS NS J 296 (1159), both ed. S. D. Goitein, *Eretz-Israel,* 7 (1964), 93–96; TS 16.122 (Ascalon, 1134–1145; twelve entries); TS 10 J 4, f. 11*v*+*. TS 13 J 14, f. 10 (+) is addressed by the Gaon Joshiah b. Aaron to "the elders of the synagogues, Fustat." Address in Arabic characters on verso.

[116] The elders and the jamāʿa, e.g., in TS 13 J 35, f. 3.

[117] ENA 2736, f. 20, a report from a provincial town to ʿAllūn b. Yaʿīsh, the parnās.

[118] TS 16.272*v*, l. 2 (Alexandria). TS 16.179, l. 51* (al-Mahdiyya). A rival Nagid states that he wants to convene an assembly of *zuʿamāʾ al-Yahūd,* the leaders of the Jews: TS Arabic Box 54, f. 60*v*, l. 8+.

[119] TS Box K 25, f. 244: *wa-mā kān ray al-ruʾasā an yuqaddimū illa 'l-rav,* "The leaders wanted to appoint the Rav as muqaddam."

[120] TS 24.6+. For Khalaf b. Jacob in al-Mahdiyya see *Tarbiz,* 37 (1968), 189.

[121] Abraham Maimuni, *Responsa,* pp. 163–164. Dropsie 344, l. 6. Mosseri A 111 (A.D. 1220).

[122] TS 13 J 28, f. 15, l. 9. *India Book* 281. Married twice: TS 24.34. Aleppo: TS 13 J 19, f. 6, margin, last but one line.

[123] See especially TS Loan 206: *ha-baḥūrīm behōd maʿamādām.*

[124] *Mittheilungen aus der Sammlung Erzherzog Rainer V* (Vienna, 1892), p. 129, l. 22. The Gaon referred to is the famous Solomon b. Judah of Jerusalem. Mez,

Renaissance, p. 33 (chap. 4), is to be corrected accordingly. Ramle: TS 10 J 32, f. 9, l. 9 *(baḥūrīm u-vūrīm u-khsilim min qeṣōt hā-'ām).* Connected with TS 10 J 32, f. 8 (falsely marked in *Sefer ha-Yishūv,* p. 60, as TS 10 J 32, f. 6).

[125] TS 13 J 37, f. 3; *shubbān,* thus far found only here.

[126] TS 18 J 2, f. 8, l. 2.

[127] Westminster College, Frag. Cairens. 51*v*.

[128] TS 16.186.

[129] TS 18 J 1, f. 5, end of a letter, dated Sept.–Oct., 1022, addressed to an allūf with pleas to renew business relations, as often found in letters to Ibn 'Awkal. For another letter sent to Ibn 'Awkal in 1022 see *Tarbiz,* 36 (1967), 369. For the revolt of the youth in Muslim society see Introduction, n. 3, above.

[130] TS 16.272, ll. 20, 23–25, 27, 35, margin, and verso, ll. 20–21. "Poor stuff," *safāsif,* not known to me from another source as a designation for people of low social standing.

[131] Lane-Poole, *History of Egypt,* p. 327.

[132] Cobblers: TS 20.170, l. 13. Potters: TS K 25, f. 244*v*, l. 33.

[133] TS NS J 24. "They exhibited the letter" is a tentative translation of *yimandilū,* cf. modern Egypt. *mandal,* magic divination.

[134] TS 20.177, l. 6.

[135] Bernard Lewis, "Ottoman Observers of Ottoman Decline," *Islamic Studies* (Karachi), 1 (1962), 85 n. 16.

[136] TS 18 J 14, f. 12, l. 42. The verb in TS 8 J 41, f. 11, l. 9 and verso, l. 2*, ed. S. D. Goitein, *Eretz-Israel,* 6 (1960), 165.

[137] TS 13 J 26, f. 18, l. 5. 'Allūn is Arabic for Eli (b. Amram).

[138] The Tail: TS 12.365, l. 5. Letter of 'Allūn: TS 20.152.

[139] ENA Uncatalogued 112; TS 12.58; TS 18 J 2, f. 6 (all addressed to Old Cairo). Bodl. MS Heb. d 65 (Cat. 2877), f. 4, ed. A. Cowley, *JQR,* 19 (1907), 256.

[140] Bodl. MS Heb. c 13 (Cat. 2807, no. 18), f. 23, l. 11, ed. S. Poznanski, *REJ,* 48 (1904), 172–173.

[141] Renting a locality for a separatist congregation: ULC Or 1080 Box 6, f. 25, ll. 19–20, ed. S. D. Goitein, *Eretz-Israel,* 10 (1970). Letter in Arabic characters of Yūsuf b. Kulayb (Joseph b. Caleb) of Ramle to the Gaon Nathan b. Abraham, the rival of Solomon b. Judah.

[142] TS K 25, f. 244*v*, ll. 28–29 (Old Cairo). TS 8 J 41, f. 11, ll. 10–11+*; TS 18 J 2, f. 3, l. 21 (both referring to Ascalon). ULC 1081 J 18, l. 11 (presumably Hebron, Palestine, ed. S. D. Goitein, *Eretz-Israel,* 6 (1960), 167. TS 24.38, ll. 39–40 (Minyat Ziftā, Egypt). Excommunication threatened: TS 16.187, ll. 13–18+*. Caliphal rescript: TS 10 J 28, f. 2*, ed. E. Ashtor, *Zion,* 30 (1965), 151–152. His text needs revision.

[143] TS 20.117*v*, ll. 5–7+.

[144] Ephraim b. Shemarya: TS 13 J 30, f. 5+*. 1028: TS 13 J 7, f. 25*. Slaughterhouses: TS 20.104. The first document contains the verb *taqqan* in its first sentence.

[145] Bodl. MS Heb. d 65 (Cat. 2877), f. 4, l. 8+: *nusaḥ mā she-qibbelū 'al 'aṣmām shetē ha-kittōt* (Heb.), "the text of the agreement between the two parties" (dated 1035). Hebrew and Arabic: TS 10 J 32, f. 9, ll. 6–7, verso, ll. 3–4 (Ramle).

[146] al-Maḥalla: TS 13 J 25, f. 16+. May, 1208: TS 13 J 3, f. 20.

[147] Tenants: TS 13 J 21, f. 31. Silk dyers: TS Box 8, f. 18*. For further statutes, especially about religious matters, see E. Ashtor, *Zion,* 30 (1965), 150.

[148] Aliens from Sicily: TS 12.371, ll. 19–21; from Tunisia: TS 13 J 23, f. 3+. Letter from Sicily: INA D-55, f. 14, ll. 3–6.

[149] TS 18 J 4, f. 19, see above, n. 47.

[150] Dropsie 389*v*, ll. 36–44.

[151] L. Finkelstein, *Jewish Self-Government in the Middle Ages* (New York, 1924), pp. 10–15.

[152] TS 16.235, ll. 7–12. The prohibition is rendered by *ḥarāmōt,* bans. *The Arabian Nights:* Mia I. Gerhardt, *The Art of Story-Telling* (Leiden, 1963), pp. 198 ff.

2. *The Officials of the Community*

[1] See S. Assaf, *Melila* (Manchester), 3–4 (1950), 224–225. Strauss, *Mamluks,* II, 245–246, and *Zion,* 30 (1965), 138–141.

[2] In the first article cited in the preceding note.

[3] I. Baer, *The Jews in Christian Spain* (Tel Aviv, 1959), pp. 126–135, (in Hebrew).

[4] TS 8.11*v,* a letter of congratulation to the notable Aaron Abu 'l-Ḥasan on the occasion of his delivery from dangerous enemies, with good wishes for the convalescence of his son Japheth and veiled solicitations for a gift.

[5] ULC Or 1080 J 258*v,* l. 17. For the authorship of this letter see *Tarbiz,* 28 (1959) 349–350.

[6] TS 8 J 4, f. 9*d,* l. 8+. Maimonides, *Responsa,* II, 367, l. 7.

[7] TS 13 J 36, f. 6, l. 5: *sa'alūnī ataqaddamhum sabt ēkhā,* "they asked me to lead them in prayer on the Sabbath preceding the ninth of Av." Bodl. MS Heb. c 28 (Cat. 2876), f. 10, l. 9: *taqaddam huwa al-qerōvōt,* "he [the Nagid] lead the congregation in prayer during the section called *qerōvōt.*" TS NS Box 320, f. 16, l. 7+ (at the seat of the academy in Jerusalem).

[8] TS 20.104, l. 7: a board of seven makes an appointment, *yuqaddimū* (ca. A.D. 1015); *muqaddam al-balad*: e.g., Bodl. MS Heb. a 3 (Cat. 2873), f. 2* (ca. 1100).

[9] Bodl. MS Heb. e 98, f. 67, *India Book* 266. In other letters the same person mentions the judges, referred to here as muqaddams, by name.

[10] TS 18 J 2, f. 11, ll. 5, 7, 12, 14. Maimonides, *Responsa,* I, p. 78 n. 5, p. 189, ll. 2, 10, p. 190, ll. 3, 23 (*rayyis* also means judge).

[11] TS 13 J 18, f. 25*, address: *jamā'at al-nuwwāb wal-muqaddamīn.*

[12] Damascus: TS 13 J 8 (so, not 18, as in the preceding note), f. 25*v,* for muqaddam as head of a synagogue, see sec. D, below.

[13] The examples given in *Med. Soc.,* I, 53–54, 404 n. 72, could easily be expanded. Shemarya b. Elhanan, the first prominent leader of the Egyptian Jews in Fatimid times was a Babylonian. His successor, Ephraim b. Shemarya, was called al-Ghazzi, i.e., from Gaza, Palestine. Muqaddam not regarded as permanent resident: *ant ghayr muqīm bihādhihi 'l-balad walā sākin fīhā,* TS 24.38.

[14] TS 13 J 7, f. 25*. The left half of the document is lost, but can be reconstructed almost in its entirety.

[15] Anatoli: TS 18 J 3, f. 15, ll. 28–31, a letter addressed to the judge Elijah b. Zachariah, and elsewhere. Muqaddams in Alexandria: e.g., TS 16.149, ll. 26–27; TS 24.21*v,* ll. 13–11 from bottom*. TS NS J 24. Abraham Maimuni, *Responsa,* pp. 182, 189.

[16] Northern Syria: TS 13 J 16, f. 17, ll. 24–25+. Joseph ha-Kohen: TS NS Box 320, f. 45, ed. S. D. Goitein, *S. W. Baron Jubilee Volume,* New York, 1970.

[17] TS 12.9; TS 16.196; TS 20.125, all emanating from the court of the Nagid Mevōrākh. The three documents are fragmentary, but complement one another.

[18] Examples for queries on liturgy in Maimonides, *Responsa,* II, 492, 496.

[19] Bodl. MS Heb. d 66 (Cat. 2878), f. 29, ll. 11–19. Damīra in Lower Egypt.

[20] TS Arabic Box 18(2), f. 4. Ed. Assaf, *Texts,* pp. 47–49. Mann, II, 199, is undoubtedly right when he says that the addressee Isaac b. Samuel is the famous Spanish scholar whom we find in Old Cairo around 1100. Moses b. Ghulayb mentioned in the letter was a grandson of a man with the same name. Cf. AIU VII D 4, where his father Ghulayb is mentioned as a boy in 1027. Assaf's dating of the letter is to be corrected accordingly.

[21] TS 18 J 4, f. 1, ll. 15–16.

[22] TS 12.6, from a locality in the vicinity of Alexandria.

[23] P. Heid. 913, ll. 10–11. The letter is exceptional, inasmuch as the writer changes occasionally from Hebrew script to Arabic, even writing Hebrew words in Arabic characters.

[24] TS 13 J 16, f. 6. The writer Isaac b. Moses was muqaddam in Sunbāṭ (cf. TS 24.25*v*), where he writes and signs a document in that townlet in 1149. (The date

1091 in E. J. Worman's *Handlist* in the University Library, Cambridge, is erroneous. He took *shtyn* as meaning *two* instead of *sixty*.)

[25] Bodl. MS Heb. a 3 (Cat. 2873), f.2, ll. 15, 52 and verso, ll. 12–13*.

[26] Bodl. MS Heb. d 66 (Cat. 2878), f. 85. The calligraphic letter contains no address and certainly was not dispatched because the writer changed his mind and wanted to formulate it differently.

[27] Maimonides, *Responsa*, II, 624–625. Alexandria: Abraham Maimuni, *Responsa*, p. 182. Abraham's statement: TS 12.597.

[28] TS 13 J 6, f. 26 (early fourteenth century, it seems).

[29] TS 16.154, addressed to the judge Abraham b. Nathan (around 1100). Incompetent: *ghayr mustaqill.*

[30] TS 8.79*v*, l. 3, written by Nathan b. Solomon, the cantor, b. Sā'ir (not *yḥyd*, as in Worman's *Handlist*). Sā'ir corresponds to Heb. She'ērīt.

[31] TS 10 J 18, f. 5.

[32] Ibn al-Muqaddam: TS K 15, f. 36*v*, ll. 2, 11, in a list of contributors, early thirteenth century (probably referring to a nonreligious office [see Dozy, *Supplement*, II, 317*a*]).

[33] To the numerous examples given in Mann, I, 258, the following may be added: Amram, son of Ezra, head of the congregation: TS 13 J 1, f. 23 (dated 1093). Samuel, the "pride of the congregations," son of Nethanel, head of the congregation: Bodl. MS Heb. e 98, f. 63 (dated 1138). Nissī, son of Samuel, "head of the congregation of God's assembly": TS 16.130 (from Persia, old). X., son of Manasse, head of the congregation: TS 16.186. Abū 'Alī Ḥasan, head of the congregation: TS 13 J 21, f. 24. Abu 'l-'Alā', head of the congregations: TS NS J 36. This man seems to be identical with "the elder of the congregations" of Alexandria who was falsely accused of having been found in the company of a woman of bad reputation (TS 13 J 13, f. 24 and TS 12.290*v*. See also n. 42, below, and E. Ashtor, *Zion*, 30 [1965], 129).

[34] Bodl. MS Heb. c 28 (Cat. 2876), f. 38: *ḍāmin al-sūq wa-dayyān al-yahūd.*

[35] Mann, I, 258. The letter TS 16.267, ed. Mann, II, 336, is old in style and script.

[36] Maimonides, *Responsa*, II, 497–498.

[37] Ephraim: JTS Geniza Misc. 1. Aleppo: Mann, I, 258.

[38] TS 13 J 6, f. 21. In Sumbuṭyā (Sunbāṭ), Lower Egypt.

[39] Gittin 59*b*-60*a*, Pesahim 49*b*, quoted by I. Baer, *Zion*, 15 (1950), 14.

[40] Mann, I, 15 n. 4.

[41] Memorial list: Mann, II, 58. Signatures: *ibid.*, pp. 98–99. There are many others.

[42] S. D. Goitein, *Tarbiz*, 34 (1965), 165. Abū Dirham Isma'īl, the head of the congregations, to whom "the answer of our Gaon" as well as the latter's responsum were conveyed in the letter JTS Geniza Misc. 1 (from Samuel b. Abraham [= Isma'īl b. Barhūn Tāhertī?] to Ephraim [b. Shemarya?], no doubt also was North African.

[43] The clash between Samuel b. Avṭaliyōn and Ephraim b. Shemarya, cf. Mann, I, *passim* (see Index), is no case in point, since the former was also a ḥāvēr.

[44] ENA 4011, ed. J. Mann, *HUCA*, 3 (1926), 295 n. 137 (the man addressed bore, in addition, the title "elder of the assembly," *ēdā*).

[45] TS NS J 183. For the Muslim usage, cf. Dozy, *Supplément*, s.v., and Brockelmann, *GAL*, Supp. II, pp. 82, 126. See also n. 92, below.

[46] Ascalon: ULC Or 1080 J 40. Qūṣ: ULC Or 1080 J 237, ll. 11–12. Old Cairo: MS Richard Gottheil, ed. by him in *Mélanges Hartwig Derenbourg* (Paris, 1909), p. 96.

[47] The word had already penetrated into Arabic in pre-Islamic times (cf. S. Fraenkel, *Die Aramaeischen Fremdwoerter im Arabischen* [Leiden, 1886], p. 280). No connection should be assumed, however, between the extremely rare occurrence of the word in ancient Arabic poetry (where it designates a lion) and its use by the Jews several hundred years later (except, of course, that some pre-Islamic poet had

heard it from Jews and misunderstood it as having the general meaning of "leader" or "strong").

48 Mann, I, 259 n. 1, and below, n. 73 *Benjamin of Tudela,* ed. Adler, p. 74.

49 TS Box 8, f. 25*, see App. B 24.

50 Mann, I, 258–259. Instead of *rōsh ha-(qāhāl), rōsh ha-(parnāsīm)* is to be restituted, as proved by another source, where the same name occurs (see n. 58, below).

51 Mishna Sheqalim, 5, 2.

52 Seven parnāsīm: TS 20.104. Over four: TS 20.96, ll. 26–27+. Four: Mann, II, 99. Small town (Minyat Ziftā): TS 12.56*v*, l. 2 from bottom.

53 TS 10 J 19, f. 16; TS 10 J 29, f. 5; TS 12.58, margin, and elsewhere.

54 TS K 15, f. 63; ULC Or 1080 J 46. Collector: *jābī.*

55 TS 10 J 9, f. 16 (from Qalahā in the Ahnasiyya district south of Fayyūm, an interesting letter, to be edited by N. Golb).

56 Bodl. MS Heb. b 3 (Cat. 2806, no. 15), f. 16, where a parnās from Alexandria collects funds in the Rīf for the maintenance of captives ransomed in the port city. MS Schechter *4, see Shaked, *Bibliography,* p. 49 (autograph of Moses Maimonides).

57 TS K 15, f. 39, d, I, l. 17. TS Box J 1, f. 4, d, l. 11*. TS K 15, f. 48.

58 1090: *Mevōrākh ha-parnās, rōsh ha-parnāsīm,* TS 12.583, and mentioned in many other documents. 1145: *Japheth ha-parnās ha-ne'emān, rōsh ha-parnāsīm,* TS 13 J 31, f. 6; Bodl. MS Heb. d 66 (Cat. 2878), f. 11.

59 TS 20.96, l. 26+: *wa-aqām al-ḥāvēr wal-jamā'a farānisa.*

60 Midrash Bamidbar Rabba 18, 9. Dinur, *Yisrael ba-Gola,* I, 2, p. 198.

61 The Aramaic term for "trustee," e.g., Bodl. MS Heb. a 3 (Cat. 2873), f. 37, l. 12+ (*parnāsīm we-hēmānīm,* dated 1028); TS 13 J 14, f. 4, *India Book* 259 *(ha-hēmān).* The Arabic plural *hayāmina*: TS 20.96, l. 18+ (1040). The office: ULC Or 1080 Box 6, f. 25, top, end+ *(tawallayt amr al-haymana,* "I was in charge of the trusteeship"); repeated in TS 13 J 17, f. 16*v*, l. 1, ed. S. D. Goitein, Eretz-Israel 10 (1970), which is the continuation of the letter. See also n. 64, below.

62 TS 20.38, ll. 46–56: The trustee Eli ha-Kohen b. Ya'īsh (above, p. 78) deposits with Nethanel ha-Levi b. Amram, a seller of potions. TS NS J 174: Sack of Old Cairo. TS 24.25: Loan given through trustee. TS Arabic Box 18(1), f. 76, contains a fragment of a notebook of a trustee, in which he lists collaterals and belongings of a foreigner from Sicily.

63 Abū Ya'qūb Joseph b. Solomon, parnās and trustee from Jerusalem: TS 12.108, l. 7; TS 16.185, l. 11; TS 13 J 14, f. 4, ll. 22–23+. The parnās Jacob ha-yerūshalmī: ENA 3793, f. 1, ll. 1–2.

64 TS 24.81 (in the hand of Judah al-'Ammānī of Alexandria). TS 20.96, l. 12+: *Ibn al-'adl.* The Muslim term *'adl* has a somewhat different meaning, see *EI*², s.v. (Tyan).

65 ENA 4011, f. 17*. A parnās is ordered by a judge to receive from a merchant (known from TS 16.158, ll. 12–13, *India Book* 159*b*) 30 dirhems every month and to deliver them to a divorcée (around 1115).

66 TS 8 J 41, f. 11, ll. 14–15+*.

67 TS 12.312, l. 5, transporting wheat to the capital.

68 ENA 191 (2559), dated 1095–1096. Reference to Deuteronomy 18:7, trans. Goitein, *Education,* pp. 188–189.

69 Westminster College, Frag. Cairens. 51*v*, ll. 1–2.

70 Grohmann, *APEL,* II, 103–106, where further literature is indicated.

71 ENA 4010, f. 1*, ed. S. D. Goitein, *Eretz-Israel,* 7 (1964), 90–92, dated 1075. TS 8 J 4, f. 9*d*+, dated 1099.

72 TS K 6, f. 106, l. 7: *khādim al-jamā'a* (Damascus).

73 TS NS J 174, l. 2: *mudh khadamt fī hādha 'l-miqdāsh* (Heb.).

74 Meridian Books edition (New York, 1958), p. 55.

[75] TS 18 J 4, f. 12, ll. 24–28.

[76] ENA 191 (2559). See n. 68, above.

[77] TS 8 J 4, f. 9 d, ll. 14–15+.

[78] TS 8 J 33, f. 10, sec. 3 (various entries).

[79] TS 13 J 31, f. 6*v*: *Sālim al-khādim ḍāmin al-rubʿ*, identical with the person referred to in nn. 62 and 73.

[80] The document cited in n. 77.

[81] ULC Or 1080 J 86 (from Sunbāṭ in Lower Egypt). TS 10 J 14, f. 20* (al-Mahdiyya). The beadle was such a good scribe that he permitted himself to write a second version of the same letter rather carelessly (TS 10 J 19, f. 20).

[82] TS 28.5. The husband was a Kohen who was not allowed to marry a divorced woman, including his own divorcée.

[83] TS 8 J 4, f. 15*a*.

[84] Silk-weaver: Bodl. MS Heb. a 2 (Cat. 2805), f. 9, ll. 19–20*, ed. S. D. Goitein, *Sefunot*, 8 (1964), 125–126. Physician: TS 8 J 5, f. 4*d*, sec. 2. Inheritance: University Museum, Philadelphia E 16510. The attorney Abu 'l-Ḥasan Eli b. Isaac ha-Kohen was a shammāsh (see TS 13 J 2, f. 14, l. 3 [Dec. 1105]).

[85] Bodl. MS Heb. c 13 (Cat. 2807, no. 17*d*), f. 22*v*.

[86] Five beadles: Bodl. MS Heb. c 28 (Cat. 2876), f. 6+. Three: TS Box 8, f. 100.

[87] ENA 4010, f. 1, l. 6+*. Here "boys" probably means "sons," not "employees."

[88] M. I. Gerhardt, *The Art of Story-Telling* (Leiden, 1963), p. 186. The complaint: TS 18 J 4, f. 12, see n. 75, above.

[89] AIU VII A 17+.

[90] TS 12.608, trans. Goitein, *Education*, pp. 134–135.

[91] Appointment of Eli b. Isaac ha-Kohen Ghazāl ("Gazelle") in summer, 1099: TS 8 J 4, f. 9*d*+. Still in office June, 1127: TS 8 J 5, f. 4*d*. Maḥfūẓ, beadle of the Palestinians, dated documents from 1159: TS NS J 296+, to Dec., 1188: Bodl. MS Heb. a 2 (Cat. 2805), f. 9*. His son (Abu 'l-)Tāhir, 1186: Bodl. MS Heb. f 56 (Cat. 2821, no. 16*f*), f. 49, ed. R. Gottheil, *Israel Abrahams Jubilee Volume* (New York, 1927), pp. 149 ff. By a strange oversight, the manuscript bears there the nonexistent mark "Cambridge MS Feb 56 C 2821." Comments in *Eretz-Israel*, 7 (1964), 96. In TS K 3, f. 11*v*, l. 1 (App. A, sec. 31, dated 1183) Ṭāhir b. Maḥfūẓ receives emoluments (the sum is not preserved), in TS NS J 375 App. A sec. 93, dated 1223) he renders communal accounts. Feb., 1227: TS 16.309, a letter from Jerusalem written by him. He might have retired by that time.

[92] ENA 3795, f. 8, a deathbed declaration. *The Arabian Nights*, Night no. 881 (reprint; Bulaq, 1252/1836–1837), II, 423, l. 14, 442, l. 2 from bottom. The female caretaker of the church is called *qayyima* (cf. the sources for *qayyim*, cited in n. 45, above).

[93] TS 13 J 20, f. 18, ll. 18, 24, ed. Mann, II, 300–301. He was called *Ibn al-ṭaffāl* or *ṭafālī*, the son of the manufacturer of fuller's earth, and *qaṣṣār* (Aramaic, written without Alif), fuller.

[94] TS 8. 79, ll. 6–7, addressed to a Nagid.

[95] TS 10 J 29, f. 4, l. 4. Further details in *Med. Soc.*, Vol. III, chap. ix.

[96] Night watchman Joseph: TS K 15, f. 50; TS Misc. Box 8, f. 9, sec. 4, l. 1, and in other lists. Mūsā (Moses): TS NS J 239. Manṣūr: TS K 15, f. 2. Thābit: TS K 15, f. 93. All these are names borne by both Muslims and Jews. They receive loaves of bread and 3/4 or 1 dirhem per week.

[97] PER H 60. In Minyat Ashnā, Lower Egypt.

[98] TS 8 K 10, f. 5, ll. 3–4, ed. Mann, II, 36: *ēdīm ne' emānīm* = Ar. *ʿudūl*.

[99] ENA 2743, f. 2, l. 11: *nawbat al-ṭawwāfīn*.

[100] Mufaḍḍal *al-mashmī ʿa*: TS K 6, f. 149, col. II, l. 16 (donates 1/2 dinar and 30 1/2 dirhems; ca. 1158). Abū Naṣr *rabīb* (foster son of al-mashmī ʿa: TS NS J 256 (donor; ca. 1220). Munajjā b. al-mashmī ʿa, his wife and two children: TS NS Box 320, f. 41*b*, l. 13, see App. B, sec. 74.

[101] The word is voweled *murahhiṭ*, in TS Misc. Box 28, f. 42. Other occurrences, e.g., TS K 15, f. 50*b*, sec. 2, l. 22, and f. 50*c*, sec. 1, l. 18, where an Ibn al-Murahhiṭ once receives one loaf of bread and once three. TS K 3, f. 34 (five). TS K 15 f. 43 (a list of names, headed "Sunday" on its upper part, and "Wednesday" on the lower section of the first page and "Monday" and "Thursday," respectively, on the second page). John Rylands Library, Manchester, Gaster Collection A 923 (the daughters of the murahhiṭ). The word is derived from Hebrew *rahaṭ*, a kind of liturgical poetry (cf. TS 16.278*v*, l. 2*).

[102] *Bulyāṭ:* (Gr. *bouleutes*, councillor) TS K 15, f. 14. He pays 1/3 dinar. *Prostatīn* (Gr. *prostatai*, leaders): A. Cowley, *Journal of Egyptian Archaeology*, 2 (1915), 212, quoted by Mann, I, 15 n. 4. *Qentōrīn* (L. *centuriones*, community officials), *Oqonomīn* (pl. of Gr. *oikonomos*, manager): TS 20.94, l. 22, ed. Mann, II, 206.

[103] Horayot 10*a*–*b*.

[104] *Khidmat al-nās* "Service of the community": Bodl. Heb. e 98, f. 76; *khidmat Yisrāel:* TS 18 J 3, f. 5, last line; *khidma:* TS 16.272*v*, l. 27. Heb. *shērūt* (same meaning: TS 13 J 13, f. 28, l. 11, ed. Mann, II, 153; TS 10 J 12, f. 17, l. 12, ed. *ibid.*, p. 128.

[105] Goitein, *Studies*, pp. 197 ff.

[106] TS Loan 40, ed. Mann, *Texts*, I, 181.

[107] TS 12.177, top (a note unconnected with the main text of TS 12.177, ed. S. D. Goitein, *Eretz-Israel*, 8 [1967], 293-297).

[108] TS 20.181, ll. 2–3, ed. Mann, II, 127: *hā-'ōmēd beshērūt hā-'ām* (Deuteronomy 6:5).

[109] TS Loan 43, ll. 33–34, ed. Mann, *Texts*, I, 319.

[110] TS 18 J 3, f. 5, bottom.

[111] Bodl. MS Heb. c 28 (Cat. 2876), f. 65, ll. 9–11 (Nathan ha-Kohen b. Mevōrākh).

[112] ULC Or 1080 J 106, l. 10, a long, but much damaged, Hebrew letter.

[113] TS 6 J 2, f. 10, *India Book* 310.

[114] Bodl. MS Heb. e 98, f. 76 (eleventh century).

[115] Bodl. MS Heb. d 66 (Cat. 2878), f. 19, ll. 6–7, 20–22. "Tossed around": *mudawdal*.

[116] Bodl. MS Heb. d 74, f. 40. For the use of "Jews" in a deprecatory sense, see p. 63, above.

[117] ULC Or 1080 J 33, ll. 9–11. The addressee is a physician Moses and his feet are kissed—like those of a judge. The cantor is called She'ērīt. One cantor with that name received a loan in al-Maḥalla in 1160 (TS 18 J 1, f. 26), another was coproprietor of a house in Fustat in 1238 (TS NS J 383).

[118] TS 13 J 21, f. 21, ed. Mann, II, 204.

[119] W. Ashburner, *The Rhodian Sea-Law* (Oxford, 1909), Introduction, p. cxxxv.

[120] TS NS J 411. The Nagid addressed is Samuel b. Hananya (1140–1159). On the principle of heredity see also E. Ashtor in *Zion*, 30 (1965), 133.

[121] Gaons: sec. A, 1, above. In a letter to the Gaon Maṣlīaḥ the wish is expressed that he should seat his sons on his throne during his lifetime (Bodl. MS Heb. d 74, f. 37, l. 8). Beadles: ENA 191 (2559)(+) and Bodl. MS Heb. f. 56 (Cat. 2821, no. 16*f*), f. 49+, where the son of the beadle of the Iraqian synagogue takes up a similar post in the synagogue of the Palestinians during his father's lifetime.

[122] BM Or 2598, f. 162, ed. J. Leveen, *JQR* n.s., 16 (1926), 395–397. Important corrections in Mann, *Texts*, I, 223.

[123] TS 20.104. Beadle: Bodl. MS Heb. f. 56, f. 49+, see n. 121. For the inheritance of public honors see sec. D. 2, n. 25, below.

[124] TS 20.100, l. 34 (dated 1006), ed. Mann, *Texts*, I. 122.

[125] See the Index s.v. "Samuel b. Eli," the Gaon, and "Hillel b. Eli," the cantor and scribe.

[126] ULC Or 1080 J 23*. The son-in-law of the judge of al-Maḥalla looks for a post in the capital.

C. THE SOCIAL SERVICES

1. *Their General Character and Organization*

[1] The subject of this section has been treated in my article "The Social Services of the Jewish Community as Reflected in the Cairo Geniza Records," *JSS,* 26 (1964), 3–22, 67–86, which is partly used here. For the background cf. I. S. Chipkin, "Judaism and Social Welfare," in *The Jews,* ed. Louis Finkelstein (New York, 1960), II, 1043–1075.

[2] See App. B secs. 12, 13, 32, App. C secs. 7, 26, 46 (hereafter in this section cited by letter and section number).

[3] Japheth b. David b. Shekhanya: e.g., A 6–9, 113–116, 119, 121–124, 169. Abu 'l-Bayān, esp. A 25–36, 101. Solomon b. Elijah: B 38, 40–43, 46–49, 77–84, 87, C 42–45, 56, 66.

[4] C 97. Cf. also TS 13 J 20, f. 27*v*, l. 7: "You make foreigners obliged to you, let alone your servants and relatives."

[5] See chap. v, A, 1, above.

[6] For Shemarya b. Elhanan see chap. v, A, 2 n. 28, above. For Aden: *Tarbiz,* 31 (1962), 366–369.

[7] *Ibid.,* p. 367.

[8] Najera: TS 12.532, ed. E. Ashtor, *Sefarad,* 24 (1964), 44–47. "The woman from Spain": B 3, verso, l. 5, first item.

[9] Granada: *Med. Soc.,* I, 405 n. 93. Arles: BM Or 5544, f. 1, ed. partially Mann, II, 191*. Complete edition in preparation by N. Golb.

[10] Details in *Med. Soc.,* I, 56–57.

[11] Fustat-Rīf: ULC Or 1080 J 87.

[12] Moses Maimonides: C 82*b*. Abraham Maimonides: TS 12.289, ed. S. D. Goitein, *Tarbiz,* 33 (1965), 189–192*.

[13] Captives: C 3, 29, 30, and subsection 3, below.

[14] Collections for Jerusalem: A 11*b*, 151, C 98, 100 ff. Before the holidays: A 11*b*, C 98.

[15] Fund raiser: A 11*a*. In this document, a cantor who was first assigned to the job was unable to travel and later replaced by a lay emissary. The post of envoy, *shālī'aḥ,* of the yeshiva was of a more permanent character and almost a vocation. The father of Eli b. Amram, the head of the Jerusalem congregation of Fustat, was regularly referred to as *ha-shalī'aḥ* long after his death.

[16] Yemenite synagogue in Jerusalem: ENA 2560, f. 32, ed. S. D. Goitein, *Eretz-Israel,* 4 (1956), 154–155; TS 8 J 16, f. 3, TS 13 J 21, f. 5, both ed. *idem, Har'el: Al-Shaykh Memorial Volume* (Tel Aviv, 1962), pp. 133–148.

[17] French rabbi in Bilbays: TS 13 J 9, f. 17, ed. J. Braslavi, *Eretz-Israel,* 4 (1956), 158. TS 13 J 20, f. 24 (dated March, 1237).

[18] The Jerusalem compound: A 11*a–c*, 13, 19, 20, 24, 40, 48 (end), 135, 136, 151. References to the *dār* or *darb al-Maqādisa* are found also in other documents. Ramle: ENA 2804, detached leaf, l. 17, ed. Mann, II, 179. Tiberias: Mann, II, 192–198, 356. TS 10 J 12, f. 22 (same matter as the document partly edited by Mann, II, 356).

[19] "With the consent of the community," *'an ra'y al-jamā'a* (Heb. equivalent: *'al da'at ha-qāhāl):* TS K 25, f. 240, sec. 12 (Abraham Maimonides, 1218).

[20] Four months: TS 20.96, ll. 36–39+. See *Eretz-Israel,* 7 (1964), 86 n. 35.

[21] The Pious: A 145, B 43. The ascetic: A 146*a*.

[22] Joint communal services: chap. *v,* B, 1, above.

[23] Cairenes in Fustat: B 12, 75, 76.

[24] The term *qōdesh* (still preferred by the Yemenite Jews) is more common in the Geniza than *heqdēsh,* which became generally used later in Europe (and in modern Hebrew); *aqdas,* e.g., A 14.

[25] Orders of payment or accounts indicating the source of revenue: A 48–92, 93, and most of the administrators' notes listed in n. 3, above.

[26] The sick foreigner: B 67.

[27] The teacher: TS NS J 434 (a letter by Solomon b. Elijah). The poor omitted from the collection: B 57*b*.

[28] Earmarking of gifts to the community chest: TS 24.25, ll. 46–48.

[29] The communal treasury: ENA 1822, f. 65 (dated 1516).

[30] The scrupulous almoner: 'Avoda Zara 17*b*.

[31] TS 13 J 24, f. 4. See C 101–112.

[32] A 21, where the qōdesh appears as party to the contract in ll. 6, 7, 10, 15, 20. A 108, l. 4: *aḥāla biha 'l-qōdesh,* "he transferred the debt to the community chest."

[33] "The trustworthy elders": *ziqnē yōsher ha-'ōmedīm be-ṣorkhē ha-heqdēsh* (this is from Ascalon, Palestine, where *heqdēsh* was used) *uv-ṣorkhē ha-qāhāl,* A 17; *ha-zeqēnīm ha-yeshārīm ha-keshērīm,* A 100.

[34] Contracts with elders: A 17, 98, 100, 109. With three people signing: A 19–21, 102, 143, 155 (in the two latter cases the signatures are only partly or not at all preserved).

[35] Parnās: A 101 (Aug., 1101). Administrator of mosques: TS Arabic Box 38, f. 119 (July, 1137).

[36] A 95*v*, ll. 3, 9, 12, 13, 16, 21, 22, 24.

[37] Almoners, *gabbā'ē ṣedāqā,* Mishna Qiddushin 4:5. The perfumer: C 81.

[38] E.g., A 41*, 100*, both referring to Abraham ha-Levi al-Najīb b. Yaḥyā. See the commentary in *Med. People.*

[39] B 29, col. III.

[40] E.g., TS 16.57 (Dec., 1121). See subsection 4*b*, below.

[41] A 24, 41, 97, 103, 104, 106, 129, 157. An early example: B 57*b*.

[42] A 48–92, B 39*b*, and many other notes. See also C 101–112.

[43] B 93, C 67, 69, 70, 75, 77, and elsewhere.

2. *Sources of Revenue and Types of Relief*

[1] TS 13 J 21, f. 30, ll. 8 and 23+.

[2] TS 12.301, l. 14. "The slaughterhouses are the city": *inn al-majāzir hī al-balad.*

[3] ULC Or 1080 J 106, l. 9: *hanā'at ha-shewāqīm* (Heb.); TS 13 J 36, f. 5, l. 6: *yu'ṭu 'l-sūq l-ibn al-shishshī.* Both are letters by the Gaon Solomon b. Judah. The second letter emphasized that because of the bad times there was no sufficient *fā'ida,* or revenue, from that source. The expression *sūq al-dhibāḥa,* "the market where animals are killed," is found in a fragment in the John Rylands Library, Manchester, Gaster Collection A 75, which speaks of a weekly revenue of 8 dirhems, parnāsīm and a dignitary styled *mesōs ha-yeshīva,* The Delight of the yeshīva, details that may point to Fustat as place of origin. "The Jewish market," *sūq al-yahūd* is mentioned as a source of income for Daniel b. Azarya, TS 20.19, l. 30, and as a place of assembly in a letter by Solomon b. Judah, TS 13 J 19, f. 16, l. 36, also referring to Ramle (see sec. D, 2, n. 43, below). Reference to the tax on meat in connection with the market of Ramle also in TS 13 J 26, f. 18*v*, ll. 21–22, a letter by the brother of the Gaon Daniel b. Azarya.

[4] Chap. vi, sec. 10.

[5] Friday the day of distribution from the *quppa:* Baba bathra 86 and parallels. On bread in the Geniza period, see *Med. Soc.,* Vol. III, chap. viii. Distribution of fresh loaves in Fustat: p. 547 n. 25, below.

[6] A 109, not ratified, probably because the judges were of the opinion that the old man had means enough to sustain himself.

[7] TS 16.272*v*, ll. 3–4. The writer was suspect of having been a follower of the self-appointed Nagid Zuṭṭā, who was believed also to have made claims to supernatural faculties.

[8] TS 8 J 17, f. 6, dated 1236, see chap. v, B, 1 n. 38, above. The writer of the letter Yeshūʿā ha-melammed (the teacher) b. Abraham reports that the income from the *quppā* was used as school fee for poor children. A man with exactly the same name signed Bodl. MS Heb. d 66 (Cat. 2878), f. 125, together with another teacher who signed Bodl. MS Heb. b 11 (Cat. 2874, no. 22) f. 23, in 1154. Therefore, not paying attention to a date mentioned in abridged form at the end of the letter in connection with another matter, I concluded erroneously in *JSS*, 26 (1964), 9 n. 34, that the letter was written around 1150. I mention this mistake of mine in order to emphasize that one should never use a relevant detail in a Geniza manuscript without examining it in its entirety—although this procedure, I must concede, is extremely time-consuming. Our schoolmaster might have been the grandson of his namesake who followed the same profession.

For a *quppā shel ṣedāqā* in Tyre, Lebanon, see the first source in n. 37, below.

[9] For *pesīqā* an Arabic term was also used: *asmā*, lit., "to put one's name on the list of donors," from which the verbal noun *tasmiya* was derived. The two terms are combined in TS 8 J 16, f. 13, l. 13 (C 84): *wa-'asmaw pesīqā yawm al-kippūr* (Heb.) *wa-ṣārat nēder* (Heb.) *ʿalayhim*, "On the Day of Atonement they made pledges for a collection which became a vow incumbent on them." In the fourteenth century *jibāya* was used also in the sense of pesīqā (C 68).

[10] ENA 4010, f. 1, ll. 9–12+*, dated 1075.

[11] Schoolmaster: TS 13 J 22, f. 9, trans. in Goitein, *Education*, p. 83. Alexandria: Dropsie 386, ed. Mann, *Texts*, I, 459–463.

[12] Poll tax: C 7. Seats of learning: chap. v, A, 1, above.

[13] ENA 4020 I, loose leaf. A similar affair in TS 8 J 17, f. 27: A debtor requests to be paid the sum collected for him, for otherwise he was unable to leave his house.

[14] TS 16.286*v*, l. 2*. The man had a rich sister in Cairo. TS 20.28. For traveling cantors see chap. vi, sec. 10, nn. 18, 19.

[15] TS NS J 35, ll. 11–13, summary in Goitein, *Education*, p. 78.

[16] Application: e.g., C 91. Nagid's permission: ENA 1822, f. 52. It is superscribed with *EMeTh*, like an order of payment, see *Med. Soc.*, I, 241. See also C 122, 123.

[17] Letters of Nagids: e.g., C 101–112, 132. Expediting collection: TS 8 J 13, f. 7; pesīqā impossible: TS 13 J 21, f. 24.

[18] TS 10 J 10, f. 9, ll. 10–12, ed. Mann, II, 111. Solomon b. Judah writes: "May our elder speak to the community [soliciting contributions for the person recommended] both in the synagogue and in the homes." TS 10 J 15, f. 27 (C 91): "Making the round of the community," *yaṭūfū ʿalā*.

[19] Women: A 15, C 17, 36, 57, 66, 77.

[20] Private charity of women: *Med. Soc.*, Vol. III, chaps. ix, x.

[21] Weddings: C 54, 62–65, 83. See also B 39*b*.

[22] Additional appeals, e.g., C 7, 38, 87, 113. "Those that have not received their share," e.g., B 65, 85.

[23] Bridegroom as collector and distributor: B 51.

[24] Sunbāṭ: TS Misc. Box 8, f. 66, col. I, ll. 17, 19; col. IV, ll. 5–7*. In the last case the donators were "the dyers from Damsīs" who probably had made pledges while attending service on a holiday in Sunbāṭ.

[25] B 39*a*, 40–43, 44*b*, 48, 49, and elsewhere. See also sec. 1, n. 31, above, where a remainder of the poll tax is paid from the item Food, *mezōnōt* (Heb.). Besides its general meaning of food, sustenance, this word has two technical applications: alimony for wife or children, and victuals *other* than bread baked from wheat and so on. Thus it seems strange that the collections for the semiweekly distributions of bread should have been called by this name. I assume that the original meaning "sustenance" was intended, and since the main constituent of food in those days and regions was bread (see sec. C, 4*b*, below), the distribution of bread was called by this name.

[26] See, e.g., C 13, 46, 47, 49, 62, 69, 70, 80.

[27] See C 22.

[28] C 38. The document enumerates 14 + 45 + 60 = 119 contributors. But 9 of these gave additional sums on the second day of the drive, so that the total of participants during the first two days amounted to 110.

[29] The Monday collection: TS 8 J 15, f. 3.

[30] The glassmaker: *Med. Soc.,* I, 94.

[31] TS Misc. Box 24, f. 137, p. 1 (1099). All three entries of the case are found on this page.

[32] The debtor: Bodl. MS Heb. b 11 (Cat. 2874, no. 35), f. 36, dated 1153.

[33] Co-owner of house: TS 16.79, l. 15+.

[34] Rabbanite husband and Karaite wife: ENA 2728, f. 2. Settlement after marital strife: TS 12.129.

[35] Karaite widow: Bodl. MS Heb. a 3 (Cat. 2873), f. 42, ll. 34–35, ed. Mann, *Texts,* II, 179.

[36] TS 13 J 6, f. 33. The bridegroom was Abū Saʿīd, son of Abū Naṣr (?) b. Isaiah, of the famous family of Karaite bankers.

[37] Tyre: TS 10 J 12, f. 25, ed. S. Assaf, *Yerushalayim* (Jerusalem, 1953), p. 109. The father-in-law of the donator was al-Dulūkī (not *'l-dlfy,* as printed twice, ll. 4 and 15), derived from Dulūk, ancient Doliche, an important frontier town on the borders of Syria and Asia Minor in Roman and early Islamic times, today a village in Turkey. Tunisia: Harkavy, *Responsen der Geonim,* p. 133, last paragraph. Freedman: *Med. Soc.,* I, 146–147.

[38] TS Arabic Box 4, f. 5*, ed. S. D. Goitein, *75th Anniversary Volume of the Jewish Quarterly Review* (Philadelphia, 1967), pp. 225–242, esp. pp. 230, 233.

[39] TS 18 J 1, f. 25. The will was made in Jan., 1143. What we have is a copy from Nov., 1153, made at the request of a nephew to whom the dying woman had willed 10 dinars. See below, chap. vii, sec. B, 3, n. 52.

[40] TS 13 J 23, f. 20, ll. 4–9. One of several legal opinions by the judge Isaac b. Samuel the Sefaradī of Fustat (around 1100). For siglaton see Heyd, *Commerce du Levant,* II, 700, and below, chap. v, sec. D, 1, n. 18.

[41] TS 10 J 16, f. 6*. The beginning of the letter is lost.

3. *Charitable Foundations (Houses and Other Communal Property)*

[1] About this institution in Islam, see *EI, s.v.* "Waḳf" (W. Heffening) and Schacht, *Islamic Law,* pp. 125–126, 371 (bibliography). About its early history see Claude Cahen, "Réflexions sur le Waqf ancien," *Studia Islamica,* 14 (1961), 37–56. A deed that is a religious endowment is called *kitāb al-ṣadaqa,* lit., document (testifying to a gift) of charity. TS 8.193, l. 4 (a fragment in the hand of Ḥalfōn b. Manasse).

[2] Women as donators of houses: A 1, 18, 38, 134, 164. Houses named after women, e.g., A 24, 94 (Muhra), A 28, 94 ('Abla). The House of Sumāna, A 3, l. 14, was bought by, not donated to, the community.

[3] See S. Klein, "Das Fremdenhaus der Synagoge," *MGWJ,* 40 (1932), 545 ff., 41, 81 ff. The spinnery and the vinegar house in A 24 (1164), the oil house in A 28 and later sections. For the funduqs, see sec. 4, n. 50, below.

[4] Both in A 39, *misṭāḥ* also in A 145, 149.

[5] Muslim partner: e.g., "one-half of the house of the Sharīf," A 25, and frequently later. A Christian: A 94.

[6] E.g., A 145: ten unoccupied apartments in ten different buildings.

[7] Special expenses for unoccupied premises: A 24, ll. 11, 13, 14.

[8] "Prepayment," *ʿalā sabīl al-taqdima,* A 102, l. 7. The term *taʿjīl,* "speeding up," common in commerce (see *Med. Soc.,* I, 199) is also used (A 161). Cases of prepayment also in A 37, 141.

[9] A 3, ll. 3, 9, 15, 18, 22, 26, 29, covering about eighty years.

[10] A 129. The office is described as *tawallī wa-naẓar,* administration and overseeing. The appointment was made "by the Nagid, his court and the elders," 1. 5.

[11] A 142. The sum of the settlement, *muṣālaḥa,* agreed upon was 80 dirhems.

[12] C 45, where in two cases 6 dirhems are paid for the collection of about 160 dirhems.

[13] TS 18 J 1, f. 25. See chap. v, sec. C, 2 n. 39 above.

[14] ULC Or 1080 J 45, 1. 16: *sū diyānatih wa-bay 'ih alheqdēshōt* (the Gaon Solomon b. Judah). See chap. vii, sec. B, 1 n. 33.

4. *Tne Beneficiaries of the Community Chest*

[1] 1075: ENA 4010, f. 1+*. 1213: TS 13 J 8, f. 11 (R. Yehiel). Schoolteacher: TS 13 J 22, f. 9+ (here the Nagid promises to pay the poll tax for him).

[2] J. M. Toledano, *HUCA,* 12–13 (1937–1938), 109, last paragraph, referring to the year 1778.

[3] TS 16.39, ll. 18–21. See *Med. Soc.,* I, 381, sec. 58.

[4] Mishna, Sayings of the Fathers, 6:2; 3:5. About the problem of the exemption of the scholars from the payment of taxes see the quotation from Maimonides Code of Law discussed in Baron, *History of the Jews,* V, 76, and M. Beer, "Were the Babylonian Amoraim exempt from Taxes and Customs," *Tarbiz* 33 (1964), 247–258. Also below, chap. vii, C, 2.

[5] TS Arabic Box 18(2), f. 4+.

[6] TS 10 J 29, f. 4 (fragment of the upper part of Sār Shālōm Gaon's letter) + TS 10 J 24, f. 7 (fragment of lower part).

[7] Bilbays: TS 13 J 20, f. 24, 1. 8 (ca. 1220).

[8] Gift: *hadiyya.* Present: *tuḥfa.* See n. 5, above.

[9] TS 24.46, see chap. vi, sec. 10, n. 10, below.

[10] See the sample contract with a private teacher translated in Tritton, *Muslim Education,* pp. 25–26. In addition to his wages, he receives every month certain quantities of meat and rice. For the *dīnār jayshī,* see, e.g., Claude Cahen, "Le régime des impots dans le Fayyūm ayyubide," *Arabica,* 3 (1956), 12.

[11] In one letter, a *yūsufī* robe is mentioned as sent as a present for a young woman (TS 12.581, ll. 6, 14). See also Dozy, *Supplément,* II, 855*b.* For *bakhāya* dirhems, *ibid.,* I, 54*b,* top.

[12] Free lodging: A 149*a.* See also A 168.

[13] A 43, col. I, ll. 5–6: Ṭāhir, the beadle, and Abu 'l-Majd, the cantor, pay rent.

[14] Office of the judge: A 46, col. I, 1. 7.

[15] Orphan of cantor: TS 13 J 6, f. 27*.

[16] Jephthah b. Jacob signed TS 10 J 4, f. 12, beneath the judge Samuel b. Saadya. Later, he was a member of the court of Abraham Maimonides (unidentified ENA manuscript, of which Professor A. S. Halkin kindly presented me with a photograph).

[17] B 40 "House (i.e., family) of judge Manasse" does not mean that he was dead at that time, for he appears again several times in that document. The wording of the account simply refers to the fact that he was absent during the week concerned and that the money was handed over to his wife.

[18] Compensation for loss of time: *sekhar baṭṭālā* (Heb.).

[19] ULC Or 1080 J 106, ll. 9–10. Details about fees for the writing of legal documents in chap. vi, sec. 11.

[20] In the early 1920's I studied Talmud with the dayyān Jacob Posen of the then very large Jewish community of Frankfurt, Germany. There were of course many professional, salaried rabbis in that city, but the dayyān did not receive any remuneration. Naturally, very few, if any, civil cases came before the rabbinical court, only matters of family law and questions of ritual, liturgical, and religious comportment. How time consuming that aspect of the dayyān's office was, I cannot

say. His teaching load, however, far exceeded that of an American professor. Every weekday morning, in winter before, and in summer after the service (which means 6:30 A.M. at latest) he gave a course to a select group of students and laymen. In addition, he read several classes in the evenings and on Saturday. The man was a rich banker and a chain smoker of choice cigars. Never in my life did I enjoy again an aroma comparable with that pervading the dayyān's study. Whenever there arose a difficult problem in the Talmud (and when does it not?), he took his cigar out of his mouth, turned it upside down, and carried it in circles around his nostrils, inhaling the exquisite fragrance of its smoke—and soon the solution was found. He personally acted also as circumciser because he strongly objected to physicians performing that little operation on newly born boys, lest it lose its religious character and become merely an act of medical treatment (as, indeed, it has in this and other countries). When I studied with him, he had already circumcised about 8,800 boys. How could a busy banker indulge in this religious sport which might require his absence from office three times a day? He had made it a matter of principle not to stay on for a single minute, even with close friends, for the reception or dinner following the ceremony. He simply came, cut, and vanished.

I have permitted myself to encroach on the reader's time and patience with this little sketch of a twentieth-century dayyān in order to impress on him that the picture emerging from the Geniza of the extremely busy merchant banker who at the same time served as religious and communal leader is not unrealistic, but natural to that type of civilization.

[21] TS 10 J 10, f. 2. The purpose of the document explains the very unusual fact that, from line 6, it passes from Hebrew script to Arabic.

[22] The often repeated talmudic maxim that the religious merit of a day of fasting is derived from the alms given on that day (Berakhot 6*b* and parallels) presumes that it was customary to hand out gifts to the poor on such days (cf. Isaiah 58:1–8). Participation of the needy in the holiday celebrations: Deuteronomy 16:11, 14.

[23] *JSS*, 26 (1964), 74; see also B 26.

[24] TS 12.244. The technical details about the desired type of bread are unfortunately not preserved.

[25] TS 8 J 4, f. 9*d*+.

[26] Lane-Poole, *History of Egypt*, p. 135.

[27] *JSS*, 26 (1964), 75.

[28] The widow of the muqaddarī and her sister each receive a jūkhāniyya, B 72, col. I, l. 9. For muqaddar = large, see Dozy, *Supplément*, II, 313*b*.

[29] Dropsie 393. The letter is incomplete, but in the same awkward hand and Hebrew style as TS 20.114, ed. Mann, II, 217–273, and addressed to the same Joshua b. Dōsā and signed Isaac b. Benveniste. There is also much similarity in the subject matter.

[30] B 25, col. I, ll. 9–10. For *thawb*, see *Med. Soc.*, I, 229.

[31] Dozy, *Supplément*, I, 230*b*.

[32] Ashtor, *Zion*, 30 (1965), 68.

[33] Subsection 1, n. 11, above. See also C 82*b*.

[34] Maimonides, *Responsa*, II, 613–614. The query is preserved only in an abridged late Hebrew translation of the Arabic original. Therefore the circumstances of the event are not known in detail.

[35] For other references to the poll tax, see B 60, 88, 92, and A and C *passim*, and esp. chap. vii, sec. C, 3.

[36] About hospitals, see chap. vi, sec. 12.

[37] A 128; TS K 25, f. 240, secs. 33–37 (A 80–86).

[38] See chap. vi, secs. 3–4.

[39] See Types of Documents at the end of App. C, item 19.

[40] C 82*a*: cash together with wheat, Alexandria, 1174. A 29: Fustat, 1183; Passover

is not expressly mentioned, but 71 dirhems are distributed by one official to the poor in Nisan, the month in which that holiday falls. A 146*b*: (the astonishingly small sum of 16½ dirhems put aside for Passover). See also A 11*b*.

[41] In lieu of clothing: A 34 (1183). A 35 (1184; Bodl. MS Heb. f 56, f. 60, 11. 2–3). Same implicitly: B 36, B 29 (some persons receive clothing, some cash).

[42] B 85 (the first group gets wheat, the second money).

[43] The sums in B 65 and 85 are irregular because they constitute arrears, payments to persons who had not yet received their full share. Still, the largest group in B 65*a* is that receiving 5 dirhems, and the "better people," such as "the widow of good family," or "the old gentleman from Jerusalem," receive 5 and 10 dirhems, respectively. The list B 92 is from a late period for which we do not have sufficient comparative material.

[44] A 104, 1. 9: *musawwagh lil-mamlūk min waqf al-heqdēsh bil-duwayra 'l-ma'rūfa b-Ibn Finḥās bi-Miṣr wa-mablaghuh fī kull sana . . .* (here the manuscript is cut off), "an allowance made to your servant from the revenue of the heqdēsh in the small house known as Ben Phinehas in Miṣr [Fustat], amounting per year to. . . ."

[45] TS 12.289+*. The addressee is required to include this item in the collection to be made for the silk-weaver.

[46] Bodl. MS Heb. d 61 (Cat. 2859, no. 3*a*), f. 9, sec. A, see *Med. Soc.*, I, 383, sec. 62. TS Misc. Box 28, f. 199*v*, 11. 2–3: a teacher in Jerusalem receives a loan of 1½ dinars out of the money destined for the poor of that city (with the written consent of the donators in Fustat!).

[47] Bodl. MS Heb. a 3 (cat. 2873), f. 2, 1. 52*.

[48] A 43, 128. See als(B 39*a*. Burial expenses are called *nawā'ib*.

[49] C 91. TS 12.289+*, where the bridegroom, himself an orphan, marries, "for Heaven's sake," an entirely destitute orphan girl.

[50] The caravanserai between the two synagogues: A 24, 1. 6 (1164), A 39*v*, 1. 2, and elsewhere. The funduq on the Great Bazaar: A 94 (1234). The small funduq: A 25, 1. 12 (1181; it brought 79 dirhems per month). "The funduq" without qualification: A 95 (1247). The innkeeper, *funduqānī*, presumably of the small funduq, paid 75 dirhems in 1183 (A 29*v*, 1. 1).

[51] A 43, page *b*, 11. 28–29: *wa'an sajn fī funduq li-aqwām min Minyat Ghamr*. Perhaps the payment was made not to a caravanserai, but to the policeman who guarded the persons confined in one of the funduqs belonging to the Jewish community.

[52] B 67. Committee of three (consisting of the cantor al-Mēvīn and two laymen): TS Arabic Box 30, f. 146.

[53] E.g., TS NS J 2*, where the transport of a nāsī from one Egyptian provincial town to another cost 40 dirhems.

[54] TS 8 J 17, f. 13 (a scholar on his way to Jerusalem).

[55] ULC Or 1080 J 34.

[56] TS 12.652, 1. 13, verso, 1. 17. Administrator of the caravanserai: *qayyim funduq al-heqdēsh*.

[57] TS 24.49, written by Evyatar ha-Kohen, the future Gaon, around 1062.

[58] TS NS J 120, 11. 8–16. The addressee is requested to approach the *me'ulle*, "the distinguished member of the academy," who is none else but Eli b. Amram.

[59] TS 16.287, written by Judah b. Aaron al-'Ammānī, the teacher. The date 168 is to be complemented by 4800 (the Heb. letters *dtt*) = 4968 Era of the Creation (*lyṣ* being an abbreviation of *la-yeṣīrā*) = 1208, as in many other letters and documents from that period, e.g., TS 13 J 21, f. 25, which is a letter by the same writer to the same addressee from the same year (summarized in Goitein, *Education*, p. 102).

[60] TS 13 J 34, f. 3, 11. 14–18, ed. Mann, II, 344–345. The fragment is in the beautiful hand of Yeshū'ā b. Joseph ha-Kohen of Alexandria, who wrote four

other letters dealing with the ransoming of captives, besides the three edited or discussed by Mann, I, 88–90, II, 87 and 240, also TS 10 J 24, f. 9, of which only the introductory phrases are preserved. Thus we have from one pen five letters concerned with this charity. The main part of Moses Maimonides' strongly worded circular to the communities of the Rīf, soliciting them to contribute to the ransom of captives, of which only the beginning had been known, TS 12.238+, is contained in TS 16.9, where a sermon in Hebrew is written between the lines. The two senior judges of Fustat, Ḥiyyā (b. Isaac) and Ephraim (b. Meshullām) had been sent to Palestine, probably to approach the Franks, who might have made captives when they sacked Bilbays on Nov. 3, 1168.

[61] S. D. Goitein, "Contemporary Letters on the Capture of Jerusalem by the Crusaders," *Journal of Jewish Studies,* 3 (1952), 162–177.

[62] TS 12.543*.

5. *Epilogue: An Appraisal of the Social Services*

[1] Muqaddasi, p. 197, l. 18.

[2] BM Or 5544, f. 2. About the letters of the Nagid Joshua see C 101–112. The Arabic term is derived from the Hebrew. The difficult problem how *ṣedāqā,* which in the Bible means *justice,* came to denote *charity* in postbiblical Judaism, is treated in a learned paper by Franz Rosenthal, *HUCA,* 23 (1950–1951), 411–430.

[3] See the Author's Note preceding Appendix A.

[4] Cf. C 3, third paragraph.

[5] There exists an even more far-reaching possibility. Sometimes, three sheets were pasted together, as in TS 13 J 6, f. 14+. (See chap. vi, sec. 11, n. 25. There, of the original 94 lines, indicated in the remaining last sheet, only 24 have been preserved. Each of the two first sheets thus had comprised an average of 35 lines. It is natural that the concluding sheet should be shorter). In view of the length of B 1, I do not regard it, however, as likely that the list consisted originally of three sheets.

[6] The details for the second, thirteenth, and fourteenth day have been preserved in their entirety (names, contributions made by each household, and daily totals). For the first day, the total (154-1/8 dinars and 385 dirhems, approximately 164 dinars) and details about the last 12 contributors (14½ dinars and 118¼ dirhems, about 17 dinars) are extant. The lost two pages referring to the first day must have comprised about 57 lines (as a comparison with those preserved shows), of which a few must have served as superscription or introduction. Since the copyist writes one name a line throughout, there is room for 50 names. The attentive reader will have noticed that the average contribution per donor on the two lost pages would be about 3 dinars (164 − 17 = 147÷50), while the last 12 donors gave an average of only 1½ (17 : 12). This, however, is perfectly in order since the lists always start with the big contributions. For the ten days for which we do not have lists, to assume a daily average of 30 households, each contributing about 2 dinars, is justified in view of the details set forth in the analysis of C 30. The totals, thus, would be:

First day (50 + 12)	62 households
Second day	39 "
Third to twelfth day	300 "
Thirteenth day	18 "
Fourteenth day	5 "
Total	424 households

Taking into consideration that contributions were occasionally made by several persons together, that some households appear twice, and, furthermore, that for some reason or other, especially travel abroad or illness, many people must have been impeded from contributing, a total of 500 heads of households seems to be reasonable.

[7] TS NS Box 320, f. 7.

[8] *Benjamin of Tudela,* ed. Adler, pp. 69–70. Benjamin visited Fustat at the time of the Gaon Nethanel b. Moses (1160–1167). The number 7,000 is given in the manuscripts, but the first printed edition (Constantinople, 1543) has 2,000.

[9] TS Arabic Box 51 (formerly marked Hirschfeld I, xv), f. 111, ed. S. D. Goitein, *Millas-Vallicrosa Jubilee Volume* (Barcelona, 1954), p. 717.

[10] B 40–43, 46–47, 49–51, 77, 79–82, 86. B 47 contains 39 households, B 86 contains 32. The possibility that some of these lists might be incomplete and represent the payments made by only one communal official (see B 40, end) must be taken into account. The large number of documents and the fact that they were written by different scribes (see B 86) make it more likely that the distributions recorded comprised all the relief recipients.

[11] See the detailed description in Lane-Poole, *History of Egypt,* pp. 215–216.

[12] Section "Gifts to the Poor," chap. 10, para. 7.

[13] *Med. Soc.,* I, 252–254, 260–261. More in *ibid.,* Vol. III, chap. viii.

[14] Kethubboth, 67*b*.

D. WORSHIP

1. *The House of Worship*

[1] If not otherwise indicated, all the sources for this section are registered in my articles "The Synagogue Building and Its Furnishings according to the Records of the Cairo Geniza," *Eretz-Israel,* 7 (1964 [L. A. Mayer Memorial Volume]), 169*–171* (Eng. section), 81–97 (Heb. section), and "Ambōl—the Raised Platform in the Synagogue," *Eretz-Israel,* 6 (1960), 162–167. On the legal situation see A. Fattal, *Le statut legal des non-musulmans en pays d'Islam* (Beirut, 1958), pp. 174–203.

[2] For a synagogue founded in Cairo shortly after its foundation see chap. vi, 12, n. 10, below.

[3] R. Gottheil, *JQR,* 19 (1906–1907), 490.

[4] TS 13 J 7, f. 6, ll. 19–22. Only the left half of the calligraphic letter is preserved.

[5] E. L. Sukenik, *Ancient Synagogues in Palestine and Greece* (London, 1934), p. 22 and *passim*; G. M. A. Hanfman, "The Ancient Synagogue of Sardis," *Fourth World Congress of Jewish Studies* (Jerusalem, 1967), pp. 38 and 40.

[6] TS 8 J 17, f. 3. Judge Elijah was asked to read out the letter to the woman.

[7] Jacob Saphir, *Iben Safir* (Lyck, 1866), p. 21*a*. Jack Mosseri, "The Synagogues of Egypt," *Jewish Review* (London), 5, no. 25 (May, 1914), 31–44.

[8] Bodl. MS Heb. f. 56 (Cat. 2821, no. 16), f. 43*v*, l. 12: *ṭāqat zujāj.*

[9] Bodl. MS Heb. b 13 (Cat. 2834, no. 22), f. 41, l. 4, ed. (incompletely) Mann, I, 222 n. 2.

[10] For Side see E. R. Goodenough, *Jewish Symbols* (New York, 1953), II, 81 ff. I owe this reference to Dr. Joseph Gutmann, Curator of the Museum of the Hebrew Union College, Cincinnati.

[11] TS Box H 12/11(*a*), f. b, l. 12. During the reading of the Esther scroll at the Purim service the Torah scroll is put into the niche of the anbōl. Dr. Ezra Fleischer of Jerusalem kindly put at my disposal a photostat of this liturgical manuscript. For the ambon in the Mu'allaqa church see Jacques Jarry, "L'ambon dans la liturgie primitive de l'église," *Syria,* 40 (1963), 147–162.

[12] TS Box H 12/11(*a*), f. 6*a*, ll. 13–14, ed. E. Fleischer, *Tarbiz,* 37 (1968), 271. Here the cantor recites on the anbōl the "sanctification of the day" (*yiqaddis,* Arabicized from Heb. *qiddūsh*), which is essentially a part of the home service and not of the

synagogue service. As late an authority as the Nagid Joshua, the great-great-grandson of Maimonides, writes in the name of his ancestor that the qiddūsh *might* be recited in the synagogue, if this was a local custom (see *Responsa of Joshua ha Nagid,* ed. A. H. Freimann [Jerusalem, 1940], p. 39). Nowadays, in the United States and most other countries, the qiddūsh forms a most solemn part of the synagogue service, but in the Yemenite synagogues it is not recited at all. In the Geniza period it was chanted in the synagogue for the benefit of the foreigners who had no home of their own, but lived in the synagogue compound. In TS 8 J 41, f. 11, l.3+, a boy chants on the anbōl the *Nishmat* ("All souls praise Your name"), an ancient hymn immediately preceding the official morning prayer.

[13] TS Misc. Box 25, f. 139, ll. 1–2 (which continues f. 132). When it was suggested to the writer to excommunicate a man for practicing masturbation, he answers: such a man is too despicable for being mentioned on the pulpits, *'ala l-manābir.* This phrase is classical Arabic and simply means: in public. In Maimonides, *Responsa,* II, 316, the editor put *al-minbar* into the text, but the manuscript has *al-anbōl.* The mistake is corrected in *ibid.,* III, 127. In *ibid.,* II, 341, *al-minbar* is used, perhaps by a writer from outside Egypt.

[14] The publications rendering the Hebrew inscription, seen by me (including the *Guide of the Israel Museum* up to 1968) provide incorrect readings and translations. The first three letters are *rwr,* with dots on the two *r*'s which are indicative of abbreviations. They stand for *(mā)r(ēnū) wer(abbēnū),* "our master and teacher," which is almost equivalent with modern Mr. The reading David (*dwd*), besides being incorrect, is impossible, for double names like "David Solomon," common in later times, were absolutely unknown to the Arabic-speaking Jews of the High Middle Ages. The eulogy on the deceased is taken from Isaiah 63:14 and should be translated "may God's spirit give *him* peace," and not "may the spirit of God bring solace to *us.*" The woodwork on the Louvre piece is more elaborate, but the Hebrew letters are less well preserved (see, e.g., L. A. Mayer, *L'art juif en terre de l'Islam* [Geneva: A. Kundig, 1959], p. 13, and fig. 6*b*). The pieces in the Louvre and the Cairo Museum were accessible to visitors and well displayed when I visited those museums last. For the turners see *Med. Soc.,* I, 423 n. 90.

[15] See *Med. Soc.,* I, 398 n. 42, where the sources for the identification of the synagogue of the Iraqians with the church building are listed. In his Ph.D. dissertation, mentioned p. 118, above, Moshe Gil arrived independently at the same result. There exists additional topographical evidence in favor of that assumption.

[16] D. S. Rice, "Studies in Islamic Metal Work V," *BSOAS,* 17 (1955), 206–231 (with many illustrations). Plates X and XI of this study show a grillwork lamp of ordinary workmanship dated 1090, which might well have been similar to those suspended at that time in the synagogue of the Palestinians in Fustat. The Star of David visible on Rice's lamp was not a Jewish emblem in those days, although the renowned Nahray b. Nissīm used it as a trademark on one of his consignments.

[17] When one reads in a letter sent from one country to another the description of a festivity detailing the numbers of wax candles (of different types!), oil lamps, and chandeliers illuminating the place one understands the importance attached in those days to proper, or, as the case would be, luxurious, lighting (ENA 4020 [detached leaf, not yet identified], ed. Mann, II, 172, ll. 18–19).

[18] The covering of columns with siglaton textiles is mentioned in TS 20.47, l. 12, ed. E. J. Worman, *JQR,* 20 (1908), 458–459 (see my note *Eretz-Israel,* 7 [1964], 92 n. 65). Certainly not all the columns were covered or covered permanently, for one account has the item: "For the polisher of the columns," TS 10 J 11, f. 26, l. 7 (App. A, sec. 113).

[19] At the time of the edition of the 1159 document in *Eretz-Israel,* 7 (1964) 94–96, I had only its left half, preserved in TS NS J 296. Because of the importance of the document I supplemented its right half by surmise. In summer, 1968, I found the missing half, contained in TS Misc. Box 28, f. 51, and had the satisfaction that most of my restitutions had been appropriate. In addition, the new manuscript

contains an otherwise unknown technical term of silversmithing whose existence could not be surmised, of course: a pair of "pomegranates" with niello work *bnwfkhtyn,* which I take as *bi-nufkhatayn,* "with two protuberances." Such grill-work is indeed common on the silver ornaments called pomegranates in the Oriental congregations up to the present day.

I should remark that on Oct. 7, 1964, which was immediately after the appearance of my article, Dr. N. Golb of the University of Chicago wrote me that, according to his notes, TS Misc. Box 28, f. 51, also contained some details about synagogue furniture. But since I did not have a photostat of that manuscript and was already occupied with entirely different topics, I disregarded and then entirely forgot his alert until a systematic survey of Box 28 (in the course of finalizing this volume) brought the lost piece to my attention. The vagaries of Geniza research!

[20] See chap. vi, sec. 10.

[21] JNUL Heb. 8° 2238, described concerning its importance for the history of the vocalization of the Bible text by H. Yalon, *Kirjath Sepher,* 30 (1955), 257–263.

[22] Alfred J. Butler, *Ancient Coptic Churches* (Oxford, 1884) I, 12–13.

[23] Maimonides, *Responsa,* II, 302 (*khizāna* meant "closet" in those days, not "shop"; *bayt* is "room," not "house").

[24] See chap. vi, sec. 4.

[25] ULC Or 1080 J 31. For the other details see the first article quoted in n. 1.

[26] See sec. C, 4, n. 50, above.

[27] TS Misc. Box 8, f. 61*v,* (App. B, sec. 46), bottom: "Gypsum for *makhzan al-qamḥ,* the storeroom of wheat—1 dirhem."

[28] TS NS J 375 (App. A, sec. 93), left col., last item: "A rope for the well, *bi'r,* 1½ dirhems." For the "basin for ablutions" see App. A, sec. 178, above.

[29] Maimonides, *Responsa,* II, 434–444. Maimonides' signature is followed by those of Samuel b. Saadya ha-Levi, Isaac b. Sāsōn (of Cairo), Mevōrākh b. Nathan, and other scholars well known from contemporary Geniza records.

[30] TS Box J 1, f. 47 (App. A, sec. 94), col. 4: *birkat al-'irāqiyīn.*

[31] Ramle: TS 13 J 20, f. 1, ed. Assaf, *Texts,* p. 28: *duwayrat al-miqwā* (Heb.), the little house of the ritual bath. The important letter TS 28.10 must have been sent from Palestine (and not from Egypt), since among many other things it reports copious rains in September which replenished the water supply in the town. The ritual bath is here referred to twice with *maṭbal,* a Judeo-Arabic noun derived from Hebrew *ṭbl,* to immerse, bathe for ritual purification.

2. *Life in the Synagogue*

[1] AIU VII E 21. The danger referred to involved "all Israel."

[2] Maimonides, *Responsa,* I, 100. See chap. vii, sec. B, 3, above.

[3] E.g., TS NS J 174, l. 2 (Old Cairo); TS 20.117*v,* l. 3, ed. Assaf, *Texts,* p. 160 (Dammūh); Mosseri L 135 *v,* l. 2, ed. Mann, *Texts,* I, 246 (*Qayrawān*); Firkovitch II, no. 210–211, f. 6*v,* l. 8, ed. Mann, *Texts,* I, 277 (Baghdad). In all four cases, the term, *miqdāsh,* sanctuary, based on Ezekiel 11:16, is used. The Temple is referred to in Hebrew by *bēth* ha-miqdāsh.

[4] N. Wieder, *Islamic Influences on the Jewish Worship* (in Heb.) (Oxford, 1957), pp. 65 and 68.

[5] Ghazālī, *Iḥyā',* Part I, chap. 4, sec. 7.

[6] ENA 151 (2557)*.

[7] Gottheil-Worrell, XXXII, p. 149. The editors' "second" and "fifth" means Monday and Thursday.

[8] TS 13 J 36, f. 6 (App. A, sec. 11*c*), ll. 19–20.

[9] TS 13 J 13, f. 13, left column (middle of eleventh century).

[10] Bodl. MS Heb. c 28 (Cat. 2876), f. 59, bottom (early eleventh century; in Heb.).

[11] TS 20.117, recto only. For the verso see n. 3, above. Both documents were written by Japheth b. David. The Damascene was called Mufarraj b. Japheth b. Shu'ayb ha-Durmasqī, a rather uncommon combination.

[12] *Siddur R. Saadja* [spelled thus] *Gaon,* ed. I. Davidson, S. Assaf, B. I. Joel (Jerusalem, 1941), p. 117. My translation differs slightly from that given in Baron, *History of the Jews,* VI, 15.

[13] TS 18 J 4, f. 12. See chap. vi, sec. 2.

[14] Maimonides, *Responsa,* I, 189–191; S. D. Goitein, "Maimonides as Chief Justice," *JQR,* 49 (1959), 197–198.

[15] Such a calligraphic invitation to the elder Suwayd and his two sons, "who love the Torah and strengthen the arms of its students" is contained in TS 8 J 13, f. 15; another, addressed by the scholar and scribe Saadya, the son of Israel the cantor, to the elder Samuel b. Shela and his sons, is found in TS NS Box 321, f. 22. The day-long *derāshā,* as it is called here, in Bodl. MS Heb. f 102, f. 52*v,* ll. 5–6.

[16] TS 8 J 15, f. 8. He quotes the story of R. Akiba and Yohanan b. Nuri ('Erkhin 16b) as being found in Baba Meṣi'a and misreads Rabban Gamliel "bar Rabbi" for "bi-Yavne."

[17] A good introduction to the subject is Shalom Spiegel, "On Medieval Hebrew Poetry," in *The Jews,* ed. Louis Finkelstein (New York, 1960), I, 854–892, esp. pp. 873 ff.

[18] See chap. vi, sec. 10. In one letter, a temporary decline of the synagogue of the Babylonians in Old Cairo was attributed to the fact that its president did not invite any guest cantor or preacher (TS Misc. Box 25, f. 106). About Obadiah the proselyte, see chap. vii, sec. A, 3, end.

[19] Moshe Perlmann, *Samau'al al-Maghribī* (New York, 1964), Ar. text, pp. 56–57, Eng. trans., p. 57. One important correction: For "the ḥazzān is assisted by the public . . . in chanting the melodies," read "is assisted by a number of persons," i.e., a choir. The text has *jamā'a,* not *al-jamā'a.*

[20] A particular devotee of synagogal poetry was the cantor Abu 'l-Majd, the confidant of Abraham Maimonides (see Index, s.v. "Abu 'l-Majd"). The interpretation of Abraham Maimuni, *Responsa,* pp. 132–133, in Baron, *History of the Jews,* VII, 103, needs some qualification. Abraham, like his father Moses Maimonides, did not object to synagogal poems as such, but to their insertion into, or replacement of, the texts of the official liturgy. Naturally, the two scholars also opposed the recitation of unworthy pieces fabricated by ignoramuses.

[21] TS 8 J 21, f. 12, addressed to Samuel, "Prince of the Levites and Pride of the Physicians," son of Solomon, "Pride of the Elders." This Samuel is not identical with the court physician Samaw'al, known from many documents dated or datable between 1214 and 1238, for the latter's father was called Japheth, e.g., TS 13 J 4, f. 14 (1214), TS 16.200 (1225). A Levite Samuel b. Solomon was a member of the noble family whose tree is found in Hebrew Union College MS Geniza 4, ll. 31–42, ed. Mann, *Texts,* I, 472, but there he bears a slight different title. Names or place of the senders are not indicated.

[22] Maimonides, *Responsa,* II, 329–330. See also n. 20, above.

[23] Solomon b. Judah: TS NS Box 320, f. 16+. The "Levi": TS NS J 66 (two drafts in Heb. of the same document). His name: Yeshū'ā ha-Levi b. Solomon. A third, final version in Arabic language, dated Iyyar (April–May), 1229, in TS 8.161.

[24] TS 8 J 22, f. 3: *al-Shīr* (Heb.). The blind man: Abu 'l-Riḍā b. Judah he-ḥāvēr.

[25] Maimonides, *Responsa,* II, 444–445.

[26] TS NS J 279, l. 9. A traveling physician is honored thus in a provincial town: *lō he'emīd le-sēfer tōrā bi-srārā ellā anī.*

[27] Haughty synagogue presidents: TS 8 J 41, f. 11+. Abraham Maimonides, *The Highways of Perfection,* Vol. I (New York, 1927), pp. 34 and 45; Vol. II (Baltimore, 1938), pp. 74–75. Honorific titles: Antonin 1154, ed. Mann, *Texts,* I, 261. Dr. Abra-

ham I. Katsh, President of Dropsie University, Philadelphia, kindly provided me with a photograph of the manuscript. In l. 14, the manuscript has *li'abūh* and not *wa'akhūh,* which solves the difficulties indicated by the editor.

[28] ULC Or 1080 J 148*, superscribed *nuskhat al-tarḥīm.* This piece, like the following three, opens with a prayer on the ancestors and other deceased relatives of the notable, but contains only his first four titles. TS 8 J 7, f. 9; TS 8 J 21, f. 3; TS NS J 39. Prayer for the notable only, containing five titles: TS Box K 21, f. 35.

[29] TS 13 J 8, f. 14 (App. C, sec. 4). Actually this is a letter that uses the phrases then in vogue in such prayers.

[30] A good example of long pedigrees with titles and praise of the merits of the ancestors is to be found in the lists TS K 15, f. 68, the first referring to the family of Moses Maimonides' wife, ed. S. D. Goitein, *Tarbiz,* 33 (1965), 183–184. Many memorial lists have been edited by Jacob Mann and others, see his remarks in Mann, *Texts,* II, 256 and the list, *ibid.,* p. 257 n. 4. But many still await publication.

[31] See n. 28, above. Dozy, *Supplément,* I, 517*b* notes the term "tarḥīm" only from the nineteenth century. But the Jews of the twelfth certainly were not the first to use it.

[32] Maimonides, *Responsa,* II, 308–309. For a detailed description of Muslim funerals see Lane, *Modern Egyptians,* chap. 28, especially, pp. 525–527.

[33] Marriage contracts could of course be made in a synagogue or mosque since both served also as courthouses. Mr. M. Friedman draws my attention to A. H. Freimann, *Seder Qiddūshīn . . .* (Jerusalem, 1945), p. 49, where the arrangement of weddings in synagogues on Saturdays (in Byzantium) is condemned in the strongest terms as an imitation of Christian usages (in addition to other reasons). Z. W. Falk, *Jewish Matrimonial Law in the Middle Ages* (Oxford, 1966), p. 49, n. 3, and p. 54, n. 1 (on which, too, Mr. M. Friedman alerted me) do not contradict the statement I make in the text. Professor Atiya writes, "My knowledge is that weddings were habitually celebrated at homes. However, I have no material evidence to prove that marriages were never contracted in a Coptic church until recent years when the Patriarch ordained that this should be the normal procedure."

[34] TS Box NS 110, f. 26*. See sec. A, 1, n. 50, above.

[35] TS NS J 165, ed. simultaneously by A. Scheiber, *Sefunot,* 8 (1964), 144 (who remarks, however, that in my book *Education,* p. 150, I had announced my intention to publish all material related to the family of Maimonides) and myself, *Tarbiz,* 34 (1965), 248–249. Scheiber arranges the text according to the rhymes; in my edition the lines are printed as they appear in the manuscript. Thus, the two editions complement each other. Scheiber's *yqbwṣ* (verso, l. 2), which is also grammatically impossible, is certainly only a misprint for *wqbwṣ (we-qibbūṣ)* (*Tarbiz,* p. 249).

David's great-grandson was also a Nagid, but the handwriting on the manuscript points to the middle of the thirteenth rather than to the end of the fourteenth century.

[36] Bodl. MS Heb. c 28 (Cat. 2876), f. 2. It is addressed to Sahlān b. Barhūn (Abraham), the Old Cairene scholar and communal leader (after 1032, since his father is referred to as dead). Gaon of Jerusalem: TS 24.43, ll. 12–33, written in the early 1020's.

[37] TS 12.26*. The document was made out in favor of the person accused.

[38] *al-Balādhurī, Ansāb al-Ashrāf,* Vol. V, ed. S. D. Goitein (Jerusalem, 1936), p. 305.

[39] Ibn 'Idhārī, *al-Bayān al-Mughrib,* ed. G. S. Colin and E. Lévi-Provençal (Leiden, 1948), I, 277.

[40] TS 12.215, Section F*; TS 13 J 34, f. 3, l. 18, ed. Mann, II, 345.

[41] Samuel Krauss, *Synagogale Altertümer,* Berlin and Vienna, 1922), pp. 182–199: "Die Synagoge als Gemeindehaus" (the synagogue as community center). *EI,* III, s.v. "Masdjid," Sec. E: "The mosque as state institution."

[42] TS 8 J 22, f. 7. The invitation is in the unmistakable hand of Eli ha-Mumḥē

b. Abraham (middle of eleventh century), see *Med. Soc.*, I, 472–473 n. 81. The addressee is Abraham b. Ḥayy (Hebraicized from Aramaic Ḥiyyā), father of Japheth. A similar invitation in TS 10 J 9, f. 28.

[43] TS 13 J 19, f. 16. Mann, I, 141 n. 1, refers to this precious, but difficult document. See sec. A, 1, n. 30, above.

[44] Karaite meetinghouses: TS 10 J 29, f. 13, l. 23 where the apprehension is expressed that many members of the Palestinian congregation might defect to the Iraqian synagogue or to the Karaites, *ila 'l-kanīsa 'l-ukhrā wa-ilā majālis al-Qarā'iyyīn*. This shows, by the way, that around 1030, the Karaites had more than one synagogue in Fustat. Private synagogues: TS 16.187+*, ll. 14–18, also TS 13 J 16, f. 21, l. 19, where the Nagid Mevōrākh prohibits the establishment of a secessionist congregation.

[45] The physician's synagogue: TS NS J 389 (App. C, sec. 90); for the physicians' morning visits, see chap. vi, sec. 12. The India trader: TS 10 K 20, f. 1+ (App. C, sec. 28).

[46] Abraham Maimonides, weddings and mourning assemblies: TS 16.187+*.

[47] Uriel Heyd, "The Jewish Communities of Istanbul in the Seventeenth Century," *Oriens*, 6 (1953), 299–314.

[48] Ascalon: TS 8 J 41, f. 11, l. 9+; Hebron: ULC Or 1081 J 18, l. 9+; Acre: TS 18 J 3, f. 5, l. 29; al-Maḥalla: TS 13 J 19, f. 6, margin, end.

[49] Krauss, *Synagogale Altertümer* (see above, n. 41), pp. 428–429.

[50] Maimonides, *Responsa*, II, 314–317, 467–468, 475. Abraham Maimonides, *Highways of Perfection* (see above, n. 27), I, 45.

[51] TS 13 J 16, f. 21 (Malīj).

[52] ENA 2736, f. 20, ll. 10–15. Cf. sec. B, 1, n. 117.

[53] TS Arabic Box 38, f. 131. The Nagid: Joseph b. Ḥāy (Arabic spelling for Ḥayy [see n. 42, above]) b. Asad. The physician: Manṣūr b. Ibrāhīm b. 'Afīf.

[54] TS 8 J 22, f. 25, ed. Braslavsky, *Our Country*, pp. 120–121. I hope to publish a revised text together with other, unedited, documents on the Palestinian Gaonate.

[55] TS 10 J 14, f. 30*. The notary: Ephraim b. Meshullām (see App. C, sec. 32).

[56] TS NS J 270+*, see App. C, sec. 93. The marriage contract of 1511 in Gottheil-Worrell, XL, p. 182, see my article in *Tarbiz*, 31 (1962), 288 n. 6.

[57] The biblical word for "justice," *ṣedāqā*, was understood in postbiblical times as meaning "charity," cf. Ketubbōt 50*a*, see sec. C, 5, n. 2, above.

[58] The text of the appeal is in Arabic, but the italicized words, including the Bible quotations, are in Hebrew.

[59] This phrase ("so that . . .") is in Aramaic and must go back to pre-Islamic times when that language was used all over southwest Asia. It appears not only here, in the appeal of a refugee, where it is appropriate, but also at the end of other appeals, e.g. ULC Or 1081 J 8* (App. C, sec. 92). In this century of displaced persons we have some understanding of this prayer, which perhaps was said first when the cruel Assyrians used the method of mass deportations to destroy a people (eighth century B.C.).

[60] ENA Uncatalogued 98+, see App. C, sec. 94. Other appeals to the community by women: App. C, secs. 92, 95, 96. Naturally, many preferred not to display their neediness in public. A circular in huge letters urging the communities to help a man who was "exceedingly bashful" asks them: "Do not force him to address the congregation. It is like shedding his blood" (TS 8.71, l. 5 [a fragment]).

CHAPTER VI: *Education and the Professional Class*

1. PRELIMINARY CONSIDERATIONS

[1] An account of Jewish education according to the Geniza papers, as far as they had been studied by me until spring, 1961, is included in my *Jewish Education in*

Muslim Countries, Based on Records from the Cairo Geniza (Jerusalem, 1962) (in Heb.). A second, enlarged, edition is in preparation. My "Jewish Education in Yemen as an Archetype of Traditional Jewish Education," *Between Past and Future* (Jerusalem, 1953), pp. 1–38 (in English) is also relevant. The *Educational Encyclopedia,* Vol. IV, *History of Education,* ed. Martin Buber, asst. ed. H. Y. Ormian (Jerusalem, 1964), contains a complete account of Jewish education, including bibliographies.

On Muslim education:

A. S. Tritton, *Materials on Muslim Education in the Middle Ages* (London, 1957), quoted hereafter as Tritton, *Muslim Education.* An original and valuable contribution.

Bayard Dodge, *Muslim Education in Medieval Times* (Washington, 1962).

——— *Al-Azhar, A Millenium of Muslim Learning* (Washington, 1961).

"Madrasa" (J. Pedersen) in *Shorter Encyclopaedia of Islam* (Leiden, 1953).

George Makdisi, "Muslim Institutions of Learning in Eleventh-Century Baghdad," *BSOAS,* 24 (1961), 1–56.

Ahmad Shalabi, *History of Muslim Education with Special Reference to Egypt* (Beirut: Dar al-Kashshāf, 1954).

G. E. von Grunebaum and T. M. Abel, *Az-Zarnūjī, Instruction of the Student: The Method of Learning* (New York, 1947).

M. Abdul Muʻid Khan, "The Muslim Theories of Education during the Middle Ages," *Islamic Culture* (Hyderabad, India), 18 (1944), 418–433.

Khalil A. Totah, *The Contributions of the Arabs to Education* (New York, 1926).

On Christian higher education in the East:

Arthur Vööbus, *History of the School of Nisibis* (Louvain, 1965).

2. ELEMENTARY STAGE

[1] Bodl. MS Heb. d 66 (Cat. 2878), f. 6*v,* ll. 5–6.

[2] TS 18 J 3, f. 19, ll. 16–19, 32–33*.

[3] TS 12.243, l. 26, *Nahray* 139.

[4] TS 10 J 19, f. 10, l. 12, and nn. 34, 40, below. Missing the school: TS NS Box 320, f. 6. The father sent a *jūkhāniyya mulḥam,* a material of silk mixed with another thread, for the boy (see *Med. Soc.,* I, 418, n. 25).

[5] Mosseri A 17, see *Med. Soc.,* I, 177.

[6] Maimonides, *Responsa,* I, 50.

[7] Education: *ḥaqq al-taʻlīm,* which might include payments for a teacher of female arts, since there were two boys and a girl. TS 16.134*v* (fall, 1044).

[8] Shabbat 119*b*; trans., e.g., *Rabbinic Anthology,* p. 520.

[9] According to the ritual of the Babylonian (Iraqian) Jews, which later was generally accepted, the Pentateuch is read in the course of one year. According to the Palestinian ritual, however, which was adhered to in the synagogue of the Palestinians in Old Cairo during the major part of the Geniza period, it was read during three and a half years. Consequently, the sections to be read each week by any of the seven or so persons called up were far shorter. This proved to be a powerful attraction for parents who wished their children to publicly chant portions of the weekly Scripture lection. TS 18 J 4, f. 12.

[10] Bodl. MS Heb. b 3 (Cat. 2806, no. 24), f. 26, margin, *India Book* 193. The copyist of the letter was of course the teacher of the boy.

[11] TS Arabic Box 30, f. 36*.

[12] Tritton, *Muslim Education,* p. 147.

[13] ULC Or 1081 J 4*. The letter was written, of course, because the desired goal was not reached.

[14] TS Arabic Box 30, f. 36*. A similarly disappointed father.

[15] TS 8 J 41, f. 11, l. 22, verso, ll. 8–9+*. An orphan boy honored with the task.

[16] TS NS J 2*. Damīra, Lower Egypt, Feb., 1244.

[17] I.e., in school. For the synagogue as a school building see below.

[18] S. Assaf, *Source-book for the History of Jewish Education* (Heb.) (Tel Aviv, 1931), II, 5. Al-Mutawakkil: discussed of late in G. E. von Grunebaum, *Studien* (Zürich, 1969), p. 343, n. 52.

[19] TS NS J 401 (21): *al-basqāt wal-dhāqāt; baqs* is no doubt Greek *abax,* abacus, accounting instrument, although I have not found the word in an Arabic dictionary; *dhāqāt,* derived from Greek *deka,* ten, as suggested by Professors Franz Rosenthal and Otto Spies.

[20] TS 13 J 23, f. 20(+)*. A facsimile of this responsum in Goitein, *Education,* facing p. 9. E. Ashtor, *Bibliotheca Orientalis,* 20 (1963), no. 314, points out that the method of teaching reading "without the alphabet" was recommended by a Jewish pedagogue in Spain in the thirteenth century (see M. Güdemann, *Das jüdische Unterrichtswesen in der spanisch-arabischen Periode* [Vienna, 1873], p. 58).

[21] Single fragments of children's exercise books are found in several collections of Geniza papers. TS Box K 5 contains a whole collection of them.

[22] To be sure, some scholars also had the habit of signing in monumental and not in cursive script. This was most probably done in order to differentiate the signature from the text (which was normally written in cursive), and perhaps also in order not to put to shame cosigners unfamiliar with the cursive script. In any case, the signature of a scholar or merchant stands out by its regularity and pleasant shape from those written by persons untrained in writing.

[23] According to Ibn Khaldūn, *Muqaddima,* chap. 6, sec. 31, this was the system of instruction in the Muslim East. In the West, according to him, calligraphy formed an integral part of the regular curriculum.

[24] TS NS Box 323, f. 13, a much effaced fragment.

[25] TS 13 J 8, f. 5, top, *Nahray* 180.

[26] Literary models: TS Arabic Box 54, fs. 25, 46; TS Arabic Box 18(1), f. 128. Also the "Common-Place Book," mentioned in sec. 11, n. 16, below. Baghdad: communication by Dr. Murad Michael, details in Goitein, *Education,* p. 45 n. 24.

[27] Antonin 1105, ed. S. D. Goitein, *Tarbiz,* 35 (1966), 274–277, with facsimile, is an exception.

[28] TS 16.179*.

[29] Bodl. MS Heb. d 37 (Cat. 2603), f. 1, dated 1044, a complete copy of the Pentateuch bought by Yiḥye b. Hillel for his "dear son Tobias, the lovely flower, the holy one"; *ibid.,* d 44 (Cat. 2624), f. 3, a section of the book of Ezekiel written for two boys by their teacher. TS 20.131: a father returns a Pentateuch which he had bought for his son at the price of 45 dirhems because its size was too small and its letters too minute.

[30] Brotherly united: *hā-'aḥīm ha-ne'eḥīm ba-tōrā.* E. Ben Yehuda, *Thesaurus Totius Hebraitatis,* I, 143, notes this form only from Piyyūṭ poetry.

[31] Antonin 521, ed. Mann, *Texts,* I, 455. First half of eleventh century.

[32] Books of teachers: TS NS J 425. Maimonides, *Responsa,* II, 424.

[33] ENA 4010, f. 1+*.

[34] TS 13 J 20, f. 3, l. 10, ed. Mann, II, 302; see *ibid.,* I, 239–240 (letter of a scholar on travel, giving detailed instructions for the education of his youngest son).

[35] DK XXIX*v*, Postscript, ll. 4–6, ed. Samuel Kandel, *Genizai kéziratok* (Budapest, 1909), p. v. Also in TS NS 320, f. 6 (see n. 4, above). Muslim schoolboys in Yemen wearing big turbans and displaying their large wooden writing boards in E. Mittwoch, *Aus dem Jemen* (Leipzig, n.d.), table xxv, an excellent photograph by the German-Jewish traveler Hermann Burchardt, who was murdered in Yemen on Dec. 19, 1909.

[36] TS Arabic Box 53, f. 65. D. H. Baneth helped me to understand this laconic note.

[37] TS Arabic Box 38, f. 1. Arabic *bswq* renders Heb. *pāsūq* in the sense of biblical text.

[38] ULC Or 1081 J 4*. See n. 13, above.

[39] TS 10 J 30, f. 9, l. 17. The writer of the letter is her husband, of course.

[40] TS 13 J 27, f. 22. The wording is noteworthy: ". . . *wahummū bi-'Elī bi'aklih wakiswatih wa'ilmih wakūnū bayyitūh 'ind 'ammih yuqrīh fi 'l-layl ziyādah 'alā 'ilm al-mu'allim walā turabbūh tarbiya radiyya.*" The writer, Ṭōviyāhū ha-Kohen b. Eli ha-Me'ulle, is the addressee of the letter listed in n. 35. The boy Eli mentioned here and there was his son. It seems, too, that this letter was sent not long after the receipt of DK XXIX and actually refers to it. But since its right half is torn off, its discussion is better deferred for the moment: the other half might turn up some day.

3. EDUCATION OF GIRLS. WOMEN TEACHERS

[1] TS 13 J 30, f. 6, l. 8* (girls attending synagogue). See also chap. v, D, 1, above.

[2] TS 13 J 22, f. 5 (a warm letter to an aunt with the request to read it to her). TS 12.262* (a woman in Tunisia, asking the mailman to read to her the letters sent by her brother from Egypt [*Med. Soc.*, I, 286]). TS 13 J 20, f. 22* (a woman "writing" to her brother, but the handwriting is of Ḥalfōn b. Manasse ha-Levi).

[3] TS 8 J 28, f. 7, ll. 13-14*. Brother and sister beat and curse each other all the time in school.

[4] Maimonides, *Responsa*, II, 524–525. See S. Assaf, *Source-book for the History of Jewish Education* (Tel Aviv, 1937), III, 2.

[5] TS 12.493*.

[6] Moshe Perlmann, *Samau'al al-Maghribī* (New York, 1964), Ar. text, p. 95, Eng. trans., p. 75.

[7] "Female copyist," *al-nāsikha*, ENA 4025, ll. 6–7, ed. S. M. Stern, *Sefunot*, 8 (1964), 149. This female copyist from the land of Kurdistan precedes another, better-known, learned Jewish woman from that remote region by 250 years (see Mann, *Texts*, I, 480–483.).

[8] Jacob Saphir, *Iben Safir* (Lyck, 1866), p. 102*a*.

[9] The sources in Baron, *History of the Jews*, V, 323 n. 89.

[10] ENA 2935, f. 17. Another dirge on that daughter praising her virtues of woman of valor *ibid.*, f. 16*v*.

[11] Tritton, *Muslim Education*, pp. 141–142.

[12] ENA Misc. 6*. When in a letter from Jerusalem (TS 8 J 19, f. 23, *Nahray* 150) a woman says: "I have also written a copy of this letter in Arabic characters," it is not certain—although it is not impossible—that she had written the letter with her own hand (see n. 1).

[13] *Med. Soc.*, I, 128.

[14] Maimonides, *Responsa*, I, 50–52.

[15] TS 13 J 6, f. 27*, l. 5, taken together with TS 8 J 11, f. 7*b*, l. 4 (App. A, sec. 32). See Goitein, *Education*, p. 90 n. 76.

[16] TS NS Box 320, f. 30*c* (App. B, sec. 63).

4. ORGANIZATION OF ELEMENTARY EDUCATION. ECONOMIC AND SOCIAL POSITION OF TEACHERS

[1] Bodl. MS Heb. c 28 (Cat. 2876), f. 52. For female relatives as assistant teachers see sec. 3, above.

[2] Partnership of teachers: first source mentioned in preceding note. Employee: TS 13 J 26, f. 7.

[3] The term "synagogue children" appears in the responsum of Hay Gaon referred to in sec. 2, n. 18, above. Our sources do not indicate whether the teaching was done

in the hall used for prayer or in adjacent rooms. Most probably, there was no uniformity of practice in this matter.

[4] Invitation of teacher and promise to pay him a minimum of 20 dirhems a week: TS 10 J 7, f. 14*v*, l. 18. ENA 4020, f. 1. Community in default of paying the teacher's salary: TS 12.55; TS 13 J 22, f. 9(+) (in both cases Qalyūb, about ten miles north of Cairo). See also n. 10.

[5] Goitein, *Education*, p. 77.

[6] Old Cairo: Bodl. MS Heb. d 66 (Cat. 2878), f. 62 (App. B, sec. 15); Jerusalem: Dropsie 392; Damascus: TS 20.92, sec. C, l. 7, ed. S. D. Goitein, *Eretz-Israel*, 8 (1967), 291. Baghdad: see chap. vii, sec. A, 3, end.

[7] TS 13 J 33, f. 8(+). Competition with a teacher from Tiberias: TS 13 J 28, f. 8, ll. 12–16.

[8] TS 12.360. The sender: (Abu 'l-Majd) "Uzziel, the servant of our late teacher and master Solomon." The judge: Moses (b. Peraḥyā, see chap. v, sec. B, 1, nn. 53, 54). Taking care of their children: *man yaṣūn awlādhum.*

[9] ENA Uncatalogued 89, App. B, sec. 44.

[10] PER H 93, ed. D. H. Baneth, *Alexander Marx Jubilee Volume* (New York, 1940), Heb. sec., pp. 77 ff. (*Ibid.*, p. 88, ll. 17–18: *limā lahū 'alā awlādina min al-tarbiya.)*

[11] TS 13 J 6, f. 27* (2 dirhems per child and month, dated 1160). ENA Uncatalogued 89 (many similar items, also the reduction for three brothers). TS NS Box 321, f. 28 (12 dirhems during two months for three boys from different families). TS NS J 434 (½ dirhem per week paid according to the instructions of the Nagid Abraham Maimonides).

The long letter TS 10 J 18, f. 5, of the half-blind teacher Japheth reports that the community used to pay 4 dirhems per month for a certain child and his demands are approved in an endorsement written in Abraham Maimonides' own hand. But this was a special case. By his teaching the old man made only 16 dirhems per month. (He certainly also received bread and clothing, and probably also money for his poll tax.)

[12] Al-Maḥalla: ENA 4020, f. 1. See also n. 4, above. In the poor little community of Qalyūb only 8 dirhems per week were offered to a religious functionary, who had to combine the offices of teacher, cantor, and ritual slaughterer. In addition, they promised to assist him in accordance with their capabilities (*yusā'idūh fī ḍarūriyyātih ḥasb mā taṣil ilayh ṭāqathum*), most probably with regard to the payment of his poll tax. The teacher Abī Sa'īd (App. B, sec. 98) made only 7½ dirhems per week.

[13] DK 121, ed. A. Scheiber, *Sefunot*, 5 (1961), 463–466. The text is to be interpreted as done here.

[14] Present to the teacher on Hanukka: TS 12.425.

[15] School fees, *khamīs:* TS Box J 1, f. 47*d*, l. 11 (App. A, sec. 94, dated 1234). TS NS J 434. Maimonides, *Responsa*, I, 50.

[16] Payment of fees after death of teacher: TS Box K 25, f. 240, sec. 26 (dated 1218). No money after holidays: TS Arabic Box 18(1), f. 33.

[17] Illness and poll tax: Dropsie 410. Poll tax: TS Arabic Box 7, f. 22*v*. The teacher: Solomon b. Elijah.

[18] TS 13 J 21, f. 3. The couple also suffered because of insufficient clothing.

[19] *Med. Soc.*, I, 53–54.

[20] France: TS 13 J 26, f. 7; Dropsie 386+. Spain: ENA 4009, f. 8. Sicily: ENA 4020, f. 1. Morocco: TS 12.3*. Algeria (Qal'at Ḥammād): TS NS J 35(+). Tunisia: Bodl. MS Heb. c 28 (Cat. 2876), f. 52; TS 13 J 25, f. 11. Libya (Nafūsa): TS 24.44 (dated 1102), TS 16.334 (dated 1126), and often. Syria: some of the teachers, described as Shāmī, or Syro-Palestinian, might have come from the country known today as Syria. Mosul: TS NS J 191, l. 20.

[21] Bodl. MS Heb. d 66 (Cat. 2878), f. 29: *qana't bita'līm al-ṣibyān ḥattā lā aḥtāj ilā makhlūq.*

[22] TS 13 J 27, f. 11. Judah b. Aaron al-'Ammānī.

[23] Loans given by teachers: TS 24.29, ed. Mann, *Texts,* I, 369 (33 dinars); ULC Or 1080 J 81 (400 dirhems); TS 12.62 (200 dirhems, dated 1224). Bequest: TS 18 J 1, f. 13 (dated 1078). Slave girl: TS 8 J 8, f. 5 (dated 1217). House: TS 16.355 (1261).

[24] TS 24.38, a letter from Minyat Ziftā addressed to Abraham II Maimonides.

[25] Scribe for private person: Bodl. MS Heb. b 3 (Cat. 2806, no. 24), f. 26+. Teacher as court scribe: TS 13 J 4, f. 8; TS 12.39; and elsewhere. As copyist of books: TS 13 J 22, f. 9(+); INA D-55, f. 13, l. 12, ed. S. D. Goitein, *Tarbiz,* 36 (1966), 59–72.

[26] Calligraphers: Isaac (ha-melammēd) b. Ḥayyīm al-Nafūsī, TS 24.44 (dated 1102); Moses (ha-melammēd) b. Judah, TS 16.151 (1130). Judah b. Aaron al-'Ammānī (see n. 22, above), from whose hand we have a great many letters, wrote gracefully even when jotting down a hurried note.

[27] Teachers as booksellers: Dropsie 394: Isaac b. Ḥayyīm Nafūsī, see preceding note. Bodl. MS Heb. d 66 (Cat. 2878), f. 119+, TS 8 J 6, f. 7: Solomon b. Elijah, appearing as bookseller also in other documents.

[28] TS 13 J 6, f. 27*. Moses b. Judah, who signs as teacher in 1130 (see n. 26, above), calls himself cantor in 1141: ENA 2558, f. 3.

[29] The Song School was called originally *schola cantorum,* the school of the choristers, cf. William Boyd, *The History of Western Education* (London, 1952), p. 104.

[30] Mez, *Renaissance,* chap. 12, p. 177.

[31] Mia I. Gerhardt, *The Art of Story-Telling* (Leiden, 1963), pp. 383–384. One story makes the fine point that even an excellent scholar when descending to teaching children turns a fool.

[32] TS 10 J 16, f. 12+*.

[33] I noted at random twelve such signatures from the beginning of the eleventh century through the late thirteenth.

[34] E.G., TS 8 J 21, f. 6, l. 6+; TS 13 J 9, 3. 2+, address.

5. VOCATIONAL TRAINING

[1] In Judaism religious law imposed on a father the obligation to let his son learn a trade (Qiddushin 19*a*). For Islam see Tritton, *Muslim Education,* p. 22.

[2] TS 12.494. Banāt, the name of the wife is abbreviated from Sitt al-Banāt, "Queen of the Girls."

[3] TS 13 J 4, f. 7.

[4] A son of Judah b. Joseph Rōsh ha-Seder of Qayrawān apprenticing with the Tustaris of Fustat: TS 12.133; Mūsā Ibn al-Majjānī with Joseph Ibn 'Awkal: TS 12.566.

[5] TS 20.127, ll. 36–38. Written by Isma'īl b. Ya'qūb (= Samuel b. Jacob) al-Andalusī (family name derived from Spain) to Abu 'l-Surūr Yūsha' b. Nathan. A very valuable letter of seventy-nine lines. The writer's father wrote TS 16.7 and TS 20.76 to the same address. By letting his boy apprentice with the addressees he would create business relations through three consecutive generations (see n. 10, below).

[6] TS 13 J 29, ll. 23, ed. S. D. Goitein, *Tarbiz,* 38 (1969), 30–37. Unfortunately, the edition is marred by a number of misprints. In l. 23, I complemented *ra'yak al-*[*sadīd*], see the translation, but *s* was omitted, which makes the reading senseless. For similar relationships see *Med. Soc.,* I, 93 and 163–165.

[7] *Tilmīdh,* pupil: TS Box K 15, f. 96, col. IV, l. 29 (App. B, sec. 8). *Mu'allim,* teacher: TS 12.566, ll. 14–15. *Tarbiya,* education: Bodl. MS Heb. a 2 (Cat. 2805), f. 17, l. 58*.

[8] Dropsie 389*v*, II. 47–55: *lī 'alayh tarbiya.*

[9] TS 10 J 9, f. 24, l. 10, *India Book* 55; TS 8 J 7, f. 23, *India Book* 219.
[10] TS 20.76, l. 37 (see n. 5, above).

6. ADULT EDUCATION

[1] Even while in school, a boy was expected to make additional studies (see sec. 2, above, end). Illumination of synagogue: chap. v, sec. B, 2, n. 76. Studying until daybreak: ENA 2804, f. ?, l. 6, ed. Mann, II, 89.

[2] TS 12.9; TS 16.196, TS 20.125, all referring to the same affair, and written around 1100. The courses are called here *fuṣūl,* lit., chapters, which is a translation of Hebrew *perāqīm.* For the latter see Mann, *Texts,* I, 195–199. About the Egyptian sycamores see *Med. Soc.,* I, 121.

[3] TS 10 J 17, f. 25, margin. A complaint that "study in the synagogue" had come to a standstill in a letter to a late Nagid, TS 28.10.

[4] TS 8 J 18, f. 29, mentioned by J. Braslavsky, *Eretz-Israel,* 3 (1954), 207*b.*

[5] Sassoon 713 (dated 1148)+.

[6] TS 16.179*.

[7] Mosseri L 268. The word lecture used here is *nawba,* "a repeated performance," which is an appropriate term, and occurs also in Dropsie 354*v,* l. 8 (early eleventh century), but seems not to be registered in any Arabic dictionary in this sense.

[8] TS 6 J 7, f. 3, ll. 14–15+. The word used here: *mī'ād,* also appears in Muslim sources in the meaning of "une leçon religieuse," Dozy, *Supplément,* II, 882*a,* bottom. For the Fatimid classes on Monday and Thursday, see al-Qalqashandī, *Ṣubḥ* (Cairo, 1913), III, 487, *EI,* (1936), III, 411, s.v. "Masdjid," F. 2.

[9] TS 20.138*v,* ll. 5–26. In Goitein, *Education,* p. 35, I took "synagogue," l. 4 from bottom, as meaning "school"; but this is unlikely since kuttāb is used in this sense a few lines before.

[10] Tinnīs: Bodl. MS Heb. d 66 (Cat. 2878), f. 58.

[11] TS 8.29. The Maecenas: Abu 'l-Munē (voweled thus) Ya'qūb b. Banīn.

[12] TS Arabic Box 7, f. 13. Abu 'l-'Alā' al-Kohen and his father Segan (ha-Kōhanīm).

[13] TS 12.190, *India Book* 108*b*; TS 10 J 9, f. 24*v,* (different from recto) *India Book* 224.

7. HIGHER STUDIES: ORGANIZATION

[1] Additional details in Goitein, *Education,* chap. 7, and *Educational Encyclopedia,* IV, 228–238 (S. D. Goitein) (see sec. 1, n. 1, above). The material contained in my articles in *Tarbiz,* 31–34 (1962–1964), was edited after the writing of those chapters.

[2] Yeshiva is Hebrew. Its Arabic name *mathība* is derived from the Aramaic *methivta,* which has the same meaning as yeshiva.

[3] *Ḥavūrā*: e.g., Westminster College, Frag. Cairens. 103*b,* ed. Mann, II, 362, l. 2 (around 1060); Mann has no MS mark. *Ḥavūrat ha-ṣedeq*: e.g., Mosseri A 43, ed. J. Mann, *HUCA,* 3 (1926), 279. S. Schechter, *JQR,* 13 (1900–1901), 365. "The Holy Corporation of Justice," *ibid.,* p. 364. For "The Great Sanhedrin" cf. H. Mantel, *Studies in the History of the Sanhedrin,* Harvard Semitic Series, 17 (Cambridge, 1962).

[4] In the Geniza period called *gemār,* as the Yemenites still do, and not gemāra, as commonly used in Hebrew today (see *Webster's New International Dictionary,* 3d ed., s.v. "Gemara"), TS 8 J 15, f. 17, l. 18+ (a letter); in booklists: TS NS Box 228, f. 3, l. 7, ed. N. Allony, *Kirjath Sepher,* 43 (1968), 135 n. 7, where additional references.

[5] The German Jewish traveler: Petaḥya of Regensburg (Ratisbon), in A. Kahana, *Jewish Historical Literature* (Warsaw, 1922), p. 221 (in Heb.). Tritton, *Muslim*

Education, p. 35. Tritton uses the word *amōrā,* which is a more ancient term for the *(me)turgeman,* the broadcaster of the words of a scholar teaching a large audience. For the Muslim office of the *mustamlī* (lit., the one who asks the lecturer to let him dictate his words to the students), see the detailed study of Max Weisweiler, "Das Amt des Mustamli in der Arabischen Wissenschaft," *Oriens,* 4 (1951), 27–57, where further literature is cited. The Muslims had other words for the broadcaster, e.g., *muballigh,* lit., the one who makes the words of the lecturer reach the audience (see *ibid.,* p. 38).

[6] See *Med. Soc.,* I, 13–14.

[7] A recent discussion of the office and title rōsh ha-sēder in Abramson, *Bamerkazim,* pp. 107–108. In the important letter TS 13 J 17, f. 16*v,* l. 14+, addressed (in Arabic letters) to the Palestinian Gaon Nathan b. Abraham around 1041, a man from Bānyās claims this title. Groups of dignitaries mentioned in letters of the Gaons: Mann, *Texts,* I, 79, 98, 108, 133.

[8] Public lecturers: *rāshē perāqīm,* see sec. 6, n. 2. Group leaders: *rāshē sī'ā.* For Oria, see *Megillat Aḥīma'aṣ,* ed. Benjamin Klar (Jerusalem, 1954), p. 36.

[9] To be sure, the European Jews also read the Talmud with a certain singsong. But this was intended to emphasize the sequence of the talmudic discussions (question, answer, new argument by a third participant, and so on), not the correct pronunciation of the words. It seems that the cantillation of the Talmud had its origin in the institution of the *(me)turgeman.* While the lecturer himself spoke in an ordinary tone, the broadcaster, who repeated the latter's words in a loud voice, accompanied them with a singsong, a custom apparently disapproved by the masters of the Talmud themselves, as may be concluded from the puns on Ecclesiastes 7:5 and 9:17: "The words of the wise are spoken quietly"—this refers to the lecturer—"[They] are more acceptable than the shouting of the preacher addressing the fools"—"This refers to the [me]turgemans, who speak in a loud voice with a singsong so that they may be heard by the masses": *Kohelet Rabba,* referring to the biblical passages cited. To be sure, the reading of a holy *text* (the Bible and the Mishnah) with cantillation is an age-old custom.

[10] D. Kaufmann and D. H. Mueller, *Mitteilungen aus der Sammlung Erzherzog Rainer,* 5 (1892), 128–129, discussed in Mann, I, 108–109; see also *ibid.,* p. 273. In this letter, ll. 30–33, the community of Fustat asks of the Gaon that his answer be signed also by the president of the court and by the Third.

[11] S. Schechter, *JQR,* 13 (1901–1902), 365, see Mann, I, 277 n. 1.

[12] Gottheil-Worrell, XLIII, pp. 196–201, see Mann, *Texts,* I, 331–332. By oversight, Gottheil-Worrell gives the date as 1043 and Mann, on p. 332, as 1041. A letter sent from Jerusalem around 1065 speaks of both the bēth ha-midrāsh and the midrāsh of the Gaon in that city (TS 13 J 9, f. 3).

[13] "At the request of the community": *'an ikhtiyār al-jamā'a* (TS 13 J 36, f. 5, l. 3). See *ibid.,* ll. 24–26. A number of other unedited letters of Solomon b. Judah were written in Ramle. But in the passage from the letter of the Gaon Joshia, TS 12.16*v,* l. 4, partly ed. Mann, II, 71, the manuscript has *'ṣl 'b,* and not *'ṣlynw,* i.e., *ēṣel āv bi-mdīnat Ramle:* the Gaon had appointed the man recommended in the letter as assistant judge to the president of the court who had his seat in Ramle.

[14] The name of the Muslim scholar, "the head of the Shāfi'īs in the whole of Palestine and Syria," was Abu 'l-Fatḥ Naṣr b. Ibrāhīm, see al-Yāfi'ī, *Mir'āt al-Janān, (Hyderabad,* 1899–1900), III, 152–153, S. D. Goitein, "Jerusalem during Its Arab Period" (Heb.), *Yerushalayim,* 4 (1952), 102.

[15] See chap. v, sec. A, 1, nn. 32, 33, above.

[16] *Med. Soc.,* I, 51–54.

[17] P. Heid. 910*v,* ll. 14–15, ed. A. S. Kamenetzky, *REJ* 55 (1908), 48–53, reedited Abramson, *Bamerkazim,* p. 110. Ban on Elhanan: TS NS Box 320, f. 16, ll. 6, 10–13+.

[18] After the death of his father Elhanan tried to reestablish his bēth ha-midrāsh at the height of al-Ḥākim's persecution (Bodl. MS Heb. a 3 [Cat. 2873], f. 21, ll.

28–41, ed. Mann, II, 39). A mat, 12 cubits long and 3-1/2 cubits wide, was made in Alexandria for Elhanan's midrāsh (TS 12.34, l. 8, ed. S. D. Goitein, *Tarbiz,* 32 [1968], 271, see Abramson, *Bamerkazim,* pp. 170–171).

[19] TS 10 J 17, f. 25*v*, ll. 5–6. I take the words *we-khol ha-talmīdīm ha-mitqabbeṣīm el midrāshō* as meaning "and all the other scholarly persons who assemble in your midrāsh."

[20] TS NS Box 246, f. 22, ll. 39–41+: *rōsh ha-medabberīm sār ha-midrāsh.* In the same list of notables, ll. 30–31, there is also a "president of the congregations" who is styled "prince of the yeshiva" namely the Palestinian yeshiva, which at that time (around 1142) had its seat in Cairo.

[21] P. Heid. 910*v*, l. 19+: *ha-shimmūsh yether min ha-limmūd.* The principle that personal contact with scholars was "greater" than mere study is of course talmudic (Berakhot 7*b*, bottom, a saying by R. Yohanan using almost the same language as that found here).

[22] TS 10 J 1 (this is a separate volume containing a copy of Sherira's pastoral letter). The passage ed. in Schechter, *Saadyana,* p. 120, see Shaked, *Bibliography,* p. 97. Discussed in detail by Mann, *Texts,* I, 86-87. Naturally, Mann's acceptance of the story of the four captives who were the founders of the schools in Spain, Tunisia, and Egypt, is to be discarded (see Gerson D. Cohen, "The Story of the Four Captives," *PAAJR,* 29 [1960–1961], 55–131).

[23] See Shraga Abramson, *R. Nissim Gaon* (Jerusalem, 1965), a monumental trial to reconstruct, mainly with the aid of a tremendous number of Geniza remnants, the works of the master, which have come down to us either in late versions or in fragments. The reader not familiar with Hebrew is referred to the important review of the book by George Vajda, *REJ,* 125 (1966), 422–426.

[24] In view of Hananel's eminence the occurrence of his name in the documentary Geniza is curiously scarce. E.g., TS 8 J 25, f. 3 (reference to a legal opinion of his [see *Med. Soc.,* I, 52]); chap. v, A, 2, n. 8 (mentioned before the Nagid and lauded for his probity); ULC Or 1080 J 7, l. 11 (his house in Qayrawān). His connections, I assume, were mainly with Spain and other European countries. According to Abraham Ibn Daud, *The Book of Tradition,* ed. Gerson D. Cohen (Philadelphia, 1967), p. 77, he had nine daughters but no son. He became very rich (leaving 10,-000 dinars, presumably after having married off most of his daughters) because the merchants of Qayrawān let him partake of their lucrative business ventures as silent partner (this, I believe, is the meaning of the Hebrew phrase, and not merely "they showered him with capital").

[25] See the newly edited Geniza letters cited in n. 1, above.

[26] ENA 191(2559)(+). For the Islamic equivalent, see *EI* (1936), III, 402, s.v. "Masdjid," D, 2, h. The question submitted to Maimonides: *Responsa,* II, 545.

[27] E.g., TS 10 J 18, f. 22*v*, ll. 6–8: the cantor Joseph b. Nādīv of Bilbays who had a grown-up son for whom he had to pay the poll tax writes to the judge Elijah b. Zechariah (whose teaching activities are often referred to): if you wish that I devote myself exclusively to study (*an naq'ud baṭṭāl,* lit., sit doing no remunerative work), I shall do so, come to Fustat and read with you Ḥullin, Qiddushim (thus!) and Giṭṭim (three sections of the Talmud, dealing with marital law and ritual killing of animals, respectively). See also sec. 8, n. 3, below.

[28] MS Schechter *9+, as cited in Shaked, *Bibliography,* p. 49. A letter from Elijah ha-Kohen b. Abraham, judge of Palmyra, to Jacob, member of the (Palestinian) academy, son of the president of the court Joseph, in Aleppo. This Jacob b. Joseph had earlier entertained the writer in Fustat, where we find him indeed signing documents in 1016 and 1018, but emigrated (or returned) to Aleppo, where he became the local dayyān (first dated document: 1028) (see Mann, I, 37). The interesting letter TS 12.252, addressed to him, seems to have been sent from the environment of Aleppo.

The phrase "appointed from the gate (i.e., the court) of *ha-nesī'ūt*" in the signature of the judge of Palmyra can only refer to the exilarch Hezekiah, who is mentioned in l. 35, and ahead of Hay Gaon. Both are credited with having sent letters of appointment to the writer.

[29] Such a case in Sassoon 713, ll. 24–25+, see sec. 6, n. 5, above.

[30] TS 16.293, ll. 20–22. "Studied with," *mushtaghil ma'a.*

8. HIGHER STUDIES: SYLLABUS AND METHODS

[1] TS K 3, f. 1, ed. S. Assaf, *Kirjath Sepher,* 18 (1941), 61–66. About the author, Joseph rōsh ha-seder b. Jacob, see N. Allony, *ibid.,* 38 (1963), 531–557, where further relevant literature and, especially, A. Scheiber, "Materialien zur Wirksamkeit des Joseph B. Jakob Habavli als Schriftsteller und Kopist," *Acta Orientalia Hungarica,* 23 (1970), 115–130.

[2] See *Med. Soc.,* I, 67.

[3] Bodl. MS Heb. c 28 (Cat. 2876), f. 28. See also Strauss, *Mamluks,* II, 392.

[4] TS 18 J 4, f. 3, ll. 13–35, ed. S. D. Goitein, *Har'el, Alshaykh Memorial Volume* (Tel Aviv, 1962), pp. 140–141.

[5] Famous examples of responsa having the size of a book are the prayerbook of Amram Gaon, sent around A.D. 870 to Barcelona, Spain, and the history of the schools of Babylonia, written in 987 by Sherira Gaon as a reply to a request from "the holy congregation of al-Qayrawān."

[6] See Baron, *History of the Jews,* VI, 115–116. Against the background revealed by the Geniza find, Baron perhaps might have judged less harshly about Ibn Migash's decision. (Baron calls him Ibn Megas, which might be more correct historically. I prefer the generally accepted traditional pronunciation of the name.)

[7] TS 13 J 26, f. 11, *India Book* 114, trans. in Goitein, *Education,* pp. 167–169.

[8] TS Loan 4, f. 5, ll. 1–4, ed. Mann, *Texts,* I, 174: "Although a student begins by 'reading' the Torah, he is obliged to memorize *(lishnōt)* the Mishnah and the Talmud and later to study *(lisbōr)* and to discuss them, as Rāvā [fourth century] has said: first learn by heart (*ligmār,* hence Gemara), then study." From a pastoral letter by Israel Gaon, son of the scholarly prominent Samuel b. Ḥofnī Gaon. It should be noted that Rāvā was famous for the excellence of his reasoning.

When the Gaon Samuel b. Eli recommended his son-in-law as spiritual leader to the community of Aleppo (1191), he noted in particular that he knew most of the Mishna and Talmud by heart (S. Assaf, *The Letters of Samuel b. Eli* [Jerusalem, 1930], p. 48, l. 4 from bottom).

[9] E.g., TS 10 J 1, ll. 9–11+, Schechter, *Saadyana,* p. 118. Sherira Gaon writes: "My son [a weak translation for *baḥūrēnū,* lit., our fine young man] Hay is very much devoted to the teaching of the students, putting into their mouth the questions, and those who do not know to ask any, he teaches the way problems are raised [in the Talmud], thus endearing to them the method of study."

[10] In this vein Sherira Gaon writes about Elhanan b. Shemarya, who had studied with him in Baghdad and was now back in Old Cairo, from where he sent his "questions" to his master: "Every letter which reaches us from him is better than the one preceding it and his new questions are continuously superior to the older ones—and all this while he is still young." Bodl. MS Heb. e 44 (Cat. 2668, no. 19), f. 81*v,* ll. 6–10, ed. Adolf Neubauer, *JQR,* 6 (1894), 222–224; re-ed. Mann, *Texts,* I, 104, who succeeded in piecing together three fragments complementing each other preserved in the University Library, Cambridge, the Bodleian, and the British Museum (but the beginning and end are still missing).

TS 20.49, ed. Abramson, *Bamerkazim,* pp. 123–130, an autograph by Elhanan b. Shemarya, addressed to Sherira Gaon and his son Hay, is an excellent example of a letter of queries: many questions from different fields, all briefly referred to in a fashion intelligible only to the initiated. Moreover, he asks for a full commentary on two tractates of the Talmud ("Vows" and "Idolatry," not belonging to the humdrum syllabus), but only of words and subject matter, not of "problems." Also see *ibid.* for second copies of certain answers sent from Baghdad via Fustat to a Qayrawānese scholar.

[11] TS 10 K 7, f. 2, ed. S. Assaf, *Tarbiz,* 11 (1940), 235 ff. About the use of the term *megillat setārīm* in general, see *ibid.*, p. 229 n. 7.

[12] The most comprehensive study on the subject: S. Abramson, *R. Nissim* (Jerusalem, 1965), xxxvi-xl, 181–360*f*. According to Abramson the title of R. Nissīm's book had the additional meaning of "Explanation of Obscure Passages."

9. SCHOLARS, JUDGES, PREACHERS

[1] Mishna Megilla 1: 3. The Arabic equivalent baṭṭāl in sec. vi, 7, n. 27, above.

[2] Instead of *benē* Torah one would also say *ba'alē* T., "those who have learning," e.g., TS 13 J 20, f. 13, l. 23+, or *anshē* T., "the men of the T," e.g., Bodl. MS Heb. e 98, f. 67, l. 9, *India Book* 266.

[3] TS 13 J 8, f. 25, l. 3 from bottom: *'ala 'l-baṭāla wal-qirāya.* Arabic *baṭāla* renders the Hebrew legal term *sekhar baṭṭāla* "compensation for not attending to one's own business."

[4] Bodl. MS Heb. c 28 (Cat. 2876), f. 6+, see *Med. Soc.* I, 54. The first word is *bn',* which can be taken either as Heb. *benē,* expressed with Imāla (i.e., *ā* for *ē*), or as an abbreviated Arabic *(a)bnā.*

The list is headed by Nahray b. Nissīm, and the first ḥāvēr mentioned is Ben Shema'ya, i.e., Abraham b. Shema'ya (App. D, sec. 12). The rayyis or Nagid heading "the Cairenes" was either Mevōrākh, or his opponent David b. Daniel. Ben Shema'ya signed documents also under the latter's authority (TS 16.77, TS 20.31).

For *'l-'sqwy* in l. 14 read *al-'Asqalānī,* no doubt identical with the cantor from Ascalon, mentioned in the contemporary list TS Misc. Box 8, f. 9, col. IV, l. 7 (App. B, sec. 18). This would bring the number of cantors to seven, if *al-ḥazzānīn* in l. 10 refers to *two* cantors only. Otherwise, their number would have been even greater.

[5] R(abbi) Abraham, l. 2, is almost certainly the Tunisian R. Abraham b. Isaac ha-Talmīd, who signed many documents in the years 1078 to 1093 as judge in Old Cairo (see App. D, sec. 10). Although he married in Old Cairo as early as January, 1050 (TS 20.7), many references in the Geniza betray him as a Tunisian. See *Med. Soc.*, I, 529, Index, s.v. Abraham, the Son of the Scholar.

[6] In Talmudic times, the term for degree was *minnuy* in Palestine and *semīkhūth* in Babylonia, see Palestinian Talmud Sanhedrin chap. 1, para. 1, p. 19*a,* l. 48. In the Geniza the terms are used interchangeably, e.g., minnuy in Babylonia in the letter cited in sec. 7, n. 28, above, and semīkhūth in Palestine in the two documents cited presently. The old usage: "In ancient times, each individual teacher licensed his own students. . . . Later on, honor was given to this house [of king David, namely to the family of the Nasi, or head of the Jewish community in Palestine during its Roman period, which claimed to be descended from the royal house of Judah]. A license issued by the Nasi was valid even without the consent of the court [namely, of the yeshiva]). Finally, it was resolved that a license had to be given both in the name of the court and the Nasi." (Palestinian Talmud, *loc. cit.,* ll. 49–56). In Geniza times: TS 12.328(+), *ha-sāmūkh ba-yeshīvā mippī rabbē ha-yeshīva,* "licensed in the yeshiva by the masters of the yeshiva"; TS 12.722+. Licensed by both the exilarch and the schools: sec. 7, n. 28, above.

[7] For Muslim "permissions" see Tritton, *Muslim Education,* pp. 40–46 and 201. In the al-Azhar of Cairo no official diploma was granted until 1872 (B. Dodge, *Al-Azhar* [Washington, 1961], p. 198).

[8] E.g., in Spain, MS Sassoon 713+, l. 20. The word used here is *minnuy* (cf. n. 6).

[9] Maimonides, *Responsa,* II, 591–592.

[10] S. Assaf, *The Letters of Samuel b. Eli* (Jerusalem, 1930), p. 49, first line.

[11] ENA 2592, ll. 3 and 11, ed. Mann, II, 313; TS 24.78*v*, l. 10*, ed. S. D. Goitein,

Gibb Presentation Volume (Leiden, 1965), pp. 270–284. The title *me'uttād la-ḥavūrā* should not be confused with *m. līshīvā,* which means candidate for the *presidency* of the academy (Mann, II, 234, bottom).

[12] TS 13 J 14, f. 16* (Mann, II, 116, provides only the address of the letter). See chap. v, B, 1, n. 95. The end of this interesting letter has not yet been found; as often happened, the second leaf which was pasted on the bottom of the first, was separated from it by moisture or otherwise.

[13] ENA 2806, f. 9*v*, ll. 7–8, *India Book* 205, ed. Mann, I, 278, where *we-liqrō bi-shmō* refers to the title conferred by the yeshiva.

[14] *Nahray,* passim: *gedōl ha-yeshīvā.* ENA 2805, f. 23: *gedōl ha-ḥavērīm.*

[15] The five leaders styled *me'ulle ba-ḥavūrā,* lit., the most prominent member of the corporation, were Nathan ha-Levi b. Yeshū'ā, Ephraim b. Shemarya, Eli b. Amram, and the brothers Judah and Mevōrākh, the sons of Saadya, who were also the first to be called Nagid. Details must be given only about the first, since the other four are mentioned throughout this book. Nathan ha-Levi he-ḥāvēr ha-me'ulle b. Yeshū'ā signed first (TS 20.7; Fustat, Jan., 1050 [see Shaked, *Bibliography,* p. 72]) above such a luminary as Judah b. Saadya, the later Nagid. He signed five other documents first, all incompletely preserved: Bodl. MS Heb. c 28 (Cat. 2876), f. 30* (fall, 1040; the name seemingly preceding his is that of the scribe who also was a party to the contract), above Ephraim b. Shemarya, the head of the Palestinians of Fustat; Bodl. MS Heb. b 12 (Cat. 2875), f. 13*b,* above Sahlān b. Abraham, head of the Iraqians in the same city; TS 8.187 (no title); TS 16.111 (he signs ḥāvēr, but is referred to as me'ulle in the validation of the court whose first signatory is [Judah b. Saady]a ha-Rōfē, the physician [see above]); TS 16.184 (signing as me'ulle). No doubt, Nathan was the head of the Cairene community who was sometimes visited and assisted by colleagues from neighboring Fustat (see chap. vii, B, 1), and, on exceptional occasions officiated in Fustat, e.g., at the wedding of Abraham, the Son of the Scholar (TS 20.7 [see App. D, sec 8]).

[16] Bodl. MS Heb. f 56, f. 130 (Cat. 2821, no. 40), l. 13, verso, 12+ (App. A 128).

[17] Tyre: TS 10 J 12, f. 25+, signed by Samuel he-ḥāvēr ha-me'ulle b. Moses he-ḥāvēr. Ascalon: TS 10 J 5, f. 21, top, l. 7: greetings from Yeshū'ā he-ḥāvēr ha-me'ulle, who is called dayyān in the signature of his son Japheth (TS 16.122 [App. A, sec. 17]). In the same document another me'ulle leads that community at a different period. Baniyas: Bodl. MS Heb. d 75, f. 13 (May, 1112), see chap. v, sec. A, 2, n. 37. Mann, II, 202–203 excerpts a few lines.

[18] Joseph of Maḥalla: sources in chap. vi, sec. 6, n. 2, above. The father of his contemporary Manasse, who was the spiritual leader of another provincial town in Egypt. Sa'adyāhū ha-me'ulle ba-ḥavūrā, was probably a Palestinian: TS 13 J 6, f. 21 (mark of MS and name wrong in Mann, II, 232).

[19] E.g., TS Box K 15, f. 8: Judah ha-me'ulle b. Ephraim ha-shōfēṭ, a father of four sons, heading a pedigree in a memorial list.

[20] TS NS Box 246, f. 22, l. 7+ (App. C, sec. 26): Nathan ha-Kohen (b. Solomon), see App. D, sec. 16; l. 13: Nathan, "the Diadem" (b. Samuel), App. D, sec. 17; Manasse al-Ṣadr (i.e., chief judge). The epithet Pious was given to dead persons, but very rarely to living ones, except when they actually adopted a pietist way of life. Sullamī (MS: *swlmy*) may mean simply a maker of ladders and wooden staircases, but could also have been the designation of a pietist, namely, one ascending on the ladder of mystical progress, as the Greek equivalent *klimax* was used by the gnostics. If this explanation applies, our me'ulle would have been the continuator of his father's work.

[21] TS 20.118*v*: Judah ha-Kohen b. Ṭōviyāhū he-ḥāvēr ha-me'ulle in Sammanūd, Lower Egypt (slightly before 1176), whose son Ṭōviyāhū was dayyān of al-Maḥalla and Sammanūd (TS 10 J 17, f. 25) and another son, David, of Malīj (Bodl. MS Heb. d 66 [Cat. 2878], f. 63). The family might have been descendants of the dayyān of

Baniyas in Palestine (see n. 17, above). TS 13 J 16, f. 5: Judge Elijah writes to David ha-Kohen ha-me'ulle, who probably was judge in Alexandria (ca. 1210).

[22] Six out of the nine instances listed by H. Z. Hirschberg for the term *talmīd* in *I. F. Baer Jubilee Volume* (Jerusalem, 1960), p. 146 n. 24, belong to one person, namely, to Abraham, "the Son of the Scholar" (see n. 5, above). Two of the remaining three belong to the thirteenth century. Other references: TS 13 J 3, f. 21 (dated 1210); TS K 15, f. 18*v*, margin (1335); TS 13 J 8, f. 25, l. 23 (before 1241). It is characteristic that in the genealogical list TS 8 K 22, f. 1, ed. Mann, II, 320, the title appears in three successive generations, preceded by three generations of fellows of the academy and one judge. Talmīd in rank below ḥāvēr: TS 20.94, l. 24, also ll. 28–29+.

[23] See sec. 7, n. 7.

[24] E.g., *Eli he-ḥāvēr ha-qavū'a be-miṣrayim,* ENA 3765, f. 8+ (ca. 1057).

[25] TS 20.141, ll. 41–42, ed. Mann, II, 235.

[26] TS Box K 3, f. 32.

[27] TS NS J 236*: the judge Nathan ha-Kohen b. Solomon asks his younger colleague, judge Nathan b. Samuel (see n. 20, above) to outline for him a funeral oration for a lady which he was supposed to deliver on the following day.

[28] See chap. v, sec. C, 1, end.

[29] See J. Mann's study about Isaac b. Samuel ha-Sefāradī in *Tarbiz,* 6 (1935), 75–78. Mann erroneously thought that he was the one who asked the questions. The full text of a long responsum sent by him to Yemen is found in *RIF, Ḥullīn,* ed. Joseph Qāfeḥ (Jerusalem, 1960), pp. 91–93. For another learned opinion of his see sec. 2, n. 20, above.

[30] For the responsa of Joseph Ibn Abitur see Assaf, *Texts,* p. 116. His famous elegy on the terrors of anarchy in Palestine refers to the events of the years 1025–1027, not to al-Ḥākim's persecution (see the article quoted in *Med. Soc.,* I, 405 n. 94). The historically correct pronunciation of the name is probably Abī Thawr, but for easier identification I retain the traditional spelling.

[31] Bodl. MS Heb. c 13 (Cat. 2807, no. 16), f. 20, ed. Mann, II, 242–245. At that time another Tunisian scholar, and not yet Nahray, was the leading Jewish scholar in Old Cairo (cf. *ibid.,* verso, ll. 13, 23). TS 13 J 21, f. 2, *Nahray* 28: this letter is superscribed *Fatwā,* i.e., (request for a) legal opinion, and, it seems, was sent from the small Egyptian town Malīj, in which reference is made to the courts of Acre, Palestine, and Tyre, Lebanon. A query to Yehiel: ULC OR 1080 J 67. Anatoli: TS NSJ 326 (only the beginning is preserved).

[32] *Med. Soc.,* I, 52.

[33] TS 20.141, ll. 24–27+.

[34] Called *darshān* and also *dārōsh* (TS Misc. Box 25, f. 106), both designating a man expounding the Scriptures.

[35] For the Muslim preachers see the extensive study of J. Pedersen in *I. Goldziher Memorial Volume* (Budapest, 1948), I, 226–251.

[36] See the source quoted by Mann, *Texts,* I, 402–403 n. 19.

[37] TS 13 J 11, f. 9+. The locality (Ṭaṭay) is well known from a considerable number of Geniza Texts. The correction suggested in Mann, I, 109 n. 1, should be dropped.

[38] TS 16.149*. Although the beginning and the end of the long letter is lost, it gives an excellent picture of the performance of a visiting preacher.

[39] TS 13 J 20, f. 13, ll. 12–14+. The writer also quotes the verse from the Prophet Isaiah with which the preacher opened his sermon and the weekly lection from the Torah, but regrets that, because of lack of space, he was unable to summarize the sermon, called here (as often) *pitrōn,* interpretation of the biblical text.

[40] ULC Or 1080 J 23*. The letter displays an unusual intimacy between husband and wife. No doubt, the receiver, who was the daughter of the dayyān of al-

Maḥalla, knew how to read (and, I am sure, also between the lines, for the husband wanted her to join him in the capital, which she refused).

[41] TS 10 J 9, f. 32 (E.b.A.). By error, two manuscripts have been given the same mark. For easier identification I added "(E.b.A.)" to this one for the signature of Eli b. Amram at the bottom of the page. The manuscript is partly effaced (as interesting manuscripts often are).

[42] See chap. v, sec. D, n. 15, above. The Arabic invitation, ULC Or 1080 J 132, is signed *berīt ḥadāshā,* "New Covenant" (Jeremiah 31:31), meaning perhaps that the writer was not known personally to the addressee. The latter, Aaron b. Ephraim b. Ṭarsōn, calls himself parnās in TS 18 J 1, f. 6 (Cairo, May, 1028), and *memunne,* "officially appointed," in TS 20.6 (Sept., 1037), ed. Assaf, *Tarbiz* 9 (1938), 32. Neither Assaf nor Mann, II, 103, notes or makes mention of the many minuscule letters, written in zigzag above and beneath Ibn Ṭarsōn's signature. In order to save others the trouble of deciphering them, here they are: *hū Ḥalfōn nīn Ephraim yeḥayyēhū ēl 'ad yāvō gō'ēl,* "identical with Ḥalfōn, offspring of Ephraim, may God keep him alive until the Redeemer comes," which means that Aaron was originally called Ḥalfōn (or vice versa) and that his name was changed during a grave illness (the charm worked). This Cairene communal leader is addressed in several notes of Elhanan b. Shemarya. The peregrine preacher certainly had received the permission to appear in the synagogue from the local dayyān (who perhaps forgot to ask the parnās, which would explain the extremely entreating tone of the letter).

[43] TS 12.608(+). Details in Goitein, *Education,* pp. 134–135. Maimonides, *Commentary on the Mishnah,* Sanhedrin, 10, Introduction, ed. J. Qāfeḥ (Jerusalem, 1965), IV, 210.

[44] TS 8 J 5, f. 25, l. 7: a legal action to be taken by "Abraham the preacher and the elders of the holy congregation" (May 1, 1261). For cantors as preachers and community leaders and al-Qalqashandī's presentation see Mann, I, 268, and the literature quoted there, and sec. 10, below.

10. CANTORS AND OTHER RELIGIOUS FUNCTIONARIES

[1] TS 12.421. Letter by Joseph b. Jacob ha-ḥazzān (he signed JNUL 5, dated 1133; the epithet refers to the father) to the cantor of Malīj, Abu 'l-Ḥasan Japheth ha-Levi b. Eli: in accordance with the instructions of the elders, the Rōsh ha-qāhāl and "The Pride," and with the approval of the Nagid, in future another cantor would substitute for him every second Sabbath and every second weekday, but would not share his other privileges. In the same provincial town there were three cantors at a time according to TS 10 J 10 f. 13: *the* cantor, probably old, because he is mentioned before the dayyān; the cantor from Ascalon, and the *young* cantor Ibn al-Jāzifīnī, who also wrote the letter (dictated to him). On the free space verso a calendar for the year 1092, written presumably shortly after the receipt of the letter.

[2] Bodl. MS Heb. c 28 (Cat. 2876), f. 6+; TS NS Box 324, f. 132 (App. B, sec. 71*a*). Maimonides, *Responsa*: see n. 20, below.

[3] Bodl. MS Heb. c 28 (Cat. 2876), f. 30*.

[4] TS 13 J 6, f. 27* (where the widow of a cantor lets her boy study with another cantor).

[5] Bodl. MS Heb. a 3 (Cat. 2873), f. 2, margin, ll. 8–18, verso, ll. 1–4*: A judge (called here shōfēṭ) is blamed by the Nagid Mevōrākh for coercing the cantor of Damīra to use a ḥizāna, or liturgy for the Day of Atonement, which was composed by the well-known cantor of Alexandria, Ibn Nufay'. The Nagid remarks that the judge himself, who was a Palestinian, was not well versed in that liturgy.

[6] TS 13 J 21, f. 25, l. 18(+), where *wayyakketū* (Deuteronomy 1:44) has the note *dargā* instead of *merkhā*. Details in Goitein, *Education,* p .102.

[7] TS 18 J 4, f. 3, ll. 15–16+.

[8] INA D-55, f. 4*v*, ll. 7–9, dated 1221 and addressed to the judge Elijah b. Zechariah.

[9] E.g., Sakan-Shekhanya, the grandfather of Japheth b. David, so frequently mentioned in this book. From a query by Dr. Ezra Fleischer, dated Dec. 2, 1968, about the name Sakan, otherwise unknown in Hebrew letters, it appears that he had identified about fifteen liturgical poems with Sakan as acronym. This Arabic name is found in the address of the letter TS 13 J 35, f. 2 (see n. 19, below).

[10] TS Arabic Box 30, f. 250.

[11] DK 16. The concluding word of the refrain was to be *Elōhīm, God,* as in Numbers 23:27 and Exodus 1:17.

[12] ENA 1822, f. 53. The receiver is Abū Sahl, which was the kunya, or by-name of the father of the cantor Ḥalfōn b. Manasse ha-Levi. But that kunya is rather common. The poems were so-called *yōṣerōt.*

[13] The poem is recorded in I. Davidson, *Thesaurus of Mediaeval Hebrew Poetry* (New York, 1924), Aleph 5658.

[14] Vigils held during the night of the New Year holiday with lamentations for Isaac's self-sacrifice, a custom due perhaps to Shi'ite influence. Details in Goitein, *Education,* p. 100.

[15] TS 13 J 27, f. 11. Judah al-'Ammānī writing to the cantor Abu 'l-Majd Meir b. Yākhīn (see the Index).

[16] TS 10 J 26, f. 7. The cantor's name: Abū Sahl ha-Levi b. al-āhūv (i.e., "Friend of the Yeshiva"). See n. 12.

[17] TS Box 28, f. 131. Isaiah 65:1: "I offered myself to those who did not ask for me and was ready to be found by those who did not seek me."

[18] TS NS J 121. The letter was sent from Malīj, where the young man had to present himself to the local dayyān. He sends greetings to his teacher, also a ḥazzān.

[19] A collection, pesīqā, for the young ḥazzān Ḥusayn b. Da'ūd b. Sakan of Old Cairo in Acre (well known under the name Japheth b. David b. Shekhanya): TS 13 J 35, f. 2. The paper with silver coins, *qirṭās darāhim*: TS 24.46. For foreign cantors in Old Cairo see n. 2, above.

[20] Maimonides, *Responsa,* II, 314, 316.

[21] TS 13 J 27, f. 11, ll. 22–24. See n. 15.

[22] In addition to the cantors designated as *mumḥe,* listed in Mann, I, 269, the following should be noted: Japheth b. David b. Shekhanya (1020–1057), see Index; Mawhūb b. Aaron, Alexandria, 1076 (TS 20.121); Ṣedāqā ha-Levi b. Solomon, Cairo 1105 (TS 16.188); Nathan ha-Kohen b. Mevōrākh (ULC Or 1080 J 74) (not to be confused with his namesake and contemporary, the judge). Cantors being scholars: Levi ha-Levi he-ḥāvēr ha-ḥazzān (TS 24.17, TS 20.119); Shela ha-Levi ha-talmīd ha-ḥazzān (TS 13 J 3, f. 21).

[23] Baghdad: TS 20.100, l. 32+. Fustat: TS 13 J 19, f. 6, l. 18. Provincial town in Egypt: TS 13 J 16, f. 6, l. 1. The writer: Isaac b. Moses (of Sunbāṭ).

[24] *Ḥazzān al-majlis:* App. B, sec. 12; he is mentioned immediately after the Nagid and before the dayyān, because he belonged to the former's entourage. The arrangement of the text as printed in Mann, II, 246, does not render the manuscript exactly. *Ḥazzān ha-keneseth*: Dropsie 392, from Jerusalem, where the Gaon prayed in his own midrāsh (TS 13 J 9, f. 3).

[25] Cantor as emissary of yeshiva: Dropsie 392, Bodl. MS Heb. c 28 (Cat. 2876), f. 15, ed. A. Cowley, *JQR* 19 (1906), 108; Bodl. MS Heb. d 76, f. 62 (a strongly worded letter of introduction for such a person); of Nagid: TS Arabic Box 18(1), f. 34 (Hillel b. Eli). A traveling cantor, asking Mevōrākh for a gift toward the holidays after a package containing his good clothing had fallen into the Nile, reminds him of his habit of being particularly generous toward cantors: Bodl. MS Heb. e 98, f. 69.

[26] TS 12.5 and 20.152, referring to the same person. TS 16.47, l. 18, *India Book* 198; TS 16.278*. The writer is the cantor Hillel b. Eli.

[27] One of the early instances: TS 10 J 2, f. 1 (1024): David b. Shekhanya; one of the late: TS NS J 297 (1290). See sec. 11, below.

[28] See chaps. vii and viii, *passim*. Matchmaker: TS 13 J 35, f. 14 (the cantor Ibn Nufay').

[29] Ban: e.g., ENA 4009, loose leaf; TS Misc. Box 8, f. 18.

[30] TS 16.272*v*, l. 8. ULC Or 1080 J 48 (App. B, sec. 57*a*). TS NS Box 31, f. 7 (App. B, sec. 91).

[31] Cantor as administrator: Japheth b. David b. Shekhanya (see n. 19), App. A, secs. 6–7, 9, 113–116, 119, 121–124; as treasurer: Abu 'l-Majd, App. A, secs. 48–92, 148, 150. Solomon b. Elijah, the ubiquitous court clerk, also served as cantor.

[32] See D. H. Baneth in *Alexander Marx Jubilee Volume* (New York, 1940), pp. 77–78, and TS 13 J 23, f. 20(+)*, TS 13 J 11, f. 9+, where a ḥazzān is addressed as leader of the local community. The ḥazzān of Taṭay also in TS 13 J 19, f. 27*v*, l. 1, *Nahray* 14.

[33] TS 18 J 3, f. 20: *ḥazzān ḍay'a*. Addressed to Isaac b. Samuel (ha-Sefāradī), ca. 1110.

[34] TS 18 J 1, f. 2 (dated 1126, see N. Golb, *JSS*, 20 [1958], 26. Same person is referred to in Bodl. MS Heb. d 66 [Cat. 2878], f. 7). TS K 15, f. 6 col. II (a contributor, son of al-meshōrēr, dated 1178). TS 13 J 4, f. 1 (in Minyat Ghamr, a man known as *ben al-m.*, dated 1226). Undated: TS 16.186 and TS K 15, f. 8. See also Mann, I, 270. For meshōrēr as poet see S. D. Goitein, *Tarbiz*, 30 (1961) 381 n. 17, which is to be corrected according to the statements made here. About the *murahhiṭ* see chap. v, sec. D, 2.

[35] App. C, secs. 70, 100. See David S. Sasson, *Massa' Bāvel*, ed. M. Benayahu (Jerusalem, 1965), p. 89. In the German jargon of the Hungarian Jews this assistant singer used to be called *Zuhälter*—a word that has a quite different meaning in regular German. Dr. I. Adler kindly drew my attention to A. Z. Idelsohn, *Jewish Music in Its Historical Development* (New York, 1929), p. 501 n. 6; H. Avenary, "The Musical Vocabulary . . . ," *Biblical and Jewish Folklore* (Bloomington, 1960), pp. 187–198; I. Adler, *La pratique musicale savante* . . . (Paris and the Hague, 1966), pp. 22–26.

[36] Ritual slaughterer: *dhabbāḥ*, e.g., TS 13 J 22, f. 2, l. 7+* (a Kohen who served as witness); more frequently circumscribed: in charge of *dhabīḥa* or *dhabāḥa* (the former perhaps to be read as *dhabēḥa*, killing) and *mināya* (from *manā*, to examine), which is a translation of Hebrew *bedīqā*, but has not yet been found in this form in a dictionary (TS 12.55 and 20.104). "Examiner" alone: *mumannī*, TS 18 J 1, f. 6, l. 17, and see *ibid.*, l. 6; TS 20.19, ll. 33, 39, 41, 43. "Cleaner": *munaqqī*, BM Or 5566 C, f. 9, l. 23+ (App. B, sec. 32). TS Misc. Box 8, f. 61 (App. B, sec. 46), where he does an errand that is not part of his intrinsic duties—he buys a shoe for the *ḥalīṣā* ceremony. Appears as recipient of emoluments also in App. B, secs. 48, l. 6, 78, l. 3 (here between a cantor and a beadle), 81, l. 1. His task is described as *niqā'at al-khawāṣir*, cleaning of the thigh of an animal (TS Misc. Box 24, f. 137, l. 8).

[37] "Guard" or supervisor: *shōmēr* in almost every list of some extent. Thus far, twelve are known also by name. The identical Arab term *nāṭūr* only in TS K 15, f. 66*v*, col. II (App. B, secs. 4–5). In TS NS J 293 (App. B, sec. 33), *shōmēr al-laban* is differentiated from *shōmēr al-maslakh* (milking and slaughterhouse). Three persons called shōmēr in TS K 15, f. 50 (App. B, sec. 22), four in TS Misc. Box 8, f. 9 (App. B, sec. 18). Mann's (I, 270) translation of the term as "constable" is to be discarded.

[38] Bodl. MS Heb. c 28 (Cat. 2876), f. 28, see sec. 8, n. 3, above.

[39] TS 20.104, l. 7. See n. 45, below.

[40] TS Misc. Box 24, f. 137, page 4. In the hand of Mevōrākh b. Nathan, (App. D,

sec. 22) but not signed. Perhaps a copy. Mentioned by E. Ashtor, *Zion,* 30 (1965), 67 n. 46.

[41] See chap. v, sec. B, 2, n. 123. Damascus: ENA 2739, f. 14 (left upper corner of a Hebrew court record in large, rectangular script). Cairo: TS 18 J 1, f. 6 (May, 1028).

[42] TS 12.427, ed. (with many mishaps) Mann, II, 342–343. Abramson, *Bamerkazim,* p. 104 n. 1, offers corrections, but his rendering of the decisive line 7 is faulty. It contains the names of the two persons concerned, Sār Shālōm and Menūḥā, the Kohens. (The latter, Menūḥā ha-Kohen b. Joseph, signs a document in Alexandria, 1033 [TS 13 J 1, f. 7]). In l. 8 the manuscript has *le-hitparnēs,* to gain one's livelihood, not *lhtprsh,* which makes no sense, as in Mann. The passage does not imply that the shohet received parts of the animal's body as compensation, but refers to Amos 3:12 and means simply: a little. The *minhāg* is mentioned in l. 20.

In ENA 4009?, ed. S. D. Goitein, *Joshua Finkel Jubilee Volume* (New York, 1970), "the son of the Exilarch" instructs Aaron b. Ephraim b. Ṭarsōn of (New) Cairo to excommunicate the shohet Ibn Shā'ūl and his son "for deviating from the law and the agreed practice," *al-qānūn wal-mustaqarr.* It is doubtful whether that dignitary had any authority to pronounce such an excommunication.

TS 8 J 13, f. 25, l. 6: *le-mannōt ṭabbāḥīm we-shōmerīm we-liqbōa' 'alēhem reshūthēnū.* The fragment is in the beautiful, but elusive hand of the Iraqian yeshivas. I assume the letter was issued by David b. Daniel b. Azarya (because of the hint to II Chron. 19:5).

[43] Moshe Perlmann, *Samau'al al-Maghribi* (New York, 1964), pp. 66–70, esp. p. 69 of Eng. trans.

[44] TS 10 J 28, f. 18. One of the signatories, Māshī'aḥ b. Ṣemaḥ, signed a marriage contract in Oct., 1029 (Bodl. MS Heb. a 2 [Cat. 2805], f. 4, ed. S. Poznanski, *REJ,* 48 [1904], 173–175), but the document discussed here is older since the congregation is lead by a ḥāvēr different from Ephraim b. Shemarya, who headed the Palestinians of Fustat as from the late 1010's. One of the "conditions": serve people coming with poultry immediately and do not let them wait. Most of the right half of the document is lost.

[45] TS 20.104, see chap. v, sec. B, 1, nn. 110, 144. David b. Shekhanya, Japheth's father, was still alive in June, 1024 (TS 10 J 2, f. 1), while the Gaon Joshia cannot have lived long after that date. "Bath of the Mice": see *Med. Soc.,* I, 293. Unsigned and much damaged.

[46] TS 16.39. After the publication of *Med. Soc.,* Vol. I, I found another part of that account, written within another text contained in TS 12.834*v* (re-marked thus [see Shaked, *Bibliography,* p. 63], but in Aug., 1968, the piece was still in TS Box J 2, as f. 77, in accordance with the original mark).

[47] TS Arabic Box 5, f. 4. It is not evident from the account how much of their weekly earnings the shohets were obliged to deliver to the community, for the amounts noted were actual payments and differ widely. It seems the writer of the document as well as the part-time shohet was Solomon b. Elijah. Price of meat: col. II, ll. 6–7. The Egyptian pound in Fatimid times had approximately the same weight as the modern U.S.A. pound. See *Med. Soc.,* I, 360.

In TS Arabic Box 4, f. 2, a shohet receives ½ dirhem per head, but kills 23–28 animals a week (during four consecutive weeks), while in TS Arabic Box 5, f. 4, the two shohets together dispatched only 14–17 in a week. The shohet of Box 4, f. 2, probably received also a small share of the meat (as was customary in other oriental communities), wherefore his cash remuneration was small.

The ancient account TS NSJ 54 deals with sheep and goats, but the payments of ½ dirhem per animal must refer to shepherds who also milked them, for the names are Muslim rather than Jewish and the number of animals far too high for a meat herd.

[48] ULC Or 1080 J 290 (Cairo; the man contracting the partnership in ritual

slaughtering mentioned *Med Soc.,* I, 163, was a cantor). Bodl. MS Heb. d 66 (Cat. 2878), f. 19, l. 6: letter of an unhappy muqaddam in Bilbays.

[49] Goitein, *Education,* pp. 80–82, three instances, but all referring to the little community of Qalyūb near Cairo. In TS 10 J 29, f. 4, fragment of a letter of the Gaon Sār Shālōm (another fragment in TS 10 J 24, f. 7), the appointment of a schoolmaster is approved who serves also as shohet in a place where other shohets and cantors were active.

[50] Five beadles in the list of the "Sons of the Torah" (Bodl. MS Heb. c 28 [Cat. 2876], f. 6+, see sec. 9, n. 4, above).

11. SCRIBES AND COPYISTS

[1] Ḥullīn, 9*a*.

[2] St. Hajnal, "Universities and the Development of Writing," *Scriptorium, International Review of Manuscript Studies* (Anvers), 6 (1952), 177 ff.

[3] Ibn al-Athīr, ed. C. J. Tornberg (Leiden, 1851–1876), 105. *The Arabian Nights,* Night no. 860, second poem, 1.3 (where the good editions have *fī khaṭṭī wa-fī qalamī,* not *ḥaẓẓī*).

[4] Tritton, *Muslim Education,* p. 195.

[5] E.g., Nathan ha-Kohen b. Solomon (dated documents: 1125–1150), Nathan b. Samuel (1128–1153), his son Mevōrakh (1150–1181), Samuel b. Saadya ha-Levi (1165–1203), Yehiel b. Eliakim (1213–1233) and his son Immanuel (1243–1265). See App. D.

[6] E.g., Abraham b. Shema'ya (1092–1132), Isaac b. Samuel ha-Sefāradī (1095–1127).

[7] E.g., the writer of TS 24.78+*.

[8] Bodl. MS Heb. c 28 (Cat. 2876), f. 23, ll. 14, 15*, ed. S. D. Goitein, *Homenaje a Millás-Vallicrosa* (Barcelona, 1954), I, 719. (The Hebrew trans. provided by me there needs revision.) ULC Or 1080 J 200, l. 5. Woman copyist: sec. 3, n. 7, above. Solomon b. Samuel b. Saadya ha-Levi: TS 8 J 6, f. 9 (dated 1231. No connection between this and TS 8 J 6, f. 9*v*, cited n. 60, below). The Bodleian Library possesses a priceless manuscript written by him: volume VI of Maimonides commentary on the Mishnah, MS Pococke 97 (Cat. 398, not from the Geniza).

[9] Scribes are common in the lists of receivers of emoluments from the public chest, e.g., TS K 15, f. 5 (App. B, sec. 19); TS K 15, f. 70+, (App. B, sec. 13). Gifts to the court clerk Ḥalfōn b. Manasse from overseas: *India Book* 33, 34, 50, 150 (by three different Adenese merchants).

[10] TS 13 J 20, f. 17. The story of the unhappy woman whose husband absconded to Spain is told in ULC Or 1080, Box 4, f. 15.

[11] Dropsie 389*v*, l. 8.

[12] ULC Or 1080 J 117. On the prices of houses, see *Med. Soc.,* Vol. III, chap. viii.

[13] TS NS Box 320, f. 6. The number 31 is to be complemented thus: (5)31 A.H. (began on Sept. 29, 1136), since the script is unmistakably of the twelfth century. Mas'ūd b. Mawhūb ("The happy one, son of the Godsent") writes to his brother Sābiq. His hand is good, almost scholarly.

[14] TS 16.164, ed. S. Assaf, in *Yerushalayim* (Jerusalem), n.v. (1953), 113.

[15] TS 13 J 3, f. 8, written and signed by Abraham b. Saadya. TS 24.25*v* (the original document), written and signed by Isaac b. Moses, Sunbaṭya. TS K 3, f. 32 (his library after his death, Oct., 1150).

[16] Bodl. MS Heb. e 74, ed. with transcription into Arabic letters and with English trans. by Richard J. H. Gottheil, "Fragments of an Arabic Common-Place Book," *Bulletin de l'Institut Français d'Archéologie Orientale* (Cairo), 34 (1933), 103–128. The facsimile shows Ḥalfōn's early style, when his script was very similar to that of his father-in-law, Hillel b. Eli.

[17] The latest document signed by Hillel b. Eli, identified thus far, is from May,

1101 (TS 10 J 2, f. 12), a *get*. But there are later documents written by him and signed by others, e.g., TS 13 J 2, f. 10 (July, 1103), TS Misc. Box 24, f. 5, first item on recto (Feb., 1108). Mr. Gershon Weiss devoted his M.A. thesis to him: "Hillel b. Eli, Documents written by Hillel b. Eli: A Study in the Diplomatics of the Cairo Geniza Documents," University of Pennsylvania, Philadelphia, 1967. (Available in the University Library.) The purpose of this thesis was not to collect all the material pertaining to Hillel b. Eli, but to reconstruct, with the use of fifty-five well-preserved documents the legal formularies on which the court clerk's work was based. See also chap. vii, sec. B, 3, n. 56, below.

[18] See A. Dietrich, "Eine arabische Eheurkunde aus der Aiyūbidenzeit," *Documenta Islamica Inedita* (Berlin, 1952), p. 123 (from the year 1207). Su'ād Māhir, "Marriage Contracts on Ancient Textiles," *Kulliyyat al-Ādāb* (Cairo, n.d.) (in Arabic). The contracts are from the years 1278, 1290, 1334. On writing materials and equipment used in Arabic countries during the Middle Ages see Adolf Grohmann, *Arabische Paläographie,* I (Vienna, 1967).

[19] How a long strip of parchment was used for a minute description of a house (a draft, of course), will be explained in *Med. Soc.,* Vol. III.

[20] Letters of recommendation, sent around 1062 by the Gaon Elijah b. Solomon from Jerusalem to Damascus, were written partly on large parchments and partly on red paper (TS 24.49, ll. 40–41, a letter by his son Evyathar to Eli b. Ḥiyya of Fustat). Red paper is repeatedly referred to in Arabic literature, but I have not yet come across any in the Geniza. To be sure, red *color* on illuminated Geniza papers, such as marriage contracts or children's exercise books, is common.

[21] TS 13 J 20, f. 18*v*, ll. 1–2+, a letter addressed to the Gaon Sār Shālōm.

[22] TS 12.583, written by Hillel b. Eli on Oct. 31, 1090, is a good example of how a page was filled with calligraphic script to the very edges so as to leave no blank space except a narrow strip on the top.

[23] Only in exceptional cases was the opposite done, namely the margin was covered with script running from top to bottom, each successive word above, and not below, the other. Such exceptions (found, e.g., in the letter of the "young" cantor writing from Malīj, sec. 10, n. 18) are usually a puzzle, especially if the handwriting is poor.

[24] This was the practice of the Fatimid chancelleries, imitated by the Jewish authorities, such as Nagids or judges.

[25] TS 20.103, end: "This power of attorney consists of two sheets (*yerī'ōt,* Heb.), its join (*ḥibbūr,* Heb.) is true and correct, and the number of its lines from the beginning to here is thirty and here is the end." The words "true and correct" are written also across the join of the leaves.

TS 13 J 6, f. 14 (Tyre): "The papers (*neyārōt,* Heb.) are three. On the join, obliquely (*'llkswnn,* for Greek *loxon*) 'true and correct' is written. The number of lines ninety-four" (of which we have only twenty-four) (ed. S. Assaf, *Eretz-Israel,* 1 [1951], 141 [one of the few cases overlooked in Shaked, *Bibliography,* where it should have been noted on pp. 117 and 266]). The Greek term (not explained by Assaf) indicates that these practices go back to Byzantine times.

[26] TS 20.121. Four leaves glued together; across the joins (ll. 1, 30, 57) the words "Truth, truth" are written twice, one beneath the other. Only fifty-seven lines are preserved, two leaves with at least fifty lines are lost. The handwriting is that of the judge Abraham b. Nathan Āv (ca. 1100, App. D, sec. 14) which makes it very likely that the scriptorial usages described were practiced in the yeshiva of Palestine.

[27] See *Med. Soc.,* I, 7 and illus. 4 (following p. 20).

[28] TS 13 J 10, f. 5 (Ṣahrajt).

[29] TS 13 J 6, f. 21, addressed to Abraham b. Nathan Āv (see n. 26).

[30] TS 8.86. A scribe writes to his father (or older colleague) that a piece of parch-

ment sent to him was sufficient for four quires, *karārīs,* less one sheet, *waraqa,* and that he would either "cook" or buy new ink since the one tried by him was worthless.

[31] TS 13 J 21, f. 21+. Four different types of ink were used in ll. 1–5, 6–8, 9–11, and 12–22, respectively.

[32] E.g., TS 20.80+. The writer took a finer pen in l. 27, but wrote altogether 92 long and about 115 short lines—and there was a second sheet that we do not have.

[33] Bodl. MS Heb. c 13 (Cat. 2807, no. 16), f. 20*v*, ll. 19–21+. Of a renowned Karaite scholar and author it was said that he was personal trimmer of reed pens to the caliph (Leon Nemoy, *Karaite* Anthology [New Haven, 1952], p. 234).

[34] Franz Rosenthal, "Al-Tawḥīdī on Penmanship," *Ars Islamica,* 13–14 (1948), 7.

[35] "The Joy of all Hearts": TS 10 J 17, f. 14.

[36] E.g., the judge Nathan b. Samuel, n. 5, above (see H. Schirmann, *Studies of the Research Institute for Hebrew Poetry in Jerusalem,* 6 [1945], 291–297). A dirge of thirty-eight lines by him on one Moses in TS 16.283. Another piece of poetry in his hand: TS 8 J 15, f. 23*v*.

[37] *Med. Soc.,* I, 11.

[38] See *Mittheilungen aus der Sammlung der Papyrus Erzherzog Rainer* (Vienna), 5 (1892), 127–132, cf. v, B, 1, n. 124, and vi, sec. 7, n. 10, above.

[39] TS 24.26, partly ed., see Shaked, *Bibliography,* p. 77. The Gaon asks the head of the community of Malīj to settle the affair locally.

[40] Eli b. Amram: TS 20.152, see *Med. Soc.,* I, 442 n. 28. The contract: TS 12.5.

[41] TS 13 J 9, f. 5. In the validation of the court, ll. 4, 6: *āmerū, nāmū.*

[42] Bodl. MS Heb. d 66 (Cat. 2878), f. 8*.

[43] Joshua: Dropsie 402. Japheth: TS 12.499, ed. S. Assaf, *Tarbiz,* 9 (1938), 19 and 205. ʿImrān: Mosseri L 10 (Mann, *Hebrew Union Jubilee Volume* [Cincinnati, 1925], p. 257); Solomon: TS 13 J 1, f. 12, ll. 1, 2. Eli: TS 13 J 1, f. 13, ll. 3, 13. Yāʾīr: TS 18 J 1, f. 10, ed. N. Golb, *JSS,* 20 (1958), 41, ll. 16, 21. Hillel: TS 24.81, l. 15 and verso, l. 29.

[44] By no stretch of the imagination could I have found out that Isaac in TS NS J 382, l. 1, was identical with Muʿāfā in l. 11 of the same document, until I identified two other fragments, TS 12.177 and TS NS J 338, as belonging to the same court record. See the facsimile of the three put together in *Eretz-Israel,* 8 (1967), 295. The father of Isaac-Muʿāfā is called first by his Hebrew name Shemarya and later by the Arabic name Muḥriz. The regular Arabic equivalent of Shemarya is Maḥfūẓ.

[45] TS Arabic Box 18(1), f. 132. Even at the end of his life the judge Nathan b. Samuel was referred to also as *sōfēr bēt-dīn,* court clerk, i.e., professional scribe. Gottheil-Worrell, VII, p. 34, l. 20 (1151).

[46] TS K 15, f. 102 (App. B, sec. 31), col. II, ll. 19–20: Arabic *ḍarīr,* blind, is written once with *ṭ* and once with *ṣ*. Many more examples could be adduced.

[47] TS 12.394. The letter is entirely in Hebrew, the family name of the writer was Pinḥāsī, the like of which was not found in Muslim countries in those days, and greetings are given to a friend from Milasā (ancient Mylasa in southwest Asia Minor, today Milas, Turkey). All this points to a man coming from Byzantium.

[48] ENA 151 (2557)+*.

[49] ULC Or 1080 J 200*. The agreement was made in the presence of the ḥāvēr Abū Kathīr, i.e., Ephraim b. Shemarya. Wages of unskilled laborers: *Med. Soc.,* I, 99.

[50] TS 13 J 20, f. 11. His name was Zakkay b. Moses; documents written and signed by him (dated 1144 and 1147) have been preserved. See about him, N. Allony, *Kiryath Sepher,* 43 (1968), 125, and S. D. Goitein, *ibid.,* 44 (1969), 127–128.

[51] TS 12.791. Codex of Pentateuch: *maṣḥaf tōrā.*

[52] Bodl. MS Heb. c 28 (Cat. 2876), f. 23+, see n. 8, above.

[53] TS 10 J 5, f. 15*. Nahray: TS 16.339*v*, l. 11, *Nahray* 179.

[54] TS 13 J 20, f. 11, l. 18, see n. 50, and *Med. Soc.,* I, 422 n. 84.

[55] Bodl. MS Heb. e 39 (Cat. 2712, no. 23), f. 136*v*, where *ṣhrwm*(?) is to be corrected to *ṣhrjt*. (The manuscript has been checked by me).

[56] To be sure, in those days, al-Jūsh was on the highroad leading to the important Mediterranean port of Tyre (see, e.g., Bodl. MS Heb. c 28 [Cat. 2876], f. 20, *Nahray*, ll. 6, 11, and Braslavsky, *Our Country*, pp. 63–67, 169, 274).

[57] E.g., Bodl. MS Heb. f 61 (Cat. 2855, no. 11), f. 49; eight generations. Of particular interest is the colophon to Bodl. MS Heb. 133 (not from the Geniza), quoted Mann, II, 204 (5), where the copyist provides details about his ancestors in the fifth and seventh generations. In the colophon mentioned in Mann, II, 103 n. 2, the long pedigree refers to the proprietor, not the scribe.

[58] E.g., Eli II ha-Kohen ha-ḥazzān (dated documents 1106–1128) b. Ezekiel II he-ḥāvēr (1074–1105) b. Eli I he-ḥāvēr (at least ten letters [see facsimile of one in Mann, *Texts*, I, 716]) b. Ezekiel I ha-ḥazzān b. Solomon he-ḥāvēr. Judge Yehiel b. Eliakim and his son Immanuel (App. D, secs. 30, 32).

[59] TS 13 J 1, f. 10 (1044). The circulars: TS 13 J 9, f. 7 (dated 1166); TS 13 J 6, f. 3^{+} (1177); TS 13 J 23, f. 7 (name of sender, the Gaon Samuel b. Eli, but no date preserved). There is of course a difference between the hasty script in a short attestation of a record dealing with a negligible sum and calligraphic circulars sent from Baghdad to Cairo. But anyone familiar with the types of writing from around 1044 found in the Geniza is struck by the family similarity between the script in that attestation and that in the circulars from Iraq. The same applies to TS 12.5, 9 (court record from Fustat, 1026) which has some Babylonian vowel signs and most probably was also written in the synagogue of the Babylonians.

[60] Outline: TS NS J 268. Full draft: TS 8 J 6, f. 9*v**, both written by Solomon b. Elijah on July 4, 1231.

12. MEDICAL PROFESSION

[1] TS 13 J 21, f. 17^{+*}.

[2] ENA 2156*v*, l. 8^{+}, see Shaked, *Bibliography*, p. 189.

[3] S. Muntner, *R. Shabbetay Donnolo* (Jerusalem, 1949) (in Heb.). *The World History of the Jewish People: The Dark Ages*, ed. C. Roth (Tel Aviv, 1966), pp. 297–301. Some of his writings have found their way into the Cairo Geniza (see A. Scheiber, *Sinai*, 62 [1968], 193-196).

[4] Ibn Saʿīd al-Maghribī, *Khiṭaṭ*, I, 367 (see Strauss, *Mamluks*, I, 202).

[5] *Maʿālim al-Qurba*, chap. 45, Eng. summary, p. 56.

[6] Abū Yūsuf, *Kitāb al-Kharāj* (Cairo, 1302/1884–1885), p. 123; Cairo, 1346/1927–1928), p. 148 (chap. "Who Is Obliged to Pay the Poll Tax?"). Big merchant: *tājir*, see *Med. Soc.*, I, 149. Practicing physician: *al-muʿālij al-ṭabīb*.

[7] Marius Canard, *Vie de l'Ustadh Jaudhar* (Algiers, 1958), p. 163.

[8] Isaac Israeli: see *Med. Soc.*, I, 54, 404 n. 74.

[9] Steinschneider, *Die arabische Literatur der Juden*, para. 55, pp. 96–97. All additional material on Moses b. Elazar and his descendants is conveniently assembled in Bernard Lewis, "Palṭiel: a Note," *BSOAS*, 30 (1967), 177–181. Lewis' ingenious conjecture that Moses b. Elazar is identical with Palṭiel b. Shefaṭya of the Aḥimaʿaṣ chronicle is vitiated by the discrepancy of the names. While it could be surmised that a person's name was changed during an illness it is hard to see why his father's name should be so different as well.

The name of Moses' father, which is known only in Arabic script, must be Elazar, and cannot be Eliezer, for only the first form occurs—and with great frequency—in the Geniza period. The reason is simple: Eliezer was familiar from the biblical account (Genesis 24) as the name of a slave, and who would give his boy such a name in a period so slavery conscious? The Arabic form *Alʿayzār* (found alongside with *Alʿāzar, Alʿazār*) is Imāla, i.e., an endeavor to express the pronunciation of ā as ā̂ approximately.

[10] R. Gottheil, "An Eleventh-Century Document Concerning a Cairo Synagogue," *JQR,* 19 (1907), 467–539. The father of this Moses was Jacob b. Isaac, the grandson of Moses b. Elazar.

[11] Chief justice: TS 13 J 19, f. 3. Governor: Bodl. MS Heb. c 28 (Cat. 2876), f. 67; TS 13 J 14, f. 5, ed. Mann, II, 83. Inner-Jewish: Bodl. MS Heb. b 11 (Cat. 2874), f. 1[(+)] (see Shaked, *Bibliography,* p. 207). The date 1088 mentioned there has nothing to do with the letter. It is a joke written by a schoolboy on the reverse side (a would-be marriage contract).

[12] See Mann, I, 84–86. The letter Bodl. MS Heb. a 3 (Cat. 2873), f. 17*, is addressed to Cairo.

[13] TS 13 J 26, f. 8, l. 8, margin. The letter was written in Alexandria in Sivan (May–June) and mentions that the receipts for the Muslim year 458 (ended Nov. 21, 1066) had not yet been received (from Tunisia).

[14] TS 13 J 9, f. 3, a letter from Jerusalem, sent around 1065 to Mubārak b. Sa'āda, alias Mevōrākh b. Saadya, containing interesting details about the latter's family. His mother is mentioned in l. 21. See Mann, II, 255–256, who assumes, however, erroneously that the elegy is dedicated to Mevōrākh's wife.

[15] Abū Manṣūr: TS 13 J 22, f. 2, l. 9+*; see Mann, I, 229, II, 281–291.

[16] Documents under his authority: 1161–1165. Ibn Abī Uṣaybi'a, II, 116. Steinschneider, *Arabische Literatur der Juden,* pp. 178–185, identified him with another Hibat Allāh, the famous Ibn Jumay'. Subsequent Geniza finds proved that Steinschneider's identification cannot be sustained (see D. H. Baneth, *Alexander Marx Jubilee Volume* [New York, 1950], Heb. sec., p. 83 n. 44).

[17] See A. Neubauer, "Egyptian Fragments," *JQR,* 8 (1896), 548, l. 2.

[18] Strauss, *Mamluks,* I, 121 n. 21.

[19] TS 8 J 26, f. 19+*, see S. D. Goitein, *JQR,* 44 (1953), 46.

[20] Tripoli: TS 16.261, l. 2; Ramle: *ibid.,* l. 27, ed. Mann, *Texts,* I, 337 ff., see also II, 1462.

[21] Aaron b. Yeshū'ā Ibn al-'Ammānī of Alexandria signed documents between 1109 (TS 10 J 26, f. 2) and 1143 (TS 13 J 3, f. 4), when he still added the word hā-rōfē (the physician, Heb.) to the name of his father, although the latter was already dead in 1109.

His grandfather Aaron b. Ṣedāqā b. Aaron hā-rōfē al-'Ammānī (the first member of the family who was called al-'Ammānī, i.e., coming from 'Ammān in Transjordania, without *Ibn*) was party to the contract TS 16.1 (Aug. 28, 1089), an enormous release containing solely legal verbiage. In l. 25, where the names are repeated, the scribe (Hillel b. Eli) added *ha-Kohen* after the name of the grandfather Aaron, but this is merely a mistake, caused by the habit of using that epithet for the biblical Aaron. It was absolutely de rigeur to refer to a Kohen as such when first introduced. The epithet might be repeated after the name of the father of the person concerned. To mention it solely after the name of the grandfather and after the three names are introduced first without it can only be due to an oversight. The name Ṣedāqā or (Ar.) Ṣadaqa = Ṣadōq recurs at least twice in the 'Ammānī family. With this, the doubts of S. Abramson in his notes to Maimonides, *Responsa,* III, 155, are resolved.

I have not yet found a Geniza document mentioning expressly one of the five sons of Aaron Ibn al-'Ammānī as physician. For the one mentioned by Mann, II, 305, was actually his great-grandson. He, Yeshū'ā hā-rōfē b. Aaron hā-rōfē, is addressed, while still a fledgling young doctor, in 1217, by his cousin and brother-in-law Judah (Ibn al-)'Ammānī (see also below, n. 44). The same Judah wrote TS 16.305 to the Nagid Abraham Maimonides, mentioning in ll. 24–27, the successful treatment of Muslim patients by a brother of his.

[22] TS 12.573. On the reverse side (unconnected) App. C, sec. 73.

[23] *EI* ², I, 1298, s.v. "Bukhtīshū'" (D. Sourdel).

[24] Cf. H. Schipperges, "Der aerztliche Stand im arabischen und lateinischen Mittelalter," *Materia Medica Nordmark* (1960), no. 12, pp. 111–112.

[25] E.g., TS 13 J 3, f. 17. Will of a physician, dated 1241.

[26] TS 13 J 19, f. 3, in the address. TS 16.176: Abū Manṣūr *al-mutaṭabbib* b. Eli *ha-rōfē* (1182). Bodl. MS Heb. a 3 (Cat. 2873), f. 3, l. 26, corresponding to *rōfē* in l. 10. See J. Schacht and M. Meyerhof, *The Medico-Philosophical Controversy between Ibn Butlan and Ibn Ridwan* (Cairo, 1937), p. 77.

[27] In the city of Tunis: TS 16.177 (tenth century); Ramle, Palestine, 1065: TS 10 J 26, f. 1, ed. S. Assaf, *Tarbiz,* 9 (1938), 201; Minyat Ziftā, 1265: TS 12.543*.

[28] Mosseri L 268. See sec. 6, n. 7.

[29] TS NS J 9, l. 22.

[30] In Arabic: *Al-Sadīd, al-Muwaffaq, al-Muhadhdhab.*

[31] *Shams al-ḥukamā',* ULC Or 1080 J 33.

[32] *'Aṭṭereth ha-rōfe'īm,* TS 8 Ja 1, f. 2. *Hadrath ha-rōfe'īm,* Bodl. MS Heb. f 56 (Cat. 2821, no. 35), f. 122, ed. Mann, II, 282.

[33] E.g., Ibn Abī Uṣaybi'a, II, 101, l. 7. This license is to be differentiated from the police certificate of good conduct (see n. 43, below).

[34] *Ibid.,* p. 109.

[35] TS K 25, f. 64* (see chap. v, sec. A, 2, n. 46).

[36] Ibn Abī Uṣaybi'a, II, 113, l. 2. Ibn Jumay' wrote a treatise about the revival of medical studies (see Paul Kraus in the Arabic review *al-Thaqāfa,* 230 [May 25, 1943] and 232 [June 8, 1943]). For lectures in a hospital see Ibn Abī Uṣaybi'a, II, 155, and A. A. Khairallah, *Arabic Contributions to Medicine* (Beirut 1946), pp. 64–65. (The name of the physician and the page of the source given there have to be corrected.)

[37] TS 16.291. The time of the writer, Meir b. al-Hamadānī, is known to us from another letter, TS 10 J 12, f. 10. The letter is addressed to the judge and physician Moses. No other person of such a description existed at that particular time. There is one difficulty in the identification with Maimonides: the writer speaks of the addressee's brother's son. But Maimonides' brother David had only a little daughter when he died on a journey to India. The solution of the difficulty is offered by the obvious fact that the letter is the calligraphic copy made by a scribe from a draft. He might easily have misread *y* for *t,* the only difference between the words "brother" and "sister" in Arabic (the letter is of course in Hebrew characters). Joseph Abu 'l-Riḍā, the son of Maimonides' sister, did indeed study with his uncle (see A. H. Freimann, *Alumma* [Jerusalem, 1935], p. 15).

[38] *Med. Soc.,* I, 80.

[39] W. Bacher, "La bibliothèque d'un médecin juif," *REJ,* 40 (1900), 55–61, and *ibid.,* p. 266, a note by S. Poznanski.

[40] TS 20.44+.

[41] TS NS J 173, ed. D. H. Baneth, *Tarbiz,* 30 (1961), 171–185.

[42] Although the title al-Muwaffaq was common (cf. n. 30, above), Ibn Jumay' may be intended here, because he is connected with Alexandria in other Geniza letters as well, and also because he wrote a treatise about the climate of that city.

[43] "Certificate of good conduct" is a translation of *tazkiya,* not found in the dictionaries in this meaning, but see *Ma'ālim al-Qurba,* p. 170: bachelors are not allowed to keep a school; even an old bachelor is permitted to do so only *bi-tazkiya murḍiya,* "on the base of a satisfactory certificate." See also Tyan, *Organisation judiciare,* pp. 238 ff.

[44] TS 24.67, ll. 7–11, 20, 24–25, 28.

[45] TS NS J 171, ll. 16–18. The reference is to the original letter found on this fragment, written in comparatively large characters. The receiver, whose hand I identify as that of Meir b. Hillel b. Ṣādōq Āv, used the sheet to write between the

lines and on the blank space a detailed letter to his son, covering fully the two pages.

[46] Abraham Maimonides: TS 10 J 14, f. 5, ed. S. D. Goitein, *Tarbiz,* 33 (1964), 192–195. (In the second word of l. 1, an Aleph has been omitted. Read: *'l-dā'ī.*) Early in the hospital: TS K 25, f. 64* (see n. 35, above). Abū Sa'd Moses b. Nethanel: An encomium was sent to him from Spain by the poet Judah ha-Levi (see Mann, I, 234–235 n. 3, where *ila 'l-rayyis ben Hibat Allāh* is to be read).

[47] See *EI* ², I, 1222–1224, s.v. "Bīmāristān" (D. M. Dunlop). Legal document: Bodl. MS Heb. e 94, f. 28. Nūr al-Dīn: Nikita Elisséeff, *Nūr al-Dīn, un grand prince musulman* . . . (Damascus, 1967), III, 838–843. Ward of dysentery: *mushaliyya,* TS 13 J 19, f. 3, address.

[48] E. Ashtor, "Saladin and the Jews," *HUCA,* 27 (1956), 311. Dr. Lawrence Berman drew my attention to similar advice given by Maimonides to Saladin's successor, where the great doctor recommends wine and music as a remedy for melancholy, although both were prohibited by the Muslim religion (see Max Meyerhof, "The Medical Work of Maimonides," *Essays on Maimonides,* ed. S. W. Baron [New York, 1941], p. 288). Maimonides stresses that it is the doctor's duty to prescribe the scientifically sound, while it is up to the patient to make his decisions according to his conscience.

[49] TS 13 J 24, f. 10*v,* ll. 12–19. R. Simḥā writes to his father-in-law, the judge Elijah b. Zechariah. The Alexandrian physician Abu 'l-Thanā' was a friend of the judge (TS NS J 29*v,* l. 7).

[50] TS NS J 354. The notable addressed bore the title *gevīr,* very uncommon in those days. It is an abbreviation of the untranslatable *gevīr ha-mevīnīm* ("the man with the strong intellect"), borne by Samuel b. Judah b. Asad, alias Abu 'l-Ma'ālī al-tājir, a great merchant and philanthropist, mentioned in many documents between 1133 (JNUL, f. 5+) and 1165 (TS 13 J 3, f. 12). The title is found in the latter document and, e.g., TS 10 J 21, f. 10, TS 13 J 3, f. 10 (1159).

[51] BM Or 5566 C, f. 10, l. 2+ (App. B, sec. 32). "In the house of the physician": App. B, sec. 1, l. 23.

[52] Old Woman: JNUL 83 c, ed. S. D. Goitein, *Kirjath Sepher,* 41 (1966), 272–274. Deathbed: TS 13 J 3, f. 2, ed. S. D. Goitein, *Sefunot,* 8 (1964), 113–115 (1142).

[53] See chap. v, secs. D, 1, and C, 4.

[54] TS 8 J 20, f. 26. Since the letter also reports that everyone appearing outside his house would be taken to forced labor on the "trench," *khandaq,* obviously the place prepared for a battle, which would explain the presence of the Christian army doctor.

Whether the Hippocratic sayings really meant that a physician should treat a poor patient gratuitously seems to be doubted today (see A. R. Hands, *Charities and Social Aid in Greece and Rome* [Ithaca, 1968], p. 131).

[55] Milk cure: TS 10 J 20, f. 5*v*+*. Dietetic problems: TS 16.290, ed. D. H. Baneth, *Gulak-Klein Memorial Volume* (Jerusalem, 1942), pp. 50–56.

[56] TS 8 J 26, f. 19+*.

[57] TS 10 J 14, f. 24. This letter, in which the writer changes from Hebrew to Arabic characters and back to Hebrew is good material for a study of the graphological problem how to establish the identity of a man using two such entirely different scripts.

[58] TS 13 J 24, f. 14, ll. 18–22. The writer regrets that the addressee, the physician Yedūthūn, had separated from his partner.

[59] ULC Or 1080 J 93*. Sign, *'alāma:* TS 8 J 14, f. 5, l. 4, where a physician is requested to pay for it.

[60] TS K 15, f. 9*v.*

[61] Al-Dimashqī, *Maḥāsin al-tijāra* (see *Med. Soc.,* I, xxi), p. 13.

[62] Bodl. MS Heb. d 66 (Cat. 2878), f. 141*.

[63] Prescriptions in Arabic characters: e.g., TS 13 J 6, f. 14 (complete and very

detailed), Arabic Box 53, f. 33; TS NS J 38*v*. In Hebrew characters: e.g., TS 12.33; TS 16.291*v*; TS 8 J 14, f. 3; TS 8 J 15, f. 20*v*; TS Arabic Box 30, f. 65*v*; ULC Or 1081 J 39; ENA 2808, f. 9; Firkovitch II, 1700, f. 21*a*. See sec. 13, nn. 29, 30, below. Many prescriptions are found in TS Arabic Boxes 38, 39 and ff. But the student of this material should discern between prescriptions actually issued for patients and others copied from books for the purpose of study.

64 Maimonides, *Responsa*, II, 302–304.

65 TS Box 25, f. 30, l. 21, *Nahray* 142. See also sec. 13, nn. 30–50.

66 TS 13 J 36, f. 6, ll. 12–13 (Eli ha-Kohen I b. Ezekiel I).

67 Bodl. MS Heb. f 56 (Cat. 2821, no. 38), f. 126, l. 4. The physician Menahem writes to his colleague, the Nagid Abraham Maimonides, about happenings when he traveled to the village Ṭanān (in the Qalyūbiyya district near Cairo) to see a patient.

68 Bodl. MS Heb. d 66 (Cat. 2878), f. 141*. The recovery: TS 13 J 25, f. 15*v*, ll. 1–2.

69 Gottheil-Worrell, III, p. 22, ll. 7–10. The last four words in l. 9: *wybs mn wrkh 'ly*. For *shy* in l. 10 read *'sy* = *'asā*, meaning "please."

70 Reminder: ULC Or 1080 J 271*v*. Death: Bodl. MS Heb. c 28 (Cat. 2876), f. 52.

71 TS 8 J 16, f. 27.

72 Oculist: *kaḥḥāl*, common, also outside the capital. For female doctors see *Med. Soc.*, I, 127–128.

73 Abu 'l-Faraj b. al-kallām: TS NS J 422 (before 1143), TS NS J 296*v* (here the *Ibn al-kallām* is referred to as "your teacher" in a letter written on the reverse side of an inventory dated 1159); Bodl. MS Heb. f 56 (Cat. 2821, no. 16*b*), f. 45* (dated 1182). It is not excluded that in all three cases the same person is referred to. In the same period lived one Abu 'l-Faḍl Ibn al-kallām: TS 10 J 17, f. 22, l. 17.

74 Cf. M. Meyerhof, "Mediaeval Jewish Physicians in the Near East," *Isis*, 77 (May, 1938) 442.

75 *Quḍā'ī:* TS Box K 15, f. 15, 50 (App. B, secs. 20, 22), 70+; Box 28, f. 42 (App. B, sec. 14); cf. S. D. Goitein in *Yerushalayim*, 2 (1955), 57 n. 14. The explanation given here was confirmed by Professor Willy Hartner in a letter to the present writer of Nov. 22, 1961.

76 Cf. J. Rasabi, *Lĕšonénu*, 20 (1956), 42, and *ibid.*, 19 (1954), 34. Franz Rosenthal, "Bibliographical Notes on Medieval Muslim Dentistry," *Bulletin of the History of Medicine*, 34 (1960), 53.

77 Phlebotomists are called in the records read thus far *fāṣid*, not *faṣṣād* as in *Ma'ālim al-Qurba*, chap. 44. Hebrew Union College, Cincinnati, Geniza MS 24, l. 6; TS NS J 416, margin; ULC Or 1080 J 29, mentioning also a *mashḥānī*, or masseur.

78 TS 8 J 26, f. 19+* (see n. 56, above).

79 Chap. v, sec. B, 1, n. 31, above.

80 TS 18 J 2, f. 1. For prices of donkeys see *Med. Soc.*, Vol. III, chap. viii.

81 ULC Or 1080 J 1.

82 TS 16.54, ll. 34–44 and 58, ed. Assaf, *Texts*, pp. 133–134.

83 Dropsy: *Med. Soc.*, I, 259. Family doctor: TS 13 J 6, f. 16, ll. 4–6. TS Arabic 4, f. 10, is an account of payments to a physician by five patients whom he visited almost daily and who paid 1–3 (dirhems?) per visit; only on Friday two patients paid 6, presumably because there usually was no visit on the Sabbath. The payments were made (or listed as not made) at the end of the week. The physician is referred to in the third person. The patients, it seems, were Muslims.

84 TS Arabic Box 40, f. 16. The fact that the petition concludes with a eulogy on the Prophet Muhammad does not indicate at all that the petitioner must have been a Muslim. The document was written by a notary in the style usual in such petitions. That the notary's Arabic was not flawless has its parallels even in books of renowned contemporary authors.

[85] *The Arabian Nights,* Night 25 (Story of the Hunchback).

[86] BM Or 5566 B, f. 15. I am indebted to Dr. Hassanein Rabie of Cairo for assistance in the reading of this document.

[87] TS 18 J 4, f. 1, ll. 15–16.

[88] Marriage contract of a poor physician: Bodl. MS Heb. f 56 (Cat. 2821, no. 16*k*), f. 54*v* (dated 1186). Will: TS 13 J 3, f. 17 (1241). In lists of contributors: *Med. Soc.,* I, 78. Letter: TS 13 J 6, f. 16 (The writer had not bought "one thread" of a new suit for two years, and his children suffered hunger).

[89] ULC Or 1081 J 5*.

[90] Ibn Abī Uṣaybi'a, II, 116–117, and 113–114.

[91] Mose ben Maimon, *Epistulae,* ed. D. H. Baneth (Jerusalem, 1946), p. 70, l. 19: *ḥāsabtuhu 'alā mā dhakarta,* "I shall make account with him according to your request." Letter of Maimonides' brother: ULC Or 1081 J 1, *India Book* 178.

[92] *Med. Soc.,* I, 252, and 463 n. 134. Also Bodl. MS Heb. e 101, f. 13 + f. 102, f. 43 (two fragments of the same document): the physician Abu 'l-Maḥāsin Japheth b. Joshiah and the sugar merchant Abu 'l-'Izz b. Abu 'l-Ma'āni declare that they had operated a sugar factory for many years together, but were now unable to pay the heavy government taxes any longer (1220–1221).

[93] TS 16.179*v,* ll. 29, 41*.

[94] Bodl. MS Heb. f 22 (Cat. 2728), fs. 25*v*–52*v* (see *JAOS,* 78 [1959], 301).

[95] Bodl. MS Heb. a 3 (Cat. 2873), f. 29 (see *Kirjath Sepher,* 43 [1969] 112–115).

[96] TS 13 J 14, f. 25. The poems are referred to as *yōṣerōt l-Ibn Shaṭanāsh,* i.e., written by Joseph Ibn Abitur (see *Med. Soc.,* I, 57). The book on Jewish law: Halākhōt Gedōlōt (of Simon Qayyārā).

[97] TS 24.38 (see sec. 4, n. 24, above).

[98] TS 8 K 22, f. 12*v.* "All this was written by its author, Samuel b. Elazar . . ."

[99] J. Schirmann, *Studies of the Research Institute for Hebrew Poetry* (Jerusalem) 6 (1945), 265–288, edited nineteen poems of Ibn al-'Ammānī and listed eight others published previously. A. Scheiber, "Unbekannte Gedichte von Aaron Ibn Al-Ammani etc.," *Sefarad,* 27 (1967), 269–281, edited six more from the David Kaufmann Collection, some accompanied by facsimiles.

[100] *Diwan,* ed. H. Brody (Berlin, 1894), I, 101, also pp. 2–3, 10–11.

[101] *Ibid.,* pp. 44–45, 175–176.

[102] Schirmann, *op. cit.* (see n. 99), p. 270.

[103] Scheiber, *op. cit.* (see n. 99), pp. 280–281. DK 164[4]. Facsimile opposite p. 271, where the manuscript is referred to as DK No. 164, p. 2b.

[104] The manuscript is damaged here. I read *be-mivṭā'ēnū.* "In our tongue," meaning, perhaps, Hebrew.

[105] Life is compared with the service of a soldier (see Job 14:14, 7:1, Isaiah 40:2). In Hebrew the words for "army," "host," and "service" are identical, a wordplay that I am unable to render in English.

[106] *Diwan* (see n. 100) I, 224–225, often quoted, e.g., J. Schirmann, *Tarbiz,* 9 (1938), 221. The pun is based on a Talmudic phrase.

[107] ENA Uncatalogued 40*, ed. S. D. Goitein, *Tarbiz,* 25 (1956) 408–412. Facsimile in *Med. Soc.,* I, between 21 and 22, illus. no. 6 (upside down in the first edition).

[108] E. Silberschlag, *Saul Tschernichowsky: Poet of Revolt* (Ithaca, N.Y.), 1968. A short, but excellent biography, accompanied by translations, and paying much attention to the poet's medical career.

[109] S. D. Goitein, "The Biography of Rabbi Judah Ha-Levi in the Light of the Cairo Geniza Documents," *PAAJR,* 28 (1959), 41–56. Some later publications, such as the edition of TS 13 J 33, f. 7, *Tarbiz,* 30 (1961), 379–384, where the poet is approached for a donation by a traveler from Badajoz, Spain, while both sojourned in Egypt, also have relevance to the topic discussed.

[110] Often quoted and translated. See *Selected Poems of Jehuda Halevi,* translated

into English by Nina Salaman (Philadelphia, 1924), p. 113. My translation tries to render the intention of the poet, as far as discernible to me.

[111] This is an allusion to the so-called *istikhāra,* "letting God choose for us," before any undertaking, such as going on a journey, doing some important business transaction, or taking a medicine. See *Med. Soc.,* I, 346, where I should have remarked perhaps that the custom was already common in Talmudic times (see Berakhot 29*b*). More about this in *Med. Soc.,* Vol. III, chap. x.

[112] The subject of this section has been treated by me in "The Medical Profession in the Light of the Cairo Geniza Documents," *HUCA,* 34 (1963), 177–194, but I have now greatly enlarged and thoroughly revised it. For the general background, see H. Friedenwald, *The Jews and Medicine* (Baltimore, 1944), and Sami Hamarneh, *Bibliography on Medicine and Pharmacy in Medieval Islam* (Stuttgart, 1964). The latter publication is to be used together with the very important study (which is partly a review of it) of Otto Spies, "Beiträge zur medizinisch-pharmazeutischen Bibliographie des Islam," *Der Islam,* 44 (1968), 138–173, and the review of Manfred Ullmann, *ZDMG,* 118 (1968), 177–179. The delightful paper by Owsei Temkin, "Byzantine Medicine: Tradition and Empiricism," *Dumbarton Oaks Papers,* 16 (1962), 97–115, is also relevant. The latest comprehensive work on the subject: Manfred Ullmann, *Die Medizin im Islam,* Handbuch der Orientalistik, Ergänzungsband VI (Leiden, 1970). About criticism, and even ridicule of the medical art and attempts of its vindication see F. Rosenthal, "The Defense of Medicine in the Mediaeval Muslim World," *Bulletin of the History of Medicine,* 43 (1969), 519–532.

13. DRUGGISTS, PHARMACISTS, PERFUMERS, AND PREPARERS OF POTIONS

[1] It is not correct to translate *sharābī* as wine merchant, as is sometimes done. A potion, *sharāb,* is frequently mentioned as bought for a sick person. Wine is called in the Geniza *nabīdh* or *khamr.* In the prescription TS Arabic Box 30, f. 65*v* (see n. 30, below) khamr is recommended as an alternative for a sharāb. Of course, wine itself served as a major medicine (often flavored with various spices or drugs, as in ENA 2808, f. 22). The *ṭabbākh sharāb,* "cooker of potions" (App. C, sec. 55), presumably produced sharābs wholesale and traded them to retail sharābīs.

A physician practicing in the store of a sharābī is mentioned in ULC Or 1080 J 93*.

[2] A *ṣaydalānī* is listed in TS 20.168 (App. A, sec. 6) and TS K 15, f. 45 (A 7) as tenant in a communal building (1043). Others are mentioned as prospective or actual proprietors of houses: TS 16.79+ (1051), TS 13 J 2, f. 3 (1093); in an Arabic document TS Arabic Box 53, f. 61. The word *ṣaydanī* seems not to appear in a dictionary, but occurs twice in App. C, sec. 19, referring to different persons (TS Misc. Box 8, f. 102, col. I, l. 16: Mubārak, *ibid.,* col. II, l. 24: Abū Naṣr b. Mukhtār). For *safūfī* see TS Misc. Box 8, f. 99, p. 6, col. VI, subcol. A, l. 5 (C 55).

The word ṣaydalānī is traditionally explained as dealer in sandalwood (the English word goes back to the same Sanskrit name of that sweet-smelling wood as the Arabic *ṣandal,* the common word for sandalwood). Thus, ṣaydalānī, like ʿaṭṭār, originally designates a perfumer.

[3] *Med. Soc.,* I, 173–179, 364, sec. 11, where, in a contract of partnership, a special stipulation is made for a popular medicine helping women to get fat. A prescription how to become stout ("not only women, but men as well") is found in the Geniza MS D. W. Amram, f. 2*v,* preserved in the Library of the University of Pennsylvania, Philadelphia, (not in the Museum, like most of the other Geniza manuscripts in the possession of the University). It is a genuine prescription, not a cabbalistic one, as stated in B. Halper, *Descriptive Catalogue of Genizah Fragments in Philadelphia* (Philadelphia, 1924), p. 218, no. 456.

[4] TS 16.70 (1095); TS 12.670* (1228).

[5] TS 16.334, written (and signed) in large calligraphic letters by Ḥalfōn b. Manasse ha-Levi. Mostly legal verbiage, forty lines preserved. Upper part missing. For Banīn, see n. 52, below.

[6] TS 10 J 4, f. 10, also written by Ḥalfōn. The lower part is irregularly torn away. A son of this 'aṭṭār, Yeshū'ā Sayyid al-Kull ("the lord of all") b. Jacob, known as Abu 'l-Munā b. Dā'ūd, received a loan of 50 dinars in TS 16.51 (two documents on one manuscript, Oct., 1128, Sept., 1129). His father was then still alive. In the part preserved Yeshū'ā's profession is not indicated.

[7] TS 10 J 5, f. 25, written by Hillel b. Eli at his best, but incomplete.

[8] *Ma'ālim al-Qurba,* Eng. summary, p. 39. See also n. 58, below.

[9] TS 13 J 1, f. 21. Mevōrākh b. Nathan, one of the two signatories, is not identical with the judge bearing this name.

[10] TS Arabic Box 40, f. 29. Christians and Jews appearing in Muslim documents are usually characterized as such.

[11] TS Arabic Box 53, f. 61. These valuable documents are incomplete.

[12] TS 16.117. In the date the hundreds are missing, but the enormous document is clearly in the hand of the judge Mevōrākh b. Nathan (App. D, sec. 22). He signs in monumental, not cursive script, wherefore his identity can be established with certainty only by his handwriting in the document itself.

[13] ULC Or 1080 J 117. Large, but incomplete.

[14] ENA 2558, f. 1 (Dec. 1126): The 'Aṭṭār al-Maḥallī gives a loan of 32 dinars. TS 10 J 26, f. 10: To another, Abu 'l-Fakhr, a balance of 4 dinars is due from a loan given by him (1146). TS 10 J 19, f. 7: A sharābī in Alexandria is bankrupt. For loans received see n. 6, above.

[15] Bodl. MS Heb. b 12 (Cat. 2875), f. 2: Two sisters certify to have received their shares in the estate of their father, namely the store of drugs, its storage room, and the goods found in both. Their brother had been a partner of their father. Bodl. MS Heb. c 28 (Cat. 2876), f. 54: After a payment of 30 dinars to the *dīwān al-mawārīth,* or Office of Inheritances, the Jewish court receives the remaining 83 dinars from the estate of an 'aṭṭār (1203). *Ibid.,* f. 44: Solomon b. Judah, the Gaon of Jerusalem writes about a man from Spain who had made a bequest for an 'aṭṭār in Egypt.

[16] Bodl. MS Heb. d 66 (Cat. 2878), fs. 47–48+*, *India Book* 287.

[17] Lane of the Lamps: Firkovitch II, 1700, f. 6 (spring, 1156), where also two other 'aṭṭārs are referred to. See Casanova, *Reconstruction,* I, 39–44, Yāqūt, II, 937.

[18] ENA 2727, f. 48. See n. 52. Sūq Wardān: also ULC Or 1080 J 2 (App. C, sec. 113).

[19] Makers of cans and canisters, *zanājil:* TS NS J 416, l. 5 (C 34). Blacksmiths: *Med. Soc.,* I, 411 n. 8.

[20] Casanova, *Reconstruction,* II, 125–132. Ephraim b. Shemarya: ULC Or 1080 J 176. Letter to Abu 'l-Ḥasan b. Sa'īd al-ṣārifī (*ā* = *ă* = *ay*) Ibn al-Maṣmūdī, *ṭabīb al-Murabba'a* ila 'l-Maṣṣāsa: Dropsie 395.

[21] *Ma'ālim al-Qurba,* Eng. summary, p. 38.

[22] TS NS J 27. The dead man is called *Ibn* al-sharābī. But the inventory of his estate shows that he had followed the profession of his father.

[23] *Ma'ālim al-Qurba,* p. 37. The article "Ibn Abi 'l-Bayān" in *EI*², II, 683 (J. Vernet) is now to be complemented by the important notes in A. Dietrich, *Medicinalia Arabica* (Göttingen, 1966), p. 216.

[24] *Minhāj al-dukkān fī adwiyat naw'i 'l-insān,* "The Store Guide [I believe purposely called thus in contrast with Ibn Abi 'l-Bayān's book "*Hospital* Handbook"]: The Medicaments for the Human Race." Brockelmann, *GAL*², I, 897, Steinschneider, *Arabische Literatur der Juden,* pp. 237–238, Dietrich, *Medicinalia Arabica* (see n. 23), pp. 148–149.

The by-name Abu 'l-Munā, "the long yearned for," was extremely common.

Abraham Maimonides (who was born when his father was fifty-two years old) was also called thus. Our druggist's personal name, Munayyir (or Munīr?, corresponding to Heb. Meir [Mē'īr]) was very rare; found, e.g., in INA D-55, f. 4: Hilāl b. Thābit (= Heb. Yākhīn) b. Munīr (I prefer this reading, since only one *y* is written), died in 1221.

[25] Max Meyerhof, *Der Bazar der Drogen und Wohlgerüche in Kairo,* Archiv für Wirtschaftsforschung in Orient, no. 3 (Weimar, 1918), p. 37.

[26] Qiddushin 82*b*: "The world cannot exist without perfumers and tanners; happy is the one who is a perfumer . . . ."

[27] Mishna Yoma 3:11. For professional secrets of Jewish dyers see *Med. Soc.,* I, 100. A recently published book of the tenth century south Arabian author al-Hamdānī on "The Yellow and The White," meaning gold and silver, contains the interesting note that only one Jewish family in Baghdad (here *ahl bayt* means "family," not "noblemen") knew how to manufacture fine, extremely thin leaves of tin, called "gold water" (Christopher Toll, *Die Beiden Edelmetalle* . . . [Uppsala, 1968], p. 297, Ar. text, p. 63*a*).

[28] The contracts of partnership (see nn. 3, 4, above) provide many interesting insights into the character and working of the druggist's activities.

[29] See n. 1, above. A prescription in Hebrew characters with the name of the patient on the top ("For the Elder Abū Yaḥyā," probably Nahray b. Nissīm) and the wish "Effective, God willing" at the bottom, both in Arabic script: ULC 1081 J 39. For other prescriptions see sec. 12, n. 63, above. TS Arabic Box 53, f. 33, in Kufesque script, seems to be particularly old, but contains no reference to a patient.

[30] TS Arabic Box 30, f. 65*v*. On the first page there is another prescription, in Arabic characters, for the same patient, but his name is written in two different hands. It was common to apply to different physicians during one illness. Some of the ingredients in the first prescription are identical with those in the second one translated here.

In the following notes Maimonides-Meyerhof (see *Med. Soc.,* I, xxiii) is abbreviated to M.-M. The numbers refer to the paragraphs (not pages) of Meyerhof's edition and French translation.

[31] Kabul, the present capital of the state of Afghanistan, has given its name to one of the various types of myrobalan, *halaylaj*. Because of the widespread use of various types of myrobalan, especially Kabul, Indian, and yellow myrobalan, the physicians, apothecaries, and overseas traders (the latter, e.g., in TS 16.7) sometimes omitted the word "myrobalan." M.-M. 112.

[32] For beleric see Sir George Watt, *The Commercial Products of India* (London, 1908), pp. 1072–1073. In 1058, 10 mann of it (approximately 20 pounds) cost 2¾ dinars in Fustat (TS 12.5, l. 6). English beleric is obviously derived from the Ar. *balaylaj,* which, through Persian, comes from an Indian word. Not in M.-M. and rare in the Geniza.

[33] Emblic, derived through Arabic *amlaj* from Sanskrit *āmālaka,* very common in the Geniza papers. M.-M. 374.

[34] English senna is Ar. *sena* (with one *n* in Ar.). M.-M. 267.

[35] About this plant, Ar. *afīthīmūn,* from Greek *epi-thymon,* from which English thyme see *Med. Soc.,* I, 47. M.-M. 23 and 186 (not 189, as misprinted in M.-M. 23).

[36] The scientific name of this plant is *Lavandula stoechas L.* The Arabic term used here, *ustukhūdus,* is the genitive of Greek *stoikhas,* the second element of the scientific name (the genitive: *stoikhodos*). M.-M. 6.

[37] Both the English and the Arabic are translations of Greek *bū-glosson,* oxtongue, a common medicament for stimulating perspiration and the flow of urine. M.-M. 211.

[38] Armenian stone and lapis lazuli are mentioned together in Dioscorides, *Materia Medica,* book 5, paragraphs 64–65 (see César E. Dubler, *La Materia Médica de Dioscorides* [Barcelona, 1955], III, 538). These easily dissolvable bluish stones,

widely used in jewelry, served also as constituents in medicaments. While lapis lazuli, as the Geniza shows, was an important item of the Mediterranean trade (East–West), the same cannot be said of Armenian stone. Or did the traders perhaps not discern between the two?

[39] English julep is derived from Ar. *julāb,* which is Persian *gul-āb,* lit., rose water. At the time of the writing of this prescription the word designated a potion different from rose water, as the continuation of the text shows and as is proved by contemporary sources.

[40] Appetizer: Ar. *ḥamaḍ*. The third letter is not clearly visible. The text says: rose sherbet *and* rose water . . . , but "and" stands in Arabic often for "or."

[41] Sherbet, an imperfect rendering of *sharāb ward.*

[42] English deodar seems to be derived directly from Hindu, where it means "God's tree." The Arabic form used here: *dyywdr* (pronounced approximately: *deyōdar)* is very similar to the English. Maimonides mentions several names of this tree, among them *shajarat Allāh,* "tree of God." The fruit is used as a diuretic. M.-M. 22.

[43] Scammony is a strong purgative. Its English and Arabic names are derived from the Greek. (The plant is indigenous in Greece.) Here it is not called by its proper name, but by a laudatory surname, *al-maḥmūda,* "the praiseworthy," so named because of its drastic effect. In commercial correspondence it is also thus referred to occasionally. M.-M. 281. Here, too, "and" may mean "or."

[44] A woman from the family of Karam, a name common in the twelfth and thirteenth centuries.

[45] DK XX. Allotment of piece against piece: *muqāyaḍa, ibid.,* verso, sec. II, l. 3.

[46] Cupboard: *khizāna wa-kursī-hā.* Settee (bench with a back): *dikka.*

[47] Among these the curious item *ṣunayjāt kibār naḥās,* "large little copper scales."

[48] Since medieval illustrations of pharmacies have been preserved (e.g., no. 57.51.21, Metropolitan Museum of Art, dated 1224, see R. Ettinghausen, *Arab Painting* [Cleveland, 1962], p. 87), the nomenclature of the details might perhaps be of interest. Pots, *barniyya,* twenty-two enumerated with their prices; short-necked bottles, *qiṭirmīz* (so pronounced, as a *y* after *q* in one case indicates), perhaps not all of them made of glass, because some are described expressly as glass bottles and one as a gilded one; flasks, *qinnīna,* in this case, too, only one is described as made of glass and costing ¼ dirhem; a high wooden case, *durj,* with a cover; a copper bowl, *qadaḥ;* a copper basin with a funnel, *kirnīb* (a Greek word) *wa-qim';* a mug, *kūz,* for ointments; and, finally, six canisters, *zanājil.* In the (temporary?) possession of this partner there were thirty other small and large pots, six copper pipes, *barbakh,* two cans, and two broken mortars.

[49] Text: *ḥiṣrim muna'na'; sikanjabīn rummānī: rubb sūs sharāb lisān al-ḥamal.* For the last item see M.-M. 213.

[50] Cassia: *khiyār shanbar,* M.-M. 387; *rībās* (spelled without *y*), M.-M. 350.

[51] TS Arabic Box 30, f. 274. Eleven items were given as *wadā'a,* "courtesy," "kindness," which, however, probably stands for classical *wadī'a,* "deposit," "charge," in the meaning of "on commission."

[52] ENA 2727, f. 48. Market police: *akhadhūhā ṣibyān al-ḥisba.* The dead druggist was called Banīn b. Dā'ūd, perhaps identical with the one mentioned in TS 16.334 (see n. 5, above).

[53] Yeshū'ā b. Joshiahu b. Shema'ya Gaon (see Mann, II, 232 [4], bottom). Court validation written by him: TS 10 J 5, f. 14. He buys a Josippon: TS 10 K 16, f. 12, and has the Pereq of R. Judah ha-Nāsī copied for himself: Bodl. MS Heb. c 18 (Cat. 2634), f. 11. ENA 4020, f. 8, *India Book* 153, is addressed to him.

[54] TS Arabic Box 54, f. 44. Samuel b. Saadya ha-Levi had at least one son (see Hebrew Union College Geniza MS 4+). About Nahray b. Nassīm as jurisconsult see chap. v, sec. C, 1, above.

[55] Exchange rate approximately 1:40, as in *Med. Soc.,* I, 381, sec. 57, also written

by Samuel b. Saadya. Since the remark "I have received" (9 dirhems) is written expressly, it stands to reason that all the other entries represent orders of payment. The use of a sprinkler, *qumqum,* for sprinkling rose oil on guests is described in lively fashion in Ḥāfiẓ Wahbe, *Jazīrat al-'Arab fi-l-Qarn al-'Ishrīn* (Cairo, 1935), p. 127.

[56] Coriander: *kuṣbara* for *kuzbara,* costing 5 dirhems, the costliest item for a spice in the second consignment.

[57] TS Arabic Box 30, f. 165. The item *qifāq,* cups, *ibid.,* verso, l. 3, could not be traced by me in any dictionary; but is found in the singular in ULC Or 1080, Box 5, f. 15, a trousseau list, written by Samuel b. Saadya's contemporary Mevōrākh b. Nathan. I take it as an Arabic rendering of Persian *qifk*—one of the many new words coming to Syria and Egypt with the invasions of the Seljuks and their successor states.

Household goods in a druggist's account also in ENA 1822, f. 24.

[58] Bodl. MS Heb. e 98, fs. 64–65* (not included in *Nahray*).

[59] DK VIII*. The writer, referred to also in other Geniza letters, is called Binyām al-Rashīdī, Benjamin of Rosetta, but it seems to me that the letter was sent from Alexandria.

[60] A. Dietrich, *Zum Drogenhandel im Islamischen Ägypten* (Heidelberg, 1954), cf. my short review in *JQR,* 47 (1957), 376–377.

Tea is regularly flavored with cardamom, *hayl,* in the Middle East, and I wonder why we do not do the same. It is delicious.

[61] TS 10 J 17, f. 12. Other letters in the same hand: TS 10 J 17, f. 3, TS 10 J 18, f. 11. There might be more—which are related to the person mentioned in the text, not to the case of rural 'aṭṭārs in general. Another good example for such an order sent by an 'aṭṭār in a small town to one in the capital is ULC Or 1080 J 101. (Eleven items, some uncommon. Both the recipient and the writer are called 'aṭṭār.)

[62] Approximately: *la'alla,* l. 7, lit., perhaps, maybe. The word is repeated before most of the prices indicated.

[63] *Fuqqā'a* designates both a vessel (e.g., "a pitcher with honey," *Med. Soc.,* I, 474 n. 18, "with mercury," *ibid.,* p. 485 n. 8) and a kind of potion. The profession of *fuqqā'ī,* frequent in the Geniza throughout, probably designated the preparer of that potion. Dozy, *Supplément,* II, 274*a,* "brasseur" (brewer), is taken from a nineteenth-century dictionary.

[64] Eye powder: *ashyāf.* On special order, bought at retail: *miswāq.*

[65] While writing *Med. Soc.,* I, 151, 241, I had order slips written only in Hebrew characters (but, of course, in Arabic language). Recently, I found a stack of such orders written in Arabic characters at the Jewish Theological Seminary, New York, ENA 3971, fs. 13–24, 31, 33, 34, fifteen altogether, but there are probably more in that collection. On these slips, the signature is always preceded by the word *wa-katab,* "written by." (Mr. M. Friedman alerted me to the fact that the volume concerned contained some documentary material.)

[66] TS Arabic Box 54, f. 19 (Dec., 1140, containing twenty slips); Westminster College, Frag. Cair., I, fs. 55–63 (10 slips). *India Book* 138, 139. One slip sometimes contains two orders.

[67] The words *ward,* roses, and *laymūn,* lemon, unaccompanied by *mā',* water, or *sharāb,* potion, are here translated rose-preserve and lemon-preserve, respectively, which, I believe, is the meaning also in various other texts studied by me.

[68] The curds were taken dissolved in water (see Dozy, *Supplément,* II, 151*b*).

[69] Plain (unflavored) potion, *sharāb sādhij.* The quantity (2 ounces!) shows again (see n. 1, above) that here sharāb cannot mean wine. Wine was consumed daily and stored in large quantities.

[70] Abu 'l-Ḥasan b. Mūsā al-fāṣid (the bloodletter) al-'aṭṭār (TS NS J 416, margin [App. C, sec. 34]).

CHAPTER VII: *Interfaith Relations, Communal Autonomy and Government Control*

A. INTERFAITH RELATIONS

1. *Group Consciousness and Discrimination*

[1] Joseph b. Shemarya ha-dayyān al-Barqī writing to Nahray b. Nissīm. ENA 2805, f. 9 (where he explains also that he is unable to travel by sea). The passage translated: ENA 2805, f. 13*v*, ll. 3–8. When a caravan arrived at a *ḥawḍ*, or water reservoir, the stronger or less considerate travelers would take all the good and clean water for themselves, leaving to the others only turbid remainders, unless special arrangements were made, as in this case. For the Jewish abhorrence of caravan travel because of the difficulties engendered by the Sabbath laws, see *Med. Soc.*, I, 280–281.

[2] For Islam, see the concise, up-to-date, and authoritative article "Dhimma" by Claude Cahen in *EI*², which registers also the relevant literature. The most detailed treatment in Fattal, *Non-Musulmans en pays d'Islam.* Some gaps in this otherwise meritorious book could have been avoided, had its author made use of the publications on the subject by E. Ashtor-Strauss and others. For the Jews in Europe, besides general books such as Baron, *History of the Jews,* see, e.g., James Parkes, *The Jew in the Medieval Community* (London, 1938), B. Blumenkranz, *Juifs et Chrétiens dans le Monde Occidental 430–1096* (Paris, 1960), Jacob Katz, *Exclusiveness and Tolerance* (London, 1961), also in Heb. (Jerusalem, 1960).

[3] Christian business friend: TS 10 J 12, f. 20, *Nahray* 144, ll. 13 and 23 (around 1060). Mistrust: TS 18 J 5, f. 5, *India Book* 149, l. 3: *lō emūnā ba-gōyīm.* For *lō,* in Aden, I heard *ēn,* which is grammatically more correct. The interpretation of Psalm 144:8 in Katz, *Exclusiveness* (see n. 2), chap. viii, n. 55.

[4] L. Brunot and E. Malka, *Textes Judéo-arabes de Fés* (Rabat, 1939), p. 393.

[5] TS 12.581*v*, ll. 8–9 (thirteenth century). TS 13 J 17, f. 3, ed. S. D. Goitein, *Tarbiz,* 36 (1967), 372–376. JNUL 7, margin (both documents eleventh century).

[6] TS 16.305*v*, l. 26. To be sure, *al-nās,* "the people," "the public," sometimes refers specifically to Jews, e.g., in TS 12.290*v*, l. 15.

[7] Two such references in TS 16.179*.

[8] Meinardus, "Orthodox Copts," p. 157.

[9] TS 12.74, l. 14: *hāʿarēlīm mithpallelīm eṣlēnū ba-bāmōth.* Ibn Jubayr, pp. 305–306.

[10] TS 8 J 26, f. 19+*. *Midrash R. David ha-Nagid,* ed. A. I. Katsh (Jerusalem, 1964–1968).

[11] Terms such as *armay* ("Aramean") for non-Jew, TS 13 J 6, f 32, l. 10, *India Book* 279, are legal parlance and not everyday phrases.

[12] E.g., TS Box J 1, f. 47, which uses *naṣārā* in col. I and *ʿārēl* in IV. The term *muslim* is even more common than *goy. Al-goy raḥimahu 'llāhu*: Westminster College, Frag. Cairens. 51*v*, l. 4.

[13] Even by such an eminent authority as Claude Cahen (in the *EI*² article quoted above, n. 2).

[14] The nomenclature does not lack a comical side. The term *sōne'ē Yisrā'ēl,* "the haters of Israel," means, in accordance with talmudic usage, "the Jews" (used when something bad or ominous is said about them). But *sōnē* without addition is an "anti-Semite" (TS 13 J 13, f. 24, ll. 23–27; DK XXVI, l. 9).

[15] TS NS J 24*v*, l. 3. *Med. Soc.*, I, 31. Āraḥ b. Nathan (= Musāfir b. Wahb) writes to his brother, the prominent notable Abraham B. Nathan, the Seventh (see App. A, sec. 171, above, and here, n. 22, below).

[16] TS 20.90, l. 15. "The first thing that God the exalted has done with you and with all Israel, of which you are the crown, is that he saved you from Ma'arra, despite the sin'ūth of its Muslim inhabitants, then that he saved your soul from the people who brought you to Fāmiya [the ancient Apamea, see *EI* ², I, 215, s.v. "Afāmiya"], which is even more terrible—having remained in the hand of the enemy in Aleppo would have been better a thousand times, . . ." A highly interesting fragment in an eleventh-century hand, possibly of the Gaon Daniel b. Azarya (see the facsimile in *Sefer ha-Yishuv,* facing p. 57, in the court validation). I have collected about ten other fragments in the same hand, which have the additional common characteristic that the writer uses occasionally the Arabic script in midst of a letter written in Hebrew characters, especially at the end of a line, when there was not space enough for the far broader Hebrew letters; e.g., here, the word *taḥaqqaq* is written at the end of l. 20 in Arabic characters, but appears in the midst of l. 21 in Hebrew script.

[17] TS 12.435*v,* ll. 24–27*. This Spanish Jew uses *sin'ā* instead of *sin'ūth,* cf. *sin'at ha-gōyīm,* TS 18 J 4, f. 26, l. 36*, ed. Mann, II, 141, and the well-known saying of the Talmud, Pesahim 49*b*, about the hatred of the ignoramuses.

[18] Baron, *History of the Jews,* I, 190–191 and 381 n. 31.

[19] TS 12.338, ed. Mann, II, 241, l. 16. (For *syqryqwn* the manuscript has rightly *syqryqyn.*)

[20] Bodl. MS Heb. c 28 (Cat. 2876), f. 34, ll. 12–18. This might be an allusion to the situation described below, where even women were not safe in Alexandria. The writer: Mūsā b. Abi 'l-Ḥayy (see *Med. Soc.,* I, Index, s.v.).

[21] TS 18 J 4, f. 6, l. 38, and verso, l. 18. Written by Isaac Nīsābūrī (see *Med. Soc.,* I, 153).

[22] TS 13 J 22 f. 23, ll. 10–16. Musāfir b. Wahb writes to his brother Abraham (see n. 15, above). The Muslim qadi was called Makīn al-Dawla. He belonged to a well-known family of judges bearing titles formed with *Makīn.*

[23] Heb. *piqqeḥīm,* which corresponds to Arabic *nuẓẓār,* mentioned before.

[24] The Arabic term used is *muḥtasib.*

[25] TS 13 J 13, f. 24, ll. 13–26. The letter deals also with personal matters.

[26] TS 13 J 33, f. 9*. The officials issued receipts, but did not enter the sums received in the government records so that the persons taxed had to pay a second time.

[27] *Histoires Coptes d'un cadi médiéval,* ed. Claude Cahen, *Bulletin de l'Institut français d'archéologie orientale,* 59 (1960), 143.

[28] TS Misc. Box 27, f. 1. Only the lower part is preserved. The manuscript is in the hand of the Alexandrian judge Shelah b. Mevassēr (dated documents identified thus far: 1075–1101). The reference to "the Nagid of blessed memory" (without name), found in the letter is used invariably of Judah, the brother and predecessor of Mevōrākh. Thus, this letter must have originated at a comparatively early stage of Mevōrākh's tenure of the office. Dr. N. Golb of Chicago has drawn my attention to this document.

[29] His full name was Abu 'l-Makārim Saniyy al-Dawla Moses b. Japheth ha-Levi (TS 16.208 [dated 1170]).

[30] TS 12.290*v,* ll. 5–18. The beginning and address of the letter are lost. But the script and style are undoubtedly those of the Alexandrian merchant Abū Naṣr b. Abraham from whose hand many letters have been preserved. The Jewish government official is referred to as al-'Amīn. Several Jewish kātibs bearing the titles Amīn al-Mulk or Amīn al-Dawla are known from that period.

[31] Gottheil-Worrell, III, 18–19. For *lā* in l. 13, read *illā.* The editors misread the address (as well as many other parts) of the letter. The addressee is Mūsā b. Abi 'l-Ḥayy, who wrote the letter referred to above, n. 20. The writer was his brother Ibrahīm.

[32] Bodl. MS Heb. b 3 (Cat. 2806, no. 15), f. 16*v*, ll. 9–10 (eleventh century).

[33] ULC Add. 3335+; often discussed and also trans. into English (see Shaked, *Bibliography*, p. 42).

[34] Bodl. MS Heb. f 56 (Cat. 2821, no. 40), f. 130+ describes the measures taken to save the pious foundations from the rapacity of "The Monk." In TS 24.78+*, a Jewish official flees the country before him. His two Jewish accomplices: TS 12.91 and TS NS J 272, which form parts of one document.

[35] *Med. Soc.*, I, 34.

[36] Mann, II, Index s.v. "Jerusalem," "Palestine," and "Shiloah." The unpublished texts enlarge, but do not change the picture substantially.

[37] For Palestine and Old Cairo, see chap. vi, sec. 10, above; Mann, I, 154, 214; Braslavsky, *Our Country*, p. 87; for Acre specifically: TS 18 J 5, f. 5+. The story of the Jewish wet nurse: Abū Yūsuf, *Kitāb al-Āthār*. Jews not permitted to ritually kill animals for Muslims in Seville, early twelfth century: É. Lévi-Provencal, *Le Traité d'Ibn 'Abdun* (Paris, 1947), p. 110, para. 157. Muslim resentment about Jews selling them meat prohibited themselves: G. Vajda, *Lévi-Provençal Memorial Volume* (Paris, 1962), p. 810 n. 20.

[38] TS 13 J 25, f. 11, ll. 15–19. Since the letter speaks of two sieges by the "Ḥijāzīs," most probably Qayrawān is referred to.

[39] TS 13 J 25, f.15, ll. 4–13.

[40] See chap. v, sec. D, 1, above. For the rebuilding of synagogues see Mann, I, 36, 72–73, 89, and my "The Synagogue Building and Its Furnishings according to the Records of the Cairo Geniza," *Eretz-Israel*, 7 (1964 [L.A. Memorial Volume]), 81–97.

[41] TS Arabic Box 18(2), f. 4, ed. Assaf, *Texts*, pp. 46–48.

[42] Westminster College, Frag. Cairens 51*v*, ll. 1–9.

[43] TS 13 J 11, f. 5, ed. Mann, II, 186. In Bodl. MS Heb. d 75, f. 20, l. 9, *Nahray* 94, the writer regrets that, owing to a grave illness, he was forced to ride up "the Mountain on the day of the Ḥajj" instead of walking in the procession.

[44] Mez, *Renaissance*, p. 54 (chap. 4, end), pp. 398–399 (chap. 23). Idris, *Zirides*, pp. 762–763.

[45] The copious Geniza material about these matters is collected in *Med. Soc.*, III, chap. viii (Burials).

[46] ULC 1080 J 93*.

[47] TS 10 J 14, f. 16, ll. 18–20, *India Book* 77x (the original text has no. 257 but was later identified as belonging together with no. 77).

[48] H. R. Idris, "Deux maîtres de l'école juridique kairounaise sous les Zirides," *Annales de l'Institut d'Études Orientales*, 13 (1955), 55–56.

[49] E.g., P. Heid. 915, l. 13: "The bearer of this letter, Isma'īl b. Nūḥ, a Muslim." The letter is written in Arabic characters, but its address in Hebrew!

[50] Lane-Poole, *Egypt in the Middle Ages*, p. 127.

[51] Ibn al-Jawzī, *Muntazam* (*Hyderabad*, 1940), IX, 228, ll. 12 ff. The source quoted in Fattal, *Non-Musulmans en pays d'Islam*, p. 104, is an abridgment and omits the detail of the Jālūt.

[52] Fattal, *op. cit.*

[53] DK, The Obadiah Scroll, ed. A. Scheiber, *Acta Orientalia Hungarica*, 4 (1954), 278, and *Kirjath Sepher*, 30 (1955), 97–98. The weights of Baghdad differed from those of Egypt, mostly referred to in this book.

[54] Bodl. MS Heb. f 56 (Cat. 2821, no. 16), f. 13*v*, ed. S. D. Goitein, *JQR*, 43 (1952), 73; see also pp. 57 ff.

[55] Ibn al-Dhahabī, *Ta'rīkh al-Islām*, MS Ayasofya 3005, Vol. XV, f. 14*b*, trans. *JQR*, 43 (1952), 62–63.

[56] TS 6 J 7, f. 3, l. 18 and verso l. 6+; see *Tarbiz*, 34 (1965), 243, and Fattal, *op. cit.*, p. 106.

[57] Chap. vi, sec. 12, n. 83, above.

[58] *Med. Soc.,* I, 345. Travel to Syria: TS NS J 279, l. 16. Customs in Cairo: ENA 2730 (Menahem). See also sec. A, 2, below.

2. *Interfaith Symbiosis and Cooperation*

[1] Qayrawān: Mosseri L 135+. Al-Maḥalla, TS 12.166. In both cases *ḥāra* is used for "quarter." Mosul: TS 20.128*v*+. "Place": *al-maḥalla.* No reference to a specifically Jewish quarter in the Jawdariyya district of New Cairo (see Mann, I, 33) has been found by me in the Geniza. The "Jewish quarter" in Alexandria (TS 12.254, margin, *Nahray* 102 [see *Med. Soc.,* I, 135]) should not be understood as the name of a locality. The Jewish neighborhoods in that city are well known by their proper names.

[2] Al-Balādhurī, *Futūḥ* (Cairo, 1932), p. 327. See also Ibn al-Faqīh, *Kitāb al-Buldān* (Leiden, 1885), p. 129, l. 3.

[3] TS 16.140*. The borders of the site are not indicated in this document.

[4] Goitein, *Studies,* p. 314 n. 5.

[5] See E. J. Worman, "Notes on the Jews in Fustāt from Cambridge Genizah Documents," *JQR,* 18 (1905), 1–39. The article provides a good general idea of the situation, although our knowledge both of Old Cairo and the Geniza naturally has much increased since its writing.

Christian neighbors of Jewish houses: TS 12.417; 12.499+ (dated 969); TS 12.641; TS 16.41 (New Cairo); TS 16.116 (dated 1[0]10); TS K 25, f. 251*v*, l. 5 (a Christian bearing the titles Fakhr al-Dawla Thiqat al-Mulk, "The Pride of the Government, the Trusted of the State"); TS NS J 3, l. 16 (a Jew describing himself as "Joseph who lives beneath the Mu'allaqa church"); Bodl. MS Heb. b 12 (Cat. 2875) fs. 9 and 29 (forming one deed, dated 959, ed. S. Assaf, *Tarbiz,* 9 (1938) 202–203*).

Muslim neighbors: TS NS J 283 (before 1040); TS 12.50; TS 16.65; TS 24.44 (dated 1102); TS 13 J 22, f. 2+*; TS Misc. Box 8, f. 61; P. Heid, 1451.

Christians and Muslims: TS 12.660 (see Worman, *JQR,* 18 [1905], 17); TS 20.85 (between 948 and 958; two Christians and one Muslim woman); TS K 25, f. 284; ULC Or 1080 J 117 (dated 1088). Three Muslims and one Christian in Minyat Ghamr: TS Arabic Box 53, f. 19. Alexandria, 1132: TS Arabic Box 30, f. 30*v*.

[Additional instances of all three occurrences were identified during my visit to England in summer, 1970.]

[6] TS 13 J 15, f. 24, ll. 12–15, addressed to Abraham b. Nathan, the Seventh (see sec. A, 1, n. 15, above), by a ḥāvēr, calling himself in the address, written in Arabic characters, simply *al-ḥābār* (written thus, to distinguish this title of the yeshiva from classical Arabic *ḥabr,* which is derived from the same Hebrew word and also means scholar, but does not have the specific connotation of "member of the Academy"). The hand is that of Solomon b. Yeshū'ā, the ḥāvēr of Damīra, who wrote the interesting (but much obliterated) letter Bodl. MS Heb. d 66 (Cat. 2878), f. 29, also addressed to this Abraham b. Nathan. It is most likely that the scene described here took place in that little town of Lower Egypt.

[7] TS 8 J 32, f. 4 (dated 1229, probably identical with the unclassed manuscript mentioned by Worman, *JQR* 18 [1905], 25 n. 3); Merx, *Paléographie hébraïque,* p. 25, which adds important details about this neighborhood (dated 1124).

[8] For the Little Market of the Jews in Fustat, see Worman, *JQR* 18 (1905), 28 and 30. The document from Tiberias, 1034: Bodl. MS Heb. c 13 (Cat. 2807, no. 9), f. 12, ed. Braslavsky, *Our Country,* p. 63. The letter: BM Or 5544, f. 9, ed. *ibid.,* pp. 44–47. (A few notes: The sender is a woman, the mother or sister of the writer. L. 10: for *'y'* read *'azā',* "may God comfort you," an expression of sympathy. L. 17: Shām is Palestine here, not Damascus. L. 22 *w'str* is not "and Esther," but Arabic *wa ('l-)sitr,* "and the curtain." The word immediately following is simply *al-kabīr,* "the large." The address "arriving, God willing" (without the name of the place),

as strange as it sounds, is correct and is found also in other letters.) Ramle: see chap. v, sec. C, 2, n. 3. Qayrawān: see Idris, *Zirides,* p. 419 n. 81.

[9] Bodl. MS Heb. a 3 (Cat. 2873), f. 35 (in Arabic script); TS Arabic Box 53, f. 61, see chap. vi, 13, n. 11; TS 12.544 (A.D. 1148); TS 16.117 (1179); Bodl. MS Heb. f 56 (Cat. 2821, no. 16), f. 43*a–c* (1181); ULC Or 1080 J 239 (1220); TS Box J 1, f. 47 (1234). Jerusalem: TS 13 J 19, f. 3. Minyat Ziftā: TS 8.4 (ca. 1140). Old Cairo, date doubtful: TS 8.150 (a physician and one Aḥmad).

[10] Maimonides, *Responsa,* I, 10, 31, 69–70. 1156: Firkovitch II, 1700, f. 2. House for the poor; TS 20.3, ll. 5–6, 25.

[11] Maimonides, *op. cit.,* II, 710.

[12] Abraham Maimuni, *Responsa,* p. 196. His grandson: Bodl. MS Heb. a 2 (Cat. 2805), f. 22, see sec. C, 1, b, n. 20, below. Charitable foundations: App. A, secs. 10, 27, 32, 33, 43, 94, and elsewhere. Christian collector: App. A, sec. 148. Protest: TS 13 J 30, f. 6*.

[13] See J. Wansbrough, *BSOAS,* (1968), 621, Fattal, *Non-Musulmans en pays d'Islam,* p. 95, and Mann, I, 33 n. 2, not mentioned by Fattal.

[14] A Muslim *faqīh* as business friend, e.g., TS 18 J 3, f. 13*v*, l. 5, *Nahray* 68 (his name: Ḥasan b. Maḥmūd al-Ḥadramī in Old Cairo).

A Christian, e.g., TS Misc. Box 28, f. 225, *Nahray* 161 (Yuḥanna, written *yḥnh,* in, or on the way to, Jerusalem).

Letter in Hebrew characters to Muslim business friend: TS 8 J 18, f. 33, margin. Muhammad's secretary: al-Balādhurī, *Futūḥ* (Cairo, 1932), p. 460. It took him two weeks to master the Hebrew script for using it in writing.

[15] Dropsie 389, ll. 30 and 31; verso, l. 40.

[16] An example of such a lasting collaboration was the *khulṭa* between Barhūn Tāhertī of Qayrawān and Abu 'l-Qāsim 'Abd al-Raḥmān, e.g., TS 20.69; TS 13 J 8, f. 13, *Nahray* 170; TS 10 J 9, f. 5, *Nahray* 171, 20.180, *Nahray* 172.

[17] Fattal, *op. cit.,* pp. 146–147. Jacob Katz *Exclusiveness and Tolerance* (Heb. ed.; Jerusalem, 1960), pp. 44 and 111. Commenda, 1141: TS 20.80*v*, ll. 42–43, *India Book* 273. 1229: TS 13 J 4, f. 4*v*, ll. 13–16 (the present recto of the manuscript is actually the verso). Trading flax: TS 28.19. See also *Med. Soc.,* I, 173. Cloth (bazz): TS 16.11, ll. 8, 27.

Query to Muslim scholar: H. R. Idris, "Commerce maritime et ḳirāḍ en Berbérie orientale," *JESHO,* 4 (1961), 233 (see also p. 228).

[18] Ibn Rajā', 1097: TS 16.87, l. 9. Nahray 1046: TS Box K 15, f. 53, I, ll. 9–11 (not in *Nahray*). Ibn 'Awkal: TS 8 J 18, f. 14, ed. S. D. Goitein, *Tarbiz,* 37 (1968), 48–50. Muslim father: Qumqum, P. Heid. 917, sec. C, ll. 6, 14, see *JESHO,* 9 (1966), 53, 54; son: Abū Sa'īd Khalaf, ENA 2805, f. 6A*v*, l. 2.

[19] Yemen: TS 16.262, *India Book* 307. Copper: TS 12.291, l. 17. Four Muslims: TS 20.180, ll. 15–19+. Muslim first: Mosseri L 209, ll. 6–8. Slave of Muslim judge: INA D-55, f. 13, ll. 31–34+. Alexandria: TS 13 J 28, f. 15+.

[20] TS 8 J 19, f. 24, ll. 17–23, *Nahray* 151.

[21] Maimonides, *Responsa,* II, 360. Muqaddasi, p. 205.

[22] TS 8 J 7, f. 18*.

[23] TS NS J 277*.

[24] ULC Or 1080 J 93*.

[25] TS NS J 150.

[26] A, 1, n. 47, above.

[27] TS Misc. Box 24, f. 66. The miller granted the loan on Ramaḍān 3, A.H. 654 (Sept. 24, 1256), and the bread baker was paid on Oct. 23, of the same year. Dr. M. A. Shaban kindly checked the former date for me.

[28] *The Code of Maimonides,* Book XII: "Acquisition," Section "Sale," chap. 18, para. 1, trans. Isaac Klein (New Haven, 1951), pp. 63–64. TS Box Misc. 8, f. 90, ed. S. D. Goitein, *Tarbiz,* 28 (1959), 190–194, reprinted in Maimonides, *Responsa,* II, 533–534.

[29] E.g., TS 8 J 39, f. 12, 10 ff., *Nahray* 127. The writer twice emphasizes that the clothes sent belonged to a gentile.

[30] DK VI, *Nahray* 146.

[31] TS 13 J 17, f. 11, ll. 14 ff., ed. S. D. Goitein, *Tarbiz,* 36 (1967), 388–390. Khallūf b. Zakariyya al-Ashqar (the Red-haired, a common family name) writes to Ibn 'Awkal. *Yawm 'Arafa* means the day before *any* holiday; the Muslim holiday concerned was 'Īd al-Fiṭr. See Goitein, *op. cit.,* p. 390.

[32] TS 13 J 14, f. 5, see Mann, I, 85, ed. Mann, II, 83. For Marja read Murajjā.

[33] E.g., *fuqahā'u 'l-muslimīn adāma 'l-lāh tawfīqahum,* the Muslim lawyers, may God give them permanent success (i.e., in always making right decisions), Maimonides, *Responsa,* I, 145. *Waffaqahu 'llāh* (same meaning), INA D-55, f. 13, l. 31+.

[34] *Med. Soc.,* I, 52.

[35] *Ibid.,* p. 253.

[36] TS 16.272, l. 25.

[37] TS 10 J 8, f. 10*v*. Postscript on top (repeated in a larger hand by a man who wanted to "try his pen").

[38] ENA 4011, f. 19. Both the beginning and the end, as well as most of the left half of the page are missing.

[39] ENA 4020, f. 6 (laminated), ed. Mann, II, 172, see chap. v, sec. D, 1, n. 17. The text implies that the scene was a private mansion, not a synagogue.

[40] AIU VII E 21.

3. *Converts and Proselytes*

[1] Mann, I, 34–38. The poem from the Geniza allegedly referring to these persecutions of al-Ḥākim (see *ibid.*) is to be explained otherwise (see Abramson, *Bamerkazim,* pp. 133–141). The document of 1016 (TS 13 J 1, f. 3) is issued by a proper court and signed by nine (see *Med. Soc.,* I, 362). It is probable that TS 12.155 (renewal of a marriage contract from spring 1013 [see sec. B, 3, n. 2, below]) was also made in Fustat, and for TS 16.245 (marriage contract, April 5, 1015) this is stated expressly, but for marriages no formal court was needed.

[2] *Med. Soc.,* I, 41.

[3] Sassoon 713+, l. 49. On the situation of the Jewish "marranos" under the Almohads see A. S. Halkin in *The Joshua Starr Memorial Volume* (New York, 1953), p. 101–110, in Heb.

[4] Renegade: *pōshēa'*. Apostasy: *pish'ūth.* The biblical word acquired this new meaning perhaps under the influence of Arabic *murtadd.*

[5] TS 12.372, l. 19. His name was Joseph b. Shabbethay. Alexandria: TS 13 J 23, f. 3*v*, ll. 11–12+.

[6] TS Box K 15, f. 95; TS 8 J 5, f. 18*c*: al-Maḥalla, 1157.

[7] Maimonides, *Responsa,* II, 657–658. Abraham Maimuni, *Responsa,* p. 177. See the notes.

[8] TS Arabic Box 40, f. 96, *India Book* 309. A similar query with regard to a woman who had neither received a bill of divorce nor been separated from her husband by a court, but had been deserted for ten years in TS 8 J 11, f. 19. The case of a woman who remained Jewish while her husband became a Christian in Strasbourg, France, May, 1229: S. Grayzel, *The Church and the Jews in the XIIIth Century* (New York, 1966), p. 181.

[9] TS 10 J 17, f. 16, where the brother-in-law of a freedman moves from Qalyūb to the Manūfiyya district in order to embrace Islam. The renegade al-Baṣrī mentioned below most probably had emigrated from Spain, where his brother lived, to Egypt.

[10] *Med. Soc.,* I, 33–34.

[11] Silk-weaver: TS NS J 277, l. 13* (see sec. A, 2, n. 23, above). The red-haired: ULC Or 1080 J 113*v*, l. 12. The letter is from Gizeh. Circumcision: Abraham Mai-

muni, *Responsa,* p. 55. The chirurgical aspect of Islamic circumcision slightly differs from the Jewish.

[12] TS Box K 15, f. 2, col. II (App. B, sec. 43).

[13] TS 20.93*a*: In reaction to a complaint by the Jewish community of Malīj the three brothers Manṣūr, Fuḍayl, and Ṭarīf, sons of Manasse, each accompanied by a son, appeared in court, insulted the judge, and threatened to embrace Islam.

[14] TS 10 J 10, f. 3, ll. 8 and 14, ed. (with facsimile) E. Ashtor, *Sefarad,* 24 (1964), 65.

[15] ULC Or 1080 J 93*.

[16] The story of Masrūr and Zayn al-Mawāṣif, *The Arabian Nights,* Nights 845–863. See its analysis in Mia I. Gerhardt, *The Art of Story-Telling* (Leiden, 1966, pp. 139–140.

[17] See *Isaac Ibn Ezra: Poems,* ed. N. Ben-Menahem (Jerusalem, 1950), especially pp. 43–47. Bibliography about him: Baron, *History of the Jews,* VII, 297 n. 35. Geniza data about his connection with Judah ha-Levi: TS 13 J 15, f. 20*v*, l. 25, *Tarbiz,* 24 (1955), 27, *India Book* 122 (report about the poet's arrival in Alexandria: "They say that the sons of Abraham Ibn Ezra came with him"). In fact, only Isaac arrived with him (see TS 13 J 14, f. 1, ll. 5–7, *Tarbiz,* 24 (1955), 36, *India Book* 120; TS 13 J 19, f. 17, ll. 9–10, *Tarbiz,* 28 (1959), 355, *India Book* 252. Isaac's brother Judah followed later. TS 10 J 24, f. 4, margin, *Tarbiz,* 24 (1955), 32, *India Book* 121. The alleged love affair: A. Mirsky, *Kirjath Sepher,* 27 (1951), 302.

[18] Bodl. MS Heb. c 28 (Cat. 2876), f. 31, *India Book* 99. The calculation made in *Tarbiz,* 24 (1955), 23, that the letter must have been sent in 1139, is correct. The qualification made *ibid.,* pp. 141–143, is to be scrapped.

[19] Gottheil-Worrell XXI, p. 94, *India Book* 107. TS 13 J 18, f. 19, *India Book* 108.

[20] Abu 'l-Barakāt al-Baghdādī: see *EI*², I, 111–113, s.v. (S. Pines).

[21] Strauss, *Mamluks,* I, 279–291.

[22] Many examples proving that this punishment was actually carried out, in particular against neo-Muslims who reverted to their previous religion, are provided by Fattal *Non-Musulmans en pays d'Islam,* pp. 165–168.

[23] TS 13 J 14, f. 1⁺; ULC Or 1080 J 258* (see *PAAJR,* 28 [1959], 45, 55).

[24] Maimonides, *Responsa,* II, 548–550, 725–728 (possibly the same person is addressed). The teachings of Christians and *jadhbhum naḥwa 'l-dīn: ibid.,* I, 284–285.

[25] TS 10 J 31, f. 13*v*, ll. 6–8.

[26] See App. B, sec. 26.

[27] TS 16.140*.

[28] TS 10 K 7, f. 1, the Evyatar Scroll, ed. Schechter, *Saadyana,* p. 90, l. 12.

[29] TS 12.458*a*, ed. Assaf, *Texts,* pp. 149–151; TS 12.458*b* and *c*: *India Book* 271.

[30] See *EI,* II, 1076, s.v. "Ḳibṭ" (G. Wiet).

[31] TS 18 J 1, f. 11 (dated 1081), ed. N. Golb, *JSS,* 20 (1958), 44–46. The phrase "for what reason do you ban the Jews" should not be understood as stressing "the difference in social status" between the proselyte and genuine Jews, as Golb (*ibid.,* p. 45) assumes. "The Jews" means simply "the people." Gottheil-Worrell XIII, p. 68, l. 35 (App. C, sec. 7): the proselyte Abu 'l-Khayr contributes a quarter dinar to a collection. His son Zayn is mentioned as an important merchant in Oriental products in TS 8 J 24, f. 7, l. 12, and margin, also in Philadelphia University Museum E 16517 (see *JQR,* 49 [1958], 46–47). See also n. 39, below.

[32] App. B, secs. 17, 26, 32, 33, 34, 66, and elsewhere.

[33] TS Box K 25, f. 166. (Another woman called Mubāraka b. Abraham in Merx, *Paléographie hébraïque,* p. 36 [dated 1094]. Her father, however, was Jewish.) *Ghālib ṣihr al-gēr:* TS 13 J 20, f. 17, l. 12.

[34] E.g., TS 12.244; TS 10 J 13, f. 1, App. B, sec. 60; TS 8 J 14, f. 6.

[35] See chap. v, sec. C, 4, n. 24, above.

[36] Private communication from October, 1968.

[37] TS NS Box 325, f. 7, ed. A. Scheiber, "A Proselyte's Letter to the Congregations

of Fostat," *Essays Presented to Chief Rabbi Israel Brodie* (London, 1967), pp. 377–380 (with facsimile).

[38] TS 12.732, ed. Assaf, *Texts*, p. 149 (see N. Golb, "Notes on the Conversion of European Christians to Judaism in the Eleventh Century," *Journal of Jewish Studies*, 16 (1965), 71 n. 1.

[39] Deathbed declaration: TS 8 J 8, f. 12. Donation: App. C, sec. 19.

[40] ULC Add 3345. For Ceuta see *Med. Soc.*, I, 64.

[41] Al-Maḥalla: see n. 27, above. Muqaddam: TS 16.154 (see chap. v, sec. B, 2, n. 29, above). Malīj: TS 8 J 14, f. 6.

[42] Malīj: TS 8 J 36, f. 5. Qūṣ: TS 13 J 26, f. 6.

[43] ULC Or 1080 J 115. Ed. N. Golb, *Sefunot*, 7 (1964), 87–104, with an important commentary. Golb tentatively identifies this proselyte with the Slovenian cleric Wecelinus, who converted to Judaism in 1005. I have the impression, rather, that he was a Christian from a city not far away from Damascus, for only two, three, or, at most, four words are missing between the statement that "he left . . ." and another saying that he fled "from them" to Damascus (l. 8), and in the next line we read "they followed him." His persecution by the Christian officials of Damascus and Jerusalem is also easier to understand if he was a native and therefore easily recognizable (speaking the local Arabic vernacular!).

[44] TS 10 J 30, f. 10*v*, ll. 3–7. The treatise: Qiddushin.

[45] After a number of previous publications, the Geniza fragments of the Obadiah Scroll were edited in toto by A. Scheiber, *Acta Orientalia Hungarica*, 4 (1954), 271–296, under the somewhat misleading title "Fragment from the Chronicle of 'Obadyah, the Norman Proselyte"; shorter version in *Kirjath Sepher*, 30 (1955), 93–98 (in Heb.), both with facsimiles. Supplement in *HUCA*, 38 (1968), 168–172. My short article "Obadya, a Norman Proselyte," *Journal of Jewish Studies*, 4 (1953), 74–84, in which I drew attention to TS 8.271, concluding that Obadiah was not a Crusader, as formerly assumed, but a south Italian cleric, and encouraging search for the scroll in the literary sections of the Geniza set into motion a real avalanche of publications. First, A. Scheiber identified the important fragment from the David Kaufmann Collection edited by him in the articles cited above. Then, N. Golb and A. Scheiber recognized that a liturgical text equipped with Italian musical notation (neumes) was in Obadiah's handwriting. Another text with neumes was identified by N. Allony in Cambridge. An unending discussion about the nature of the music represented in these neumes ensued. See N. Golb, "Obadiah the Proselyte: Scribe of a Unique Twelfth Century Hebrew Manuscript Containing Lombardic Neums," *Journal of Religion*, 45 (1965), 153–156; A. Scheiber, "Der normannische Proselyt Obadja, der Aufzeichner der ersten Hebräischen Melodie," *Studia Musicologica*, 8 (1966), 173–187; Israel Adler, "Les Chants synagogaux notés au XIIe siècle (ca. 1103–1150) par Abdias, le proselyte Normand," *Revue de Musicologie*, 1 (1965), 19–51; Leo Levi, "Le due piu antiche transcrizioni musicali di melodie ebraico-italiane," *Scritti sull' Ebraismo in memoria di Guido Bedarida* (Florence, 1966), pp. 105–136, plus 10 tables. For the lively discussion of the subject at the Fourth World Congress of Jewish Studies see its *Papers* (Jerusalem, 1968), II, 395–408. Latest bibliographical note on further literature on Obadiah in A. Scheiber, *HUCA*, 38 (1968), 168 n. 44.

The Cambridge text found by Allony in 1965, TS Box K 5, f. 41, has been known to me for many years and is quoted in my book *Education* (1962), p. 43. When I saw it first, I noted: "Italian neumes, late" (i.e., of little value for me), a view shared by the eminent musicologist Eric Werner (see *Papers of Fourth World Congress of Jewish Studies*, p. 406). But what seems unimportant to one scholar may be most exciting for twenty others. This example shows again that the only way to make the Geniza treasures accessible to the scholarly world is by complete editions accompanied by facsimiles.

[46] "Pamphlets": Heb. *quṭrās* (from Lat. *commentarius*), more usually *qunṭrās*,

pronounced today *kuntres*. The word may also designate a set of sheets, and not a separate pamphlet.

[47] Especially TS 12.732+ (see n. 38, above).

[48] Cf. TS NS J 397: He remained in Atfīḥ and passed there the Sabbath. Normally, one did this only where it was possible to attend a service.

[49] "They will proselyte you": *yughayyirūki*.

[50] "The Jews," rendered here, as often, by the word "Israel."

[51] "I made an appeal": *taqaddamt*.

[52] Literally, "by the place God occupies in your heart," *bi-mawdiʿ Allāh min qalbak*.

[53] TS 8 J 27, f. 3. Written in strange large characters, half-cursive and half-monumental, with a stroke above *d, k, t* if they are to be read as *dh, kh, th*, respectively, and a dot in them when they denote *d, k, t*. The lines are not straight, but move up and down like waves. Hand of a village clerk.

[54] TS NS Box 325, f. 50, ed. A. Scheiber, "Von den Gebetbüchern der Proselyten," *In Memoriam Paul Kahle* (Berlin, 1968), pp. 208–213. Shorter Hebrew version, *Tarbiz*, 35 (1966), 269–273. Both with facsimiles. Scheiber rightly notes the similarity of Obadiah's poems with medieval Latin hymns. The main point, however, is not the sequence of rhymes (*a a a b, c c c b*), the like of which is found in the Arabic and Hebrew *muwashshaḥ*, but the freedom of treatment, with only the last vowel rhyming occasionally (*mōde-ʿōse; ḥayy-sīnay*) and with random disregard of the meter. Naturally, there are here Hebrew expressions inspired by Arabic, such as "our lord Moses" (which is Arabic, despite Numbers 11:28), or "the first of the warners," said of Abraham (read: *le-mazhīrīm*). After all, Obadiah learned all his Hebrew in the East.

"Judah, the pure proselyte," described in the two articles cited in this note as the copyist of TS NS Box 325, f. 64, is nonexistent. The manuscript has "Judah, the son [*bar*, not *gēr*] of Ṭāhōr," a common name.

[55] *JQR*, 49 (1958), 46 n. 28.

[56] Note 38, above.

B. COMMUNAL JURISDICTION

1. *The Judiciary*

[1] Tyan, *Organisation judiciaire*, pp. 212–218. S. D. Goitein, *An Introduction to Muslim Law* (Jerusalem, 1957), pp. 34–36 (in Heb.).

[2] *The Code of Maimonides*, Book XIV: "Judges," Treatise I, chap. ii, para. 11, trans. A. M. Hershman (New Haven, 1949), p. 10. "None may judge alone save One," quoted by the Gaon Solomon b. Judah in TS 13 J 19, f. 16*v*, ll. 18–22, in a passage strongly criticizing a judge who wished to dispense the law in splendid isolation like his Muslim colleagues.

[3] E.g., ENA 4011, f. 56, dated 1125. (See *Med. Soc.*, I, 363, sec. 7. During the process of binding the loose leaves of ENA 4011 into a volume, the shelf mark was changed from 57 to 56.) In TS 8 J 10, f. 17*, a short note about a settlement between a husband setting out on a journey and his wife, and TS 8 J 10, f. 18, another short note, no room was left for the word *we-shālōm*. Bodl. MS Heb. a 2 (Cat. 2805), f. 15, ed. S. Assaf, *Tarbiz*, 9 (1938), 218, is a validation, which may be, and is occasionally, given by the "Court" alone (see TS 16.124 [dated 1017]), signed by the same Elhanan b. Shemarya, calling himself here "Court for all Israel."

[4] *The Code of Maimonides* (see n 2, above), para. 13. The settlement of spring, 1092: TS 20.31. The ten signatures are rendered (with some mishaps) in Schechter, *Saadyana*, p. 81 n. 2. When Maimonides writes "judgment by eleven men is preferable to one rendered by ten," he might have had cases like this one in mind.

[5] *India Book* 1–18. Only three of the twelve signatories of the document from

spring, 1092 (see preceding note) reappear in the court records of 1097–1098 referred to in the text.

[6] E.g., Bodl. MS Heb. a 2 (Cat. 2805), f. 4+ (Old Cairo, 1029); TS 20.89 (Ephraim b. Shemarya, signing last, as in the preceding document); Bodl. MS Heb. a 2 (Cat. 2805), f. 23, ed. S. Assaf, *Tarbiz,* 9 (1938), 217 (Qayrawān, 1050).

[7] E.g., TS 13 J 1, f. 2 (Ramle, 1015), ed. Mann, II, 49. ENA 3011, f. 1 (Jerusalem, 1037), ed. *ibid.,* p. 65; ENA 2804, f. 1, ed. *ibid* , p. 115. TS 20.126 (Palestine, 1066). Bodl. MS Heb. c 28 (Cat. 2876), f. 49+ (Baghdad, 997, a copy), ed. J. Mann, *JQR,* n.s. 8 (1917–1918), 359. TS 13 J 5, f. 2(+) (Old Cairo, 1085), where the Nāsī David b. Daniel signs last. Ceremonial of the Palestinian yeshiva, *rusūm mathībat al-Shām:* Mosseri L 290, part C, ll. 35–36.

[8] Bodl. MS Heb. a 3 (Cat. 2873), f. 6 (Old Cairo, 1169), l. 33. Certain types of documents, namely writs of divorce and bills of manumission, do not represent contracts or settlements made before a court, but are legally one-sided declarations in which the husband or master frees his wife or bondman from any allegiance to him. Therefore, they may be witnessed by only two signatories.

[9] ULC Add. 3339, sec. C, l. 26 (Bilbays, Lower Egypt, 1218).

[10] See chap. vi, secs. 8, 9, 11, especially 11, nn. 3–6; chap. v, B, 2, and C, 4, a.

[11] TS 13 J 5, f. 1, sec. 3*.

[12] E.g., TS 13 J 2 f 24 (see Mann, I, 217 n. 2 [read 24 for 14]). Bodl. MS Heb. a 3 (Cat. 2873), f. 5, l. 10*. ULC Or 1080 J 112*v*, l. 4. TS 13 J 18, f. 18, l. 8: *mawāliya battē dīnīm.*

[13] The situation in Ramle was of a specific nature since the high court of the yeshiva and its president mostly had their seats there and not in Jerusalem.

[14] Sijilmāsa: Sassoon 713+, l. 49. Barqa: Mosseri L 130*v*, l. 16. Palermo: TS 10 J 15, f. 15, l. 12 (*Nahray* 230). Alexandria: ULC 1080 J 112, ll. 15–19; TS 13 J 24, f. 8, l. 16, *Tarbiz* 28 (1959), 354, and often.

[15] TS 12.338+: Joseph *bēth-dīn* (referred to as such in a letter of his son Yeshū'ā). TS 20.129: Shelah (b. Mevassēr) *bēth-dīn* (1075–1101). "My colleagues, the judges": TS 16.251, l. 10+.

[16] TS 13 J 26, f. 16, ll. 5–7+. One judge is called *shōfēṭ* and one *dayyān.*

[17] The common abbreviation of the title "president [in Hebrew *āv,* 'father'] of the court" is *āv; bē rabbānān* for *rēsh bē rabbānān,* "Head of the School" (see Mann, I, 192); *sādatuna 'l-mathā'ib,* "our lords, *the heads* of the academies," TS 13 J 36, f. 1, ll. 5 and 30+. A. Grohmann, *Studien zur historischen Geographie und Verwaltung des frühmittelalterlichen Ägypten* (Vienna, 1959), p. 36: *majlis* = President of the court. Hebrew literary source: "several scholars living in one city, all being battē dīnīm" (Derekh Ereṣ Zuṭṭā 9 [see Mann, II, 137 n. 2]).

[18] Harkavy, *Responsen der Geonim,* pp. 80–81. Cf. chap. v, B, 2, above.

[19] For the twelfth century, cf. the circular of the Nagid Samuel (1140–1159) to officials called *dayyān, muqaddam, shōfēṭ,* and *ḥazzān* (TS 13 J 18, f. 25)*. Joseph, the shōfēṭ of Damietta (1106); Bodl. MS Heb. d 66 (Cat. 2878), f. 8*.

[20] TS 24.73, end (dated 1047), ed. S. Assaf, *Yerushalayim,* (1953), 115 (where the words put in brackets should be replaced by the phrase: *umikkēwān shehū,* "and considering he is").

[21] Damascus: TS 16.181, l. 18+ (dated 933). See also TS 16.14, ll. 12 and 33 (dated 1007). Ramle: Gottheil-Worrell XLIII, p. 200*v*, l. 4. Alexandria: n. 16, above. Old Cairo: TS 20.104, l. 25, referring to Ephraim b. Shemarya. Sijilmāsa: TS 20.6, l. 5+ (see S. Assaf, *Tarbiz,* 9 (1938), 30 n. 1*a*).

[22] E.g., in Rafaḥ, southern Palestine (see Mann, I, 265).

[23] TS 12.16+: Solomon ha-shōfēṭ b. Saadya ha-shōfēṭ (ca. 1010). Dropsie 337: Joseph ha-kohen ha-shōfēṭ b. Solomon ha-kohen ha-shōfēṭ signs together with Ephraim b. Shemarya. He seems at some time to have been in charge of the then still small Jewish community of New Cairo (see TS 18 J 1, f. 6). TS K 15, f. 8: Shabbāt ha-shōfēṭ and his brother Ephraim ha-shōfēṭ. The son of Ephraim, Judah,

became a distinguished member of the yeshiva. TS 8 J 21, f. 29: "The illustrious shōfēṭ Azhar, son of Abraham, son of the shōfēṭ Azhar." The "Lane of Azhar the shōfēṭ" in TS 20.16 (see E. Worman, *JQR,* 18 [1906], 27). This family is mentioned in many Geniza documents, e.g., Joseph, another grandson of the first Azhar in TS 20.83 (dated 1066), Bodl. MS Heb. d 66 (Cat. 2878), f. 133*v* (1085), Dropsie 341. The whereabouts of the shōfēṭ Amram (TS 8.245, early eleventh century) are not indicated.

[24] See chap. v, A, 1, above.

[25] ENA, Uncatalogued 109*, ed. S. D. Goitein *JQR,* 44 (1954), 301, l. 18. Maimonides, *Responsa,* I, 54, 132, 148, 152, 153 and, in particular, p. 78 n. 3, where further literature.

[26] E.g., TS 12.125. The letter is from Sammanūd, which is a considerable distance from Cairo. The judge is promised payment of his expenses.

[27] TS 13 J 18, f. 25*, issued by the Nagid Samuel in 1143. The word *dayyānīn* is spelled in the Arabic way.

[28] For *nā'ib,* see TS 18 J 4, f. 10, ll. 16 and 39, with regard to the Babylonian congregation in Old Cairo; *khalīfa,* chap. v, sec. A, 1, n. 6, above.

[29] ULC Or 1080 J 29, l. 12. ULC Or 1080 J 112, ll. 12 and 19; verso, l. 5 (the "courts," i.e., the judges are referred to in the plural in the preceding line). Judge in Fustat "deputy" of Nagid: TS Box J 1, f. 47 (1234): *R. Yiftaḥ nā'ibnā.*

[30] Mann, *Texts,* I, 103, last line: Sherira Gaon reports that he had once appointed Shemarya b. Elhanan as his *mishne* (ca. 1000). TS 16.191: signature of the judge (of Ṣahrajt) Manasse ha-mishne be-Rabbi (Judah, see TS 16.267+). TS 28.6, l. 22: "The mishne, known as Ibn al-Maghrebi, behaved toward his partner [in a piece of land] not quite properly." Presumably a Muslim judge.

[31] Tyan, *Organisation judiciaire,* pp. 308 ff.

[32] The divorcée: Bodl. MS Heb. d 66 (Cat. 2878), f. 133, l. 9. Ramle: TS 10 J 32, f. 8. Partly ed. in *Sefer ha-Yishuv,* p. 60, where, however, the main point, the demotion of the judge, is missing. See v, B, 1, n. 124. *Sefer ha-Yishuv,* p. 60 n. 42, read for 10 J 32, f. 3: 10 J 32, f. 9. There, instead of the senseless *wyshkbm* the manuscript has *wyskrm,* "he hired them."

[33] The nāsī of Alexandria: TS NS J 29 (shortly before 1227). Solomon b. Judah: ULC Or 1080 J 45, l. 16 (see chap. v, sec. C, 3, n. 14, above). There are other, preposterous, accusations in this letter.

[34] Tyan, *Organisation judiciaire,* pp. 293–332. Claude Cahen, *Der Islam,* I, in *Fischer Weltgeschichte,* Vol. XIV (Frankfurt, 1968), p. 107. A French or English edition will certainly be on the market soon. TS 12.16, l. 19(+): "The qadi is just." TS 13 J 25, f. 15, ll. 11–12: "The situation of the Jews became precarious only when the qadi was deposed" (letter from the Rīf).

[35] See chap. v, sec. B, 2, nn. 61–64, above. Complaint to Mevōrākh: TS 18 J 4, f. 12, ll. 38-45. Solomon b. Judah: ULC Or 1080 J 106, ll. 11–12.

[36] Cairo: see App. D, secs. 24–26. Alexandria: see chap. v, sec. B, 1, n. 95. Al-Mahdiyya: four generations of the Ibn Sighmār family (details in *India Book*). Gabes: Mann, *Texts,* I, 185–186. Ascalon: Mann, II, 202 (read TS 16.122 for 16.22), TS 18 J 2, f. 3, and TS 18 J 4, f. 4. Egypt (Minyat Ziftā): see chap. v, B, 1, nn. 19, 21, 39–42, above. Barqa: TS K 6, f. 47, taken together with ENA 2805, f. 13, see sec. A, 1, n. 1, above. The father and grandfather of Joseph b. Shemarya had also been judges, see Mann, II, 339(7).

[37] For al-Nu'mān see *EI,* s.v. (A. A. A. Fyzee), and R. Gottheil, "A Distinguished Family of Fatimid Cadis (al-Nu'mān) in the Tenth Century" (not listed in *EI*), *JAOS,* 27 (1906), 217–296; Kamal S. Salibi, "The Banū Jamā'a: A Dynasty of Shafi'ite Jurists in the Mamluk Period," *Studia Islamica,* 9 (1958), 97–109.

[38] ULC Or 1080 J 29, where documents deposited with the late judge Aaron Ibn al-'Ammānī of Alexandria were in the possession of his sons living in Old Cairo. Aaron's great-grandson: Judah b. Aaron al-'Ammanī. Grandson succeeding: As far

as we know, Abraham (II), the son of Nathan (I) b. Abraham (I), the Gaon who was later demoted to āv, never attained any judicial rank (see *Tarbiz,* 36 [1967], 62–63). His son Nathan (II) was again president of the court, while his grandson Abraham (III) b. Nathan āv (II) had tremendous initial difficulties before he obtained his position of judge in (New) Cairo (see TS 10 J 13, f. 11, ENA 1822, fs. 44–45). Public office, how far hereditary: chap. v, A, 1, nn. 34–35, B, 2, nn. 120–126.

[39] E. Tyan, *Le Notariat dans la pratique du droit musulman* (Beirut, 1959). Scribes: (1) Japheth ha-ḥazzān b. David ha-ḥazzān b. Shekhanya (1020–1057). (2) Aaron ha-Mumḥē weha-ḥazzān b. Ephraim (1058–1066). (3) Hillel ha-ḥazzān b. Eli (1066–1108). (4) Abraham b. Aaron ha-Mumḥē (1102–1107. Son of no. 2. He had probably held a post outside Old Cairo for most of his life. (5) Ḥalfōn ha-ḥazzān b. Ghālib ha-ḥazzān (1116–1126). The date 1088 in Mann, II, 232, is erroneous. (6) Ḥalfōn ha-ḥazzān b. Manasse (1100–1138. Son-in-law of no. 3 [see chap. vi, sec. 11, above]). Later examples: Ḥalfōn b. Elazar ha-Kohen (1208–1222), and Solomon b. Elijah (as from 1224, see Index).

[40] TS NS Box 297, f. 1*; TS Arabic Box 39, f. 170.

[41] Such a diary of a notary who was mainly a bookseller (*warrāq*) has been preserved (see *JAOS,* 78 [1959], 301–302). TS 24.81 is a complete copy of agreements made before a notary who indicates (in his own hand) who had signed with him.

[42] TS NS J 51: *fasu'ila bēth dīn ithbāt dhālika liyakūn fī shimmūshā* (dated 1037). Sixty dinars: TS 13 J 2, f. 13 (dated 1106).

[43] E.g., Japheth b. David (TS NS J 51) and Judah b. Aaron al-'Ammanī of Alexandria (see n. 38, above). Judge: Mevōrākh b. Nathan, TS 13 J 1, f. 21 (July, 1150), ENA 4011, f. 55, dated 1153.

[44] Bodl. MS Heb. b 13 (Cat. 2834, no. 23), f. 42, ed. S. Poznanski, *REJ,* 48 (1904), 171–172. This document is in Hebrew; the governor is called mōshēl (ll. 18, 22). TS 13 J 5, f. 1, sec. A*.

[45] TS 16.45. In the first record (introduced by the words "There appeared before the court instituted in the synagogue of the Palestinians in Fustat by the High Court of Jerusalem") Abraham ha-Levi b. Samuel is the plaintiff, in the second he signs first (he also signed other documents [see Mann, II, 99]). Ḥalfōn ha-Levi b. Solomon signs the first record and appears as party (with his Arabic name Khalaf ha-Levi b. Solomon) in the third record. The first two records are in the hand of Japheth b. David.

[46] E.g., Bodl. MS Heb. c 28 (Cat. 2876), f. 37*v*, l. 18, *Nahray* 188, where the judge of al-Mahdiyya regrets that Nahray b. Nissīm (in Old Cairo) ceased to give his opinion on a case when he learned that his colleague in Tunisia was involved in it.

[47] TS 10 J 29, f. 1, ed. Assaf, *Texts,* p. 29, a letter of a Gaon to "the three elders" in a small town in Palestine with the instruction to act in a matter of inheritance, and above chap. v, A, 1, *passim.*

[48] Damietta: Bodl. MS Heb. a 2 (Cat. 2805), f. 3*, ed. S. Assaf, *Tarbiz,* 9 (1938), 208. Baniyas: Assaf, *Texts,* p. 62 (read 13 J 1, f. 15 for 13 T 1 (15)). Zawīlat al-Mahdiyya: TS 28.6 C. Fustat, 1120: TS 12.163. Fustat, 1203: Bodl. MS Heb. c 28 (Cat. 2876), f. 54.

[49] TS 12.587, written in the hand of Mevōrākh b. Nathan b. Samuel he-ḥāvēr. The signatures are not preserved. See *Med. Soc.,* I, 182.

[50] See chap. v, sec. B, 1, n. 116, above.

[51] PER H 2, ed. S. Assaf, *Sepher ha-Yovel Alexander Marx* (New York, 1943), pp. 74–76.

[52] TS 13 J 16, f. 3, ll. 9 and 12. See also chap. v, sec. B, 1, n. 57, where *qāhāl* is also used.

[53] TS 13 J 5, f. 1*v*, l. 9*: *bijam' al-yahūd.* Cf. also the Hebrew expression *'ad sheyithwā'adū we-yir'ū* (= Ar. *wa-yanẓurū*) *ba'asāqēnū,* in Bodl. MS Heb. b 13, f. 42, l. 18+ (see n. 44, above).

[54] (1) TS NS J 133, l. 11: *istaghāthat ila 'l-yahūd.* (2) A second case in the same

court record, verso l. 2. (3) TS 13 J 5, f. 1*, in abbreviated form (without *ila 'l-yahūd*). (4) Bodl. MS Heb. a 3 (Cat. 2873), f. 26, ll. 6–10*, where also the Hebrew equivalent *ṣōʿēq qōvēl*. (5) PER H 160, ll. 13–14* (dated Aug. 1, 1038): *mustaghīth ilā yisrāʾēl*, "calling Israel for help." (6) TS 18 J 3, f. 2: *yā maʿāshir yisrāʾēl al-mustaghāth billāh wa-bikum*, "O assemblies of Israel, God and you are approached for help." (7) TS 13 J 18, f. 18: "I am bringing my complaint before God and the congregation." (8) TS 10 J 5, f. 5 (only the beginning preserved).

[55] Preceding note, no. (5).

[56] ULC Or 1080 J 112, l. 12.

[57] N. 54, nos. (1), (6), and (7). See also chap. v, sec. D, 2, nn. 56–60, above.

[58] ENA 2348, f. 1. The appeal is in Arabic. Hebrew words of the original are rendered here in italics.

[59] This is not a literal translation, but renders the meaning of the verse as intended in accordance with the subsequent appeal.

[60] Although this phrase is common in the Bible, it is rarely used in the Geniza letters. It must be regarded as a translation of the corresponding Arabic formula, usually heading a document.

[61] On the Mount of Olives, east of Jerusalem, public announcements used to be made every year at the festive assembly during the Sukkot Holiday (see sec. A, 1, n. 43, above). About the prohibition to apply to a Muslim court, see sec. D, below.

[62] Whenever one had to tell something unpleasant, etiquette required an addition to the effect that the hearer might be spared similar situations.

[63] N. 54, above, nos. (2) and (5).

[64] TS 12.26*.

[65] See Tyan, *Organisation judiciaire*, pp. 219–230. The word *muftī* is indeed used in Geniza letters in a nontechnical sense with regard to Jewish scholars: "As to the advice of the *muftī* that peace and mutual understanding should prevail—let him who gave this advice, achieve it." TS NS J 344, ll. 7–8. In TS Arabic 54, f. 66*v*, l. 10, the "muftī" is requested to pray for the writer. Most probably the judge Hananel b. Samuel is intended here (May, 1235).

[66] Fatwā: TS 13 J 21, f. 2+. Bodl. MS Heb. c 13 (Cat. 2807, no. 16), f. 20+. Reference to question submitted to him: TS 12.371, ll. 4–6.

[67] 1050: TS 20.7 (see Mann, II, 245). 1080: TS 8.251, *Nahray* 25. 1055: TS 12.634 and TS 24.18, *Nahray* 24 and 26; the two fragments are part of one document. 1075: ENA 4010, f. 1*v*.

[68] When Abraham (III) b. Nathan (II) is also occasionally styled "the Great Rāv" (TS 18 J 1, f. 8), it is perfectly appropriate, since any "court" had the ius respondendi. The same applies to Shemarya b. Elhanan and his son Elhanan.

[69] Cf. S. Schwarzfuchs, *Études sur l'origine et le développement du rabbinat au Moyen Age* (Paris, 1957).

[70] E.g., TS 13 J 3, f. 21*v* (dated 1210); TS 13 J 3, f. 27*v* (1218).

[71] TS NS J 259 (1095). *India Book* 3 and 11 (1098). Bodl. MS Heb. d 66 (Cat. 2878), f. 46 (1099). ENA 4020, f. 2 (1115/6).

[72] Mann, I, 266 and 266 n. 2. Similar address in TS 20.135; Bodl. MS Heb. c 28 (Cat. 2876), f. 64. In DK IX he is styled *dayyān Miṣr* (Old Cairo). Cf. chap. v, sec. B, 2, n. 34, where a "head of the Congregation" in the address is informally called *dayyān al-yahūd*. The document in Arabic characters: TS Arabic Box 38, f. 131.

2. *The Law*

[1] "The Jews" instead "of Israel" is found in Palestinian documents, bills of divorce from Ramle, dated 1027, and Jaffa, 1077, and a marriage contract from Tiberias (see S. Assaf, *Tarbiz*, 9 [1938], 28, and *Texts*, p. 28, l. 1). "The Jews" without "Moses" in a marriage contract from Ramle TS 16.123, dated 1052, ed. S.

Assaf, *Yerushalayim* (Jerusalem), n.v. (1953), 104–106. The latter formula was already in use in the second century A.D.

[2] TS 13 J 1, f. 3 (dissolution of partnership; dated 1016). Dropsie 335 (gift; 1041). TS 12.178 (power of attorney; in, or around, 1041). TS 20.160 (promise of bridegroom to fulfill certain conditions during his married life; 1047). See also next n.

[3] Antonin 637, ed. S. Assaf, *Shetaroth Hay Gaon* (Jerusalem, 1930), p. 58. PER H 24, ed. S. Assaf, *Sepher Ha-Yovel Alexander Marx* (New York, 1943), p. 77 (Damsīs, 1083). TS NS J 283 (eleventh century or earlier).

[4] Mastaura, Asia Minor, 1022: TS 16.374+ (see Mann, II, 96 n. 2). Damietta: Bodl. MS Heb. a 2 (Cat. 8205), f. 3+*. Damsīs: second item in preceding n.

[5] *Med. Soc.,* I, 176, 242. Harkavy, *Responsen der Geonim,* p. 216, no. 423.

[6] This principle is emphatically cited and illustrated by a number of examples in Harkavy, *op. cit.,* p. 274, no. 552.

[7] *The Code of Maimonides,* Book XII: "Acquisition," trans. Isaac Klein (New Haven, 1951), pp. 4–21. The little technicality of the actual delivery of an object (here: a piece of clothing with ritual fringes, Book of Numbers 15:38) was, however, obligatory. A foreigner from Persia who believed that a mere agreement accompanied by handshake was binding learned to his dismay that he was mistaken. TS Arabic Box 49, f. 166*.

[8] Moses ibn al-Maqdisī (the son of the Jerusalemite) "gives" the threshold of his house to the attorney appointed by him in 1215 (TS 13 J 3, f. 25). A similar expression in Maimonides, *Responsa,* I, 56. The contracts of "conveyance of land [in Palestine]" mentioned in E. J. Worman's handlists of the Taylor-Schechter Collection, Cambridge, are mostly powers of attorney using the formulas alluded to. Alexandria: TS 13 J 1, f. 7, l. 17, *we-qānīnū mē-'aṣmēnū* (1033).

[9] TS 18 J 1, f. 6. See chap. vi, sec. 10, n. 41, above.

[10] TS 8 J 7, f. 18*.

[11] PER H 160, l. 9* (dated 1038). See *Eretz Israel,* 6 (1960), 167.

[12] Alexandria: TS 8 J 22, f. 6. Apprehension: see chap. v, sec. B, 2, n. 85.

[13] ULC Or 1080 J 93*.

[14] TS Misc. Box 25, fs. 132, 139.

[15] Abraham Maimuni, *Responsa,* p. 26. For fines, see chap. v, sec. C, 2, nn. 30–36.

[16] TS 16.213. See chap. v, sec. B, 1, n. 57.

[17] TS 12.320, ll. 14–17, *India Book* 51.

[18] TS 18 J 2, f. 5.

[19] TS 13 J 30, f. 3, ed. Mann, II, 173. The first word is to be read: *wesheyavdīlah.* The name of the woman: Mubāraka; also marred by a misprint. The Muslim chief justice is called *shōfēṭ ha-shōfeṭīm* (see sec. B, 1, n. 21, above).

[20] TS 12.239.

[21] TS 8 J 22, f. 14*v*, ed. S. D. Goitein, *Joshua Finkel Jubilee Volume* (New York, 1970).

[22] TS 8 J 32, f. 6*.

[23] Bodl. MS Heb. e 94, f. 28. Representative: *rasūl* (corresponding to Heb. *shālī'aḥ*); errand boy: *ṣabī.*

[24] A somewhat ridiculous example: chap. v, B, 1, n. 45, above. Private person (a proselyte!): TS 18 J 1, f. 11, ll. 15–16+.

[25] TS 12.657*. The cantors are the promulgators of bans (see chap. vi, sec. 10, n. 29).

[26] E.g., TS 13 J 24, f. 4, ll. 18 ff.; TS 13 J 26, f. 6*v*, l. 17.

[27] TS 13 J 12, fs. 1–5. These are forms of excommunication.

[28] TS 8 J 5, f. 10, sec. A: *an yakhruj yunaẓẓif shughluh min al-ḥerem.* The fragment contains four court records from Sept., 1133, in the hand of Nathan ha-Kohen b. Solomon.

[29] TS 13 J 26, f. 6*v*, ll. 16–23. The (scholarly) writer uses the Hebrew terms for ban, *ḥerem* (in the Arabic verbal form *aḥramūh*) and *niddūy,* indiscriminately.

[30] TS 16.154 (a muqaddam in an Egyptian provincial town). The statute mentioned in n. 15 rules that only a proper court of three was entitled to proclaim a ban.

[31] TS 8 J 10, f. 19: Abraham Maimonides acceding to a ban pronounced against Evyatar al-Kohen al-Āmidī. The document is incomplete.

[32] See K. Reinhardt, "Eine koptisch-arabische Kirchenbannurkunde," *Ägyptiaca,* G. Ebers Jubilee Volume (1897), pp. 89 ff.

3. *Procedures*

[1] Minutes are normally called *zikhrōn 'ēdūth,* "record of witness," or *ma'ase (she-hāyā be-fānēnū),* "[report of] what has happened [in our presence]." The very common *shimmūsh (bēth dīn),* lit., "[for] use [in court]," perhaps originally designated the copy retained by the judge (see below and Mann, II, 231 n. 1). The Arabic *maḥḍar,* "minutes," is used in letters while referring to a court record, but occurs rarely in an official document, such as PER H 160* (Aug. 1, 1038), a report about happenings in a synagogue.

[2] Quoting the law, e.g., in Bodl. MS Heb. c 28 (Cat. 2876), f. 49+, a judgment given in Baghdad under the authority of Sherira Gaon in Oct., 997 (a matter of inheritance between people from Damascus and Baalbek). In l. 15 read: *liyazīd al-am*[*r wa*]*ḍāḥan,* "for an additional clarification of the case." TS 18 J 1, f. 1, notification about the minutes, maḥḍar, of a lawsuit written in Damascus and signed by fourteen persons. One of these, Zur'a[h] ha-Levi b. Abraham, appears as witness in TS 16.370, dated 995 (also a case of inheritance). The legal maxims quoted in these documents are rather commonplace. The same in TS 16.115+*, a will made in Nov., 1006, and in the decision by Elhanan b. Shemarya (Bodl. MS Heb. a 2 [Cat. 2805], f. 15, ed. S. Assaf, *Tarbiz,* 9 [1938], 217, see Abramson, *Bamerkazim,* p. 133). Likewise in TS 12.155, renewal of the marriage contract of David b. Shekhanya (spring, 1013).

[3] For acquittance the Aramaic (*sheṭār*) *avīzāryā* is normally used, e.g., TS 20.16 (from which Heb. *avīzār,* "free of obligation" [TS 13 J 1, f. 7, l. 15] is derived, not noted, I assume, in any Hebrew dictionary). Arabic *ibrā'* is also very common. Hebrew *piṣṣūy* (entirely different from the modern meaning of the word) occurs less frequently.

[4] Acknowledgment, Ar. *iqrār,* Heb. *hōdā'ā.* Normally neither of these terms is used, but the acknowledgment is introduced by the symbolic purchase: *uqniya minhu,* "he made a legally binding declaration by performing the symbolic purchase."

[5] Legal opinion by Shemariah b. Elhanan, ed. L. Ginzberg, *Geniza Studies* (New York, 1929), II, 265.

[6] Maimonides, Code of Law, *The Book of Judges* I, chap. 23, para. 9, trans. A. M. Hershman (New Haven, 1949), p. 70. These are quotations from talmudic sources.

[7] Joseph Caro, *Shulhan Arukh,* Part 4, section "Judges," chap. 12, para. 20.

[8] Ginzberg, *Geniza Studies,* II, 137, ll. 3–5 and 13–16 (*'al menāth she'ēnō pōsēq dīn bemā shehū ḥōtēkh*).

[9] Maimonides, *Responsa,* I, 56–57. Abraham Maimonides was asked a similar question and answered that the defendant was obliged to respond to claims and arguments made by an attorney, but questions addressed by the defendant to the claimant had to be answered by the latter in person. Abraham does not refer to the responsum of his illustrious father. TS 12.204 (in course of publication by S. D. Goitein).

[10] TS 13 J 5 f. 1*, see sec. B, 1, n. 44.

[11] E.g., TS 8 K 20, f. 1; TS 8 J 4, f. 1 (both dated 1028). TS 20.6 (1037)+.

[12] TS 8.14 (second third of eleventh century).

[13] Tyan, *Organisation judiciaire,* p. 267.

[14] PER H 160*. Bodl. MS Heb. a 3 (Cat. 2873), f. 26*.

[15] Maimonides, Code of Law, The Book of Judges, I, chap. 21, para. 9, trans. (see above, n. 2), p. 65. The beadle taking down the recapitulation of the depositions: TS 8 J 4, f. 9 d, ll. 14–15+.

[16] Extremely frequent. E.g., Dropsie 351. TS 16.47, *India Book* 198. ULC Add. 3416 c, *India Book* 17.

[17] TS NS J 366.

[18] Judge writing both the deposition and the validation: Bodl. MS Heb. d 75, f. 11, Damascus, Sept., 1084. *Ibid.,* d 68 (Cat. 2836), f. 106, ca. 1100.

[19] E.g., in Cretes, MS Christ College, Cambridge, Abrahams Collection, no. 10. For validation see, e.g., *Med. Soc.,* I, 260.

[20] TS 13 J 1, f. 4 (dated 1018).

[21] Two signatures out of four validated: TS 13 J 2, f. 19 (1136); two out of six: TS 28.7 (1060). All six: TS 13 J 1, f. 14 (Ramle, 1057). All seven: TS 12.53.

[22] Two pairs of witnesses testified in Old Cairo that they knew the handwriting of two out of three witnesses who had signed a testimony in Zawīlat al-Mahdiyya, Tunisia, in 1047: TS 13 J 9, f. 5. In 1063, two out of three witnesses who had signed a document in the same Tunisian town appeared in court in Old Cairo and identified themselves by writing down their signatures in the presence of the judges: TS 20.187.

The formulas of attestation by the court differ widely in legal parlance. Of particular interest is TS 13 J 1, f. 10, made out in the court of the Iraqis in Old Cairo, but written in Hebrew. In Mann, I, 38 n. 1, *zō ʿēdūth (ber)ūrā,* "this is a well attested witness," is to be read for *(ka-t)ōrā,* as may be seen in the manuscript and is evident from other documents validated by Elhanan b. Shemariah. In Mann, *loc. cit,* the number 13 is omitted from the shelf mark 13 J 1, f. 3.

[23] TS 8 J 18, f. 18 (see *Med. Soc.,* I, 254).

[24] Harkavy, *Responsen der Geonim,* p. 27, no. 59, cf. Ginzberg, *Geonica,* II, 280 and 284.

[25] Bodl. MS Heb. a 3 (Cat. 2873), f. 26 (dated 1042), sec. F*. ULC Add. 3416, l. 11, *India Book* 16.

[26] *Med. Soc.,* I, 209.

[27] Robert Brunschvig, "Le système de la preuve en droit musulman," *Recueils de la Société Jean Bodin* (Brussels), 18 (1964), 183–184.

[28] TS 16.277*v*, ll. 4, 9, 15, 16, 20*, a letter from Bilbays. As I learned from Joseph Schacht, the term *amāra* was used in the sense of circumstantial evidence also in Islamic law.

[29] E.g., ULC Add. 3422 (spring, 1098), a long series of allegations about transactions made by the claimant's father.

[30] INA D-55, f. 13, ll. 24–27+. Claim: over 100 dinars. Settlement: 10 dinars. See *Tarbiz,* 36 (1967), 70 n. 36.

[31] *India Book* 1–13 (the last item is a letter referring to the ninth session of the court, the proceedings of which have not been preserved. Nahray: TS 12.371 (not in *Nahray*).

[32] TS 10 J 17, f. 6.

[33] TS 8 J 25, f. 3. A memo, *tadhkira,* by Isḥāq b. Eli Majjānī.

[34] TS NS J 7*v*, ll. 10–18, *India Book* 206.

[35] TS 24.51 (Damīra, around 1150). For *ten* persons composing a board or council see chap. v, sec. B, 1, nn. 103–109, above.

[36] TS NS J 7, ll. 19–20+: *wala 'l-ḥukkām yaqṭaʿū fīh amr walā jakhrujū ʿan il-muṣālaḥa.* The reference is to a lawsuit different from that referred to in n. 34. "Settlement" is normally designated by the Hebrew term *peshārā.*

[37] Oath in the synagogue: ENA 4020 I (dated 1091). TS 16.44, l. 34 (1126). TS

16.243. Syracuse: Bodl. MS Heb. d 79, f. 36 (dated 1020, see chap. v, sec. B, 1, n. 3, above). Oath of a woman: TS 13 J 3, f. 10, l. 17 (date 1159). *Three* Torah scrolls clad in black: TS Misc. Box 29, f. 44*a*, l. 5.

[38] Maimonides, *Responsa,* I, 101–102.

[39] The first source mentioned in n. 37. ULC Add. 3339, sec. C, l. 24 (Bilbays 1218).

[40] TS 8 J 4, f. *3v** (ban in presence of the accused), Bodl. MS Heb. a 3 (Cat. 2873), l. 3* (the Gaon's letter), TS 13 J 12, f. 4 (another *ḥerem setām* in Arabic). Maimonides, *Responsa,* II, 534 (the accused answering "Amen"). TS 10 J 29, f. 5, ll. 7–12 (Ibn al-Ḥijāziyya).

In TS Arabic Box 41, f. 79, a letter written on particularly thin paper (ladies' stationery?) and in beautiful, large Arabic characters, the widow of Mubārak b. Mundhir b. Sābā asks a ḥāvēr in the name of her orphaned children to pronounce a ban. It should be directed against anyone falsifying documents affecting her late husband and submitting them to a Muslim court. She accused a definite person, of course, but asked for the proclamation of a ban in general terms, and on the little fast (the Ninth of Av), when everyone attended the service. The letter is connected with TS 18 J 1, f. 1. The writer emphasizes twice that the pronouncement of the ban was a matter of public concern and not only for the benefit of the orphans.

[41] TS Misc. Box 24, f. 42, sec. III. The person suspected was none other than the notable Rāṣūy (see App. C, 39, 40, 44, and elsewhere).

[42] Qadi: Gottheil-Worrell, VII, p. 34. See *Med. Soc.,* I, 442 n. 31 (dated 1151). Denunciation: TS 13 J 4, f. 12 (1269). Duress: TS 13 J 5, f. 4 (1174), and Bodl. MS Heb. e 101, f. 14 (1231). Slave girl: TS K 27, f. 45. Minyat Ziftā: Bodl. MS Heb. c 28 (Cat. 2876), f. 68 (1125). See G. Horowitz, *The Spirit of Jewish Law* (New York, 1953), pp. 459–460. In TS Arabic Box 39, f. 476, sec. 3, a woman makes payments to a Samaritan under duress (fall, 1130).

[43] A good example in ENA Uncatalogued 112, ll. 15–19.

[44] TS 13 J 1, f. 10 (dated 1044). An ancient example: TS 28.3 (July, 1004). Thus, the assumption that the custom had already fallen into disuse in talmudic times (G. Allon, *Tarbiz,* 4 [1933], 291) cannot be sustained.

[45] G. Vajda, *HUCA,* 12–13 (1937–1938), 380–384.

[46] Lane-Poole, *History of Egypt,* p. 170. *The Arabian Nights,* Night no. 25 (Būlāq, 1252), I, 77, l. 9.

[47] JNUL 5, ll. 3 and 52 (Jan., 1133); ed. in *Kirjath Sepher,* 41 (1966), 267–271.

[48] See chap. vi, sec. 12, n. 40, above.

[49] TS 8 J 5, f. 1* (1114), TS 12.531*v* (1157).

[50] TS 13 J 1, f. 3 (1016; Friday, eve of the Day of Atonement; settlement between husband and wife). TS 13 J 1, f. 4 (1018; Wednesday; same judge; a trifling case). TS 8 J 32, f. 3 (1162; the Gaon Nethanel in person; as court physician, he possibly happened to be free only on that Tuesday). TS 8 J 32, f. 4 (1229; regular business: sale of part of a house).

[51] Sessions of the court in Qayrawān, Tunisia, in 977–978 (TS 12.468, ed. Mann, *Texts,* I, 363) and in Denia, Spain, in 1083 (TS 12.570, ed. E. Ashtor, *Sefarad,* 24 [1964], 77) were held on Tuesdays. Too few dated documents have been preserved from these countries to allow generalization.

[52] TS 28.6, sec. A (Old Cairo, 1079). TS 13 J 1, f. 22 (Tyre, 1091). TS 18 J 1, f. 25 (Alexandria, 1153; the original document had been written in 1143).

[53] Firkovitch II, 1700. While in Leningrad in summer, 1965, I transcribed parts of this manuscript and summarized others, leaving a copy of my notes with the gifted assistant librarian Victor Lebedev, who had drawn my attention to it. I confidently hope that this valuable source of social history will soon be edited, accompanied by a complete facsimile.

[54] E.g., the sons of the Alexandrian judge Aaron al-'Ammānī, who lived in Fustat, kept documents related to a case of inheritance of a man from Sanhūr (ULC Or 1080 J 29. The heirs (at least grandsons or grandnephews) of the Gaon Nethanel

b. Moses, who died in the 1180's, possessed around 1250 the letter of appointment of R. Isaiah, the administrator of the properties of the Jewish community of the Egyptian capital, who had been appointed in 1150 by Nethanel's predecessor (TS 16.63, P.S., l. 2+* [see App. A, sec. 157]).

[55] A most interesting fragment of such a book of formularies, based on actual documents, is found in Bodl. MS Heb. f 27 (Cat. 2642), ed. Assaf, *Texts,* pp. 100 ff. (from Lucena, Spain, 1021).

[56] Mr. Gershon Weiss, whose M.A. thesis was a study of the documents written by Hillel b. Eli (see chap. vi, sec. 11, n. 17), has written his Ph.D. dissertation on those of Ḥalfōn b. Manasse (over 250), University of Pennsylvania, 1970.

[57] Hay Gaon's Book of Formularies was edited by S. Assaf as a supplement to *Tarbiz* (1930) (see Shaked, *Bibliography,* where the manuscripts are listed). But many more fragments of this book seem to be extant in the Geniza collections, and a new examination of all the material seems to be advisable. In TS 8.143*v* there is a note to the effect that the nāsī had borrowed that book (on the front page of a draft dated 1250). Mr. M. Friedman (see n. 59) writes in his Ph.D. dissertation that the marriage contracts of the thirteenth century seem to adhere to Hay's forms more closely than the earlier ones.

[58] TS Box J 3, f. 27.

[59] Milton (Mordechai) Friedman, "Jewish Marriage Contracts in the Palestinian Tradition from the Cairo Geniza," Ph.D. dissertation, University of Pennsylvania, 1969.

C. THE STATE

1. *The Government and Its Servants*

a. RULERS AND THEIR ENTOURAGE

[1] TS 13 J 20, f. 22, l. 12*.

[2] TS Arabic Box 48, f. 270v, l. 24+.

[3] See chap. vi, sec. 12, nn. 10, 12, and chap. v. sec. A, 1, nn. 28–30.

[4] TS 24.67, ll. 28–29.

[5] TS 24.72*, ed. S. D. Goitein, *Yerushalayim,* 2 (1955), 62–65. This oculist seems to be identical with Abu 'l-Barakāt Ibn al-Quḍā'ī, whose biography is given in Ibn Abī Uṣaybi'a, p. 147.

[6] TS 13 J 22, f. 24. The sultan's palace: *dār al-sulṭān.*

[7] TS Arabic Box 51, f. 111+. See sec. D, 2, n. 15, below.

[8] Text in Samuel Kandel, *Genizai kéziratok* (Budapest, 1909), pp. i–ii. Later marked: DK 245. The name of the official addressed: Judah ha-Kohen *sōfēr ha-malkhūth* b. Elazar. The dated and datable documents related, or addressed to him are from Saladin's time.

[9] Bodl. MS Heb. a 3 (Cat. 2873), f. 17.

[10] TS 12.215*.

[11] See sec. A, 1, n. 34.

[12] DK 129, ed. Alexander Scheiber, *Tarbiz,* 32 (1963), 273–276 (with facsimile).

[13] TS 18 J 4, f. 26, l. 11+*.

[14] Ibn Muyassar, p. 60.

[15] *Ibid.,* p. 30, l. 11, p. 58, last line, and p. 80, bottom. For Fatimid propaganda see *Med. Soc.,* I, 34.

[16] TS 13 J 24, f. 7 (in al-Afḍal's time). TS 18 J 3, f. 19, *v,* l. 3* (1089, during the rule of al-Afḍal's father). TS 8 J 22, f. 23* (from Tlemçen, Morocco).

[17] TS 20.93, sec. A, where a rambunctious litigant from Malīj in the Nile Delta threatens to apply to al-Malik al-Afḍal in person.

[18] Ibn Muyassar, p. 59, ll. 1–4. For *ḥaḍara* read *ḥaṣara.*

[19] ULC Or 1080 J 86, l. 23. Bodl. MS Heb. c 28 (Cat. 2876), f. 59, l. 33+.

[20] TS NS J 277*.

[21] TS 18 J 4, f. 6, margin and verso, l. 1. Bodl. MS Heb. b 11 (Cat. 2874), f. 7, ll. 19–20, ed. *Zion*, 17 (1952), 145. TS 18 J 4, f 5, l. 32+. ENA 4010, f. 15. TS NS J 272, l. 10.

[22] Bodl. MS Heb. f 56 (Cat. 2821, no. 16), f. 18*a*, ed. *JQR*, 43 (1952), 57–76.

[23] Goitein, "Attitudes towards Government in Islam and Judaism," *Studies*, pp. 197 ff.

[24] According to Jacob Katz (see sec. A, 1, n. 2, end), chap. 5, n, 15, p. 60.

[25] TS NS 110, f. 26*.

[26] TS 18 J 4, f. 26, ll. 19–27+*. Seljuks: TS Loan 174+; see App. D, sec. 11.

[27] Goitein, *Education*, pp. 61–62.

[28] TS 13 J 13, f. 2*v*, l. 2 (this part is in Arabic script). TS 13 J 21, f. 14, ll. 11–14: *faqad shana'u* (in a meliorative sense, cf. Dozy, *Supplément*, I, 791*b*, and found elsewhere in the Geniza in this meaning) *an qad khuli'a 'ala l-ḥaḍra l-makhdūma laylat al-khamīs . . . allah yuḥaqqiqhū wayaqḍī fīhi lahu walanā bil-khayr wal-khayra*, "Rumor had it that a robe of honor was bestowed on your Excellency, of whom I am the servant, on Wednesday night. . . . May God let this be true and may He ordain through you for you and for us everything good." From the letters addressed to this man it appears that he belonged to the class of the merchants rather than to that of the government officials.

[29] Bodl. MS Heb. a 3 (Cat. 2873), f. 17. The extremely deferential way in which Abraham b. Isaac ha-Kohen Ibn al-Furāt is addressed here (by the Gaon Daniel b. 'Azarya) shows that he must have occupied at this time a very powerful position.

[30] Mann, I, 79-80.

[31] ULC Add. 3335+, see *JQR*, 9 (1897), 36. TS 12.230, see Mann, II, 251. Scanty information: *EI*, s.v. "Al-Afḍal" (C. H. Becker).

[32] ULC Or 1080 J 27, l. 17: *wayūjidka 'l-ḥazz 'ind hādha l-ṣulṭān* (!) *wa-ḥāshiyatih* "and let you find favor with this sultan and his entourage" (said to a young and still unmarried man). The ladies of the court: Bodl. MS. Heb. c 28 (Cat. 2876), f. 26, l. 7, ed. Mann, II, 340.

[33] Jacob b. Amram: see S. D. Goitein, *Zion*, 27 (1962), 19. Samuel's son: TS 10 H 3, f. 11*v*, ed. Mann, II, 369.

[34] *Peraqim* (New York), 4 (1966), 31–33.

[35] ULC Add. 3335+.

[36] TS 10 J 17, f. 13. The person addressed probably was Abu 'l-Munajjā Solomon b. Sha'ya. See Mann, II, 264 ff., where similar poems dedicated to this Solomon are printed.

[37] TS NS J 29. The name of the governor was al-Mu'tamid. The stipend is referred to as *jāmikiyya*.

[38] TS 20.24+.

[39] TS 13 J 20, f. 5*, a petition addressed to (al-Malik al-'Ādil, i.e.) Ibn al-Salār, the vizier, written in December, 1150, to release such an estate.

[40] TS NS J 52.

[41] TS 32.4, ll. 28-30, ed. Mann, II, 12. See Mann, I, 19–22.

[42] Bodl. MS Heb. e 108, f. 70, l. 14. The place is called *armōn* (Heb.).

[43] ENA 4020, f. 6 (lamenated)+, see sec. A, 2, n. 39, above.

b. GOVERNMENT OFFICIALS AND AGENTS. TAXFARMERS

[1] Mosseri L 135*v*, l. 7, ed. Mann, *Texts*, I, 247: *aṣḥābna 'l-ladhī fī 'amal Ben Ḥabbūs*. TS 13 J 2, f. 25, l. 4*: *lays tuṭliq lahu khidma*. TS 18 J 3, f. 9, l. 31, ed. Mann, II, 178: *'ōsē melekhet ha-melekh*.

[2] For Abu 'l-Barakāt and his grandson see below nn. 4–5. Al-kātib al-Tinnīsī: TS 20. 116. Sitt al-Kuttāb: TS 16.61; TS 24.81; Bodl. MS Heb. b3 (Cat. 2806), f. 4; *ibid.*,

f 56, (Cat. 2821, no. 1, *h*) f. 15. The families of three of these four women are known to us from other documents.

[3] Chap. vi, sec. 12, n. 30. Abu 'l-Barakāt al-kātib al-sadīd (he was already dead in 1169, and is thus not identical with the government official bearing the same name mentioned in the preceding note, who lived slightly later): Bodl. MS. Heb. a 3 (Cat. 2873), f. 6, ll. 14–15.

[4] Bodl. MS Heb. b 13 (Cat. 2834), f. 20 (dated 1175). TS 13 J 20, f. 6.

[5] TS 12.425, trans. Goitein, *Education*, pp. 48-51. In TS 13 J 33, f. 3, a letter addressed to him, nine Hebrew titles and epithets, but no Arabic ones are attached to his name.

[6] Ibn Duqmāq, V, 46–47. See Mann, I, 215–217, and sec. C, 1, a, n. 36.

[7] TS 8 J 4, f. 14*a*.

[8] Bodl. MS Heb. a 3 (Cat. 2873), f. 22, ed. Mann, II, 269, ll. 26–27.

[9] Ibn Muyassar, p. 59, ll. 10–14, and p. 62, l. 16.

[10] *Ibid.*, p. 54, l. 8.

[11] See also sec. C, 1, d, below.

[12] Damascus: TS 13 J 2, f. 25* (dated 1140). Cf. n. 1, above. Ascalon: sec. C, 1, a, n. 12, above.

[13] DK 245+ (see sec. C, 1, a, n. 8), ll. 30–35. The term for emoluments: *'awn*. The *mushārif* of the village Sandafā, who received 1½ dinars per month: TS 10 J 18, f. 13*v*, l. 10. See n. 32, below. The mushārif fixed the amount of the poll tax and of other impositions: TS 10 J 10, f. 7.

[14] Dropsie 395*v*, l. 8. Here, and in the source quoted in the next note, the salary is called *al-jārī*.

[15] Bodl. MS Heb. f 22 (Cat. 2728), f. 39*v*.

[16] E.g. Gottheil-Worrell XXXVI, pp. 164–166*, see *Med. Soc.*, I, 339–342. TS K 15, f. 53 (dated 1046), ll. 13–14, "gift to the 'boys' of the *'āmil* and seven qirāṭs to the scribe." The shipment consisted of fourteen bales, having a total value of 226 dinars. The scribe thus received half a qirāṭ per bale.

[17] Maimonides, *Responsa*, I, 128. TS NS J 259, ll. 16, 19, 25+ (dated 1095).

[18] TS 16.148+ (dated 1086): *mutawallī dār al-ḍarb*. TS 12.1: *ṣāḥib dār al-ḍarb wamin qibal al-shilṭōn* [Heb.] *'āmil*.

[19] TS 12.1, l. 18: *Abu 'l-Qāsim, mutawalli* [the text has: *mtly*] *'l-sikka*. TS NS J 259+, court record no. *d*; *ḍāmin dār al-ḍarb*. The name in the first source and the context in the second prove that the official was a Muslim. The *Director of Coinage* was different from the *Director of the Mint* and his superior, as evident from TS 12.1.

[20] Bodl. MS Heb. a 2 (Cat. 2805), f. 22. The incomplete letter is most probably from al-Maḥalla and approximately from the year 1308. The name of the Nagid to whom it is addressed is not preserved, but it must be Abraham II b. David Maimonides, for greetings are given to a son Moses, who was married but did not yet have children (Moses b. Abraham was born in 1290) and to Obadiah, who was still a boy (born 1297), while Joshuah (b. 1310) is not yet mentioned.

[21] The term "ḍāmin" for a person leasing property from the Jewish community is used in the documents described in App. A, secs. 99 and 103. In sec. 100 *muḥtakir* is used instead. A ḍāmin collecting rents and executing repairs in buildings belonging to the Jewish community in Old Cairo in App. A, sec. 24. TS Arabic Box 54, f. 93, margin, l. 3: *hunā mutaqabbil al-dabāgha Yahūdī*, "here [Fustat] the farmer of the taxes on tanning is a Jew."

[22] E.g., ULC 1080 J 258* is a letter to a *nā'ib* and deals with tax farming. The person is mentioned in *Tarbiz*, 24 (1955), 46, l. 15.

[23] TS 13 J 20, f. 11. An Arabic commentary on the Five Books of Moses is copied for the ḍāmin Abu 'l-Bishr Mevassēr ha-Kohen b. Salmān.

[24] Examples of places whose tax farmers are referred to without any further qualifications:

1) Atfīḥ (thus, not, as often, Aṭfīḥ): TS 13 J 2, f. 24, dated 1139.
2) Benhā: TS 13 J 3, f. 12 (1165). Lawsuit not connected with tax farming.
3) Fuwwa: TS NS J 257. The tax farmer is asked to forward a letter.
4) Maḥallat al-Ymn: TS 8 J 22, f. 22. The ḍāmin is the father of a woman submitting a complaint against her husband, who also happened to be a ḍāmin.
5) Manūf: Bodl. MS. Heb. d 66 (Cat. 2878), f. 63. Greetings extended to the ḍāmin of Manūf who happened to live in Malīj.
6) al-Maṭariyya (Heliopolis): (*a*) TS NS Box 297, entry *d*, dated 1289. Agreement between two partners in tax farming. (*b*) DK XXXI. One tax farmer outbidding the other.
7) al-Minya: TS 13 J 14, f. 14+. Complaint of a ḍāmin about competitors, submitted to the Nagid Mevōrākh.
8) Minyat Ashna: TS 24.25, ll. 44–45. The ḍāmin mentioned as a debtor.
9) (Jazīrat) Qawsaniyya: TS 13 J 26, f. 19, l. 10*. The tax farmer sells beehives.
10) Sanhūr: TS 8 J 22, f. 22, and TS 18 J 3, f. 12. The husband of the woman mentioned above in no. 4.
11) Snyh: TS 24.25, l. 38. Mentioned as a debtor, cf. no. 8.
12) 'tfhn': TS 12.543 (dated 1266)*. The ḍāmin makes a contribution to a collection made in Minyat Ziftā.
13) Ḥmtyh: TS 13 J 19, f. 4, l. 12. His name: Furrayj ("pullet").
14) Sharbīn: TS 10 J 13, f. 3, ll. 6–7. Rashīd b. Mufaḍḍal, recipient of letter.

See also n. 32, below.

In TS Arabic Box 40, f. 153, a Muslim farms "the two zakāts of the village Qabīl" (see Ibn Duqmāq, V, 110, Omar Toussoun, *La géographie de l'Égypte a l'époque arabe,* Vol. I [Cairo, 1924], p. 275) for 8 dinars per month from the caliph al-Mustanṣir, the viceroy Amīr al-Juyūsh and their various underlings (dated 1086).

[25] Maimonides, *Responsa,* I, 175. Abraham Maimuni, *Responsa,* p. 150.

[26] TS 24.78*v*, l. 22+*.

[27] TS 13 J 3, f. 6* (dated 1147).

[28] TS NS J 7*v*, ll. 4–5+.

[29] See above, n. 24, no. 1. TS Misc. Box 8, f. 18*. Qalyūb: Bodl. MS. Heb. c 28 (Cat. 2876), f. 69, l. 5.

[30] Manbij: Bodl. MS Heb. c 28 (Cat. 2876), f. 38. TS 13 J 26, f. 18, a letter from Ramle, Palestine, referring to the market in Old Cairo.

[31] Dropsie 351, l. 3.

[32] Sūq Sandafā: TS 10 J 18, f. 13*v*, ll. 4–6. Fragmentary. Bodl. MS Heb. d 74, f. 42*v*, ll. 5–6. The *ḍāmin birsīm* was Jewish.

[33] TS 18 J 2, f. 6*v*.

[34] Port of New Cairo (Maqs): TS 13 J 13, f. 10, *India Book* 125. Old Cairo (Ṣinā'a): TS NS J 7+. 'Aydhāb: TS NS J 117, *India Book* 256. Ibn Jubayr, p. 302, ll. 16–21.

[35] ENA 2743, f. 2, ll. 18–19: *mā bi'īqnī 'ani 'l-dukhūl illā nawbat al-jāliya, bi'an mā ṣaḥḥ 'indna ḍāmin yaktub al-barāwāt.* Maimonides, *Responsa,* III, 137: *mutawalli l-jawālī . . . al-gōy al-ḍāmin.* Isaac b. Samuel: TS 8.21, top. The tax farmer was Jewish, for an action was brought against him before a Jewish court.

[36] *Arabica,* 3 (1956), 21.

[37] Badr al-Jamālī, referred to as *dhū riyāsatayn,* "the man with the two commands," because he was *wazīr al-sayf wal-qalam,* "vizier of the sword and the pen," i.e., chief commander as well as head of the civil administration. TS 13 J 14, f. 14*, see above, n. 24, no. 7.

[38] Bodl. MS Heb. d 66 (Cat. 2878), f. 8*: *al-tawqī' al-'ālī.*

[39] DK XXIX+*, plus 10 J 5, f. 17*, which is its direct continuation.

[40] TS 16.22+.

[41] Firkovitch II, 1700, f. 13, item *c.* For Būsh and dependencies.

[42] See n. 38. The name of the town: Ibwān. A similar license for Būsh and

environments brought 3½ dinars in the month of Muḥarram (June) 1147, Bodl. MS Heb. d 66 (Cat. 2878), f. 17*. Same district in TS NS 138 (1149).

43 TS 13 J 20, f. 2, ll. 10, 15, and verso, ll. 3–4.

44 In addition to those mentioned here, e.g., TS 8 J 16, f. 4+. TS 13 J 16, f. 8, l. 15: "coming from Ṣahrajt, *hārib min al-ḍamān,* fleeing because of his inability to make the payment for the farming."

45 TS 16.293, ll. 26 ff.

46 The source quoted in n. 27.

47 TS K 15, f. 91*.

48 Ibn al-Athīr, ed. C. J. Tornberg (Leiden, 1851 ff.), X, 75 (under the year 1079/80).

49 See n. 33 above. Fruit trees: TS NS J 42*, cf. *Med. Soc.,* I, 118.

50 TS Arabic Box 40, f. 126*v.*

c. JUDICIARY AND POLICE

1 ULC Or 1080 J 26 (around 1100).

2 TS 13 J 3, f. 4* (dated 1143).

3 Bodl. MS Heb. c 28 (Cat. 2876), f. 36. TS 13 J 19, f. 3 (both around 1040).

4 ULC Or 1080 J 39 (around 1100). The qadi is called *Thiqat al-Dawla ṣāḥib al-tartīb.* The term *tartīb* has not yet been found elsewhere in the Geniza in such a connection. For the procedure cf. also S. M. Stern, "Three Petitions of the Fatimid Period," *Oriens,* 15 (1962), 172–209.

5 E.g., Sassoon 713, l. 30+, (a case of a debt of 8 dinars!).

6 DK 245+, see sec. C, 1, a, n. 8, above. "Bribe of over 40 dinars": TS 12. 212, ll. 12–13, ed. Abramson, *Bamerkazim,* p. 167.

7 TS K 15, f. 95. The qadi's attendant received 1½ dirhems (called *ju'l,* pay, not *shōḥad,* the Hebrew word for bribe, as said of the qadi's share). May, 1150.

8 TS 16.272, ll. 8–9. *ḥujjāb* and *ghilmān.*

9 TS 12.16+.

10 See sec. A, 1, n. 22, above.

11 TS 20.114, l. 36+. The last word in the line should be read haqāṣ(īn, no Aleph).

12 Ibn Muyassar, p. 91, ll. 1–2.

13 *Ibid.,* p. 77, ll. 3–6.

14 See *Med. Soc.,* I, 311.

15 BM Or 10126, f. 19, see *JQR,* 51 (1960), 41.

16 TS 10 J 5, f. 12*v,* l. 10, *Nahray* 157: *dār al-qāḍī.* TS 8 J 22, f. 10, top, *Nahray* 3: *al-qāḍī aw'adhum bikull jamīl yakhzun riḥālāthum ilā awwal al-zamān yusāfirū wamā yaṭlub min aḥad falt illā an arād al-bay'.*

17 TS 16.87 (dated 1097). Mosseri L 161 (mercury). TS 8 J 25, f. 13, l. 9, *Nahray* 234: *al-wakīl al-qāḍī* (reference to his warehouse).

18 TS 16.179, Section D*, TS 12.215, sec. A*. The former passage refers to Tunisia, the latter to Old Cairo.

19 TS 16.272, l. 30, and verso, ll. 16–17.

20 E.g., TS 12.290, l. 9, and sec. C, 1, a, n. 5, above.

21 TS NS J 344*v,* ll. 7–9.

22 Chap. v, sec. B, 2, nn. 98, 99.

23 TS 13 J 3, f. 4*. Maimonides, *Responsa,* II, 488.

24 TS 24. 78*v,* l. 4+*.

25 TS 13 J 19, f. 3, l. 14. Maimonides, *Responsa,* I, 179, l. 2; II, 685, l. 21.

26 Gottheil-Worrell, XIII, p. 68, l. 30 (a Jew who works *'ind al-shurṭa*). AIU VII A 23, l. 20. TS 18 J 1, f. 11, l. 24+ (confined one night in the *shurṭa*). For *ṣāḥib al-shurṭa* as title see *Tarbiz,* 24 (1955) 143; as an office: Bodl. MS Heb. d 74, f. 47 (seems to refer to a locality in Syria).

[27] E.g., TS 13 J 20, f. 5, l. 2 and verso, l. 7*: *mutawalli l-ma'ūna*. Cf. Dozy, *Supplément*, II, 192*a*.

[28] Cf. Marius Canard, *Vie de l-Ustadh Jaudhar* (Algiers, 1958), p. 149 n. 336, where this meaning is assumed for the Mamluk period.

[29] TS 28.19, l. 36 *(wālī hādhihi 'l-ḍay'a)*. Around 1110.

[30] TS 13 J 15, f. 10 (object of request not stated). The section edited in *Eretz Israel*, 4 (1956), 152, deals with another matter. TS 18 J 4, f. 19 (competition by a newcomer). TS 16.277* (for retrieving a prayer book claimed by someone else.) TS 12.290*v*, ll. 11–14. See sec. A, 1, n. 30, above.

[31] TS 13 J 21, f. 24*v*, ll. 1–3.

[32] "Gift of honor," *makruma*: Bodl. MS Heb. f 102, f. 52*v*, ll. 8–10. Brawl: ULC Or 1080 J 86 (Sumbāṭ).

[33] TS 13 J 19, f. 17, ll. 6–9. *Tarbiz*, 28 (1959), 355. See sec. A, 3, n. 23, above.

[34] See sec. A, 1, n. 24, above. About the *muḥtasib* in Fatimid times see E. Ashtor-Strauss, *Rivista degli Studi Orientali*, 31 (1956), 83–84, and Tyan, *Organisation judiciaire*, p. 624. About the pre-Islamic history of this office see Benjamin R. Foster, "Agoranomos and Muḥtasib," *JESHO*, 13 (1970), 128–144, very instructive, but it entirely disregards the rich talmudic material on the subject.

[35] AIU VII A 23, l. 19.

[36] TS K 6, f. 44*v*, l. 30, App. A, sec. 95: *ṣāḥib rub' ḥaqq mā jama 'a 'l-yahūd yawm khurūjhim lil-sulṭān* (dated 1247). Also *ibid.*, l. 19.

[37] E.g., Bodl. MS Heb. b 11 (Cat. 2874), f. 5, ll. 7 and 28, App. A, sec. 5. Pentecost (Shavuot) is called here *'anṣara*, as in Christian Arabic. TS Box J 1, f. 47*v*, App. A, sec. 94. In TS Box J 1, f. 32*v*, l. 5, App. A, sec. 46, the *ḥāmi 'l-ḥāra*, the environment police, receives 2 dirhems. Good terms: TS 18 J 4, f. 10*v*, l. 1.

[38] TS 12.1, ll. 13–14: *rikābiyya warajjāla* (in, or around 1082). Maimonides, *Responsa*, II, 457, l. 13 *(al-rajjāla wal-tawkīl ma'a 'Abd al-Salām min 'ind al-qāḍī*, "the footmen and a power of attorney in the hands of A. given by the qadi"). TS 10 J 9, f. 21, *Nahray* 86, and TS 13 J 7, f. 5 (with the customs offices in Old Cairo and Rosetta). TS 13 J 16, f. 10 (poll tax).

[39] *Med. Soc.*, I, 94–96. In TS 18 J 1, f. 11, l. 22+, *raqqāṣīn* is identical with *rajjāla*, *ibid.*, l. 31. Dozy, *Supplément*, I, 515*a*, notes that *rajjāla* also may mean "workmen" (like *raqqāṣ*). It has not been found in this meaning in the Geniza. ULC Or 1081 J 13, l. 6 (raqqāṣīn sent by a mushārif).

[40] E.g., MS. Frankfurt, ed. J. Horovitz, *Zeitschrift für Hebraeische Bibliographie*, 5 (1905), 155: *waṣalu 'l-ḥushshār yaṭlubu 'l-mamlūk*. Dropsie 358, l. 4, and 398, l. 17. TS Box 25, f. 62, l. 9, *Nahray* 118. See sec. C, 2, n. 19, below.

[41] TS 12.1, ll. 6–14: *al-ḥāmī*: in TS 13 J 17, f. 3, l. 11+, and TS 13 J 19, f. 29, l. 19 ed. S. Assaf, *Epstein Jubilee Volume* (Jerusalem, 1950), p. 187, for soldiers as opposed to sailors on warships. Cf., however, n. 37, third source.

[42] *EI*², I, 256, s.v. (Cl. Cahen). Besides ENA, Uncatalogued 112, and Mann, II, 190, l. 35, quoted in Cl. Cahen, *Mouvements populaires et autonomisme urbain* (Leiden, 1959), p. 260 (86), see TS 13 J 11, f. 5, l. 14+. For Aleppo: Bodl. MS Heb. d 66 (Cat. 2878), f. 3*v*, l. 5, ed. S. Assaf, *Tarbiz*, 19 (1948), 107, where *al-aḥdāth* is to be read for *'l-'hd'h*. These "young men" had occupied a Jewish house on the corner of the bazaars of the furriers and the tanners (around 1100). Sfax: Gottheil-Worrell, XXXVI, p. 166, ll. 30 and 33*, payments made at a customs office to *sulṭān waṣibyān*, where, however, "waṣibyān" may mean simply "underlings." Lambert of Hersfeld: J. D. Ross and M. M. McLaughlin, *Medieval Reader* (New York, 1956), p. 457.

[43] Chief of secret police: *ṣāḥib khabar*, in the sources quoted sec. A, 3, n. 23, above. His messengers: *rusul*. Detectives: *nuẓẓār*, for which Hebrew *piqqeḥīm* ("those who see") is mostly used (TS 13 J 13, f. 24, l. 16, where "nuẓẓār" equals "piqqeḥīm" in l. 22. TS 20.122*v*, l. 40 (Palermo). TS 12.435 (Fez). TS 8 J 19, f. 25, l. 5 (Old Cairo; a Jew employed as detective).

[44] TS Misc. Box 28, f. 137. In TS 13 J 20, f. 5*, a *mutawalli 'l-ma'ūna,* which also means "chief of police," puts his seal on all items of an estate.

[45] TS 16.231, ll. 12–27 (probably around 1240).

[46] ENA 4010, f. 15. The letter is in Hebrew and renders *rassam 'alayh* with *piqqēd bō.* The word *popmē* is either a mispronunciation or a scribal error for *pompē,* an ancient loanword from Greek (from which English "pomp" is also derived).

[47] Bodl. MS Heb. d 66 (Cat. 2878), f. 6, ll. 5–7. TS 8 J 35, f. 1, l. 1 (1144). ULC Or 1080 J 167, ll. 9–10, *Nahray* 97. TS 12. 434, l. 20. See also *Med. Soc.,* I, 243.

[48] Sassoon 713+. TS Misc. Box 28, f. 137. TS 13 J 20, f. 5, l. 15*.

[49] TS 12.248*v,* ll. 15–21, *Nahray* 75.

[50] Dropsie 379, l. 13.

[51] Alfred J. Butler, *Coptic Churches of Egypt* (Oxford, 1884), I, 127.

[52] Assaf, *Texts,* p. 60, ll. 8–10. TS NS J 36. Diyā' asks her relative, the parnās Eli-'Allūn (see chap. v, sec. B, 2, n. 49) to obtain from the Nagid Mevōrākh a note to the qadi al-Makīn.

[53] This is the meaning of *lil-rajjāla walil-shurṭa dīnārayn* in TS 18 J 1, f. 11, l. 31+ (see n. 26, above). The second word refers to the personnel of the guardhouse.

[54] In addition to the examples mentioned before: ULC Or 1080 J 36: "almost two gold pieces," approximately the same amount as the one mentioned in the source quoted in n. 53. Ralph B. Pugh, *Imprisonment in Medieval England* (Cambridge, 1968), reviewed by Donald W. Sutherland in *Speculum,* 45 (Jan., 1970), 159.

[55] TS 8 J 22, f. 30. TS Box G 1, f. 1, cf. *Ginze Qedem,* 5 (1934), 62. TS 13 J 21, f. 5, l. 26+. The first two sources mention *hanbāzayn,* perhaps pincers. ULC Or 1081 J 13. The most detailed description of tortures in TS 10 J 7, f. 4 (beyond imagination. Late).

[56] In the first source mentioned in the preceding note.

[57] TS NS J 4, ll. 5–14. S. D. Goitein, *From the Land of Sheba* (New York, 1947), pp. 20–21.

d. NON-MUSLIM GOVERNMENT OFFICIALS

[1] Fattal, *Non-musulmans en pays de l'Islam,* pp. 257 ff. The references to literary sources provided there could easily be expanded.

[2] Government servants, *khuddām al-sulṭān,* mentioned together with the head of the yeshiva and the dayyānīm in Bodl. MS Heb. c 28 (Cat. 2876), f. 31, margin, ll. 11–13+.

[3] Ibn Muyassar, pp. 61–62. Fischel, *Jews,* pp. 88–89. As our interpretation of the pun contained in verse 3 proves, the verses were first promulgated in Abū Sa'd's time.

[4] Ibn Muyassar, pp. 61–62.

[5] *Kitābat al-kharāj,* the source quoted in chap. vi, sec. 12, n. 4, above.

[6] E.g., in a list of donors from this period (around 1230) among sixteen persons whose profession is indicated, four were physicians, but only one was a *kātib* and none was a *ṣayrafī:* TS K 15, f. 61 (App. C, sec. 40).

[7] Bodl. MS Heb. a 3 (Cat. 2873), f. 24, l. 64+*. The name of the Nafīs was Amram and that of the qadi al-Fāḍil, which was rather common in those days.

[8] *Amīn al-dawla ṣāḥib dār al-wakāla:* Bodl. MS Heb. c 28 (Cat. 2876), f. 54 (dated 1203). *Dār wakālat al-shaykh al-'Amīd b. Kushik:* TS 20. 80*v,* ll. 20–24, *India Book* 273.

[9] *Med. Soc.,* I, 188.

[10] TS 13 J 6, f. 5, ll. 13–14*, trans. *JESHO,* 9 (1966), 33–35. Tax office: *dīwān al-kharāj,* ENA 2935, f. 14 (fragment).

[11] Mann, I, 228. Ibn Muyassar, p. 74, l. 5. TS 24.25: Abu 'l-Makārim al-Sadīd b. Bu 'l-Dimm al-Ṭabīb (1164).

[12] Fischel, *Jews,* pp. 78–87, esp., p. 79 n. 4, quoting Ibn Ṣayrafī: *sāra nāẓiran fī jamī'i umūri 'l-dawlati.*

[13] Ibn Muyassar, p. 32, ll. 20–21. The vizier who engineered Abū Sa'd's assassination also seems to have been a Jew converted to Islam (see Fischel, *Jews,* p. 89 n. 1).

[14] TS 13 J 3, f. 6*.

[15] Ibn Muyassar, p. 36, l. 9. Al-Makīn: the source cited in the preceding note.

[16] Ibn Duqmāq, V, 46–47.

[17] ULC Or 1080 J 86, l. 15.

[18] TS 24.78*v*, 29+*. TS 13 J 21, f. 18, addressed to Eli, the son of Hillel b. Eli, who was *nā'ib al-nāẓir fī Bahnasā.* Revenue office: ENA 4020, f. 30*.

[19] ULC Or 1081 J 13, l. 5.

[20] Bodl. MS Heb. c 28 (Cat. 2876), f. 43, ll. 16–19. The letter was addressed to 'Allūn b. Ya'īsh, and the court physician referred to was Abraham b. Isaac b. Furāt. The full name of the Karaite 'āmil was Abū Sa'd Isḥāq b. Khalaf b. 'Allūn, al-kātib al-miṣrī (TS 8.14 and TS 20.187, the latter dated 1063).

[21] TS 13 J 14, f. 9, *Nahray* 205: Dalāṣ. DK VI, l. 3, *Nahray* 146: Manyamūn.

[22] TS 13 J 33, f. 9, l. 13* (Alexandria). TS 16.296, l. 9* and TS K 15, f. 53, col. I, l. 13 (both Old Cairo).

[23] Westminster College, Frag. Cairens. 51 (rent). TS 13 J 26, f. 21 (mules and camels). Ibn Jubayr, p. 302 (customs). Whether *mudawwin,* an official mentioned only with reference to Tunisia, had the same function cannot yet be decided: TS 12.372*v*, l. 2. Dropsie 389, l. 24. TS 10 J 6, f. 2*v*, l. 1, *Nahray* 219.

[24] TS 12. 281, *Nahray* 4: *jahbadh al-dīwān.*

[25] Alexandria: Bodl. MS Heb. c 28 (Cat. 2876), f. 35, ll. 25–28, ed. Mann, II, 274. "My father served the government in the city of Alexandria, being put over the gate of the sea for fifteen years" (in Heb.). Denia: Yāqūt, II, 938, 11–19. For the *mushrif 'alā marākib al-sulṭan,* see TS 24.78+*.

[26] TS K 15, f. 58, l. 20 (App. C, sec. 67): *Ibrāhīm ibn al-ḥāshir* (a contributor). TS 8 J 19, f. 25: *Manṣūr ibn ukht al-piqqē'aḥ* (Manṣūr, the nephew of the member of the secret police). For night watchmen see chap. v, sec. B, 2, nn. 96–99. Jews called raqqāṣ: TS NS J 41, B, l. 13 (App. B, sec. 17), TS NS J 293 (App. B. sec. 33, dated 1140).

[27] TS 10 J 13, f. 10, and TS 10 J 14, f. 12. TS Arabic Box 18 (1), f. 137, contains a letter of the same man to his son, but no reference to the army.

[28] Mann, *Texts,* II, 278–279.

[29] Christian surgeon: chap. vi, sec. 12, n. 54. Army camp: TS 13 J 21, f. 17+*.

[30] ULC Or 1080 J 138.

[31] TS NS J 29. A letter to him: Dropsie 398. A letter to his father expressing regret about the son's prolonged absence: TS 18 J 3, f. 5, l. 6.

[32] TS 13 J 18, f. 20. The name of the locality: Salmūn.

[33] Bodl. MS Heb. a 3 (Cat. 2873), f. 29.

[34] Steinschneider, *Arabische Literatur der Juden,* p. 183.

2. *The Poll Tax and Other Impositions*

[1] The topic of this subsection has been discussed in my article "Evidence on the Muslim Poll Tax from Non-Muslim Sources: A Geniza Study," *JESHO,* 6 (1963), 278–295. For the sources and previous treatments see *EI*², s.v. *"Djizya"* (Claude Cahen). For the earlier history of the jizya in Egypt see the detailed exposition of A. Grohmann, *Die Arabischen Papyri aus der Giessener Universitaetsbibliothek* (Giessen, 1960), pp. 19–28, 82–83.

[2] TS 13 J 22, f. 9. See chap. vi, sec. 4, n 17.

[3] TS 12.3*.

[4] ULC 1081 J 13.

[5] TS 12.192, ll. 3–9+, App. C, sec. 82.

[6] TS 13 J 4, f. 7.

[7] Abraham Maimuni, *Responsa,* pp. 161–162. Maimonides, *Responsa,* I, 50.

[8] S. Kandel, *Genizai kéziratok* (Budapest, 1909), p. vi, now marked DK XXX: a father of a boy of fourteen declares to have paid for him jāliya for five years. Judge Joseph ha-Levi b. Samuel to whom the query is addressed is hardly identical with the recipient of TS 20.141+, a letter dated 1094. A man with the same name, but apparently different script, signed TS 10 J 4, f. 7* (Aug., 1181).

[9] TS 13 J 3, f. 2+. The declaration contained other provisions too.

[10] Maimonides, *Responsa,* I, 103.

[11] TS 8 J 26, f. 18*.

[12] Brother-in-law: Dropsie 398.

[13] Maimonides, *Responsa,* I, 36–37. Syria: TS 13 J 6, f. 30.

[14] TS 13 J 28, f. 15*v*, l. 14, *India Book* 291.

[15] TS NS J 3, l. 16. The traveler had left Egypt in 1156.

[16] Bodl. MS Heb. c 28 (Cat. 2876), f. 65, margin: *barā'a dīwāniyya.*

[17] E.g., TS 13 J 15, f. 2, l. 11. See *Med. Soc.,* I, 300.

[18] See chap. v, sec. B, 1, n. 148, above. TS Arabic Box 41, f. 109.

[19] TS Misc. Box 25, f. 62, ll. 3–11, *Nahray* 118.

[20] TS 13 J 14, f. 18*v*, ll. 5–10, *Nahray,* 54.

[21] See, however, n. 27, below.

[22] Bodl. MS Heb. f. 56 (Cat. 2821, n. 16), f. 19, ll. 7–11, see *JQR,* 43 (1952), 76 and 59–60. S. Schechter, "A Geniza MS.," *A. Berliner Jubilee Volume* (Frankfurt am Main, 1903), Heb. sec., pp. 108–112. About the payment of the poll tax by the community for its scholarly officials see chap. v, C, 4, n. 4.

[23] Dropsie 393, l. 13. The European traveler obviously thought that Heb. *zimiya* (from Greek *zemia,* fine) is derived from Arabic *dhimmī,* "protected non-Muslim."

[24] TS 18 J 3, f. 1: *man yaskun fīhā mā yazin jāliya.* TS 13 J 36, f. 2: *kitāb an yaṭlubūh fi 'l-'amal wamā mskh (miska) thamma 'alā jaliya.*

[25] TS 10 J 10, f. 10: Ibrahīm b. Isḥāq of al-Maḥalla writes to Abū Sa'd Hibat Allāh, alias Nethanel Rōsh ha-qāhāl (twelve lines of exquisite Hebrew proem, the rest in Arabic characters) about Yākhīn ha-meshōrēr (see chap. vi, sec. 10, n 34). The Geniza document: TS 16.353, ed. H. Hirschfeld, *JQR,* 15 (1093), 167–181. The Yemenite version: "Kitāb Dhimmat al-Nabī," ed. S. D. Goitein, *Kirjath Sepher,* 9 (1933), 507–521. Discussion of all the literary material about the Khaybarīs in Braslavsky, *Our Country,* pp. 1–52. One Ibn al-Khaybarī contributes to the collection ENA 2348, f. 1*v*, App. C, sec. 121. Another is mentioned in TS 12.245, l. 7, a letter in a Spanish hand, as transmitting a message from Egypt to the West. A Saadya b. Benjamin Khaybarī is accused in an old court record by Rayyisa b. Joseph Bīmī (a strange name, perhaps abbreviation of talmudic Avīmī), the wife of Yeshū'ā b. Nissīm, to have retained 4 dinars due her (TS NS J 73).

[26] Ibn Mammātī, *Qawānīn al-dawāwīn* (Cairo, 1943), p. 318. Bodl. MS Heb. f 56 (Cat. 2821, no. 16), f. 45, l. 7*, called here *jizya.*

[27] DK XXI: "one and two thirds dinars" (1-16/24 for 1-15/24; the man most probably had to pay a qirāt as fine; see below). TS 16.272*v*, l. 7: "five prisoners who have to pay eight dinars," which is 1-24/40 per person (1⅝ equals 1-25/40). TS 8 J 19, f. 1, ll. 5–6: 1 - 1/3 plus ¼ plus ½ qirāṭ, which would be 1½ ḥabbas instead of 2 ḥabbas. For payment to a special office for foreigners in the capital, see n. 21, above.

[28] See A. Scheiber and J. L. Teicher, *Journal of Jewish Studies,* 5 (1954), 37.

[29] ULC Or 1080 J 258, ll. 22–28*: *tawqī' mukammal* [cf. Dozy, *Supplément,* s.v.] *. . . yataḍamman an yujraw fi 'l-jizya 'alā mā hum 'alayh . . . wa an yujraw 'ala mā kān qarrarhu al-qāḍi 'l-makīn.*

[30] TS 12.290*v*, l. 9.

[31] Cf. Cl. Cahen, "Histoires Coptes," *Bulletin de l'Institut français d'archéologie orientale,* 59 (1960), p. 140, l. 2.

[32] MS Frankfurt, ed. Joseph Horovitz, *Zeitschrift für Hebraeische Bibliographie,* 4 (1900), 155–158. The writer bears the extremely rare name Mishael b. Uzziel, although it was a name that was common in the family of Maimonides' Egyptian wife. The very wording *al-mamlūk yazin 'an Damīra l-qibliyya* shows that he did not live in that place. The addressee, R. Hananel, is well known. Documents signed by him from 1223 have been preserved. Flat rate: C. H. Becker and Claude Cahen, *Bulletin d'Études orientales Damas,* 16 (1958–1960), 29, 71. TS 12.581, l. 13. ULC Add 3417 (b). See also n. 9, above.

[33] TS 16.39 (The account is most probably from 1183).

[34] TS 8 J 11 f 7 d, margin, App. A, sec. 27.

[35] ENA 4020, f. 30*: "I sold the old kerchief *(mandīl),* which I used to wear, for 13½ dirhems and with it paid the poll tax." ULC Or 1080 J 80, l. 8: a father sends to his son 11 dirhems for the jāliya. TS 16.286*: "They took 12 dirhems from me and left me alone for a while" (Alexandria 1219). Also, 13 + 11 dirhems in TS Arabic Box 30, f. 129.

[36] E.g., TS 8 J 21, f. 6, l. 15+, "Talk for me to the *ba'al ha-mas*" (Heb. for Arabic, *ṣāḥib al-jāliya*).

[37] Dropsie 358, ll. 4–5, and 398, l. 7. Fine: *maghram,* TS 16.296, l. 7*.

[38] TS 13 J 26, f. 13, ed. Mann, II, 174–175 (where f. 11 is printed for f. 13).

[39] See n. 35, Maimonides, *Responsa,* I, 116 and 92.

[40] Advance: Dropsie 410. Loan: above, n. 26.

[41] TS 10 J 17, f. 19*v*; TS 10 J 18, f. 22*v*, ll. 5–6; TS 13 J 34, f. 8. Other examples: TS 12.289+*; Westminster College Frag. Cairens. 43.

[42] Bodl. MS Heb. d 66 (Cat. 2878), f. 135: *ḥaṣalat lil-nās shadā'id min ajli 'l-jāliya wakunna jamī' mukhabbayīn fi 'l-buyūt.*

[43] TS 13 J 36, f. 2, ll. 12–14. TS 10 J 17, f. 20. Here, the writer complains that others owed him money too.

[44] ULC Or 1081 J 61. See n. 11, above.

[45] See n. 18, above.

[46] TS 13 J 11, f. 5, ll. 18–20+: *pittāqē* (from Greek *pittakion*) *ha-mas* is the Heb. equivalent for Ar. *riqā' al-jāliya,* warrants of arrest for nonpayment of the poll tax. See p. 382 and n. 4, above.

[47] Dropsie 392. Some of the ten persons signing the document are known from other sources.

[48] TS K 25, f. 240, nos. 11, 12, and 1. The Trusted: *al-Thiqa,* a common title in those days.

[49] TS 13 J 33, f. 9, ll. 10 and 13*. For *ṣayrafī* attending to the collection of the jāliya in the fourteenth century, see TS 16.296, l. 9*. One talked also generally about *ṣāḥib* and *aṣḥāb al-jāliya* (TS NS J 290, l. 10; Dropsie 379, l. 9; cf. Heb. *ba'al ha-mas* in n. 36).

[50] The first source mentioned in n. 49.

[51] TS Box G 1, f. 1.

[52] TS 16.286*v*, l. 4*: *tabarru'*. TS 20.133; share: *qaṭī'a.*

[53] TS 8 J 20, f. 16: *yu'khadh lil-khandaq.*

[54] Maimonides, *Responsa,* I, 199. Strauss, *Mamluks,* I, 223.

[55] Bodl. MS Heb. d 74, f. 47, see *Med. Soc.,* I, 85. Before reporting that they were dragged to the corvées, *sukhar* (in the plural), they write: *qad ṣāb al-'abīd al-taṣdīr.* Could *taṣdīr* mean the same as *muṣādara?*

[56] Employee: *musta'mal:* App. C, sec. 31 (four in the Bazaar of Threads); App. A, sec. 24, l. 17; sec. 43, l. 32. App. C, sec. 46, *Zion,* 7 (1942), 143; ULC Or 1080 J 200, l. 5*.

[57] Ibn Muyassar, p. 59, 11, 6 ff.

[58] TS 18 J 4, f. 6, l. 38; verso, l. 18.

D. COMMUNAL AUTONOMY AND GOVERNMENT CONTROL

1. *The Interplay of Laws*

[1] TS 12.5: the contract of 1058. TS 20.152: the clean copy of the appeal. The draft Bodl. MS Heb. a 3 (Cat. 2873), f. 9, ed. S. Assaf, *Responsa Geonica* (Jerusalem, 1942), pp. 125–127.

[2] TS 16.133, ed. Assaf, *Texts*, pp. 140–142. Assaf says (p. 140, last line) he died without leaving heirs, but the document says expressly that he had (l. 20, where the manuscript has *hywrshym,* not *hwwrshym.* In l. 9 *ha-mit'akhsēn* is to be read for *ha-mit'abbēq*). L. 12 states that he had no *male* heir.

[3] Maimonides, *Responsa,* I, 102.

[4] Gottheil-Worrell, VIII, pp. 37–43.

[5] Bodl. MS Heb. c 28 (Cat. 2876), f. 54. After the payment of all the liabilities there remained 83 dinars, while the flat sum taken by the qadi before was 30 dinars. Most probably the widow's indemnity was 50 dinars, while the only daughter took the remaining 33 dinars.

[6] DK XXVI.

[7] ULC Or 1080 J 26, ll. 4–11. In a letter from Qūṣ 'Arūs b. Joseph is admonished to expedite the matter in the capital.

[8] Westminster College, Frag. Cairens. 43.

[9] TS 12.666. The right half of the document is torn away. The qadi: Ibn Abī 'Aqīl. Ephraim b. Maḥfūz, i.e., Shemarya, is addressed, and the Nagid (of Tunisia) and R. Hananel are referred to.

[10] Strauss, *Mamluks,* I, 223, who provides a detailed survey of the development of this question in Islamic law.

[11] TS 13 J 3, f. 4*.

[12] *Med. Soc.,* I, 63. TS 13 J 21, f. 5, l. 17+ (ca. 1215).

[13] Mosseri A 11, ll. 12–13*, ed. Assaf, *Texts,* p. 172. For the marriage portion see *Med. Soc.,* Vol. III, chap. IX. Shares to the families of sisters: PER H 94+.

[14] TS 13 J 30, f. 3+, quoted by H. Z. Hirschberg in his Hebrew study on Muslim courts in the gaonic period, *Herzog Memorial Volume* (Jerusalem 1962), p. 15.

[15] Bodl. MS Heb. a 2 (Cat. 2805), f. 9+*.

[16] In the source quoted in n. 5, ll. 12–13.

[17] TS 8 J 4, f. 17*b–c*.

[18] Maimonides, *Responsa,* II, 625, no. 349.

[19] TS 13 J 8, f. 31. Interesting, but extremely complicated.

[20] *Ibid.,* f. 1. The boy stayed with his mother, while the father was permitted to have him on the Sabbath.

[21] Bodl. MS Heb. d 66 (Cat. 2878), f. 133. The Karaites used to include in a marriage contract the condition that none of the two parties ever apply to a Muslim court, e.g., TS 16.67, l. 25 (Cairo, 1200).

[22] E.g., Bodl. MS Heb. a 3 (Cat. 2873), f. 26, sec. A*. See also next note.

[23] TS Misc. Box 28, f. 246, margin, *Nahray* 169; TS 12.215, sec. A* (both commercial matters).

[24] This is in accordance with Muslim law (see Schacht, *Islamic Law,* p. 132).

[25] App. A, sec. 21.

[26] E.g., TS 8 J 4, f. 17*a*; Bodl. MS Heb. b. 11 (Cat. 2874, n. 35) f. 36, dated 1153 (both granting of payment in installments). TS 20.32: renouncement of part of debt, dated 1057. TS 12.594: settlement of debt, dated 1143.

[27] TS 16.238. Maimonides, *Responsa,* I, 38.

[28] ENA 4011, f. 57*v*.

[29] Maimonides, *Responsa,* I, 178.

[30] BM Or 10 126, f. 6* (see *JQR,* 51 [1960], 39). Arabic *ḥujja* (Fustat, 1150): ENA

4011, f. 33. Alexandria: JNUL 3*, ed. S. D. Goitein, *Kirjath Sepher,* 41 (1966), 264–265.

[31] Sec. B, 1, n. 61, above. Sec. B, 2, nn. 18–19, above. Mez, *Renaissance,* chap. 4, pp. 40–41. Hirschberg's study quoted in n. 14. Cf. in particular Maimonides, *Responsa,* II, 624, referring to the statute about excommunication, promulgated in 1187.

[32] 1052: above n. 20. 1117: Bodl. MS Heb. a 3 (Cat. 2873), f. 42+. 1055: Mosseri A 43/2+. 1027: TS 13 J 5, f. 1. Commercial matters. 1052: JNUL f. 1, *Nahray* 23, cf. A. Yellin, *Kirjath Sepher,* 2 (1926), 292. 1098: ULC Add. 3420*d*, l. 7, *India Book* 8. Al-Maḥalla: TS 10 J 17, f. 25, ll. 21–24.

[33] E.g., TS NS J 27, paged, no. 7: a man deposits his *ḥujaj,* Muslim documents, with the *bēth dīn* and is permitted to bring his brother before a Muslim court, in the event he does not accept the settlement offered (payment of a debt of 27 dinars in installments of a quarter dinar per month; 1143). TS 13 J 5, f. 3 (1150). I counted about thirty such documents, but there are certainly many more. See also Maimonides, *Responsa,* II, 685.

[34] TS 13 J 9, f. 7, cf. chap. v, sec. A, 1, n. 28, above.

[35] Sec. C, 1, c, n. 45, above.

[36] *Med. Soc.,* I, 136.

[37] Bodl. MS Heb. d 68 (Cat. 2836, no. 21), f. 99.

[38] TS 28.19.

[39] Maimonides, *Responsa,* II, 353.

[40] TS 13 J 26, f. 21*v* (not connected with recto).

[41] Oath: also Mosseri L 39*e*, l. 5 (even under duress). TS 13 J 14, f. 1*v*, l. 7+.

[42] ENA. Uncatalogued 89, ll. 8–10 (a Christian). The same perhaps Assaf, *Texts,* p. 101, where *'ngṭ* most probably is the name of a Christian. TS 13 J 20, f. 21 (al-Maḥalla, 1217: a Muslim).

2. *How Much Autonomy?*

[1] TS 16.64, margin, ed. S. D. Goitein, *Tarbiz,* 38 (1968), 22–26.

[2] TS 10 J 28, f. 2+*, see chap. v, B, 1, n. 142, above.

[3] ENA Uncatal. 109+*. The leader of the dissenting group bears the name Joseph both here and in the source mentioned in the preceding note.

[4] Bodl. MS Heb. d 79, f. 34*v*, (different from recto), ed. S. D. Goitein, *J. Schirmann Jubilee Volume* (Jerusalem, 1969). This is not a letter, as stated by Mann, II, 218, but a record of a public meeting. The fragment TS 8 J 26, f. 3, referring to a speech by Abū Isḥāq, allūf, or distinguished member, of the Iraqian yeshiva (i.e., Abraham b. Sahlān) concerning the eclipse of the exclusive juridical authority of the Palestinian yeshiva (*infasadat reshūth al-shāmiyyīn fi 'l-ḥāvēr Abū Kathīr,* i.e., Ephraim b. Shemarya), seems to be connected with the same affair.

[5] S. M. Stern, *Fatimid Decrees* (London, 1964), pp. 23–34, re-editing and discussing previous editions by R. Gottheil and S. D. Goitein. TS Arabic Box 30, f. 278+. Bodl. MS Heb. b 18, f. 21, ed. S. M. Stern, *REJ,* 128 (1969), 203–222. See also chap. v, A, 1, nn. 29 and 37, above.

[6] TS 13 J 9, f. 2, l. 15+; TS 18 J 4, f. 26, ll. 6–16+*.

[7] TS 10 J 16, f. 8, *India Book* 254.

[8] TS 10 J 13, f. 11 (not in *Nahray*). "Government papers": *istanjiz* [a technical term for securing something from the government] *kutub sulṭāniyya bismī.* He asks also that an insubordinate shohet who, in addition, was incompetent (*yuṭ'im al-aṭrāf,* for Heb. *ṭerēfōt*) be threatened with excommunication (*petīḥīn*).

[9] TS 16.272, l. 10.

[10] Gottheil-Worrell, II, pp. 12 ff., see chap. v, B, 1, n. 47, above.

[11] TS 10 J 24, f. 8*v* (no continuation of recto), l. 8, ed. Mann, II, 373. Strangely, Mann gives as shelf mark TS 13 J 34, f. 2. But this manuscript is edited by him

(*ibid.*, p. 349, where, however, 13 J 34, f. 1, is erroneously printed). "Gentile writ". I prefer this translation to "Arabic script," which makes no sense here, while the "government papers," n. 8, above, appear in a similar context.

[12] TS NS J 29, ll. 8, 24: an *iṭlāq* from the sultan is sought for the judge Elijah; *ibid.*, margin: the nāsī, who served as judge in Alexandria received a *jāmikiyya*, or salary, from the sultan al-Malik al-Kāmil.

[13] See chap. v, D, 2, n. 21, above.

[14] AIU, undefined (see Shaked, *Bibliography*, p. 298, ed. Richard Gottheil, *Mélanges H. Derenbourg* [Paris, 1909], p. 98). The text has to be re-edited. Other queries, written in Arabic letters and addressed by Jews to Muslim jurisconsults in this period: TS Arabic Box 38, f. 87 (someone frightened an old man so that he fell ill); Bodl. MS Heb. a 3 (Cat. 2873), f. 16*v* (separate from recto, although connected with it by topic, a question of inheritance). TS Arabic Box 39, f. 173 (alimony for orphans): TS Arabic 39, f. 417 (partnership in a house, a case dealt with before by other Muslim scholars); TS Arabic Box 41, f. 105 (reform of the synagogue liturgy) seems to be another, and better, version of the AIU query.

[15] TS Arabic Box 51, f. 111+.

[16] Meinardus, *Orthodox Copts*, p. 163. B. Spuler, *Die morgenländischen Kirchen*, Handbuch der Orientalistik, I, (Leiden and Cologne, 1961), viii, 2, p. 294.

General Index

(Owing to the frequency of their occurrence, the following have not been indexed: Cairo, Egypt, Fustat, Islam, Jew[ish], Judaism, Muslim, Old Cairo. The appendixes and notes are not indexed. J.-A. stands for Judeo-Arabic.)